Andrew's Previews 2021

The year 2021, told through parliamentary and local by-elections

Andrew Teale

A publication of the

"All the right votes, but not necessarily in the right order"

First published by Britain Elects 2021
First published in paperback by Local Elections Archive Project 2022

Local Elections Archive Project
`https://www.andrewteale.me.uk/leap/`

ISBN 978 1 9998345 5 5

Front cover: Map of Hartlepool constituency (page 153) by the author
Back cover: Picture of a polling station at the Camperdown by-election, 9th September 2021 (page 364) by the author
Picture of Scott's View (page 19) by "Kharasho2", and licensed for reuse under `creativecommons.org/licenses/by-sa/3.0`
Maps of the Furness Peninsula ward (page 75) and the Oakham North West ward (page 455) © OpenStreetMap contributors and licensed for reuse in accordance with `openstreetmap.com/copyright`
Tweet of Greater Manchester mayoral election booklet (page 85) originally published at `tinyurl.com/54nhpdrc` and reproduced with permission from Jane Healey-Brown.
Picture of the *Amarna Princess* (page 436) by "geni" and licensed for reuse under `creativecommons.org/licenses/by-sa/4.0`
Pictures of the Cursing Stone (page 71), the Falkirk Wheel (page 426) and the Kinver Rock Houses (page 442) and constituency maps (pages 166, 204, 220, 252, 537 and 577) by the author.

With thanks to David and Heather Teale
and Ken Leadbeater
for the proofreading
and for spotting all the words which left out of the first draft

Erratum

Andrew's Previews 2016, page 90: LD vote should read 154 and Lab vote should read 38.

Contents

Other books in the Andrew's Previews series:

Andrew's Previews 2016 (ISBN 978-1-9998345-0-0)

Andrew's Previews 2017 (ISBN 978-1-9998345-1-7)

Andrew's Previews 2018 (ISBN 978-1-9998345-2-4)

Andrew's Previews 2019 (ISBN 978-1-9998345-3-1)

Andrew's Previews 2020 (ISBN 978-1-9998345-4-8)

Andrew's Previews is published (normally) weekly by Britain Elects,
`britainelects.com`

The Local Elections Archive Project is the longest-running online repository of UK local election data, and can be browsed at
`www.andrewteale.me.uk/leap`

Introduction

Welcome to the sixth annual collection of Andrew's Previews, another compilation of weekly articles published by the *Britain Elects* website to cover by-elections to the UK's local councils in 2021.

This was not a normal year—but then, what is a normal year these days? As December 2020 turned into January 2021 the pulse of democracy had stopped, the country closed down by lockdowns to fight coronavirus. But this time there was a difference: vaccines which could show us the way out of the pandemic.

Matters improved fast enough that the May 2021 local elections could go ahead as scheduled, forming the most complicated set of UK local elections ever attempted. The fact that these elections happened at all was an important step back to normality. Local by-elections in England had been suspended because of the pandemic restrictions; polls did go ahead in Scotland and Wales, but there are no polls in this volume until March 2021. January and February were dark months, in every sense.

And then it was back to normal politics. The May 2021 local elections saw big gains for the Conservative government, enjoying its "vaccine bounce" in the polling. The party even gained an opposition seat in a parliamentary by-election, in Hartlepool (page 153), whose 2021 election results grace the cover of this book. Five more parliamentary by-elections took place that year, in Airdrie and Shotts (page 195), Chesham and Amersham (page 212), and Batley and Spen (page 242) during the summer, and in Old Bexley and Sidcup (page 527), and North Shropshire (page 567) in December. We also had two county-wide by-elections for police and crime commissioners, in Wiltshire (page 329) and in North Yorkshire (page 495).

In between those, we had a host of local by-elections. After what was effectively a fallow year in 2020, 2021 was the busiest year yet for Andrew's Previews. Overall, this column previewed 450 by-elections or postponed polls, compared with just 36 in 2020.

These by-elections are our democracy's weekly pulse check, bringing into sharp relief the local consequences of the national opinion polls and whatever else is going on. Any opinion pollster will tell you that there is an awful lot of error and noise in a single poll, and this is even more true for local by-elections where local factors can often amplify or cancel the underlying national signal. Trying to tease out these effects is half of the fun of writing these previews. The government's polling ratings went on a steady downward slide as 2021 went on: see if you can pick that up in the results as the book progresses.

Thanks are due to everyone involved, starting first and foremost with a round of applause for our returning officers and electoral services teams, who work so hard behind the scenes to keep the democratic show on the road for your benefit.

My thanks also to the team at *Britain Elects*, on whose website these columns were originally published, and to all those people—you know who you are—who donated their own time and knowledge to help with the writing and the research.

During his own preview session for the 2021 local elections Michael Thrasher was kind enough to describe *Andrew's Previews*, in my own hearing, as "wonderful reports". All British psephologists are forever in debt to both him and Colin Rallings for their work over many years in collecting and analysing the UK's local election results. Rallings and Thrasher's annual *Local Elections Handbooks* are the primary sources for pre-2002 election results where they are quoted here; results since then are taken from my own collection which you can browse online at the *Local Elections Archive Project*[*]. As before, the hard work of the Ordnance Survey and the 2011 census team have been extensively relied on.

And don't forget: if you voted in Great Britain in 2021, you contributed towards the making of this book in some small way.

I am also grateful to those who took the time to read the early drafts of this book. Anything which is still incorrect is of course my own fault.

By buying this book, you have very kindly made a donation to support future Previews, and I hope that this book will be a fitting permanent reminder of your donation. If you get to the end of this book and would like to read more, well, you can: there are five previous collections in the series, *Andrew's Previews 2016* to *2020*, and you can stay up to date with by-elections and future columns as they happen by keeping an eye on the *Britain Elects* website.

Without further ado, let me now bring you fun and sunshine as Andrew's Previews looks back at "all the right votes, but not necessarily in the right order"...

Andrew Teale
Little Lever, Bolton
July 2022

[*] `www.andrewteale.me.uk/leap/`

4th March 2021

"All the right votes, but not necessarily in the right order"

Spring is in the air. The days are drawing longer. The skies have dried up and the sun occasionally shines. The daffodils are sprouting from the ground. Nature is reasserting itself.

Democracy is also returning to our attention. Welcome out of hibernation (or, as it's called these days, furlough) to a new year of Andrew's Previews, that weekly column for Britain Elects whose aims are amply summed in the above misquote from Eric Morecambe to the original Andrew Preview. As well as the UK set pieces of general elections, devolved parliament elections and the local government elections which take place every May, the meat and drink of this column is by-elections. These don't just happen for vacancies in Parliament. Incidentally, tomorrow we will break the record for the streak of time between parliamentary by-elections: the last one was Brecon and Radnorshire in August 2019,* and despite everything that has happened since every one of the 650 MPs elected in the December 2019 general election are still with us and still in post.

We are also in a record-breaking streak of time between local by-elections in England. The last poll to take place in England or Wales was a by-election to Coventry city council on 19th March 2020, at the start of the first lockdown.† Since then we have only had occasional Scottish local by-elections to entertain us while the vacancy list in England and Wales has grown like topsy. After a year of electoral inactivity, your columnist's latest count of vacancies in British local councils stands at over 390, of which at least 15 are a direct result of COVID-19. Some councils stand more than 10% short of their full membership. Once the notices for the 6th May elections are published at the end of this month, my estimate is that the final vacancy count will be somewhere between 450 and 500.

---

* *Andrew's Previews 2019*, page 227. † *Andrew's Previews 2020*, page 79.

Even those May elections will not fully resolve this democratic deficit. Last week it was announced that the county and district council elections due this year in Cumbria, North Yorkshire and Somerset would be postponed by a year while a consultation takes place on local government reorganisation in those counties. The Cabinet minister responsible, Robert Jenrick, has defended this decision on the grounds that it would prevent councillors being elected for short terms, which is not a statement that stands up to scrutiny particularly well.

Consider: at one end of the scale, every winner in this year's Reading council elections will only serve a one-year term, because the whole of Reading council will come up for re-election in May 2022 on revised ward boundaries. At the other end of the scale, the eleven members of Craven district council in North Yorkshire who were elected in 2016 and were due for re-election in 2020 have already seen their terms extended by one year due to COVID, and are now to see their terms extended by a further year due to this consultation, and probably by a further year on top of that if reorganisation actually happens. That's a four-year term extended to six years, potentially seven years, which is unfair on the councillors concerned and a denial of democracy to their constituents. All this when there's not even an indication in any of these areas that there is a settled plan for what form reorganisation should take. Maybe the better option would have been to allow the local elections in Cumbria, North Yorkshire and Somerset to proceed and sort out the consequences afterwards.

In support of that opinion, your columnist would point out that there's not even a financial saving to be made from postponing this year's local elections in Cumbria, North Yorkshire and Somerset. The electoral services teams within those counties still have elections to organise in May regardless: those for the police and crime commissioners. These form just one part of the polls on the 6th May 2021 which will be the most complicated set of local elections ever staged. All the remaining county councils and the elections to the Senedd and the Scottish Parliament will be combined with everything held over from last year: the police and crime commissioners, most of the combined authority mayors, those English unitary and second-tier districts which hold elections by thirds or halves, and the Mayor and Assembly in Greater London. Once by-elections, parish councils and a few local referendums are added into that mix, we can see that most voters will have a large number of ballot papers to juggle and most counters will have a large number of ballot papers to separate before they can even start on the vote counting.

All of this, of course, has to be done under the terms of the current emergency which has occasioned some changes to the normal rules. If you are required to isolate at the time of the poll due to a COVID-related reason then you will qualify for an emergency proxy vote; your polling card will tell you how to organise that. The signature requirement for candidate nomination papers in England and Wales has been drastically reduced. The polling stations will be run in a safe manner; but if for whatever reason you don't want to attend the polling station then you can apply for a postal vote, and I would recommend that you do that now and beat the rush.

Given the number of simultaneous elections involved, it will probably take a few days to finish the count. The Electoral Management Board for Scotland have already decided that they will not attempt an overnight count for the Scottish Parliament this year, and this column would expect many returning officers outwith Scotland to come to the same decision in organising their counts.

So this May's counts will probably be a slow process, but accuracy is more important than speed and we can have confidence in the abilities and accuracy of our counting teams. A recent case in the Election Court has borne this out. Back in January 2020 a by-election took place for two seats in the Barnhill ward of the London Borough of Brent*, which the Labour slate of Mansoor Akram and Gaynor Lloyd held with unusually small majorities of 112 and 70 votes over the lead Conservative candidate Kanta Mistry. Mistry and her running-mate Stefan Voloseniuc launched a legal case to request a recount, which was duly held in July and found no significant error in the original result. They could and probably should have applied to withdraw the case at that point, but that would have involved paying the legal costs of the Labour slate and the returning officer; so it appears that Voloseniuc and Mistry did nothing more to resolve the case until the returning officer escalated the matter to the High Court in London. Voloseniuc and Mistry comprehensively lost in the High Court last month, and their legal bill has doubled to an estimated £60,000.

Let the experience of Voloseniuc and Mistry stand as an expensive lesson to those who believe the Wild Twitter Rumours which habitually fly around from counting centres and elsewhere early on election night. As we saw over the pond in November, partial counts can be very unrepresentative of the final result. The Britain Elects team are of course here to cut through all that nonsense and bring you cold, hard facts as they emerge from the declarations, and your columnist encourages you to follow us on the nights and days after 10pm on 6th May while we make sense of it all. We have some exciting things lined up.

Before then, we have some by-elections to bring you. There are nineteen polls in Scotland and Wales scheduled over the next five weeks to ease us back into the democratic routine, and here are the first two of these. Not necessarily in the right order...

* *Andrew's Previews 2020*, page 11.

Fortissat; and Thorniewood

North Lanarkshire council, Scotland; caused respectively by the resignations of Tommy Cochrane and Steven Bonnar. Both were originally elected for the Scottish National Party, but Cochrane had left the party in 2018 and was sitting as an independent councillor. Cochrane resigned in March 2020 due to pressure of work, having represented the ward since 2012. Bonnar, who is now the MP for Coatbridge, Chryston and Bellshill, had served since winning a by-election in 2015.

So, we kick Andrew's Previews off for 2021 in North Lanarkshire to see whether the Scottish National Party can overcome a recent bout of infighting. There are two by-elections in North Lanarkshire district today, both of which were originally scheduled for November but were postponed at the last moment due to increased COVID restrictions in the Central Belt. Both of these are wards which have appeared in this column before but whose names may not be immediately helpful to the outsider.

Such as the Thorniewood ward, which lies just outside the eastern edge of Glasgow between the M 8 and M 74 motorways. This is an area where the population boomed after the Second World War due to new industry coming in, such as a coalmine and a large Caterpillar factory. To house the people needed to run these industries, the town of Viewpark was born.

Viewpark combines with the neighbouring areas of Tannochside and Birkenshaw to form the Thorniewood ward. In case you have never heard of these places and are wondering why that is, none of these areas are recognised as towns by the Royal Mail, which classifies almost every address within the ward as "Uddingston, Glasgow". To confuse matters further, Uddingston proper is in South Lanarkshire, beyond the district boundary and the M 74 motorway. The postal boundaries of Uddingston have caused some confusion for outsiders, as this column will discuss in more detail in a couple of weeks' time. The ward name "Thorniewood" is shared by Thorniewood United, a local junior football team. Your columnist has been confused by this concept before, so let me explain: in Scottish football "junior" refers not to the age of the players but to the level of football, roughly equivalent to non-league in the English system.

Further to the east the M 8 motorway passes through Fortissat ward. Despite the name (which refers to an old estate that covered most of the area), this ward is based on the town and hinterland of Shotts, located on high ground roughly halfway between Glasgow and Edinburgh. Shotts was traditionally an ironworking and mining town, but with the end of industry its population has declined; one of the major local employers now is HMP Shotts, a high-security prison. The town lies on a recently-electrified railway line between Edinburgh and Glasgow.

These wards in the heart of the Central Belt were created in 2007 when Scottish local elections moved to using proportional representation. Until the Indyref Thorniewood was one of the strongest Labour wards in Scotland, with the party polling over 68% of the first preferences and winning two out of three seats in the 2007 and 2012 elections. The remaining seat was held by the SNP, who successfully defended it in a by-election in 2015 at the height of the party's powers: that by-election saw the Nationalists' candidate Steven Bonnar lead Labour candidate Hugh Gaffney 47–43 in the first round and win by 52–48 after transfers.

Gaffney eventually got elected to North Lanarkshire council two years later. On revised boundaries in May 2017 Labour polled 50% in Thorniewood ward and the SNP 39%, the seat count remaining at 2–1 to Labour. A month later Gaffney was elected to the Westminster Parliament, defeating single-term SNP MP Phil Boswell by 1,586 votes on a swing of over 13% in the local seat of Coatbridge, Chryston and Bellshill. The SNP hold the local Scottish Parliament constituency of Uddingston and Bellshill, having gained it from Labour in 2016.

The Fortissat ward also originally elected three councillors, and in 2007 it returned one Labour councillor, one SNP member and independent Charlie Cefferty. The 2012 election here is notable for Labour candidate Francis Fallan topping the poll but not getting elected. On first preferences he was one vote ahead of his running-mate Jim Robertson and two votes ahead of Cefferty, but there was an SNP quota, Cefferty was elected on Conservative transfers and Robertson (who was seeking re-election) picked up more transfers from the Tories and SNP than Fallan did.

The 2017 boundary review for North Lanarkshire expanded Fortissat ward from three councillors to four, with the addition of the village of Morningside from Murdostoun ward. In May 2017 the expanded ward gave 36% to Labour, 29% to the SNP, 13% to the Conservatives, 11% to a "No Referendum Maintain Union Pro-Brexit" candidate (that is a registered description of the British Union and Sovereignty Party, now the British Unionist Party) and 10% to Cefferty. Labour won two seats, the SNP one and the Conservatives one; during the count Cefferty overtook the pro-Brexit candidate on SNP transfers and the pro-Brexit transfers went strongly to the Conservatives. Labour and the Tories followed up that good performance in June's general election in the local seat, Airdrie and Shotts, which the SNP held over Labour by just 195 votes.

Since June 2017 both Fortissat and Thorniewood wards have had by-elections. Fortissat was first out of the blocks, because the newly-elected Conservative councillor Sandy Thornton appears to have decided that he didn't actually want to be a councillor after all. He didn't sign his declaration of acceptance of office, and once the deadline for doing so had expired his seat was declared vacant.

The resulting Fortissat by-election in September 2017* saw the Labour vote increase from 36% to 38%, the British Union and Sovereignty Party move into second place with 23% and the SNP fall to 21%. The Conservatives, who were defending the seat, finished fourth with just 11%. Labour picked up most of the SNP transfers to comfortably defeat the BUSP 62–38 in the final count and gain the seat.

The Thorniewood by-election came two years later in September 2019† after Labour councillor Hugh Gaffney MP decided to concentrate on his parliamentary duties. Labour held the resulting by-election with a clear swing to the SNP since May 2017: the Labour lead was 44–39 on first preferences and 55–45 after transfers. In retrospect, that was a bad move for Gaffney: when a general election came around three months later he saw his majority of 1,586 over the SNP turn into a 5,624-vote majority for his former ward colleague Steven Bonnar. Bonnar has now resigned from North Lanarkshire council in his turn, and given the changed parliamentary arithmetic he can reasonably expect a longer term on the green benches than Gaffney enjoyed.

The Nationalists may be riding high in the polls but they will be doing well if they hold either of these by-elections—and they will need to win both to become the largest party on North Lanarkshire council, which currently stands at 30 Labour councillors (who form a minority administration), 29 for the SNP, eight Conservatives, eight independents and these two vacancies.

For the Thorniewood by-election the Scottish National Party have reselected Eve Cunnington, who was the runner-up in the previous by-election. The Labour candidate is Helen Loughran, a Tannochside community councillor. Also standing in Thorniewood are Oyebola Ajala for the Conservatives, Rosemary McGowan for the Greens, independent candidate Joseph Budd and UKIP's Daryl Gardner. ‡

The defending SNP candidate for Fortissat is Sarah Quinn, a third-year university student who until recently represented the local constituency of Airdrie and Shotts in the Scottish Youth Parliament. Labour, who won the previous by-election, have selected Peter Kelly who is described as a local community activist. Despite their second-place finish last time there is no British Unionist Party candidate now, so it will be interesting to see what happens to their

* *Andrew's Previews 2017*, page 242. † *Andrew's Previews 2019*, page 292. ‡ *North Lanarkshire, Thorniewood*: first preferences Lab 998 SNP 944 Ind 518 C 212 Grn 53 UKIP 15; final Lab 1263 SNP 1160 [Lab gain from SNP]

Parliamentary constituency: Airdrie and Shotts
Scottish Parliament constituency: Airdrie and Shotts (almost all)
Sept 2017 by-election Lab 1420 British Union and Sovereignty Party 858 SNP 761 C 424 Ind 184 Grn 24 UKIP 18
May 2017 first preferences Lab 1840 SNP 1465 C 670 No Referendum Maintain Union Pro-Brexit 559 Ind 509

Figure 1: North Lanarkshire, Fortissat

Parliamentary constituency: Coatbridge, Chryston and Bellshill
Scottish Parliament constituency: Uddingston and Bellshill
Sept 2019 by-election Lab 1362 SNP 1202 C 296 LD 168 Grn 46
May 2017 first preferences Lab 2354 SNP 1811 C 519

Figure 2: North Lanarkshire, Thorniewood

vote. Perhaps it could end up predominantly with one of the other candidates: the Conservatives' Ben Callaghan, the Greens' Kyle Davidson or UKIP's Neil Wilson.*

All of these candidates were originally selected for the aborted by-elections in November and have been renominated for these polls. If they had gone ahead the November by-elections would also have had Lib Dem candidates, but that party appears to have decided not to bother this time round.

* *North Lanarkshire, Fortissat*: first preferences Lab 1071 SNP 965 C 656 Grn 69 UKIP 31; final Lab 1408 SNP 1026 [Lab gain from SNP]

11th March 2021

Three local by-elections in Scotland on 11th March 2021:

Aird and Loch Ness

Highland council; caused by the death of Conservative councillor George Cruickshank who had served since 2017.

Welcome to the heart of the Scottish Highlands. We're in the Great Glen, a massive geological fault which runs in a straight line from Inverness to Fort William and creates a natural travel route through the mountains. The Great Glen is navigable to vessels on the Caledonian Canal, which links together a series of lochs along the route of which the largest is Loch Ness.

It's difficult to overestimate the scale of Loch Ness. This is the second-deepest loch in Scotland and the largest body of water by volume in the UK, containing more water than all the lakes in England and Wales put together. The water is extremely murky thanks to all the peat in the surrounding soil. Over the years a large number of people who should probably have known better have claimed to see something unexplained swimming in the loch's waters, and the so-called Loch Ness Monster has been a boon to Scottish tourism for decades.

The Loch Ness Monster has had political consequences as well. In 1962 the Loch Ness Phenomena Investigation Bureau was founded, with a brief of looking for the monster, by a group of worthies including the WWF conservationist Sir Peter Scott and the naval war hero David James. At the time James was the Conservative MP for Brighton Kemptown, which you might notice is quite a long way from Loch Ness. Legend has it that his neglect of his constituency in favour of searching for a non-existent Scottish animal was one factor in James losing his seat to Labour by seven votes in the 1964 general election.

The area around Loch Ness is sparsely populated compared to the Aird, which lies immediately to the west of Inverness along the south bank of the Beauly Firth. The Beauly Firth terminates at Beauly, which as its French name (*beau lieu*) suggests is a beautiful place. Beauly is the railhead for the Aird and Loch Ness ward, being the first stop out of Inverness on the Far North Line.

This area was controlled for centuries by the Lords Lovat from their base at Beaufort Castle near Beauly. Unfortunately aristocracy doesn't pay what it used to, and the 15th Lord Lovat, Simon Fraser, sold Beaufort Castle to the Stagecoach millionaire Ann Gloag in 1995 to meet an inheritance tax bill. Lovat's Second World War service was even more high-profile than James'; as an officer in the Commandos, he was involved in the Lofoten, Hardelot and Dieppe raids, and he was piped ashore at Sword Beach on D-Day by his personal piper. Hitler put a price of 100,000 Reichsmarks on his capture, dead or alive.

That prize was never claimed, and once the war was over Lovat served for decades on the Inverness county and district councils. These were swept away in 1996, the year after his death, in favour of the modern Highland Council. Originally this was elected by first-past-the-post, which led to an independent majority and a large number of unopposed returns. The introduction of proportional representation in 2007 led to contested elections throughout and resulted in established parties winning seats.

Aird and Loch Ness ward dates from the introduction of PR in 2007. Its first two elections, in 2007 and 2012, both returned two independent councillors (Margaret Davidson and Helen Carmichael) and one each from the SNP (Drew Hendry) and the Lib Dems (Hamish Wood). SNP councillor Drew Hendry became leader of the Highland council after the 2012 election, and in May 2015 he was elected as MP for Inverness, Nairn, Badenoch and Strathspey. He resigned from the Highland council to concentrate on his Westminster duties, and the resulting by-election in October 2015 was won by the Lib Dem candidate Jean Davis.

Going into the 2017 election, fought on slightly revised boundaries, the Lib Dems were defending two seats here and lost them both. Independent councillor Margaret Davidson topped the poll with 28% of the first preferences and was re-elected on the first count; the SNP polled 22% with Emma Knox avenging her defeat in the by-election; the Conservative candidate George Cruickshank polled 20% and was elected here after two previous failed attempts; and independent councillor Helen Carmichael was re-elected to the final seat with 12% of the vote, ahead of the Lib Dems' Jean Davis who polled 10%. On the decisive fifth count, Carmichael was 289 votes ahead of Davis with only an SNP surplus of 258 left to transfer.

The 2017 Highland council election returned a hung council, with 28 independent councillors, 22 for the SNP, 10 each for the Tories and Lib Dems, 3 Labour and a single Green councillor. The current administration is a coalition

Parliamentary constituency: Inverness, Nairn, Badenoch and Strathspey (part: former Kirkhill, Loch Ness East and Loch Ness West wards); Ross, Skye and Lochaber (part: former Beauly and Strathglass ward)
Scottish Parliament constituency: Skye, Lochaber and Badenoch
May 2017 first preferences Ind 1405 SNP 1128 C 998 Ind 625 LD 515 Grn 388

Figure 3: Highland, Aird and Loch Ness

of the main independent group, the Lib Dems and Labour, and is unlikely to be affected by the outcome of this by-election.

The usual Scottish disclaimers apply here: Votes at 16 and the Alternative Vote are in use, and with a political scene as fragmented as that transfers could turn out to be very important. Defending for the Conservatives is Gavin Berkenheger, a geologist who runs a company looking for gold in Scotland. Berkenheger failed to strike gold with his previous attempt to win election to the Highland council, finishing as runner-up in the 2018 Wester Ross, Strathpeffer and Lochalsh by-election[*]. Maybe this area will prove to be a better prospect? With 40% of the first preferences going to independent candidates you cannot rule out a challenge from the single independent this time: David Fraser gives an address in Drumnadrochit on Loch Ness, where he is chair of the Glen Urquhart community council. The SNP have selected Gordon Shanks, who came to the Highlands over 20 years ago to study forestry and never left. The Lib Dem candidate is Martin Robertson, and completing an all-male ballot paper are Ryan Mackintosh for the Scottish Greens and the ward's first Labour candidate since 2012, Bill Moore.[†]

Leaderdale and Melrose

Scottish Borders council; caused by the death of Scottish National Party councillor Kevin Drum at the age of 60. He had served since 2017.

From the Highlands we come south to the border region, an upland area dividing Scotland from Northumberland. Part of the border between England and Scotland is formed by the River Tweed, whose valley forms an easy route into the interior. This may not have the grandeur of the Highlands, but the Borders have a charm all their own.

As is demonstrated by Scott's View (Figure 4), a favourite place of the author Sir Walter Scott whose baronial pile at Abbotsford is somewhere beyond the Eildon Hills in the middle distance. To the right of those hills is the town of Melrose, which grew up in the twelfth century around a Cistercian abbey

[*] *Andrew's Previews 2018*, page 428. [†] *Highland, Aird and Loch Ness*: first preferences Ind 997 SNP 994 C 824 LD 300 Grn 272 Lab 133; final Ind 1663 SNP 1211 [Ind gain from C]

Figure 4: Scott's View

founded by King David I. The abbey thrived up to the wars of religion in the 17th century, and a number of Scottish kings are buried there including the heart of Robert of Bruce; the casket containing his heart was twice excavated in the twentieth century before being reinterred.

In recent years Melrose has been opened up to tourists without access to road transport. The Borders Railway opened in September 2015, terminating at Tweedbank station a couple of miles away from the town and within the boundary of this ward. Although Tweedbank doesn't get a namecheck in the ward name, it is now the area's largest population centre.

To the right of Scott's viewpoint is the valley of the Leader Water, called Leaderdale in this ward name and Lauderdale in nearly every other context. With its north-south orientation Lauderdale was a natural route for Dere Street, the main Roman road from Hadrian's Wall to the Antonine Wall; Dere Street and its modern replacement, the A 68 Edinburgh–Jedburgh–Carter Bar road, have formed a major transport link through the borders for centuries. The major population centre in the valley is Lauder, which is just about within commuting distance of Edinburgh and as such has a fast-growing population.

Lauderdale had been covered by a number of Conservative wards in the 2003 elections to Scottish Borders council, but Melrose and Tweedbank had voted for independent candidates that year. In 2003 independent councillor David Parker thrashed the Conservative candidate in Lower Langlee and Tweedbank ward by 1,113 votes to 69, and Parker has continued in that vein by topping the poll in all three ordinary elections to the expanded ward since 2007. In 2007 he polled 30% of the first preferences, far ahead of a packed field for the other two seats: the Conservatives started in second place in 16%, the Lib Dems and the Borders Party, a localist group opposed to the planned rail link to Edinburgh, polled 15% each and the SNP 14%. In the final count the SNP were eliminated, and their transfers gave the final two seats to the Lib Dem candidate John Paton-Day and the Borders Party candidate Nicholas Watson. The Conservatives missed out. Paton-Day lost his seat to the SNP in 2012 by the narrow margin of 21 votes.

In 2013 the Borders Party councillor Nicholas Watson resigned, prompting a by-election. Without David Parker on the ballot, this time the Conservatives' Rachael Hamilton polled the most first preferences: 28%, to 23% for the new Borders Party candidate Iain Gillespie, 21% for the Lib Dems and 18% for the SNP. The SNP and Lib Dem transfers went to Gillespie, who overtook the Conservatives to hold the by-election for the Borders Party by a 53–47 margin over Hamilton. Rachael Hamilton has bounced back from that disappointment: she is now the MSP for the Ettrick, Roxburgh and Berwickshire constituency, the safest Conservative seat in Scotland (although that might not be saying much these days).

The most recent election for this ward was in May 2017 and saw the Conservatives finally break through here: they had 32% of the first preferences against 25% for David Parker, 18% for the new SNP candidate Kevin Drum, and 11% for the outgoing Borders Party councillor Iain Gillespie who sought re-election as an independent candidate and nearly got it when the Unionist transfers lined up behind him. Drum eventually won the final seat by a margin of 44 votes.

Again, this is a ward with a large independent vote. Had the May 2017 votes been for one seat then David Parker would have won it with a 406-vote margin over the lead Conservative Tom Miers; if we exclude Parker from the reckoning, then Iain Gillespie would have beaten Miers by 100 votes. In neither case are the SNP particularly close to winning, which will concern the Nationalists as they are the ones defending this by-election. A Nationalist loss here would likely be a boost to the Conservative-Independent coalition running Scottish Borders council; the 2017 election here returned 15 Conservatives, 9 for the SNP, 8 independents and two Lib Dems.

The defending SNP candidate is John Paton Day, who has contested every previous election in this ward as the Liberal Democrat candidate and was a Lib Dem councillor here from 2007 to 2012. The Conservatives have selected Jenny Linehan, a lawyer from Melrose. There are two independent candidates: Mary

Parliamentary constituency: Berwickshire, Roxburgh and Selkirk
Scottish Parliament constituency: Midlothian South, Tweeddale and Lauderdale
May 2017 first preferences C 1457 Ind 1149 SNP 811 Ind 510 LD 426 Ind 202
May 2013 by-election C 956 Borders Party 814 LD 744 SNP 613 Lab 235 UKIP 105; final Borders Party 1444 C 1283
May 2012 first preferences Ind 1304 Borders 621 SNP 558 C 441 LD 439 Lab 225
May 2007 first preferences Ind 1362 C 713 LD 703 Borders Party 692 SNP 640 Ind 394 Ind 78

Figure 5: Scottish Borders, Leaderdale and Melrose

Douglas gives an address in Galashiels, while Karen Wilks works for the Citizens' Advice Bureau in Musselburgh. Also standing are Jonny Adamson for the Liberal Democrats, Michael Needham for the Greens and Scott Redpath for Labour.*

Livingston South

West Lothian council; caused by the resignation of Scottish National Party councillor Peter Johnston, who retired last year after a 35-year career in local government. He was first elected in 1985 to the former West Lothian district council, had led the West Lothian SNP group since 1992, and twice served as Leader of the Council.

And now for something completely different. We return to the Central Belt of Scotland for a trip to the southern of three wards covering the town of Livingston. This is a New Town, built in the 1960s on land whose main previous use had been for mining shale oil. In the days before the discovery of liquid oil reserves West Lothian was the centre of the world's first oil boom, and by 1870 shale was being mined here at the rate of 3 million tons a year.

Shale mining finally ended in 1962 with the designation of Livingston as a new town. After six decades of development, Livingston is now the eighth-largest settlement in Scotland and has a diverse economic base, with electronics, distribution, a Sky TV call centre being major employers. Much recent attention has focused on the Valneva biotech factory, which is busily making a proposed new COVID-19 vaccine that's currently at the clinical trials stage.

Valneva's factory is within the boundary of this ward, next to the Edinburgh–Shotts–Glasgow railway line. On this line is the Livingston South railway station, which has recently been rebuilt as part of an electrification scheme. The railway station is some distance from the town centre, which lies within this ward on the south bank of the River Almond. Transport geeks will also note that along the

* *Scottish Borders, Leaderdale and Melrose*: first preferences C 1380 SNP 1042 LD 538 Douglas 159 Grn 152 Lab 115 Wilks 69; final C 1653 SNP 1297 [C gain from SNP]

Parliamentary constituency: Livingston
Scottish Parliament constituency: Almond Valley
May 2017 first preferences SNP 3359 Lab 2919 C 1594 Grn 200 LD 144
May 2012 first preferences Lab 3288 SNP 2890 C 374 Action to Save St John's Hospital 312
May 2007 first preferences Lab 3665 SNP 3422 C 527 LD 420 Ind 341 SSP 115

Figure 6: West Lothian, Livingston South

ward's eastern boundary is the Cousland Interchange, Scotland's only surviving cloverleaf road junction and one of only two in the UK.

The boundaries of this ward have been unchanged since 2007. In its first two elections Labour and the SNP were very close to each other and both above 40% of the vote, which gave both parties two seats: Lawrence Fitzpatrick (the current council leader, who has topped the poll here in every election to date) and Danny Logue for Labour, Peter Johnston and John Muir for the SNP. In 2017 the Labour vote fell below 40% and Danny Logue lost the second Labour seat to the Conservative candidate Peter Heggie; on the SNP side John Muir retired and was replaced by Moira Shemilt. Shares of the vote were 41% for the SNP, 36% for Labour and 19% for the Conservatives. Had the votes been counted for one seat, Labour's Fitzpatrick would have benefited from Conservative transfers to beat the SNP's Johnston by 54–46.

The SNP are in opposition on West Lothian council, which is run by a Labour administration with Conservative support. Going into this by-election the Nationalists and Labour are on 12 seats each with 7 Conservatives and an independent holding the balance of power, so a Labour gain will result in them overtaking the SNP to become the largest party on the council.

Defending for the SNP is Maria MacAulay. Labour have selected Gordon Connolly, a former bandsman in the Royal Scots who manages the village hall in Murieston. The Conservatives had to re-run their selection after their original candidate Eddie Millar was dropped for dubious social media posts; the replacement Tory candidate is Douglas Smith. Also standing are Cameron Glasgow for the Scottish Green Party, Caron Lindsay for the Liberal Democrats, the aforementioned Eddie Millar as an independent candidate, and John Mumford for UKIP.*

* *West Lothian, Livingston South*: first preferences SNP 2465 Lab 1382 C 989 Ind 332 Grn 234 LD 185 UKIP 29; final SNP 2703 Lab 1579 C 1124

18th March 2021

There are seven local by-elections on 18th March 2021. In contrast to last week's Scottish polls where the SNP went backwards in the seat count, this week the Nationalists are on the front foot with opportunities for gains in Glasgow from Labour and the Conservatives, while the Lib Dems and an independent will defend two seats in Argyll and Bute. But Andrew's Previews starts this week by returning to Wales for the first time in twelve months, with Labour, Plaid Cymru and independent defences in the former county of Clwyd. Read on...

Corwen

Denbighshire council; caused by the death of Plaid Cymru councillor Huw Jones.

Things are looking up in Wales. The rugby is going well. The daffodils are in bloom. The fields are filling with lambs. Spring is in the air, and the first shoots of democracy are starting to sprout. Welcome to the first Welsh local by-elections in over twelve months.

I'm going to start this week with a seat which has been vacant throughout that 12-month period. Huw "Chick" Jones died in February 2020 at the age of 62. He was president of and a coach at Corwen FC, and committed to local sport and leisure; earlier this year Corwen's leisure centre was renamed in his honour.

The town of Corwen lies on the old road from London to Holyhead, in the Dee valley under the shadow of the Berwyn mountains. This was an important place in Welsh history: Owain Glyndŵr had a manor in the valley at Glyndyfrdwy,

---

Parliamentary and Senedd constituency: Clwyd South
May 2017 result PC unopposed
May 2012 result PC unopposed
May 2008 result PC 531 Ind 311 C 77 Ind 43
June 2004 result Ind 307 PC 276 C 142 Ind 97 Ind 95

Figure 7: Denbighshire, Corwen

and it was here in September 1400 that he was proclaimed Prince of Wales. A statue of Glyndŵr on horseback was erected in Corwen in 2007.

Glyndyfrdwy is now a stop on the preserved Llangollen Railway, which runs down the valley to Llangollen linking together several villages within the Corwen ward. The preservationists have almost reached Corwen, but the original Corwen station site and buildings are unavailable due to new ownership: it's now the showroom for Corwen's largest employer, Ifor Williams Trailers.

Although Corwen was part of Merionethshire back in the day, it was included within Clwyd in the 1970s reorganisation and has been within the county of Denbighshire since 1996. Huw Jones had represented Corwen for Plaid Cymru since 2008, when he defeated the previous independent councillor Nigel Roberts by a 55–32 margin; Jones and Roberts had also been the top two at the previous election in 2004, when Roberts won narrowly. Nobody had opposed Huw Jones' re-elections in 2012 and 2017, so this will be the first contested local election in Corwen for 13 years. The Returning Officer has been so keen to get this vacancy filled that the by-election was originally rescheduled for 18th February this year, before changes to the rules in Wales forced a four-week postponement.

The 2017 election to Denbighshire council returned 16 Conservative councillors, 13 Labour, 9 Plaid Cymru, 8 independents and a Lib Dem (who sits within the Independent group on the council). Every group except Labour is represented in the administration, with the independent group supplying the council leader. Corwen is part of the Clwyd South constituency, which was fought in 1997 by a Conservative candidate called Boris Johnson. (Anybody know what happened to him? Answers on a postcard, etc. etc.) Johnson's successors have had better luck in that Clwyd South was one of the Welsh seats which fell to the Conservatives in December 2019; it looks safe enough for Labour in the Senedd based on the 2016 results, but then 2016 was a much better Labour performance. Not that you should try to read too much into national trends from this result of course, particularly as this by-election has no Conservative candidate.

Defending for Plaid Cymru is Alan Hughes, a married father-of-two working in the health and social care sector. He is up against two Corwen town councillors: Lisa Davies for the Liberal Democrats and Gordon Hughes for Labour.*

Eirias

Conwy council; caused by the death of independent councillor Dave Cowans in September 2020 at the age of 73.

* *Denbighshire, Corwen*: PC 480 Lab 148 LD 104

Our two other Welsh by-elections today are rather more urban in character. We start on the north coast with the Eirias division, which is the western of the two electoral divisions covering the village of Old Colwyn. This was the original village from which the seaside resort of Colwyn Bay, a couple of miles to the west, grew; the beach does extend to the seafront of Old Colwyn, but you have to cross the busy A 55 road and railway line to get there.

The Eirias division extends south along the Llanelian Road to take in Ysgol Bryn Elian, the local secondary school, and the home ground of Colwyn Bay FC. Despite the name, the division does not include the public open space and sports complex of Eirias Park, which is within the Colwyn Bay community boundary.

Colwyn Bay was the home of a district of its own until 1996, when it was incorporated within the Conwy county borough along with Llandudno, Conwy itself and a rural hinterland which is large but sparsely populated. Nearly all of Conwy county borough's population lives along the coastal strip. Eirias division elects two members of the council.

Colwyn Bay is the major town in the Clwyd West parliamentary constituency, which since 2007 has been Conservative-held at both Westminster and Senedd level. However, the largest proportion of Conwy's local councillors are independents. The 2017 election returned 21 independents against 16 Conservatives, 10 Plaid Cymru councillors (mostly from the interior), 8 Labour and 4 Lib Dems. The independents are not a united bloc: in fact there are currently four independent groups on the council, which is run by the Conservatives in coalition with some of the independent councillors.

Throughout this century elections in Eirias have been dominated by independent councillor Bob Squire, who has topped the poll in every election from at least 2004 to date with very large shares of the vote. Dave Cowans had sat on Conwy council since 1999, originally being elected as a Labour councillor for the other Old Colwyn division (which is simply but confusingly called Colwyn). After losing that seat in 2008, he transferred here as an independent candidate in 2012 and won with a majority of 22 votes over the Conservatives. In the 2017 Welsh local elections Squire and Cowans were opposed only by a single Conservative candidate, whom Cowans defeated by an increased but still small majority of 58 votes.

There will be rather more choice for the electors in this by-election. One independent candidate has come forward to replace Cowans; she is local resident Gail Jones, who is married with three grown-up children and "has engaged with local community issues, such as scrutinising local planning applications". The Conservatives have selected Debra Jones, a businesswoman who sits on the Bay of Colwyn town council (which fuses together Old Colwyn, Colwyn Bay

Parliamentary and Senedd constituency: Clwyd West
May 2017 result Ind 707/458 C 400
May 2012 result Ind 687/293 C 271/185 LD 185 PC 161
May 2008 result Ind 820/686 C 355 BNP 102
June 2004 result Ind 807 LD 543 PC 256 Lab 183

Figure 8: Conwy, Eirias

and Rhos-on-Sea). Also standing are former social care and housing worker Patrick Cahill for Plaid Cymru, Bay of Colwyn town councillor and former Metropolitan and North Wales police officer Paul Richards for Labour, town planner Adam Turner for the Green Party (who hit the headlines* during the campaign after North Wales police briefly stopped his leaflets being distributed) and childminder Lisa Wilkins for the Liberal Democrats.†

Maesydre

Wrexham council; caused by the resignation of Labour councillor Paul Jones in September 2020 for family reasons. He had served since 2017.

We finish our tour of Wales in the largest town within North Wales. Wrexham has been a market town and a place of industry for centuries: the traditional brewing and leather industries were joined in the Industrial Revolution by ironworking and coalmining. By the late twentieth century all this was gone, leaving behind a town with an attractive town centre, some high-technology manufacturing and a growing sideline in finance. And maybe a bit of Hollywood sparkle as well: last month the North American actors Ryan Reynolds and Rob McElhenney completed their takeover of the local football club, Wrexham FC.

The Maesydre division of Wrexham runs north-east from the town centre, between the Chester Road and the Holt Road. Included within the boundaries are the Waterworld leisure centre, the town's law courts, a couple of supermarkets and a residential area along Park Avenue.

The first three Welsh local elections this century had elected Liberal Democrat councillors for Maesydre division, quite comfortably. This changed in 2017, when the Lib Dems fell to third place and Labour went from third to top; shares of the vote were 44% for Labour, 24% for the Conservatives and 21% for the Liberal Democrats.

This was a rare bright spot for Labour in Wrexham 2017, which was an election where they made a nett loss of eleven council seats. Following the 2017 elec-

* `https://tinyurl.com/f3y6ptt4` † *Conwy, Eirias*: Ind 235 C 180 Grn 91 Lab 85 PC 66 LD 33

Parliamentary and Assembly constituency: Wrexham
May 2017 result Lab 249 C 137 LD 119 Ind 59
May 2012 result LD 242 Ind 134 Lab 132 C 45
May 2008 result LD 434 Lab 210
June 2004 result LD 337 Forward Wales 161 Lab 114

Figure 9: Wrexham, Maesydre

tion half of the 52 Wrexham councillors were independents, with Labour holding 12 seats, the Conservatives 9, Plaid Cymru 3 and the Lib Dems 2. Wrexham was one of the "red wall" parliamentary constituencies to fall to the Conservatives in 2019; it will undoubtedly be a seat to watch in the Senedd election campaign over the next month and a half.

Defending for Labour is Tom Stanford, who already represents the Maesydre area on the Acton community council (which covers the five north-eastern electoral divisions of Wrexham town). The Conservatives have selected Cathy Brown, a retired NHS nurse and former Clwyd county councillor. The Lib Dem candidate also has previous local government experience: Royal Navy veteran and former schoolteacher Roger Davies has previously sat on Devon county council and Exeter city council. Completing the ballot paper are independent candidate Clive Ray, and Becca Martin for Plaid Cymru.*

Baillieston; and Partick East/Kelvindale

Glasgow council; caused respectively by the disqualifications of Labour councillor Jim Coleman and independent councillor Tony Curtis, who had originally been elected for the Conservatives. Both had failed to attend any meetings of the council in six months.

We travel north to Scotland for the remaining four by-elections this week. All of these are linked together by the River Clyde; we shall come presently to two wards on the shore of the Firth of Clyde, but before that there is Glasgow to consider.

There is also the six-month non-attendance rule to consider. At first sight, this is pretty simple. If you are a member of a local authority and you don't attend a meeting of the council for six months, then you get disqualified and your council seat is automatically vacated.

However, there are a number of wrinkles in the definition of those trouble-

* *Wrexham, Maesydre*: PC 150 Lab 133 C 123 LD 47 Ind 36 [PC gain from Lab]

some words "attend" and "meeting". Full council can resolve to give leave of absence to any councillor who may need it (for example, because of long-term illness) and that overrides the non-attendance rule, although such leave has to be given before the disqualification kicks in. At the start of the current pandemic, a number of councils gave leave of absence to their entire membership because of concerns over when the next meeting would be.

The Coronavirus Act 2020 answered those concerns, and took a major step towards bringing our local authorities into the twenty-first century, by allowing council meetings to be held remotely using your networking suite of choice. This has kept us entertained by bringing to prominence the critically-acclaimed satirical drama known as Handforth Parish Council Planning and Environment Committee, but the serious point of this change is that remote meetings have allowed our councils to keep functioning. Any councillor who logs into a remote meeting of Full Council or a committee which they sit on counts as having attended a meeting for the purposes of the six-month non-attendance rule.

With this change having made life significantly easier for many councillors, it's rather strange that Glasgow city council has had two of its members fall foul of the non-attendance rule in the last couple of months. I'll come to former councillor Curtis in a moment, but the suggestion in respect of Jim Coleman's disqualification is that he simply couldn't make the technology work.

It's a sad end to a council career that has lasted for decades. Coleman was the longest-serving member of Glasgow city council, having been first elected all the way back in 1988 with continuous service in the council chamber since then. A stalwart of the local Labour party, he had served for a number of years as deputy leader of the city, stepping up to interim leader for a short period in 2015; he had also served in the past as the chair of Strathclyde Regional Transport.

Since 2007 Jim Coleman's ward was Baillieston, at the eastern end of the Glasgow city council area. Baillieston was a small mining village until the twentieth century, when the Garrowhill housing estate was built between the Edinburgh and Glasgow Roads; this was a private development, and almost a century on Garrowhill is still one of the least-deprived areas of Glasgow. The area was annexed by the city in 1975 and has filled with houses since then, playing on the good railway and motorway links to the city centre. Much of Springhill went up in the 1980s and 1990s, as did a sculpture by Andy Scott next to the M 8 motorway, "Heavy Horse". Modern Glasgow's largest industrial area, the Queenslie Industrial Estate, lies within the ward boundary. All this development led to Baillieston giving its name to a parliamentary constituency from 1997 to 2005 (for Westminster) and 2011 (for Holyrood).

Development was still going on in the twenty-first century in the Broomhouse area, to the south of the Glasgow–Whifflet railway line. Broomhouse gets its post from Uddingston which has led to some confusion over whether it's part of Glasgow or not; administratively, it's definitely within the city boundary. Much of the area around Broomhouse was occupied by the estate of Calderpark House, which in 1939 was bought by the Zoological Society of Glasgow and West of Scotland. The result was Glasgow Zoo, which occupied the site from 1947 until 2003, when financial problems forced its closure. Much of the zoo's site has now been redeveloped for new housing. One of Broomhouse's most famous residents is someone you might be seeing a lot of on the television at the moment: the First Minister of Scotland and Scottish National Party leader, Nicola Sturgeon, is an elector here.

Nicola Sturgeon worked her way up to her current position through a number of unsuccessful election campaigns, starting all the way back in April 1992 when she was the SNP candidate for the local Glasgow Shettleston parliamentary seat. At the time, she was a 21-year-old law student at Glasgow University and she was the youngest parliamentary candidate in Scotland that year. Her other failed early attempts to gain elected office include the last Strathclyde Regional Council election in 1994, when Sturgeon was the SNP candidate for the Baillieston/Mount Vernon ward which had a similar area to the present-day Baillieston ward; on that occasion she lost to Labour candidate Douglas Hay by 4,908 votes to 2,140.

In 1997 Nicola Sturgeon narrowly and controversially lost in the Glasgow Govan constituency to Mohammed Sarwar, who became the first Muslim MP for Scotland and the first British MP to swear the Oath of Allegiance on the Koran. Sarwar was subsequently charged with electoral offences, but acquitted at trial. He served in the Commons until 2010, then left the UK to continue his political career in Pakistan where he currently serves as Governor of the Punjab. Anas Sarwar, Mohammed's son, will lead the Scottish Labour Party against Nicola Sturgeon's SNP in May's forthcoming Holyrood election.

Sturgeon did eventually make the SNP breakthrough in Glasgow, winning the Govan constituency at the 2007 Holyrood election after serving for eight years as an SNP regional MSP for the city. On the same day the Baillieston ward of Glasgow held its first election, with Labour leading the SNP 46–33 on first preferences and both parties winning two seats . Jim Coleman and the aforementioned Douglas Hay were the Labour councillors; John Mason and David McDonald were the SNP winners.

The following year David Marshall, the Labour MP for the local Glasgow East constituency, resigned due to a stress-related illness. This forced a Westminster by-election. In 2005 Marshall had enjoyed the third-largest Labour majority in Scotland at 13,507 votes; but this was overturned in the by-election by SNP councillor John Mason, who won the by-election by 11,277 votes to 10,912, a majority of 365. Mason promptly resigned from Glasgow council, and the SNP held the resulting September 2008 Baillieston ward by-election with a majority of 198 votes after transfers. Labour councillor Douglas Hay resigned shortly afterwards, and Labour held the resulting November 2008 Baillieston ward by-election with a majority of 190 votes after transfers. John Mason lost his seat in Westminster in 2010, but returned to elected politics a year later as the SNP member of the Scottish Parliament for the local seat of Glasgow Shettleston.

There were major changes to Glasgow's ward map for the 2017 election, with an increase in the number of councillors forcing the creation of two new wards. The knock-on effects saw Baillieston ward reduced in size with a cut from four councillors to three. This time the SNP topped the poll with 45% of the first preferences, to 29% for Labour and 21% for the Conservatives. The SNP and Labour both had one seat, and Labour transfers ensured that the Conservatives won the final seat with a margin of 170 votes over the second SNP candidate David Turner. Turner had won the September 2008 by-election, but now lost his seat to his running-mate Elaine Ballantyne.

One of the new Glasgow wards created in the 2017 redistribution was Partick East/Kelvindale, which took in territory from the former wards of Hillhead, Maryhill/Kelvin (which was renamed Maryhill) and Partick West (which was renamed as Victoria Park). The northern boundary of the ward is the River Kelvin and the Forth and Clyde canal; the western boundary is the Partick–Anniesland railway line. Features of the ward include much of the Glasgow Botanic Gardens, the Hamilton Crescent cricket ground which back in 1872 hosted the first ever international football match (Scotland 0 England 0, since you asked), and the upmarket Byres Road which forms the ward's eastern boundary. The Partick and Kelvinhall subway stations link the ward to the city centre as does its main thoroughfare, the Great Western Road. And it would be remiss of me not to namecheck one of the ward's famous former residents: Hermes, the Hyndland Station cat, retired to the countryside in 2018.

Unfortunately Hermes was never eligible to vote, on account of being a cat; but as in Baillieston we do have a notable elector in this by-election. That's Allan Faulds, editor of the Scottish polling aggregator *Ballot Box Scotland**, which this column strongly recommends you include in your social media along with our very own Britain Elects.

If you were asked to draw the least economically deprived ward within the Glasgow city limits, it would be difficult to do better than Partick East/Kelvindale.

* `http://ballotbox.scot/`

Parliamentary constituency: Glasgow East
Scottish Parliament constituency: Glasgow Shettleston (part south of Glasgow–Airdrie railway line), Glasgow Provan (part north of Glasgow–Airdrie railway line)
May 2017 first preferences SNP 3090 Lab 1998 C 1454 Grn 159 LD 133 SSP 81 Libtn 20

Figure 10: Glasgow, Baillieston

Much of this area was once within the burgh of Partick (hence the Partick East part of the name), but this is really the western part of Glasgow's trendy West End. The major boundary changes since the last Scottish census in 2011 make demographic figures difficult to obtain, but in 2011 42% of the adults in the old Partick West ward were in managerial or professional occupations (compared to 25% for the city as a whole), with 17% being full-time students (compared to 14% for Glasgow as a whole).

The West End of Glasgow has not been well served by the Boundary Commissions in recent years. Partick East/Kelvindale is split between two Westminster constituencies and three Holyrood constituencies, and as stated before 2017 there were three Glasgow wards here. The 2017 election was contested by three outgoing Glasgow councillors: on the Nationalist side Kenny McLean (SNP) and Martin Bartos (Green Party) who had both previously represented Partick West, on the Unionist side Martin Rhodes (Lab) who transferred from Maryhill/Kelvin. All of them were re-elected in this politically diverse ward: shares of the vote were 34% for the SNP, 22% for the Conservatives' Tony Curtis, 18% for Labour and 16% for the Greens, with Bartos picking up transfers from the Lib Dems (who, way back in 2003, dominated this area's representation) to win the final seat very comfortably ahead of the second SNP candidate.

Tony Curtis joined Messrs McLean, Rhodes and Bartos as the Conservative councillor for Partick East/Kelvindale. Unfortunately Curtis is one of those people for whom lockdown has been a disaster: he is a gym owner, and as such he has been unable to earn a living for many months through no fault of his own. He left the Conservative party last year over that issue, and appears to have ceased to perform his council duties after that.

The 2017 election to Glasgow city council returned 39 SNP councillors, 31 Labour, 8 Conservatives and 7 Greens. The SNP topped the poll in all 23 wards of the city, and run the council in coalition with the Green Party. With the opposition defending both these by-elections from a position of weakness, there is a good chance here for the administration to increase its majority.

The usual Scottish disclaimers need to be read out here: Votes at 16 and the Alternative Vote apply, and with the fragmented political scene in Partick East/Kelvindale in particular transfers could be crucial. If we re-run the 2017

Parliamentary constituency: Glasgow North (eastern part), Glasgow North West (western part)
Scottish Parliament constituency: Glasgow Kelvin (Partickhill and Hyndland), Glasgow Maryhill and Springburn (north of Great Western Road), Glasgow Anniesland (Gartnavel Hospital and housing immediately to its north)
May 2017 first preferences SNP 3607 C 2336 Lab 1848 Grn 1727 LD 889 Ind 109

Figure 11: Glasgow, Partick East/Kelvindale

votes for one vacancy then the Tories get overtaken by Labour thanks to Green transfers, and the two-party preferred vote is 55–45 for the SNP.

This will be of some concern to the Conservatives, who are defending the seat. Their candidate is Naveed Asghar, a self-employed political analyst and interfaith champion according to his Twitter. The SNP have also selected an ethnic minority candidate: Abdul Bostani came to Glasgow 20 years ago as an Afghan refugee from the Taliban, and is hoping to become the first former refugee to win an election in Scotland. He now works as an accountant. The Labour candidate is Jill Brown. The Scottish Greens have selected Blair Anderson, a law student at the University of Glasgow (now where have we heard that before?) Completing the ballot paper are Tahir Jameel for the Lib Dems and the leader of UKIP Scotland Donald Mackay, who gives an address quite a long way from Glasgow in the Lanark area.*

Labour will also have an uphill struggle to hold their by-election in Baillieston ward, where they trail the SNP 45–29 on first preferences and 56–44 in the two-party preferred count. Their defending candidate is William Docherty, a UNISON activist and chair of the Scottish TUC's LGBT+ committee. The SNP have reselected David Turner, winner of the September 2008 Baillieston by-election and councillor for this ward from 2008 to 2017. Standing for the Conservatives is John Daly, a former headteacher. Completing the ballot paper are Lorraine McLaren for the Green Party, Daniel Donaldson for the Liberal Democrats and Christopher Ho for UKIP.†

Helensburgh and Lomond South; and Isle of Bute

Argyll and Bute council; caused respectively by the deaths of Liberal Democrat councillor Ellen Morton at the age of 76 and independent councillor Len Scoullar

* *Glasgow, Partick East/Kelvindale*: first preferences SNP 2084 Lab 1836 Grn 1200 C 1084 LD 259 UKIP 33; final Lab 2927 SNP 2812 [Lab gain from C] † *Glasgow, Baillieston*: first preferences SNP 1980 Lab 1278 C 946 Grn 200 LD 90 UKIP 26; final SNP 2133 Lab 1868 [SNP gain from Lab]

at the age of 81. Morton had served since 1999, originally for Helensburgh North ward; she had served as Depute Leader of the council, and her daughter Aileen went one better by serving as Leader of the Council from 2017 until last year. Scoullar also had continuous service since 1999, originally being elected for Bute South ward; since 2013 he had chaired Argyll and Bute's meetings as the council's Provost.

We finish with two wards on the shores of the Firth of Clyde, which form part of the Argyll and Bute council area. However, it would be rather incorrect to describe either of these as Argyll.

Consider the ward of Helensburgh and Lomond South, which covers a rural and mostly upland area on the north bank of the Firth of Clyde. The main population centre here is Cardross, on the North Clyde railway line to Helensburgh; this was the location where Robert the Bruce died in 1329, but Cardross is perhaps best known these days for St Peter's Seminary, a Brutalist building which currently lies derelict despite its huge architectural interest.

The railway continues to the Helensburgh suburb of Craigendoran, and the ward boundary wraps around the eastern side of Helensburgh to take in the town's north-east corner. The Lomond South section of the ward name refers to a few villages on the western side of Loch Lomond, including the road junction at Arden; this part of the ward lies within the Loch Lomond and the Trossachs National Park.

Cardross is only a few miles from Dumbarton, and until the 1970s this whole area (including Helensburgh) was part of the county of Dunbartonshire rather than Argyll. Indeed this ward is still part of the Dumbarton constituency of the Scottish Parliament. By contrast, Helensburgh to the Argyll and Bute council headquarters in Lochgilphead is a road journey of 65 miles, via the mountain pass at Rest and be Thankful which is often impassable in winter.

Further down the Firth of Clyde we come to the Isle of Bute. Unlike some areas this column has discussed over the years, Bute is a genuine island and the only way here is by ferry. The main ferry link to Bute doesn't go to Argyll at all: it's the regular service from Rothesay, Bute's only town, to Wemyss Bay in Renfrewshire on the far side of the Firth of Clyde. As the crow flies, Rothesay to the Argyll and Bute council headquarters in Lochgilphead is only around 20 miles, but the road journey around Loch Fyne is 75 miles, via the ferry over the Kyles of Bute at Colintraive.

Until the 1970s the Isle of Bute was the centre of a county of its own. Buteshire was based on three inhabited islands in the Firth of Clyde, taking in Arran and Great Cumbrae as well as Bute. However, since the 1990s Arran and the Cumbraes have been included within the North Ayrshire local government district, effectively splitting Buteshire up.

Parliamentary constituency: Argyll and Bute
Scottish Parliament constituency: Dumbarton
May 2017 first preferences C 1149 LD 651 SNP 525 Lab 250 Ind 248 Ind 94 UKIP 32
May 2012 first preferences LD 1195 SNP 584 C 558
October 2007 by-election LD 642 C 627 Ind 493 SNP 356; final LD 1014 C 839
May 2007 first preferences LD 1009 C 835 Ind 713 SNP 572

Figure 12: Argyll and Bute, Helensburgh and Lomond South

Since 2007 Scottish local councils have been elected using proportional representation, with each ward electing either three or four councillors. The three-councillor minimum caused some problems with respect to offshore islands, as some islands which had previously supported a single councillor found themselves merged into a larger area a ferry ride away. In response to these concerns the Islands (Scotland) Act 2018 was passed by Holyrood, and the Local Government Boundary Commission for Scotland is working away on new maps for those councils which contain populated islands.

With the three-councillor minimum removed in those cases, the draft proposals for the old Buteshire involve restoring Arran as a single-member ward of North Ayrshire; Great Cumbrae, which is too small for a councillor of its own, will continue to be linked with the mainland. There are no boundary changes proposed for the Isle of Bute ward, but in response to its falling population the LGBCS has proposed a cut in its representation from three councillors to two. It's fair to say this proposal has not found favour on Bute.

In 2003, 2007 and 2012 Bute returned two SNP councillors, Robert MacIntyre and Isobel Strong, and independent councillor Len Scoullar who topped the poll in 2007 and 2012. The 2017 election saw much change. The SNP vote fell from 42% to 33%, and they lost one of their two seats: Isobel Strong retired, and Robert MacIntyre lost his seat to his running-mate Jim Findlay. New independent candidate Jean Moffat polled 19% and was elected in second place; the Conservatives polled 17%; and Len Scoullar, despite losing half of his vote and starting in fifth place with 14%, scraped together enough transfers to beat the Conservatives for the final seat by 537 votes to 504.

Helensburgh and Lomond South ward has a very different political dynamic, being much more right-wing. Since its creation in 2007 two of its three councillors have been the late Ellen Morton for the Liberal Democrats and David Kinniburgh for the Conservatives; the third seat originally went to independent candidate Ronald Kinloch, but he died within weeks of his election in 2007 and the resulting by-election returned Lib Dem candidate Andrew Nisbet. Nisbet lost his seat in 2012 to the SNP's Richard Trail, who was re-elected in 2017. The

Parliamentary constituency: Argyll and Bute
Scottish Parliament constituency: Argyll and Bute
May 2017 first preferences SNP 828 Ind 472 C 427 Ind 340 Ind 325 Ind 85
May 2012 first preferences SNP 968 Ind 707 Lab 351 C 216 Christian Party 45
May 2007 first preferences SNP 1390 Ind 868 Ind 238 Lab 225 LD 218 C 143

Figure 13: Argyll and Bute, Isle of Bute

shares of the vote here in May 2017 were 39% for the Conservatives, 22% for the Lib Dems and 18% for the SNP; had the Tories run two candidates they might have knocked the SNP out here.

That 17-point deficit will concern the Helensburgh Lib Dems as they try to hold this by-election. They have selected Henry Boswell, who has spent 25 years working on product innovation for Proctor and Gamble. The Conservative candidate is Gemma Penfold, who runs a local dance studio. Standing for the Scottish National Party is Math Campbell-Sturgess, who has local government experience as a former councillor for Inverclyde North ward on the far side of the water. Mike Crowe, who was runner-up here in 2017 as an independent candidate, now has the Green nomination; Labour have selected Jane Kelly; and Paul Burrows is the first election candidate for the Workers Party of Britain, a left-wing group founded in 2019 by George Galloway.*

The by-election on the Isle of Bute to replace Len Scoullar has two defending independent candidates. Fraser Gillies has stood here twice before, polling 13% and finishing sixth out of seven candidates in May 2017; Liz McCabe is a local cafe-owner. The SNP have selected Kim Findlay, a solicitor who is doing her bit for the current emergency with some contact tracing work for NHS Scotland. Also standing are Peter Wallace for the Conservatives and Dawn Macdonald for Labour.†

The SNP are the largest party on Argyll and Bute council, but have been shut out of the administration by a coalition of independent councillors, the Conservatives and the Liberal Democrats. The 2017 election returned 11 SNP councillors, 10 independents, 9 Conservatives and 6 Lib Dems. As in Glasgow, it doesn't seem likely that these by-elections will disturb the ruling administration; but stranger things have happened.

* *Argyll and Bute, Helensburgh and Lomond South*: C 1206 SNP 562 LD 333 Lab 133 Grn 123 Workers Party of Britain 22 [C gain from LD] † *Argyll and Bute, Isle of Bute*: first preferences SNP 658 McCabe 411 Gillies 382 C 338 Lab 224; final McCabe 772 SNP 767

25th March 2021

There are three local by-elections on 25th March 2021, and it's a Nationalist Special with all three seats being defended by Plaid Cymru or the Scottish National Party. With whom we start, as Andrew's Previews considers the last two local by-elections in Scotland before the Holyrood elections on 6th May. Read on...

Midlothian East

Midlothian council; caused by the resignation of Scottish National Party councillor Kenneth Baird, who had served since 2017.

We start south-east of Edinburgh with the county of Midlothian. The Midlothian council area has six electoral wards, of which three cover the district's major towns of Bonnyrigg, Dalkeith and Penicuik and the other three are more rural areas. Such as Midlothian East, which stretches north-west from Soutra Hill (a summit on the A 68 road from Edinburgh to Lauderdale), and runs between Bonnyrigg and Dalkeith to the Sheriffhall Roundabout on the Edinburgh city bypass. The six-way roundabout at Sheriffhall is a notorious traffic blackspot and the powers that be have been talking about rebuilding it for years, but the fact that the junction is built on unstable ground over old mineworkings makes grade separation difficult to achieve.

It's the mineworkings that have traditionally been the mainstay of this area's economy. In fact, they spawned a new village. Mayfield was built in the 1950s to house workers for the collieries at Newtongrange and Easthouses; the collieries are gone, but the village remains.

East ward's other principal population centre is rather different in character. Eskbank is a suburb of Dalkeith and traditionally a well-heeled area; and that will only have increased with the reopening of the Borders railway line, which includes a station at Eskbank. With trains to central Edinburgh twice an hour, Eskbank handled 367,000 passengers in 2018–19 just three years after it had opened.

With a *bona fide* commuter area, a pit village and a large rural hinterland Midlothian East has something for everyone. The ward was created in 2007, when it elected one councillor each from the SNP, Labour, and the Lib Dems. The Lib Dem councillor then defected to Labour and stood for re-election in 2012 as a Labour candidate, but polled poorly and lost her seat to independent candidate Peter de Vink. The SNP and de Vink formed an administration to run Midlothian council, and East ward's SNP councillor Lisa Beattie briefly served as leader of the council following the 2012 election.

The Labour councillor for Midlothian East resigned in 2014, and the resulting by-election resulted in a narrow Labour hold; the first preferences were 33% for Labour, 32% for the SNP and 20% for independent candidate Robert Hogg, and a 34-vote lead for Labour on first preferences turned into a 69-vote lead over the SNP in the final count. This by-election came two months after the independence referendum while Scottish politics was in the middle of realigning, and was generally seen at the time as an impressive Labour performance. Mind, given that the winning Labour candidate had previously worked for the then party leader Ed Miliband as a press officer, perhaps a positive spin on the result was to be expected.

It was all change here for the May 2017 Midlothian council election, with all three incumbent councillors for East ward standing down and boundary changes removing a small corner of the ward into Bonnyrigg ward. There was a very close four-way result on the first preferences, with the Conservatives coming from nowhere to top the poll on 27%, the SNP polling 26%, Labour 23% and independent Robert Hogg on 19%. The three seats went to the Conservatives, Labour and the SNP with the Tories picking up Peter de Vink's seat. Labour went on to pick up the Midlothian constituency at the Westminster general election a month later, but lost the seat back to the SNP in December 2019. Colin Beattie, husband of former SNP ward councillor Lisa Beattie, has represented the ward in Holyrood since 2011 as part of the Midlothian North and Musselburgh constituency.

In last week's four Scottish by-elections we saw two occasions in which the candidate trailing on first preferences came from behind to win in the final count. Transfers can be crucial, and this could well be the case here as well given the fragmented political scene we start with. The usual Scottish disclaimer of Votes at 16 applies, too.

The 2017 Midlothian council election resulted in a three-way split on the council, with seven Labour councillors, six SNP and five Conservatives. The SNP subsequently became the largest party by winning a by-election in Penicuik, gaining the seat from Labour. Despite that, Labour run Midlothian council as a

Parliamentary constituency: Midlothian
Holyrood constituency: Midlothian North and Musselburgh
May 2017 first preferences C 1522 SNP 1481 Lab 1284 Ind 1064 Grn 301

Figure 14: Midlothian, Midlothian East

minority with Conservative support.

Defending for the SNP is Stuart McKenzie, from Dalkeith. The Conservatives have selected Alan Symon, who sits on the community council for Eskbank and Newbattle. The Labour candidate is Hazel Flanagan, a senior childcare practitioner who grew up in Mayfield. There is no independent candidate this time, so completing the ballot paper are Joy Godfrey for the Greens and Margaret Davis for the Liberal Democrats. The *Midlothian Advertiser* has interviewed all the candidates, and you can find out more at `https://tinyurl.com/59r5kpk6`.*

Almond and Earn

Perth and Kinross council; caused by the death of Scottish National Party councillor Henry Anderson who had served since 2012.

For other Scottish by-election we return to another ward which has appeared in Andrew's Previews before. The Almond and the Earn are two rivers in Perthshire, the Almond flowing into the Tay immediately north of Perth and the Earn reaching the sea at the head of the Firth of Tay.

The two rivers give their name to an electoral ward which covers the southern and western hinterland of the city of Perth. The largest population centre is Bridge of Earn, a commuter village south of Perth at the lowest crossing-point of the Earn. To the west of Perth on the road to Crianlarich is Methven, a village which was the location of a victory for England in 1306 in the days when England and Scotland faced off on the battlefield instead of the rugby field.

Methven (then part of the Strathalmond ward) voted SNP in the 2003 Scottish local elections, but the Almond and Earn ward took in better Conservative territory in Bridge of Earn and its first election in 2007 was a Conservative win on first preferences, with 46% against 37% for the SNP and 17% for the Liberal Democrats. However, with three seats available 46% was short of two quotas, and the SNP surplus ensured that the final seat went to the Lib Dems rather than the second Conservative candidate.

The winning Conservative here was Alan Jack, who had represented Bridge

* *Midlothian, Midlothian East*: first preferences SNP 1538 C 1279 Lab 1070 Grn 282 LD 178; final SNP 1963 C 1656

Parliamentary constituency: Ochil and South Perthshire
Holyrood constituency: Perthshire South and Kinross-shire
May 2017 first preferences C 2441 SNP 1212 LD 230 Grn 214
April 2016 by-election C 1651 SNP 1327 Lab 219 LD 157 UKIP 77
May 2012 first preferences SNP 1520 C 1112 Ind 444 Lab 369 LD 244
May 2007 first preferences C 2255 SNP 1790 LD 849

Figure 15: Perth and Kinross, Almond and Earn

of Earn since 1999. He fell out with the Tories in the 2007–12 term and stood for re-election in 2012 as an independent. The first preferences split 41% for the Conservatives, 30% for the SNP and just 12% for Jack, but the Conservatives had only stood one candidate and Jack picked up transfers from all over the place to be re-elected. His final margin was 14 votes over the second SNP candidate. This was not without controversy: Alan Jack was subsequently fined £450 for going over the campaign spending limit, but for reasons which this column doesn't fully understand he was allowed to keep his seat.

Alan Jack died in 2016 at the age of 76, and the resulting by-election[*] was a gain for the Conservatives who led the SNP 48–39 on the first count and 51–41 after transfers (with a Labour vote of 8% still to distribute). The Conservatives confirmed that by-election gain in the May 2017 local elections; on unchanged boundaries, their first preference lead over the SNP was a whopping 60–30, resulting in two seats for the Conservatives and one for the SNP.

Overall the Conservatives won the 2017 Perth and Kinross elections, with 17 seats against 15 SNP, 4 Lib Dems, 3 independents and 1 Labour councillor (for the unlikely-looking Labour area of Carse of Gowrie). The Conservatives run the council as a minority and have successfully defended two previous by-elections in this council term.

In December 2020 the SNP councillor for Almond and Earn, Harry Anderson, had put a strongly-worded post on his Facebook aimed at anti-vaxxers, subsequently telling the *Perthshire Advertiser* that he and his family would get the COVID-19 vaccine as their "civic duty"[†]. He never got the chance. By the end of the month, Harry Anderson was dead from COVID-19.

This is the first council by-election to be a direct result of the current pandemic. It will not be the last. This column maintains a list of local councillors who were taken from us by COVID-19; that list currently has seventeen names on it, including Anderson's. Given that the demographic upon which COVID wreaks the greatest havoc is the same demographic that tends to serve in our council chambers, the list could have been a lot longer.

---

[*] *Andrew's Previews 2016*, page 75. [†] `tinyurl.com/k6snxam4` (story from the *Daily Record*)

It will be an uphill struggle for the SNP to hold the 2021 Almond and Earn by-election from a 30-point deficit on first preferences. Their defending candidate is Michelle Frampton. The Tories will have reasonable hopes that they can win here in the first round; they have selected former golf professional Frank Smith. Also standing are Claire McLaren for the Lib Dems and Craig Masson for Labour.*

Llanrug

Gwynedd council, North Wales; caused by the death of Plaid Cymru councillor Charles Wyn Jones.

Croeso and welcome to the Welsh-speaking capital of the world. We're in Llanrug, a village on the northern slopes of the Snowdon massif about four miles east of Caernarfon, which was listed by the 2011 census as having 87.8% of its population able to speak Welsh—the highest proportion of any electoral division in the principality. Figures from the 2021 census, taken last weekend, will take a couple of years to come through so Llanrug's title is safe for a little while yet.

With a population of just under 2,000, Llanrug is the largest population centre in the Arfon constituency outside Bangor and Caernarfon, and it's big enough to support a secondary school, Ysgol Brynrefail, with over 700 pupils on the roll. Notable people who studied at Ysgol Brynrefail include the rugby player Rhun Williams, who was the star player in the Wales Under-20 grand slam-winning team in 2016 and subsequently made 28 appearances for Cardiff Blues, but was forced to retire from rugby last year aged 22 due to a nerve injury. As we saw at the weekend, rugby can be a cruel game sometimes. Two knights of the realm, the Chief Bard Sir T H Parry-Williams and the cycling coach Sir David Brailsford, also went to school in Llanrug, as did the former Welsh MEP Eurig Wyn.

Wyn served in the European Parliament from 1999 to 2004 as a member of Plaid Cymru, who are the dominant political force in this corner of North Wales. Charles Wyn Jones, who had represented Llanrug since the establishment of the modern Gwynedd council in 1995 and also sat on Arfon council before that, was also a Plaid Cymru member. He had served as chairman of Gwynedd council in 2004–05. Away from local government, Jones had a 30-year career with British Telecom, co-founded the Gwynedd branch of the Alzheimer's Society, and was secretary of the Llanrug Silver Band.

The present Llanrug division was created in 2004 as the northern half of the previous two-seat Llanrug division (the rest becoming Cwm-y-Glo division).

* *Perth and Kinross, Almond and Earn*: C 1819 SNP 1327 LD 267 Lab 143 [C gain from SNP]

Parliamentary and Assembly constituency: Arfon
May 2017 result PC unopposed
May 2012 result PC unopposed
May 2008 result PC 477 Ind 128
June 2004 result PC unopposed

Figure 16: Gwynedd, Llanrug

On its current boundaries, Charles Wyn Jones only once had to fight a contested election: that was in 2008, when he polled 79% of the vote in a straight fight with independent candidate Dafydd Ifan.

In the 2017 Gwynedd elections Jones was counted among the 41 Plaid Cymru councillors returned, against 26 independents, 6 councillors for the localist group Llais Gwynedd, and one each for Labour and the Lib Dems. The ruling Plaid group is now down to 38 councillors plus this vacancy - if the Llanrug by-election is lost, that will be a majority of one.

This by-election sees a record choice for the local electors with four candidates standing. Defending for Plaid Cymru is Beca Brown, a Llanrug community councillor currently working for SaySomethinginWelsh, an online language teachers' firm. To take the other candidates in alphabetical order, independent (as the ballot paper says, "Independent") candidate Martin Bristow gives an address in Y Felinheli on the Menai coast; the Lib Dems' Calum Davies is a local resident and was their parliamentary candidate for Clwyd South in 2019; and independent (as the ballot paper says, "*Annibynnol*") candidate and Ysgol Brynrefail school governor Richie Green has recently retired as a police superintendent. The Local Democracy Reporting Service have interviewed all the candidates, and you can find out more at `tinyurl.com/rxzutu4j`.*

* *Gwynedd, Llanrug*: PC 431 Green 221 LD 16 Bristow 13

1st April 2021

One by-election on 1st April 2021:

St Kingsmark

Monmouthshire council; caused by the death of Conservative councillor David Dovey.

Do not adjust your calendar. Today is April Fool's Day, and it is also Maundy Thursday. It's not so long since Maundy Thursday was a day on which elections were not allowed to be held, and even since this was legalised not that many by-elections have been scheduled for the Thursday before Easter. The proximity of the May local elections—now just five weeks away—and the prospect of paying bank holiday rates to the count staff makes a Maundy Thursday by-election a generally unappealing proposition for everyone involved.

There are now just four local by-elections left before the ordinary May elections, all of which are in south-east Wales. We will have three polls to discuss next week in the Torfaen district, but first we cross the border over the tidal River Wye to come to the town of Chepstow.

Chepstow is an important location in both English and Welsh history. It is the lowest point at which the Wye can be crossed, and as such it was fortified immediately after the Norman conquest: Chepstow Castle was founded in 1067 by the Earl of Hereford, William fitz Osbern. As a free port under the jurisdiction of the Marcher Lords, mediaeval Chepstow was the largest port in Wales and the town remained as an important shipping centre into the nineteenth century. The decline in trade was offset by the late 18th-century "Wye Tour", the prototype from which the modern tourist industry grew. After all, as this column has often pointed out, sometimes multiple times in the same sentence, the Welsh Marches are beautiful and the Wye Valley particularly so. We are only a few miles downstream from the picturesque and ruined Tintern Abbey.

Tintern Abbey dates from the twelfth century, but religion has been going on in this corner of Britain a lot longer than that. Six centuries before Tintern's foundation St Dubricius was preaching the good word in the kingdom of Ergyng, based on the Wye Valley. Dubricius' disciples included a rather obscure figure called Cynfarch or Kynemark, who was renowned for his holiness. Under the Anglicised name of Kingsmark, a number of churches in Wales and the West Country are dedicated to him, one of which—founded in the 7th century—was in Chepstow. This was replaced in 1270 by an Augustinian priory, which was dissolved in the sixteenth century along with all the other monasteries and has since disappeared without trace.

Except for this ward name. St Kingsmark is the northern of the five electoral divisions covering Chepstow, and has somewhat unusual demographics for Wales. According to the 2011 census, 51% of the workforce are in managerial or professional occupations, while 47% of adults living here have a degree-level qualification. This is the sort of demographic that in England, on the other side of the river, would scream "middle-class commuter centre", and that is what Chepstow has become. The opening of the Severn Bridge in 1966 (and the removal of its tolls in December 2018) brought the town within easy commuting range of Bristol on the far side of the river, while Newport and Cardiff are easily accessible via the railway and the M 4 motorway.

St Kingsmark division turns in the sort of election results you would expect for that demographic. It has voted Conservative at all six local elections since the present Monmouthshire council was established in 1995, and also voted Conservative at all six local elections to the predecessor Monmouth district council. David Dovey had represented the division from 2008 until his death in January 2021. At his last re-election in May 2017 he defeated an independent candidate, Lia Hind, by the relatively narrow margin of 45–40.*

This Tory win is quite typical of Monmouthshire, which is the only county or county borough council in Wales with a Conservative majority. The May 2017 elections here returned 25 Conservatives against 10 Labour, 5 independents and 3 Lib Dems. The Monmouth constituency, which covers a very similar area, has been Tory-held at Westminster since 2005 and is the only Welsh constituency which has voted Conservative in every Senedd election to date. However, the outgoing Tory MS Nick Ramsay has been deselected for the 2021 election in favour of the council leader Peter Fox; Ramsay has not taken this well, and is threatening to seek re-election as an independent.

Will these ructions have an effect on the St Kingsmark by-election? We

* The original version of this column had stated that Hind had tied with the Labour candidate for second place on 13%, which was the result of an error in the Local Elections Archive Project. That error has now been corrected.

Westminster and Senedd constituency: Monmouth
May 2017 result C 456 Ind 407 Lab 94 LD 62
May 2012 result C 422 LD 257
May 2008 result C 474 LD 270 Lab 110
June 2004 result C 422 LD 385 Lab 87
May 1999 result C 539 Lab 223 LD 176
May 1995 result C 456 Lab 390
(Earlier results are for Monmouth district council)
May 1991 result C 570 Lab 227 LD 145
May 1987 result C 497 All 220 Lab 149
May 1983 result C 551 Lab 176
May 1979 result C 823 Lab 322
May 1976 result C 423 Lab 191
May 1973 result C 286 Lab 102

Figure 17: Monmouthshire, St Kingsmark

shall see. Defending for the Conservatives is Christopher Edwards, who fought his home division of Trellech United (further up the Wye Valley) in 2017 and narrowly failed to unseat an independent councillor. Labour have selected Tom Kirton, who was Mayor of Chepstow in 2019–20. Completing the ballot paper is the Lib Dem candidate, Jenni Brews.*

* *Monmouthshire, St Kingsmark*: C 439 LD 230 Lab 119

8th April 2021

In the last contests before the 6th May local elections, there are three by-elections on 8th April 2021:

Abersychan; Cwmyniscoy; and New Inn

Torfaen council, Gwent; caused respectively by the death of independent councillor Raymond Williams and the resignations of Labour councillor Neil Waite and Conservative councillor Raymond Mills.

There are four weeks to go until local elections resume in England on 6th May 2021. Before then, we have three local by-elections to bring you from the Torfaen district of south-east Wales. Torfaen district is based on the New Town of Cwmbran and the older town of Pontypool, in which general area all three of today's by-elections are concentrated.

The village and division of Abersychan can be found north of Pontypool, in the Lwyd valley on the way to the World Heritage Site of Blaenavon. Like Blaenavon, the Abersychan area started out with an ironworking industry, which gave way to coalmining by the twentieth century. By the 1920s one of the major local figures in the mineworkers' unions was Arthur Jenkins, who was elected in 1935 as Labour MP for Pontypool; his son Roy Jenkins, born in Abersychan in 1920, became one of the most significant politicians of the late 20th century.

The modern Abersychan division covers a number of villages in the valley, including Cwmavon and Varteg. Varteg made the headlines around the world a few years back with a proposal from the Welsh Language Commissioner to change the spelling of its name to the Welsh-language *Y Farteg*, which it's fair to say caused a bit of a stink among the locals. In the 2011 census Abersychan came in the top 100 divisions or wards in England and Wales for population born in

Westminster and Senedd constituency: Torfaen
May 2017 result Ind 1242/906 Lab 1000/706/504 C 338
May 2012 result Lab 845/679/623 Ind 570/244/238/199/175/137 PC 252 Grn 178
May 2008 result Ind 1148/810/734 Lab 862/725/465 Grn 446
June 2004 result Lab 1062/970/614 Ind 773/661/568/398 Grn 265
May 1999 result Lab 1348/1327/1204 Ind 732/611
May 1995 result Lab 1559/1313/1104 Ind Communist 822 Ind 593 Ind Lab 565 Grn 167

Figure 18: Torfaen, Abersychan

the UK.

Immediately to the south of Pontypool can be found the Cwmyniscoy division, which is based on the Cwmfields area along Cwmynyscoy Road. This division includes the local campus of the further education college Coleg Gwent. However, most of the division's acreage is upland, pockmarked with quarries.

Very different in character is New Inn, on the eastern side of the valley. Pontypool is rather unlike other Valleys towns in that it was an important railway centre, and New Inn was once at the centre of that: there were extensive marshalling yards here, and a steelworks down the hill at Panteg also offered employment. The only survivor of this industry is the railway station on the Marches Line, now an unstaffed halt called Pontypool and New Inn with irregular trains to Newport, Hereford and beyond.

These three divisions have contrasting political traditions. New Inn division was created by boundary changes in 2004, which merged together the previous New Inn Lower and New Inn Upper divisions. The division was gained by the Conservatives in 2008, and these days it votes as if it was in Monmouthshire over the border: New Inn has become one of two reliable Conservative divisions in Torfaen. (The other is Llanyrafon East and Ponthir, on the eastern edge of Cwmbran). In May 2017 the Conservative lead over Labour here was 55–31, with the division's councillors accounting for three-quarters of the Conservative group on Torfaen council. Raymond Mills had sat for New Inn since 2008.

The other two divisions go back to the founding electoral arrangements of Torfaen council in 1995. Cwmyniscoy is a single-member division which took until 2008 to see a contested election; in that year Neil Waite, who had sat since 1999, lost his seat by 19 votes to People's Voice. This was one of three seats won in Torfaen that year by People's Voice, which was a political party associated with Peter Law, the Labour-turned-independent MP and AM for Blaenau Gwent, and which continued after Law's death until being wound up in 2010. Neil Waite got his seat back in 2012, and was re-elected in 2017 with a 56–44 margin in a straight fight with UKIP.

Westminster and Senedd constituency: Torfaen
May 2017 result Lab 192 UKIP 150
May 2012 result Lab 274 Ind 225 PC 10 C 9
May 2008 result People's Voice 232 Lab 213
June 2004 result Lab unopposed
May 1999 result Lab unopposed
May 1995 result Lab unopposed

Figure 19: Torfaen, Cwmyniscoy

Westminster and Senedd constituency: Torfaen
May 2017 result C 1171/1067/1013 Lab 655/594/576 Ind 314
May 2012 result C 1086/1061/1050 Lab 739/724/671 PC 219
May 2008 result C 977/913/813 Ind 805 Lab 667/630/570 People's Voice 609
June 2004 result Lab 934/933/916 UKIP 811 C 711 LD 368

Figure 20: Torfaen, New Inn

Recent elections in Abersychan have tended to be a free-for-all between Labour and a large number of independent candidates. The late independent councillor Ray Williams was first elected in 2004, lost his seat in 2012 and got back in 2017 by winning the last of the division's three seats with a 200-vote majority over the second Labour candidate, Wayne Tomlinson. Sadly, Williams died in December 2020 from COVID-19, aged 84.

Former Labour councillor Wayne Tomlinson is one of two independent candidates seeking to succeed Raymond Williams in the Abersychan by-election. Tomlinson has contested every election in this division from 1999 onwards, being elected as an independent candidate in 2008 and as a Labour candidate in 2012. The other independent candidate is Charlotte Hill, who runs a specialist cheese shop in Blaenavon. Labour have selected Lynda Clarkson, who represents part of the division (Garndiffaith and Varteg ward) on Pontypool community council. Also standing in Abersychan are Tristan Griffin for the Conservatives and Kieran Gething, in the first election for a new political party: Gething is standing for Propel, a Welsh nationalist movement led by the former Plaid Cymru MS Neil McEvoy.*

In Cwmyniscoy the defending Labour candidate is John Killick, the deputy leader of Pontypool community council. Killick has been a Torfaen councillor before: he won a by-election in Pontypool division in 2011 partly thanks to six independent candidates splitting the opposition vote, but lost his seat there in 2012. With no UKIP candidate this time, Killick is opposed in Cwmyniscoy by

* *Torfaen, Abersychan*: Lab 503 Hill 176 Tomlinson 175 C 138 Propel 19 [Lab gain from Ind]

Propel candidate Ben Evans and independent Bridgette Harris.*

Finally, the defending Conservative candidate for New Inn is Keith James, a solicitor. Labour have reselected IT worker Farooq Dastgir, who was on their slate here in 2017. Completing the New Inn ballot paper is independent candidate Ross Attfield.†

* *Torfaen, Cwmyniscoy*: Lab 155 Ind 30 Propel 16 † *Torfaen, New Inn*: C 641 Lab 344 Ind 206

6th May 2021 Part I: Scotland, Wales and London

Welcome to Andrew's Previews' countdown to the May 2021 elections, which promise to be the biggest electoral event of this Parliament. The whole of Great Britain is due to go to the polls. And there's not just one type of election involved: many voters will have two, three or (in some cases) four or more ballot papers to juggle, and multiple electoral systems abound. It's complicated.

Because of its extraordinary length this Preview will be split into four parts, set out as follows:

I. Introduction, Scotland, Wales and London.

II. The North and Midlands.

III. The South and East.

IV. The Parliamentary Special; and concluding remarks.

Introduction

The hybrid nature of the May 2021 elections means that any comparison is inevitably going to be confusing. There are two different baselines to consider.

Most of the posts up for election next year were last filled in 2016, which was a very close set of local elections in England. The BBC's Projected National Share put Labour under Jeremy Corbyn on 31%, the Conservatives under David Cameron on 30%, the Lib Dems on 15% and UKIP on 12%. In the Scottish Parliament, the SNP gained vote share but lost its overall majority; the party has been running Holyrood as a minority since. Labour fell short of a majority in the National Assembly for Wales (as it was then), but stayed in power with the support of the single Liberal Democrat member. Sadiq Khan gained the London mayoralty for Labour following the retirement of Boris Johnson who had chosen to re-enter politics on the national stage, with some success. Finally, the second set of Police and Crime Commissioner elections saw a bonfire of many of the independents who had been elected on comedy turnouts in November 2012.

May 2016 was very much another time, and by May 2017 things were very different. This set of local elections came slap-bang in the middle of Theresa May's snap election campaign, and very much in her honeymoon period. The BBC's Projected National Share had an eleven-point Conservative lead, with 38% against 27% for Labour and 18% for the Liberal Democrats. With 2017 being (in England) essentially a county council year, and with UKIP having done well in the 2013 county elections, that resulted in big seat gains for the Conservatives who gained Derbyshire from Labour and won majorities in Cambridgeshire, East Sussex, Gloucestershire, Lancashire, Lincolnshire, Norfolk, Suffolk, Warwickshire and the Isle of Wight.

These previews will make a lot of comparisons with 2019, for the purpose of establishing something of a "par score". The May 2019 local elections took place in a political scene much more like May 2016 than May 2017 and, unusually, happened at a time when *both* major parties were in a weak position but while the new forces taking votes off them, the Brexit Party and Change UK, were not ready for prime time. While there was a lot of anti-incumbent sentiment about, those new parties were unable to take advantage as they had no candidates; so that anti-incumbent sentiment manifested itself in many areas with large shares for independent candidates and localist parties. These small groups had been mostly swamped in 2015 by general election turnout, so 2019 marked something of a renaissance for them.

Since March 2020, local by-elections in England have been suspended due to reasons which are obvious. Some local by-elections have taken place in Wales, and the Scottish returning officers have efficiently cleared their vacancy backlog, but in England we have no information from real-life elections as to how things are going. We only have the national opinion polls, which suggest a national picture closer to 2017 than to 2016. How this will translate into a series of local pictures is extremely difficult to predict, but one reasonable guess might be that the Conservatives consistently do better than the 2019 "par scores" set out in this preview.

The merging together of the 2020 and 2021 local elections, together with the filling of 352 casual vacancies, means that a total of exactly 5,000 councillors are up for election on 6th May. In councillor terms, this is not the largest set of local elections in the UK—2019 was larger—but in vote terms that definitely is the case. Everybody in Great Britain has something to vote for, even if it's only the

Police and Crime Commissioners.

Because of the limited space and time available and the extraordinary number of by-elections, I have applied a much stronger than usual filter when naming candidates in the 6th May previews. All mayoral and PCC candidates have been namechecked, but by-election candidates are generally only named in this text if their party was within 10% last time out. If you're a by-election candidate and you're not happy with not having your name in this preview, then I would love you to prove me wrong by going ahead and winning your contest.

I am fully aware that there will be mistakes in this preview. Have fun finding them.

To start off, here is Part I covering the three parts of Great Britain where there are no ordinary council elections this year: Scotland, Wales and London.

Scotland

Scottish Parliament

This piece is not going to look in any great detail at the Scottish Parliament elections. There are plenty of other people doing this in far more detail than I can provide; I shall instead point you to Allan Fauld's *Ballot Box Scotland* blog[*], which is doing a sterling job in previewing this year's Holyrood polls. The Britain Elects team have also been working on a prediction model.

The last Holyrood elections in May 2016 returned 63 Scottish National Party MSPs, 31 Conservatives, 24 Labour, 6 Greens and 5 Lib Dems. The SNP formed a minority administration. The Conservative MSP for Ettrick, Roxburgh and Berwickshire resigned in 2017 to seek election to the House of Commons, and the Conservatives held the resulting by-election.[†] The Liberal Democrat MSP for the Shetland Islands resigned in 2019 to take up a new job and the Lib Dems held the resulting by-election.[‡] Five regional MSPs (four Conservatives and one Labour) have been replaced since 2016 by candidates from their party's list.

The Scottish Parliament election is being extensively polled. At the time of writing, the polling indicates that the SNP government will be re-elected and there will probably again be a nationalist majority in the chamber, although whether the SNP can achieve an overall majority of their own or would need to rely on the Greens or other nationalist parties to govern remains an open question.

[*] `https://ballotbox.scot` [†] *Andrew's Previews 2017*, pages 143 to 150. [‡] *Andrew's Previews 2019*, pages 260 to 268.

Local elections

Scotland's returning officers have efficiently filled all the vacancies which arose last year. The Scottish Parliament election for 2021 is combined with just one local by-election, in the *Forth and Endrick* ward of STIRLING council. This is a large rural ward with no towns to speak of, located about 20 miles north of Glasgow beyond the Campsie fells. The eastern bank of Loch Lomond, the Munro of Ben Lomond and the village of Drymen lie within the boundaries of the Loch Lomond and the Trossachs National Park, while the ward extends east down the Forth valley as far as Gargunnock. It's part of the Stirling constituency at both Holyrood and Westminster level. The Stirling Holyrood seat has been SNP-held since 2007, but the Conservatives carried this ward in 2017 with a 45-30 vote lead and a 2-1 seat lead over the SNP. The ward's SNP councillor Graham Lambie has died, and the Conservatives (who are the largest party on Stirling council, but in opposition to an SNP/Labour administration) are in a good position to gain a seat here. The defending SNP candidate is Paul Goodwin, while Jane Hutchison challenges for the Conservatives.[*]

Wales

Senedd Cymru

Senedd Cymru holds its fifth election in 2021, but the first under its current name: until last year, when the body was upgraded to a Parliament, it was known as the National Assembly for Wales. The last elections in 2016 returned 29 Labour members, 12 Plaid Cymru, 11 Conservatives, 7 UKIP and a single Liberal Democrat who is not seeking re-election; the administration is a coalition of Labour, the Lib Dem and a Plaid Cymru defector who is not seeking re-election either. The Labour AM for Alyn and Deeside took his own life at the end of 2017, and Labour held the resulting by-election in 2018.[†] Four regional MSs (two from Plaid and one each from the Conservatives and UKIP) have been replaced since 2016 by candidates from their party's list. It may not surprise to learn that the UKIP group has fallen apart: Neil Hamilton, the notorious former Conservative MP for Tatton, is the only MS still in the party, while the former Conservative and UKIP MP Mark Reckless is seeking re-election to the Senedd for the single-issue Abolish the Welsh Assembly Party.

This Senedd Cymru election is also being extensively polled, but Wales is a difficult country to poll well and this is reflected in a lot of volatility in the

[*] *Stirling, Forth and Endrick*: first preferences C 3195 SNP 2636 Lab 1172 Grn 754 LD 332; final C 3717 SNP 3445 [C gain from SNP] [†] *Andrew's Previews 2018*, pages 38 to 46.

pollsters' readings. Although proportional representation is in use, forty of the sixty seats are single-member constituencies which can provide a big bonus for any party which does well in the constituencies. Traditionally this is Labour, which won 27 of the 40 constituencies in 2016; however in the December 2019 general election the party only won 22 constituencies here, against 14 Conservatives and 4 for Plaid. As such, any fall in the Labour constituency vote (which was 35% in 2016) could result in disproportionate seat changes. The First Minister, Mark Drakeford, is sitting on a particularly small majority over Plaid Cymru in his Cardiff West constituency; but he's safer than he looks, partly because he has a huge national profile now, and partly because the Plaid candidate from 2016, Neil McEvoy, has been thrown out of the party and taken a large chunk of the local Plaid activists with him into his new pro-Welsh independence party, Propel. If the polling is to be believed (and, as I say, it is volatile), then Welsh Labour are likely to continue in office with some form of support from Plaid Cymru.

Police and Crime Commissioners

Most of the focus of the 2021 elections in Wales will be on the Senedd, and with good reason. However, Wales also has four police and crime commissioners to elect. The 2016 Welsh PCC elections, also held alongside a Senedd poll, saw quite a lot of change due to the fact that they were contested by Plaid Cymru, who hadn't stood in 2012.

Plaid ended up gaining two PCC positions. One of those was *North Wales* PCC, covering the old counties of Clwyd and Gwynedd and thus not quite the same as the North Wales electoral region of the Senedd. That position was open following the retirement of 2012 winner Winston Roddick, who had won that year as an independent candidate despite being a Lib Dem party member. (Roddick's political career went all the way back to the 1970 general election, in which he was the Liberal candidate for Anglesey.) In 2016 the North Wales police area gave 31% to Plaid Cymru candidate Arfon Jones, 26% to Labour candidate David Taylor, 20% to the Conservatives and 12% to UKIP; Plaid picked up a lot of transfers to win the runoff against Labour 58–42.

Arfon Jones is standing down after one term and is replaced as Plaid candidate by Ann Griffith, an Anglesey county councillor. Labour have selected Flintshire councillor Andy Dunbobbin, the Conservative candidate is former Mayor of Ruthin Pat Astbury, and UKIP have not returned. Completing the ballot paper are independent Mark Young and Lisa Wilkins of the Lib Dems.*

* *North Wales PCC*: first preferences C 75472 Lab 69459 PC 67672 Ind 15907 LD 10149; final Lab 98034 C 90149 [Lab gain from PC]

The 2012 election for *Dyfed-Powys* PCC had been a straight fight between the Conservatives and Labour, with the Tories' Christopher Salmon prevailing against former Welsh agriculture minister Christine Gwyther. There was a wider field for the 2016 election, with Plaid Cymru candidate Dafydd Llywelyn leading the first count on 28% against 25% for Salmon, 19% for Labour and 11% for UKIP who narrowly beat the Lib Dems for fourth place. In the runoff Llywelyn defeated Salmon by a 56–44 margin. Llywelyn is seeking re-election against Conservative candidate Jon Burns (a former Welsh city and county councillor) and Labour's Philippa Thompson (a former diplomat who contested Preseli Pembrokeshire in December 2019). Again, UKIP have not returned, so Tomos Preston of the Lib Dems completes the ballot paper.[*]

The two PCC positions in industrial south Wales were both safely Labour. A three-cornered contest last time in *Gwent* saw Labour lead in the first round with 46% against 31% for the Conservatives and 23% for Plaid; Plaid's transfers gave Labour a 62–38 win over the Conservatives in the runoff. Incumbent Labour PCC Jeff Cuthburt is seeking re-election; the Tory candidate is Iraq veteran Hannah Jarvis, and Plaid have selected Caerphilly councillor Donna Cushing. Also standing are independent candidate Paul Harley, Clayton Jones of the pro-Welsh independence party Gwlad, and John Miller of the Lib Dems.[†]

In the *South Wales* police area (corresponding to the old county of Glamorgan) former First Minister Alun Michael was re-elected for a second term as PCC in 2016 without fuss. Michael led in the first round with 41% of the vote. A three-way contest for the other place in the run-off saw the Conservatives and Plaid poll 18% each with independent Mike Baker in fourth on 17%; the Tory candidate Timothy Davies finished second, just 29 votes ahead of Plaid (70,799 to 70,770). That put Davies into the runoff, where he was duly crushed 68–32 by Michael. Michael is seeking re-election for a third term; the Conservative candidate is Swansea councillor and former police officer Steve Gallagher; Plaid have selected criminal justice campaigner Nadine Marshall, whose son was murdered six years ago by a person who was on probation at the time; and independent Mike Baker is trying again. Completing a six-strong ballot paper are Callum Littlemore of the Lib Dems and Gail John of Propel.[‡]

It should be noted that the elections in Wales on 6th May have different franchises. If you are aged 16 or 17, or you are resident in Wales but not a citizen of a Commonwealth or EU country, then you cannot vote for your Police and Crime

[*] *Dyfed-Powys PCC*: first preferences C 69112 PC 68208 Lab 48033 LD 17649; final PC 94488 C 77408 [†] *Gwent PCC*: first preferences Lab 75775 C 52313 PC 29392 Ind 13601 LD 7640 Gwlad 2615; final Lab 92616 C 60536 [‡] *South Wales PCC*: first preferences Lab 177110 C 102465 PC 82246 Ind 37110 LD 19907 Propel 13263; final Lab 225463 C 127844

Commissioner but you can vote for the Senedd and in any local by-elections. Which we shall come to next.

Local elections

There are no local elections in Wales this year, but there are ten council by-elections taking place. One of these is a direct result of COVID-19, which has taken from us FLINTSHIRE county councillor Kevin Hughes. He had served since 2017 as an independent councillor for *Gwernymynydd* division, taking over an open seat after a long-serving Liberal Democrat councillor retired; the Lib Dems didn't put up a candidate to defend the seat, and Hughes picked it up with a 58–29 lead over the Conservatives. Gwernymynydd is a village just south-west of Mold on the main road towards Ruthin, and the division includes a number of other hamlets to the south of Mold. Kevin Hughes' son Andy is seeking to follow in his father's footsteps as an independent candidate, and is opposed only by Plaid Cymru's Bob Gaffey.*

At the far end of North Wales there are two by-elections to the ISLE OF ANGLESEY council. *Seiriol* division is the eastern end of the island, covering the town of Beaumaris and surrounding villages; *Caergybi* division is the town of Holyhead, and as such is on the front line of Brexit as the main port of embarkation for Dublin and Dún Laoghaire. The Caergybi division split its three seats between two independents and a Labour candidate in 2017; the late councillor Shaun Redmond was the second independent candidate, gaining his seat from Labour. Independent candidate Jeff Evans will seek to succeed Redmond, as will Labour's Jennifer Saboor.† Seiriol returned a full slate of Plaid Cymru candidates in 2017 and looks safe enough for the party, whose defending candidate is Gary Pritchard.‡

The other seven by-elections are in the industrial south of the country. NEWPORT's *Victoria* division is on the east bank of the Usk immediately opposite the city centre; the division is centred on Rodney Parade, the home ground of the Dragons Pro14 rugby side. Victoria was the first division in Wales to elect a Muslim local councillor, Mohammad Asghar, who was returned here as a Plaid Cymru representative in 2004 and was subsequently elected to the Senedd on their ticket in 2007. Asghar was still an MS at the time of his death last year, although he had defected to the Conservatives in 2011. Victoria division is now safe for Labour, whose defending candidate is Farzina Hussain.§ The previous coun-

* *Flintshire, Gwernymynydd*: Ind 639 PC 171 † *Isle of Anglesey, Caergybi*: Ind 788 PC 636 Lab 629 LD 107 ‡ *Isle of Anglesey, Seiriol*: PC 1113 Lab 789 Ind 588 LD 161 § *Newport, Victoria*: Lab 1138 LD 402 C 259 Grn 167. For a later by-election here in December see page 547.

cillor Christine Jenkins resigned over a year ago, and the Victoria by-election was originally due to take place in April 2020 as were a number of other by-elections listed in this section.

The old county of Mid Glamorgan has given us three by-elections which have all generated varying degrees of controversy. BRIDGEND councillor David Owen has got his name firmly into the Councillors Behaving Badly file after he was sentenced to three years' imprisonment in March 2020: he was found guilty of conspiracy to steal and handling stolen goods, in relation to the theft of an agricultural vehicle worth £9,000 from a farm in Abergavenny. His resignation letter to the council was sent from his prison cell, shortly before he was due to be disqualified from office (this kicks in when the deadline for appeals expires, or once any appeal is disposed of).

Owen had served since 2012 as an independent councillor for *Nant-y-moel* division, at the head of the Ogmore Valley, and had beaten Labour 62–38 in 2017. The Nant-y-moel by-election features an all-female ballot paper: new independent Mary Hughes is challenged by Labour's Lee-Anne Hill and the Tories' Clare Lewis.*

In the large RHONDDA CYNON TAF district, Conservative councillor Mike Diamond has fallen out with his former party and resigned as councillor for the Cardiff commuter area of *Llantwit Fardre* division, which is the only safe Tory division in the district; while the council's only member from the Cynon Valley Party, Gavin Williams, has been controversially disqualified under the six-month non-attendance rule, leaving a vacancy in the village with Wales' highest rates of child poverty according to official 2019 figures, *Penrhiwceiber*. Labour still hold the other seat in Penrhiwceiber division. Gavin Williams is seeking re-election in the by-election caused by his disqualification, this time as an independent candidate; Ross Williams will try to gain his seat for Labour.† The defending Conservative candidate in Llantwit Fardre is Sam Trask.‡

Over in Port Talbot, Labour have the tricky task of defending the *Aberavon* division of NEATH PORT TALBOT under the shadow of the M 4 motorway. This is an electoral division of two parts, with the Aberavon and Baglan Moors areas divided from each other by the Neath Port Talbot Hospital and a large industrial estate. Aberavon division was a stronghold of the continuing SDP into the twenty-first century, long after they had disappeared from the national scene; but the SDP are now extinct here and the division's three seats split two to Plaid Cymru and one to Labour in 2017. Labour's Stephanie Lynch has the

* *Bridgend, Nant-y-moel*: Ind 437 Lab 315 C 46 † *Rhondda Cynon Taf, Penrhiwceiber*: Lab 954 Ind 384 PC 194 [Lab gain from Cynon Valley Party] ‡ *Rhondda, Cynon Taf, Llantwit Fardre*: C 1011 Lab 656 PC 464 Williams 162 Tizard-Lee 80 LD 73

task of defending this by-election; Plaid's Andrew Dacey will look to gain.*

Finally, Labour also have two by-elections to defend in the city of SWANSEA. *Castle* division (in the Swansea West constituency) covers the city centre, while *Llansamlet* division (in the Swansea East seat) is in the north-east of the city and takes in the villages of Llansamlet and Birchgrove together with the Swansea Enterprise Park. Both of these returned full slates of four Labour councillors in May 2017 and should be safe for the party's candidates: Hannah Lawson in Castle (which has a field of nine candidates)† and Matthew Jones in Llansamlet.‡

Greater London

Mayor and Assembly

A quick mention of the biggest single election in the country. The fifth *Mayor of London* election will grab a lot of the headlines; this was a Labour gain at the most recent poll in 2016 after Conservative mayor Boris Johnson stood down. (Anybody know what happened to him after that? Answers on a postcard to the usual address.) The Labour candidate, then Tooting MP Sadiq Khan, led the Conservative candidate Zac Goldsmith by 44–35 in the first round, and increased that lead to 57–43 in the runoff: 1,310,143 votes to 994,614.

Khan is seeking a second term, and a number of opinion polls suggest he will not struggle to get it. The Conservatives have selected Shaun Bailey, who has been a London Assembly member since 2016 and has stood twice for Parliament: he fought Hammersmith in 2010, and Lewisham West and Penge in 2017. Also standing are (deep breath): Siân Berry for the Green Party, Luisa Porritt for the Liberal Democrats, Peter Gammons for UKIP, Mandu Reid for the Women's Equality Party, Kam Balayev for Renew (an anti-Brexit group), Count Binface (who needs no introduction) for his self-titled party, Valerie Brown for the Burning Pink party (an Extinction Rebellion splinter group), Piers Corbyn for Let London Live (an anti-lockdown group), independent Max Fosh (a YouTuber), Laurence Fox for the Reclaim Party (another anti-lockdown group), Richard Hewison for a group called Rejoin EU, Vanessa Hudson for the Animal Welfare Party, Steve Kelleher for the Social Democratic Party, outgoing Assembly member David Kurten (who was originally elected for UKIP) for the Heritage Party, independent Farah London (a businesswoman), independent Nims Obunge (pastor of an evangelical church and head of an anti-crime charity), independent

* *Neath Port Talbot, Aberavon*: Lab 677 PC 647 C 199 Ind 144 Gwlad 121 Propel 34 † *Swansea, Castle*: Lab 1637 LD 694 C 424 PC 423 Grn 185 UKIP 120 Independents @ Swansea 105 Ind 73 TUSC 58 ‡ *Swansea, Llansamlet*: Lab 2492 PC 887 Grn 426 LD 351

Niko Omilana (another YouTuber), and Brian Rose of the London Real Party (another anti-lockdown group).*

The GREATER LONDON ASSEMBLY is the only English elected body to use proportional representation. In the 2016 election Labour polled 40% of the vote on the Londonwide list ballot and won 12 seats; the Conservatives polled 29% of the vote and won 9 seats; the Greens and UKIP polled 8% and 7% respectively and won 2 seats each; and the Liberal Democrats won 1 seat with 6%, just coming in over the 5% threshold which applies to the list vote. 13 seats would be an overall majority, and if Labour can improve their list vote that could be in range.

Local elections

There are forty-six local by-elections in the capital on 6th May, all of which are being dealt with by the London Elects team as part of the centralised Mayor and Assembly count. This is being split over two days, with seven GLA constituencies due to declare on Friday 7th, and the other seven constituencies and the list votes to come in on Saturday 8th. Accordingly, it may take some considerable time for these by-election results to come through after the poll. It could be worse: Tower Hamlets could be running the show.

I'll go through these polls in an anti-clockwise direction, starting with two by-elections to REDBRIDGE council. *Seven Kings* ward has a name which has nothing to do with seven kings; it was originally something like *Sevekings*, and as such probably referred to a settlement of people associated with a man called Seofoca. This ward lies to the north of the Great Eastern railway line and Roman road, while *Loxford* ward lies to the south of those communication links on the east bank of the River Roding. Both of these wards were over 75% Labour in the 2018 local elections, so quite why Chaudhary Mohammed Iqbal, elected on the Labour slate in Loxford, thought it was necessary to commit electoral fraud to get elected there is difficult to fathom. Iqbal, who was living in Barking at the time of the election, had lied about his address on his nomination papers; he resigned from the council after pleading guilty to four criminal charges, and he is now serving a 68-week prison sentence. The defending Labour candidates are Sahdia Warraich in Loxford† and Pushpita Gupta in Seven Kings.‡

The River Roding flows into the Thames estuary at Barking Riverside, which

* *Mayor of London*: first preferences Lab 1013721 C 893051 Grn 197976 LD 111716 Omilana 49628 Reclaim 47634 London Real 31111 Rejoin EU 28012 Count Binface 24775 Women's Equality 21182 Let London Live 20604 Animal Welfare 16826 UKIP 14393 Farah London 11869 Heritage Party 11025 Obunge 9682 SDP 8764 Renew 7774 Fosh 6309 Burning Pink 5305; runoff Lab 1206034 C 977601 † *Redbridge, Loxford*: Lab 2184 C 756 LD 197 ‡ *Redbridge, Seven Kings*: Lab 2227 C 791 TUSC 551 LD 313

forms the *Thames* ward of BARKING AND DAGENHAM council. Barking and Dagenham has had a full slate of 51 Labour councillors since 2010, and don't expect any change to that here: in 2018 Thames ward gave 83% of the vote to Labour in a straight fight with the Conservatives. This time there is more choice for the ward's voters with five parties and an independent candidate standing; although the Tories have put up a high-profile candidate in the form of Andrew Boff, who stood here in 2014 and has contested the Hackney mayoralty on a number of occasions, don't bet against Labour candidate Fatuma Nalule.*

Barking and Dagenham's Thames ward is served by Dagenham Dock railway station, from which change at Barking for an Underground train to *East Ham Central* ward in the London Borough of NEWHAM. Similar considerations to Thames ward apply here, with Farah Nazeer as the defending Labour candidate.†

The poor voters of East Ham Central will have five ballot papers to juggle: three votes for the GLA, this by-election and the *Newham governance referendum* on whether to abolish the elected mayoralty and move to the committee system of governance. This was not without controversy: a group looking to move back to the leader and cabinet model had put a petition in for a referendum to that effect, which was ruled out of order because it had been delivered during the middle of pandemic restrictions. If the people of Newham decide to vote for a change in their governance, that would commence after the current Mayor Rokhsana Fiaz' term expires next year.‡

Another *governance referendum* has turned up in neighbouring TOWER HAMLETS, on scrapping the directly elected mayoralty (which, it's fair to say, has not proven an unqualified success here) and reverting to the Leader and Cabinet model of governance. Any change would happen from 2022 when current mayor John Biggs comes to the end of his term.§

Rather different in character is the remaining by-election east of the Lea, in the *Hatch Lane* ward of WALTHAM FOREST. This is the south-eastern of the three wards covering Chingford, a Tory holdout which returns Iain Duncan Smith to Parliament. Hatch Lane was safe enough for the Conservatives in May 2018, and their defending candidate is Justin Halabi.¶

Waltham Forest is part of the North East constituency of the London Assembly, along with two Middlesex boroughs which have turned up with a large number of by-elections. There are four polls in the borough of HACKNEY, with

* *Barking and Dagenham, Thames*: Lab 1545 C 939 Ind 574 TUSC 345 CPA 158 LD 81
† *Newham, East Ham Central*: Lab 2297 C 1288 Grn 283 LD 239 CPA 115 TUSC 91 ‡ *Newham, governance referendum*: Mayor 45960 Committee 36424 § *Tower Hamlets, governance referendum*: Mayor 63029 Leader and Cabinet 17951 ¶ *Waltham Forest, Hatch Lane*: C 2072 Lab 1565 Grn 266 LD 170

Labour defending the trendy *Hoxton East and Shoreditch* ward on the edge of the City and also *King's Park* ward in the Lea Valley (the ward which includes the Hackney Marshes), both within the Hackney South and Shoreditch constituency. Both of the vacating councillors have gone on to greater things: Tom Rahilly (King's Park) now has a politically-restricted job, while Feryal Clark (Hoxton East and Shoreditch, elected under her maiden name of Feryal Demirci) was elected in December 2019 as the Labour MP for Enfield North. The wards are safe, and the defending Labour candidates are Anya Sizer in Hoxton East and Shoreditch*, and Lynne Troughton in King's Park.†

In the Hackney North and Stoke Newington constituency, we have two fascinating by-elections in the Hasidic enclave of Stamford Hill. At the time of the 2011 census, Hackney's New River and Lordship wards both turned in a Jewish population of over 25%, ranking 12th and 13th of all the wards in England and Wales for Judaism. Since 2011 Hackney's ward boundaries have changed; much of this area is now covered by the *Woodberry Down* ward (very safe Labour in 2018) and the *Stamford Hill West* ward (a Conservative gain from Labour in 2018). Both of these wards have by-elections on 6th May. In Woodberry Down the defending Labour candidate is Sarah Young‡, while Stamford Hill West sees Conservative Hershy Lisser challenged by Labour's Rosemary Sales.§

ISLINGTON borough has outdone Hackney with five by-elections. *Bunhill* ward runs from the northern edge of the City to the Angel, and takes in the Silicon Roundabout at Old Street underground station; *St Peter's* ward runs north-east from the Angel between Essex Road and the Grand Union canal; *Mildmay* ward is centred on the Overground station at Canonbury; *Highbury West* ward includes Arsenal football grounds old and new; and *Holloway* ward is based on the northern end of the Caledonian Road. The Bunhill by-election is to replace controversy magnet Claudia Webbe, who was elected in 2019 as a Labour MP for Leicester. Despite the presence of independent candidates in Bunhill and St Peter's standing on anti-Low Traffic Neighbourhoods tickets, none of these polls should give the defending Labour candidates (respectively Valerie Bossman-Quarshie,¶ Toby North,‖ Angelo Weekes,** Bashir Ibrahim†† and Jason Jackson‡‡) any cause for concern.

---

* *Hackney, Hoxton East and Shoreditch*: Lab 1504 Grn 454 C 307 LD 253 Ind 222 TUSC 47
† *Hackney, King's Park*: Lab 2484 Grn 636 C 279 Battaglino 151 LD 136 Mathis 120 TUSC 72
‡ *Hackney, Woodberry Down*: Lab 1680 Grn 535 C 530 LD 167 § *Hackney, Stamford Hill West*: C 1456 Lab 1192 Grn 189 LD 59 ¶ *Islington, Bunhill*: Lab 1960 C 744 Grn 590 LD 572 Ind 181 ‖ *Islington, St Peter's*: Lab 1885 LD 876 C 749 Grn 567 Ind 318 ** *Islington, Mildmay*: Lab 2307 Grn 883 C 603 LD 349 †† *Islington, Highbury West*: Lab 2465 Grn 1799 LD 776 C 773 ‡‡ *Islington, Holloway*: Lab 2852 Grn 792 C 720 LD 548

Things are different in ENFIELD district where Labour are defending three by-elections. *Chase* ward, the northernmost ward within the Greater London boundary, takes in some genuinely rural areas within the M 25 motorway; Crews Hill railway station, on the Hertford Loop, links the ward to the centre of the Great Wen. This ward has swung a mile to the left over the last two decades, although not far enough for Labour to consider the ward safe yet. Chris James defends for Labour, Andrew Thorp is the Conservative candidate.* Also within the Enfield North constituency is *Southbury* ward straddling the Great Cambridge Road, which is safer for Labour; as is *Jubilee* ward, immediately to the south of Southbury and located within the Edmonton constituency. Ayten Guzel† and Chinelo Anyanwu‡ are respectively the defending candidates.

Also on the northern edge of Greater London is the *Edgware* ward of BARNET, where the Northern Line terminates; included within this ward is the Scratchwood or London Gateway motorway service area on the M 1, assuming that the guns of HMS *Belfast* (which are aimed at Scratchwood) haven't destroyed it yet. This is a safe Conservative ward with a very large Jewish population; the defending candidate is Nick Mearing-Smith.§ Barnet by-election watchers are more likely to be focused on the poll in *East Barnet* ward, to the east of the East Coast main line and served by Oakleigh Park and New Barnet stations; this was narrowly gained by Labour in 2014, but the Tories took one of the ward's three seats back in a close 2018 result. Labour candidate Linda Lusingu is defending the East Barnet by-election, the Tories' Nicole Richer will try to gain.¶

Another Labour-held marginal to watch is the BRENT ward of *Brondesbury Park* in Willesden, which has returned slates from all three major parties in the last three local elections. Labour gained this ward from the Tories in 2018 by the narrow margin of 45% to 43%. Three by-election results in Brent in January 2020‖ were very poor for Labour, but things may have changed since then. Gwen Grahl defends for Labour, Sapna Chadha will try to gain for the Conservatives.**

Also keep an eye on the *Churchill* ward of WESTMINSTER city council. Located at the southern end of Westminster either side of Grosvenor railway bridge, this ward includes the Victoria coach station and Chelsea Barracks but is based on Churchill Gardens, a highrise postwar housing estate on the far

* *Enfield, Chase*: C 2138 Lab 1775 LD 517 Grn 374 TUSC 58 [C gain from Lab] † *Enfield, Southbury*: Lab 1961 C 1380 Grn 470 LD 246 TUSC 82 We Matter 37 Taking the Initiative Party 36 ‡ *Enfield, Jubilee*: Lab 2170 C 1070 Grn 321 LD 171 Taking the Initiative Party 100 TUSC 63 § *Barnet, Edgware*: C 3427 Lab 1456 Grn 343 LD 254 ¶ *Barnet, East Barnet*: C 2549 Lab 2257 Grn 547 LD 415 For Britain Movement 49 [C gain from Lab] ‖ *Andrew's Previews 2020*, page 11. ** *Brent, Brondesbury Park*: Lab 1871 C 1227 Grn 469 LD 448

side of the river from Battersea Power station. As with East Barnet, Churchill ward was Conservative up to 2010, voted Labour in 2014, and split its three seats two to Labour and one to the Conservatives in 2018. If Labour can repeat their good December 2019 result in the local Cities of London and Westminster constituency, this by-election should be a comfortable hold for them. Labour's Liza Begum is challenged by the Conservatives' Shaista Miah.*

Moving into west London, we come to three by-elections in the EALING borough. Two of these are caused by Conservative councillors being elected to Westminster: Alex Stafford (of *Ealing Broadway* ward) is now the MP for Rother Valley in Yorkshire, Joy Morrissey (of the neighbouring *Hanger Hill* ward, running from North Ealing underground station to the notorious Hanger Lane gyratory) has taken on the task of representing Beaconsfield in the Commons. These were the only two Ealing wards which the Tories carried in the 2018 local elections, and both of these by-elections should be safe Conservative holds for Julian Gallant† and Fabio Conti‡ respectively. Labour should just as easily defend *Hobbayne* ward, which runs north from Hanwell station on the Great Western main line to Ruislip Road East; their candidate here is Louise Brett.§

Further out we come to the *Charville* ward of HILLINGDON borough, a perennial marginal in Hayes to the north of the Uxbridge Road. Unusually for a London ward, Charville has swung to the right over the last two decades: it returned a full slate of Labour councillors in 2002 and a full Conservative slate in 2018, with split representation at the three elections in between. Defending Tory candidate Darran Davies, who got himself into trouble during the campaign for some offensive stuff on his Facebook, is challenged by Labour's Steve Garelick.¶

Mrs Gaskell's charming literary village of *Cranford* is located (checks notes) at the eastern end of the Heathrow Airport runways within the borough of HOUNSLOW, and its economy is dependent on the airport—not good news at the moment. Poonam Dhillon was one of the local residents who once drew a wage from services related to air travel (in her case, catering); in January 2021 she died from COVID-19, aged 58, during her third term as a councillor. The by-election to replace her takes place at the same time as another by-election to Hounslow council, in the neighbouring *Hounslow Heath* ward. Both of these are safe for Labour, whose candidates are Devina Ram‖ and Madeeha Asim**

* *Westminster, Churchill*: Lab 1340 C 1016 LD 295 Grn 186 For Britain Movement 99 † *Ealing, Ealing Broadway*: C 2076 Lab 1601 LD 977 Grn 716 Workers Party 58 TUSC 32 ‡ *Ealing, Hanger Hill*: C 1762 Lab 1397 LD 1100 Grn 611 TUSC 33 § *Ealing, Hobbayne*: Lab 2345 C 1477 Grn 609 LD 366 TUSC 56. For a later by-election in this ward in September see page 371. ¶ *Hillingdon, Charville*: C 2098 Lab 1799 Grn 164 LD 107 Ind 61 ‖ *Hounslow, Cranford*: Lab 2129 C 1191 Ind 355 Grn 284 LD 133 ** *Hounslow, Hounslow Heath*: Lab 2179 C 1150 LD 386 Grn 322 TUSC 154

respectively.

Our final by-election north of the river takes place in *Hampton Wick* ward, across the water from Kingston upon Thames. This ward in the borough of RICHMOND UPON THAMES was safe Conservative up to 2014, when the councillors elected on the Tory slate here included Tony Arbour and Tania Mathias. Arbour is a veteran of local government who was first elected to Richmond council as far back as 1968, won one of the last by-elections to the Greater London Council in 1983, and has represented the South West constituency of the London Assembly since the establishment of the Assembly in 2000. (He retires from the Assembly this year.) Mathias was elected in 2015 as the MP for the local Twickenham constituency, defeating cabinet minister Vince Cable; she promptly resigned from Richmond council, and the resulting by-election surprisingly went to the Liberal Democrats. This was a harbinger of things to come: Richmond upon Thames was comprehensively taken over by the Liberal Democrats at the 2018 election. A number of wards in that election saw joint slates of Lib Dem and Green Party candidates, and Hampton Wick was one of them; this by-election is one of them, and this by-election is caused by the resignation of Hampton Wick's Green councillor Dylan Baxendale. He won the final seat in 2018 with a majority of 98 votes over Tony Arbour, a long way behind the Lib Dem slate. This one looks interesting, particularly as the Lib Dems are standing a candidate. Chas Warlow defends for the Greens, Petra Fleming challenges for the Lib Dems, Nina Watson stands for the Conservatives.*

If Richmond's by-election is interesting, the by-election in KINGSTON UPON THAMES looks bizarre. This is in *Chessington South* ward, the salient of Greater London between Esher and Epsom. Chessington South is safe Lib Dem, and the by-election has come about due to the resignation of their councillor Patricia Bamford who has topped the poll here in every election this century. Her son Charles Bamford is contesting the by-election—for the Labour Party, while the former Labour MP for Thurrock Andrew Mackinlay (who was a Labour member of Kingston council many years ago) is also contesting the by-election—as the defending Liberal Democrat candidate. This may be the constituency of the Lib Dem leader Ed Davey, but Chessington South ward also contains the pub run by the Official Monster Raving Loony Party's deputy leader Jason "Chinners" Chinnery, and Chinners has recruited not one, not two, but *thirteen* OMRLP candidates for this by-election, which deserves some sort of award (the Turner Prize would probably be the most appropriate one). On the other hand, I suppose it's *possible* that all those Loonies might end up splitting the vote.

* *Richmond upon Thames, Hampton Wick*: LD 2447 C 1232 Grn 538 Lab 446 [LD gain from Grn]

Overall the ballot paper has nineteen candidates, which must be a record for a single-member local by-election.[*]

Labour have a seat to defend in each of the boroughs of Merton and Wandsworth. The MERTON by-election is in Merton's half of the *St Helier* estate; this ward has had a few by-elections in previous years[†] which have given Labour no trouble, and neither should this poll. Helena Dollimore defends.[‡]

The WANDSWORTH seat is vacated by Fleur Anderson, who scored the only Labour gain from the Conservatives in December 2019 by winning the Putney constituency. Her former *Bedford* ward is in the Tooting constituency; it's named after the Bedford Hill and includes much of Tooting Common. Anderson gained her council seat from the Conservatives in 2014 alongside Rosena Allin-Khan, who now represents Tooting in Parliament. Bedford ward swung further to Labour in 2018 to return a full Labour slate for the first time, but the defending Labour candidate Hannah Stanislaus shouldn't forget that when it comes to local elections Normal Rules Do Not Apply within the borough of Wandsworth.[§]

The troubled finances of the London Borough of CROYDON will not be helped by having to organise five council by-elections this May. Two of these are due to the resignations of the former Labour council leader Tony Newman and former finance cabinet member Simon Hall, on whose watch the borough ran out of money. Newman and Hall, who are suspended from the Labour party, have respectively vacated *Woodside* ward (south-east of Norwood Junction station) and *New Addington North* (the northern half of the isolated quasi-New Town of New Addington). Labour are also defending a by-election in *South Norwood* ward (west of Norwood Junction station), while the Tories have seats to defend in *Park Hill and Whitgift* ward (south-east of Croydon town centre) and *Kenley* ward (on the road and railway lines towards Warlingham and Caterham on the southern edge of Greater London). None of these should give the defending parties much cause for concern in ordinary course, although with the special circumstances that apply in Croydon at the moment there is the potential for some big swings. The defending Tory candidates are Ola Kolade in Kenley[¶] and Jade Appleton in Park Hill and Whitgift[‖], while the Labour candidates for

---

[*] *Kingston upon Thames, Chessington South*: LD 1387 C 1278 Lab 451 Kingston Ind Res Group 378 Grn 139 Loonies 92 (Undertaking Director Brunskill 16 Colonel Cramps 14 Captain Coily 13 A.Gent Chinners 12 Baron von Achenbach 8 Duke Diddy Dodd 8 Casual Count of Corinthian 6 Kingstonian Newt 6 Landlord Rover 3 Landlady Lucky 2 Lady Dave Pither 2 Sam Squatch 1 Rev Robbie the Radical Recyclist 1) TUSC 7

[†] *Andrew's Previews 2016*, page 81; *2017*, page 196.

[‡] *Merton, St Helier*: Lab 1859 C 907 Grn 409 LD 241

[§] *Wandsworth, Bedford*: Lab 2714 C 1778 Grn 815 LD 310. Stanislaus resigned shortly afterwards prompting a further by-election, for which see page 503.

[¶] *Croydon, Kenley*: C 2220 Lab 618 LD 455 Grn 372 Heritage Party 52

[‖] *Croydon, Park Hill and Whitgift*: C 1188 Lab 724 Grn 199 LD 153

New Addington North[*], South Norwood[†] and Woodside[‡] are respectively Kola Agboola, Louis Carserides and Michael Bonello. Independent candidate Mark Samuel, a regular fixture in Croydon local by-elections who sometimes achieves the dizzy heights of ten votes, put in nomination papers for all five by-elections but was only allowed to contest one: he has chosen Woodside ward. Croydon council have recently received a petition for a mayoral referendum, which will be held over until the autumn.

Greenwich and Lewisham have turned up with four by-elections each, all of them Labour defences. In Lewisham, promising young Labour councillor Tom Copley is now a Deputy Mayor of London in Sadiq Khan's administration, while Joe Dromey (the son of Jack Dromey and Harriet Harman) has also taken up a new job which is politically restricted. They have vacated *Sydenham* and *New Cross* wards respectively. There are also by-elections in the south of the borough in the *Bellingham* ward[§] and the neighbouring ward of *Catford South*. All of these were safe for Labour in 2018. The defending Labour candidates are Rachel Onikosi in Bellingham[¶], James Royston in Catford South[‖], Samantha Latouche in New Cross[**] and Jack Lavery in Sydenham.[††]

Turning our attention to Greenwich, a mention is due to the first Muslim to become a UK local council leader. Mehboob Khan led the Labour group on Kirklees council in West Yorkshire from 2003 to 2014, and was leader of that council from 2009 to 2014. In 2015 he resigned from Kirklees council and transferred to Greenwich, taking over the seat in *Greenwich West* ward vacated by the newly-elected Greenwich and Woolwich MP Matthew Pennycook. Khan has now taken a politically-restricted job and accordingly a by-election needs to be held in Greenwich West. This is the core of historic Greenwich, taking in the town centre, the Royal Naval College, Greenwich Park and the old Observatory building, whose position defines the Greenwich Meridian of 0° longitude.

The by-election in Greenwich's *Glyndon* ward, covering the area between Plumstead and Woolwich, is less savoury. Tonia Ashikodi, who won a by-election here in May 2016 and was re-elected on the Labour slate in 2018, had accepted a council house in the borough in 2012 without revealing that she was the owner

---

[*] *Croydon, New Addington North*: Lab 1214 C 985 Ind 109 Grn 95 BNP 55 LD 38 [†] *Croydon, South Norwood*: Lab 2276 C 1173 Grn 423 LD 288 Taking the Initiative Party 251 Ind 154 [‡] *Croydon, Woodside*: Lab 2375 C 1315 Grn 515 LD 368 Taking the Initiative Party 219 Bone 125 Samuel 40 [§] For more on Bellingham ward see *Andrew's Previews 2016*, page 133. [¶] *Lewisham, Bellingham*: Lab 2118 C 738 Grn 336 Lewisham People Before Profit 303 LD 210 CPA 80 [‖] *Lewisham, Catford South*: Lab 2473 LD 891 C 761 Grn 590 CPA 114 Young People's Party 52 [**] *Lewisham, New Cross*: Lab 3038 Grn 862 C 526 Lewisham People Before Profit 219 LD 214 TUSC 111 [††] *Lewisham, Sydenham*: Lab 2634 C 982 Grn 820 LD 513 Lewisham People Before Profit 188

of three other properties. She was found guilty of two charges of fraud by false representation, and in March 2020 she resigned from the council after being given an 18-month suspended sentence. A by-election was immediately called to replace her but the pandemic intervened before it could be held, and Ashikodi's dishonesty has meant her council has had a vacant seat for over a year.

The other two Greenwich by-elections are also Labour defences, in the wards of *Kidbrooke with Hornfair* and *Shooters Hill* along the Roman road towards the Channel ports. On paper, none of these should give Labour any cause for concern. The defending Labour candidates are Sandra Bauer in Glyndon*, Pat Slattery in Greenwich West†, Odette McGahey in Kidbrooke with Hornfair‡, and Clare Burke-McDonald in Shooters Hill.§

The final two by-elections in London are both the result of councillors moving on to greater things. Conservative councillor and London Assembly member Gareth Bacon was elected in 2019 as the MP for Orpington, and he has vacated his BEXLEY council seat in *Longlands* ward (the western end of Sidcup). Labour councillor Marina Ahmad is contesting and is favourite to win the Lambeth and Southwark constituency in this year's London Assembly elections, and she has resigned her BROMLEY council seat in *Crystal Palace* ward. These should be safe defences for their respective parties' candidates: Lisa-Jane Moore for the Conservatives in Longlands¶, Ryan Thomson for Labour in Crystal Palace.‖

* *Greenwich, Glyndon*: Lab 2520 C 687 Grn 546 LD 402 TUSC 87 † *Greenwich, Greenwich West*: Lab 3203 C 1228 Grn 1135 LD 1121 Loony 110 ‡ *Greenwich, Kidbrooke with Hornfair*: Lab 1928 C 1519 Grn 621 LD 261 Ind 225 § *Greenwich, Shooters Hill*: Lab 2479 C 1286 Grn 548 LD 262 ¶ *Bexley, Longlands*: C 2467 Lab 859 Grn 323 LD 275 Heritage Party 49 ‖ *Bromley, Crystal Palace*: Lab 2235 Grn 820 C 783 LD 370

6th May 2021 Part II: North and Midlands

So now, here is Part II, covering the north of England and the English Midlands. With the exception of the Cleveland police area, which will be the focus of Part IV.

Northumbria

Police and Crime Commissioner

Vera Baird, the former Labour MP for Redcar, was Northumbria PCC from 2012 until 2019 when she resigned to become Victims' Commissioner for England and Wales. The resulting by-election, held in July 2019, saw Labour's Kim McGuinness, a Newcastle upon Tyne city councillor, take the lead on first preferences: 38%, against 22% each for two Northumberland councillors, independent candidate Georgina Hill and Conservative Robbie Moore; the Lib Dems coming in fourth and last with 19%. Having placed second narrowly ahead of Moore, Hill got into the runoff and picked up most of the transfers, meaning that McGuinness was elected in the final reckoning by the narrow margin of 52–48.

McGuinness is seeking re-election. Georgina Hill has not returned but there is a new independent candidate, NHS doctor Julian Kilburn. The Tories have had to change candidate after Robbie Moore got elected to Parliament in December 2019 (more on that story later) and they have selected Duncan Crute. Completing the ballot paper is Gateshead councillor Peter Maughan, standing for the Lib Dems.*

* *Northumbria PCC*: first preferences Lab 179021 C 118543 Ind 45567 LD 40955; runoff Lab 206467 C 139875

Local elections

The whole of Northumberland county council is up for election along with one-third of the seats in the five Tyne and Wear boroughs and the elected mayoralty of North Tyneside.

The Conservatives almost won an overall majority in NORTHUMBERLAND in May 2017. Their 12 net gains, for a total of 33 seats, were mostly due to a collapse by the Lib Dems who lost all their seats in the Berwick upon Tweed constituency. However, the Conservatives did also gain two seats in Cramlington (one of them from an obscure Labour councillor called Laura Pidcock, who subsequently had an ill-starred Parliamentary career in North West Durham) and they tied for first place in the South Blyth division whose Lib Dem councillor was re-elected on the returning officer's drawing of lots. This was a sign of things to come: Cramlington and Blyth are both in the Blyth Valley constituency which was the first declared Conservative gain of the December 2019 general election. With 33 seats against 24 for Labour, 7 independents and 3 Lib Dems the Conservatives formed a minority administration, although they're a man down at the moment after Robbie Moore went off to become MP for Keighley. His seat in Alnwick is vacant, and this was crucial in 2020 when the then Conservative leader Peter Jackson lost a confidence vote over a whistleblowing scandal by 33 votes to 32.

The largest of the five Tyne and Wear boroughs is another early declarer: the city of SUNDERLAND. This column wrote in 2019 that Sunderland has a Labour administration which is very locally unpopular while also having a very secure majority, and despite the fact that Labour lost 12 councillors in 2019 that's still true. The Labour group currently has 51 seats (three of which are vacant), against 12 Conservatives, 8 Lib Dems, 3 UKIPpers and 1 Green (whose seat is vacant). There are 10 wards with split representation and Labour are defending every single one of them; but for the party's majority to be in serious danger they'd have to do far worse even than in 2019..

NORTH TYNESIDE is different to the other four Tyne and Wear boroughs in that it has an *elected mayor*. The mayoralty has been held by both Labour and the Conservatives in the past with a number of very close results, but the last mayoral election in 2017 had a big lead for Labour's Norma Redfearn who was re-elected in the first round with a 56–31 lead over the Conservatives.

Redfearn is seeking re-election for a third term as Mayor. The Conservatives have selected Steven Robinson, a Royal Marine turned British Gas engineer. Also standing are John Appleby for the Lib Dems, Jack Thomson for UKIP and Penny Remfry for the Green Party.*

* *Mayor of North Tyneside*: Lab 33119 C 19366 Grn 4278 LD 3549 UKIP 1753

Including vacancies, Labour hold 51 of the 60 seats on North Tyneside council against 7 Conservatives, a Lib Dem and an independent. A repeat of the 2019 results would result in no change to the Labour total, as they would pick up the Lib Dem seat in Northumberland ward to offset a net loss to the Conservatives. In the event that the Conservatives gain the mayoralty, it's likely that the new mayor will have to cohabit with a Labour-majority council.

Labour are secure in the other three Tyne and Wear boroughs, although they may suffer a net loss of seats in SOUTH TYNESIDE, where there has been some infighting in the Labour group, and in NEWCASTLE UPON TYNE where the Lib Dems and localists did reasonably well in 2019.

Durham

Police and Crime Commissioner

Ron Hogg, who had led the English police response against football hooliganism during the 2002 FIFA World Cup in Japan and South Korea, had been the Durham PCC since 2012. In 2016 he was re-elected in the first round, defeating the Conservatives 64–24. Hogg died in December 2019 and his deputy, Steven White, has been serving as PCC in an acting capacity since then.

The Labour Party have selected Joy Allen as their new candidate for Durham PCC; she is the Mayor of Bishop Auckland and a cabinet member on Durham county council. The Tories' George Jabbour, who claims to be the only candidate ever to run for election in all four nations of the UK, adds a PCC run to his previous attempts at elections to Parliament (in Inverclyde), the Senedd (in Bridgend), the Northern Ireland Assembly (in Belfast South) and three local authority mayoral elections (in Doncaster, Mansfield and Watford). He's never been particularly close to winning on any of those occasions. Anne-Marie Curry completes the ballot paper for the Lib Dems.*

Local elections

There are whole council elections this year for DURHAM council. The last elections here were in 2017 and left Labour with a reduced majority. They won 74 seats against 25 for various categories of independents and localists, 14 for the Liberal Democrats (who are particularly strong in Durham city), 10 Conservatives and 3 seats for the North East Party, a regionalist movement with a powerbase in the New Town of Peterlee. None of the ten Conservative councillors were

* *Durham PCC*: first preferences Lab 71084 C 69748 LD 21376; runoff Lab 80510 C 77352

elected in the North West Durham constituency, which the party now holds in Westminster. There have been six by-elections since 2017, with Labour holding three, the Lib Dems holding one* and gaining one from Labour†, and a very fragmented by-election in Spennymoor in May 2019 which saw an independent candidate finish in first place with just 19% of the vote, succeeding a different independent.‡

There are no scheduled local elections this year in DARLINGTON, but that borough will take part in the Tees Valley mayoral election which is discussed in the forthcoming Part IV of the preview. Darlington council does have two by-elections: Paul Howell, the new Conservative MP for Sedgefield, has vacated his seat in *Hummersknott* ward on the western edge of town, while on the eastern edge of town Labour are defending the *Red Hall and Lingfield* ward which Howell unsuccessfully contested in 2015. Both of those wards were safe in 2019, although Red Hall and Lingfield was fairly close in a November 2017 by-election§. The defending candidates are Jack Sowerby for the Conservatives in Hummersknott¶ and Mandy Porter for Labour in Red Hall and Lingfield.‖

Cumbria

Police and Crime Commissioner

The Cumbria PCC position has been held by the Conservatives since 2012. Peter McCall, a former Army officer who commanded a squadron during the Bosnian war, has served since 2016. On the first count he had 34% of the vote against 24% for Labour, 17% for the Lib Dems and 15% for an independent candidate; in the runoff McCall defeated the Labour candidate by 58–42.

McCall is seeking a second term. Labour have selected former Allerdale councillor Barbara Cannon. The Liberal Democrat candidate is Loraine Birchall, chair of the party's Barrow and Furness branch. The independent from last time has not returned, so those are your three candidates.**

Local elections

When it comes to discussion of Cumbrian local elections, there's really only one place we can start.

---

* *Andrew's Previews 2019*, page 66. † *Ibid.*, page 106. ‡ *Ibid.* § *Andrew's Previews 2017*, page 343. ¶ *Darlington, Hummersknott*: C 971 Grn 809 Lab 120 LD 32 For Britain Movement 14 ‖ *Darlington, Red Hall and Lingfield*: C 466 Lab 360 Ind 201 Grn 38 LD 27 For Britain Movement 11 [C gain from Lab] ** *Cumbria PCC*: C 56753 Lab 27687 LD 21506

Figure 21: The Cursing Stone

Figure 21 is your columnist's photograph of the Cursing Stone. Located in a pedestrian subway just outside Carlisle Castle in the city centre, and installed in 2001, it's a polished granite boulder inscribed with a 1,069-word curse placed on border reivers in 1525 by Gavin Dunbar, then archbishop of Glasgow. It has cursed CARLISLE.

That's a strong statement to make, but consider: in the year the Stone was installed the farms of Cumberland were devastated by foot-and-mouth disease. The city has suffered a series of devastating floods, in 2005 and the Storm Desmond flood of 2015, which took out the McVitie's factory and led to a national biscuit shortage which lasted for months. The Cursing Stone has taken the blame for a series of well-publicised crimes, hits to the local economy and even Carlisle United's relegation from the football league in 2004. Coincidence?

Consider also: after the 2005 flood Jim Tootle, city and county councillor for Castle ward which then covered the Cursing Stone, proposed to the city council that it be removed or destroyed to prevent any further nasty things happening. The council voted to keep it. Seven years later Tootle was dead at the age of 59, and since then a series of other councillors for Castle ward have died at an early age or resigned. Since the Cursing Stone was installed, Carlisle's Castle ward has had a horrific councillor attrition rate, with nine by-elections here (either at city or county level) in the fifteen years from 2001 to 2016.* Coincidence?

Consider also: the scheduled elections this year for the whole of Cumbria county council and one-third of Carlisle and South Lakeland councils have been

* See most recently *Andrew's Previews 2016*, pages 192 and 294.

cancelled, pending a possible reorganisation of local government in the area. As a result, only the PCC elections and a series of by-elections are taking place in the county on 6th May. One of these is a by-election to Carlisle city council for the renamed and redrawn ward of Cathedral and—you guessed it—Castle.

Coincidence?

Cathedral and Castle, Carlisle's city-centre ward, is just one of three by-elections in Carlisle which Labour have the task of holding on 6th May. These days it's a safe Labour ward, as is *Newtown and Morton North* ward in the inner west of the city; Labour also have a full slate of councillors in *Harraby South and Parklands* ward, along the London Road at the south-eastern entrance to the city, but the Conservatives and UKIP were both fairly close behind at the only previous poll on these lines in 2019. UKIP haven't returned, but the Conservatives have selected Linda Mitchell in Harraby South and Parklands, while the defending Labour candidate there is Abdul Harid.[*] The Labour defences in the other two Carlisle city by-elections are led by Pete Sunter (Cathedral and Castle)[†] and David Graham (Newtown and Morton North).[‡]

The Carlisle returning officer also has the task of organising a by-election to Cumbria county council in the *Brampton* division. This covers the town of Brampton, on the road and railway line from Carlisle to Newcastle, as well as six other parishes to the north-east of the town. Brampton division was safe Conservative at the last county council elections in 2019, and their defending candidate is Mike Mitchelson.[§]

The returning officer for ALLERDALE is even busier, with seven by-elections to arrange. Two of these arise from the death of Joe Holliday, who was an independent member of both the district and the county councils. His district council ward was *St John's*, the eastern ward of Workington town; his county council seat of *St John's and Great Clifton* added two villages to the east of Workington. St John's returned two independents and a Labour councillor in 2019, while the county division was close between Holliday and Labour in 2017. Independent district councillor Paul Scott is standing to replace Holliday in the county by-election[¶], while the district by-election has two defending independent candidates (George Campbell and Andrew Eccles)[‖]; the Labour candidate for both by-elections is Antony McGuckin, who was runner-up to Holliday in 2017.

---

[*] *Carlisle, Harraby South and Parklands*: C 1028 Lab 752 Grn 132 [C gain from Lab] [†] *Carlisle, Cathedral and Castle*: Lab 673 C 599 Grn 299 LD 95 Reform UK 49 [‡] *Carlisle, Newtown and Morton North*: C 883 Lab 767 Grn 101 TUSC 40 [C gain from Lab] [§] *Cumbria CC, Brampton*: C 933 LD 272 Lab 246 Grn 208 [¶] *Cumbria CC, St John's and Great Clifton*: C 621 Lab 603 Ind 368 LD 54 Grn 41 [C gain from Ind] [‖] *Allerdale, St John's*: Lab 513 C 451 Eccles 250 Campbell 55 LD 41 Grn 30 [Lab gain from Ind]

Facing St John's ward across the River Derwent is the *Seaton and Northside* ward of Allerdale council, which has been vacated by the new Workington MP Mark Jenkinson. Jenkinson was first elected to the predecessor Seaton ward in 2015 as a UKIP candidate, the other two seats in Seaton going to his Kipper running-mate Joe Sandwith and Labour's Celia Tibble. In the revised ward in 2019 Sandwith again topped the poll, this time as an independent candidate; a second independent was elected; and Jenkinson was re-elected to the final seat with the Conservative nomination and a massive personal vote. He polled 582 votes, enjoying a majority of 36 over the Labour slate, while his Tory running-mates only scored 117 and 97. Can all that Conservative vote transfer to another candidate? The Tories' Colin Sharpe will hope it can, while independent Aileen Brown and Labour's Beth Dixon will attempt to prove otherwise.*

The Conservatives will fancy their chances of gaining two by-elections in the town of Cockermouth. One is for the county council in *Cockermouth North*, which was a Lib Dem gain from the Conservatives in 2017; Fiona Jayatilaka is the defending Lib Dem candidate here, while the Tories have selected Catherine Bell.† The Allerdale district ward boundaries divide Cockermouth east–west rather than north–south, with Labour defending a by-election in *Christchurch*, the town's western ward; this was close between Labour and Conservative in 2019, and Labour's Helen Tucker has work to do to hold off the Tories' Alan Kennon.‡

Another chance of a Conservative pickup arises in the *Ellen and Gilcrux* ward, covering three parishes along the River Ellen to the east of Maryport. This ward elected the Labour slate in 2019, but one of the Labour councillors has been kicked off for non-attendance and the Tories are just about within marginal range. Martin Harris is the defending Labour candidate, while Patrick Gorrill will try to gain for the Conservatives.§ The neighbouring ward of *Aspatria* (pronounced a-SPAY-tree-a, for those who weren't aware) was the only seat won in 2019 by the localist movement Putting Cumbria First; the localist councillor defected to the Conservatives before resigning, and with no new Putting Cumbria First candidate the Tories' Lucy Winter will attempt to convert their defection gain into a by-election gain.¶

There are enough by-elections here that they could make a significant difference to control of Allerdale council, which currently stands at 17 independent

* *Allerdale, Seaton and Northside*: C 629 Ind 415 Lab 395 Grn 48 LD 27 † *Cumbria CC, Cockermouth North*: C 807 Lab 546 LD 411 Grn 135 Ind 54 [C gain from LD] ‡ *Allerdale, Christchurch*: C 623 Lab 378 LD 248 Ind 21 For Britain Movement 12 [C gain from Lab] § *Allerdale, Ellen and Gilcrux*: C 343 Lab 285 Ind 193 Grn 38 LD 12 [C gain from Lab] ¶ *Allerdale, Aspatria*: Ind 531 C 344 Lab 158 Workers Party 21 [Ind gain from Putting Cumbria First]

councillors, 15 Conservatives, 12 Labour and 5 vacancies. An Independent–Conservative coalition was formed after the 2019 elections, but this has recently collapsed leaving the Conservatives in minority control.

In COPELAND district, we finally get around to the by-election in *Whitehaven Central* ward which was postponed from March 2020. For those who haven't been to Whitehaven, you should: despite the predations of John Paul Jones it's a rather handsome port full of nice Georgian buildings. Whitehaven Central ward was created for the 2019 election, at which it split its three seats between two Labour candidates and an independent with the Conservatives not far behind. Joseph Ghayouba defends for Labour, Richard Donnan stands as an independent candidate, and there may be some confusion generated by the Conservatives and the Heritage Party nominating two different candidates both called William Dixon.*

We finish our tour of Cumberland as was by travelling to EDEN district. A few years ago Andrew's Previews visited the most White British ward in England and Wales, *Hartside* ward on the western slopes of the High Pennines†; on that occasion Robin Orchard succeeded his late wife Sheila as the ward's Conservative councillor. Sheila Orchard, incidentally, had taken the seat over from John Lancaster, the father of the former England rugby head coach Stuart Lancaster. I am sorry to report that councillor Robin Orchard has since passed away in his turn. Orchard won the 2018 by-election easily and nobody opposed his re-election in 2019; for this by-election the defending Conservative candidate is Raymond Briggs (no, not that one).‡ There is also a poll in *Skelton* ward, covering two far-flung parishes on the road from Penrith to Wigton and taking in the village of Unthank, which is vacated by the former Conservative council leader Kevin Beaty. Beaty had represented the ward since 2011 but only faced one contested election, defeating the Lib Dems easily in 2019; Colin Atkinson will try to hold his seat for the Conservatives.§ The Conservatives lost control of Eden council in 2019, and a recent attempt by them to topple a rainbow anti-Conservative coalition failed.

Two by-elections take place to BARROW-IN-FURNESS council. *Hindpool* ward, covering part of the town centre and points west, is a very safe Labour area where their candidate Jo Tyson should knock out the opposition.¶ The Conservatives' Jay Zaccarini should have few problems defending the village of *Roosecote*, just to the east of the town.‖

* *Copeland, Whitehaven Central*: Lab 633 C 542 Ind 90 Heritage Party 45 LD 18 † *Andrew's Previews 2018*, page 47. ‡ *Eden, Hartside*: C 194 Castle-Clarke 101 Lab 94 Parks 41 § *Eden, Skelton*: C 302 LD 131 Grn 81 Lab 41 ¶ *Barrow-in-Furness, Hindpool*: Lab 600 C 359 ‖ *Barrow-in-Furness, Roosecote*: C 881 Lab 564

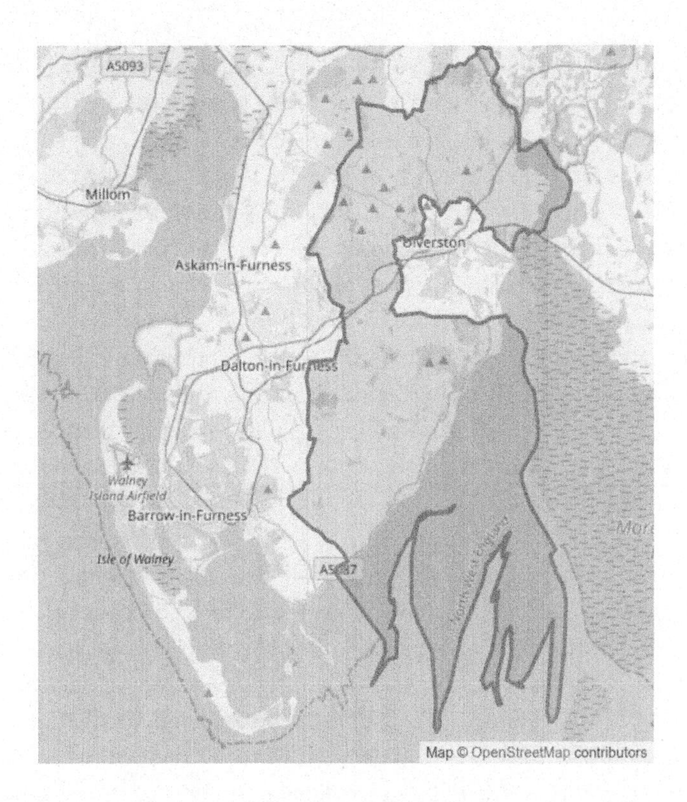

Figure 22: *Ph'nglui mglw'nafh Cthulhu R'lyeh wgah'nagl fhtagn.*

The Conservative challenge to the Tim Farron political machine in South Lakeland may have been dented by the retirement from frontline politics of James Airey, who was leader of the Conservative group on the county council and had also previously led the Conservative group on Lancaster council. Airey was the Conservatives' parliamentary candidate for Westmorland and Lonsdale in 2017 and 2019, losing narrowly to Farron on both occasions. He has taken up a new position with the National Farmers' Union.

Accordingly we have by-elections for Airey's seats on Cumbria county council and South Lakeland council. His county seat was *Ulverston West*. The town of Ulverston is developing a bit of a counter-culture vibe, but Airey had a large majority in 2017 and Andrew Butcher, the Conservative candidate for the county by-election, will start as favourite.*

Ulverston West has no overlap with Airey's district seat of *Furness Peninsula*, which must be a strong candidate for the UK's most cthulhoid ward. I mean, just look at Figure 22. Thankfully Cthulhu is not qualified to be a councillor

* *Cumbria CC, Ulverston West*: Grn 885 C 869 Lab 380 LD 102 [Grn gain from C]

because the house at R'lyeh is outside the boundaries of South Lakeland district; as such the electors will be unable to vote for the greater evil on this occasion. In the real world Furness Peninsula ward returned three Conservative councillors in 2018, the first contest on these boundaries, with the Lib Dems close behind; and the 2019 election saw the Lib Dems gain a seat. So this is one to watch between the defending Conservative candidate Ben Cooper and the Lib Dems' Loraine Birchall, who is also standing in the Ulverston West county by-election and for Police and Crime Commissioner.*

There are three other by-elections to South Lakeland council on 6th May, two of which are difficult Conservative defences within the Lake District National Park. *Broughton and Coniston* ward split its three seats between two Conservatives and a Lib Dem in 2018 and was a Lib Dem gain in 2019. The final Conservative seat is up in this by-election, with their candidate Matt Brereton (who lost his seat in 2019) up against the Lib Dems' Heather Troughton.† *Kendal Rural* ward wraps around the north of the town to take in the Lune Gorge, which travellers on the motorway and railway line to Carlisle and Glasgow will traverse; the largest settlement here is Staveley-in-Kendal. This ward returned two Lib Dems and a Conservative in 2018 with the Lib Dems holding one of their two seats easily in 2019; the other Lib Dem seat is up in this by-election, and the party's defending candidate is Ali Jama.‡

We finish our tour of Cumbria's by-elections on the county's south coast, in the Victorian seaside resort of Grange-over-Sands. This forms the *Grange* ward of South Lakeland council, which was close between the Lib Dems and Conservatives in 2018 but was safe Lib Dem in 2019. Pete Endsor is their defending candidate.§

Lancashire

Police and Crime Commissioner

The Lancashire police and crime commissioner is Labour's Clive Grunshaw. In May 2016 he polled 44% in the first round against 32% for the Conservatives and 17% for UKIP, and went on to win the run-off by a 56–44 margin.

Grunshaw is seeking re-election for a third term. The Conservatives have selected Lancashire county councillor Andrew Snowden. UKIP's 2016 candidate

* *South Lakeland, Furness Peninsula*: C 939 LD 790 Lab 216 Grn 111 † *South Lakeland, Broughton and Coniston*: LD 1317 C 977 Grn 136 Lab 108 [LD gain from C] ‡ *South Lakeland, Kendal Rural*: LD 1206 C 794 Grn 239 Lab 74 § *South Lakeland, Grange*: LD 1427 C 627 Grn 163 Lab 155. For a subsequent by-election here in August see page 319.

James Barker stands again with the Reform UK nomination, and the ballot paper is completed by Neil Darby for the Liberal Democrats.*

Local elections

There are elections this year for the whole of Lancashire county council, the whole of Chorley and Pendle councils on new ward boundaries, and one-third of Blackburn with Darwen, Burrnley, Hyndburn, Preston, Rossendale and West Lancashire councils.

Lancashire county council has swung rather wildly in recent years: Labour in 2005, Conservative in 2009, hung in 2013 with Labour as the largest party, Conservative in 2017. That election returned 46 Conservative councillors against 30 Labour, 4 Lib Dems, 2 independents, a Green councillor and the only UKIP councillor returned in 2017 (in Padiham and Burrnley West; he is now in the Conservatives, and leads the Tory group on Burrnley council as we shall come to later). The Tories had a majority of 8 seats which rests on particularly good results in marginal Rossendale and Colne and the New Town territory of Leyland. There are a large number of marginal divisions in these areas, and on current polling this will be a difficult council for the Conservatives to defend.

The Conservatives did particularly well in East Lancashire at the 2019 general election, but generally this wasn't off a strong local government base. Their strongest council is Pendle covering the towns of Nelson and Colne, but the Conservatives lost control here in May 2019 to a Labour/Lib Dem coalition. There are new ward boundaries in Pendle this year with all the seats up for election; at the time of writing the Conservatives hold 22 seats (two of which are vacant), Labour 16 (one of which is vacant), the Lib Dems have 9 (one of which is vacant) and there is one independent. One of the Tory vacancies is in respect of the new Bury South MP Christian Wakeford, who was the group leader here before he entered the Commons; Wakeford was subsequently thrown off Pendle council under the six-month non-attendance rule, which doesn't say much for his organisational skills.

Further down the Calder valley we come to Burrnley, which elected MPs from all three main parties in the last decade but whose council elections tell a rather different story. Labour lost their majority on Burrnley council in May 2019, and the council currently stands at 22 Labour seats against 8 Lib Dems, 6 members of the Burrnley and Padiham Independent Party, 6 Tories (three of whom were elected for UKIP, whose council group have effectively performed a

* *Lancashire PCC*: first preferences C 166202 Lab 154195 LD 32813 Reform UK 17926; runoff C 181354 Lab 172362 [C gain from Lab]

reverse takeover of the Burrnley Conservatives), 2 Greens and an independent. A rainbow anti-Labour coalition was formed after the 2019 election, but this fell apart in September 2020 and Labour are back in minority control. If the 2019 results are repeated, Labour would lose Trinity ward to the Greens and Rosegrove with Lowerhouse to the localists.

HYNDBURN district (based on Accrington) has a Tory MP now but a large Labour majority on its council, which currently stands at 26 Labour seats (one of which is vacant) and 8 Conservative seats (two of which are vacant). The vacant seats are in the politically split wards of Barnfield (in eastern Accrington), Overton (in Great Harwood) and St Andrew's (in Oswaldtwistle). The Overton ward has a rather tasty candidate list, with the defending Labour candidate being former council leader and Lancashire MEP Michael Hindley, and the Conservatives having selected Gareth Molineux who has previously been a Labour councillor for the area at both district and county level. A repeat of the 2019 results would result in two seats swapping to give no net change here.

By contrast Labour have a difficult defence of ROSSENDALE council over the moors in the upper Irwell valley. They currently hold 19 out of 36 councillors, against 13 Tories and 4 independents and localists. This time Labour are defending two wards (plus one held by a councillor who was expelled from Labour and isn't standing again) which voted Conservative in 2019 together with Eden ward, a normally-Tory area which surprisingly went Labour in 2016 in the aftermath of severe flooding in Irwell Vale on Boxing Day 2015. This is one to watch.

South-facing Rossendale is paired for parliamentary purposes with north-facing Darwen, which is part of the borough of BLACKBURN WITH DARWEN. This is strongly Labour (34 out of 51 seats at present) and if the 2019 results are repeated Labour would gain one seat from the Conservatives. The councillors up for election here were last elected in 2018 following boundary changes.

Perhaps surprisingly Labour have an even larger majority on CHORLEY council (37 out of 47 seats), having gained five seats here from the Conservatives in 2019. There are new ward boundaries in Chorley this year with all the seats on the council up for election, which may give the Tories some chance of fighting back although they start a long way behind.

New ward boundaries came in last year for PRESTON, resulting in a Labour majority with 30 seats against 9 each for the Tories and Lib Dems. Only one ward could be reasonably described as marginal on the basis of the 2019 results (Tory-held Sharoe Green ward in Fulwood) so we shouldn't expect much if any change here.

WEST LANCASHIRE elections are normally a snoozefest, this being an extremely polarised district where two-party swings are low; however, this year promises to be interesting. Currently Labour have 29 seats, the Conservatives have 19 and there are 6 councillors from the OWL group. The OWLs are not what they seem: the initials represent Our West Lancashire, a localist group which won all three wards in Ormskirk in the 2019 election. This time round Labour are defending two of the Ormskirk wards, and if they lose them both it will probably be No Overall Control time.

There are nine other local by-elections to report. In the politically-balanced SOUTH RIBBLE council Labour defend the *St Ambrose* ward in central Leyland, while the Conservatives defend the *Longton and Hutton West* ward off the Preston–Liverpool road; these are safe wards and should return Labour's Kath Unsworth[*] and the Tories' Julie Buttery[†] respectively.

Further up the Ribble Valley we come to three Tory-held wards in the RIBBLE VALLEY local government district. *Mellor* ward covers three parishes immediately to the north-west of Blackburn; *Billington and Langho* ward is the northern terminus of the Devil's Highway, the A 666 from Blackburn; *West Bradford and Grindleton* covers two villages north of Clitheroe which were once part of Yorkshire. All of these are very safe Conservative wards. The defending Tory candidates are Steve Farmer in Billington and Langho[‡], Robin Walsh in Mellor[§] and Kevin Horkin in West Bradford and Grindleton.[¶]

BLACKPOOL council has recently lost two veteran councillors. Lily Henderson may have been the oldest serving local councillor in the UK when she died in January at the age of 94; she had first been elected to Blackpool council in 1983 as a Conservative, and since 2000 she had represented *Highfield* ward in the south of the town. Her death leaves a tricky by-election in a marginal ward which has split its two seats between Labour and the Conservatives since 2011. Bradley Mitchell defends for the Conservatives, Christine Wright is the Labour candidate.[‖]

At the other end of Blackpool it is my sorry duty to have to take you to Norbreck. At the time of writing the Norbreck Castle Hotel was rated by Tripadvisor as 75th out of 81 hotels in Blackpool, and having had the dubious pleasure of staying there on several occasions (at someone else's expense, thank goodness) I am not going to disagree with that assessment except to say that the Britannia group were lucky to find six worse hotels in the resort. This dilapidated building on the seafront, a tram ride away from anywhere better, dominates the northern

[*] *South Ribble, St Ambrose*: Lab 517 C 398 LD 249 [†] *South Ribble, Longton and Hutton West*: C 1301 Lab 353 LD 151 Reform UK 70 Grn 61 [‡] *Ribble Valley, Billington and Langho*: C 638 Lab 254 Grn 81 [§] *Ribble Valley, Mellor*: C 712 LD 200 Lab 109 Grn 50 [¶] *Ribble Valley, West Bradford and Grindleton*: C 416 Lab 90 LD 77 [‖] *Blackpool, Highfield*: C 982 Lab 498 Ind 192 Grn 55 Reform UK 40 LD 22

end of Blackpool with discoloured crenellations that bring to mind a set of bad teeth.

The *Norbreck* ward which shares that hotel's name had been represented throughout this century by Maxine and Peter Callow, who were originally Conservatives. Peter Callow was the leader of Blackpool council from 2007 to 2011, overseeing a huge investment programme which saw the council buy the Blackpool Tower and the Winter Gardens, and upgrade the trams with modern vehicles. The Callows were deselected by the Blackpool Conservatives for the 2019 election, but were easily re-elected as independent candidates. Peter Callow died in November at the age of 81; he was in hospital for general observations, but is listed as another victim of COVID-19. The by-election to replace him is contested by new independent candidate Pam Haslam, a recent jackpot winner on the People's Postcode Lottery, while Julie Sloman will seek to recover the ward for the Conservatives.[*] These two by-elections are the only council polls in Blackpool this year.

Finally, there are two by-elections to LANCASTER council. One of these is for *Bulk* ward, the north-eastern ward of the city itself along the road towards Caton. This is one of the few safe wards for the Green Party, who are strong in Lancaster, and their defending candidate is Jack Lenox.[†] Outside the urban area we come to *Kellet* ward, covering five rural parishes east of Carnforth; this was safely Conservative in 2015 but the Lib Dems came from nowhere to win in 2019 with a majority of six votes. Ross Hunter is the new Lib Dem candidate, Stuart Morris will look to recover the seat for the Conservatives.[‡]

Merseyside

Police and Crime Commissioner

The Merseyside PCC position is held by Labour's Jane Kennedy. In 2016 she won in the first round with 62% of the vote, the Conservatives being her nearest challengers on 18%.

Kennedy has retired this year. Labour have selected Liverpool councillor Emily Spurrell. The Conservative candidate is Bob Teesdale, who is from Southport. Also standing are Kristofor Brown for the Lib Dems and Malcolm Webster for Reform UK.[§]

[*] *Blackpool, Norbreck*: C 963 Ind 480 Lab 378 LD 82 [C gain from Ind] [†] *Lancaster, Bulk*: Grn 1283 Lab 824 C 209 LD 45 [‡] *Lancaster, Kellet*: C 447 LD 271 Ind 161 [C gain from LD]
[§] *Merseyside PCC*: Lab 178785 C 71961 LD 51979 Reform UK 11662

Liverpool City Region mayoral election

The Liverpool City Region mayoralty covers a larger area than just Merseyside, with the Halton borough also included; this covers the towns of Runcorn and Widnes up the Mersey estuary. The first mayoral election was held in May 2017 and was a convincing win for the outgoing Liverpool Walton MP Steve Rotheram, who defeated Tory candidate Tony Caldeira in the first round by 59% to 20%.

Rotheram is seeking re-election. The Conservatives have changed candidate to Jade Marsden, who was their parliamentary candidate for Bootle in 2015 and Sefton Central in 2017. Also standing are David Newman for the Lib Dems and Gary Cargill for the Green Party.[*]

Local elections

There are elections this year for one-third of all the Merseyside boroughs plus the elected mayoralty of Liverpool.

The Liverpool mayoralty (not to be confused with the Liverpool City Region mayoralty, or the Lord Mayor of Liverpool) is likely to be the main point of interest in the big city. Labour's Joe Anderson performed poorly in 2016 relative to PCC Jane Kennedy; Anderson won in the first round with 53% compared to 20% for the Liberal Democrats and 11% for the Green Party. Recent well-publicised legal troubles, which prompted central government to send in the Commissioners, have forced him out of office. A controversial Labour selection produced Joanne Anderson; no relation of Big Joe, Joanne has appeared in this column before[†] when she won a by-election to the city council in Princes Park ward. She is not seeking re-election as a councillor this year, so the stakes are high for her. The Liberal Democrats have reselected their council group leader Richard Kemp, and the Green candidate is also their council group leader, Tom Crone. Completing the city mayoral ballot paper are Roger Bannister for the Trade Unionist and Socialist Coalition, Katie Burgess for the Conservatives, Steve Radford for the Liberal Party and independent candidate Stephen Yip.[‡]

Regardless of the mayoral result, the Commissioners will continue to work with a Labour-majority city council. Labour currently hold 72 out of 90 seats; a repeat of the 2019 results would see them lose one seat nett to the Greens.

Labour control of Knowsley is also secure, despite a poor performance in the 2019 election—if those results happen again the Green Party would gain

---

[*] *Mayor of the Liverpool City Region*: Lab 198736 C 66702 Grn 40211 LD 35049 [†] *Andrew's Previews 2019*, page 321. [‡] *Mayor of Liverpool*: first preferences Lab 38958 Ind 22047 LD 17166 Grn 8768 Lib 7135 C 4187 TUSC 2912; runoff Lab 46493 Ind 32079

two seats and an independent would gain one. A similar story played out in ST HELENS in 2019, where the Greens won two wards from nowhere and were close in a number of others; a repeat of those results would see Labour lose four seats. This will be the last thirds election to St Helens council, which is going over to whole-council elections on new ward boundaries from next year.

By contrast Labour are on the rise in SEFTON, having finally broken through into the traditional Lib Dem stronghold of Southport. They have a good chance of four seat gains this year (two from the Lib Dems in Southport, two from independents in Maghull) to increase the Labour majority. Currently Labour hold 43 out of 66 seats here, which is a mark of how far this area has swung to the left: Sefton had never had a Labour majority before 2012.

The Labour majority over the water in WIRRAL council has disappeared since the 2019 election partially as a result of infighting following a left-wing takeover. There are three wards with split representation, and this year Labour are defending all of them: Birkenhead/Tranmere and Prenton voted Green in 2019, whereas Pensby and Thingwall voted Conservative.

Cheshire

Police and Crime Commissioner

David Keane gained the Cheshire PCC post for Labour from the Conservatives in 2016. On first preferences he had 40% of the vote to 38% for the Tories and 12% for UKIP; in the run-off Cheshire went Labour by the narrow margin of 51% to 49%, a majority of 2,949 votes.

This election will be a rematch between Labour's David Keane and the Conservative PCC he beat in 2016, John Dwyer. With UKIP not standing again, the other candidates are Jo Conchie for the Lib Dems and Nick Goulding for Reform UK.*

Local elections

Following the 2019 local elections Labour, for the first time, have a monopoly on local government in Cheshire, running as a majority or as a minority all the local government districts which cover the county. And this is true whatever current or historical definition of Cheshire you use. Rather striking for the county that includes the richest areas of north-west England.

* *Cheshire PCC*: first preferences C 99565 Lab 83329 LD 32348 Reform UK 8258; runoff C 111962 Lab 99463 [C gain from Lab]

There are elections this year for all the councillors in HALTON and WARRINGTON, with new ward boundaries coming in for Halton. Both of these councils have strong Labour majorities at present (51 out of 56 seats in Halton, 45 out of 58 seats in Warrington), and Labour have a number of seats in Halton guaranteed due to insufficient opposition candidates. The Conservatives gained the Warrington South parliamentary seat in December 2019 but that wasn't based on local government strength: in 2016 the party won just two seats on Warrington council, in the Real Housewives territory of Lymm South, and one of those has since gone Lib Dem in a by-election.[*]

There are no local elections of any sort this year in Cheshire East or in Cheshire West and Chester apart from three by-elections. In CHESHIRE WEST AND CHESTER Labour currently have half of the seats, and that shouldn't change even with a by-election to defend in the town of *Neston* at the foot of the Wirral; Neston was safely Labour in 2019 and their candidate Keith Millar should be favoured to hold.[†] The opposition Conservatives should also have little trouble defending a by-election in *Frodsham*, after their councillor Andrew Dawson left these shores to take up a job with the Falkland Islands government; Christopher Basey can be expected to defend that poll.[‡] In the unlikely event that Labour hold Neston and gain Frodsham, they will gain an overall majority on the council. Over in CHESHIRE EAST the ruling Labour group should have little trouble holding a by-election in *Crewe West* ward, where their candidate is Connor Naismith.[§]

Greater Manchester

Mayor of Greater Manchester

The Greater Manchester mayoralty was created in 2017, subsuming the Police and Crime Commissioner post. Andy Burnham had a big win in the inaugural GM mayoral election, crushing the Tory candidate Sean Anstee by 63% to 23% in the first round. Unusually, a ward-level breakdown of the count was published, and the number of wards Anstee carried in the county (out of a possible 214) can be counted on the fingers of two hands.

Burnham is seeking re-election to (among other things) complete his bus franchising policy, and little which has happened since 2017 suggests that he will struggle to achieve re-election. The Tories have selected Laura Evans, a

[*] *Andrew's Previews 2018*, page 142. [†] *Cheshire West and Chester, Neston*: Lab 875 C 579 LD 80 [‡] *Cheshire West and Chester, Frodsham*: C 1481 Lab 1296 LD 384 Grn 176 [§] *Cheshire East, Crewe West*: Lab 724 C 539 Putting Crewe First 184 Grn 126 Ind 72 LD 55 Workers Party 13

former Trafford councillor. Also standing are Simon Lepori for the Lib Dems, Melanie Horrocks for the Green Party, Stephen Morris for the English Democrats, independent candidates Marcus Farmer, Alec Marvel and David Sutcliffe, and Nick Buckley for Reform UK.*

The Returning Officer has sent a booklet to all households with candidate statements. Its front cover carried a map of Greater Manchester's ten boroughs. As can be seen from Figure 23, this resulted in an unlikely viral Twitter hit...†

Local elections

There are elections this year for the whole of Goldfish ... sorry, Salford council on new ward boundaries, the Mayor of Salford, and one-third of the councillors in the other nine Greater Manchester boroughs.

The only Conservative-run metropolitan borough in the North of England is the Greatest Town in the Known Universe. Following a decisive rejection of Labour in the 2019 BOLTON council election a minority Conservative administration was installed by a gaggle of localist groups, the Lib Dems and UKIP. After a confusing series of defections, the composition of Bolton council is now (deep breath) 18 Labour, 17 Conservatives (1 elected as LD, 1 elected as UKIP), 6 Lib Dems (1 elected as Labour), 4 Farnworth and Kearsley First, 3 for the Bolton Independent Group (all elected as Conservative), 2 Horwich and Blackrod First Independents, 2 UKIP, 1 "One Kearsley" councillor (who was elected for Farnworth and Kearsley First), 4 ex-Labour independents (including all three councillors for Crompton ward), 1 ex-Conservative independent, and 2 vacancies following the deaths of Conservative councillors Christine and Paul Wild. Christine was due for re-election this year in Westhoughton North and Chew Moor ward, while there will be a by-election in Astley Bridge ward to replace Paul. We finally see the back of the infamous former Labour council leader Cliff Morris, who is standing down in Halliwell ward.

Students of Bolton politics have been greatly helped over the last year by the Twitter account *Bolton Elects*‡, run by a group of students who have bravely commissioned monthly polling of the Greatest Town. Their final pre-election poll, released on 30th April 2021, had topline figures of 34% for Labour, 26% for the Conservatives, 15% for the Lib Dems, 7% for the Greens and 14% for localist and other parties, which is a 3-point swing towards Labour since the 2019

* *Mayor of Greater Manchester*: Lab 473024 C 137753 Grn 30699 LD 22373 Reform UK 18910 EDP 9488 Farmer 6448 Sutcliffe 2182 Marvel 1907 † I was the second person to retweet this and I accept some responsibility for its going viral. At the time this book was put together Figure 23 had attracted over 600 retweets and over 2,700 likes, together with some press interest...

‡ `https://twitter.com/boltonelects`

GM mayoral election flyer amended by my 8year old:

Wigan: elephant
Bolton: cat
Bury: owl
Rochdale: rhino
Oldham: fox
Tameside: pig
Stockport: sideways man(?!)
Manchester: dog
Trafford: Harry Potter sorting hat
Salford: goldfish

What do other local authorities look like?

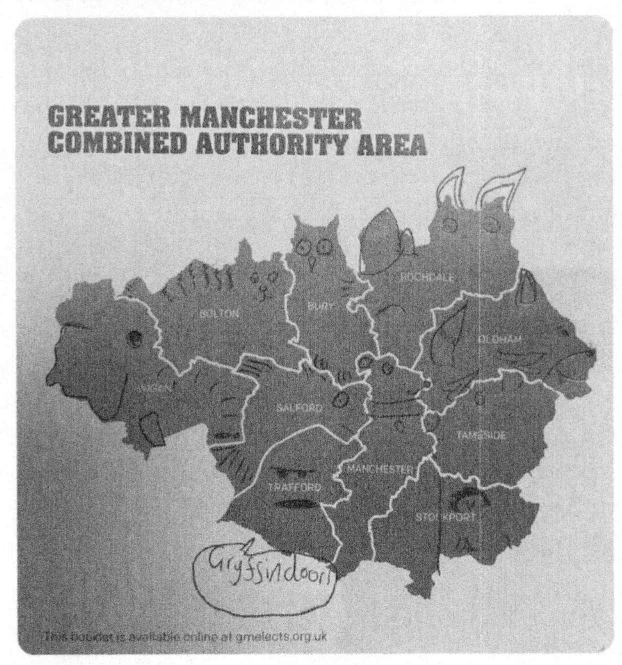

8:22 AM · Apr 22, 2021 · Twitter for iPhone

Figure 23: It's a jungle out there...

elections but a 3-point swing to the Conservatives since 2016, the year these seats were last contested.

Of the 12 wards Labour won in 2016, Farnworth and Hulton wards have already gone to the localists and the Conservatives in by-elections, while Breightmet, Crompton and Westhoughton South wards have been lost to defection. Of those, only Crompton is likely to come back and that will probably be offset by further losses in the two Horwich wards (to Horwich and Blackrod First). Even with the Lib Dems having withdrawn support for the minority Conservative administration, it should continue after these elections. The localists are continuing to multiply: a new "Bolton for Change" slate (containing a number of ex-UKIP figures) is standing in a number of wards, and there are now two competing localist parties in Keawyed City (namely "Active for Westhoughton" and the "Westhoughton First Independents"). Of the two UKIP councillors who won in 2016, Mark Cunningham in Kearsley is seeking re-election as a Conservative (although he'll probably lose to Farnworth and Kearsley First), while Rees Gibbon in Little Lever and Darcy Lever is seeking re-election in what's clearly going to be a close contest with Labour and the Conservatives, judging from the deluge of leaflets coming through this column's letterbox. One other thing: the Bolton Elects team have published ward subsamples, which with sample sizes of just over 100 aren't much better than noise but are consistently showing the Green Party in contention to win their first ever Bolton council seat in Hulton ward, the centre of a championship golf course planning controversy. Their final poll also has Bolton for Change running Labour very close in Tonge with the Haulgh ward. Watch this space.

The localist surge we have seen in Bolton could also spill over and cost Labour control of neighbouring BURY this year. This is a council to watch, as Bury is a small but perfectly formed metropolitan district. You can find everything here from Red Wall territory (Radcliffe) to trendy suburbs (Prestwich) to thriving towns (Bury) to well-off commuter areas (Tottington, Ramsbottom) to deprived estates (Dickie Bird). All human life is here.

Bury currently has 27 Labour councillors plus one vacancy, 14 Conservatives plus one vacancy, 4 Lib Dems, 1 independent elected as a Conservative and 3 independents elected on a localism ticket in the forgotten town of Radcliffe, giving a Labour majority of 3. In 2019 Labour lost Radcliffe North ward to the Conservatives, Radcliffe East ward to the localists and St Mary's ward in Prestwich to the Lib Dems; the localists subsequently took a by-election off Labour in working-class Radcliffe West. Labour are defending all those wards this year. There are several other marginal Labour wards which the Tories will have their eyes on, such as Elton and Unsworth in western and southern Bury; and of course this is a borough with two extremely marginal Conservative parliamentary seats. The Bury Conservatives have made the headlines with their nomination of Jihyun Park, the first North Korean defector to stand for election in the UK, on their slate for the Moorside ward of northern Bury; there are two seats up for election there this year following the resignation of a Labour councillor, but the Conservatives haven't won Moorside since 2006 and a gain this time would be a tall order.

On the positive side for Labour, they have a good chance of offsetting any losses in the previous paragraph by gaining marginal Conservative seats in Ramsbottom and Prestwich's Sedgley ward. Sedgley ward is 34% Jewish, the sixth-largest Jewish population for any ward in England and Wales, and was gained by the Conservatives in 2016; this was seen as a shock result at the time, and subsequent comfortable Labour holds in 2018 and 2019 suggest it might have been a fluke. The Tory defence here will be not be helped by the fact that their new candidate has put out a leaflet which managed to misspell "Prestwich" in three different ways. A Labour gain of Sedgley ward will likely be spun as an indication that the party is sorting out its anti-Semitism problem, but remember the 2018 and 2019 results before you accept that line.

The other major battle in Greater Manchester would appear to be for Stockport council. This is currently tied at 26 seats each for Labour and the Lib Dems, with 8 Conservatives and three Heald Green ratepayers holding the balance of power. In 2019 the Lib Dems gained five seats from the Conservatives and they have a chance of a further gain this year in Marple South and High Lane ward; that would probably make them the largest party on the council and could result in a change of control.

The other seven Greater Manchester boroughs have impregnable Labour majorities, and that includes Salford where all 60 councillors are up for re-election on new ward boundaries this year. The new lines have created a completely new ward in the inner city, reflecting large housing developments under construction in the Quays area; the new Quays ward is hugely undersized at the moment in population terms but this should resolve itself over the next few years.

Salford has an *elected mayor* of its own, currently Labour's Paul Dennett who won the 2016 mayoral election in the first round: he polled 51% against 26% for the Conservatives and 16% for UKIP. Dennett is standing for a second term. The Conservative candidate is Arnie Saunders, who has appeared in this column before: a rabbi from Broughton Park, he was the Tory candidate who won the Kersal by-election in 2017* and has subsequently turned Kersal, the number 1 Jewish ward in England and Wales. into a Conservative stronghold. Saunders

* *Andrew's Previews 2017*, page 66.

was the Conservative parliamentary candidate for Worsley and Eccles South in 2019. UKIP haven't returned, so completing the Salford mayoral ballot paper are Wendy Olsen for the Green Party, independent candidates Stuart Cremins and Stephen Ord, and Jake Overend for the Lib Dems.*

West Yorkshire

Mayor of West Yorkshire

The latest piece in the devolution jigsaw will slot into place in these elections with the first poll for the West Yorkshire mayoralty. This position covers the five metropolitan boroughs of Bradford, Calderdale, Kirklees, Leeds and Wakefield, and will replace the West Yorkshire police and crime commissionership.

The outgoing PCC is Labour's Mark Burns-Williamson, who has overseen the county's police force almost continuously since 2003 when he became chairman of the former West Yorkshire police authority. In the 2016 election he came very close to winning in the first round, polling just under 50% against 23% for the Conservatives and 14% for UKIP, and increased his lead to 66–34 in the runoff.

Burns-Williamson is not standing again. For the new mayoralty Labour have selected Tracey Brabin, a former *Coronation Street* actress who has been MP for Batley and Spen since winning the 2016 by-election after Jo Cox' murder†. The Conservative candidate is Matt Robinson, a Leeds city councillor. There's no UKIP candidate this time, so completing the ballot paper are Stewart Golton for the Lib Dems, Thérèse Hirst for the English Democrats, Waj Ali for Reform UK, Bob Buxton for the Yorkshire Party and Andrew Cooper for the Green Party.‡

Local elections

There are elections this year for one-third of the councillors in all five West Yorkshire boroughs. All of these had Labour majorities following the party's gain of CALDERDALE in May 2019; that council's Labour group (currently 28 councillors out of 51) has the chance to substantially increase its majority this year, as the Conservatives are defending 6 wards which voted for Labour, Lib Dem or an independent candidate in 2019.

The Labour majority in KIRKLEES district, however, disappeared in November 2020 after three councillors walked out of the party and went independent.

* *Mayor of Salford*: Lab 30892 C 12234 Grn 4585 Ord 1890 LD 1716 Cremins 1036 † *Andrew's Previews 2016*, page 251. ‡ *Mayor of West Yorkshire*: first preferences Lab 261170 C 176167 Yorkshire Party 58851 Grn 55833 LD 30162 Reform UK 14943 EDP 8969; runoff Lab 310923 C 209137

The party also faces a relatively difficult ward map—a repeat of the 2019 results would see Labour make a net loss of one seat. Two of the Conservative gains in West Yorkshire at the December 2019 election are within Kirklees district (Colne Valley and Dewsbury) but the party has some catching up to do at the local level. Also watch out for the Heavy Woollen District Independents, who won the closely-knit ward of Dewsbury East in 2019.

The other three West Yorkshire boroughs have comfortable Labour majorities, particularly so in WAKEFIELD where the party holds three-quarters of the seats. The Conservatives made no impression at all here in May 2019: they held the four seats they were defending but fell short in their target ward of Wrenthorpe and weren't particularly close anywhere else. Despite this, the party broke through to gain the Wakefield parliamentary constituency in December 2019. The council's ward map is better for the Conservatives this year, as they will have the chance to gain the two Ossett wards which Labour are now defending. Labour are also in trouble in Knottingley ward, which has suddenly turned into a Lib Dem hotspot. Regrettably, Wakefield has an entry for the Councillors Behaving Badly file: Alex Kear, elected two years ago as an independent councillor for Airedale and Ferry Fryston ward, is now serving a four-year prison sentence for paedophile offences, and there will be a replacement for him elected at this election.

North Yorkshire

Police and Crime Commissioner

The North Yorkshire PCC position is Conservative-held. The incumbent is Julia Mulligan, who in the 2016 election polled 40% against 26% for Labour and 23% for an independent candidate, beating Labour 59–41 in the runoff.

Mulligan is not standing again and the Conservatives have selected Philip Allott, a former leader of the Conservative group on Harrogate council and their parliamentary candidate for Halifax in 2015. Away from politics he runs a PR agency. The Labour candidate is Alison Hume, an award-winning TV screenwriter who was on the Labour list for Yorkshire and the Humber in the 2019 European Parliament elections. Also standing are independent candidate Keith Tordoff and the Lib Dems' James Barker.*

* *North Yorkshire PCC*: first preferences C 73656 Lab 40803 Ind 22338 LD 19773; runoff C 83737 Lab 53442. For a subsequent by-election for this position see page 495.

Local elections

The scheduled elections this year for the whole of North Yorkshire county council and one-third of Craven council have been postponed to 2022, to allow time for a consultation on local government reorganisation. As a result, only by-elections are taking place to the county's local councils. Two of these are for the COUNTY COUNCIL. The Liberal Democrats defend their seat in the two-member county division of *Harrogate Bilton and Nidd Gorge*, covering the northern end of Harrogate town; the other seat in this division was Lib Dem in 2005 and 2009, UKIP in 2013 and Conservative in 2017, so we can expect an interesting contest here. Andrew Kempston-Parkes is the defending Liberal Democrat candidate, Matt Scott will seek to gain for the Conservatives.*

In the Yorkshire Dales National Park the Conservatives defend two by-elections in beautiful Ribblesdale, following the death of Richard Welch who sat on both the county council and CRAVEN council. His county seat of *Ribblesdale* runs from the source of the Ribble all the way to the Lancashire border, with the town of Settle as the major population centre. Craven's *Penyghent* ward covers Ribblesdale from Stainforth northwards, together with the village of Giggleswick on the main road from Skipton to Kendal. Welch had large majorities in both wards, and the succeeding Tory candidates David Staveley (for the county seat)† and Robert Ogden (for the district seat)‡ will be favoured.

Staying in the Yorkshire Dales National Park, there is a second by-election to Craven council for the *Barden Fell* ward. This is based on Wharfedale around the village of Bolton Abbey, taking in the ruined Bolton Priory, and also extends west to cover the quarrying village of Rylstone. Barden Fell had been a Conservative-held ward until 2016, when it was gained by independent candidate David Pighills. Pighills was subsequently thrown off the council under the six-month non-attendance rule, but he is seeking re-election in the by-election caused by his own disqualification. That by-election is a straight fight with the Tories' John Dawson.§

Our final North Yorkshire by-election couldn't be in a more different landscape. The *Camblesforth and Carlton* ward of SELBY district takes in nine parishes on the flat agricultural land between the Aire and the Ouse before their confluence just north of Goole. The ward is dominated in every way by the massive Drax power station, which supplies 6 per cent of Britain's electricity; Drax was once the third-largest coal-fired power station in Europe, but its

* *North Yorkshire CC, Harrogate Bilton and Nidd Gorge*: C 1991 LD 1639 Lab 434 Grn 430 Yorkshire Party 136 Ind 46 [C gain from LD] † *North Yorkshire CC, Ribblesdale*: C 1537 Lab 475 LD 430 Grn 395 ‡ *Craven, Penyghent*: C 392 LD 295 Lab 103 § *Craven, Barden Fell*: Ind 500 C 142

conversion to biomass fuel is well under way. Camblesforth and Carlton ward voted Conservative in 2015, but one of its councillors, Mike Jordan, subsequently defected to the Yorkshire Party and was re-elected in 2019 under the colours of the White Rose. Jordan is now back in the Tory fold, and following the resignation of his running-mate Paul Welburn the Yorkshire Party have not put up a candidate to defend this by-election. Camblesforth and Carlton can be expected to revert to the Conservatives, whose candidate is Charles Richardson.*

Humberside

Police and Crime Commissioner

Labour gained the Humberside PCC position at the 2016 election, defeating Tory incumbent Matthew Grove 60-40 in the runoff; the first round had given 40% to Labour, 27% to the Conservatives and 18% to UKIP. Grove had won narrowly in 2012, defeating the UKIP MEP Godfrey Bloom and former Deputy Prime Minister John Prescott.

The Labour incumbent PCC is former police chief superintendent Keith Hunter, who is seeking re-election. The Conservatives had to change candidate at the last minute after Craig Ulliott, who was originally selected over a year ago, stood down just nine days before the nominations deadline; Hunter has since passed a file to Humberside Police with electoral fraud allegations against Ulliott. Jonathan Evison, the present Mayor of North Lincolnshire, is picking up the pieces of the Conservative campaign. With no UKIP candidate this time Bob Morgan, of the Liberal Democrats, completes the ballot paper.†

Local elections

Two of the four Humberside boroughs are holding elections this year. NORTH EAST LINCOLNSHIRE, based on Grimsby, Cleethorpes and surrounding villages, has swung a mile to the right in recent years at both parliamentary and council level; the Tories won an overall majority here in 2019, and a repeat of those results would see them gain four more seats.

Things are rather different over the Humber estuary in the big city of KINGSTON UPON HULL. This has a rather narrow Labour majority of 31 seats out of a possible 57, with a significant Liberal Democrat opposition of 24. The city got

* *Selby, Camblesforth and Carlton*: C 996 Lab 342 Grn 162 [C gain from Yorkshire Party]

† *Humberside PCC*: first preferences C 71554 Lab 61859 LD 23640; runoff C 79534 Lab 71615 [C gain from Lab]

new ward boundaries in 2018, and a repeat of the 2019 results would result in no net changes.

There are no local elections this year in North Lincolnshire or in the East Riding except for by-elections. The amazing story of the *Broughton and Appleby* ward of NORTH LINCOLNSHIRE is too long to tell here, but I have related it before in an extraordinary edition of Andrew's Previews in April 2020*, because I researched for it for a March 2020 double by-election that never happened. We are now having another go at filling the seats vacated by the late Ivan Glover and the new Scunthorpe MP Holly Mumby-Croft; Janet Lee and Carol Ross will defend this ward which is now safely Conservative.† Also postponed from March 2020 is a by-election in the *Ashby* ward of eastern Scunthorpe, which is safe for the defending Labour candidate Christopher Skinner.‡ Regrettably, the pandemic has added a fourth vacancy to the list in North Lincolnshire: Derek Longcake, Conservative councillor for the *Bottesford* ward of southern Scunthorpe, died in the first wave of COVID-19. His widow Janet Longcake is the Conservative candidate for the resulting by-election, and she will start as favourite.§

COVID-19 has also taken from us Mike Bryan, a Conservative member of the EAST RIDING council. His ward was *South West Holderness*, based on the town of Hedon just east of Hull; this ward returned Lib Dem councillors until 2007 and an independent until 2011, but is now safe Conservative. David Winter is their defending candidate.¶ There is also a by-election in the neighbouring ward of *South East Holderness*, a large rural area based on Withernsea and running to the now-island of Spurn. This ward has had a full slate of Conservatives at every election this century, but Labour came close in by-elections in 2012 and 2016‖ and UKIP were a strong second in 2015. Despite this history, the Conservative candidate Claire Holmes should be favoured.**

South Yorkshire

Police and Crime Commissioner

The South Yorkshire police and crime commissionership is held by Labour's Alan Billings, an academic and priest who has served since winning a by-election

* *Andrew's Previews 2020*, page 84. † *North Lincolnshire, Broughton and Appleby*: C 1217 (Ross)/ 1141 (Lee) Lab 450 (Watson)/412 (Ladlow) Grn 99 (Baker)/82 (Watson) For Britain Movement 34 ‡ *North Lincolnshire, Ashby*: C 1137 Lab 980 Grn 119 [C gain from Lab] § *North Lincolnshire, Bottesford*: C 2984 Lab 1088 ¶ *East Riding, South West Holderness*: C 1304 Lab 814 LD 626 Ind 525 ‖ For the latter by-election see *Andrew's Previews 2016*, page 149. ** *East Riding, South East Holderness*: C 1624 LD 691 Lab 396 Yorkshire Party 317 Reform UK 89

in 2014. He was re-elected in the first round in 2016, polling 52% against 20% for UKIP and 11% for the Conservatives.

Although he is now well into his seventies, Billings is seeking a third term. He won't face a UKIP candidate this time. The Conservatives have selected former senior police officer David Chinchen, and Joe Otten completes the ballot paper for the Liberal Democrats.*

Local elections

There are elections this year for the whole of Rotherham council on new ward boundaries, the whole of Doncaster council and one-third of Barnsley and Sheffield councils.

ROTHERHAM council has had a troubled recent history, being taken over by Commissioners in 2014 following a huge child sexual exploitation scandal. In that year's local elections the UK Independence Party won 10 seats on Rotherham council, which they increased to 14 at a whole-council election in 2016: Labour won 48 seats that year, and the remaining seat went to an independent candidate in Anston and Woodsetts ward. This year's election will be on new ward boundaries. The Rother Valley parliamentary seat, which the Conservatives gained in December 2019, is one of several constituencies with a Tory MP but no Tory local councillors; the party will have a chance to do something about that now. Rotherham UKIP have since rebadged as the "Rotherham Democratic Party" and are not giving up their seats on the council without a fight.

DONCASTER went over to the elected mayoral system some years ago. The current mayor is Ros Jones of the Labour party, who narrowly defeated the English Democrats mayor Peter Davies in 2013; Jones had a much easier time in the 2017 mayoral election, winning in the first round with 51% of the vote against 21% for the Conservatives and 12% for UKIP. She is backed up by a large Labour majority on Doncaster council: the simultaneous 2017 council election returned 43 Labour councillors, 7 Conservatives, 3 localists from Mexborough and two independents.

Jones is seeking re-election for a third term as Mayor. The Conservatives have selected James Hart, a businessman and former leader of the Conservative group on the council, who is seeking to return to public office after standing down in 2017. There's no UKIP candidate this time; the other candidates are independents Joan Briggs and Frank Calladine, Andy Budden for the Yorkshire Party, Warren Draper for the Greens and Surjit Singh Duhre for Reform UK.†

* *South Yorkshire PCC*: Lab 165442 C 98851 LD 42462 † *Mayor of Doncaster*: first preferences Lab 27669 C 17980 Calladine 5166 Yorkshire Party 4073 Briggs 3904 Grn 3370 Reform UK 1012; runoff Lab 31232 C 21019

Despite some extremely wacky results in 2019, including two seat gains for the Democrats and Veterans Party (the "gay donkey" UKIP splinter group), the Labour majority in BARNSLEY looks completely safe.

The big city of SHEFFIELD should, however, be hotly contested. Following a row over tree-felling which led to major losses in 2019, the ruling Labour group is currently on 45 councillors plus four vacant seats, with 43 being a majority. A repeat of the 2019 results would see Labour lose seven seats nett to the Lib Dems and Greens, putting that majority in danger. Sheffield also has a *governance referendum*, on whether the council should abolish the leader and cabinet system and move to the committee system of governance.*

Derbyshire

Police and Crime Commissioner

The Derbyshire PCC election in 2016 was very close. In the first round Labour's Hardyal Singh Dhindsa led with just 37% of the vote, against 35% for the Conservatives' Richard Bright and 17% for UKIP. Bright picked up most of the transfers in the runoff, but it wasn't enough as Dhindsa prevailed by 50.5% to 49.5%, a majority of 1,613 votes out of over 150,000.

Dhindsa is seeking re-election for Labour. The Conservatives have selected Angelique Foster, a Derbyshire county councillor and leader of Dronfield town council. UKIP haven't returned, so completing the Derbyshire PCC ballot paper are Stan Heptinstall for the Lib Dems and Tim Prosser for UKIP.†

Local elections

There are elections this year for the whole of Derbyshire county council and for one-third of Amber Valley and Derby councils.

AMBER VALLEY is a very swingy council based on the towns of Belper and Heanor to the north of Derby. This was a Labour gain from the Conservatives in 2019, but the party will have a difficult time defending their majority; this year all the traditionally Labour-voting wards in the east of the district are due to poll. and the party is defending 11 of the 15 wards up for election. If the Conservatives are having a good night, they have a realistic chance of making the gains they need for outright control.

---

* *Sheffield governance referendum*: Leader and Cabinet 48727 Committee 89670 † *Derbyshire PCC*: first preferences C 137884 Lab 104700 LD 25811 Reform UK 10721; runoff C 149749 Lab 117564 [C gain from Lab]

The Conservatives do currently run DERBY city council as a minority. The city has become very politically balanced, with currently 19 Conservative councillors, 15 Labour, 8 Lib Dems, a five-strong Reform Derby group (who were elected on the UKIP ticket, and are standing in these elections with the joint nomination of Reform Derby and Reform UK), and three independents. A repeat of the 2019 results would see the Conservatives lose 1 seat and Labour lose 2. Derby is one of the few councils which will declare its ward results overnight, so expect some desperate spinning of its results on the Friday morning.

Derby city is not covered by DERBYSHIRE COUNTY COUNCIL, which has swung wildly between the two main parties at the last three elections: it was a Tory gain in 2009, a Labour gain in 2013 and a Tory gain again in 2017. In seat terms the Conservative win four years ago looks pretty large—37 seats against 24 Labour and 3 Lib Dems—but in vote terms it won't take that much of a swing for many of those seats to change hands. For example, in the High Peak district the Conservatives hold three county seats in Buxton and Glossop on very small majorities; and the party hasn't performed particularly well there since, only narrowly gaining the High Peak constituency in December 2019 and resoundingly losing a by-election in the Whaley Bridge county division to the former Labour MP Ruth George two months later*. The Tory candidate to take Whaley Bridge back in this election certainly has name recognition: she is the former Conservative MP Edwina Currie, giving us a rare former MP versus former MP contest in a council election. Labour may have lost Dennis Skinner's Bolsover seat in December 2019, but given the majorities involved it will take another special Tory performance for them to gain any county divisions in that corner of Derbyshire.

This is borne out by the 2019 elections to BOLSOVER council, as while Labour did lose their majority there in 2019 it was mostly independent candidates who benefited from that. Labour have a crucial by-election to defend here in the *Bolsover North and Shuttlewood* ward, where they were opposed in 2019 only by a candidate from the left-wing Socialist Alternative; Donna Hales defends the seat for Labour, while the Socialist Alternative's Elaine Evans tries again with the nomination of the Trade Unionist and Socialist Coalition.† The village of *Pinxton* voted strongly for independent candidate James Watson in 2019, with Labour winning the ward's other seat; Watson's death has resulted in a free-for-all by-election, with Kevin Rose looking to succeed him as an independent and Labour nominating Stan Fox.‡ If Labour hold Bolsover North and Shuttlewood and gain Pinxton, they will regain their overall majority on the council.

* *Andrew's Previews 2020*, page 30. † *Bolsover, Bolsover North and Shuttlewood*: Lab 351 C 254 TUSC 38 Ind 38 ‡ *Bolsover, Pinxton*: Lab 442 C 299 Ind 140 LD 14 [Lab gain from Ind]

The neighbouring district of NORTH EAST DERBYSHIRE now has a Conservative majority, as the memory of mining fades and towns like Eckington and Killamarsh continue their transition from industrial and pit settlements into dormitory towns for Sheffield just to the north. The two Killamarsh wards now have a full slate of Conservative councillors, although in 2019 they did win the second seat in Killamarsh East by a majority of just one vote over Labour. Both Killamarsh wards have by-elections following the resignations of Conservative councillors Kevin and Patricia Bone; in *East* ward David Drabble defends against Labour candidate John Windle,* while in *West* ward the Conservative and Labour candidates are Alex Platts and Stuart Mullins respectively.† The neighbouring ward of *Eckington South and Renishaw* was Labour in 2019, but is having a by-election after Labour councillor Clive Hunt was disqualified under the six-month non-attendance rule; I'm not sure of the circumstances behind this, but Hunt is seeking re-election while the Conservatives have selected Philip Wheelhouse.‡

The Conservatives also have a majority on EREWASH council, where Labour are defending two by-elections. *Hallam Fields*, the southern ward of Ilkeston, was very close in 2015 and 2019 between Labour and the Conservatives; Labour won both seats in 2019, gaining one from the Conservatives, and their defending candidate is Jo Ward while the Conservatives have selected Jon Wright. Accordingly, the Lib Dems' Angela Togni is in the unusual position for a T of first on the ballot paper.§ Labour have a larger majority in the *Nottingham Road* ward of Long Eaton, based on the Trent railway junction, where their defending candidate is Adam Thompson.¶

"Some might say we will find a brighter day", according to the song by Oasis. The cover photograph for their single *Some Might Say* was taken at Cromford railway station, which is part of the *Masson* ward of the DERBYSHIRE DALES district. In addition to Cromford, Masson ward also takes in the Little Switzerland of Matlock Bath, a spa village which is a huge tourist trap but worth a visit nonetheless. This beautiful scenery is the backdrop to one of the crucibles of the Industrial Revolution: it was at Cromford in 1771 that Richard Arkwright set up the world's first water-powered textile mill, using his revolutionary spinning frame. Arkwright's mill still stands today and is a UNESCO World Heritage Site.

* *North East Derbyshire, Killamarsh East*: C 519 Lab 359 LD 42. For a later September by-election in this ward see page 366. † *North East Derbyshire, Killamarsh West*: C 748 Lab 479 LD 111 ‡ *North East Derbyshire, Eckington South and Renishaw*: C 657 Lab 547 LD 70 [C gain from Lab] § *Erewash, Hallam Fields*: C 683 Lab 507 LD 73 [C gain from Lab] ¶ *Erewash, Nottingham Road*: C 707 Lab 509 Grn 110 LD 47 [C gain from Lab]

Arkwright's legacy to Cromford and the neighbouring town of Wirksworth is an engineering history and a large Labour vote. Masson ward consistently turns in close results between Labour and the Conservatives, and has split its two seats between Labour and the Tories since 2011. Labour are defending the Masson by-election on 6th May; their candidate is Nicholas Whitehead, while the Conservatives have selected Dermot Murphy.[*] *Wirksworth* is the safest Labour ward within the Derbyshire Dales district, and their candidate Dawn Greatorex should be favoured to hold the by-election there.[†]

Earlier in this section I mentioned Edwina Currie, who was the Conservative MP for SOUTH DERBYSHIRE from 1983 to 1997. This is the sort of area which has swung strongly to the Conservatives in recent years; the December 2019 general election gave the Conservative candidate Heather Wheeler a majority of over 19,000 votes, and the May 2019 re-elected the Tory administration on South Derbyshire council (which has the same boundaries as the parliamentary seat) with a 22–14 majority over Labour. All seemed set fair; but in December 2020 the ruling Conservative group on the council suffered a huge split, and Labour have taken over as a minority administration.

The four South Derbyshire council by-elections on 6th May—and the Conservatives are defending all four of them—will be the electorate's first chance to make their views clear on this right-wing split and left-wing takeover. The Conservatives will be helped by the lack of any candidates from the dissident group. They are safe in *Hilton* ward (covering eight parishes on the main road towards Uttoxeter), where two of the three seats are up for election and are defended by Gillian Lemmon and Peter Smith.[‡] *Seales* ward, the southernmost point of Derbyshire, covers six parishes including the village of Coton in the Elms; this is recognised as the farthest point in the UK from the sea, being 70 miles from the Wash, the Dee Estuary and the Severn Estuary. Seales ward is also safe Conservative, with Simon Ackroyd defending.[§] Things are politically very different in the *Church Gresley* ward of Swadlincote, which split its three seats between two Labour candidates and one Conservative in both 2015 and 2019; the Tories' Roger Redfern will defend this marginal against Labour's Sue Taylor.[¶] If Labour can gain the Church Gresley by-election, they will remain as the largest party on South Derbyshire council unless the Conservatives and ex-Conservatives can settle their differences.

---

[*] *Derbyshire Dales, Masson*: C 447 Lab 444 Grn 192 [C gain from Lab] [†] *Derbyshire Dales, Wirksworth*: Lab 1109 C 741 Grn 373 [‡] *South Derbyshire, Hilton*: C 1364 (Lemmon)/1097 (Smith) LD 467 Lab 457 (Peacock)/428 (Timmins) Reform UK 105 [§] *South Derbyshire, Seales*: C 1070 Lab 527. For a later by-election in this ward in September see page 368. [¶] *South Derbyshire, Church Gresley*: C 994 Lab 625

Nottinghamshire

Police and Crime Commissioner

The Nottinghamshire PCC since 2012 has been Paddy Tipping, the former Labour MP for the Sherwood constituency who served for a time as Deputy Leader of the Commons during the last Labour Government. Tipping was re-elected quite easily in 2016: in the first round he led with 47% against 28% for the Conservatives and 12% for UKIP, and he increased his lead to 62–38 in the runoff.

Tipping is seeking a third term of office. He is up against Conservative candidate Caroline Henry, a businesswoman. UKIP have not stood again, so completing the ballot paper is David Watts for the Lib Dems.*

Local elections

There are elections this year for Nottinghamshire county council only. There are no local elections this year in the city of Nottingham.

The Conservatives have had spectacular success in Nottinghamshire at parliamentary level in recent years. They now hold all eight constituencies in the area covered by the COUNTY COUNCIL, having taken Ashfield and Bassetlaw in 2019 to add to the gain of Mansfield in 2017. The task now for the party is to make this dominance stick at county council level, as the Tories do not have a majority at the county hall in West Bridgford and are governing in coalition with the Mansfield Independent Forum. That group along with the Zadroznyite Ashfield Independents will form a large independent bloc on the new county council, so for the gains they need for a majority the Tories will likely have to look elsewhere: perhaps in the northern Nottingham suburbs of Arnold and Carlton, where there are a number of marginal Labour divisions. The Tories must have carried a number of divisions in Worksop in December 2019 given their huge majority in Bassetlaw, but as in neighbouring Bolsover the Labour county councillors there are sitting on very large majorities from May 2017.

In fact the May 2019 local elections in BASSETLAW were pretty poor for the Conservatives, who lost all but one of their seats within the Bassetlaw constituency. They have a good chance to get two of those seats back on 6th May. *Sutton* ward, covering a number of villages to the west and north of Retford, was gained from the Conservatives in 2019 by independent candidate Rob Boeuf; no independent candidate has come forward to succeed Boeuf, and the seat should

* *Nottinghamshire PCC*: first preferences C 131318 Lab 119271 LD 23794; runoff C 138658 Lab 131302 [C gain from Lab]

revert to the Conservatives who have selected Denise Depledge.* Immediately to the north of Sutton ward is *Ranskill* ward, which was a very surprising gain in 2019 for Labour partly thanks to the outgoing Tory councillor Michael Gray seeking re-election as an independent and splitting the right-wing vote. Labour haven't found a candidate to replace Nicholls, so the Ranskill by-election is likely to be gained by either the Tories' Gerald Bowers or by Michael Gray, who is standing again.† Within Bassetlaw district but part of the Newark constituency is the *Tuxford and Trent* ward, which takes in the former power station site at High Marnham and one of Network Rail's test tracks for new rail vehicles; this was close in 2019 between the Conservative slate and an independent, but with the independent not returning the Tories' Lewis Stanniland should be favoured to hold the seat.‡

The Conservatives defend two other Nottinghamshire by-elections caused by newly-elected MPs vacating their district council seats. Brendan Clarke-Smith, the new Bassetlaw MP, was a NEWARK AND SHERWOOD councillor for *Boughton* ward, located a few miles west of Tuxford and on the border of his constituency. This is part of the Nottinghamshire coalfield, which was operating round here until just a few years ago; Boughton ward was very close between the Tories and Labour in both 2015 and 2019, with Clarke-Smith gaining it in the latter year. Another close contest between defending Conservative candidate Tim Wildgust and Labour's Derek Batey can be expected.§ The Tories don't have many council seats in MANSFIELD, but one of them was held by Lee Anderson who is now the MP for Ashfield; Anderson represented the *Oakham* ward on the southern edge of Mansfield, which he gained from the Mansfield Independent Forum in 2019. The Tories have selected Robert Ellman to hold the Oakham by-election, while the result of the Forum's candidate Kevin Brown may be an early pointer as to whether they can get the Mansfield mayoralty back from Labour in 2023.¶

Lee Anderson had got elected to Parliament the hard way, as he had to defeat Jason Zadrozny who bestrides ASHFIELD politics like a colossus. Zadrozny is the leader of Ashfield council at the head of his own party, the Ashfield Independents, and most of the candidates on his slate were elected with enormous shares of the vote in 2019. This column has seen nothing like it since the Lib Dem takeover of Kendal nearly twenty years ago. The Ashfield Independents are defending two by-elections: in *Skegby* ward (the north-eastern ward of Sutton-in-Ashfield), after

* *Bassetlaw, Sutton*: C 422 Lab 134 LD 107 [C gain from Ind] † *Bassetlaw, Ranskill*: C 454 Ind 193 LD 74 [C gain from Lab] ‡ *Bassetlaw, Tuxford and Trent*: C 745 Lab 472 LD 75 § *Newark and Sherwood, Boughton*: C 542 Lab 283 Ind 60 ¶ *Mansfield, Oakham*: C 428 Lab 228 Mansfield Ind Forum 104 Ind 69

the council chairman Anthony Brewer died of COVID; and in *Annesley and Kirkby Woodhouse* ward next to the M 1 motorway. Both of these wards were over 70% Zadroznyite in 2019, so it will take a lot for the defending candidates Jamie Bell (Annesley and Kirkby Woodhouse)* and Will Bostock (Skegby)† to lose these.

Things are more politically normal in the final three Nottinghamshire by-elections. Labour have two safe wards to defend in the BROXTOWE district, covering a number of towns to the west of Nottingham; in Stapleford Sue Paterson defends the *South West* ward‡, while in Beeston Shaun Dannheimer is the party's candidate to hold *Rylands* ward.§ Over the Trent we have a safe Conservative defence to RUSHCLIFFE council: Matt Barney should be favoured to hold the ward based on the village of *Sutton Bonington*.¶

Lincolnshire

Police and Crime Commissioner

The 2016 Lincolnshire PCC election turned in a fragmented first-round result after the independent incumbent retired. In a field of four candidates the Conservatives' Marc Jones led with 35% against 26% for UKIP candidate Victoria Ayling, 23% for Labour and 17% for the Lincolnshire Independents, a long-standing group of independent county councillors. Jones and Ayling went into the runoff, which Jones won 56–44 to gain the position for the Conservatives.

Marc Jones is seeking re-election for a second term, and this time he won't have to face a UKIP candidate. Labour have selected Lincoln city councillor Rosanne Kirk. The Lincolnshire Independents have returned with their candidate David Williams, a former army officer who chairs the Lincolnshire Police Independent Advisory Group. Also standing are Ross Pepper for the Liberal Democrats and Peter Escreet for Reform UK.‖

Local elections

There are elections this year for the whole of Lincolnshire county council and for one-third of Lincoln council. These shouldn't see much excitement. LINCOLN city council is the only Labour-controlled district in Lincolnshire; their majority

* *Ashfield, Annesley and Kirkby Woodhouse*: Ashfield Ind 1630 Lab 547 † *Ashfield, Skegby*: Ashfield Ind 1137 C 426 Lab 310 ‡ *Broxtowe, Stapleford South West*: Lab 696 Ind 305 C 287 LD 170 § *Broxtowe, Beeston Rylands*: Lab 709 C 545 Grn 183 LD 154 ¶ *Rushcliffe, Sutton Bonington*: C 402 Lab 143 LD 62 ‖ *Lincolnshire PCC*: C 102813 Lab 34310 Lincs Ind 18375 LD 10172 Reform UK 6101

over the Conservatives is 24–9, and a repeat of the 2019 results would see three Tory seats flip to Labour. LINCOLNSHIRE COUNTY COUNCIL returned a large Tory majority in the 2017 election, after a sizeable UKIP caucus in the 2013–17 term fell apart; unless something similarly seismic happens the Conservatives are in no danger at the county hall this time.

The Tories are defending four of the five by-elections to Lincolnshire's district councils. The odd one out is the *Bassingham and Brant Broughton* ward of NORTH KESTEVEN district, which covers nine rural parishes east of Newark and south of Lincoln; this ward was taken over by the Lincolnshire Independents in 2019, and their defending candidate Penelope Bauer will seek to defend against the Tories' Russell Eckert.* In SOUTH KESTEVEN district the Tories defend *Glen* ward, which covers a number of villages to the west of Bourne including Little Bytham on the East Coast main line; this is very strongly Conservative and their candidate Penny Robins is opposed only by Labour.†

The one genuinely urban Lincolnshire by-election on 6th May has given this column an awful lot of grief in trying to sort out what is going on. *Skirbeck* ward covers the docks of BOSTON, straddling both sides of the River Witham. In 2015, the first contest on the present boundaries, it elected one councillor each for UKIP, the Conservatives and Labour; in 2019 UKIP gave up their seat without a fight and Labour were defeated, the three councillors elected being Alistair Arundell for the Conservatives and independent candidates Anne Dorrian and Colin Woodcock. Arundell resigned shortly afterwards, and a by-election was held alongside the December 2019 general election‡ which was convincingly held by new Conservative candidate Martin Howard. Howard announced in July 2020 that he would step down to allow a by-election to be held in May 2021. Independent councillor Colin Woodcock then handed in his resignation in October 2020, prompting this column to put a double by-election on my vacancy list. As it turns out, Martin Howard never followed through on his resignation announcement and he is still a Boston councillor, so this Skirbeck by-election is for Woodcock's seat only. Two independent candidates, Dale Broughton and Christopher Cardwell, are seeking to succeed Woodcock, but if the December 2019 by-election is any guide the Tories' Katie Chalmers should start as favourite here.§

Things have got even more complicated on the beaches of Lincolnshire's east coast. There is a localist party here, the Skegness Urban District Society, which is

* *North Kesteven, Bassingham and Brant Broughton*: C 721 Lincs Ind 616 Lab 254 [C gain from Lincs Ind] † *South Kesteven, Glen*: C 585 Lab 167 ‡ *Andrew's Previews 2019*, page 398.
§ *Boston, Skirbeck*: C 338 Broughton 307 Lab 210 For the People Not the Party 88 Cardwell 36 [C gain from Ind]

seeking self-governance for Skeggy and won six seats in the 2019 East Lindsey council elections. The SUDS are now looking to clean up at Lincolnshire county council level, and they have nominated seven candidates—rather ambitious given that Skegness only has two county council seats and the other five candidates are standing for divisions outside the town. Two of these candidates are Steve Walmsley, who was nominated for Ingoldmells Rural county division; and Danny Brookes, who was nominated for both Ingoldmells Rural and Mablethorpe divisions. The deputy returning officer will have pointed out to Brookes that he could only stand for one of those, so he withdrew—from Mablethorpe, leaving SUDS with two candidates for one seat in Ingoldmells Rural.

The plot thickens when you consider that Ingoldmells Rural includes the East Lindsey ward of *Chapel St Leonards*. One of the oldest wards in England by population (in 2011 71% of the population were aged 45 or over—the place must be almost fully vaccinated by now), the seaside resort of Chapel St Leonards can be found about five miles north of Skegness. This is within range for the Skegness Urban District Society, and they have nominated a candidate for the East Lindsey council by-election here—but that candidate is not Danny Brookes or Steve Walmsley. Instead, the SUDS candidate for the Chapel St Leonards by-election is Ady Findley, while Steve Walmsley is contesting the by-election as an independent. Confused? You will be. The Conservatives are defending the by-election with Graham Williams as their candidate, while Labour (who won a by-election here in 2013 and weren't far off holding their seat in 2015) have selected Isaac Bailey to complete the ballot paper.[*]

Thankfully our final by-election within Lincolnshire is strange only in the sense that the voters of *Kelsey Wold* ward will be electing a successor to the late Tory district and county councillor Lewis Strange. Strange had won his final term in 2019 in this ward of West Lindsey, based on the villages of North and South Kelsey between Brigg and Market Rasen, comfortably enough that new Conservative candidate Peter Morris should have few problems in holding the by-election.[†]

Northamptonshire

Police and Crime Commissioner

Northants' police and crime commissioner election in 2016 was a three-way fight. The first round was relatively close with 41% for the new Conservative candidate

[*] *East Lindsey, Chapel St Leonards*: C 795 Lab 206 Skegness Urban District Society 121 Ind 58

[†] *West Lindsey, Kelsey Wold*: C 565 LD 243 Lab 94

Stephen Mold, 36% for Labour and 24% for UKIP; UKIP's transfers broke for the Conservatives giving them a 54–46 win in the final reckoning.

Stephen Mold is seeking a second term. Labour have selected Claire Pavitt, who was their parliamentary candidate for Kettering in December 2019. UKIP have not returned, so completing the ballot paper are Ana Gunn for the Liberal Democrats and Mark Hearn for Reform UK.*

Local elections

Northamptonshire's local government has been reorganised this year following the financial failure of Northamptonshire county council. 2021 sees the inaugural elections for the two new councils of North Northamptonshire and West Northamptonshire.

WEST NORTHAMPTONSHIRE is the larger of the two with around 307,000 electors on the roll. The county town of Northampton accounts for slightly under half of the electorate, and should be comfortably outvoted by the former rural districts of Daventry and South Northamptonshire which are generally true blue. Similar considerations apply in NORTH NORTHAMPTONSHIRE, which succeeds the former districts of Corby, East Northamptonshire, Kettering and Wellingborough. Corby is a strongly Labour-voting town, and the party can also perform decently in Kettering, but politically these will be red islands in a large blue lake. Mind, we only have parliamentary election data from Northamptonshire in recent years, because the May 2019 elections for all the districts here were cancelled in advance of the reorganisation.

Leicestershire

Police and Crime Commissioner

Leicestershire's police and crime commissionership was gained by Labour in the 2016 election. Lord Bach, who served as a junior minister for much of the Blair and Brown years in the defence and environment departments and the whip's office, led in the first round with 45% against 31% for the Conservatives and 13% for the Liberal Democrats; in the final reckoning he beat the Conservatives 57–43.

Bach is not standing again. The Labour candidate here is local government veteran Ross Willmott, who was first elected to Leicester city council in 1983. Willmott was leader of that council from 1999 until 2010, when he resigned the leadership to unsuccessfully contest North West Leicestershire in that year's

* *Northamptonshire PCC*: C 102752 Lab 53166 LD 29621 Reform UK 7715

general election. The Tories have selected Rupert Matthews, a former Kingston upon Thames councillor and prolific author on paranormal subjects; Matthews was a Conservative MEP for the East Midlands from 2017 to 2019. Completing the ballot paper is the Lib Dems' James Moore, a former Hinckley and Bosworth councillor who currently teaches history and politics at Leicester University. One thing to look out for in the Leicestershire PCC count is differential turnout, because there are no scheduled local elections in the Labour stronghold of Leicester to boost turnout for the PCC contest.[*]

Local elections

There are, however, elections this year for LEICESTERSHIRE COUNTY COUNCIL. Unlike the PCC position this has a large Conservative majority thanks to the absence of Labour-voting Leicester city, which has unitary status; the Lib Dems form the main opposition on the county council thanks to their strength in Oadby, Wigston and Hinckley. The 2017 election returned 36 Conservatives, 13 Lib Dems and 6 Labour councillors. Not much is likely to change here.

As stated, there are no local elections this year in the city of LEICESTER apart from a by-election in the *North Evington* ward. At one point named as the UK's COVID hotspot, North Evington is a majority-Asian area about a mile east of Leicester city centre, which returned very high Labour votes in 2015 and 2019. Nine candidates have come forward for the by-election, but it will probably take a lot for any of them to defeat Labour's Vandevi Pandya.[†]

There are four local by-elections within the Leicestershire county council area, and we should start our discussion with the *Worthington and Breedon* ward of NORTH WEST LEICESTERSHIRE which covers a number of villages between East Midlands Airport and Ashby de la Zouch. The ward's Conservative councillor David Stevenson, who had sat on North West Leicestershire council for all but one term since the council's first election in 1973, passed away in early November of 2019. No move was made by the local Conservatives to call a by-election over the winter, and the subsequent suspension of by-elections means that Worthington and Breedon's residents have now been without a councillor for almost eighteen months. Even given the exceptional circumstances of the last year and a bit, this should not have been allowed to drag on so long. Stevenson enjoyed a large majority in Worthington and Breedon, and while his successor as Tory candidate Raymond Morris might not serve for quite as long he shouldn't

[*] *Leicestershire PCC*: first preferences C 121252 Lab 81898 LD 42951; runoff C 135566 Lab 102211 [C gain from Lab] [†] *Leicester, North Evington*: Lab 3306 C 2565 Grn 241 LD 240 TUSC 117 Reform UK 89 For Britain Movement 69 Ind 61 Comm 33

have much trouble holding the by-election.*

Things are rather different in *Ibstock East* ward on the same council. This has been a Labour-inclined marginal in recent years, with Labour increasing their majority over the Conservatives to 10 points in 2019; but the outgoing Labour councillor Daniel Tebbutt, who was elected to the council at the age of just 18, defected to the Conservatives after four months in office and then resigned. The resulting Ibstock East by-election looks set to be an interesting contest between Labour's Carissma Griffiths and the Tories' Jenny Simmons.†

Another relatively young Leicestershire councillor to have resigned recently is Frankie McHugo, who was first elected to HARBOROUGH council in 2011 at the age of 21. A blog post on *Conservative Home* from the time‡ listed her among twelve Conservative councillors under the age of 23. At least three of the people who were on that list (Jack Brereton, Jonathan Gullis and Gary Sambrook) are now MPs, although the presence of Gary Sambrook there is an error: as long-term readers of Andrew's Previews will know, Sambrook wasn't first elected to Birmingham city council until he won a by-election in February 2014. Keep an eye on this column after 6th May, you might just be seeing the stars of the future (as I described Jonathan Gibson, the new *Mastermind* champion, back in September 2019§).

Anyway, Frankie McHugo served until 2015 when she stood down from Harborough council, then returned in 2019 as one of the two councillors for *Market Harborough—Little Bowden* ward, which is the south-eastern of Market Harborough's four wards. Her resignation creates a by-election in a marginal ward, as the other councillor here is was elected for the Liberal Democrats. The defending Conservative candidate is Peter Critchley, while the Lib Dems' James Ward will look to gain.¶

Our final Leicestershire by-election takes place in the *Stanton and Flamville* ward, which covers five parishes between Hinckley and the Fosse Way but is administered as part of the BLABY local government district. This ward is sufficiently safe for the Conservatives that nobody bothered to oppose their slate here in 2019; the defending Conservative candidate Mike Shirley will, however, face a contest in this by-election.‖

The Leicestershire police area includes Rutland, where there are no council elections this year.

* *North West Leicestershire, Worthington and Breedon*: C 696 Lab 139 Grn 104 LD 60 † *North West Leicestershire, Ibstock East*: C 355 Lab 164 LD 54 Grn 41 [C gain from Lab] ‡ `https://tinyurl.com/2p8znpw3` § *Andrew's Previews 2019*, page 288. ¶ *Harborough, Market Harborough—Little Bowden*: C 727 LD 507 Lab 213 Women's Equality 149 Grn 122 Ind 61 ‖ *Blaby, Stanton and Flamville*: C 1651 LD 552 Lab 265 Grn 197

Warwickshire

Police and Crime Commissioner

Independent Warwickshire PCC Ron Ball retired at the 2016 election leaving the position open. On the first count the Conservatives led with 31%, Labour had 25%, UKIP 13% and independent candidate Dave Whitehouse 11%; the Tories and Labour went through to the runoff where the Conservatives won by 55–45.

Conservative PCC Philip Seccombe is seeking re-election. Labour have selected Ben Twomey, who was an independent candidate for this post in 2016; on that occasion Twomey polled 8% and finished last out of six candidates. UKIP have not returned, so completing the ballot paper are Louis Adam for the Liberal Democrats and Henry Lu for Reform UK.[*][†]

Local elections

There are elections this year for the whole of Warwickshire county council, for one-half of Nuneaton and Bedworth council, and for one-third of Rugby council.

The main contest here will be in NUNEATON AND BEDWORTH which is currently on a knife-edge. The ruling Labour group has 17 seats—half of the council—with the Conservatives on 14, the Greens on 1 and two independents (who were elected for the Conservatives). This is one of the handful of councils which renew half of their members at every election, so the last local elections here were in May 2018; a repeat of those results would see the Conservatives gain six seats and a comfortable majority to go with their lead in the Nuneaton and North Warwickshire parliamentary seats.

The good Conservative result in Nuneaton and Bedworth in May 2018 was also seen at the WARWICKSHIRE COUNTY COUNCIL elections in May 2017 and allowed the Tories to gain overall control of the county hall in Warwick. The 2017 elections in Warwickshire returned 36 Conservatives, 10 Labour, 7 Lib Dems, two Greens and two localist independents. Labour will need to do a lot better in Nuneaton and Bedworth to force a hung council here.

The North Warwickshire constituency includes Bedworth together with the whole of the NORTH WARWICKSHIRE local government district, which is based on the towns of Atherstone and Polesworth. Both of those towns see by-elections to the district council with Labour defending. *Polesworth East* is a safe Labour ward which shouldn't give their defending candidate Emma Whapples too much

[*] This paragraph was missed in error from the originally-published version of this column.
[†] *Warwickshire PCC*: C 85963 Lab 45768 LD 26660 Reform UK 6692

trouble.* *Atherstone Central* ward has had a full slate of Labour councillors since a 2009 by-election, but it remains marginal in vote terms and promises to be a close contest between Sara Bishop (Labour, defending) and Mark Jordan (Conservative).† Although their resigning councillor had previously left the party and gone independent, the Conservatives should be given very little trouble in *Curdworth* ward, covering a number of villages east of Sutton Coldfield and south of Tamworth together with the Belfry golf club; their defending candidate is Sandra Smith.‡

RUGBY council has a small Conservative majority which looks safe enough. A repeat of the 2019 results would see just one seat change hands, the Conservatives picking up the rural Dunsmore ward from an independent councillor.

The only other poll to report on here is a by-election to WARWICK council from *Leamington Clarendon* ward. This is the town centre ward for Leamington Spa, taking in all the glorious Georgian buildings on the Parade and a fair amount of deprivation and student lets in the terraces behind. Clarendon was close in 2019 between Labour and the Liberal Democrats, and it will be interesting to see whether the student vote appears here at all given that Warwick University is generally closed to in-person teaching. The defending Labour candidate is Colin Quinney, while Hugh Foden challenges for the Lib Dems.§

West Midlands

Mayor of the West Midlands

Both of the West Midlands metropolitan area's major elected officials will be up for election this year. On paper the mayoralty is the more interesting position, as this was very close in 2017. The first count gave Conservative candidate Andy Street, a former head of the John Lewis Partnership, a 42–41 lead over Birmingham Labour MP Siôn Simon; Simon got slightly more transfers, but it wasn't enough to take the lead in the runoff which Street won by 50.4–49.6, a majority of 3,766 votes across the county.

This election is significant enough that two opinion polls have been commissioned for it. Over the Easter weekend a poll by Find Out New and Electoral Calculus for the *Daily Telegraph* gave Andy Street a 45–38 lead over the Labour candidate on first preferences, narrowing to 52–48 in the runoff. Redfield and Wilton were in the field from 18th to 21st April, giving Street a 46–37 lead on

* *North Warwickshire, Polesworth East*: C 477 Lab 396 [C gain from Lab] † *North Warwickshire, Atherstone Central*: C 367 Lab 258 Grn 45 [C gain from Lab] ‡ *North Warwickshire, Curdworth*: C 875 Lab 198 § *Warwick, Leamington Clarendon*: Lab 1370 C 761 LD 539 Grn 431 Ind 103 SDP 16

first preferences. These polls will be rather discouraging to the Labour candidate, who is another Birmingham Labour MP: Liam Byrne has represented the Hodge Hill constituency since winning a by-election in 2004, and is perhaps best known for the "I'm afraid there is no money" note which he left for his successor as a Treasury minister after the Labour government's defeat in 2010. Also standing this time are Jenny Wilkinson for the Lib Dems, Pete Durnell (who was the UKIP candidate four years ago) for the Reform Party, and Steve Caudwell for the Greens.*

Police and Crime Commissioner

By contrast the West Midlands police and crime commissionership, despite covering the same area, has always been safe for Labour. This post has been held by Michael Jamieson since he won a by-election in 2014. At the 2016 election Jamieson was less than a thousand votes short of being re-elected in the first round, polling 50% against 26% for the Conservatives and 17% for UKIP; in the final reckoning he beat the Conservative candidate 63–37.

Jamieson is standing down, and Labour have selected Simon Foster, a solicitor. The Conservative candidate is Jay Singh Sohal, a former TV journalist who is now a communications director. Also standing are independent candidate Jools Hambleton, Mark Hoath for Reform UK, Jon Hunt for the Liberal Democrat and Desmond Jaddoo, leader of the newly-formed We Matter Party.†

Local elections

As in 2019, DUDLEY council is the West Midlands borough to watch. This currently stands at 35 Labour councillors, 34 Conservatives, two independents and one vacancy; the Conservatives have a minority administration, and the casting vote of the mayor helps in that. This year the ward map is in the Tories' favour; the 2016 results here had Labour winning 14 wards, the Conservatives 9 and UKIP 1, while in 2019 the Conservatives won 13 wards to Labour's 11. That would suggest that the Conservatives should be favoured for an overall majority here.

The Tories already have a majority in WALSALL, although only a thin one: 31 councillors against 26 Labour, two Lib Dems and an independent. Again, this

* *Mayor of the West Midlands*: first preferences C 299318 Lab 244009 Grn 35559 LD 21836 Reform UK 13568; runoff C 314669 Lab 267626 † *West Midlands PCC*: first preferences Lab 276743 C 239288 LD 38594 Ind 27664 Reform UK 18002 We Matter 7745; runoff Lab 301406 C 259839

year the ward map is in their favour: a repeat of the 2019 results would see the Conservatives gain 3 Labour wards and all 3 of the seats held by other parties.

A sterner test for the government party will be to see whether they can make any headway in SANDWELL. This is the Black Country council which includes the two West Bromwich constituencies, both of which were Tory gains in December 2019; however, the last three Sandwell council elections have returned 72 Labour councillors out of a possible 72. Judging from the May 2019 results the Tories should have their eyes on gaining Blackheath ward (based on Rowley Regis), but anything else looks a very tall order.

On the far side of Birmingham, the Conservatives have suddenly found themselves in trouble in SOLIHULL where their majority is down to 26 seats out of 51. The opposition here is an unlikely one: it's the Green Party, who have broken through in some of the bourgeois ex-Liberal parts of Solihull proper *and* the tower blocks of Chelmsley Wood and Castle Bromwich. A repeat of the 2019 results would see the Conservatives lose Castle Bromwich ward to the Greens; although they should pick up a safe ward from a defector who is not standing again, if the Tories lose anything else then their majority on the council would go.

There are no local elections this year to BIRMINGHAM city council apart from four by-elections. In the north of the city we have the 1930s and 1940s estates of *Oscott* ward; in the west former Labour council leader John Clancy has vacated *Quinton* ward, off the main road towards Hagley and Kidderminster; while in the south of the city there are by-elections in the neighbouring wards of *Billesley* and *Hall Green North*. All of these are Labour defences with only Hall Green North (defended for them by Saima Suleman) looking completely safe.* At the last city council elections in 2018 Labour had a 2-point lead in Quinton, and leads of just over 10 points in Billesley and Oscott. Quinton will be defended for Labour by Elaine Kidney, with the Conservatives selecting Dominic Stanford†; in Oscott the two major-party candidates are Uzma Ahmed for Labour and Darius Sandhu for the Tories.‡ The Billesley by-election has attracted no fewer than nine candidates, with Katherine Carlisle as the defending Labour candidate and Clair Felton challenging for the Tories.§

The Labour majorities in COVENTRY and WOLVERHAMPTON are impregnable.

---

* *Birmingham, Hall Green North*: Lab 2542 Ind 833 C 819 Grn 246 LD 242 TUSC 55 † *Birmingham, Quinton*: C 2728 Lab 2344 Grn 323 LD 182 TUSC 27 [C gain from Lab] ‡ *Birmingham, Oscott*: C 1981 Lab 1086 LD 238 Grn 165 Ind 112 TUSC 58 [C gain from Lab] § *Birmingham, Billesley*: Lab 2553 C 1534 Grn 252 Rashid 107 LD 91 Dalton 64 Freedom Alliance 49 Reform UK 42 TUSC 34

Staffordshire

Police and Crime Commissioner

The Staffordshire PCC position has been held since 2012 by the Conservatives' Matthew Ellis. In 2016 Ellis led the first round rather narrowly with 36% against 31% for Labour and 16% for UKIP; he increased his lead in the final round, but only to 53–47.

This year Ellis is standing down. The Conservatives have selected Ben Adams, a long-serving Staffordshire county councillor who was their parliamentary candidate for Stoke-on-Trent North in 2015 and 2017. The Labour candidate is Tony Kearson, a Newcastle-under-Lyme councillor and criminologist. UKIP haven't returned, so completing the ballot paper are independent candidate Deneice Florence-Jukes, Michael Riley for Reform UK and Richard Whelan for the Lib Dems.*

Local elections

There are elections this year for the whole of Staffordshire county council and for one-third of Cannock Chase and Tamworth councils.

STAFFORDSHIRE COUNTY COUNCIL has had a large Conservative majority since 2009, when the ruling Labour group crashed from 32 seats to just 3. The local Labour party has never really recovered from that experience, although they didn't do quite as badly in the 2017 election which returned 51 Conservatives, 10 Labour and an independent. Any Labour recovery would need to start in Cannock, Tamworth and Newcastle-under-Lyme, and pre-pandemic results from Newcastle do not give much indication of that happening. What about Cannock and Tamworth, though?

Well, Labour do retain CANNOCK CHASE council, but only as a minority after losing overall control in 2019. Going into these elections there are 17 Labour councillors, 15 Conservative seats (one of which is vacant), 2 Lib Dems and 7 others, most of whom were originally elected for the Green Party which has suffered a split here. More than half of the Labour group is up for re-election this year, and a repeat of the 2019 results would see the Conservatives become the largest party on the council.

And there's not much sign of a Labour revival in TAMWORTH either. The Conservatives have had a large majority here for a long time now: the council currently has 21 seats against 5 Labour, 2 UKIP and 2 independents. A repeat of the 2019 results would see the Conservatives gain one seat each from Labour

* *Staffordshire PCC*: C 136024 Lab 67050 Ind 19102 LD 10690 Reform UK 5504

and UKIP, who are still active in Tamworth and have nominated a full slate of candidates for the borough elections.

There are no local elections this year in STOKE-ON-TRENT apart from a by-election following the abrupt resignation in May 2020 of councillor Mohammed Pervez. He had been leader of the Labour group on the council since 2010, and until 2015 was leader of the council. Pervez had a strong majority in *Moorcroft* ward, which covers the southern end of Burslem, and new Labour councillor Javed Najmi will be hoping to defend that. Regrettably, the voters of Moorcroft will not have the chance to vote for the Official Monster Raving Loony Party's candidate Sir Honkey Tonk James, who had turned 18 by polling day but was underage on the day his nomination papers went in; the Returning Officer, on the time-honoured principle of "I'd love to help you son, but you're too young to vote", rejected James' nomination.[*]

Outside the Potteries we have four by-elections for five seats. Two of these occur in the town of Cheadle, within the STAFFORDSHIRE MOORLANDS district. Cheadle's three wards returned a full set of independent councillors in 2019 with large majorities, but both of these by-elections see multiple independent candidates who could split the vote. In *Cheadle North East* ward those are Liz Whitehouse—niece of the late councillor Ian Whitehouse whose death caused the by-election—and Paulette Upton,[†] while *Cheadle South East*'s independent candidates are Jamie Evans, Colin Pearce and Alan Thomas.[‡]

EAST STAFFORDSHIRE district has a double by-election for both seats in *Eton Park* ward. This is not as bucolic as it sounds. Eton Park ward is the northern end of Burton upon Trent, and the area is dominated by a large Pirelli tyre factory. The ward was safe Labour until 2019 when one of its two seats was taken by independent candidate Dale Spedding.

Long-time readers of Andrew's Previews may recognise that name. Spedding won a by-election to the East Staffordshire council in the neighbouring Stretton ward in 2017, with the Conservative nomination[§], then resigned two months later over harassment he was getting from his constituents[¶]. He lasted a little longer on the council second time round, but still didn't make it into a second year before resigning: the double by-election to replace Spedding and the late Labour councillor Sonia Andjelkovic was originally scheduled for 26th March 2020 before the pandemic intervened.

[*] *Stoke-on-Trent, Moorcroft*: C 769 Lab 702 TUSC 77 [C gain from Lab] [†] *Staffordshire Moorlands, Cheadle North East*: C 308 Whitehouse 163 Lab 117 Upton 33 Grn 31 [C gain from Ind] [‡] *Staffordshire Moorlands, Cheadle South East*: C 359 Lab 206 Evans 153 Pearce 87 Thomas 24 Grn 18 [C gain from Ind] [§] *Andrew's Previews 2017*, page 263. [¶] *Andrew's Previews 2018*, page 50.

There is no independent candidate this time to replace Spedding so his seat is open, and it should revert back to Labour: the Labour slate here is Louise Walker (who was runner-up in the 2019 election) and Thomas Hadley.*

Finally, we come to the *Summerfield and All Saints* ward of LICHFIELD district, which again is less scenic than the name might suggest: this is the central of the five wards covering the former mining town of Burntwood. Summerfield and All Saints elected a full slate of three Conservative councillors in 2015, but Labour gained two seats in 2019 and are defending this by-election. A closely-watched contest can be expected between defending Labour candidate Michael Galvin and the Tories' Heather Tranter.†

West Mercia

Police and Crime Commissioner

The West Mercia police area covers three counties in the Severn and Wye valleys in the west of England: Worcestershire, Shropshire and Herefordshire. The 2012 PCC election returned an independent candidate, Bill Longmore, who didn't seek re-election in 2016. Five years ago the Conservatives topped the poll here with 33% against 21% for Labour, 17% for UKIP and 14% for an independent candidate; the Conservatives' John-Paul Campion and Labour's Daniel Walton went through to the runoff, which Campion won 60–40.

Campion is seeking re-election for a second term. The Labour candidate this time is Telford and Wrekin councillor Kuldip Sahota. Peter Jewell, who was the UKIP candidate five years ago, now has the Reform UK nomination. Completing the ballot paper is Margaret Rowley of the Liberal Democrats.‡

Local elections

There are elections this year for the whole of Shropshire council and Worcestershire county council and for one-third of Redditch and Worcester councils.

To start in REDDITCH, which is a New Town with voting patterns to match. The Conservatives run Redditch council with an 18–11 lead over Labour, and no fewer than seven of the Labour councillors are up for re-election this year. A par score for the council is difficult to assess, because of the way Redditch's wards come up for election, but would involve significant Conservative gains.

---

* *East Staffordshire, Eton Park*: Lab 660 (Hadley)/656 (Walker) C 330 (Ackroyd)/247 (Gould) LD 53 (Goldsworthy)/43 (Warner) [1 Lab gain from Ind] † *Lichfield, Summerfield and All Saints*: C 783 Lab 392 LD 191 [C gain from Lab] ‡ *West Mercia PCC*: C 179411 Lab 77664 LD 50699 Reform UK 16419

Worcester city council is currently hung: the Conservatives have 16 seats, Labour 15, the Greens 3 and the Lib Dems 1. An all-party administration is in place. The Conservatives will have their eye on gaining the city-centre Cathedral ward which they won two years ago, but the second gain they require for an overall majority may prove elusive.

Worcestershire county council has a big Conservative majority and that looks unlikely to change. The 2017 election here returned 40 Conservative councillors, 10 Labour, 3 Lib Dems, 2 Greens, 1 Kidderminster Health Concern and an independent.

The only local by-election within Worcestershire has fallen in the by-election-prone ward of *Elmley Castle and Somerville*, covering seven parishes in the Vale of Evesham to the north and east of Bredon Hill. This is a safely Conservative ward of Wychavon council which has generated a number of casual vacancies in the last decade. Elmley Castle and Somerville was represented by Anna Mackison until she died shortly before the 2011 election; it appears that nobody was planning to oppose her that year as no candidates were nominated for the ward, so a by-election had to be held in June 2011 which was won by the Tories' Roma Kirke. Kirke resigned shortly before the 2015 election, which was held for the Conservatives by Anna's widower George Mackison. George has now resigned in his turn, and Emma Kearsey will look to defend the ward for the Tories in a straight fight with the Green Party.*

The ruling Conservative group on Shropshire council attracted rather a lot of bad publicity over the last decade, although the last term does seem to have been significantly quieter on that front suggesting things may have calmed down somewhat. The Tories are defending a large majority from the 2017 election which returned 49 Conservatives, 12 Lib Dems, 8 Labour (all from Shrewsbury and its satellite village of Bayston Hill), three independents, a Green councillor and a representative of Kidderminster Health Concern (in Cleobury Mortimer, for which Kidderminster is the main service centre). The Conservative defence will be helped by the fact that they have held Albrighton division unopposed. Albrighton is the only uncontested seat on the British mainland in this year's local elections.

There are no local elections this year in Herefordshire or Telford and Wrekin apart from three by-elections. In Herefordshire we pay a visit to *Newton Farm* ward on the south-western edge of Hereford, which elected independent candidates in the 2015 and 2019 elections; two new independents have come forward here in the shape of Alan Jones and Glenda Powell. Jones appears to be fighting his first election campaign; Powell was the runner-up here in 2015 as an

* *Wychavon, Elmley Castle and Somerville*: C 632 Grn 316

independent, and finished fourth in 2019 with the Democrats and Veterans Party nomination. Second in this ward last time were the Lib Dems, whose candidate Jacqui Carwardine is standing again. The Labour candidate Steve Horsfield also deserves a mention thanks to his TikTok campaign video, which has become an unlikely viral hit[*].[†]

Finally in this section, Labour have two by-elections to defend in TELFORD AND WREKIN. *Dawley and Aqueduct* ward is in the south of the New Town (which was originally going to be called Dawley), while *Donnington* ward is in the north-east corner of Telford on the way to Newport. Both of these wards were safe Labour in 2019, and the defending candidates are Ian Preece[‡] and Sophie Thompson[§] respectively.

[*] The campaign video can be found at `https://tinyurl.com/2p82dfvz` [†] *Herefordshire, Newton Farm*: C 282 LD 190 Lab 64 Jones 62 Powell 45 Woods 16 TUSC 9 [C gain from Ind] [‡] *Telford and Wrekin, Dawley and Aqueduct*: Lab 1310 C 1192 LD 72. For a later by-election in the same ward see page 586. [§] *Telford and Wrekin, Donnington*: C 851 Lab 658 LD 66 [C gain from Lab]

6th May 2021 Part III: South and East

So now, here is Part III, covering the south of England outside London (for which, see Part I). We will start in the South West, and then flip over to East Anglia and the Home Counties.

Gloucestershire

Police and Crime Commissioner

The post of Gloucestershire PCC has been held since 2012 by retired senior police officer Martin Surl, who was elected in 2012 and 2016 as an independent candidate. At the 2016 election Surl led in the first round with 41%, to 35% for the Conservatives and 24% for Labour; the Labour transfers broke heavily for Surl who won the run-off by the comfortable margin of 59–41.

Surl is seeking a third term. The Conservatives have selected Chris Nelson, a retired Army officer and former Cheltenham councillor. The Labour candidate is Simon O'Rourke, from Tewkesbury, and the ballot paper is completed by Lib Dem Christopher Coleman and independent candidate Adrian "Stratts" Stratton.*

Local elections

There are elections this year for the whole of Gloucestershire county council and Gloucester and Stroud councils, and for one-half of Cheltenham council.

GLOUCESTERSHIRE COUNTY COUNCIL was a Conservative gain in 2013 and has a relatively small majority: there are 31 Conservative seats against 14 Lib Dems, 5 Labour, 2 Greens and one county councillor for the People Against Bureaucracy

* *Gloucestershire PCC*: first preferences C 79086 LD 37024 Surl 34286 Lab 31347 Stratton 13131; runoff C 91097 LD 59838 [C gain from Ind]

Group, a long-standing localist group based in northern Cheltenham which is not standing again this year. With a number of Tory-held divisions across the county having small majorities, it won't take much of an unwind for a No Overall Control result.

GLOUCESTER city council is in a similar position. It last polled in 2016, when the Conservatives won 22 seats in Gloucester against 10 for Labour and 7 Lib Dems. The ruling group has since lost a by-election to the Lib Dems and has two further vacancies; unfortunately one of these is an entry for the Councillors Behaving Badly file, because Conservative councillor Lee Hawthorne resigned after becoming one of the first people to be charged under recently-enacted laws against upskirting. Despite that scandal, the Conservative majority in Gloucester is probably stronger than it appears as most of their wards look fairly safe.

In STROUD district, which also last polled in 2016, the Conservatives are the largest party but the administration is a coalition of Labour, the Greens and the Liberal Democrats. The Tories will have to improve their position here significantly to take over the council. One-half of CHELTENHAM council is also up for election; this borough has a large Lib Dem majority which does not look in serious danger.

The four local by-elections in Gloucestershire consist of two either side of the Severn. On the east side, the Conservatives defend a by-election in the *Fosseridge* ward of COTSWOLD district, covering a number of villages to the north and east of Stow-on-the-Wold. Cotswold council was taken over by the Lib Dems in 2019 following a scandal over the Cotswold Water Park which has been ongoing for some years, but Fosseridge ward has remained firmly in the Conservative column and their candidate David Cunningham should be favoured to hold.* The highest point of the Cotswolds is Cleeve Hill, which is not in the Cotswold district at all: *Cleeve Hill* gives its name to a ward of TEWKESBURY district which wraps around the eastern side of the fast-growing settlement of Bishop's Cleeve, north of Cheltenham. Again, this is safely Conservative and their defending candidate Keja Berliner should be confident of election.†

Things are rather different to the west of the Severn in the FOREST OF DEAN. The Forest's council is run by a coalition of independent and Green councillors, with the main parties in opposition. *Berry Hill* ward, the birthplace of Dennis Potter, returned two independent councillors in 2019 with the Conservatives in second place; one of the independent seats is up in this by-election. Jamie Elsmore has come forward as a new independent candidate, while the Tories have nominated Terry Hale.‡ Labour are defending a by-election in *Cinderford*

* *Cotswold, Fosseridge*: C 641 LD 251 Grn 114 † *Tewkesbury, Cleeve Hill*: C 910 LD 842 Grn 114 Lab 107 ‡ *Forest of Dean, Berry Hill*: Ind 561 C 400 Grn 199 Lab 185 LD 33

East ward, which was safe for them two years ago; Shaun Stammers leads their defence.*

Avon and Somerset

West of England Mayoralty

It's metro mayor time again as we come to the mayoralty for the Bristol area, generally known as the West of England Mayoralty. This is voted for by the voters of the city of Bristol and the districts of South Gloucestershire, and Bath and North East Somerset. North Somerset, on the far side of the Clifton suspension bridge, is not included.

The inaugural election for this position turned in a fragmented result on the first count. The Conservatives' Tim Bowles led with 27% of the vote; Labour candidate Lesley Mansell placed second with 22%; former Lib Dem MP Stephen Williams finished third with 20%; independent candidate John Savage polled 15% and the Green Party 11%. The Conservatives and Labour went through to the runoff, which Bowles won 52–48.

Tim Bowles is not seeking re-election. The Conservatives have selected Samuel Williams, who runs a communications consultancy. The Labour candidate is Dan Norris, who was the MP for Wansdyke from 1997 to 2010. The Lib Dems have reselected Stephen Williams; not to be confused with the Conservative candidate of a similar name, Stephen was the MP for Bristol West from 2005 to 2015. John Savage has not returned, so completing the ballot paper is the Green candidate Jerome Thomas, a member of the outgoing Bristol city council.†

Police and Crime Commissioner

There is a wider electorate for the Avon and Somerset police and crime commissioner, whose remit covers the three boroughs in the West of England mayoralty, the Somerset county council area and the unitary district of North Somerset. Since 2012 the PCC has been independent figure Sue Mountstevens, who in 2012 was the only police and crime commissioner to receive a vote from more than 10% of their electorate: such was the awful turnout in those comedy elections. Things were different in 2016, when Mountstevens topped the poll in the first round with just 26% of the vote; Labour polled 24%, the Conservatives 19%,

* *Forest of Dean, Cinderford East*: Lab 362 C 319 Grn 152 Ind 83 † *Mayor of the West of England*: first preferences Lab 84434 C 72415 Grn 54919 LD 41193; runoff Lab 125482 C 85389 [Lab gain from C]

UKIP 9% and three other candidates all saved their deposits with 7% each. Sue Mountstevens and Labour candidate Kerry Barker went through to the runoff, which Mountstevens won 54–46.

Sue Mountstevens is not seeking re-election, but her deputy John Smith is standing as an independent candidate. Criminal barrister Kerry Barker tries again for Labour. The Conservatives have selected Mark Shelford, an Army officer of 32 years' service. UKIP have not returned, so completing the PCC ballot paper are Heather Shearer for the Lib Dems and Cleo Lake for the Green Party.*

Local elections

For some reason, BRISTOL has ended up with three major single-member elected posts. As well as the Avon and Somerset Police and Crime Commissioner and the Mayor of the West of England, the Mayor of Bristol is up for re-election. This is currently Labour's Marvin Rees who had a big win here in 2016; on the first count he led with 40% against 23% for the outgoing independent mayor George Ferguson and 14% for the Conservatives, and Rees increased his lead in the runoff to beat Ferguson 63–37 in the final reckoning.

Rees is seeking re-election for a second term. Ferguson has not returned. The Conservatives have selected Alastair Watson, a businessman and former city councillor (serving as ceremonial Lord Mayor in 2014–15). Also standing are Sandy Hore-Ruthven for the Green Party, Caroline Gooch for the Lib Dems, Tom Baldwin for the Trade Unionist and Socialist Coalition, independent candidates Sean Donnelly, John Langley and Oska Shaw, and Reform UK candidate Robert Clarke.†

Along with Rees' mayoralty, Labour are defending an overall majority of four seats on BRISTOL city council. In 2016 they won 37 seats against 14 Conservatives, 11 Greens and 8 Lib Dems.

There are no local elections this year in Bath and North-East Somerset, North Somerset or South Gloucestershire apart from by-elections. In SOUTH GLOUCESTERSHIRE the suburban Bristol ward of *Frenchay and Downend* is defended by the Conservatives; this is a safe ward which should return their candidate Liz Brennan.‡ Things are politically rather different in the *Portishead East* ward of NORTH SOMERSET, which voted strongly for the localist Portishead

* *Avon and Somerset PCC*: first preferences C 136988 Lab 93495 Grn 64790 LD 52839 Ind 46379; runoff C 161319 Lab 146293 [C gain from Ind] † *Mayor of Bristol*: first preferences Lab 50510 Grn 36331 C 25816 LD 15517 Donnelly 4956 TUSC 3194 Langley 1528 Reform UK 806 Shaw 389; runoff Lab 59276 Grn 45663. Langley was accidentally omitted from the original version of this preview. ‡ *South Gloucestershire, Frenchay and Downend*: C 1819 LD 1598 Lab 1049 Grn 347

Independents in 2019; their defending candidate is Caroline Goddard.*

The scheduled election for Somerset county council has been postponed to 2022 due to the possibility of further local government reorganisation in the county. As a result there are no local elections within the Somerset county council area apart from two by-elections. We have already had one recent reorganisation with the formation in 2019 of Somerset West and Taunton council, where there is a by-election to the ward of *Trull, Pitminster and Corfe* covering three rural parishes immediately south of Taunton. This was safely Lib Dem in 2019, and their candidate Dawn Johnson should be favoured to hold.†

Things are rather different in the city of Wells, where there is a by-election in the *Wells St Thomas'* ward of Mendip council. This was a longstanding Lib Dem-Tory marginal, the Liberal Democrats normally having the better of the results, including in a 2018 by-election‡; the ward then became safe Lib Dem in 2019. The party had selected Wells city councillor Tony Robbins to defend the by-election, but they cocked up his nomination papers and as a result there is no Lib Dem candidate on the ballot. Accordingly, this Wells St Thomas' by-election is an unexpected free-for-all between the Conservatives' Tanys Pullin and Labour's Adam Fyfe.§

Wiltshire

Police and Crime Commissioner

The Wiltshire PCC is Angus Macpherson of the Conservatives, who was re-elected for a second term in 2016 comfortably. In the first round he had 47% of the vote against 23% for Labour and 16% for the Liberal Democrats; this lead was extended to 64–36 in the runoff.

Macpherson is standing down, and to replace him the Conservatives have selected Wiltshire councillor Jonathan Seed. The Labour candidate is Swindon councillor Junab Ali. Standing for the Lib Dems is Liz Webster, who fought North Swindon and The Cotswolds in the 2017 and 2019 general elections respectively. Also standing are Julian Malins (a former City of London alderman, former Conservative parliamentary candidate, and brother of the former Conservative MP Humfrey Malins) for Reform UK, Brig Oubridge for the Greens

* *North Somerset, Portishead East*: Portishead Ind 768 C 609 LD 303 Lab 219 † *Somerset West and Taunton; Trull, Pitminster and Corfe*: LD 781 C 583 Lab 44 ‡ *Andrew's Previews 2018*, page 380. § *Mendip, Wells St Thomas'*: C 887 Lab 642 [C gain from LD]

and independent candidate Mike Rees.*

Local elections

There are elections this year for the whole of Wiltshire council and one-third of Swindon council.

The present WILTSHIRE council dates from 2009 when the county's local government was reorganised and its district councils were abolished. All three Wiltshire elections to date have returned Conservative majorities, with the party winning 68 seats out of a possible 98 in 2017. Although new division boundaries make comparisons difficult, there's no real reason to expect a change of control here.

Instead attention within the county will focus on the town of SWINDON. This has a small Conservative majority that rests on a particularly good result in May 2019, when the Tories converted a 39.6–39.2 lead over Labour in votes into a 12–7 win in seats; this seat tally was impressive enough in its own right but was actually an improvement on the 11–8 Tory lead recorded on general election day in 2015. This year Labour and the Tories are defending nine wards each, plus a Conservative-defended by-election in the safe Chiseldon and Lawn ward, and a par score would be for the Conservatives to increase their majority on the council.

Dorset

Police and Crime Commissioner

The Dorset PCC since 2012 has been Martyn Underhill, a long-serving senior police officer who worked on (among other things) the Sarah Payne child murder investigation. Underhill was elected in 2012 as an independent candidate, being re-elected in 2016; in the first round he had 38% of the vote to the Conservatives' 29% and UKIP's 17%, and in the runoff he defeated Tory candidate Andrew Graham 60–40.

Underhill is not seeking re-election. He has endorsed new independent candidate Dan Hardy, a former Grenadier Guardsman and police officer. David Sidwick, according to his unimprovable Twitter description, is a "husband, dad, boardgame geek, wildlife lover, sci-fi nut, teacake fan, strategic leader and Conservative PCC candidate for Dorset". UKIP have not returned, so the ballot

* *Wiltshire PCC*: first preferences C 84885 LD 35013 Lab 34147 Ind 31722 Grn 16606 Reform UK 4348; runoff C 100003 LD 58074. Seed was returned while ineligible and a by-election subsequently had to take place, for which see page 329.

paper is completed by Patrick Canavan for Labour, Mark Robson for the Lib Dems and Claire Seymour for the Green Party.[*]

Local elections

Following the reorganisation of Dorset's local government in 2019, the only local elections in the county this year are two by-elections to BOURNEMOUTH, CHRISTCHURCH AND POOLE council.

BCP council dates from the 2019 reorganisation as a merger of the former unitary districts of Poole and Bournemouth with the non-metropolitan district of Christchurch. This seems to have gone down very badly in Christchurch in particular. At parliamentary level Christchurch is one of the safest Conservative constituencies, but the Tories were thrashed in most of that town's wards by an independent slate and, largely as a result of that, failed to win a majority on the council. An anti-Conservative rainbow coalition with a slim majority was set up under the leadership of Lib Dem councillor Vikki Slade.

In April 2020 Colin Bungey, a former mayor of Christchurch and independent councillor for *Commons* ward (covering northern Christchurch and Bournemouth Airport), died. Because of the pandemic, no by-election could be held. The Conservatives promptly launched a no-confidence motion against Slade, which resulted in a tie and was rejected on the council chair's casting vote. Then in July 2020 Pete Parish, Lib Dem councillor for *Canford Heath* ward in Poole, died. Because of the pandemic, no by-election could be held. Another no-confidence motion was launched against the rainbow coalition, and this time Vikki Slade was ousted and a Conservative council leader installed.

The Conservatives now run a minority administration in BCP with 36 councillors, two short of a majority; if they can gain both of these by-elections they will have half of the seats. Will they manage that? Judging from the 2019 results, that seems like a tall order. The Christchurch Independents had a large majority in Commons ward two years ago, and they have since filed the paperwork with the Electoral Commission to register as a political party and use the name "Christchurch Independents" on the ballot paper. Their defending candidate is Vanessa Ricketts.[†] Canford Heath has been a safe Lib Dem area for many years and their candidate Jennie Hodges will be a short-priced favourite.[‡]

---

[*] *Dorset PCC*: first preferences C 64071 Ind 31112 Grn 21283 LD 17837 Lab 16379; runoff C 70353 Ind 43427 [C gain from Ind] [†] *Bournemouth, Christchurch and Poole; Commons*: Christchurch Ind 1310 C 822 Ind 296 LD 242 Lab 214 UKIP 48 [‡] *Bournemouth, Christchurch and Poole; Canford Heath*: C 1406 LD 1365 Lab 335 Ind 132 Grn 128 UKIP 105 [C gain from LD]

Devon and Cornwall

Police and Crime Commissioner

The Devon and Cornwall PCC election turned in a close result in 2016. Top in the first round was Alison Hernandez of the Conservatives with just 24%; Gareth Derrick of Labour was second with 23%; UKIP polled 17%, independent candidate Bob Spencer got 15% and former Lib Dem MP Richard Younger-Ross finished fifth with 12%. Hernandez and Derrick went through to the runoff, and transfers from the other four candidates were very even which resulted in a Conservative win by 51.1–48.9, a majority of 3,794 votes.

Hernandez is seeking re-election in a reduced field of four candidates. Labour have reselected Plymouth councillor Gareth Derrick for another go, the Lib Dem candidate this time is former police officer Brian Blake, and the Greens' Stuart Jackson completes the ballot paper.*

Local elections

There are elections this year for the whole of Devon county council, Cornwall council and the Isles of Scilly council, together with one-third of Exeter and Plymouth councils.

Both the cities of Exeter and Plymouth have Labour majorities. Labour control PLYMOUTH with 30 seats out of 57. A repeat of the May 2019 results would see that majority wiped out with four losses to the Conservatives; however the opposition Conservative group have since suffered a major split. In the event that Labour lose their majority, the Tories would probably need to sort their own house out first before challenging for the council leadership.

The Labour majority in EXETER does not look in serious danger. As Plymouth is a unitary council, Exeter supplies the entire Labour group on DEVON COUNTY COUNCIL which has a large and secure-looking Conservative majority.

Things are different over the Tamar in CORNWALL, where the Conservatives are the largest party but the administration is a Lib Dem–Independent coalition. There are major boundary changes in Cornwall with no fewer than 36 seats disappearing, which should shake things up quite a lot.

The tiny ISLES OF SCILLY council is non-partisan. Sixteen candidates have come forward for the sixteen seats; there will be an election for the 12 seats on St Mary's as 13 candidates are standing there, but there will not be an election for the other four islands in the archipelago. Harry Legg has been elected unopposed

* *Devon and Cornwall PCC*: first preferences C 247173 Lab 99894 LD 88318 Grn 59242; runoff C 275217 Lab 146979

in St Agnes, Tony Tobin-Dougan in St Martin's and Robert Dorrien-Smith in Tresco. No candidates came forward to represent the island of *Bryher*, and a by-election will have to be held there in due course—assuming, that is, that one of the locals (and Bryher's population is comfortably under 100) wants to be a councillor.

With all of Cornwall's local government being renewed this year, for local by-elections we have to cross back to Devon. There have been shenanigans in Mid Devon district over the last year: the Conservatives lost their majority in 2019 and an Independent-Lib Dem-Green administration took over, but following disagreements within the ruling coalition the Lib Dem cabinet ministers were sacked in August 2020 and the Conservatives have taken their place in the administration. Mid Devon council has three by-elections on 6th May, two of which are in Tiverton: *Castle* ward, covering the north of the town, returned two Lib Dem gains from the Conservatives in 2019 in a close a three-way marginal result, and the Lib Dems' David Wulff will face competition from the Tories' Elizabeth Slade (who lost her seat here in 2019) and Labour's Richard Cornley.[*] *Westexe* ward, covering the west of Tiverton, has returned independent, Conservative, Labour and UKIP councillors this century and voted Conservative in a September 2017 by-election[†]; in 2019 a full slate of independent councillors was elected, and three independent candidates have come forward for this by-election (Stephen Bush, Claire Hole and Adrian Howell). If they split the independent vote between them, that could present an opportunity for the Conservatives' Stephen Pugh or the Greens' Rosie Wibberley.[‡] Finally, the Conservatives defend the deeply-rural *Taw* ward, covering seven parishes on the western side of the Taw valley from Wembworthy to Zeal Monachorum; the Tories were unopposed here in 2019, and their candidate Peter Heal should have little trouble holding the Taw by-election.[§]

In the South Hams district we have an intriguing by-election in the *Ivybridge West* ward, which returned two Conservatives in 2019 against opposition from a single Labour candidate and a single Lib Dem. The candidate list this time is the unusual combination of Conservative, Green Party, and Trade Unionist and Socialist Coalition; Louise Jones defends for the Tories, while the Green candidate Katie Reville was a strong runner-up here in 2015 but didn't stand in 2019.[¶]

[*] *Mid Devon, Castle*: C 513 LD 319 Lab 213 Ind 213 [C gain from LD] [†] *Andrew's Previews 2017*, page 248. [‡] *Mid Devon, Westexe*: C 567 Lab 274 Grn 263 Howell 179 Hole 126 Bush 108 [C gain from Ind] [§] *Mid Devon, Taw*: C 418 LD 234 [¶] *South Hams, Ivybridge West*: C 933 Grn 768 TUSC 149

There are no local elections this year in TORBAY apart from a local by-election in *Clifton with Maidenway* ward, which is located in western Paignton. Long-time readers of Andrew's Previews will remember a by-election here in November 2015 which was a big win for Adrian Sanders, the former Lib Dem MP for Torbay. Sanders didn't seek re-election to the council in 2019, but his old ward (on revised boundaries) remained safely Lib Dem, and their new candidate Cat Johns starts as favourite.*

Our final Devon by-election takes place east of Exeter in the EAST DEVON district, which was taken over by an independent-led administration after the 2019 election. One of the wards which voted independent was *Whimple and Rockbeare*, a few miles west of Ottery St Mary, but that will change in this by-election as there is no defending independent candidate. Richard Lawrence of the Conservatives takes on Lib Dem Todd Olive in a straight fight.†

Norfolk

Police and Crime Commissioner

The outgoing Norfolk PCC is former Canadian diplomat Lorne Green. In the 2016 election he was top of the first round with 28%, against 24% for Labour and 17% each for UKIP and the outgoing independent PCC Stephen Bett, who finished fourth in his re-election attempt. The runoff saw Green beat the Labour candidate by 54–46.

Green is not seeking re-election and the Conservatives have selected the wonderfully-named Giles Orpen-Smellie, an Army veteran of 34 years' service including tours in Northern Ireland, the Falklands, the Gulf War, the Balkans, Sierra Leone and Iraq. The Labour candidate is Michael Rosen; this Michael Rosen is not the former Children's Laureate and near-casualty of COVID of that name, rather he is the former director of children's services for Norfolk county council. Also standing are John Crofts for the Lib Dems, independent David Moreland and the Greens' Martin Schmierer.‡

Local elections

There are elections this year for the whole of Norfolk county council and for one-third of Norwich council.

* *Torbay, Clifton with Maidenway*: LD 1014 C 983 Lab 149 Grn 69 † *East Devon, Whimple and Rockbeare*: C 502 LD 392 [C gain from Ind] ‡ *Norfolk PCC*: first preferences C 103980 Lab 51056 LD 31666 Grn 23469 Ind 20473; runoff C 119994 Lab 69552

NORFOLK COUNTY COUNCIL was hung in the 2013–17 term thanks to a very good UKIP performance in May 2013; this has since unwound and the 2017 election gave the Conservatives 55 seats here against 17 Labour, 11 Lib Dems and one independent. It's difficult to see that changing, although the Green Party (which was wiped out here in 2017) will want to get back on the council.

The Green powerbase is in NORWICH, whose city boundaries are rather weird thanks to the council holding harbour rights for most of the River Wensum. All of Norwich city council was up in 2019 on slightly-revised ward boundaries; that election gave 27 seats to Labour, 9 to the Greens and 3 to the Lib Dems, and none of the city's 13 wards look marginal so it will take a lot of effort for that seat count to change.

The Norfolk and Norwich elections this year will not be complete on 6th May. Eve Collishaw, who was standing as the Conservative candidate for the Sewell county division and ward, sadly died during the election campaign and the polls there have been postponed to 17th June.*

Norfolk's four local by-elections on 6th May are defended by four different parties. GREAT YARMOUTH council moved off the thirds cycle in 2019, but there are two by-elections here this year: in *Claydon* ward within the town, and *Ormesby* ward covering two parishes some distance to the north. Claydon has voted Labour in every election since 2004 with the exception of a UKIP win in 2014; Labour were well ahead here in 2019 and their candidate Jo Thurtle should be favoured.† Ormesby's independent councillor Steven Scott-Greenard has resigned and the by-election to replace him is a straight fight between the Ron Hanton of the Conservatives (who hold the ward's other seat) and Alison Green of Labour.‡

Further along the Norfolk coast we come to the *Coastal* ward of NORTH NORFOLK council, based on Cley next the Sea and Blakeney. This ward was a big win for the Liberal Democrats in May 2019, but their councillor Karen Ward contracted COVID and is yet to regain her health. The Lib Dem candidate Phil Bailey should be favoured in the Coastal by-election.§ In May 2019 Coastal ward was part of a Lib Dem constituency, but the Liberal Democrats failed to defend it in the December 2019 general election; new Conservative MP Duncan Baker has vacated his North Norfolk council seat resulting in a by-election in the ward immediately to the south, *Holt* ward. Holt split its two seats between the Conservatives and the Liberal Democrats in 2019, but the Lib Dems have failed to find a candidate for the resulting by-election. Defending Conservative Eric

* See page 222. † *Great Yarmouth, Claydon*: C 728 Lab 648 [C gain from Lab] ‡ *Great Yarmouth, Ormesby*: C 939 Lab 320 [C gain from Ind] § *North Norfolk, Coastal*: C 585 LD 303 Lab 108 [C gain from LD]

Vardy* will instead take on Labour's Jasper Haywood and two independents, Nick Coppack (a former Conservative North Norfolk councillor) and Jono Read (digital editor of the *New European* newspaper).†

Suffolk

Police and Crime Commissioner

In 2016 Suffolk easily re-elected the Conservatives' Tim Passmore as its police and crime commissioner. On the first count Passmore had a big lead with 44% of the vote, against 25% for Labour and 17% for UKIP; his lead in the run-off against Labour was 62–38.

Passmore is seeking re-election for a third term. The Labour candidate this time is Elizabeth Hughes, an Ipswich councillor who fought safe-Conservative Suffolk constituencies at the 2017 and 2019 general elections. UKIP have not returned, so completing the ballot paper are Andy Patmore for the Green Party and James Sandbach for the Liberal Democrats.‡

Local elections

There are elections this year for the whole of Suffolk county council and for one-third of Ipswich council.

Unlike its northern neighbour, SUFFOLK COUNTY COUNCIL narrowly re-elected its Conservative administration in 2013 with a 39-36 lead over the opposition; however, by 2017 that Tory majority had disappeared in a series of poor by-election results. The 2017 election marked a return to form for the Tories with 52 seats, against 11 Labour, 5 Lib Dems, 4 independents and 3 Greens. Local elections in the county two years ago were not that promising for the Conservatives, who lost control of Babergh and Mid Suffolk districts and performed particularly poorly in the rural west of the county (the constituency of the health secretary Matt Hancock, although that underperformance probably wasn't his fault). Despite that, there should be enough headroom for the Conservative administration to continue.

A lot of that underperformance in western Suffolk was a large independent vote resulting from the abolition of the former Forest Heath council, based on Newmarket and Mildenhall, whose area is now administered by WEST SUFFOLK

* Vardy sat on Charnwood council until 2019, and in the resulting preview (*Andrew's Previews 2019*, page 306) I mistakenly reported that he had died. For the avoidance of doubt, Mr Vardy is alive and well. † *North Norfolk, Holt*: C 837 Read 738 Lab 112 Coppack 63 ‡ *Suffolk PCC*: C 112139 Lab 47159 Grn 27965 LD 17801

council from Bury St Edmunds. Independent candidates did very well in the old Forest Heath area, as can be seen from the result in *Lakenheath* ward where independent David Gathercole, the only opposition to a two-man Conservative slate, topped the poll. This ward includes the RAF Lakenheath airbase occupied by the US Air Force; very few if any of the Americans here will have the right to vote, so Lakenheath ward shouldn't suffer the turnout problems seen in other military-dominated wards. Two independent candidates, David Chandler and Gerald Kelly, will try to take over the late David Gathercole's seat; while Colin Noble will seek to gain for the Conservatives.*

That's just one of six local by-elections to West Suffolk council, the most for any council on 6th May. Two of these are in sprawling wards covering villages between Bury St Edmunds and Haverhill. *Whepstead and Wickhambrook* ward had a big Tory lead in May 2019 and their candidate Sarah Pugh should have few problems.† *Clare, Hundon and Kedington* ward returned two Tories and an independent in 2019, but this by-election (which follows the death of the independent councillor) is a straight fight between the Conservatives' Nick Clarke and Kerry Rogers for Labour, who didn't stand here last time.‡

That leaves three local by-elections in Bury St Edmunds. Beyond the A 14 on the eastern edge of the city lies *Moreton Hall* ward, which extends outside the city boundary to take in Rougham Airfield. Local elections here are dominated by independent councillor Trevor Beckwith; he topped the poll in 2019, with the other two seats going to independent Frank Warby and a Conservative. The by-election here is in respect of Warby, who had joined the Conservatives before resigning from the council; his replacement is likely to be a contest between independent Barry Thomas and Conservative Birgitte Mager.§ The Tories will also be looking to gain the city-centre *Abbeygate* ward, which returned one councillor each for the Greens and Conservatives in 2019; the Greens' Julia Wakeham will be looking to hold against the Tories' Nick Wiseman.¶ Finally, Bury St Edmunds' *Southgate* ward was safe Conservative last time and should be an easy hold for their candidate Sarah Stamp.‖

Another new council created in 2019 was East Suffolk district, which stretches along the littoral from Felixstowe to Lowestoft. The Green Party will fancy their chances in both East Suffolk by-elections today. *Framlingham*, a tiny market town about 16 miles north-east of Ipswich, is the location of the "castle

* *West Suffolk, Lakenheath*: C 573 Kelly 434 Lab 119 Chandler 64 [C gain from Ind] † *West Suffolk, Whepstead and Wickhambrook*: C 645 Lab 142 Grn 137 ‡ *West Suffolk; Clare, Hundon and Kedington*: C 1814 Lab 697 § *West Suffolk, Moreton Hall*: C 1098 Ind 496 Lab 495 [C gain from Ind] ¶ *West Suffolk, Abbeygate*: Grn 751 C 606 Lab 279 ‖ *West Suffolk, Southgate*: C 814 Lab 251 Grn 186 LD 148

on the hill" in that song by Ed Sheeran, who is an elector here; Framlingham Castle is notable in its own right as the place where Mary Tudor was proclaimed Queen in 1553. The Conservatives won both seats here at the first East Suffolk council elections in 2019 with the Greens close behind; defending Tory candidate Lydia Freeman will be challenged this time by Green Party nominee Beth Keys-Holloway.* The Greens have turned the Broads town of Beccles into a stronghold at local level, and Sarah Plummer should have little trouble defending the *Beccles and Worlingham* by-election.†

Beccles lies on the northern boundary of Suffolk, while the Sudbury suburb of *Great Cornard* lies on the county's southern boundary. This is one of the strongest Labour areas within the BABERGH district of southern Suffolk, although the Conservatives still won all three seats here in 2019. Simon Barrett is the defending Conservative candidate in the Great Cornard by-election, Jake Thomas will hope to gain for Labour.‡

Despite having a Tory MP since December 2019, IPSWICH council has a large Labour majority which looks in no serious danger, although a repeat of the May 2019 results would see Labour lose two seats. in Holywell and Stoke Park wards, to the Conservatives.

Cambridgeshire

Mayor of Cambridgeshire and Peterborough

The most rural of the metro mayoralties set up to date is that for Cambridgeshire and Peterborough, which covers an area which is fast growing in population but still has a lot of green space (although quite a lot of that is fenland). The inaugural mayoral election in 2017 saw the Tories' James Palmer lead in the first round with 38%, with 23% for the Lib Dems and 19% for Labour. Palmer and the Lib Dem candidate Rod Cantrill went through to the runoff, which Palmer won by the easy margin of 57–43.

Palmer is seeking re-election for a second term as mayor. The Lib Dems have selected Aidan van de Weyer, the deputy leader of South Cambridgeshire council. Completing the mayoral ballot paper is Labour candidate Nik Johnson, an NHS consultant paediatrician and Huntingdonshire councillor.§

* *East Suffolk, Framlingham*: C 1508 Grn 1036 Lab 318 † *East Suffolk, Beccles and Worlingham*: Grn 2374 C 2062 Lab 418 ‡ *Babergh, Great Cornard*: C 971 Lab 602 LD 287 Grn 234 § *Mayor of Cambridgeshire and Peterborough*: first preferences C 93942 Lab 76106 LD 61885; runoff Lab 113994 C 108195 [Lab gain from C]

Police and Crime Commissioner

A year earlier, the Cambridgeshire PCC election (which covers the same area) had a rather different result. Conservative PCC Jason Ablewhite was re-elected for a second term, polling 36% in the first round against 31% for Labour and 17% for UKIP; on this occasion the run-off was Tory versus Labour, with Ablewhite prevailing by the narrower margin of 53–47. Ablewhite resigned as PCC in November 2019 under something of a cloud, and his deputy has been acting in the role since then.

For this election the Conservatives have changed candidate to Darryl Preston, a former police officer now working for the Association of Police and Crime Commissioners. Labour have selected Cambridge city councillor Nicky Massey. UKIP have not returned, so completing the PCC ballot paper are Susan Morris for Reform UK and Rupert Moss-Eccardt for the Liberal Democrats.*

Local elections†

There are elections this year for the whole of Cambridgeshire county council, for the whole of Cambridge city council on new ward boundaries, and for one-third of Peterborough council.

CAMBRIDGESHIRE COUNTY COUNCIL was a Conservative gain in 2017, with new division boundaries helping the party to 36 seats against 15 Lib Dems, 7 Labour councillors and 3 independents. The Tories have since performed very badly in the south of the county: the Lib Dems won a majority in South Cambridgeshire district in 2018, weren't far off winning control of East Cambridgeshire in May 2019 and weren't far off taking the South Cambridgeshire parliamentary seat in December 2019. Some of these trends were already evident in May 2017 (six of the 15 Lib Dem wins that year were in South Cambridgeshire district) so we shouldn't overstate the chance of major seat changes, but the Tories must be looking at their majority on the county council with some concern.

PETERBOROUGH council is currently hung, with a minority Conservative administration on 28 out of 60 seats (two of which are vacant) supported by the 3 Werrington localist councillors. A repeat of the May 2019 results would see the Conservatives lose three further seats and could result in Labour challenging for the council leadership. Mind, Peterborough is a city that had three different MPs in 2019, which shows a volatile local political scene firmly in keeping with

* *Cambridgeshire PCC*: first preferences C 99034 Lab 72313 LD 51490 Reform UK 8031; runoff C 114053 Lab 102195 † The four by-elections in South Cambridgeshire district were omitted from this section in error. See page 189 for information on those.

the volatile events of that year. It would take a brave person to predict what will happen here.

Outside Peterborough we have a by-election to FENLAND council from *Lattersey* ward, covering the south-east corner of Whittlesey around Whittlesea station. (When it comes to spelling, there's the right way, the wrong way and the railway.) The Conservatives won this ward unopposed in 2015—Fenland district is like that—and they had a 2–1 margin over Labour in 2019, so the defending Tory candidate Jason Mockett can be confident of his election chances.*

Peterborough was once linked with the former county of HUNTINGDONSHIRE, which is now a district under Cambridgeshire county council and sees four by-elections on 6th May. I mentioned earlier that the Police and Crime Commissioner Jason Ablewhite had resigned in November 2019; he had also resigned as a Huntingdonshire councillor, and a by-election was sneaked in during the winter of 2019–20 which resulted in a Conservative hold in the East ward of the town of St Ives.† The other *St Ives East* councillor has now resigned, and the Conservatives should hold this seat with their candidate Craig Smith.‡ The Tories also defend by-elections in *St Ives South* ward and in the *Warboys* ward in the fens between Huntingdon and Ramsey (with respectively Rianna d'Souza§ and Michael Haines¶ as the defending candidates), and might fancy their chances in the Labour-held ward of *Huntingdon North* (covering most of Huntingdon town), although Labour's candidate Marion Kadewere is defending a large enough majority from the last Huntingdonshire elections in 2018.‖

Finally, Labour are firmly in control of CAMBRIDGE city council, where all 42 seats are up for election this year on slightly-revised ward boundaries.

Essex

Police and Crime Commissioner

The 2016 Essex PCC election was open following the retirement of Tory PCC Nick Alston. New Conservative candidate Roger Hirst topped the poll in the first round with 33% of the vote, against 24% for former Conservative MP Bob Spink standing as the UKIP candidate, 20% for Labour and 13% for "Zero Tolerance Policing Ex Chief" Martin Terry. Hirst and Spink went through to the runoff, with Hirst winning comfortably by 57–43.

* *Fenland, Lattersey*: C 449 Lab 267 † *Andrew's Previews 2020*, page 33. ‡ *Huntingdonshire, St Ives East*: C 824 Lab 374 Grn 302 § *Huntingdonshire, St Ives South*: C 970 LD 599 Lab 441 Grn 246 ¶ *Huntingdonshire, Warboys*: C 1235 LD 382 Lab 352 ‖ *Huntingdonshire, Huntingdon North*: Lab 902 C 799 LD 498 UKIP 142

Roger Hirst is seeking re-election for a second term, and this time he won't have to face a UKIP candidate or Martin Terry. Labour have re-selected their 2016 candidate Chris Vince, a Harlow councillor and maths teacher. Also standing are Jon Whitehouse for the Lib Dems and Robin Tilbrook for the English Democrats.*

Local elections

There are elections this year for the whole of Essex county council and for one-third of Basildon, Brentwood, Castle Point, Colchester, Epping Forest, Harlow, Rochford, Southend-on-Sea and Thurrock councils.

ESSEX COUNTY COUNCIL is one of the safest county councils for the Conservatives. The 2017 election returned 56 Conservative councillors against 7 Lib Dems, 6 Labour, 3 localists (2 from Canvey Island, the other from Loughton), 2 independents and a Green.

Instead attention within the county should focus on the districts and boroughs. To start with England's oldest town, COLCHESTER council is currently hung; the Conservatives are the largest party with 23 seats (including one vacancy) out of 51, but the administration is a coalition of the Lib Dems, Labour and an independent group which has a lock on Highwoods ward. A repeat of the 2019 results would see that coalition increase its majority, with Stanway ward falling to the Lib Dems.

Moving to the towns on the north side of the Thames estuary, a similar rainbow coalition controls SOUTHEND-ON-SEA council where the Conservatives are currently the largest party on 20 seats out of 51. The Tories did very poorly here in May 2019, carrying only four of the borough's 17 wards; they are defending eight seats this year so there is the potential for some large changes on this council.

ROCHFORD council, based on Rayleigh and the rural area to the north of Southend, has a strong Conservative majority which can be expected to increase. To the west of Southend, CASTLE POINT council is stuck in a rut, with the Conservatives holding all the wards on the mainland in Benfleet and an independent group dominating offshore on Canvey Island; because Benfleet has more councillors than Canvey, this means a small but very stable Conservative majority. The Castle Point returning officer has taken the unusual step of filling casual vacancies in *Boyce*† and *St George's*‡ wards, on the mainland, with separate elections rather than combining them into a double vacancy election like every other RO in a thirds or halves council does, so if you are voting in those wards

* *Essex PCC*: C 235246 Lab 99712 LD 58131 EDP 42831 † *Castle Point, Boyce*: C 979 Edwards 654 Lab 219 Roberts 189 ‡ *Castle Point, St George's*: C 952 Lab 535

you will receive two ballot papers for the district council election (plus one for the county council and one for the PCC).

Billericay and Wickford are covered by the large BASILDON council where the Tories lost control in 2019; Labour and a number of independent groups are now running the show. In 2016 Basildon returned three UKIP councillors, none of whom are still in the party; their respective wards returned one Conservative, one Labour and one independent councillor in 2019, so the Tories probably can't rely on a UKIP unwind here.

The UKIP factor was much larger in THURROCK in 2016. The Kippers topped the poll across the 17 wards up for election that year with 39% of the vote, and won 6 wards; Labour polled 32% and won 4 wards, and the Conservatives won 7 wards despite coming in third in votes with just 28%. Isn't England's first-past-the-post system wonderful? A number of those UKIP councillors (after a "Thurrock Independents" interlude) have ended up in the Conservative group since the 2019 election, which has resulted in the Tories gaining, albeit by defection, a majority on Thurrock council for the first time since 2007. Judging from the 2019 results, that majority could well be endorsed by the electorate this time round.

BRENTWOOD has a rather small Conservative majority of 20 seats out of 37, following a good Lib Dem performance in 2019, but the scope for further Conservative losses is limited as they are only defending six wards this year. The Conservative majority in EPPING FOREST looks safe, as does the Labour majority in HARLOW where the Tories have yet to make their dominance at parliamentary and county council level stick. Harlow council currently has a 20–13 lead for Labour, who are defending 7 wards this year to the Conservatives' 4.

The standalone by-elections (other than the ones in Castle Point already mentioned) are an interesting bunch. We start in the county town of CHELMSFORD where the Lib Dems defend *Moulsham Lodge* ward, in the south of the city proper; although the Tories won one of the two seats in 2015, this was safely Lib Dem in 2019 and the defending candidate is Hazel Clark.*

To the east of Chelmsford is the deeply rural and very small MALDON district, which returned a tiny Conservative majority of 16–15 over independent councillors in 2019. That majority has since fallen apart thanks to a damaging split in the Tory group, and the independents took over the council leadership in November last year. Things could get worse for the Maldon Conservatives if they fail to defend the by-elections in *Heybridge East* ward (immediately north-east of Maldon, and including a large swathe of saltmarsh in the Blackwater estuary)

* *Chelmsford, Moulsham Lodge*: C 790 LD 652 Ind Network 183 Lab 122 Grn 89 [C gain from LD]

or *Tollesbury* ward (a remote village in the marshes which returned a Labour councillor in a 2012 by-election, but was safe Conservative in 2019). The defending Conservative candidates are Bruce Heubner in Heybridge East[*] and Debbie Keating in Tollesbury.[†]

UTTLESFORD district, covering a large rural area in the north-west of Essex, was one of the councils where the Conservatives lost control in 2019: the ruling Residents for Uttlesford party has a large majority on the council which is not in danger even though they are defending two by-elections: in *The Sampfords* ward, covering five parishes east of Saffron Walden, which was a Residents gain in 2019 on a big swing; and in *Newport* ward on the railway line from Stansted to Cambridge which R4U have held since 2015. On the other hand, the R4U councillor who vacated Newport had jumped to the Greens before leaving the council, so some debate can be had about whether the defending candidate there is Judy Emanuel for the Residents or Edward Gildea for the Greens.[‡] The Residents have nominated Uli Gerhard to hold the by-election in The Sampfords.[§]

The Green Party have had a presence for some time in the BRAINTREE district, but the two wards holding elections there on 6th May were both safely Conservative in 2019. These are *Witham South* ward, defended for the Tories by William Korsinah;[¶] and *Hatfield Peverel and Terling* ward, a rural area to the west of Witham town, where the Conservatives have nominated Darren White.[‖]

Saving the best till last, we come to the TENDRING district which covers everything in Essex east of Colchester, including the town of Clacton-on-Sea which, seven long years ago, was the first constituency to elect a UKIP member of parliament. UKIP won a large number of seats on Tendring council at the following elections in May 2015; despite the inevitable split and a seventh-place finish in the 2019 elections, the Kippers did still hold on to five council seats here in May 2019. One of those was in the *West Clacton and Jaywick Sands* ward, based on the village of Jaywick.

When your own council leader describes your village as "an embarrassment to the whole country", as the then Tendring leader Neil Stock said in 2012[**], you know you've got problems. Notorious for consistently being right at the bottom of the English indices of multiple deprivation, worse-off than anywhere in inner-city London or Manchester, Jaywick started off in the late 1920s as summer

[*] *Maldon, Heybridge East*: C 510 Perry 202 Lab 123 Outlaw 111 LD 87 [†] *Maldon, Tollesbury*: Ind 531 C 224 Lab 39 LD 18 [Ind gain from C] [‡] *Uttlesford, Newport*: R4U 892 C 322 Grn 63 LD 62 Lab 61 [§] *Uttlesford, The Sampfords*: C 384 R4U 361 Grn 52 Lab 46 LD 21 [C gain from R4U] [¶] *Braintree, Witham South*: C 623 Lab 339 Grn 157 LD 91 [‖] *Braintree, Hatfield Peverel and Terling*: C 1009 Grn 315 Lab 195 Ind 124 [**] `https://tinyurl.com/4dydpmce`

holiday homes for East Enders, and is now occupied year-round with increasingly dilapidated housing stock, mostly unadopted roads, a serious coastal flooding risk and intractable economic problems following the closure of the nearby Clacton Butlins camp in the 1980s. Despite this, there is clearly a community spirit in the village: Jaywick residents successfully fought off an attempt by the local council to bulldoze the place in 1970, and the use of the village in an attack ad by a 2018 US congressional Republican candidate resulted in uproar here[*] and a climbdown from the candidate concerned. Those who would sneer at people who live in UKIP-voting areas (of whom your columnist is one) would do well to put those sneers away.

And a UKIP-voting area this is: West Clacton and Jaywick Sands ward elected an independent (easily) and a UKIP candidate (narrowly) as its two councillors in 2019. The UKIP councillor has resigned and the party is not defending the resulting by-election giving us a free-for-all. Andy White, who was the runner-up here in 2019 as an independent candidate, has returned for another go and this time he has the nomination of the localist group Tendring First; two other independents are standing (Brad Thompson and Andy Wood), while the ruling minority Conservative group on the council have nominated Jayne Nash for this by-election.[†]

The Tories may have better chances in the other Tendring by-election, at the other end of Clacton-on-Sea. *Eastcliff* ward was close in 2019 between the localist group "Holland-on-Sea and Eastcliff Matters" and the second-placed Conservatives. The localists have nominated Rick Speller to hold the Eastcliff by-election, while former Tory councillor Mick Skeels senior will seek to make a comeback.[‡]

Hertfordshire

Police and Crime Commissioner

The Hertfordshire PCC since 2012 has been David Lloyd of the Conservatives. He was re-elected in 2016, polling 42% against 27% for former Labour MP Kerry Pollard and 16% for the Lib Dems. Lloyd's lead over Pollard in the final reckoning was 59–41.

[*] `https://tinyurl.com/ydfek5a8` [†] *Tendring, West Clacton and Jaywick Sands*: C 500 Thompson 395 Tendring First 140 Lab 110 Wood 32 LD 21 [C gain from UKIP] [‡] *Tendring, Eastcliff*: Baker 414 C 294 Holland-on-Sea and Eastcliff Matters 118 Lab 44 Mayzes 18 LD 13 [Ind gain from Holland-on-Sea and Eastcliff Matters]

The 2021 PCC election will feature only those three parties on the ballot. The Conservatives' Lloyd is seeking a third term, and is opposed by Labour's Philip Ross (a cybersecurity consultant) and the Lib Dems' Sam North (a North Hertfordshire councillor and former police officer).*

Local elections

There are elections this year for the whole of Hertfordshire county council and for one-third of Broxbourne, North Hertfordshire, St Albans, Stevenage, Three Rivers, Watford and Welwyn Hatfield councils. The only one of those which looks completely safe for the Tories is BROXBOURNE, based on the towns of Cheshunt and Hoddesdon in the Lea Valley.

The A1/East Coast Main Line corridor is another matter entirely. The Conservatives lost their majority on WELWYN HATFIELD council in 2019, but still run the district as a minority with 23 seats against 13 Labour and 12 Lib Dem councillors. If the 2019 election is repeated the Tories would lose three of the ten wards they are defending and fall further from overall control.

Similar considerations apply in NORTH HERTFORDSHIRE district, which is based on Hitchin, Letchworth and Royston; however, here the 22-strong Conservative group is in opposition to a coalition of Labour (16) and the Lib Dems (11). STEVENAGE council has had a Labour majority continuously since the 1974 reorganisation and that will not change this year.

Following a Tory bloodbath in 2019 ST ALBANS council is tied, with the Conservatives and Lib Dems both on 24 seats; the balance of power is held by 5 Labour councillors, 4 independents and a single Green councillor. Since then the Lib Dems have gained the St Albans parliamentary seat after decades of trying. A repeat of the May 2019 results would result in four Lib Dem gains, mostly from the small parties, which would make their present minority administration more secure. The Liberal Democrats are more firmly in control of WATFORD (where they hold the elected mayoralty) and the THREE RIVERS district which wraps around the western side of Watford.

HERTFORDSHIRE COUNTY COUNCIL has a large Conservative majority at present (51 councillors against 18 Lib Dems and 9 Labour), but there are enough marginal divisions for this majority to be in some real danger if the poor Conservative performance in 2019 is repeated two years down the line.

There are five standalone by-elections taking place. In EAST HERTFORDSHIRE district the Lib Dems have the task of defending *Bishop's Stortford All Saints* ward, covering the east of the town on the road towards the motorway

* *Hertfordshire PCC*: first preferences C 155144 LD 87524 Lab 76941; runoff C 167905 LD 135696

and Stansted Airport; this ward has seesawed between the Tories and Lib Dems over the last couple of decades, but the Liberal Democrat win in 2019 was by a big enough margin that their defending candidate Richard Townsend should be favoured.*

The Liberal Democrats also performed well in the 2019 elections to DACORUM council at the western end of Hertfordshire, making the *Tring Central* ward safe; Sheron Wilkie is their defending candidate there.† The Dacorum district is based on the new town of Hemel Hempstead, which also hosts a by-election in *Leverstock Green* ward on the eastern edge of the town; this ward was safe Conservative in 2019 and their defence is led by Neil Harden.‡

Finally, on the southern boundary of Hertfordshire two by-elections are being held in marginal wards of HERTSMERE council.§ The Liberal Democrats defend *Bushey North* ward, immediately to the east of Watford town centre: this was a traditional area of strength for the party at local level, which went Conservative during the coalition years but where the Lib Dems made a comeback in 2019. Alan Matthews defends this marginal ward for the Liberal Democrats, Jane West will try to gain for the Conservatives.¶

We also return to *Borehamwood Kenilworth* for the second by-election in that ward since 2019, and the third in four years.‖ Appropriately for a ward much of whose housing was built on the former site of the MGM Elstree studios, there has been a lot of drama here in recent years. Borehamwood Kenilworth, which has significant Jewish and black populations, split its representation in 2019 between two Labour councillors and one Conservative; the second and third Labour candidates Kumail Jaffer and Dan Ozarow tied for the final seat on 819 votes each, and Jaffer won that seat on the returning officer's drawing of lots. Jaffer subsequently got a job with the *Daily Mail* under a Stephen Lawrence Scholarship, a scheme to give jobs in national journalism to people from deprived and/or BAME backgrounds; the *Mail* then transferred him to Glasgow as a Scottish affairs correspondent. The Conservatives gained the resulting by-election in February 2020**. This by-election is caused by the resignation of the other Conservative councillor. David Neifeld defends for the Conservatives, while Labour's Dan Ozarow is back for another go after losing the 2020 by-election and losing the drawing of lots two years ago.††

* *East Hertfordshire, Bishop's Stortford All Saints*: LD 1194 C 821 Lab 392 † *Dacorum, Tring Central*: LD 925 C 438 Grn 172 Lab 137 ‡ *Dacorum, Leverstock Green*: C 1459 Lab 470 LD 298 Grn 185 § The Hertsmere by-elections were in error from the originally-published version of this column. ¶ *Hertsmere, Bushey North*: LD 1136 C 785 Lab 265 Grn 125 ‖ For the 2017 by-election, which was on slightly different boundaries, see *Andrew's Previews 2017*, page 272. ** *Andrew's Previews 2020*, page 35. †† *Hertsmere, Borehamwood Kenilworth*: Lab 1119 C 828 LD 152 [Lab gain from C]

Bedfordshire

Police and Crime Commissioner

In the 2016 police and crime commissioner elections Bedfordshire was the only police area which the Conservatives gained from Labour, whose win in 2012 had been rather surprising. Former TV presenter and journalist Kathryn Holloway topped the poll in the first round with 37% against 35% for outgoing Labour PCC Olly Martins and 12% for the Lib Dems; in the runoff Holloway won by 51.6–48.4, a majority of 2,883 votes.

Holloway is standing down after one term, and the Conservatives have selected Festus Akinbusoye, who runs a security business and briefly served as a special constable before his nomination papers went in. Akinbusoye was the Conservative candidate for West Ham in the 2015 general election. Labour have selected David Michael, who has 30 years' service as a Metropolitan Police officer under his belt. Akinbusoye and Michael are both black, and the Lib Dems make it a trio of BAME candidates from the major parties—not something you see very often in a shire county election—with their nomination of Jas Parmar, a postmaster and former police officer. Also standing are independent Patrick Hamill and the English Democrats' Antonio Vitiello.*

Local elections

The only local elections this year in Bedfordshire are two by-elections to Luton council. *High Town* ward, immediately to the north of the town centre, has been vacated by the new Luton South MP Rachel Hopkins; as described in *Andrew's Previews 2016*, page 106, this is a safe Labour ward and their candidate Umme Ali shouldn't have much trouble holding it.† The neighbouring *Round Green* ward is a very different matter, having returned candidates from all three main parties in the last two elections; the 2019 poll returned two Labour councillors and one Lib Dem, and this by-election promises to be closely fought between the defending Labour candidate Fatima Begum and the Lib Dem challenger Steve Moore.‡ The pandemic has led to huge financial difficulties for Luton council, which wholly owns Luton Airport and funded a number of its services out of the airport's dividend payments; central government have effectively been forced to bail the council out to the tune of £35 million.

---

* *Bedfordshire PCC*: first preferences C 51700 Lab 42708 LD 15983 Ind 8279 EDP 3387; runoff C 59793 Lab 50815 † *Luton, High Town*: Lab 717 C 327 Grn 202 LD 202 Comm 36 ‡ *Luton, Round Green*: LD 1041 Lab 910 C 520 Grn 173 Ind 60 [LD gain from Lab]

There are no local elections this year to Bedford or Central Bedfordshire councils.

Thames Valley

Police and Crime Commissioner

The Thames Valley is one of the largest of England's police areas, covering the counties of Berkshire, Buckinghamshire and Oxfordshire to the north-west of London. The PCC since 2012 has been Anthony Stansfeld, a Falklands veteran and Conservative representative. In the 2016 PCC election Stansfeld led in the first round with 40% against 33% for Labour and 15% for the Lib Dems, winning the run-off over Labour by the relatively small margin of 54–46.

Stansfeld is standing down and the Conservatives have selected Matthew Barber, who is a former leader of Vale of White Horse council in Oxfordshire and presently serves as Stansfeld's deputy PCC. The Labour candidate is Laetisia Carter, a West Oxfordshire councillor and mental health practitioner. The Lib Dems have selected Oxfordshire county councillor John Howson, and completing a ballot paper of four Oxfordshire-based candidates is independent Alan Robinson.*

Local elections

There are elections this year for the whole of Oxfordshire county council, the whole of the new Buckinghamshire council, the whole of Oxford council on new ward boundaries, and for one-third of Cherwell, Milton Keynes, Reading, Slough, West Oxfordshire and Wokingham councils.

To start in BUCKINGHAMSHIRE, which holds its first local elections since May 2017 following a reorganisation of the county's local government. Four years ago the old Buckinghamshire county council returned 41 Conservative councillors against an opposition of four Lib Dems (all from Aylesbury), three independents and a single Labour councillor. The new unitary council carries over the electoral divisions from the old county council but will have three times as many councillors, so for a par score those numbers should be scaled up accordingly.

The reforms in Buckinghamshire have left untouched the New City of MILTON KEYNES, whose council is very politically balanced; the ruling minority Labour group has 22 seats (one of which is vacant) against 19 Conservatives

* *Thames Valley PCC*: first preferences C 267404 Lab 175123 LD 110072 Ind 77210; runoff C 313148 Lab 233446

(including two vacant seats), 15 Lib Dems and an independent. The Conservatives lost five seats here in May 2019, which doesn't look good at first sight but that actually outperformed expectations given that they were defending ten marginal wards; the ward map this year is much more friendly to the Tories, and a repeat of the 2019 results would see them gain three seats from Labour and become the largest party.

The Conservatives did pretty poorly in the 2019 Oxfordshire council elections, but that underperformance was concentrated in the districts south of Oxford. The Tory vote generally held up better in CHERWELL district, based on Banbury and the fast-growing town of Bicester; a repeat of the 2019 results for Cherwell council would see them lose one seat in Bicester and two seats in the Oxford satellite town of Kidlington, but that won't significantly threaten the Conservative majority on the council. Similar considerations apply in WEST OXFORDSHIRE district, where the Conservatives are defending four wards (mostly in Witney town) which voted for the opposition in 2019; however they will have to do worse than that for the district to fall into No Overall Control.

There has been no Conservative local government presence for many years in the city of OXFORD, where the whole council is up for election this year on revised ward boundaries. Oxford is, of course, more than just dreaming spires; there's a significant technological and manufacturing base to the city's economy, and that produces a safe Labour council.

That Tory underperformance in Oxford cost them a majority on OXFORDSHIRE COUNTY COUNCIL in both 2013 and 2017, the latter election resulting in 31 Conservative councillors against 14 Labour, 13 Lib Dems, 4 independents and a localist from Henley-on-Thames. The Conservatives rely on three of the independent councillors for control of the county. It will be interesting to see whether the party's poor May 2019 performances in the Vale of White Horse (Abingdon and Wantage) and South Oxfordshire districts are repeated, particularly with the Lib Dems and Greens in South Oxfordshire having apparently renewed their electoral pact.

Those two districts also see three local by-elections. One of these is in the home of the Williams Formula 1 team, the village of Grove, which can be found immediately north of Wantage in the VALE OF WHITE HORSE district. *Grove North* was a ward gained by the Lib Dems in their takeover of that council in 2019, and Lib Dem candidate Andy Przybysz will look to defend a seat which should be safe for them now.*

Further up the Great Western main line is the boom town of Didcot, within the SOUTH OXFORDSHIRE district. In the town's *North East* ward a Tory slate

* *Vale of White Horse, Grove North*: C 704 LD 575 Lab 191 Grn 98 [C gain from LD]

was cleared out in 2019 and replaced by two Lib Dems and independent Simon Hewerdine; Hewerdine has resigned and his seat is open with no independent candidate contesting the resulting by-election. Paul Giesberg contests for the Lib Dems, while the Tories' Andrea Warren will hope to gain a seat back.*

At the other end of South Oxfordshire district we come to the third contest Andrew's Previews has covered between the Tories' John Walsh (an accountant with Oxford University Press) and the Lib Dems' Tim Bearder (a former BBC journalist and son of the former Lib Dem MEP Catherine Bearder). Walsh and Bearder have previously faced off within this column in a 2013 by-election for the North ward of Oxford city council (which Labour won) and in a 2018 by-election for the Wheatley division of Oxfordshire county council (which Bearder won†). With Bearder holding a 1–0 lead in the series, round 3 will take place immediately to the east of Oxford in the *Forest Hill and Holton* ward of South Oxfordshire. Walsh lost his district council seat here to the Lib Dems rather soundly in 2019, and following the withdrawal of Labour this by-election is a straight Lib Dem-Tory fight.‡

Berkshire county council disappeared in the 1990s, but three of its former districts are holding elections. In the county town of READING, where boundary changes have been deferred until next year, Labour have a strong majority on the council and got a rare swing in their favour in the Reading East constituency at the 2019 general election. The Reading East constituency includes a large amount of territory which is part of the town's urban area but administered separately by WOKINGHAM council; this is a council where the ruling Conservatives have been underperforming throughout the last electoral cycle, and a repeat of the 2019 results would see the Lib Dems gain five seats here and wipe out the Tory majority. Finally, the Labour majority on SLOUGH council is in no danger whatsoever.

There are no local elections this year in Bracknell Forest, West Berkshire or Windsor and Maidenhead.

Hampshire

Police and Crime Commissioner

Hampshire's police and crime commissioner elections have been unusually interesting, with the inaugural contest in 2012 won by independent candidate Simon Hayes who defeated former Conservative MP Michael Mates. For the 2016 election the Tories changed candidate to Michael Lane, whose 29% of the

* *South Oxfordshire, Didcot North East*: C 1113 LD 953 Lab 670 [C gain from Ind] † *Andrew's Previews 2018*, page 420. ‡ *South Oxfordshire, Forest Hill and Holton*: LD 907 C 503

vote was enough for a big lead in the first round. A four-way pileup for the other place in the runoff was won by Labour candidate Robin Price on 16%, ahead of outgoing independent PCC Hayes who finished third with 15%; close behind were the Lib Dems and UKIP on 14% each. The runoff between Lane and Price resulted in an easy Conservative gain with a 64–36 margin.

Lane is not seeking re-election, and the Conservatives have selected former Portsmouth council leader Donna Jones. The Labour candidate is Tony Bunday, who is fighting his first election campaign, runs an events company and is a former social worker. The Lib Dems have selected Richard Murphy, a businessman from Winchester, and completing the ballot paper is Steve James-Bailey for a new party called the Hampshire Independents.*

Local elections

There are elections this year for the whole of Hampshire county council, for the whole of Isle of Wight council on new ward boundaries, for the whole of Basingstoke and Deane council on new ward boundaries, for one-half of Fareham and Gosport councils, and for one-third of Eastleigh, Hart, Havant, Portsmouth, Rushmoor, Southampton and Winchester councils.

To take the big one first, HAMPSHIRE COUNTY COUNCIL has a strong and long-standing Conservative majority, the 2017 election returning 56 Conservative councillors against 19 Lib Dems, 2 Labour councillors (both from Basingstoke) and one councillor from the Community Campaign in Hart district, of which more later.

The 2017 election also saw the Tories gain overall control of the ISLE OF WIGHT council after four years of independent-led administration. Wight returned 25 Conservative councillors, 11 independents, 2 Lib Dems and one councillor each from Labour and the Greens. There have been no local elections on the Isle of Wight since then. The Labour slate for this year's Wight council election includes a former MP: Sarah McCarthy-Fry, who represented Portsmouth North in the 2005–10 parliament, is standing for the party in the Conservative-held Lake South division.

The districts which face Wight across the Solent are an interesting bunch. To start at the eastern end, HAVANT council was a rare bright spot for the Conservatives in the May 2019 elections: the party was defending every seat up for election that year, and did so successfully. The Tory majority there is under no danger. Things were different over the water in the city of PORTSMOUTH which was

* *Hampshire PCC*: first preferences C 262667 Lab 101832 LD 93581 Hants Ind 68895; runoff C 312933 Lab 145731

taken over by a minority Lib Dem administration; the most recent breakdown has 17 Lib Dems, 15 Conservatives, 6 Labour and 4 others (all of whom were elected on one of the above tickets). A repeat of the 2019 results would see the Lib Dems lose some ground: they are defending Eastney and Craneswater ward which voted Conservative in 2019, and St Jude ward which voted Labour in 2019. The Tories will also have their eye on the Labour seat in the volatile estates of Paulsgrove ward.

Over the water again, the Tories are defending a majority of two seats on GOSPORT council. This has bizarre voting patterns: in the 2018 election the Conservatives polled 52% of the vote across the district to the Lib Dems' 23%, but the Tories and Lib Dems won eight wards each. A repeat of those results would result in two Conservative losses and No Overall Control. To reach the rest of the country from Gosport you have to pass through FAREHAM district, whose Conservative majority is under no danger. The Lib Dem majority on the neighbouring EASTLEIGH council is even more impregnable.

The only Labour-controlled local authority in Hampshire is SOUTHAMPTON city council, where Labour have a 30–18 majority over the Conservatives. A repeat of the May 2019 results would see the Conservatives gain three seats nett.

Moving to the M3 corridor of inland Hampshire, the Tories performed very poorly in 2019 in WINCHESTER district which now has a Lib Dem majority. Although the district does include a large rural area around the city, the Winchester Conservatives will be doing well if they can stem further losses. All the seats on the BASINGSTOKE AND DEANE council are up for election on new ward boundaries; this district is currently hung, with 28 Conservatives forming a minority administration against 13 Labour councillors, 10 independents (a number of whom have split from Labour) and 7 Lib Dems.

In the north-east of the county, HART district (based on Fleet and Yateley) is run by a coalition of the Liberal Democrats and the aforementioned Community Campaign, and that coalition's majority is in no danger. The Conservatives will remain in control of RUSHMOOR district, based on the aerospace and military towns of Aldershot and Farnborough.

Most Hampshire districts hold elections by thirds, but there are also five local by-elections to discuss. Three of these are in the TEST VALLEY district, which runs all the way from Andover to the edge of Southampton. The edge-of-Southampton ward is called *Chilworth, Nursling and Rownhams* and represents some closure for your columnist, because I previewed a by-election here on 19th March 2020 which was called off at the last moment due to COVID.* That by-election was to replace the late councillor Nigel Anderdon; since then a

* *Andrew's Previews 2020*, page 80.

second councillor for the ward, Alison Finlay, has also died. Both of them were Conservative councillors for a safe ward. This double by-election is a straight fight between the Conservatives and Lib Dems; on the defending Conservative slate, Terese Swain returns from the aborted 2020 by-election and is joined by Mike Maltby.*

The other two by-elections to Test Valley council are in Andover, where a localist slate called the Andover Alliance won seven seats in 2019 and appears to have since fallen apart in Handforthesque scenes. Both these by-elections will be free-for-alls as the Andover Alliance are not defending them. *Andover St Mary's* is a contest between the three main parties, with the Tories' Jan Budzynski possibly favourite although Nigel Long, who polled decently as an independent in 2019, is back for another go and now has the Lib Dem nomination.† In *Andover Millway*, which was very close between the Conservatives and Andover Alliance in 2019, the localist torch has been taken up by Susana Ecclestone of the breakaway Andover Independents, while Jim Neal will seek to gain for the Conservatives.‡

Finally, we come to the two by-elections in East Hampshire district, both of which are in wards on the boundary with Surrey. *Grayshott* is essentially an extension of the Surrey village of Hindhead, while the large village of Liphook on the London–Portsmouth railway line anchors the *Bramshott and Liphook* ward. These are very safe Conservative wards and should be easily defended by Nick Scar (Bramshott and Liphook)§ and Tom Hanrahan (Grayshott).¶

Surrey

Police and Crime Commissioner

If you thought the Conservatives could never lose a county-wide election in true-blue Surrey, think again. It happened as recently as November 2012, when the first Surrey police and crime commissioner election was won by "Zero Tolerance Policing Ex Chief" candidate Kevin Hurley. For the 2016 election the Conservatives got their act together, and their Surrey PCC candidate David Munro led in the first round with 35% against 18% for Hurley, 13% for the Lib Dems and 12% for Labour. Munro and Hurley went through to the runoff which Munro won by the wide margin of 63–37.

* *Test Valley; Chilworth, Nursling and Rownhams*: C 1391 (Maltby)/1365 (Swain) LD 742 (Dunleavey)/674 (Beesley) † *Test Valley, Andover St Mary's*: C 790 Lab 439 LD 377 [C gain from Andover Alliance] ‡ *Test Valley, Andover Millway*: C 1246 LD 359 Grn 259 Lab 251 Andover Ind 249 [C gain from Andover Alliance] § *East Hampshire, Bramshott and Liphook*: C 1470 LD 754 Lab 378 ¶ *East Hampshire, Grayshott*: C 453 LD 239 Grn 64 Lab 55 UKIP 19

For the 2021 election the Conservatives have deselected David Munro in favour of Lisa Townsend. Munro has not taken this well, and is seeking re-election as an independent. Zero Tolerance Policing Ex Chief Kevin Hurley is also trying to get his old job back. The Lib Dems have selected Mole Valley councillor Paul Kennedy, and train driver and Labour candidate Howard Kaye completes a five-strong ballot paper.*

Local elections

There are elections this year for the whole of Surrey county council and for one-third of Elmbridge, Mole Valley, Reigate and Banstead, Runnymede, Tandridge and Woking councils.

The 2019 local elections were generally horrific for the Tories in Surrey, with the party losing more than 100 councillors across the county. 60 of them disappeared in Guildford and Waverley districts alone. In GUILDFORD the Conservatives have a chance to recover from that with three local by-elections. They are defending the Army-dominated *Pirbright* ward, which was the safest Tory ward in the district in 2019 but where the previous Tory councillor, Gordon Jackson, had gone independent before resigning from the council; Keith Witham is the defending candidate.† *Friary and St Nicolas* ward, covering Guildford town centre, was safe Lib Dem in 2019 and is defended by their candidate Cait Taylor.‡ *Send* ward, between Guildford and Woking, has been held since 2015 by the Guildford Greenbelt Group and gave that party 71% of the vote in 2019; Guida Esteves is their defending candidate.§

There are two other standalone by-elections in Surrey to mention. One of these arises out of the death in January 2020, at the horribly young age of 33, of a luckless man called Sam Kay.¶ Readers may remember a controversy from 2009 involving the quartet from Corpus Christi College, Oxford, memorably captained by Gail Trimble and including Kay, which won the final of that year's series of *University Challenge*. Now, when your columnist did *UC* in the 2002–03 series it was made clear in the selection meeting that, because of the timing of the series recordings, final-year students were not eligible. Kay was a final-year student at the start of the 2008–09 series, but was intending to stay on at Oxford by applying for a PhD. That fell through. By the time the quarter-finals and later

* *Surrey PCC*: first preferences C 112360 LD 69412 Zero Tolerance Policing Ex Chief 59554 Lab 53013 Ind 40597; runoff C 155116 LD 112215 † *Guildford, Pirbright*: C 440 Grn 119 Residents of Guildford and Villages 109 Lab 56 ‡ *Guildford, Friary and St Nicolas*: LD 1056 Residents of Guildford and Villages 660 C 548 Lab 430 § *Guildford, Send*: Guildford Greenbelt Group 851 C 500 Grn 206 Lab 68 ¶ Kay's life is covered in more detail in *Andrew's Previews 2020*, page 90; a piece which was not published at the time it was originally written in May 2020.

stages were recorded, Kay had left Corpus and found work as an accountant, but he still took part in the recordings in breach of the series rules. After the final was broadcast news of this got out, and the programme-makers Granada disqualified Corpus and stripped them of their title.

Regrettably, Sam Kay's local government career didn't last much longer than his reign as a *University Challenge* champion. He had been elected in May 2019 as a Liberal Democrat member of Surrey Heath council representing the town of *Bagshot*, beating the alphabet to top the poll and riding the anti-Tory wave in that election. Kay's death leaves the local Lib Dems with a tricky defence in a marginal ward within Michael Gove's constituency. Richard Wilson is the defending Lib Dem candidate, opposed in a straight fight by the Tories' Mark Gordon.*

Surrey's other standalone by-election comes over the river in Spelthorne district, which is based on Staines-upon-Thames and was one of the few parts of Middlesex that escaped incorporation into Greater London in the 1960s. The Conservatives lost a large majority here in the 2019 election and now run the district as a minority; one of the wards which fell was *Staines South* ward, which returned two Liberal Democrats and one Labour councillor. You get the impression that the opposition parties didn't see this result coming, as the Lib Dems finished with a big lead in votes but only had a slate of two for the three available seats. Over the last two years Spelthorne council has suffered a number of defections and regroupings, including Lib Dem Staines South councillor Nichola Cornes who went independent and then resigned from the council altogether. For the resulting by-election Rob Millist is the defending Lib Dem candidate, Harriet Digby stands for Labour and Sinead Mooney for the Conservatives.† The sort of defection level seen in Spelthorne often indicates a slightly dysfunctional council, and this political dysfunctionality may soon be joined by financial dysfunctionality. Spelthorne council has invested massively in commercial property in recent years; their position is rather different to that of Croydon, who have made similar investments and run out of money, in that Spelthorne's portfolio is mostly generating rent, but whether the buildings are still worth what the council paid for them is another matter.

Of the Surrey councils holding elections by thirds this year, Mole Valley council (based on Leatherhead and Dorking) flipped straight to the Liberal Democrats in 2019; Elmbridge council (outer London suburbia around Weybridge and Walton-on-Thames) was taken over that year by a coalition of the residents groups and Lib Dems; while in Tandridge (the eastern end of the county,

---

* *Surrey Heath, Bagshot*: C 1225 LD 1038 [C gain from LD] † *Spelthorne, Staines South*: C 675 LD 668 Lab 319 Ind 154 TUSC 30 [C gain from LD]

including Caterham and Oxted) and in WOKING the Conservatives now have to rely on independent councillors for control. In those areas, the primary focus for the Surrey Conservatives must be to stop the rot. So far as Elmbridge is concerned, the Conservatives may be helped by what appears to be a breakdown in the Residents/Lib Dem pact: most of Elmbridge district is covered by the Esher and Walton parliamentary seat where the Lib Dems came close to knocking out foreign secretary Dominic Raab in December 2019, and the party appears to be trying to build on that success by contesting several Resident-held marginal wards. The election to fill a casual vacancy in the Felbridge ward of Tandridge has been called off after the Labour candidate died, and will be held at a later date.*

The Tories do still retain overall control of REIGATE AND BANSTEAD council (the M 23/Brighton Line corridor) and the RUNNYMEDE district at the northern end of the county. All of the seats on those councils were up in 2019 with new ward boundaries, and there don't appear to be many opportunities for opposition parties in the seats up for election there.

One interesting question will be whether this May 2019 underperformance feeds through to SURREY COUNTY COUNCIL. However, given that the Tories won 61 seats out of a possible 81 here in May 2017, it will take a lot for that majority to disappear.

Sussex

Police and Crime Commissioner

There was little of interest in the 2016 election for Sussex police and crime commissioner, which easily re-elected Conservative PCC Katy Bourne. In the first round she led with 42% against 22% for Labour and 16% for UKIP; the run-off against Labour produced a Tory majority of 62–38.

Bourne is seeking a third term for the Conservatives. Labour have selected Paul Richards, a former Whitehall special adviser. UKIP have not returned, so completing the Sussex PCC ballot are Jamie Bennett for the Lib Dems, Kahina Bouhassane for the Greens and independent candidate Roy Williams.†

Local elections

There are elections this year for the whole of East Sussex and West Sussex county councils, for one-half of Adur and Hastings councils and for one-third of Crawley

* See page 225. † *Sussex PCC*: first preferences C 214523 Lab 84736 LD 63271 Grn 60781 Ind 30408; runoff C 244810 Lab 128259

and Worthing councils.

The stand-out one of these to watch is CRAWLEY. This New Town got new ward boundaries in 2019 putting all 36 council seats up for re-election; in vote terms there was a photofinish with the Tories and Labour polling 42.6% each across the borough, while in seat terms Labour eked out a win by 19 to 17. Since then two Labour councillors have died and two more have left the party, which at one point left the Conservative group holding half of the seats; a highly unusual situation has developed, with the Conservatives declining to seek control of the council for themselves and instead shoring up the Labour administration in advance of these elections. Control of Crawley council is likely to come down to a handful of votes in one or more wards.

Things are on the other foot in the south coast resort of WORTHING where Labour have made strong gains over the last electoral cycle. Worthing council currently stands at 23 Conservative councillors against 10 Labour, 3 Lib Dems and a UKIP councillor; nearly half of the Tory group is up for re-election this year, and a repeat of the 2019 results would result in five Labour gains and a sharply-reduced Conservative majority.

The Tories have much less margin for error in the neighbouring ADUR district, based on towns such as Shoreham on the coastal strip between Worthing and Brighton; they currently hold 16 seats (including vacancies) out of a possible 29. Adur last went to the polls in 2018, and a repeat of those results would see the Conservatives gain two seats with UKIP wiped out.

The four local by-elections in West Sussex are all defences for the opposition. ARUN council, which stayed Conservative throughout the lean times of the 1990s, is now run by a minority Lib Dem administration following impressive results in 2019. Among the Lib Dem gains that year were *Brookfield* ward (in Littlehampton) where the party holds both seats, and *Pevensey* ward (in Bognor Regis) where they split the two seats with an independent councillor. The Lib Dems are defending both by-elections: Bob Woodman should be favoured to hold Brookfield,* while John Barrett is the defending candidate in Pevensey but may face a challenge from independent Jan Cosgrove.†

There is more long-standing Lib Dem strength in the *Trafalgar* ward of HORSHAM, which covers the west of the town and where their candidate Martin Boffey is favoured.‡ In MID SUSSEX district the 2019 election saw the Conservatives lose *Copthorne and Worth* ward (immediately to the east of Crawley) to an independent slate; Norman Mockford has come forward as a new independent

* *Arun, Brookfield*: C 680 LD 526 Lab 152 Workers Party 45 [C gain from LD] † *Arun, Pevensey*: C 357 LD 210 Lab 140 Ind 132 Grn 93 [C gain from LD] ‡ *Horsham, Trafalgar*: LD 1581 C 529 Lab 307

candidate for this by-election against the Tories' Bruce Forbes.*

The Conservative majority on WEST SUSSEX COUNTY COUNCIL is in no danger. EAST SUSSEX COUNTY COUNCIL is however more balanced, with the 2017 election returning 30 Conservatives against 11 Lib Dems, 5 independents and 4 Labour councillors. Since then the Tories have performed pretty poorly in the 2019 local elections in Bexhill-on-Sea and the 2018 local elections in Hastings, where all of the Labour county councillors come from. One-half of HASTINGS council is up for election this year, and the Labour majority there looks safe.

Of the nine council by-elections in the East Sussex council area, eight are Conservative defences. The new Hastings and Rye MP Sally-Ann Hart has vacated her seat on ROTHER council, provoking a by-election in *Eastern Rother* ward which covers the villages around Rye. This ward is safe Conservative and should return their candidate Lizzie Hacking.† The Tories are defending four by-elections in the sprawling WEALDEN district, including both wards in Heathfield and two of the six wards in Hailsham. Three of these look safe and should be defended without fuss by their candidates Mike Baker (*Heathfield North*),‡ Tom Guyton-Day (*Heathfield South*)§ and Kevin Balsdon (*Hailsham South*),¶ but *Hailsham North* ward was a three-way marginal in 2019 and could again be closely contested between Chris Bryant of the Conservatives, Paul Holbrook of the Lib Dems and Rachel Chilton of the Greens.‖

Over on the coastal strip, the Conservatives are defending two of the five Seaford wards in by-elections to LEWES council. Both *Seaford East* (defended by Richard Turner)** and *Seaford West* (defended by Linda Wallraven)†† look safe enough; the Greens ran second in both wards last time, but the decision by the Lib Dems to contest these by-elections may split their vote. Lewes shares a lot of its services with EASTBOURNE council, where Conservative MP Caroline Ansell has vacated *Sovereign* ward; this is based on a relatively new marina development and as such is very unlike the rest of Eastbourne. Sovereign ward is safe Tory and their defending candidate is Kshama Shore.‡‡ Finally, in the north of Eastbourne the Lib Dems defend a by-election in the very safe *Hampden Park* ward; their candidate is Josh Babarinde.§§

There are no scheduled local elections this year in BRIGHTON AND HOVE, but there are two by-elections to the city council from wards in Caroline Lucas'

* *Mid Sussex, Copthorne and Worth*: C 810 Grn 284 Ind 221 [C gain from Ind] † *Rother, Eastern Rother*: C 999 Lab 300 LD 273 ‡ *Wealden, Heathfield North*: C 733 Grn 268 Lab 179 § *Wealden, Heathfield South*: C 661 Ind 441 ¶ *Wealden, Hailsham South*: C 411 LD 332 Ind 90 Grn 77 ‖ *Wealden, Hailsham North*: LD 360 C 293 Ind 152 Grn 66 SDP 17 [LD gain from C] ** *Lewes, Seaford East*: C 820 Grn 452 LD 347 Lab 109 †† *Lewes, Seaford West*: C 1028 LD 401 Grn 277 Lab 120 ‡‡ *Eastbourne, Sovereign*: C 1996 LD 1160 Lab 257 UKIP 124 §§ *Eastbourne, Hampden Park*: LD 1080 C 857 Lab 418

Pavilion constituency. *Hollingdean and Stanmer* ward runs out along the railway line towards Lewes up to and including the University of Sussex campus. This has been a Labour-Green marginal for the last decade, and in 2019 the ward split its representation between two Labour councillors and one Green. Labour's Leila Erin-Jenkins will defend the by-election, the Greens' Zoë John will hope to gain.* *Patcham* ward lies on the northern edge of the city at the point where the road and railway line from London break through the South Downs; this is a safe Conservative ward which Anne Meadows should defend for the party.†

Kent

Police and Crime Commissioner

Our final English PCC election is for the county of Kent, which returned independent candidate Ann Barnes as its first police and crime commissioner in 2012. Barnes retired in 2016 and the first round of the election to replace her saw Matthew Scott of the Conservatives top the poll with 33%. Second with 27% was UKIP candidate Henry Bolton, who subsequently had his fifteen minutes of fame as leader of that party. Labour's Tristan Osborne finished third with 19% of the vote, while independent candidate Gurvinder Singh Sander polled 10%. Last of the six candidates that year was Steve Uncles of the English Democrats, who polled 3% and lost his deposit; Uncles was subsequently sent to prison for seven months for electoral fraud in the 2013 Kent county council elections, having submitted seven sets of nomination papers for English Democrats "candidates" who either hadn't consented to their nomination or never existed in the first place. The run-off for the 2016 Kent PCC election was Conservative versus UKIP, with Scott beating Bolton by 54–46.

Matthew Scott is seeking re-election, and is opposed this time by two other candidates: Lola Oyewusi (who is also standing for the county council, in Sittingbourne South) for Labour and Graham Colley for the Lib Dems.‡

Local elections

There are elections this year for the whole of Kent county council and for one-third of Maidstone and Tunbridge Wells councils. There are no local elections this year in the Medway towns.

* *Brighton and Hove, Hollingdean and Stanmer*: Grn 1542 Lab 1262 C 745 TUSC 54 LD 47 UKIP 35 Ind 24 [Grn gain from Lab] † *Brighton and Hove, Patcham*: C 2011 Grn 1733 Lab 879 LD 174 UKIP 50 ‡ *Kent PCC*: C 237278 Lab 103807 LD 69464

TUNBRIDGE WELLS was extensively discussed by this column at the end of 2019,[*] after that year's local elections saw the Conservatives lose 13 of the 18 seats they were defending; one of the seats they held was won on the toss of a coin following a tied result in Paddock Wood West ward. To cut a long story short, a lot of that was down to proposals by the council for a new civic centre/theatre/underground car park complex which went down with the locals with, for want of a better word, disgust. That cunning plan has since fallen by the wayside, but the ruling Conservatives will have to rebound a heck of a lot from last year's performance to hold onto their council majority.

MAIDSTONE council is hung and likely to remain so; a Lib Dem and Independent administration is currently in place. Maidstone is also home to KENT COUNTY COUNCIL, whose Tory majority shouldn't be in danger. The county council candidate lists have revealed a mistake by Labour who have managed to nominate two candidates for the Malling Central division (based on East and West Malling together with Larkfield off the M 20 motorway); mind, Labour only polled 5% there in 2017 so this probably won't cost them a seat. Sadly, the Labour candidate for Elham Valley division (a large swathe of the North Downs to the north of Folkestone) has died, and the poll there will be postponed.[†]

The Conservative revival in the polls in late 2019 saw its first fruits on 17th October that year with a by-election gain in the *Westcourt* ward of GRAVESHAM[‡], a downmarket residential area in eastern Gravesend. That Westcourt poll was the first council by-election the Conservatives had gained from Labour in over a year. Well, we are back here again for a crucial local by-election to Gravesham council; if Labour lose this one as well, their council majority will go with it and they will be down to half of the seats. Karina O'Malley defends this Westcourt by-election for Labour, Samir Jassal challenges for the Conservatives.[§]

The Conservatives have three other local by-elections to defend in western Kent. In the Darent valley there are by-elections to DARTFORD council from *Darenth* ward (Maria Kelly defending)[¶] and from the cumbersomely-named neighbouring ward of *Wilmington, Sutton-at-Hone and Hawley* (Ellenor Palmer defending).[‖] In SEVENOAKS district the Tories defend a by-election in *Brasted, Chevening and Sundridge* ward, covering villages immediately to the west of Sevenoaks at the south-east corner of the M 25 (Keith Bonin defending).[**] None of these look in any danger.

[*] *Andrew's Previews 2019*, page 370. [†] See page 224. [‡] *Andrew's Previews 2019*, pages 323 and 329. [§] *Gravesham, Westcourt*: C 577 Lab 534 LD 56 [C gain from Lab] [¶] *Dartford, Darenth*: C 252 Lab 218 Reform UK 35 [‖] *Dartford; Wilmington, Sutton-at-Hone and Hawley*: C 1465 Lab 445 Reform UK 88 [**] *Sevenoaks; Brasted, Chevening and Sundridge*: C 1051 LD 704 Lab 182

East Kent's by-elections have a rather left-wing bias to them. The by-election-prone *Beaver* ward in the south of ASHFORD town comes to the notice of this column for the fourth time in ten years,[*] following the death of one of the Labour councillors; Dylan Jones is the defending Labour candidate for a ward that should be safe enough for them.[†] In DOVER district Labour defend *Mill Hill* ward, the western of the four wards covering Deal: Jeffrey Loffman is the Labour candidate here in a ward that had good showings in 2019 for both the Conservatives (who have selected David Hawkes) and the Greens (Mike Eddy).[‡]

We finally get around to the by-election in the *Newington* ward of THANET, which I previewed all the way back on 19th March 2020[§] but which was pulled by the returning officer due to the pandemic. All four candidates who were nominated in that aborted poll have returned, with Mary King favoured to hold for Labour.[¶] Newington ward is in Ramsgate, as is *Central Harbour* ward which split its three seats between Labour and the Greens in 2019; confusingly, the defending Labour candidate has the name David Green, while the Greens have selected Tricia Austin.[‖] Over in Margate we have a by-election in the *Dane Valley* ward which is defended by the Thanet Independents, the main remnant of the UKIP group which won a majority on Thanet council in 2019. Dane Valley voted Conservative in 2007, Labour at a December 2009 by-election and in 2011, then UKIP in 2015 before splitting its three seats in 2019 between the two Thanet Independents candidates and Labour, with the Tories close behind. All three candidates for this Dane Valley by-election will feel they have realistic chances of winning: Mark Websper defends for the Thanet Independents, Martin Boyd is the Labour candidate, David Wallin stands for the Conservatives.[**]

These three by-elections could be crucial to the future direction of Thanet council. The 2019 Thanet election returned 25 Conservative councillors, 20 Labour, 7 Thanet Independents, 3 Greens and 1 independent; a Conservative minority administration was originally installed, then deposed in favour of a Labour minority administration. The Labour council leader has recently resigned in an attempt to stave off a counter-coup attempt; a new leader will be elected on 13th May once the results of these by-elections are known.

Further along the north Kent coast Labour defend the town of *Sheerness*, where they have held two out of three SWALE council seats since the current

---

[*] For the most recent previous by-election (on boundaries which have since been replaced) see *Andrew's Previews 2016*, page 155. [†] *Ashford, Beaver*: C 468 Lab 402 Ind 105 Grn 70 LD 64 [C gain from Lab] [‡] *Dover, Mill Hill*: C 716 Lab 608 Grn 292 Ind 103 LD 59 [C gain from Lab] [§] *Andrew's Previews 2020*, page 81. [¶] *Thanet, Newington*: C 265 Lab 260 Grn 144 Ind 43 [C gain from Lab] [‖] *Thanet, Central Harbour*: Grn 776 Lab 631 C 480 [Grn gain from Lab] [**] *Thanet, Dane Valley*: C 491 Lab 461 Thanet Ind 294 [C gain from Thanet Ind]

ward was introduced in 2015. The other seat went to UKIP in 2015 and to an independent candidate in 2019, so this by-election could be tricky to hold given the presence of a candidate from the Swale Independents council group. Nicola Nelson is the Labour candidate, Dolley White stands for the Swale Independents.*

The only Conservative by-election defence in East Kent is the *Swalecliffe* ward of Whitstable, after Ian Thomas—who represented the area on both Canterbury council and Kent county council—took his own life after being arrested on suspicion of sexual assault. The by-election is for Canterbury council only, and the defending Conservative candidate is Mark Dance.†

In Canterbury proper we have a by-election for the city-centre *Westgate* ward. This was the destination point for many pilgrimages to the shrine of Thomas Becket over the centuries, so it's fitting that our tour of England's local by-elections on 6th May 2021 ends here. Since it was redrawn in 2015 Westgate ward has returned councillors from all three main parties, with a Labour gain from the Conservatives at a by-election on 8th June 2017‡ presaging the Labour gain of the parliamentary seat later on that election night. The May 2019 poll here returned one Lib Dem and two Labour councillors, with the Conservatives now out of the running. Pip Hazelton defends for Labour, Alex Lister will try to gain for the Lib Dems.§

* *Swale, Sheerness*: C 648 Lab 504 Grn 209 Swale Ind 201 [C gain from Lab] † *Canterbury, Swalecliffe*: C 616 Grn 527 Lab 278 Ind 24 ‡ *Andrew's Previews 2017*, page 157. § *Canterbury, Westgate*: Lab 842 LD 661 C 404 Grn 242

6th May 2021 Part IV: Hartlepool

Without further ado, here is Part IV: the Cleveland police area, starting with the Parliamentary Special.

Hartlepool

House of Commons; caused by the resignation of Labour MP Mike Hill.

Including the Mayor of the Tees Valley; the Cleveland Police and Crime Commissioner; and local by-elections within the Cleveland Police area.

> "The contest in Hartlepool will be very important, and no-one knows how it will turn out."
>
> —*The Spectator*, 10th January 1891

It all started on the headland. The coast of Durham, like that of many counties on the east coast on England, is notably smooth; but a few miles north of the Tees estuary a small but solid peninsula juts out into the North Sea. Since ancient times this peninsula has been an obvious stopping-point for coastal trade. There's nothing to indicate that the Romans were ever here, but the Anglo-Saxons definitely were in residence; and the headland played its part in the survival of Christianity in these islands.

A lot of that survival is down to St Aidan, the Apostle of Northumbria. Aidan was originally based at the monastery of Iona along with a young and pious lad called St Oswald. Oswald was of royal stock, and in AD 634 he became king of Northumbria with a mission from God: a mission to bring Christianity back to his people. He sent for Aidan, who based himself at Lindisfarne and set about his missionary task with gusto.

One of Aidan's works, in 640, was to help with setting up an abbey on the headland. He installed as its first abbess St Hieu, an Irishwoman who is the first recorded woman to rule over a mixed religious settlement of both men and women. Hieu's foundation became known as *Hereteu*, a name of unclear origin. "Stag island" is the generally-accepted modern translation from the original Old English, although if you squint a bit it is possible to read Hieu's name into it.

St Hieu moved to Tadcaster nine years later and was replaced as abbess of Hereteu by one of the most important figures of the seventh century. St Hilda was by now in her mid-thirties. Although she was of royal stock, she had become a nun and her star was rising under the influence of Aidan. It was at Hereteu—modern Hartlepool—that Hilda first gained her reputation for wisdom and skilled administration. This was recognised in 655 by King Oswiu of Northumbria, who sent his one-year-old daughter Ælfflæd to be brought up as a nun under Hilda's guidance.

However, the placename that comes to mind for many people when St Hilda is remembered these days is not Hartlepool. In or around 658 Hilda founded a new double monastery further down the North Sea coast at Streanæshalch, modern-day Whitby, and continued the Lord's work from there. Hilda hosted the Synod of Whitby, convened in 664 by King Oswiu, which settled a dispute over the *computus*—the calculation of the date of Easter—by resolving that the Northumbrian church would celebrate Easter on the same day as the Roman Catholic church rather than follow the Celtic reckoning used at Iona. Hilda died in 680, and Ælfflæd succeeded her as abbess of Whitby.

Following Hilda's departure nothing more is heard of the abbey at Hartlepool, and nothing remains of it today. The abbey's cemetery has been excavated on the headland, and was the subject of an episode of Channel 4's *Time Team* broadcast in early 2000. On that occasion one of their trenches obliterated the car park of the local Conservative club, which will have given some satisfaction to the series presenter Tony Robinson, a noted Labour Party supporter.

The modern-day church on the headland dedicated to St Hilda, which occupies roughly the same site as the old monastery, is a Norman building whose size and quality clearly shows that there was a fair amount of money in Old Hartlepool in the twelfth century. It's not too fanciful to suggest that some of this will have been due to the patronage of the de Brus family, which controlled the town along with large estates in the north of England. Robert I de Brus had come over from Normandy in the 1090s, and was made Lord of Hartness in 1153, but his family also ended up with a Scottish peerage as Lords of Annandale. It was Robert I's son William de Brus, the 3rd Lord of Annandale, who persuaded King John to give Hartlepool a market charter in 1185. The de Brus family, however, left the story of Hartlepool in 1306 when Robert VII de Brus was crowned king of Scotland; that prompted Edward I to confiscate his English landholdings and fortify the town.

The market, together with Old Hartlepool's fishing industry and its status as the major port of County Durham, ensured the town's survival through the centuries. There was even a minor spa industry: the poet Thomas Gray turned up here in the eighteenth century for the waters. To this day Hartlepool has its own water company, now a subsidiary of Anglian Water, which—unusually for the north of England—supplies hard water to the town's homes and buildings.

However, the headland was a constrained site with little room for expansion, and the Industrial Revolution threatened to leave Hartlepool behind. By the early 1830s the town's population was only around 900, and its position as Durham's major port was under threat from new harbours at Seaham to the north, Port Clarence on the Tees estuary to the south, and a tiny but fast-growing settlement called Middlesbrough on the Yorkshire side of the river opposite Port Clarence. Something needed to be done to ensure Hartlepool's survival in this brave new modern industrial world.

The borough council's answer was to establish the Hartlepool Dock and Railway Company, to build a railway connecting the town with the Durham collieries and to build new, large docks for modern ships. The railway part of the plan worked pretty well. The dock part of the plan was another matter.

Enter Ralph Ward Jackson.

Hartlepool council had engaged railway entrepreneur Christopher Tennant to set up the Hartlepool Dock and Railway Company. Tennant died in 1839 and Ward Jackson, a solicitor from Stockton-on-Tees, took over the company's running with the dock part of the plan in some trouble. The fault lay with the council, which had placed onerous restrictions on the redevelopment of the existing port and the surrounding area.

Rather than work within these constraints, Ward Jackson decided to go it alone. He bought an area of sand-dunes just to the south-west of the headland, and built there a brand-new 8-acre dock, a brand-new railway to bring coal to the dock, and a brand-new town to serve the industries. The business venture paid off, and in the end there was nothing Hartlepool council could do about it.

Thus was born the town of West Hartlepool, which grew from nothing in 1841 to a population of 28,000 in the 1881 census, more than twice the size of Old Hartlepool. West Hartlepool was incorporated as a borough in 1887, and promoted to a county borough in 1902.

To the south of the two Hartlepools lay Seaton Carew, which was very different in character from the two industrial ports to the north. This is a small but perfectly formed seaside resort, originally developed in the eighteenth century for wealthy Darlington Quaker families. Seaton Carew's wide and sandy beach and art-deco bus station deserve to be better known, so it's a shame that the place has most recently come to public attention thanks to the 2002 canoeing accident in which local resident John Darwin faked his own death. The sands at Seaton Carew hide the remains of *Doris*, a Danish schooner which was wrecked here in a storm in 1930. Also washed up on the beach, by every tide, is a fine black powder: this is sea coal, from an open seam on the seabed.

Old and West Hartlepool, together with Seaton Carew, were enfranchised in the 1868 redistribution as the parliamentary borough of The Hartlepools. Thus was born a constituency whose boundaries are little changed to this day. Appropriately enough, its first MP was Ralph Ward Jackson who stood as the Conservative candidate and won—but only by 1,550 votes to 1,547, a majority of 3 over the Liberals' Thomas Richardson.

The following general election in 1874 was a rematch between Ward Jackson and Richardson, with Richardson winning handily to gain the seat for the Liberals. He was a major employer in West Hartlepool through the firm of T Richardson and Sons, which made marine engines. Unfortunately, shortly afterwards Richardson ran into financial trouble and was forced to leave the Commons.

The resulting first Hartlepools by-election, held in July 1875, was held for the Liberals by Lowthian Bell. An alderman of Newcastle upon Tyne, Bell had been elected in the 1874 general election as one of the two MPs for North Durham, but that election was voided by the Election Court for intimidation by agents of the Liberal campaign, and Bell had lost the resulting by-election. Lowthian Bell had also been elected in 1874 as a Fellow of the Royal Society and as the first recipient of the Bessemer Gold Medal; as well as being a metallurgist of some renown, he ran an enormous ironworks in Port Clarence with a number of associated quarries, was a director of the North Eastern Railway and had set up the UK's first aluminium smelter in Washington.

The 1880 general election in the Hartlepools featured two official Liberal candidates, with Thomas Richardson (his money problems now resolved) seeking to get his seat back and Bell looking for re-election. This did not cost the Liberals the seat. Richardson won with 1,965 votes, against 1,717 for Bell and 1,597 for the Conservative candidate, to return to the Commons after five years away.

The Liberal Party split in 1885 over the issue of Irish Home Rule, and Richardson was on the breakaway side of the split. He was re-elected in 1886 under his new Liberal Unionist colours, with a 58–42 lead over the replacement Liberal candidate.

Thomas Richardson died at the end of 1890, aged 69. The resulting second Hartlepools by-election in January 1891 pitted together two men who both symbolised what West Hartlepool had become. Defending the seat for the Liberal Unionists was Sir William Gray, who employed 2,000 men as a shipyard owner in this maritime town. Gray's shipyard had launched 18 ships in 1878, a British record at the time, and went to claim the title of the UK's most productive shipyard six times in the years between then and 1900. Gray had been knighted the previous year for his charitable work and service as Mayor of West Hartlepool.

In 1877 William Gray and Company had built a number of steamships for Thomas Furness and Company, a Hartlepool provision merchants firm which had decided to operate its own shipping fleet rather than rent space on other people's ships. Thomas Furness and Company split up in 1882, with Thomas keeping the provision merchants side of the business and his younger brother Christopher Furness spinning off the shipping line under the name of Christopher Furness and Company. Furness Line merged in 1891, the year of this by-election, with the Edward Withy shipyard in Hartlepool to form Furness Withy, which would grow into one of the UK's largest transport businesses and become the biggest employer in the two Hartlepools.

With little to choose between Gray and Furness on background—they were both huge local employers with public profiles to match—many outside observers thought that the Irish Home Rule issue would decide the by-election. Not so, as it turned out: Furness successfully wooed the town's working-class (or at least those of them who had the right to vote) by saying that he would employ only union labourers. Furness won the 1891 Hartlepools by-election by 4,603 votes to 4,305, a majority of 298, and gained the seat for the Liberal Party. The Liberal Unionists cried foul and threatened to launch legal action against the result, but eventually thought better of it. As we shall see, this wasn't the only dodgy campaign associated with Christopher Furness, who holds the dubious distinction of being one of the few people to appear before the Election Court more than once.

The 1892 and 1895 elections in the Hartlepools were close contests between Furness for the Liberals and Thomas Richardson II, son of the late Hartlepools MP Thomas Richardson, for the Liberal Unionists. Thomas II had taken over the marine engineers T Richardson and Sons following his father's death. Furness won the 1892 contest by 4,626 votes to 4,550, a majority of 76; Richardson gained the seat in 1895 by 4,853 votes to 4,772, a majority of 81.

Sir Christopher Furness, as he was by now, then tried to get back into Parliament by contesting the York by-election of January 1898. After losing by 11 votes to the Conservative candidate, Rear-Admiral Lord Charles Beresford, he launched proceedings in the Election Court to force a recount. The recount resulted in a tie on 5,643 votes each with a number of dubious ballot papers reserved for the Court to adjudicate on; Furness was advised he wouldn't get enough of them to win, and the Court allowed him to withdraw the case.

The third Richardson v Furness contest in 1900 was a big win for Furness who recovered the Hartlepools seat he had lost five years earlier. Having defeated Thomas Richardson II at the ballot box, Sir Christopher Furness then took over his company: a series of mergers transformed T Richardson and Sons into the marine engineers Richardsons Westgarth and Company, with Furness Withy holding a controlling stake. This effectively neutralised the Liberal Unionist threat in the Hartlepools, and Furness was re-elected unopposed in the Liberal landslide of 1906.

Sir Christopher Furness finally over-reached himself in the January 1910 general election, at which he was opposed by W G Howard Gritten of the Conservatives. Furness won by 6,531 votes to 5,754, a majority of 777, but then found himself back in the Election Court over campaign irregularities. A wide variety of allegations were made against the Liberal campaign, particularly that it had gone over the election expense limit (Furness' election expense return was just a few shillings below the maximum), but the only such allegation that could be made to stick was that £5 of postage stamps had been omitted from the return, and the judges granted Furness relief for that. However, it was proven that Christopher Furness' election agent had hired a band of miners to go around the streets intimidating voters, and the verdict of the Court was that Furness, by his agents, was guilty of the electoral offence of undue influence. Accordingly he was unseated. That was the end of his Commons career, although he found himself translated to the Lords in short order as the first Lord Furness.

The resulting third Hartlepools by-election in June 1910 had a very similar look to the January 1910 ballot paper, because the Liberals selected Stephen Furness, Sir Christopher's nephew. Stephen already had two winning election campaigns under his belt, having been elected to West Hartlepool borough council in 1897 and to Durham county council in 1898. W G Howard Gritten returned as Conservative candidate. Stephen Furness won the by-election by 6,159 votes to 5,993, a reduced Liberal majority of 166, and then won the Hartlepools' third parliamentary election in a year that December by 6,017 votes to 5,969, a majority of just 48 votes.

In 1912 Lord Furness died, and Stephen took over his uncle's business interests and became the new chairman of Furness Withy. He was made a baronet the following year. However, Sir Stephen didn't get to savour this power for very long. He died in 1914, having suffered an accident while on holiday, aged just 42.

The resulting fourth Hartlepools by-election in September 1914 took place during the wartime political truce, and was uncontested. The winner was Sir Walter Runciman of the Liberals, the father of the long-serving Liberal MP of the same name.* Walter senior had run away to sea at 11 and by 1914 he was a shipping magnate, having founded the South Shields Shipping Company (later the Moor Line) in 1889.

Shortly afterwards, the war came to Hartlepool. The Imperial German Navy raided a number of east coast towns, including Hartlepool and West Hartlepool, between 8:10am and 8:50am on 16th December 1914. 1,150 shells were fired into the two towns; over a hundred civilians were killed as were seven soldiers. Private Theophilus Jones, Durham Light Infantry, was the first British soldier to die from enemy action on British soil for two centuries.

Runciman didn't seek re-election once the First World War was over. For the 1918 general election the coalition government endorsed the Liberal candidate Charles Macfarlane, but he was soundly beaten by the Conservative candidate W G Howard Gritten who had narrowly lost all three Hartlepools elections in 1910. This election broke the mould in many ways. It was the first Hartlepools election to feature a Labour candidate (locally-born trade unionist Will Sherwood, who polled 19% and saved his deposit), and it was the first Hartlepools election not to return a major player in the engineering or maritime industries. The first Conservative (as opposed to Liberal Unionist MP) for the seat since Ralph Ward Jackson, Gritten was the vice-president of the Tariff Reform Federation and was best known as a barrister and writer.

The Liberals bounced back from their disappointing performance in 1918 to defeat Gritten in 1922 by 18,252 votes to 17,685, a majority of 567. The new Liberal MP was William Jowitt. A schoolfriend of Clement Attlee (in whose cabinet he served as Lord Chancellor, many years later), Jowitt was a barrister who had made it to KC on the day before polling. He was re-elected in 1923 with a reduced majority, defeating Gritten again by 17,101 votes to 16,956, a majority of 145.

William Jowitt represented three different constituencies in the Commons (he was later elected for Preston and Ashton-under-Lyne), and he lost his seat in 1924 to another MP who represented three different constituencies. After service in the Royal Engineers in the Great War, Bolton-born engineer Wilfrid Sugden had been elected as MP for Royton in Lancashire in 1918, but had lost that seat in 1923. In 1924 he turned up as Conservative candidate for the Hartlepools, and defeated William Jowitt quite soundly. Sugden didn't seek re-election here in 1929, instead choosing to return to Lancashire by contesting Rossendale (which

* For more on Walter Runciman junior see page 244.

he lost); he later served as MP for Leyton West in the 1931–35 Parliament.

Sugden's move to Lancashire cleared the way for W G Howard Gritten to return as Conservative MP for the Hartlepools in 1929, although he was pushed all the way by Stephen Furness junior, the son of the 1910–14 MP of the same name. Gritten won by 17,271 votes to 17,133, a majority of 138, with Labour polling over 10,000 votes here for the first time. Furness, as a supporter of the National Government, didn't contest the 1931 election and that didn't go unnoticed; he went on to be elected in 1935 as a Liberal National MP for Sunderland, without Conservative opposition, and served as a junior minister in the Chamberlain administration.

W G Howard Gritten wasn't seriously challenged in the Hartlepools constituency after 1929. He was still in office when he died in 1943, aged 73. The resulting fifth Hartlepools by-election in June 1943 again took place during the wartime political truce, but this time there was a contest. The Tories' Thomas Greenwell, owner of a Sunderland shipyard, put the work in against independent Labour, independent Progressive and Common Wealth candidates and was rewarded with a 64% vote share—one of the better Conservative performances in a contested by-election during the Second World War. The Hartlepools' first female parliamentary candidate, Elaine Burton of Common Wealth (who would later serve as a Labour MP for Coventry), finished second and saved her deposit.

The 1945 general election broke the mould again with the first Labour win in the two Hartlepools. D T Jones, a railway signalman from south Wales who had been selected as Labour candidate for the 1939–40 general election that never happened, rode the Attlee landslide to defeat Greenwell by the narrow margin of 16,502 votes to 16,227, a majority of 275.

Labour quickly consolidated their position, and the Hartlepools swung strongly to Labour in 1950 against the national trend. That increased majority helped D T Jones to survive marginal results in 1951 (by 2,710 votes) and 1955 (by 1,585 votes).

It didn't help him in 1959 when the British film industry intervened. Ten years earlier, during the Chinese Civil War, the frigate HMS *Amethyst* had been travelling up the Yangtse River, to relieve another ship guarding the British Embassy at Nanking, when it was fired on by the People's Liberation Army with heavy casualties. 22 men aboard were killed, including the captain, and 31 men and the ship's cat were wounded. Lt-Cdr John Kerans, the assistant British naval attaché at Nanking, took over command of *Amethyst* and, after three months of fruitless negotiations with the PLA, pulled off a daring night-time escape down the river to the open sea. Kerans was subsequently awarded the Distinguished Service Order, while the ship's cat Simon became the only cat to date to be awarded the Dickin Medal for animal bravery.

Kerans, now promoted to Commander, acted as a technical advisor for the 1957 war film *Yangtse Incident: The Story of HMS Amethyst*, in which he was played by Richard Todd and *Amethyst* was brought out of retirement to play herself.

Two years later John Kerans was in Parliament, having defeated D T Jones to become, to date, the last Conservative MP for the Hartlepools. His margin of victory in the 1959 general election was 25,463 votes to 25,281, a majority of 182. He clearly didn't harbour a grudge against the People's Liberation Army, speaking in Parliament in favour of Communist China being admitted to the United Nations.

Kerans did not seek re-election in 1964, and the seat reverted to Labour whose successful candidate was Ted Leadbitter. A teacher from Easington, Leadbitter went on to serve as a backbench MP for the constituency for 28 years. While his judgment may occasionally have been suspect (accusing Commander Kerans, of all people, of cowardice for not seeking re-election was unwise), he was noted for his parliamentary work and for his efforts on behalf of the towns. His parliamentary question in 1979 led to the revelation that Anthony Blunt, the Surveyor of the Queen's Pictures, was a Soviet spy.

My grandad lived in Hartlepool for many years. He was a senior firefighter and a strong Labour man who knew and respected Leadbitter. God knows what Grandad would have made of what has happened in the town since he died in 1997. My dad cast his first vote in one of the last elections for Hartlepool county borough council, and claims that his first ballot paper was a choice of Labour versus Independent Labour. Having looked at the county borough election results for the relevant period, all I can say is that I cannot verify this.

It was during Leadbitter's tenure that the two Hartlepools became one. Hartlepool borough and West Hartlepool county borough were merged into a single Hartlepool county borough in 1967, a move that did not go down well on the headland. In February 1974 the constituency's name was changed to "Hartlepool" to reflect this. Two months later Hartlepool town was transferred out of County Durham into the new county of Cleveland, a move that did not go down well among any Hartlepudlian. This was followed in 1983 by the only change of any significance to the parliamentary boundaries since 1867, with the transfer in of eight small rural parishes which were previously in the Easington constituency. This boosted the constituency's electorate by only about 3%, so describing the Hartlepool constituency as "semi-rural" is not accurate. (The present Rural West ward, as I shall discuss later, is misleadingly named.) The seat has had unchanged boundaries since 1983 and, having the same boundaries as

Hartlepool council, is likely to escape the next boundary review unscathed.

The town has changed over the postwar years as well. The shipyards closed down in the 1960s, and the associated industries went into decline. There's still a lot of industry here: the nuclear power station is one of the town's largest employers, and the Liberty Steel factory makes pipes for the energy and construction industries, but the industries don't employ anything like the number of people they used to in the old days, the power station is coming to the end of its useful life and the steel mill is threatened by the recent collapse of Greensill Capital, its major lender. Unemployment has been a major and chronic problem here for decades, and this has led to an increase in the town's average age as young people leave to find work elsewhere.

Ted Leadbitter was run fairly close at his first election by the Tories' Geoffrey Dodsworth (later an MP for Hertfordshire in the 1970s), winning with a margin of 2,867. After that he made the seat safe, only being seriously challenged in February 1974 and 1983.

Leadbitter retired in 1992 and passed the seat on to one of the most influential figures in the Labour Party over the last 40 years. A grandson of the former London County Council leader and Attlee cabinet member Herbert Morrison, Peter Mandelson first came to prominence in 1985 when he was appointed as director of communications for the Labour party. He was elected as MP for Hartlepool in 1992, served as director of the Labour campaign for the 1997 general election with some success, and served in Cabinet in 1998 as trade and industry secretary and as Northern Ireland secretary from 1999 to 2001. Mandelson has long had a reputation as a master of the dark political arts—the character of Malcolm Tucker in *The Thick of It* was partially based on him—so it's ironic that both of those spells in Cabinet were terminated by scandal-induced resignations.

During this period a fair amount of regeneration money flowed into Hartlepool. The docks are still suitable for large ships, but much of the space in them was turned into a marina for pleasure boats. The town's main shopping parade, Middleton Grange, was given a roof to keep the weather out. The oldest Royal Navy warship still afloat, HMS *Trincomalee*, became the focus of a new maritime museum (now part of the National Museum of the Royal Navy) to bring in the tourists. The seafront at Seaton Carew was improved.

It was also during Mandelson's time in office that the county of Cleveland was dissolved and Hartlepool became a unitary council. It was also during Mandelson's time in office that Hartlepool council started to turn in weird election results. The fun begin in earnest in 2000 when the Liberal Democrats suddenly won seven out of 15 wards, a figure they have never matched before or since, and Labour lost overall control of the council. This wasn't caused by freak vote splits:

six wards in that election were straight fights between Labour and the Lib Dems and, ironically in view of what was to come, there wasn't a single independent or minor-party candidate to be seen.

A referendum in October 2001 then produced a very close vote in favour of introducing an elected mayor (10,667 in favour, 10,294 against). Hartlepool's first mayoral election, held in May 2002, turned in an infamous result. The first round was very close between Labour, on 28%, and two independent candidates: Ian Cameron on 27% and Stuart Drummond on 29%. Drummond, a 28-year-old who had previously worked as the mascot for Hartlepool United football club and was standing as a publicity stunt for the club, went on to win the runoff against Labour by a 52–48 margin.

Peter Mandelson resigned in 2004 to become the UK representative on the European Commission. The resulting sixth Hartlepool by-election, held in September 2004, returned Labour's Iain Wright by a relatively narrow margin over the Lib Dems. At the time of his election Wright was a Hartlepool councillor (representing Rift House ward) and working as a chartered accountant. The UK Independence Party crept over 10% of the vote, beating the Conservatives into fourth place—something that was noteworthy at the time.

Back to the council. Mayor Drummond never did implement his only election pledge—free bananas for the town's schoolchildren—but his governing style proved to be sober and professional. He was re-elected in 2005 and 2009, and it took the passing of a mayoral abolition referendum in 2012 for the Labour council group to get rid of him and take back control of the council. In the meantime, UKIP broke through in the council chamber: their by-election candidate Stephen Allison won the headland ward of St Hilda in 2006, and UKIP won a second seat in 2008 in Foggy Furze ward. Neither UKIP councillor was re-elected, and a whole council election in 2012 on new ward boundaries (with a significant cut in the number of councillors, reflecting the mayoral structure that was about to be abolished) returned a Labour majority of 21 councillors against 5 independents, 4 councillors for the localist party Putting Hartlepool First, and 3 Conservatives in Rural West ward.

As this column has previously examined in detail*, this ward is misnamed. Although Rural West does include most of Hartlepool's rural parishes, the core of the ward is the West Park area. West Park combines mansions for the shipyard owners of olden days with a series of privately-developed housing estates to add up to by far the most middle-class and most expensive part of Hartlepool proper. In 2018 the median house in West Park went for around £300,000, compared to asking prices of £100,000 or less in most of the rest of the town. This is the only

* *Andrew's Previews 2018*, page 241.

part of Hartlepool that consistently votes Conservative at local elections.

The Kippers struck back in 2014, winning the Seaton ward (Seaton Carew) and the Jesmond ward in the north of the town. They took the 2015 general election seriously, selecting the former semi-professional wrestler Philip Broughton who finished second with 28% of the vote. Iain Wright's majority was cut to 3,024 and the seat became marginal. UKIP won nothing on the council that year, but in the 2016 Hartlepool council elections they gained three wards and followed up with a by-election gain in Headland and Harbour ward.* The EU membership referendum in June 2016 saw Hartlepool turn in a Leave vote of 69.6%, the highest figure for any local authority in the north-east.

Iain Wright, who had become chairman of the Business, Innovation and Skills select committee after the 2015 election, didn't seek re-election in 2017. The Labour Party selected Mike Hill to hold the seat: the political officer for the Northern region of UNISON at the time, Hill had been the Labour candidate for Richmond (Yorkshire) in 2015. He won the June 2017 election very comfortably, with an 18-point lead over the Conservatives.

Then the wheels *really* started to come off the clown car that is Hartlepool council. This is complicated, please bear with me. In 2018 the five UKIP councillors walked out of the party and, eventually, rebranded as a new party called the Independent Union. Just before the May 2019 elections the ruling Labour group suffered a huge split, with most of the leadership group walking off to join the Scargillite Socialist Labour Party. The electorate were not impressed, and in May 2019 Labour lost six of the nine wards they were defending and overall control of the council.

The Local Elections Archive Project's map of the Hartlepool 2019 results has two wards coloured in far-right navy blue, representing two different parties. This column is open to persuasion that the Veterans and People's Party (which won Foggy Furze ward) may be better characterised as populist right than far-right, but there can be little doubt that the For Britain Movement (which won De Bruce ward) is on the far side of that dividing line.

Following the implosion of Hartlepool Labour, a coalition of the Independent Union, Conservatives, and Veterans and People's Party was formed to run the town, with support from the Socialist Labour Party group. (Hands up whoever expected to see Scargillites supporting Conservatives.) John Tennant, a former leader of the Independent Union group, joined the Brexit Party and was elected as a Brexit Party MEP for north-east England three weeks later. The Independent Union and VPP councillors followed suit in September 2019, suddenly giving the Brexit Party control of Hartlepool council in coalition with the

* *Andrew's Previews 2016*, page 219.

Conservatives.

Also in September 2019, Labour MP Mike Hill was suspended from the party over sexual harassment allegations. He was reinstated a month later, stood for re-election in December 2019 as an official Labour candidate, and was re-elected with a greatly reduced majority: 38% of the vote, against 29% for the Conservatives and 26% for the Brexit Party, whose candidate was the party chairman and MEP Richard Tice.

Following the December 2019 general election, the Brexit Party councillors walked out of the party as suddenly as they had walked in and (with the exception of former MEP John Tennant, who is now in Reform UK) reverted to their previous allegiances. What was left of the Labour group on the council then split *again*, with several councillors walking off to form a new localist group called Hartlepool People.

It would appear that the majority of Hartlepool councillors have taken to heart the unimprovable words of Groucho Marx: "those are my principles, and if you don't like them … well, I have others." If this sort of defection level had happened in a foreign parliament, the words "basket case" or even "banana republic" would not be far from commentators' lips. We should hold the clown car that is Hartlepool council up to the same standards. What has gone on here over the last three years is an embarrassment to British local government.

The last three ordinary elections to Hartlepool council have returned 14 Labour councillors, 5 independents, 4 UKIP, 3 councillors from Putting Hartlepool First (which is now defunct), 3 Conservatives, 2 councillors for the Independent Union, 1 For Britain Movement and 1 Veterans and People's Party. Following this dizzying series of defections (and the description above is nowhere near being an exhaustive list of everything that has happened) there are now 6 Labour councillors, 5 councillors for the Independent Union, 4 Conservatives, 4 Socialist Labour, 3 Hartlepool People, 2 Putting Seaton First, 2 independent councillors, 2 Veterans and People's Party, 1 For Britain Movement, 1 Reform UK and three vacant seats. (Checks arithmetic: yes, this does add up to 33 as required.) The Independent Union, Conservative, VPP and For Britain Movement councillors form the ruling coalition with 12 councillors, currently 4 short of a majority.

The usual medicine which central government administers to dysfunctional councils like Hartlepool is to send in the Commissioners and/or hit the factory reset button by holding a whole-council election, preferably with new boundaries to shake things up a bit. As luck would have it the Local Government Boundary Commission have been in town recently, so the May 2021 Hartlepool council election will be all-up with new ward boundaries (Figure 24) and an increase from 33 councillors to 36. To be honest, it's a wonder the Commissioners haven't

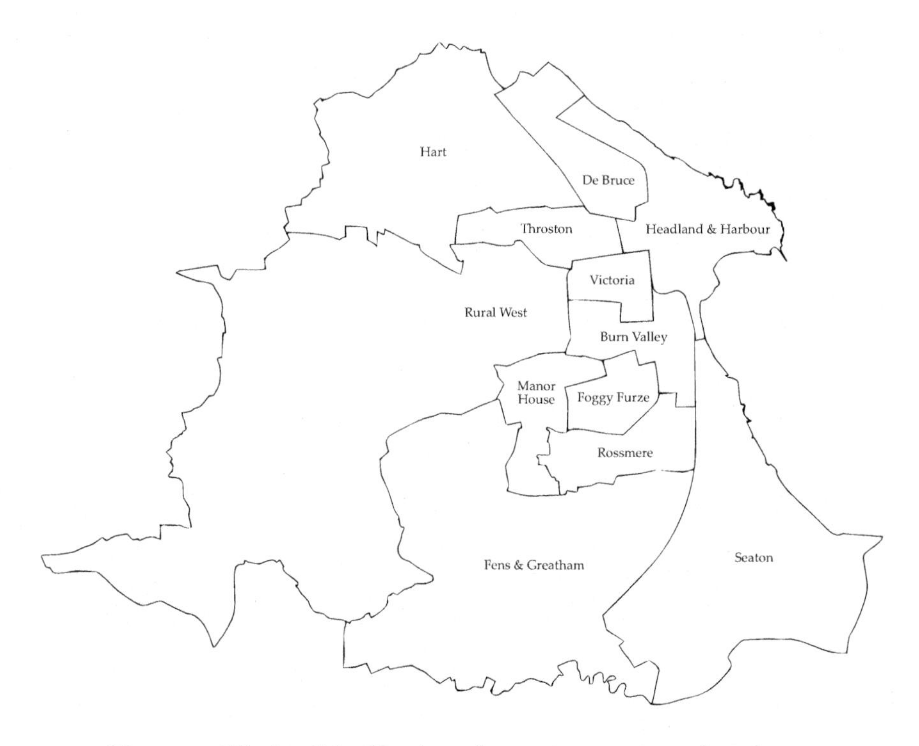

Figure 24: Wards of the Hartlepool constituency, introduced 2021

gone in already; perhaps the cabinet minister responsible for local government would prefer to pick fights with easier targets like Liverpool.

The only party that is standing enough candidates to win an overall majority on the new Hartlepool council is Labour, with 31 candidates for 36 available seats. There are 25 independent candidates (including the three Hartlepool People councillors and the two Putting Seaton First councillors), 15 candidates for the Veterans and People's Party, just 13 Conservative candidates, 9 Reform UK, 7 Independent Union, 3 For Britain Movement, 3 Lib Dems, and one candidate each for the Heritage Party, the SDP and the Socialist Labour Party. None of the four current Socialist Labour councillors are seeking re-election.

In the meantime, the sexual harassment allegations against the Labour MP for Hartlepool Mike Hill have not gone away and he is due to answer them later this year in an employment tribunal. He has resigned as an MP prompting the *seventh* Hartlepool by-election, which will be the first parliamentary by-election of the 2019 parliament and the first since Brecon and Radnorshire in August 2019.

The Hartlepool parliamentary by-election and whole council election will both be held on 6th May alongside elections for the Mayor of the Tees Valley

Combined Authority and the Cleveland Police and Crime Commissioner. That's four ballot papers for the electors to fill out and for the counting team to juggle. And we do need to mention those county-wide elections before we come to the parliamentary candidate list.

The Cleveland Police and Crime Commissioner since 2012 has been Barry Coppinger, a Labour man who had previously sat on Middlesbrough council. Having already announced his retirement, Coppinger resigned as PCC in 2020 and his deputy has taken over for the rest of his term. At Coppinger's re-election in 2016 he polled 41% of the first preferences against 23% for the Conservative candidate Matt Vickers and 21% for UKIP, and his lead over the Conservatives in the runoff was a handy 62–38.

The Tees Valley mayoral election the following year told a completely different story. The electorate here consists of the four Cleveland boroughs plus Darlington, and the addition of Darlington made all the difference in 2017. Ben Houchen, who had previously been leader of the Conservative group on Stockton-on-Tees council, was elected as the first Mayor of the Tees Valley by the narrow margin of 51.1% to 48.9% over Labour in the runoff, having led 39.5–39.0 on first preferences.

Almost nothing has gone right for Labour in the Tees Valley councils since then. We have already discussed Hartlepool council for quite long enough. In 2019 Middlesbrough council elected an independent mayor, Darlington council was gained by the Conservatives, the ruling Labour group in Stockton-on-Tees lost its majority, and as for Redcar and Cleveland—well, you would be hard pressed to guess from the map of the 2019 results that Redcar and Cleveland now has two Conservative MPs. In the 2019 election the ruling Labour group there crashed to 15 councillors, against 14 independents, 13 Lib Dems, 11 Conservatives, 2 UKIP and 4 localists. The ruling coalition is now made up of independent and Lib Dem councillors. Interestingly, the Conservative group on the council has fallen apart and there are now just two official Tory councillors left; the party will have a chance to do something about that on 6th May as they are defending three by-elections to Redcar and Cleveland council. Two of these are in *Guisborough* ward (covering the northern half of the town of the same name) and on the edge of the North York Moors National Park in *Hutton* ward (covering the western end of Guisborough together with the mini-Matterhorn of Roseberry Topping and the village of Newton under Roseberry).* Hutton is safe Conservative and their candidate Stephen Waterfield should be favoured to hold,† but Guisborough ward split its three seats in 2019 between an indepen-

* For a longer discussion of Hutton ward, on earlier boundaries, see *Andrew's Previews 2017*, page 68. † *Redcar and Cleveland, Hutton*: C 1318 LD 566 Ind 332 Lab 256

dent, the Conservatives and Labour. The defending Conservative candidate for Guisborough is Andrew Hixon, two independents have come forward (Sheila Berry and Fred Page) and the Labour candidate is Lisa Belshaw.* *Longbeck* ward, based on New Marske,† was the only ward within the Redcar parliamentary seat to return Conservative councillors in May 2019; the Tory slate had a narrow majority over an independent councillor, and new Conservative candidate Andrea Turner may have work to do to hold off new independent candidate Judith Findley.‡

There are five local by-elections on 6th May to STOCKTON-ON-TEES council. All of them are defended by the opposition to the minority Labour administration, but none of them are in wards where Labour are in contention. In *Yarm*§ the three seats available in 2019 split between an independent and two Conservatives; the Tories' Dan Fagan will seek to hold off independent candidates Tony Bell-Berry, Alan Gallafant and Christopher Johnson to defend this by-election.¶ On the Durham side of the Tees we have a free-for-all in *Billingham West* ward which voted strongly for an independent slate in 2019; three different independents are standing (Mark Bellerby, Giles Harris and Paul Henderson), with the Tories' Lee Spence ready to pounce on any resulting freak vote split.‖ The rural *Western Parishes* ward sees a bizarre by-election after Conservative councillor Andrew Stephenson was disqualified under the six-month non-attendance rule; Stephenson is seeking re-election as an independent in the poll caused by his own disqualification, while the Tories have selected Steve Matthews.** On the western edge of Stockton proper, Lib Dem candidate Matthew Eves will seek to hold the borough's only Liberal Democrat ward of *Bishopsgarth and Elm Tree*.†† Finally, the Tories' Niall Innes will attempt to take over the seat in the safe-Conservative *Hartburn* ward vacated by Matt Vickers, who bounced back from losing the Cleveland Police and Crime Commissioner election in 2016 to become the MP for Stockton South in 2019.‡‡

The December 2019 general election results within the Tees Valley mayoral area were just as dire for Labour, if not more so. As well as Stockton South already mentioned, the Redcar and Darlington constituencies were also gained

* *Redcar and Cleveland, Guisborough*: C 879 Lab 406 Berry 398 Page 195 LD 69 † For a longer discussion of Longbeck ward, on earlier boundaries, see *Andrew's Previews 2018*, page 110. ‡ *Redcar and Cleveland, Longbeck*: C 710 Lab 440 Ind 399 LD 29 § For more detail on Yarm see *Andrew's Previews 2017*, page 169, a by-election for a seat vacated by Ben Houchen after his mayoral election. ¶ *Stockton-on-Tees, Yarm*: C 2757 Gallafant 759 Lab 644 Bell-Berry 149 LD 76 Johnson 59 ‖ *Stockton-on-Tees, Billingham West*: C 863 Bellerby 791 Lab 429 Reform UK 53 Henderson 32 LD 7 Harris 4 [C gain from Ind] ** *Stockton-on-Tees, Western Parishes*: C 928 Lab 362 Ind 136 †† *Stockton-on-Tees, Bishopsgarth and Elm Tree*: C 1055 LD 730 Lab 386 Ind 165 [C gain from LD] ‡‡ *Stockton-on-Tees, Hartburn*: C 1999 Lab 620 Reform UK 112

by the Conservatives as was the Sedgefield constituency, part of which is in Darlington borough. Ben Houchen's election as Mayor of the Tees Valley Combined Authority in May 2017 was seen at the time as a surprise, but given what has happened since he must be considering the prospect of re-election with some confidence. The 2021 Tees Valley mayoral election will not go to transfers because it is a straight fight: Houchen seeks re-election from the blue corner, while former charity CEO Jessie Joe Jacobs challenges from the red corner.*

Labour had originally selected the former Stockton South MP Paul Williams as their candidate for Cleveland Police and Crime Commissioner, but had to reselect at the last minute after Williams got the nomination for the Hartlepool by-election. Their replacement defending candidate is Matthew Storey, the leader of the Labour group on Middlesbrough council. The Conservatives have selected Steve Turner, who was elected in 2015 as a UKIP member of Redcar and Cleveland council; he defected to the Conservatives in 2017, but lost re-election in 2019. UKIP have not returned, so completing the PCC ballot paper are independent candidate Barry Cooper and the Lib Dems' Christopher Jones.†

Which finally brings us to the Hartlepool parliamentary ballot paper of sixteen candidates. Right at the bottom, thanks to his position at the wrong end of the alphabet, is the Labour candidate Paul Williams. Williams has previous parliamentary experience as the MP for Stockton South from 2017 to 2019; away from politics he is a general practitioner and as such has been hard at work on the COVID front line for the last year and a bit. In the 2021 New Year Honours Williams was appointed OBE for services to Parliament and to healthcare in Stockton-on-Tees.

The Tories, having added together the Conservative and Brexit Party shares from December 2019 and concluded that they are in with a realistic chance of a rare government gain in a parliamentary by-election, have selected Jill Mortimer. Mortimer is a member of Hambleton council in North Yorkshire, representing the Raskelf and White Horse ward to the south and south-east of Thirsk in the Vale of York.

Third here in 2019 was Richard Tice of the Brexit Party, who have since morphed into Reform UK. Tice is seeking election to the London Assembly (he is top of the Reform UK list there and also contesting the Havering and Redbridge constituency), and the Reform UK candidate for the Hartlepool by-election is John Prescott. No not that one (the former Deputy Prime Minister of the same name is now in the Lords); this John Prescott is an IT consultant from the Houghton-le-Spring area. It will be interesting to see whether Prescott

* *Mayor of Tees Valley*: C 121964 Lab 45641 † *Cleveland PCC*: C 74023 Lab 39467 Ind 16667 LD 6540 [C gain from Lab]

gets the same support from the Hartlepool council ruling group that Tice got in 2019.

No other candidates saved their deposit here in December 2019. The only minor party to return from that election is the Liberal Democrats, who have reselected their parliamentary candidate from 2017 and 2019 Andrew Hagon.

There are twelve other candidates to list. First alphabetically is David Bettney who has the nomination of the Social Democratic Party. The modern SDP is a very different beast to the one formed by the Gang of Four forty years ago, having been taken over by Euroseceptics. Nick Delves stands for the Monster Raving Loony Party under his *nom-de-guerre* "The Incredible Flying Brick"; his policies include relocating the Houses of Parliament to the Hartlepool marina, which would solve the town's unemployment problem at a stroke. The North East Party, a serious regionalist movement with a local government powerbase in nearby Peterlee, have nominated their party chairman Hilton Dawson; he is best known as the Labour MP for Lancaster and Wyre from 1997 to 2015. The Women's Equality Party have selected Gemma Evans, who fought Bury South in December 2019 and gives an address in the Sunderland area. Another Sunderland-based candidate is the Green Party's Rachel Featherstone, who was top of the Greens' list for north-east England in the 2019 European Parliament elections and is also seeking election to Sunderland council on 6th May. Adam Gaines, a former technology worker who now runs a pub on the Hartlepool marina, is standing as an independent candidate. Steve Jack is the candidate of the Freedom Alliance, an anti-lockdown group. Independent candidate Chris Killick, a former shop assistant, was revealed during the campaign to be on the sex offenders' register following a voyeurism conviction in 2020; he did not receive a custodial sentence and as such he is not disqualified from elected office (and even if he was disqualified the returning officer could not have rejected his nomination on that basis), but in the unlikely event Killick is elected it seems doubtful whether he could properly fulfil the role of an MP. Another Hartlepool-based independent candidate is Sam Lee, a businesswoman and former sports journalist. The Heritage Party, an anti-lockdown group whose most prominent personality would appear to be the outgoing ex-UKIP London Assembly member David Kurten, have selected Claire Martin. Thelma Walker, the Labour MP for Colne Valley from 2017 to 2019, is standing as an independent candidate with the support of the Northern Independence Party, which I would like to describe as a serious regionalist movement but whose conduct of the campaign has been rather too trollish to justify the adjective "serious". (Or "regionalist", given that they appear to be run out of the noted Northern city of Brighton. Or even "movement", given that the Electoral Commission threw out their application to register as

Hartlepool council wards: all
December 2019 result Lab 15464 C 11869 Brexit Party 10603 LD 1696 Ind 911 Soc Lab 494
June 2017 result Lab 21969 C 14319 UKIP 4801
May 2015 result Lab 14076 UKIP 11052 C 8256 Picton 2954 Grn 1341 Save Hartlepool Hospital 849 LD 761 Hobbs 201
May 2010 result Lab 16267 C 10758 LD 6533 UKIP 2682 BNP 2002
May 2005 result Lab 18251 LD 10773 C 4058 UKIP 1256 Soc Lab 373 Grn 288 Ind 275 Loony 162
September 2004 by-election Lab 12752 LD 10719 UKIP 3193 C 3044 Respect 572 Grn 255 NF 246 Fathers4Justice 139 Soc Lab 95 Common Good 91 Ind 90 Loony 80 Rainbow 45 EDP 41
June 2001 result Lab 22506 C 7935 LD 5717 Soc Lab 912 Cameron 557 Booth 424
May 1997 result Lab 26997 C 9489 LD 6248 Referendum Party 1718
April 1992 result Lab 26816 C 18034 LD 6860
June 1987 result Lab 24296 C 17007 Lib 7047 Ind 1786
June 1983 result Lab 22048 C 18958 SDP 7422

Figure 25: House of Commons, Hartlepool

a political party.) Finally, it's appropriate that we finish our discussion of the Hartlepool by-election candidates by going full circle back to the beginning of the town: Ralph Ward-Jackson, a businessman who is a great-nephew of the West Hartlepool founder of the same name, is standing as an independent candidate.

Two opinion polls of the constituency have been carried out during the campaign, both by Survation. Their first poll for the Communication Workers Union, with fieldwork from 29th March to 3rd April and a sample size of 502, showed the Conservatives in a position to win Hartlepool for the first time since 1959, with a 49–42 lead over Labour and no other named party with more than 2%. A further poll for ITV's *Good Morning Britain* programme, with fieldwork from 23rd to 29th April and a sample size of 517, showed an increased Conservative lead of 50–33.

The Hartlepool acting returning officer is going for an overnight count for the parliamentary by-election, but with verifications for four different elections having to be sorted out before the by-election count can commence it seems unlikely that the declaration will come much before dawn. Nevertheless, with very little other overnight counting taking place for this year's local elections it seems likely that the Friday morning breakfast TV bulletins will be dominated by the result from the Pool. Who will win? I don't know, but I'll be interested to find out.*

* *House of Commons, Hartlepool*: C 15529 Lab 8589 Lee 2904 Heritage 468 Reform UK 368 Grn 358 LD 349 Walker 250 Killick 248 North East Party 163 Ward-Jackson 157 SDP 140 Women's Equality 140 Gaines 126 Loony 108 Freedom Alliance 72 [C gain from Lab]

In memoriam

Before wrapping this marathon 6th May preview up, I would like to pause here to remember and to pay tribute to the local councillors who have passed away over the two municipal years since May 2019. Some of these people were veterans of local government, others only just beginning their careers in our council chambers; in some cases their family, friends and colleagues left behind can reflect on a long life well lived, in others we mourn those who passed before their time. Some of these names have already appeared in this column over the last two years; but in too many cases, the pandemic has left insufficient space for their stories to be told here.

Where a councillor's name is marked by a † symbol, that signifies that the councillor was reported to have died of COVID-19.

Mona Adams, Richmond upon Thames
Jean Adkins, Somerset West & Taunton
Les Alden, Adur
Derek Allcard, Reigate and Banstead
Pete Allen, Kingston upon Hull
George Allison, Newcastle upon Tyne
Nigel Anderdon, Test Valley
†Henry Anderson, Perth and Kinross
Sonia Andjelkovic, East Staffordshire
Dick Angel, Wealden
Steffan ap Dafydd, Neath Port Talbot
Adrian Axford, Isle of Wight
Sucha Singh Bains, Coventry
Bob Band, Perth and Kinross
Cynthia Barker, Hertsmere
Peter Barnes, Stratford-on-Avon
Clarence Barrett, Havering
Malcolm Barron, Lancashire CC
George Barton, West Sussex CC and Adur
Ronen Basu, Tunbridge Wells
Margot Bateman, Pembrokeshire
Rajinder Bath, Hounslow
Jane Baugh, Trafford
Ruth Baxter, Ribble Valley
Stuart Bellwood, Redbridge
Pat Beresford, Adur
Peter Billson, Wolverhampton
Douglas Birkinshaw, Barnsley
John Blackie, North Yorkshire CC and Richmondshire
Chris Blakeley, Wirral
Chris Blanchard-Cooper, Arun
Chris Bond, Enfield
Joy Broderick, Tendring
John Bowden, Dacorum
Ray Bowker, Trafford
†Anthony Brewer, Ashfield
Alan Bristow, Fenland
†Mike Bryan, East Riding
Norman Bull, Amber Valley
Colin Bungey, Bournemouth, Christchurch and Poole
Mary Butcher, Corby
Colin Caller, Gravesham
†Peter Callow, Blackpool
Peter Campbell, Thanet
John Caswell, Northampton
Henry Caunce, Chorley
John Chatt, Hounslow
Richard Chattaway, Warks. CC
Julia Cherrett, Stockton-on-Tees
Imelda Clancy, Basildon
Elizabeth Clare, Telford and Wrekin
Colin Clark, South Ribble

Richard Clayton, Wigan
†Louise Coles, Peterborough
John Collinson, North Lincolnshire
Wendy Congreve, Cardiff
Paul Connor, Eden
Peter Connor, Salford
Norah Cooney, Redcar and Cleveland
Anne Court, Basingstoke and Deane
Dave Cowans, Conwy
Gary Crookes, Coventry
Leonard Crosbie, Horsham
Sybil Crouch, Swansea
George Cruickshank, Highland
Terry Cutmore, Essex CC and Rochford
Ray Darby, Broxtowe
Des Davies, Neath Port Talbot
John Davies, Huntingdonshire
Tim Davies, Cardiff
Andrew Davis, Elmbridge
John Daw, Mid Devon
Stephen Dehnel, Ashford
Stuart Denleigh-Maxwell, Worcester
†Poonam Dhillon, Hounslow
Tony Dobson, Hyndburn
Ian Doggett, Torbay
David Dovey, Monmouthshire
Dawn Downes, North Warwickshire
Kevin Drum, Scottish Borders
Mark Ellen, Swale
Martin Ellis, Neath Port Talbot
Mike Ellis, Bradford
†Keith Evans, Hampshire CC and Fareham
Nuala Fennelly, Doncaster
John Ferguson, Salford
Alison Finlay, Test Valley
Lawrence Fisher, Cumbria CC
Dorothy Flude, Cheshire East
Hilary Flynn, West Sussex CC
Alison Fox, Derbyshire CC
Nadine Fudge, Kingston upon Hull
Neil Fyfe, Hillingdon
Mike Garrett, Luton
David Gathercole, West Suffolk
Roger Glithero, East Northamptonshire
Ivan Glover, North Lincolnshire
Janet Goodwin, Peterborough
Brian Gordon, Barnet
Gill Gower, Canterbury
Michael Greatorex, Staffordshire CC and Tamworth
Lord Greaves, Pendle
Marilyn Greenwood, Calderdale
Christine Grice, Greenwich
Carmel Hall, Leeds
Andy Harland, Manchester
Richard Harrap, East Riding
Allan Harvey, Knowsley
Ken Harwood, Tandridge
Terence Haslam-Jones, Rossendale
Lily Henderson, Blackpool
†Sandra Hevican, Sandwell
Austin Hicks, Gosport
Pattie Hill, Worcestershire CC and Redditch
Wendy Hinder, Maidstone
Ron Hogg, Durham Police & Crime Commissioner
Joe Holliday, Cumbria CC and Allerdale
Anna Holloway, Tewkesbury
Fergus Hood, Aberdeenshire
Sue Hordijenko, Lewisham
Len Horwood, Tunbridge Wells
Diane Hoy, Rochford
†Kevin Hughes, Flintshire
†Abid Hussain, Bradford
Bernard Hunt, Herefordshire
Paul James, Ceredigion
David Jennings, Leicestershire CC
Charles Wyn Jones, Gwynedd
Huw Jones, Denbighshire
Ken Jones, South Ribble
Sam Kay, Surrey Heath
John Kerslake, Brentwood

Jean Khote, Leicester
Hina Kiani, Hounslow
Graham Lambie, Stirling
Mike Langley, Bristol
Jack Lee, Waverley
Geoff Lewis, Sandwell
Keith Linnecor, Birmingham
Bob Lloyd, Sandwell
Thomas Lloyd, Wellingborough
†Derek Longcake, North Lincs.
Gerald Luxton, Mid Devon
Brian Lyttle, Amber Valley
Rory McClure, Barrow-in-Furness
†Richard McLinden, Liverpool
Ruth Martin, Gravesham
†Frances Mason, Harlow
Brian Mattock, Swindon
David May, South Hams
Jim Meikle, West Suffolk
†Pat Midgley, Sheffield
Des Moffatt, Swindon
Keith Morley, Halton
Ellen Morton, Argyll and Bute
Michael Mumford, Lancaster
Sue Murphy, Manchester
Pauline Nelson, Warrington
Graham Nicol, Dumfries and Galloway
Lise Noakes, Gloucester
Susan Nuttall, Bury
Michael O'Brien, Sefton
†Bill Olner, Warwickshire CC
Terry O'Neill, Warrington
Robin Orchard, Eden
John Orrick, Tandridge
Pete Parish, Bournemouth, Christchurch and Poole
Judith Pattison, Exeter
Joyce Pawley, Derbyshire Dales
Graham Payne, Wiltshire
John Pearson, Blackburn with Darwen
Charles Petts, West Sussex CC and Crawley
Ron Pinnock, East Northamptonshire
Shaun Redmond, Isle of Anglesey
Peter Rippon, Sheffield
Brian Roberts, Cheshire East
†Frank Rust, Rushmoor
†Shabnum Sadiq, Slough
Jenny Samper, Canterbury
Len Scoullar, Argyll and Bute
Raj Sharma, Crawley
Patrick Sheard, Guildford
Alan Smith, South Tyneside
Norman Smith, Castle Point
Robert Smith, Rhondda Cynon Taf
Ralph Snape, Chorley
David Soans, Kettering
Syd Stavrou, Epping Forest
Bob Stevens, Warwickshire CC
David Stevenson, North West Leicestershire
Alan Storah, Uttlesford
Lewis Strange, Lincolnshire CC and West Lindsey
Sandy Stuart, Aberdeenshire
Graham Sutton, Dacorum
Hazel Sweet, Coventry
Tony Swendell, St Albans
Dennis Teasdale, Redcar and Cleveland
Geraint Thomas, Crawley
Ian Thomas, Kent CC and Canterbury
Nigel Todd, Newcastle upon Tyne
Christopher Tranter, Sandwell
Chriss Triandafyllou, Wealden
Paul van Looy, Southend-on-Sea
Geoff Walker, Waltham Forest
Geoffrey Walker, Sunderland
Noel Walsh, Ribble Valley
Alex Ward, Ashford
Sheena Wardhaugh, South Lanarkshire
Alan Wassell, Wakefield
James Watson, Bolsover

Geoffrey Watt, Wirral
Neil Weatherley, Gateshead
Geoff Webber, North Yorkshire CC
Richard Welch, North Yorkshire CC and Craven
Ian White, Lewes
Ian Whitehouse, Staffordshire Moorlands
Christine Wild, Bolton
Paul Wild, Bolton
Gerald Wilkinson, Leeds
Andy Williams, Cheshire West and Chester
†Raymond Williams, Torfaen
Roger Wilson, Gloucestershire CC
†Brian Wood, Castle Point
Kevin Woodbridge, Orkney Islands
Bill Wright, Blaby

Requiescat in pace.

Final remarks

The UK's electoral services teams, who work their socks off all year round to put this show on for your benefit, have been hard at work to make sure that these elections are being run in line with the current public health restrictions. If you are attending a polling station this year, you can have confidence that you can cast your vote safely. If you find yourself unable to attend a polling station due to self-isolation, contact your local council's elections office immediately (and definitely before 5pm on Thursday) as you will qualify for an emergency proxy vote.

The deadline to apply for a postal vote has passed. If you have a postal vote you should have received one by now. In Scotland almost a quarter of the electorate have secured postal votes for this election, which is the highest proportion on record; there's no reason to believe that similar increases won't happen in England and Wales.

The Britain Elects team have put a huge amount of work into preparing for these local elections. We are here to give you cold hard facts, facts which may turn out to be surprising. In fact I fully expect that some of the results will surprise, and that at least one ward will produce a result which makes my jaw drop. These previews have been researched to the best of my ability, in line with the Andrew's Previews policy of covering "all the right votes, but not necessarily in the right order"; but they can't and won't all turn out as expected. Any errors are, of course, my own.

We have never previously tried holding ordinary county council and district council elections together. Even in 1973, when the current local government structure was set up in many parts of England, the county and district elections were staggered with different tiers polling on different dates. Add the other polls on top of that, and this is going to make for some horribly complicated and protracted counts at a time when space in our counting halls is at a premium. Very few returning officers are going for a traditional overnight count this year; final results for the Scottish Parliament and the London Assembly won't be available until Saturday, and the count for several of the Police and Crime Commissioners won't even start until the Monday after the election. The election-watcher's vigil this May is going to be a long one. There will be plenty of time to hunker down with your snacks of choice and to read this primer on what to look out for in the results.

It only remains for me to wish the very best of luck to everybody participating in these elections—whether as a voter, as a candidate or as an administrator. Whoever you support, whoever you vote for, do have an enjoyable election, and I'll see you on the other side.

6th May 2021 Part V: Debrief

After four hard days and nights of counting, the largest ever set of UK local elections (in terms of ballot paper numbers) is over. Let's summarise what happened.

The Britain Elects team have mapped all the results beautifully[*], and you may wish to refer to this map when looking at the text below, as I haven't had time to prepare maps of my own. Results will go onto your columnist's own Local Elections Archive Project[†] in the usual slow timescale, although the by-election results are already there.

Scotland

Possibly the most consequential poll of all last week was that for the Scottish Parliament. This saw relatively little change, with the Scottish National Party having won 63 seats in 2016, two short of an overall majority; this time they finished on 64 seats, one short of a majority. That seat gain was the result of the retirement of the former Scottish Conservative leader Ruth Davidson, who is retiring to the Lords; the SNP picked up her former constituency of Edinburgh Central. The Conservatives offset that loss by gaining a seat from Labour in the Highlands and Islands region. The other party to gain seats in the Holyrood elections was the Greens, which took a seat from the Lib Dems in the North East region and from Labour in the Central region.

Overall the Scottish National Party now have (as stated) 64 MSPs, the Conservatives have 31, Labour 22, the Greens 8 and the Lib Dems 4. The SNP minority administration looks set to continue. With an increased majority for the pro-independence SNP and Greens, another referendum on independence for Scotland could be on the cards.

On the undercard, the Forth and Endrick by-election to Stirling council was

[*] `https://tinyurl.com/2p8w2wb7` [†] `https://www.andrewteale.me.uk/leap/`

won by the Conservatives, gaining a seat from the SNP.

Wales

The sixth Senedd Cymru elections (not the fifth, as I said in the preview) were a convincing win for the Labour party which now holds half of the seats in the Welsh Parliament. Labour's net gain of one seat was a result of unseating the former Plaid Cymru leader Leanne Wood in the Rhondda constituency. The Conservatives gained two constituencies, Brecon and Radnorshire from the Liberal Democrats and Vale of Clwyd from Labour, but the Lib Dems and Labour offset those losses by picking up regional seats which had been won by UKIP in 2016. UKIP were wiped out, with the Conservatives and Plaid as the main beneficiaries.

The new Senedd has 30 Labour MSs, 16 Conservatives, 13 Plaid and 1 Lib Dem. Labour intend to govern alone. In the last Senedd Elin Jones, the Plaid Cymru MS for Ceredigion, acted as Llywydd (equivalent to the Speaker of the Commons); if she wishes to continue in that role then Labour would have a working majority in the chamber, otherwise they would be forming a minority administration.

Plaid Cymru failed to defend the North Wales Police and Crime Commissionership, but their transfers ensured that Labour came from behind on first preferences to defeat the Conservatives 52–48 in the runoff. There was another come-from-behind victory for Plaid in Dyfed-Powys; the Conservatives had led 34.0–33.6 on first preferences but Plaid won the runoff convincingly. Labour had no trouble defending the PCCs for Gwent and South Wales.

The only seat to change hands among the Welsh local by-elections was in Rhondda Cynon Taf, where Labour gained the Penrhiwceiber division convincingly from the Cynon Valley Party. Their outgoing councillor, who had been controversially disqualified for not attending any meetings in six months, sought re-election but finished a distant second. The closest result was in the Aberavon division of Neath Port Talbot, where Labour held off Plaid Cymru by 30 votes, 677 to 647.

Greater London

Labour's Sadiq Khan was re-elected as Mayor of London as expected, although the result was closer than anticipated. On first preferences he led the Conservatives' Shaun Bailey by 40–35, increasing that lead to 55–45 in the runoff: 1,206,034 votes to 977,601.

The Labour party also went backwards in the London Assembly, losing one of the twelve seats they were defending. UKIP came nowhere near holding their two seats, and all the other parties in the Assembly picked up an extra London-wide seat. The new Assembly will have 11 Labour members, 9 Conservatives, 3 Greens and 2 Lib Dems.

On the undercard, three of London's 46 council by-elections resulted in a seat change. The Conservatives gained two seats from Labour, Chase ward in Enfield and East Barnet ward in Barnet, while the Green Party came nowhere near defending their Richmond council seat in Hampton Wick ward which went convincingly to the Liberal Democrats. The thirteen Official Monster Raving Loony candidates in the Chessington South ward of Kingston upon Thames polled 92 votes between them, with Undertaking Director Brunskill having the best score of 16 and Sam Squatch and Rev Robbie the Radical Recyclist sharing the wooden spoon on one vote each; six of the Loonies finished ahead of the Trade Unionist and Socialist Coalition candidate, who polled seven votes.

North East

Kim McGuinness was re-elected as the Labour PCC for Northumbria without fuss, defeating the Conservatives 60–40 in the runoff.

In vote terms, Northumberland council swung to Labour compared with May 2017, but England's first-past-the-post electoral system had other ideas. In 2017 the Conservatives had won 33 seats, one short of a majority, tied for first place in South Blyth and lost the drawing of lots to the Liberal Democrats. This year they won 33 seats, one short of a majority, tied for first place in Berwick West with Ord and lost the drawing of lots to the Liberal Democrats—and also tied for first place in Hartley and won the drawing of lots against Labour. That tiebreak means that Northumberland now has a Conservative overall majority. Don't let anybody tell you your vote never changed anything.

Labour remain in control of the five Tyne and Wear boroughs, but they lost another nine seats in Sunderland. Another year like that and it'll be No Overall Control time there. Norma Redfearn was re-elected as the Labour mayor of North Tyneside in the first round, with a 53–31 lead over the Conservatives.

The Labour vote in County Durham collapsed and they very nearly lost the police and crime commissionership. Labour's Joy Allen led the Conservatives' George Jabbour in the first count by 43.8% to 43.0%, going on to increase her lead in the runoff to 51–49. Labour have lost control of Durham council, losing 21 seats mostly to the Conservatives; the new council has 53 Labour councillors, 31 independents, 24 Conservatives, 17 Lib Dems and a Green Party member.

The Conservatives scored a clean sweep of the elections in the Tees Valley. Ben Houchen was re-elected as Mayor with a stonking 73–27 lead over Labour; the Tories gained the Cleveland PCC from Labour in the first round, Steve Turner enjoying a 54–29 lead over Labour; the Conservatives gained the Hartlepool parliamentary by-election, which was not close; all 13 Conservative candidates for the all-out council election in Hartlepool were elected, making them the largest party against 12 independents and 11 Labour councillors (it would appear that most of the clowns have now left the circus); and they won all ten local by-elections in the area, gaining Red Hall and Lingfield ward in Darlington from Labour, Billingham West ward in Stockton from independents and Bishopsgarth and Elm Tree ward in Stockton from the Lib Dems. The new Tory councillors for those wards are David Willis, Lee Spence and Hugo Stratton respectively. Interestingly the Greens had a go at the Darlington by-election in Hummersknott ward, normally a safe Conservative area, but they fell short.

North West

The Conservatives held the Cumbria PCC position in the first round, polling 54% against 26% for Labour and 20% for the Lib Dems.

With the cancellation of Cumbria's county and district council elections there were only by-elections to look forward to. Three of these were for Carlisle city council, and the Conservatives gained two of them: the marginal Harraby South and Parklands and the previously safe-Labour ward of Newtown and Morton North. Neville Lishman is the new councillor there. Those two gains mean that the Conservative minority administration in Carlisle is much more secure: they now have nineteen seats, just one short of a majority.

A flurry of by-elections in Allerdale has left the council finely balanced. The Conservatives held their marginal seat in Seaton and Northside ward, and gained seats from Labour in Christchurch, and Ellen and Gilcrux wards, but they lost Aspatria (a defection gain) to independent candidate Kevin Thurlow. The remaining district by-election in St John's ward saw Labour pick up a seat which had previously been held by an independent. That leaves Allerdale council with 18 Conservatives, 18 independents and 13 Labour councillors and a Conservative minority administration.

The Conservatives also made two county council gains in Allerdale. Candidate Debbie Garton picked up the independent-held seat in St John's and Great Clifton division, defeating Labour by 18 votes; while the Lib Dems finished third in their defence of Cockermouth North.

However, the Tories didn't have it all their own way on the county council, with the Ulverston West by-election going to the Green Party's Judy Filmore. Elsewhere in South Lakeland, the Conservatives lost the by-election in Broughton and Coniston ward which was picked up by the Lib Dems.

Over the sands in Lancashire, the Police and Crime Commissionership was a gain for the Conservatives whose candidate Andrew Snowden defeated Labour's Clive Grunshaw 51–49 in the runoff. The Conservatives increased their majority on the county council, which now stands at 48 Conservatives, 32 Labour, 2 Lib Dems and 2 Greens. They also picked up by-elections in Norbreck ward, Blackpool (from an independent) and Kellet ward, Lancaster (from the Lib Dems).

Some MRP-based polling before the election had suggested that Labour might win a majority on Burrnley council with Hyndburn going hung. This would have required Labour to gain seats in Burrnley at the same time as the Tories taking a clean sweep in Hyndburn, which seemed unlikely at best given that the two towns are demographically very similar. And indeed "no change" was the outcome in those two boroughs. Burrnley is now more hung than it was before, with 18 Labour councillors, 9 Conservatives, 8 Lib Dems, 5 Greens and 5 localists; the Tories did gain four seats in Hyndburn, but Labour are still comfortably in control with 22 seats against 12 Conservatives and an independent who has broken the borough's two-party duopoly. All of Pendle council was up for election and the Conservatives are back in control there with 18 councillors to 10 Labour and 5 Lib Dems. As I suggested, Rossendale council is now hung although Labour still hold half of the seats.

There wasn't much change in Blackburn with Darwen, but the election of the Tories' Tiger Patel (whose campaign video* went viral during the campaign) has already resulted in an improvement for his Audley and Queen's Park constituents. The broken swings in the video have now been fixed. Despite an all-out election being held the Tories failed to make much headway in Chorley which now has a 29–13 Labour lead. More gains for Our West Lancashire, and a surprise Labour loss to an independent in Skelmersdale, mean that West Lancashire council is now hung: Labour have 26 seats, the Conservatives have 20 and the OWLs and independents have 8.

Merseyside didn't see many shocks, although Labour put in an embarrassing performance in the Mayor of Liverpool election. Joanne Anderson (no relation of Big Joe) polled just 38% of the first preferences across the city and was taken to a runoff against independent candidate Stephen Yip, although she did win that runoff easily. By contrast, Steve Rotheram was re-elected as Mayor of the Liverpool City Region in the first round with 58%, and Labour's Emily Spurrell

* https://youtu.be/B3KBajUoEjo

is the new Merseyside PCC with 57% of the vote in the first round. Wirral council remains hung with Labour losing three seats to the Greens and one to the Conservatives; the council now stands at 30 Labour councillors, 23 Conservatives, 6 Lib Dems, 5 Greens and 2 independents.

The rematch between the Tories' John Dwyer and Labour's David Keane for the Cheshire PCC position resulted in a gain for Dwyer, who won the runoff 53–47. The other main change in Cheshire is that the Conservatives have become the main opposition on Warrington council, which now has 36 Labour councillors, 11 Conservatives, 8 Lib Dems and 3 independents.

Andy Burnham was re-elected as mayor of Greater Manchester with a whopping 67–20 lead over the Conservative candidate Laura Burns and a majority of over 335,000 votes. The bus companies had better watch out. Paul Dennett was re-elected as mayor of Salford in the first round with a 59–23 lead over the Tories' Arnie Saunders, who was re-elected to the council in his renamed ward of Kersal and Broughton Park. Saunders is a prominent rabbi and Kersal and Broughton Park is the most Jewish ward in England; however, the Tories' tactic of running a religiously balanced slate of two Jews and a Muslim there backfired as the voters elected the two Jewish Tory candidates and a Jewish Lib Dem, giving the Liberal Democrats their first Salford council win since 2008.

Over the border in Bury, the Conservatives also lost the strongly-Jewish ward of Sedgley (in Prestwich) and failed to gain Unsworth. The ruling Labour party lost Elton ward to the Tories and all three wards in Radcliffe, but gained Sedgley and Ramsbottom and held St Mary's ward in Prestwich to stay in control of Bury council with a majority of one seat.

The Conservatives have consolidated their position as the largest party on Bolton council, winning nine of the borough's twenty wards to equal the record they set (on the current boundaries) in 2008. Bolton council now stands at 21 Conservative councillors, 19 Labour, 14 localists, 5 Lib Dems and a UKIP councillor. The Conservative minority administration in the Greatest Town should continue.

Despite a dubious performance in Oldham where the council leader lost his seat, the worst news for Labour in the 2021 Greater Manchester elections came from Stockport where the Liberal Democrats are now the largest party. Stockport council now stands at 26 Lib Dems, 25 Labour, 8 Conservatives, 3 Heald Green residents and one Green Party councillor. The Liberal Democrats look set to take over the council leadership from Labour and form a minority administration.*

* In fact the Labour minority administration continued, with Conservative support.

Yorkshire and the Humber

Labour's Tracy Brabin is the new Mayor of West Yorkshire, defeating the Tories' Matt Robinson by a 60–40 margin in the runoff. This will have consequences: Brabin has resigned her seat in Parliament, and a by-election will be held for the Batley and Spen constituency in due course.*

Batley and Spen is the northern constituency covering the Kirklees metropolitan district, which remains hung following the elections. There are now 33 Labour councillors, 19 Conservatives, 9 Lib Dems, 3 Greens and 5 independents of various hues. The Conservatives had a very good election in Wakefield, gaining six wards including parts of the old coalfield, but Labour remain firmly in control there as they are in the other three West Yorkshire boroughs.

Sheffield city council has fallen into no overall control after another bad performance by Labour, who lost eight seats to the Greens and Lib Dems. The council now stands at 41 Labour councillors, 29 Lib Dems, 13 Greens and a Conservative—that's the first council seat the Conservatives have won in Sheffield since 2004. In 2004 the Tory ward was middle-class Dore and Totley; this year they gained the isolated steelworking ward of Stocksbridge and Upper Don from UKIP. The results in neighbouring Barnsley this year weren't as wacky as those in 2019, but again we have a Conservative win in unusual territory for them: the Tories and Labour tied for first place in Rockingham ward, with the Conservatives winning the drawing of lots. Hopefully they celebrated their Rockingham win with some wine gums.†

There were big changes on Rotherham council, which returned a much-reduced Labour majority. Labour now have 32 councillors, the Conservatives (who didn't have a single seat before the election) are now the main opposition on 20, the independent ex-UKIP group held just 4 of their seats and the Lib Dems won 3. The Labour mayor of Doncaster Ros Jones was taken to a runoff but was easily re-elected with a 60–40 margin over the Conservatives. Alan Billings was re-elected as the Labour PCC for South Yorkshire in the first round.

In North Yorkshire there was almost a clean sweep for the Conservatives, with Philip Allott becoming PCC with a 61–39 margin over Labour in the runoff and the Tories sweeping all but one of the local by-elections. They gained a county council seat in Harrogate Bilton and Nidd Gorge from the Lib Dems, and picked up the open seat on Selby council vacated by the Yorkshire Party. The one that got away was the Barden Fell by-election to Craven council, where independent councillor David Pighills was re-elected in the by-election caused

* See page 242. † `https://youtu.be/wioh5qUj7fM`. For more on Rockingham ward see *Andrew's Previews 2017*, page 383.

by his own disqualification under the six-month non-attendance rule.

Having only been selected at the last possible moment, the Conservatives' Jonathan Evison is now the Humberside Police and Crime Commissioner. He gained the position from Labour's Keith Hunter by a 53–47 margin. There was more good news for the local Conservatives, whose candidate Joanne Saunby gained a by-election in the previously safe-Labour Ashby ward of Scunthorpe, while the party held the other by-elections they were defending in North Lincolnshire and the East Riding and greatly increased their majority on North East Lincolnshire council. The Labour majority on Hull city council is now down to three seats: they have 30 councillors against 26 Lib Dems and one Conservative.

East Midlands

In the East Midlands PCC elections the Conservatives scored a clean sweep. They convincingly gained Derbyshire from Labour, winning the runoff 56–44; gained Leicestershire from Labour by the even more convincing margin of 57–43; held Lincolnshire and Northamptonshire in the first round; and gained Nottinghamshire from Labour by 51.4–48.6.

Nottinghamshire county council now has a Conservative overall majority, with 37 seats against 15 Labour, 13 independents (most of whom are Zadroznyite) and a Lib Dem. The party performed particularly well in Bassetlaw, where the Labour group leader on the county council lost his Worksop North seat; the Conservatives also picked up two open seats in by-elections to Bassetlaw council. Ben Bradley, the Tory MP for Mansfield, will take over as leader of the county council.

In Derbyshire a Conservative administration was re-elected for the first time as the party increased its majority. As I suggested Labour gained seats in High Peak, where Ruth George defeated Edwina Currie in the Whaley Bridge battle of ex-MPs, but they lost all their county seats in Amber Valley and performed badly in the Bolsover district. The new council has 45 Conservative councillors against 14 Labour, 4 Lib Dems and a Green.

The Conservatives also gained Derbyshire's Amber Valley council directly from Labour, with Labour holding only two of the wards they were defending. Amber Valley now stands at 28 Conservatives, 16 Labour and a Green. In the county's local by-elections the Conservatives gained four wards from Labour: Masson ward in Derbyshire Dales (by three votes), the Hallam Fields ward of Ilkeston and the Nottingham Road ward of Long Eaton, both in Erewash district (Nottingham Road was a safe ward taken by the Conservatives' Bryn Lewis), and the Eckington South and Renishaw by-election in North East Derbyshire district. There is one bright spot for Derbyshire Labour amidst this wreckage: following a by-election gain from an independent in Pinxton ward, they now have overall control of Bolsover council.

In by-elections in Lincolnshire and Leicestershire the Conservatives gained Bassingham and Brant Broughton ward in North Kesteven from the Lincolnshire independents, Skirbeck ward in Boston town from an independent, and Ibstock East ward in North West Leicestershire from Labour. North West Leicestershire council also had a by-election in Worthington and Breedon ward for the longest-standing vacancy in the UK's local government, the previous Conservative councillor having died in November 2019; it's fitting that this was one of the first results to come through on Thursday night.

The two new Northamptonshire councils delivered large Conservative majorities. North Northamptonshire has 60 Conservative seats against 14 Labour, 3 Greens and an independent; West Northamptonshire's ruling Tory group will have 66 seats opposed by 20 Labour, 5 Lib Dems and two independents.

West Midlands

The standout story in the West Midlands is the re-election of the Conservative West Midlands mayor Andy Street, the former chairman of the John Lewis Partnership. Street nearly won on first preferences, with a 49–40 lead over Labour's Liam Byrne MP; Byrne narrowed the margin to 54–46 in the runoff, but that was too far behind to come back from. Clearly the West Midlands' voters really like John Lewis. The West Midlands Police and Crime Commissioner election, with the same boundaries and the same franchise, returned the same 54–46 margin—but for Labour's Simon Foster.

The good performance by Andy Street was mirrored by good Conservative performances in the Black Country. They gained 12 seats on the hung Dudley council, with Labour holding only three of the wards they were defending, to take a large majority of 46–24 (with two independent councillors). The Tories increased their majority in Walsall, made significant gains in Wolverhampton and broke through in Sandwell where the Labour monopoly has been broken: Sandwell now has 58 Labour councillors, 9 Conservatives, 4 independents and one vacant seat. Two of the Birmingham by-elections, in Oscott and Quinton wards, also fell to the Conservatives.

In Nuneaton and Bedworth, which was hung before the elections, the Conservatives gained ten seats and now have an overall majority with 24 councillors against just seven for Labour, two independents and a Green. Six of the seven Labour councillors are up for re-election next year—can they afford another year like this? The Conservatives also gained two seats from Labour in by-elections to North Warwickshire council.

There was another bloodbath for Labour in Staffordshire. The party held only four seats on the county council, and lost every seat they were defending on Cannock Chase council which now has a Conservative majority for the first time. The Conservatives gained four by-elections, two from independents in Cheadle, one from Labour in Brownhills and one from Labour in the Moorcroft ward of Stoke-on-Trent. The only bright spot for Staffordshire Labour was that they gained a seat from an independent in the Eton Park by-election to East Staffordshire council, in one of the grottier parts of Burton upon Trent.

To the south of Birmingham, the Conservatives won a clean sweep of all nine seats up for election in Redditch, gaining seven seats from Labour. Redditch council now stands at 25 Conservatives and just four for Labour—fewer Labour councillors than neighbouring Bromsgrove. Worcester council now has a Conservative majority, although the all-party administration might well continue there. Despite losing six seats in Shropshire, including that of the council leader, the Conservatives remain in control there; and elsewhere in the Marches they picked up by-elections in the Donnington ward of Telford (from Labour) and the Newton Farm ward of Hereford (from an independent).

The three PCC elections here outside the West Midlands metropolitan area (Warwickshire, Staffordshire and West Mercia) were all Conservative holds in the first round.

South West

As we now enter the south of England, the story of the 2021 local elections starts to change. Whereas the North and Midlands were characterised by Conservative gains, the South was a much more patchy picture. We can see this in Gloucestershire, where the Conservatives lost three seats on the county council and only narrowly remain in control: they have 28 seats against 16 Lib Dems, 5 Labour and 4 Greens. Gloucester council is listed by the BBC as a Conservative gain from No Overall Control, but it was only hung because two of the previous Tory seats were vacant; the Conservatives benefited from a Labour collapse here to increase their majority. Stroud council remains hung with the Green Party having made significant gains; the Labour-Green-Lib Dem coalition may well continue here. There was good news for the Tories in the Gloucestershire PCC contest: the independent outgoing PCC Martin Hurl finished third, and the Conservatives beat the Lib Dems 60–40 in the runoff.

Eleven years after losing his seat in the House of Commons to Jacob Rees-

Mogg, Labour's Dan Norris is back on the frontline of politics as the new mayor of the West of England. He led in the first round with 33% against 29% for the Conservatives, 22% for the Green Party and 16% for the Lib Dems, and ran away with the transfers to win the runoff by a 60–40 margin. Norris' win owes a lot to a good performance in Bristol, whose Labour mayor Marvin Rees was re-elected; he led on the first round with 36% against 26% for the Greens, 19% for the Conservatives and 11% for the Liberal Democrats, and went on to beat the Greens 56–44 in the runoff. However, Rees will have to work hard to get his programme through Bristol city council after the Greens made significant gains there: the new Bristol council has 24 Labour councillors against 24 Greens, 14 Conservatives and 8 Lib Dems, and all 24 Labour councillors will have to vote to avoid the council reaching the two-thirds majority needed to block the mayor's budget.

There was better news for the Bristol Conservatives, in that they gained the post of Avon and Somerset Police and Crime Commissioner from independent PCC Sue Mountstevens who didn't seek re-election. The Tories' Mark Shelford led in the first round with 35% against 24% for Labour, 16% for the Greens and 13% for the Lib Dems; Labour picked up most of the transfers but were too far behind, and Shelford won the runoff 52–48. The Conservatives also picked up the by-election in the Wells St Thomas' ward of Mendip council, gaining the seat from the Lib Dems who messed up their nomination papers and failed to get on the ballot.

This column is going to have to come back to Wiltshire very soon* as we have *already* had the ludicrous Police and Crime Commissioner by-election rules triggered. Jonathan Seed, the Conservative candidate for PCC who won the runoff 63–37 against the Lib Dems, is ineligible for that office due to a previous drink-driving conviction. He will have to settle for being one of the 61-strong ruling Conservative group on Wiltshire council—that's a loss of seven seats in 2017, although boundary changes make it difficult to pinpoint exactly which seats have changed hands. By contrast the Conservatives increased their majority in Swindon, whose council now stands at 36 Conservatives, 20 Labour and an independent ex-Conservative who has resigned from the council since the election.

The Dorset PCC election went to a runoff between the Conservatives' David Sidwick and independent Dan Hardy, who had the endorsement of the previous independent PCC. Sidwick won the runoff by 62–38. The Conservatives gained the safe Lib Dem ward of Canford Heath at a by-election to Bournemouth, Christchurch and Poole council, shoring up the Conservative minority adminis-

* See page 329 for the Wiltshire PCC by-election.

tration which remains two seats short of a majority.

The Conservatives held the Devon and Cornwall PCC election very comfortably indeed, beating Labour 65–35 in the runoff. This comes off the back of a good result in Plymouth where they gained six seats from Labour and are now the largest party; the city council stands at 26 Conservative councillors, 24 Labour and 7 seats for a Tory splinter group. There should be enough votes here for the Conservatives to form an administration to run Plymouth. In Devon by-elections the Conservatives picked up an open seat on East Devon council in Whimple and Rockbeare ward, and gained two seats on Mid Devon council in Tiverton's Castle and Westexe wards (from the Lib Dems and an independent respectively).

The Tories also took back control of Cornwall council from a Lib Dem-Independent coalition. Cornwall now has a small Tory majority with 47 seats, against 16 independents, 13 Lib Dems, five Labour, five seats for the Cornish nationalist party Mebyon Kernow, and a Green councillor. Britain's smallest principal council by population, the Council of the Isles of Scilly, is non-partisan.

Eastern

The ordinary elections in Norfolk saw little change, but the by-elections were another matter. The Conservatives won all four of them, gaining two seats in Great Yarmouth (Claydon ward from Labour, the open Ormesby ward from an independent) and picking up a Lib Dem seat in the Coastal ward of North Norfolk. This column is scheduled to return to Norfolk next month to cover the contests in the Sewell division of the county council and the Sewell ward of Norwich city council, which were postponed after the Conservative candidate died.

Over the border in Suffolk the Conservatives did well in Ipswich this year, gaining six seats; however, Labour still have a comfortable majority there. The Tories improved their position on West Suffolk council, gaining the Lakenheath by-election from an independent and confirming a defection gain from an independent councillor in the Moreton Hall ward of Bury St Edmunds.

Cambridgeshire, on the other hand, provided one of the sensations of the election with the Cambridgeshire and Peterborough mayoralty. On the first count the outgoing Conservative mayor James Palmer led with 41% of the vote against 33% for Labour's Nik Johnson and 27% for the Lib Dems' Aidan van der Weyer, but the Lib Dem transfers went strongly to Johnson giving him a 51.3–48.7 win in the runoff. Nik Johnson's election as Mayor of Cambridgeshire and Peterborough means he has vacated his seat on Huntingdonshire council, and Andrew's Previews will be back to cover the resulting by-election in St Neots in due course.

The Conservatives also lost control of Cambridgeshire county council thanks to the Liberal Democrats winning all but two of the county seats in the South Cambridgeshire district, which surrounds the city of Cambridge and includes all the villages in the city's hinterland; as such it's full of people associated with Cambridge's universities who are very annoyed at a number of the current government's policies. When I draft the annual megapreviews there always seems to be one district that gets accidentally left out, and this year I'm afraid it was South Cambridgeshire: there were four by-elections to the district council on 6th May, with the Liberal Democrats gaining *Girton*[*] ward from an independent councillor, and holding the wards of *Harston and Comberton*[†], *Melbourn*[‡], and *Milton and Waterbeach*[§]. My apologies for not mentioning these in Part III of the 6th May Preview.

Cambridgeshire county council doesn't include the city of Peterborough, which saw very little change this year. The Tories did manage to hold on to the Cambridgeshire PCC, but only by 53–47 in the runoff over Labour.

To the south, the county of Essex presents a mixed picture. To start at the eastern end in Tendring district, the Conservatives picked up the open seat left behind by UKIP in West Clacton and Jaywick Sands ward, while the Holland-on-Sea and Eastcliff Matters group lost Eastcliff ward to an independent candidate. Neighbouring Colchester remains hung with very little nett change: the current rainbow coalition of Lib Dems, Labour and independents may well be joined by the Green Party which won its first seat on the council.

The Conservatives struck back in Chelmsford district, gaining the Moulsham Lodge by-election from the Lib Dems. Things were different in neighbouring Maldon, which now officially has an independent majority following an independent gain from the Conservatives in the Tollesbury by-election. In Uttlesford district in the north of the county, the ruling Residents for Uttlesford group recovered a seat in Newport ward which they had lost to defection, but lost a by-election to the Conservatives in The Sampfords ward.

The South Essex councils were a mixed bunch. The Tories did well in the hung council of Southend-on-Sea, but they were facing a difficult map this year and an overall majority was never likely. Neighbouring Castle Point is suddenly on a knife-edge after an independent group gained three seats on the mainland

[*] *South Cambridgeshire, Girton*: LD 967 C 621 Lab 344 Grn 246 [LD gain from Ind] [†] *South Cambridgeshire, Harston and Comberton*: LD 1785 C 1459 Lab 519 Grn 335 [‡] *South Cambridgeshire, Melbourn*: LD 1510 C 992 Grn 256 [§] *South Cambridgeshire, Milton and Waterbeach*: LD 1255 C 1069 Lab 915 Grn 424

in Benfleet; with Canvey Island in the hands of a localist party, the council now stands at 21 Conservative councillors against 20 independents and localists. The Conservatives confirmed their majority in Thurrock and gained control of Basildon council, which had previously been run by Labour and a number of independent groups.

The standout result for the Essex Conservatives, however, was that in Harlow where they won ten of the borough's eleven wards and gained the council from Labour. The Tories have done the clean sweep of Harlow's county seats on a number of occasions, but in an even year the district ward boundaries tend to concentrate Conservative voters in four safe wards so this is an even more impressive performance than it looks. The new Harlow council has 20 Conservative councillors, 12 Labour and one vacant seat.

Over in Hertfordshire we saw a similarly impressive Conservative result in Welwyn Hatfield district. The Tories had been underperforming here in the last electoral cycle, but unexpectedly won 14 of the 16 wards up for election with Labour wiped out. The new council has 28 Conservative councillors, 11 Lib Dems and 9 Labour.

Hertfordshire also includes the only council where the Liberal Democrats gained majority control this year: St Albans, where they picked up all the seats Labour were defending and broke through in the traditionally-Tory town of Harpenden. The new St Albans council has 30 Lib Dem councillors, 23 Conservatives, 2 independents, 2 Labour and a Green. These gains were reflected at county council level too, but the Conservatives are still in control of Hertfordshire county council with a reduced majority of 46 out of 78 seats. The only local by-election in Hertfordshire to result in a seat change was another Conservative loss: Labour gained the Hertsmere ward of Borehamwood Kenilworth.

The Conservatives held all the Police and Crime Commissioner contests in the Eastern region, including Bedfordshire where there were no local elections apart from two by-elections to Luton council. The Liberal Democrats gained the Round Green by-election from Labour, who held the High Town by-election.

South East

For our final region in this review of the 6th May elections, we start with a Conservative win in the brand-new Buckinghamshire council. The ruling Conservative group here is the largest outside of the House of Commons, with 113 (count em!) councillors; the opposition is made up of 15 Lib Dems, 14 independents, 4 Labour and a Green councillor. On the previous Buckinghamshire county council the Conservatives held 41 out of 49 seats; the new council is three times the size of the old, so 113 councillors, while an impressively large number, is ten seats behind the Conservatives' notional performance four years ago. Andrew's Previews will travel to Buckinghamshire in the near future for the parliamentary by-election in Chesham and Amersham, for which I hope to be able to offer more coherent analysis.

The best Conservative result in the Thames Valley police area came in the new city of Milton Keynes, where they gained six seats and are now the largest party again. The new MK council has 24 Conservative councillors, 19 Labour, 13 Lib Dems and an independent. Although they held the relevant seat in Woughton and Fishermead without fuss, Labour's campaign in Milton Keynes will not have been helped by an entry for the Councillors Behaving Badly file: former Labour councillor Shammi Akter had resigned in February 2021 after receiving an eight-month suspended sentence for child neglect. Labour run a minority administration in MK which the Conservatives may now attempt to overturn.

The Conservatives also did well to lose only one seat in the Cherwell district of northern Oxfordshire, given the carnage that took place on the county council. The 2013 and 2017 results had left the Conservatives one seat away from an overall majority; this year they lost nine seats to leave the county council at 22 Conservatives, 21 Lib Dems, 15 Labour, 3 Greens and 2 independents. This Conservative total includes a gain from Labour in Banbury Ruscote division, where it appears that the Tory candidate was wrongly declared elected after the Conservative and Labour vote totals were accidentally transposed. Labour have indicated that they will go to the Election Court to have the result overturned. More news on that as we get it.*

Despite the general Tory bloodbath in southern Oxfordshire the party did gain two by-elections in that area: Didcot North East (in South Oxfordshire district) from an independent and Grove North (in Vale of White Horse district) from the Lib Dems. The Conservatives also did well enough to hold onto West Oxfordshire and the Wokingham district of Berkshire, although they are still losing seats in those areas.

In Hampshire the Conservatives impressively won control of Southampton city council, gaining seven wards from Labour to take a 25–23 lead. However, on the Tory side this was offset by the loss of Isle of Wight council which is now hung, with 18 Conservative councillors, 17 independents, and 2 Greens, 1 Labour and 1 Lib Dem councillor holding the balance of power. The Conservatives are now again the largest party on the hung Portsmouth council after the ruling Lib Dems lost two seats: the Tories now have 16 seats there, the Lib Dems 15, and there are 7 Labour and four independent councillors. The other hung council

* For the outcome of this petition see page 334.

in Hampshire is the Hart district, based on Fleet and surrounding towns on the M 3 corridor, where the ruling Lib Dem-Community Campaign coalition lost a seat to the Conservatives.

On the local by-election front, the Conservatives gained two seats on Test Valley council from a now-collapsed Andover localist party. The St Michael ward of Winchester was the last ordinary district council ward to declare its result: it was originally supposed to be counted on Friday, but was delayed until Saturday due to a fire alarm at the count venue, and the count then had to be adjourned until Monday after a recount was requested.

The performance of the Surrey Conservatives was nothing to write home about, given the high expectations psephologists have of them. Following three Liberal Democrat gains in Woking the Conservative minority administration there is now in trouble: the new council is finely balanced with 13 Conservatives, 12 Lib Dems, 3 Labour and 2 independent councillors. The Tories remain in control of Surrey county council but lost fourteen seats: the new council has 47 Conservatives against 16 Residents and independents, 14 Lib Dems, and two each from the Greens and Labour. There was good news for the Conservatives in Surrey's local by-elections: they gained Staines South ward in Spelthorne district and Bagshot ward in Surrey Heath district, both from the Liberal Democrats.

In Sussex, the strange situation in Crawley has not been resolved. Labour did rather better here than a few other New Towns we have covered, as they held their losses to one seat: the new Crawley council is finely balanced at 18 Conservatives, 17 Labour and one ex-Labour independent. I indicated in the Preview that Labour were on course for major seat gains in Worthing, and they delivered on that: the Conservatives now have a majority of one on the council, with 19 Conservative councillors against 15 Labour and 3 Lib Dems.

This poor Conservative performance wasn't repeated in the coastal districts outside Worthing. In Arun district the Tories gained two by-elections from the Liberal Democrats (one in Littlehampton, the other in Bognor Regis) to improve their position as the largest party, and they may now make another attempt to depose the minority Lib Dem administration. In Adur district, based on Shoreham-by-Sea between Worthing and Brighton, the collapse of UKIP was to the benefit of the Conservatives who increased their majority. Other local by-elections saw the Conservatives gain a seat in Mid Sussex from an independent in Copthorne and Worth ward.

The ruling Conservatives lost seats on both Sussex county councils, with Labour the main beneficiaries in West Sussex and the Greens breaking through in East Sussex. East Sussex county council is now very close with 27 Conservative councillors, 11 Lib Dems, 5 Labour, 4 Greens and 3 independents. The Greens also performed well in two by-elections in Brighton, picking up Hollingdean and Stanmer ward from Labour to shore up their minority administration on Brighton and Hove council. Other by-elections in East Sussex saw the Liberal Democrats gain the Hailsham North ward of Wealden council from the Conservatives.

The main story in Kent comes from Tunbridge Wells, where the Conservatives have lost another six seats and control of the council. There are 24 Tory councillors left, half of the council. against 13 Lib Dems, 6 Labour, 5 members of the Tunbridge Wells Alliance and an independent.

The other Kent district council up for election this year was Maidstone, where by contrast an excellent Conservative performance saw them gain five seats and a majority of the council. Maidstone now stands at 29 Conservatives, 17 Lib Dems, 5 independents and 4 Labour councillors.

Thanet council might also see a change in control following three seat changes in by-elections. The Conservatives gained Newington ward in Ramsgate from Labour and Dane Valley ward from the ex-UKIP Thanet Independents, while Labour lost Central Harbour ward in Thanet to the Green Party. Thanet council now has 27 Conservative councillors, 17 Labour, 6 Thanet Independents, 4 Greens and 2 other independents, with the leadership currently vacant and to be decided at a full council meeting this week. Other Kent local by-elections saw four more Conservative gains from Labour: Beaver ward in Ashford, Mill Hill ward in Deal (Dover council), Westcourt ward in Gravesham and Sheerness ward in Swale.

That completes our review of what changed in the May 2021 local elections. This was a marathon in every sense, and an enormous vote of thanks is due to all the people who made these elections happen: the hard-pressed returning officers, electoral services teams and poll staff recruited and employed by our local councils. They have had a horrible job to do this year, and (with the possible exception of the deputy returning officer for Cherwell district) have performed it with the high standards we have come to expect. Thank you. Thank you all.

Thanks are also due to those who participated: the candidates, and the voters. I had been asked before the election whether I thought that turnout would fall as a result of public health restrictions; based on what had been happening in the Scottish and Welsh local by-elections I never believed this would happen, and indeed the final reckoning is that turnout has generally been at or above the average for these types of election. The Scottish Parliament elections had the highest turnout on record, with more electors casting votes in Scotland than in London.

The district councillors elected this year, the police and crime commissioners, and most of the combined authority mayors will serve short terms of only three years and will be due for re-election in 2024. This is so that we can get back to the electoral cycle which we had before democracy paused in March 2020. May 2024 is also the scheduled date of the next general election, so the administrators' nightmare may well be repeated on steroids in three years' time. Watch this space.

In the meantime, for the first time since the winter of 2019–20 your columnist can now finally see the bottom of the list of future council vacancies. That feels *so* good. The only dates scheduled at the moment are for the two postponed polls in Norwich and a forthcoming by-election in Aberdeenshire, which will take place on 17th June, and Andrew's Previews will return then. Before that, we have this week's parliamentary by-election in Airdrie and Shotts for which there is a separate Parliamentary Special preview. I hope you will join me for those polls, and after a short recovery period from these elections I look forward to restarting Andrew's Previews in earnest, to once again bring you all the right votes—but not necessarily in the right order. Stay tuned.

13th May 2021: Parliamentary Special

After the excitement of last week, there is one by-election on 13th May 2021:

Airdrie and Shotts

House of Commons; caused by the resignation of Scottish National Party MP Neil Gray.

> An honest man's the noblest work of God.
>
> —Alexander Pope, *An Essay on Man*

It all started with the monks. In 1140 a group of monks came to the Lothian area from Melrose abbey, under the patronage of King David I, and founded a Cistercian religious house called Newbattle Abbey. The abbey thrived, with many kings of Scotland making generous bequests, including (in 1160) a grant from Malcolm IV of extensive lands in central Scotland. That area became known as the Monklands.

The largest town in the Monklands was traditionally Airdrie, located on high ground in the middle of the Central Belt. Airdrie became a market town in 1695 by an Act of the old Scottish Parliament, and by the early nineteenth century it was an important weaving and coalmining centre. Following the Radical War of 1820 the town became an independent burgh with a rather wide franchise for the time: anybody who could scrape together three guineas was entitled to vote here, and in the first local elections here in 1821 a boy under the age of 10 is recorded as having cast a vote.

Airdrie marks the eastern end of what might be termed the Greater Glasgow area, and the area to the east of Airdrie is still mostly agricultural with no large towns until Livingston. This rural area is at a relatively high altitude, which explains why Airdrie was bypassed by the original railway and canal links between Edinburgh and Glasgow (which ran on lower ground via Falkirk). The railway line through Airdrie is very much a secondary route between the two major cities, and wasn't fully reopened until 2010.

The only other significant population centre in this area is Shotts, where Andrew's Previews has been very recently. Shotts was primarily a mining town with some ironworking, but one of the major local employers now is the high-security prison HMP Shotts. The town lies on a different Edinburgh-Glasgow railway line, which has recently been electrified.

Normally in these Parliamentary Specials I start in 1885, because the redistribution of that year arising from the Third Reform Act more or less created the single-member constituency system which we have in Westminster to this day. Lanarkshire was a big winner from the Third Reform Act: its representation went up from two MPs to six, while the city of Glasgow (which was physically much smaller then than it is today) increased from three to seven members of Parliament. Part of this increase was masterminded by Donald Crawford, a Fellow of the Royal Society of Edinburgh, who was an advocate and political secretary to the Lord Advocate. Crawford was appointed to the Boundary Commission for Scotland in 1884 by Sir Charles Dilke, who was the president of the Local Government Board, one of the prime movers behind the Third Reform Act, the MP for Chelsea and a rising star of the Liberal Party. A year later Crawford was elected as an MP for the newly-drawn constituency of North East Lanarkshire, covering most of the area around Airdrie.

Donald Crawford wasted no time at all in making his mark in public affairs. In 1881 he had married Virginia Smith, a daughter of the Liberal MP and shipping magnate Thomas Smith. The marriage was not a happy one. By the time of the 1885 election, which Donald Crawford won with a narrow majority of 159 over the Unionists, Donald had sued for divorce on the grounds of an affair between Virginia and Sir Charles Dilke. A sensational trial in early 1886 granted the divorce and essentially destroyed the political career of Dilke, who lost his seat in the 1886 general election and never returned to the frontbenches. (By contrast, Virginia's representation did recover: she became a prominent feminist and suffragist.) Crawford was re-elected as MP for North East Lanarkshire in 1886 with an increased majority of 279 over the Liberal Unionists, although his seat was still very marginal. In 1892 he won a third term by 5,281 votes to 5,184 for the Unionists, a majority of 97.

Donald Crawford left the Commons in 1895 to become Sheriff of Aberdeen, and his seat was taken over in that year's general election by John Colville with a 537-vote majority over the Unionists. The father of the future Scottish secretary of the same name, John Colville was the Provost of Motherwell, a Lanarkshire county councillor, and ran an iron and steel manufacturing firm in Motherwell. He was re-elected easily in 1900 and the seat looked safe.

Not so. John Colville died in 1901 at the early age of 49, and the resulting North East Lanarkshire by-election was contested by John Smillie as the Scottish Workers candidate. Smillie, who by this time already had a number of parliamentary campaigns under his belt, was the president of the Scottish Miners' Federation and a founder member of the Independent Labour Party. The defending Liberal candidate was Cecil Harmsworth, the younger brother of the newspaper proprietors Alfred and Harold Harmsworth. Harmsworth and Smillie split the left-wing vote, allowing the Liberal Unionist Sir William Rattigan to win with a majority of 904. The 1901 North East Lanarkshire poll goes down as something which had become increasingly rare in recent years: a government gain in a parliamentary by-election.

Sir William Rattigan had come to the UK from a prominent legal career in India, having previously been vice-chancellor of Punjab University and a member of the Punjab's legislative council. One wonders whether the Scottish weather was all that agreeable to him. He died in 1904 at the age of 61, and by this time the Liberals were on the up. The Liberal Unionists had passed the right-wing nomination over to their Unionist partners who selected George Touch for the second North East Lanarkshire by-election. Touche, as George changed his name to a couple of years later after getting tired of people mispronouncing his surname, was a chartered accountant whose name survives as the Touche in the modern Big 4 accounting firm Deloitte Touche Tohmatsu (to give it its full name). The Scottish Workers candidate was the up-and-coming trade unionist John Robertson, who had started work down the pits at 13 and eventually rose to become MP for Bothwell. However, the winner on this occasion was the Liberals' Alexander Findlay, who ran a structural engineering firm in Motherwell and was provost of the town. Findlay won with a majority of 942, reversing the Liberal Unionists' gain in the 1901 by-election.

Findlay stood down at the January 1910 election and his seat was taken over by Thomas Wilson, a Glasgow solicitor and long-serving Lanarkshire county councillor who had been a Liberal election agent for many years. Wilson was re-elected in December 1910 but resigned from the Commons almost immediately, forcing a third North East Lanarkshire by-election in March 1911. James Millar, who held the by-election for the Liberals with a reduced majority of 1,200, was a prominent advocate who had been the MP for the St Andrews Burghs in the January–December 1910 Parliament; this by-election represented a quick return for him.

The mention of St Andrews Burghs brings up one of the more curious aspects of Scottish elections during this period: the use of District of Burghs constituencies grouping together a number of disconnected towns. One of these was the Falkirk District of Burghs, which from 1885 to 1910 connected together Falkirk (in Stirlingshire), Linlithgow (in the county now called West Lothian) and three Lanarkshire burghs: Lanark, Hamilton, and Airdrie. This separation could cause some tension, as was seen in 1885 when there was a dispute over the Liberal selection and the Hamilton Liberal Association nominated its own candidate (who subsequently withdrew, but was credited with 14 votes at the declaration). The Falkirk Burghs were generally Liberal during this period, but did return Liberal Unionist candidates in 1886 (by 19 votes), 1895 and 1900 and a number of other elections were marginal.

The 1918 redistribution dissolved the Falkirk Burghs and placed Airdrie in a new constituency with the name of Coatbridge, while most of the rural area around it (from Shotts to Easterhouse) became part of the North Lanarkshire constituency. The blast furnaces of the Industrial Revolution had created Coatbridge from almost nothing in the middle of the nineteenth century; the town grew up on a site west of Airdrie which was low-lying, relatively flat, and thus much easier for the canals and railways to serve than Airdrie was. Immigration from Ireland caused Coatbridge to boom and turned it into a strongly Catholic town, in contrast to Airdrie which remained a Protestant centre.

But by 1918 Coatbridge was already on the economic slide. All the ironstone under the Monklands had been worked out, raw materials were having to be imported from elsewhere, and the town's housing stock—which was horrifically overcrowded from the day it was built—had never been improved. Even in the 1930s, when the blast furnaces ceased firing and after a large proportion of the population had decamped south of the border to Corby, Coatbridge was still the most overcrowded town in Scotland.

It's in this context that we start to look at Airdrie's parliamentary history, as part of the Coatbridge constituency. Coatbridge's first election in 1918 was a Unionist versus Labour contest, with the government endorsing the Unionist candidate Arthur Buchanan who won easily. Buchanan came to the Commons from a long career in the Army including 25 years serving with the Gordon Highlanders; he had fought in the Boer War, and had spent the Great War at the Gordon Highlanders' depots in Aberdeen and France.

Buchanan was defeated in 1922 by the first Labour MP for Coatbridge. James C Welsh had started work in the pits at 12 and was a full-time mining official by this point. He was also a published novelist, drawing on his experience down the pits for his books *Songs of a Miner* and *The Underworld*. Buchanan won four terms as MP for the seat, being re-elected in 1924 by the narrow margin of 12,782 votes against 12,725 for the Unionist candidate Thomas Moore (later a long-serving MP for the Ayr Burghs).

In 1929 the Unionists changed candidate to a talented young sportsman called Lord Dunglass, who had played first-class cricket for Oxford University, Middlesex and MCC (on their tour of Argentina in 1926–27). The heir to the Earl of Home, Dunglass had joined the TA and by this point he was a captain in the Lanarkshire Yeomanry. Today we know him better as Alec Douglas-Home. This was the first parliamentary contest for the future Conservative prime minister, who lost Coatbridge in 1929 by 7,669 votes but learned valuable lessons for his later election campaigns.

The Labour collapse of 1931 swept away James C Welsh, who lost his seat to the Unionists' William Templeton by 1,501 votes. Templeton had been the MP for Banffshire in the 1924–29 parliament. He stood down in 1935 and Coatbridge resoundingly returned to the Labour fold: their candidate was the Reverend James Barr, who had been the MP for Motherwell from 1924 to 1931. Barr was a Presbyterian minister who had been strongly opposed to the 1929 merger of the United Free Church with the Church of Scotland, which may have helped him to pick up some extra votes in Airdrie.

Barr retired in 1945 and handed a safe seat on to Labour's Jean Mann, a campaigner for better housing and planning. This was not without controversy. At the time of the election Mann was a remunerated member of the Rent Tribunals established under the Rent of Furnished Houses Control (Scotland) Act 1943, and a select committee subsequently decided this was an "office of profit under the Crown" which disqualified her from being an MP. A special Act of Parliament (the Coatbridge and Springburn Elections (Validation) Act 1945) had to be rushed through to confirm her election and regularise her position.

The Coatbridge constituency's electorate grew from 31,557 in 1918 to 40,104 in 1945, partly as a result of the granting of the vote to women under 30 during this period. However, there was much higher population growth in the North Lanarkshire seat, which went from 40,014 electors in 1918 to 69,064 at the 1945 election—by far the largest seat in the county—thanks to the development of Glasgow suburbs within its boundaries. The former North East Lanarkshire Liberal MP James Millar didn't seek re-election here in 1918, choosing to contest Motherwell (which he lost), and the seat went to the Unionists' Robert McLaren who had the coalition's coupon. McLaren lost his seat in 1922 to Labour's Joseph Sullivan, the president of the Lanarkshire Miners' County Union and the first Labour MP for the area.

Sullivan lost his seat in 1924, the Unionists' Sir Alexander Sprot winning

North Lanarkshire with a majority of 2,028. Sprot had a distinguished military career, serving in Afghanistan and the Boer War, and he had the distinction of defeating the former Prime Minister Herbert Asquith in the 1918 general election. He went on to serve as MP for Asquith's old seat of East Fife until 1922.

Sir Alexander Sprot died in February 1929 at the age of 75, forcing a tricky by-election for the government. The Unionists nominated Lord Scone, the 29-year-old heir to the earldom of Mansfield and Mansfield. Joseph Sullivan had by now returned to Parliament by winning a by-election in Bothwell, and Labour needed a new candidate: they selected a 24-year-old schoolteacher from Fife called Jennie Lee who, like Scone, was fighting her first election campaign. Scone was old enough to vote; Lee was not, because only women aged 30 or over had the vote at the time. By the time the by-election took place on 21st March it was clear that a general election was imminent and the by-election winner would not serve for long. Jennie Lee won with a majority of 6,578, gaining the seat for Labour with a swing of almost 16%, and became the Baby of the House. She was re-elected in the general election two months later with a reduced majority over Scone, following the withdrawal of the Liberals.

Jennie Lee started as she meant to go on as a fiery left-winger. Her maiden speech was an all-out attack on the Conservatives' budget which included accusing Winston Churchill, then the Chancellor of the Exchequer, of "cant, corruption and incompetence". Churchill was impressed by the style, if not the content. Lee was opposed to the formation of the National Government under Ramsay MacDonald; she sought re-election in 1931 for the Independent Labour Party, but was one of many left-wingers swept away by the National Government landslide.

The Unionist candidate who defeated Lee was even younger than she was. Aged 26 at the time of the 1931 election, William Anstruther-Gray came from a military family and had gone from Eton and Oxford into the Coldstream Guards, serving in the Shanghai Defence Force in 1927–28. He enjoyed a majority of 4,693 over Jennie Lee in 1931, which increased to 5,034 at the 1935 election when the left-wing vote was split between Lee and an official Labour candidate.

Anstruther-Gray, who later represented Berwick and East Lothian for thirteen years, was the last Conservative or Unionist MP for North Lanarkshire. He was defeated in the 1945 Attlee landslide by Labour's Peggy Herbison, an English and history teacher who had been born and brought up in Shotts. Her father had recently died in a colliery accident, and his colleagues had put Herbison forward for the Labour nomination.

Peggy Herbison went on to serve as MP for North Lanarkshire for 25 years, retiring in 1970 from a seat where she had never been seriously threatened. She was a member of Harold Wilson's first Cabinet as Pensions and National Insurance minister (renamed to Social Security minister in 1966), serving at the top table until 1967. Herbison is also thought to have been the only woman to attend the first parliamentary assembly of the Council of Europe in 1949.

The neighbouring Coatbridge seat—which was renamed in 1950 as Coatbridge and Airdrie—also developed into a safe Labour constituency after the Second World War, with the exception of the 1959 election when Jean Mann retired and Labour changed candidate. James Dempsey won his first election by 22,747 votes to 21,953 votes for the Unionists, a majority of 794, but was not threatened thereafter.

Dempsey served seven terms as MP for Coatbridge and Airdrie, dying in office in 1982 at the age of 65. The resulting Coatbridge and Airdrie by-election in June 1982 returned Labour's Tom Clarke, who had started his political career in that 1959 election, aged 18, as James Dempsey's election agent. Clarke had served on Coatbridge town council from 1964 until its abolition in 1975, and had been provost of the successor Monklands council—covering Airdrie and Coatbridge—from 1974 to 1982. He won the by-election with no fuss whatsoever.

Tom Clarke went on to serve in the Commons until 2015, and is still with us at the age of 80. In the last New Year honours list he was knighted for his political and public service. However, he now leaves the story of Airdrie and Shotts. The 1983 redistribution radically redrew the parliamentary boundaries in this corner of Lanarkshire, placing Airdrie and Coatbridge into separate constituencies. The North Lanarkshire seat disappeared, with Shotts becoming part of the new constituency of Motherwell North, and much of the area to the north of Shotts joining with Airdrie to become the Monklands East constituency. Tom Clarke sought re-election in the Coatbridge-based seat of Monklands West, leaving Monklands East free for the Labour MP who had represented North Lanarkshire since 1970.

That man had also started his electoral career early, fighting the 1961 East Fife by-election as the Labour candidate while he was a 23-year-old law student. He graduated from Glasgow University in 1962 and became an advocate at the Scottish bar in 1967. John Smith was 31 years old when he was elected in 1970 as MP for North Lanarkshire, and he quickly rose through the ranks. He got on the ministerial ladder in October 1974 in the Department of Energy, and had the responsibility of getting the Callaghan government's bills for Scottish and Welsh devolution through the Commons. In November 1978 John Smith made the Cabinet, as President of the Board of Trade. It was his only Cabinet position.

John Smith served in the Shadow Cabinet throughout the 1979, 1983 and 1987 Parliaments, and he was elected leader of the Labour Party in 1992. With his election coming straight after Britain's ignominious exit from the European Exchange Rate Mechanism, Smith quickly took the Labour Party to a big lead in the opinion polls. The local elections on 5th May 1994 saw huge losses for the Major government.

Seven days later, on 12th May 1994, John Smith suffered a fatal heart attack. He left behind a wife, three daughters (one of whom, Sarah, is now the Scotland editor of BBC News) and a very tricky by-election for Labour to defend. While John Smith had dominated the national stage, things were not going well for the ruling Labour group on Monklands council. A well-publicised scandal, inevitably dubbed "Monklandsgate" by the press, alleged that there was a sectarian bias in the council's spending in favour of Coatbridge (it may be relevant to note here that all 17 Labour councillors were Catholics, although I should point out that the sectarian allegations were never proven) and that relatives of Labour councillors had been given preference for council jobs. The controversy led to a big increase in support for the Scottish National Party, which had run a distant second here in April 1992. They selected social worker Kay Ullrich who was standing for Parliament for the fourth time, while the Labour candidate was Helen Liddell, a former journalist and former aide to the press baron Robert Maxwell. Liddell won with a majority of just 1,640 votes over the SNP.

The constituency name of Airdrie and Shotts was created for the 1997 general election, with the Shotts area added to the Monklands East constituency. On the new boundaries, Liddell's seat reverted to safety in 1997 and 2001. Helen Liddell's parliamentary career peaked in 2001–03, when she served in Cabinet as Scottish secretary. She retired from the Commons in 2005 to become the British High Commissioner to Australia, and now sits in the Lords.

The most recent Scottish redistribution, in 2005, had reduced the number of constituencies in Scotland following the establishment of the Scottish Parliament. Airdrie and Shotts was left relatively untouched by this process, losing a small area to Motherwell and Wishaw and gaining the Holytown area from the abolished seat of Hamilton North and Bellshill. It also gained the MP for Hamilton North and Bellshill, John Reid. An MP since 1987 (originally representing Motherwell North), Reid was one of the big hitters of the Blair government and held a remarkable number of government posts. He entered Cabinet in 1999 as Scottish secretary, and served successively as Northern Ireland secretary (the first Catholic to hold that role), Labour Party chairman, Leader of the Commons, and Health Secretary. Following the 2005 election he was reshuffled to Defence Secretary, and finished his time in government with a year as Home Secretary—his seventh Cabinet position in eight years. Reid stepped down from the frontbenches at the end of the Blair administration, and retired to the Lords in 2010.

John Reid passed his seat on in 2010 to his parliamentary assistant Pamela Nash. She was 25 years old at the time of the election and became the Baby of the House. Iain Gray, then leader of the Labour group in the Scottish Parliament, went so far as to say that Nash had a "big future in Scottish politics".

To date that hasn't come to pass, thanks to the political realignment in Scotland following the 2014 independence referendum. Nash was defeated in 2015 on a 27% swing by the Scottish National Party candidate Neil Gray, who enjoyed a majority of almost 20%. A former athlete who had represented Scotland in the 400 metre race, Gray was 29 at the time of his election and had worked as a reporter for BBC Radio Orkney and as the office manager for the Nationalist MSP Alex Neil.

Which is a good point to discuss what has happened to this area in the Scottish Parliament. When the Holyrood Parliament was originally set up its 73 constituencies were the same as the Westminster seats (except that Orkney and Shetland were given separate representation), and as such there has been an Airdrie and Shotts constituency in that Parliament since 1999. Its first MSP was Karen Whitefield, who won easily in 1999 and 2003 but saw her majority fall to 1,446 votes in 2007.

The SNP's Alex Neil gained the seat in 2011 with a majority of 2,001 votes, and was re-elected easily in 2016. He retired at last week's Holyrood election after 22 years in office, having been elected from the SNP list for Central Scotland in 1999, 2003 and 2007. Neil served in the Scottish cabinet from 2011 to 2016, holding the Infrastructure and Capital Investment, Health and Wellbeing, and Social Justice portfolios. He was the only Scottish National Party MSP to have declared on the record a Leave vote in the 2016 EU membership referendum.

In the six years since 2015 Neil Gray has been re-elected twice to the House of Commons. His majority was cut to just 195 votes over Labour in June 2017, but recovered to 5,201 votes in December 2019. On that occasion he polled 45%, with Labour's Helen McFarlane on 32%, the Conservatives' Lorraine Nolan on 18% and no other candidate saving their deposit.

Following Alex Neil's retirement, Neil Gray sought and won the SNP nomination for the Holyrood Airdrie and Shotts constituency. On the Holyrood boundaries (which are slightly smaller than the Westminster seat, excluding Holytown and the village of Newmains) he beat Labour last week by 51% to 33%, a reduced majority of 5,468 votes. The Labour candidate here was Richard Leonard, who was leader of Scottish Labour from 2017 until January this year; Leonard is, however, back in Holyrood as one of the seven MSPs for the Central Scotland region.

The seat is entirely within the North Lanarkshire council area. The most

Figure 26: Wards of the Airdrie and Shotts constituency

recent Scottish council elections were in May 2017; as can be seen from Figure 26 the ward and parliamentary boundaries don't quite match up, but across the four wards wholly in the seat (the three Airdrie wards and Fortissat) the SNP polled 33% of the first preferences against 32% for Labour and 18% for the Conservatives. With proportional representation in effect, this translated into six SNP councillors, five Labour, four Conservatives and an independent. The seat also contains part of the Mossend and Holytown ward, which was close between Labour and the SNP in May 2017, and a small corner of the Murdostoun ward which had a large independent vote in May 2017. The independent councillor for Murdostoun ward, Robert McKendrick, has recently died and this column will return to North Lanarkshire in due course once the by-election to replace him is held.*

The Scottish National Party had required Gray to resign his Westminster

* See page 232.

seat in order to stand for Holyrood. The original plan had been to hold the two polls at the same time, but the returning officer for North Lanarkshire was unhappy with this citing public health grounds. As a result, the voters of Airdrie and Shotts are having to travel to the polls two weeks in succession.

Due in part to the high turnover of Scottish MPs at the last three Westminster elections, this is the first Westminster by-election in Scotland since Inverclyde in June 2011. It's also the first ever parliamentary by-election at which the Scottish National Party are defending. Their candidate is Anum Qaisar-Javed, a modern studies teacher and (in a previous political life) a former general secretary of Muslim Friends of Labour. She was an SNP candidate for Murdostoun ward in 2017, finishing in sixth place.

The Scottish Labour Party have selected Kenneth Stevenson, who has been a North Lanarkshire councillor since 2017 representing the Fortissat ward (based on Shotts and the surrounding rural area). In May 2017 the council seats in Fortissat split two to Labour and one each to the SNP and Conservatives; Labour have since gained both the Conservative and the SNP seats in by-elections (in September 2017[*] and March 2021[†] respectively). Stevenson defeated Pamela Nash for the Labour nomination.

The Conservative candidate is Ben Callaghan, who has appeared in this column very recently as the Conservative candidate in the March 2021 Fortissat by-election. On that occasion he polled 23% of the vote and finished in third place; his transfers ensured that Labour won the election very comfortably over the SNP. However, the usual Scottish disclaimers do *not* apply here: this is a Westminster election, so it's Votes at 18 and there is no transferable voting.

There are a total of eight candidates for the Airdrie and Shotts by-election. The Lib Dems have selected Stephen Arrundale, who was their parliamentary candidate for Midlothian in December 2019; according to his Twitter he's the treasurer of the party's Scottish branch and a (presumably long-suffering) Hartlepool United fan. (Up the Pools!) The other four candidates are all from fringe Unionist parties. Reform UK's Martyn Greene was an election agent for the party in last week's Holyrood elections. Donald Mackay turned up in this column back in March as the leader of Scottish UKIP, contesting a council by-election in Glasgow (page 27). On that occasion he polled 0.5% in Partick East/Kelvindale ward, finishing last out of six candidates; last week he topped the UKIP list for the Lothian region, which polled 0.11% and finished 17th out of 19. One of the two lists which UKIP Lothian beat was that of the Social Democratic Party, which polled 0.06% and finished in eighteenth place; second on the SDP's Lothian list was Neil Manson, one of two candidates in this by-election (along with Labour's

[*] *Andrew's Previews 2017*, page 242. [†] See page 12.

Scottish Parliament constituency: Airdrie and Shotts (most), Motherwell and Wishaw (part), Uddingston and Bellshill (part)
North Lanarkshire wards: Airdrie Central, Airdrie North, Airdrie South, Fortissat, Coatbridge North (part), Coatbridge South (part), Mossend and Holytown (part), Motherwell North (part), Murdostoun (part)
December 2019 result SNP 17929 Lab 12728 C 7011 LD 1419 Grn 685
June 2017 result SNP 14291 Lab 14096 C 8813 LD 802
May 2015 result SNP 23887 Lab 15108 C 3389 UKIP 1088 LD 678 Ind 136
May 2010 result Lab 20849 SNP 8441 C 3133 LD 2898 Ind 528
May 2005 result Lab 19568 SNP 5484 LD 3792 C 3271 SSP 706 Scottish Independence Party 337

Figure 27: House of Commons, Airdrie and Shotts

Kenneth Stevenson) to give an address in this constituency. Finally, former UKIP figure Jonathan Stanley, who was second on the All for Unity list which polled 0.8% in the Central Scotland region last week, has the nomination of the Scottish Unionist Party.*

This column will now take a rest before returning in mid-June for our next by-elections.

* *House of Commons, Airdrie and Shotts*: SNP 10129 Lab 8372 C 2812 LD 220 SDP 151 Scottish Unionist Party 59 Reform UK 45 UKIP 39

10th June 2021

Two by-elections on 10th June 2021:

Grove Green; and Lea Bridge

Waltham Forest council, London; caused respectively by the death of Chris Robbins and the resignation of Yemi Osho. Both were Labour councillors.

Welcome to the first Andrew's Previews of the 2021–22 municipal year. For those who haven't been here before, this is a theoretically-weekly blog for Britain Elects which covers the most low-profile elections that take place in the UK: by-elections to our local councils. Our remit is to travel up and down the country every week, shining a spotlight on parts of the country which you might know well or not at all, giving a sense of what the area is like and whether you might want to visit. Or not, as the case may be.

At least, that's what's supposed to happen. However, for pandemic-related reasons there have been no standalone local by-elections in England since March 2020, when Gurdev Singh Hayre was elected as a Labour councillor for the Upper Stoke ward of Coventry.* Some local by-elections have taken place in Scotland and Wales since, but all English council vacancies which were unfilled on that date, and everything after that date, had their polling days postponed to May 2021 or cancelled altogether.

The cutoff date for by-elections to be called for May 2021 was the end of March. A number of vacancies have arisen since then, and there is also some unfinished business from 6th May which will be taken care of next week. Your columnist has a list of (at the time of writing) 45 vacancies in our local government, of which 33 have polling dates set over the next two months. There are a lot of interesting races still to come.

---

* *Andrew's Previews 2020*, page 79.

Two further by-elections also need to be noted. There was due to be a poll next week in the Caerphilly district of south Wales for the *Aber Valley* division; this is one of the smaller Valleys, with the division's population concentrated in the villages of Abertridwr and Senghenydd north-west of Caerphilly town. These are pit villages, and Senghenydd was the scene of the UK's worst-ever mining disaster: an underground explosion at the Universal Colliery on 14th October 1913 killed 439 miners and a rescuer, a huge loss in a valley whose modern-day population is under 7,000. Subsequent negligence charges led to fines of £24 for the colliery manager and £10 for the colliery company, which was calculated as equivalent to 1s 1¼d per life lost. In more recent times Senghenydd is notable as one of the areas covered by the Caerphilly Heart Disease Study, which since 1979 has tracked the health of adult males in the area who were born in 1918–1938. Aber Valley division has had a full slate of Plaid Cymru councillors since 2008, and Plaid enjoyed a 66–20 lead at the most recent Welsh local elections in May 2017. When nominations for the by-election closed Charlotte Bishop, of Plaid, was the only candidate, and she has been declared elected unopposed.

We have also filled the first vacancy among the class of 2021, which arose offshore on the Isles of Scilly. This arises from the retirement of Marion, Lady Berkeley, who had served for many years as a Scilly councillor for the island of *Bryher*. A few years ago Marion married Anthony Gueterbock, the 18th Lord Berkeley; as this column has previously noted* Lord Berkeley is an active Labour member of the House of Lords, and even in these days of remote sittings it's rather difficult to do that from the Isles of Scilly. Lord and Lady Berkeley now divide their time between Cornwall and London. Lady Berkeley didn't seek re-election to the Council of the Isles of Scilly in May's election, and no candidates came forward to replace her so nominations for Bryher had to be reopened with a new election date set for 24th June. Bryher is one of the smallest electoral units in the UK, with a population comfortably under 100, so a contested election was never likely; when nominations closed for the second time there was just one candidate, local fisherman Andrew Frazer, who was accordingly declared elected unopposed. As with all Scilly councillors, he stood as a non-party candidate. This column sends its congratulations to newly-elected Councillors Bishop and Frazer.

So, for our first standalone local by-elections in England for 15 months we have to go to that London and the borough of Waltham Forest. In order to reach there we travel to one of the UK's newest railway stations. Lea Bridge station, after being closed in 1985, reopened in May 2016 with regular trains south to Stratford and north up the Lea Valley. The Lea Bridge itself was originally built

* *Andrew's Previews 2019*, page 44.

in 1745 over the river Lea or Lee (the spelling, like the river, is a little bit fluid), and the Lea Bridge Road over it is the only road link between Hackney and Walthamstow. Unusually for London, Lea Bridge ward includes a significant amount of wild open space: the Leyton and Walthamstow Marshes, much of which are given over as nature reserves or for sport.

If you came to Grove Green ward expecting similar open space, then you'd be disappointed. The name refers to a road running along the eastern end of the ward, which has been almost entirely built-up for more than a century. This is a residential area lying between Leyton to the west and Leytonstone to the east; Leyton Midland Road station, on the Gospel Oak–Barking line of the Overground, lies on the ward's northern boundary.

Like much of East London, the demographic profiles of these wards have been transformed by London's becoming a world city. In the 2011 census, the most recent census for which these figures are available, Grove Green ward was in the top 20 wards in England and Wales for population born in the countries which joined the EU this century (16.2%) and within the top 75 in England and Wales for White Other population (24.2%). Lea Bridge is even more of a melting-pot, being in the top 100 wards for those born in EU accession countries (10.6%) and for black population (24.0%), although Asians in fact form the largest ethnic group here (30.3%). Both wards have significant Muslim populations, mostly of Pakistani heritage.

Both wards are also very safe for the Labour party these days. Lea Bridge ward has returned a full slate of Labour councillors at every election this century; Grove Green ward split its three seats between Labour and the Lib Dems in 2002, but has been solidly Labour since 2006. At the most recent Waltham Forest council elections in May 2018, Labour beat the Lib Dems 54–24 in Grove Green and enjoyed a 59–17 lead in Lea Bridge over the Green Party. The 2018 elections returned a strong Labour majority in Waltham Forest, with 46 councillors against 14 Conservatives (all of whom represent wards in the Chingford area), and the safe Labour theme is continued at parliamentary level with both of these wards being (for the moment) in safe Labour parliamentary seats. At present Lea Bridge is part of the Walthamstow constituency, with Grove Green in Leyton and Wanstead; the Boundary Commission for England's provisional map for the next redistribution of seats doesn't change that.

In the London Mayor and Assembly elections just five weeks ago, Sadiq Khan beat Shaun Bailey 59–14 in Grove Green and 55–18 in Lea Bridge. The Greens ran second here in the London Members ballot for the Assembly: Grove Green had 54% for Labour against 17% for the Greens and 10% for the Conservatives, while the shares of the vote for those three parties in Lea Bridge were 56%, 16%

Parliamentary constituency: Leyton and Wanstead
London Assembly constituency: North East
May 2018 result Lab 2052/2047/1997 LD 897/725/623 Grn 456/416 C 247/216/200 TUSC 128
May 2014 result Lab 1858/1751/1686 LD 1009/865/856 Grn 507/485 C 345/335/335 TUSC 160/86
May 2010 result Lab 2342/2271/2178 LD 1681/1639/1563 C 608/599/594 Grn 429/383
May 2006 result Lab 1517/1430/1356 LD 1286/1173/1171 Grn 480 C 270/265/235
May 2002 result Lab 1169/1081/949 LD 1103/1052/1048 Grn 265/218/167 C 235/226/191 Socialist Alliance 163
May 2021 GLA results (excludes postal voters)
Mayor: Lab 1776 C 415 Grn 350 LD 111 Omilana 78 London Real 45 Count Binface 44 Women's Equality 34 Rejoin EU 29 Reclaim 27 Let London Live 23 Animal Welfare 16 Farah London 16 Heritage 15 Burning Pink 11 Obunge 8 SDP 6 Renew 5 UKIP 5 Fosh 4
London Members: Lab 1671 Grn 511 C 317 LD 183 Women's Equality 83 Animal Welfare 69 Rejoin EU 60 Reform UK 29 TUSC 28 London Real 24 CPA 19 Comm 19 Let London Live 17 Heritage 13 UKIP 12 SDP 11 Londonpendence 7 Nat Lib 4

Figure 28: Waltham Forest, Grove Green

and 13% respectively. As usual with GLA results quoted by this column, these figures are only for those voting on the day and do not include postal votes, which are tallied at borough level and traditionally skew to the right; however, the May 2021 elections saw a much higher uptake of postal votes than normal, and many boroughs reported unusually little difference between their postal and on-the-day returns.

So we shouldn't expect too much of a surprise in these two by-elections. The Grove Green by-election is to replace the previous mayor of Waltham Forest, Labour councillor Chris Robbins, who died in April at the age of 76. He had sat on the council since 2002, and became leader of the Labour group in 2009 and Leader of the Council in 2010. Robbins served as council leader for seven years, being appointed CBE in 2017 for his public service, and was elected as mayor for 2019–20; his term was extended to two years on account of the pandemic. Lea Bridge ward is also vacated by a former mayor of Waltham Forest: that's Yemi Osho, a long-serving nurse who was first elected to the council in 2014 and was the borough's first citizen in 2017–18.

Defending Lea Bridge for Labour is Jennifer Whilby, a black rights activist and local party officer. The Green candidate for the ward is the unusually-capitalised RoseMary Warrington, who was their parliamentary candidate for Ilford South in December 2019. Also standing are Sazimet Imre for the Conservatives, Naomi McCarthy for the Lib Dems and independent candidate Claire Weiss who has lived in the ward for more than forty years.*

* *Waltham Forest, Lea Bridge*: Lab 1176 Ind 441 C 436 Grn 181 LD 116

Parliamentary constituency: Walthamstow
London Assembly constituency: North East
May 2018 result Lab 2313/2131/2036 Grn 660 C 408/262/222 LD 252/240/175 TUSC 214 Duma Polska 97
May 2014 result Lab 2259/2020/1871 Grn 619 LD 429/375/233 C 379/370/289 TUSC 276
May 2010 result Lab 2891/2850/2730 LD 1810/1435/618 Grn 711 C 661 Ind 215
May 2006 result Lab 1375/1327/1240 LD 517/509/471 C 451/360/320 Grn 429
May 2002 result Lab 1207/1126/1110 LD 536/427/356 C 463/445/436 Socialist Alliance 120
May 2021 GLA results (excludes postal voters)
Mayor: Lab 1690 C 559 Grn 323 Omilana 93 LD 52 London Real 50 Reclaim 44 Let London Live 44 Count Binface 36 Rejoin EU 35 Women's Equality 30 Farah London 26 UKIP 18 Obinge 17 SDP 14 Animal Welfare 13 Burning Park 11 Heritage 6 Renew 5 Fosh 3
London Members: Lab 1794 Grn 507 C 403 LD 90 Women's Equality 79 Animal Welfare 56 Rejoin EU 52 CPA 50 Let London Live 29 London Real 27 TUSC 26 UKIP 24 Comm 16 Reform UK 12 SDP 11 Heritage 9 Londonpendence 7 Nat Lib 2

Figure 29: Waltham Forest, Lea Bridge

In Grove Green the defending Labour candidate is Uzma Rasool, a teacher, researcher and long-standing local resident. The Liberal Democrats have reselected Arran Angus who was runner-up here in 2018; he is currently taking a career break to bring up his children. Completing the Grove Green ballot paper are Mark Dawes for the Green Party, Shahamima Khan for the Conservatives and Kevin Parslow for the Trade Unionist and Socialist Coalition.*

So, there you are. Not the most exciting of Previews this week, but at least we are back to considering local by-elections in England after too long away. And stay tuned for next week's Previews, which will include a Parliamentary Special.

* *Waltham Forest, Grove Green*: Lab 1301 LD 541 Grn 205 C 142 TUSC 40

17th June 2021: Parliamentary Special

Eight polls on 17th June 2021, and we start with a Parliamentary Special:

Chesham and Amersham

House of Commons; caused by the death of Conservative MP Dame Cheryl Gillan.

> Through Amersham to Aylesbury and the Vale,
> In those wet fields the railway didn't pay.
> The Metro stops at Amersham today.
>
> —John Betjeman, *Metroland*

I'd like to start this piece by paying tribute to someone who was taken from us at the very start of the current pandemic. Jon Jacob was a property lawyer by trade, but I knew him as a quizzer. What Jon didn't know about classical music wasn't worth knowing, and his general knowledge was good enough to compete at the highest level.

Jon was one of four people (to date) to have beaten your columnist on BBC *Mastermind*, doing so in the heats of the 2013–14 series with his subject "The Life and Work of Sir Arthur Sullivan". Two of the other three people to have beaten me on that series are a former Brain of Mensa and a *Fifteen-to-One* champion, which tells you just how good Jon was. When he died of COVID in March 2020, aged 69, tributes came in from all over the quiz community. We all miss him.

Jon played quiz league for many years, competing both in London where he worked and in the Chiltern quiz league, near where he lived. His team was the Hen and Chickens B, from Botley just outside Chesham, which despite the name was for many years the strongest team in the league. The Chiltern quiz league comprises a number of teams in the general area of Chesham, Amersham and Rickmansworth, and they are always looking for new players and teams. If you are local to the area and at a loose end on a Tuesday evening, you could do worse than to visit their website* and get in touch.

Prospective Chiltern quiz league players will find themselves in some rather nice licensed premises in some rather nice towns in some rather nice countryside. The largest of these towns is Chesham, whose history can be nearly summed up by four words beginning with the letter B: boots, beer, brushes and Baptists. Not many of these industries are left now, with the possible exception of Baptists.

Chesham is rather tucked out of the way in the Chess valley, and the town of Amersham is much better connected. This is another market town, located in the Misbourne valley on the railway line from London to Aylesbury. Brewing was a traditional key industry here, but this was supplanted during the Second World War by an unusual new trade: the Radiochemical Centre, Amersham (since spun off and now part of the GE Healthcare empire) made radioactive products for the pharmaceutical industry.

The railway linking Chesham and Amersham to London is an unusual one. It was built by the Metropolitan Railway, which started out in central London in 1863 as the world's first underground railway, and then built a branch line north from Baker Street. The railway soon came to see this branch line as its main route, and they extended it to Chesham in 1885, to Aylesbury via Amersham in 1892, and then onwards into the Aylesbury Vale as far as Brill and Verney Junction. The Metropolitan aggressively promoted the development of new suburbs along its route, resulting in the creation of "Metroland" and giving a commuter profile to its catchment area. It escaped the railway grouping of the 1920s, but ended up in the hands of London Transport from the 1930s; as a result of that, Chesham and Amersham are London Underground stations—the western termini of the Metropolitan line—despite being a very long way out of Greater London. London Transport sold everything beyond Amersham to British Rail in the 1960s, and mainline Chiltern Railways services between Marylebone and Aylesbury also call at Amersham.

There are other towns in the area. West of Amersham on the road and railway to Aylesbury can be found Great Missenden, for many years the home of the author Roald Dahl and now the location of a museum in his memory. To the south-east of Amersham are the Chalfonts, some of the most expensive and exclusive villages in the country. Chalfont St Giles was the place where John Milton completed his poem *Paradise Lost* after the Great Plague forced him out of London; while Chalfont St Peter can be heard around the world as the home of BFBS Radio, which broadcasts around the clock to British service personnel.

---

* `https://chilternquizleague.uk/`

All this is in the county of Buckinghamshire which is a surprisingly diverse area, running a long way from the banks of the Thames in the south, through the Chiltern Hills, to the Aylesbury Vale. Like much of the English county system, it is of Anglo-Saxon origin; but the ancient county town of Buckingham, tucked away at the northern end of the county it gave its name to, never grew into a significant town and is now rather a backwater. Since its creation in the 1880s the Buckinghamshire county council has been based in Aylesbury, while the county's largest urban centre isn't old enough to be drawing a pension yet: that's the New City of Milton Keynes.

Buckinghamshire has played its part in politics over the years. John Hampden, one of the prime movers behind the English Civil War, was from a prominent Buckinghamshire family and was one of the two MPs for the county from 1640 until his death in 1643. In those days Bucks enjoyed fourteen members of Parliament, two for the county and two each for the six boroughs of Wycombe, Wendover, Great Marlow, Buckingham, Aylesbury and a "thriving little market town" in the Chilterns called Amersham.

The Amersham parliamentary borough had a relatively democratic franchise, with all householders paying the local tax of scot and lot having the right to vote. However, in practice it was a pocket borough controlled by the wealthy Drake family of the nearby Shardloes stately home. The last contested election for the borough was a by-election in February 1735, and from 1768 onwards all the town's MPs were Drakes (later Tyrwhitt-Drakes). This was exactly the sort of abuse which the first Reform Act of 1832 intended to put a stop to, and Amersham was one of the many boroughs which were disenfranchised by that Act in 1832.

Following the passage of the third Reform Act in 1885, all of the parliamentary boroughs in Buckinghamshire were swept away and the county was reduced to just three MPs, elected from single-member constituencies. The Buckingham constituency covered the vale at the northern end of the county; the Wycombe seat covered the western Chilterns and the southern end of Buckinghamshire, including a small place on the Great Western Main Line called Slough; while in the middle lay the Aylesbury constituency. The Aylesbury seat of 1885–1945 was much larger than the seat of the same name which exists today, covering a large swathe of central Buckinghamshire and the eastern Chilterns, including the whole of the modern Chesham and Amersham constituency.

The pre-reform Amersham constituency may have been dominated by the wealthy Drakes, but the Aylesbury constituency at this time was dominated by an even more wealthy and far more influential family. The first election for the new Aylesbury constituency at the end of 1885 was won easily by the Liberal candidate, Baron Ferdinand de Rothschild. "Ferdy" had entered the

Commons just a few months earlier, contesting and winning a by-election for the old Aylesbury borough in July 1885 after his cousin Sir Nathan Rothschild MP was elevated to the peerage. Nathan, the first non-baptised Jew to enter the Lords, had been a partner in the London branch of the Rothschild banking empire, financing ventures including the Suez Canal and Cecil Rhodes' adventures in southern Africa as a well as a number of philanthropic schemes and good (or at least less-dubious) works.

Ferdinand de Rothschild's country house, Waddesdon Manor to the west of Aylesbury, was nearing completion at the time and already filling up with the Baron's extensive art collection. It also quickly became a place of political intrigue. The Rothschilds left the Liberals over the Irish Home Rule controversy, joining the breakaway Liberal Unionists, and Ferdy hosted a number of prominent Conservative politicians in meetings which led to the Conservatives and Liberal Unionists forming an alliance. Ferdy was re-elected in 1886 under his new Liberal Unionist colours with a massive 74–26 lead over the new Liberal candidate, and he was never seriously challenged in Aylesbury after that. His last re-election as MP for Aylesbury, in 1895, came without a contest.

Ferdinand de Rothschild died in December 1898, on his 59th birthday. The resulting Aylesbury by-election of January 1899 was won by the Liberal Unionist candidate Walter Rothschild, son and heir of the 1st Lord Rothschild, who was declared elected unopposed after the Liberals decided not to contest the by-election. Aged 30 at the time, Walter had been put to work in the family banking business even though he had little aptitude for finance, and he was best known at this time as a zoologist. Walter's zoological collection was opened to the public in 1892, and now forms the basis of the Natural History Musuem at Tring in Hertfordshire.

Walter Rothschild only faced one contested election in Aylesbury, holding out against the Liberal landslide of 1906 with a 56–44 majority (the Liberal candidate that year was Silas Hocking, a Methodist preacher and bestselling novelist). Walter decided to retire from politics in 1910 and he left the Commons, although as it turned out that retirement was short-lived. He inherited his father's titles and entered the Lords in 1915 as the 2nd Lord Rothschild, was the recipient of the 1917 Balfour Declaration, and served from 1925 to 1926 as president of the Board of Deputies of British Jews.

Walter Rothschild was a prominent Zionist, but his successor as MP for Aylesbury was anything but. Lionel de Rothschild, who took over the seat in January 1910, came to prominence in 1915 as vice-chairman of the Central Jewish Recruiting Committee, attempting to persuade Jews to enlist for military service; for this he was in the very first tranche of military OBEs when the Order of the

British Empire was established in 1917. In response to the Balfour Declaration, Lionel was a co-founder of the League of British Jews, an anti-Zionist organisation which opposed the idea of a Jewish homeland in Palestine (although it was in favour of helping Jews who wanted to settle there). Away from politics, Lionel de Rothschild was a noted gardener whose legacy today is the Exbury Gardens in Hampshire.

The Aylesbury seat experienced boundary changes in 1918, with the town of Beaconsfield being transferred in from the Wycombe constituency and Linslade, now part of Leighton Buzzard, moving into the Buckingham seat. This didn't change things immediately, as Lionel de Rothschild was re-elected unopposed in 1918; but in 1922 he was run very close by the Liberals' Thomas Keens who lost by 13,406 votes to 12,835, a majority of 571. Lionel chose to retire in 1923, breaking the Rothschild family's hold on the Aylesbury constituency.

The stage was set for two contests in Aylesbury between the new Unionist candidate Alan Burgoyne, who had lost his seat in Kensington North the previous year, and the reselected Liberal candidate Thomas Keens, an accountant who was active in local politics in his native Luton. Keens served on Bedfordshire county council from 1901 to 1952, and went on to be knighted in 1934 for his public service. Despite the intervention of a Labour candidate (Fred Watkins, who went on to serve two non-consecutive terms as MP for Hackney Central), Keens won the 1923 election by 13,575 votes to 13,504, a majority of 71. He was, to date, the last Liberal MP for the area: Burgoyne won the rematch in 1924 very easily.

Alan Burgoyne retired in 1929 and was replaced as Unionist MP for Aylesbury by Michael Beaumont, a former Coldstream Guards officer who was the son and grandson of Liberal MPs. He enjoyed a majority of 2,844 over Keens in 1929, and wasn't seriously challenged in 1931 or 1935. In 1935 the second-placed Liberal candidate was Margaret Wintringham, who fourteen years earlier had become the party's first female MP by winning the 1921 Louth by-election. Many years later, Michael Beaumont's son Timothy became the first Green Party member of the Houses of Parliament, joining the party three decades after entering the Lords as a life peer.

Michael Beaumont resigned as MP for Aylesbury in May 1938. The resulting by-election later that month was held for the Conservatives by Stanley Reed, a journalist who had retired to the UK after a long career in India: he was editor of *The Times of India* from 1907 to 1924. Reed enjoyed a large majority over the Liberal candidate Atholl Robertson, a fine arts publisher who had been MP for Finchley in 1923–24.

Stanley Reed was re-elected as MP for Aylesbury in 1945, with Labour moving into second place in the constituency for the first time. Unusually, the Aylesbury seat was subject to a boundary change that year. The town of Slough had seen huge growth in its population since 1918, resulting in the Wycombe constituency becoming hugely oversized, and Wycombe was one of the seats which was split up in the emergency wartime redistribution of that year. Most of Wycombe's electors went into a new seat with the establishment-friendly name of "Eton and Slough", while the rump Wycombe seat grabbed the Princes Risborough area from Aylesbury to make up the numbers.

Having been granted a fourth MP in the 1945 wartime review, Buckinghamshire got a fifth MP in 1950 with the division of Aylesbury into two new seats. The northern end of the old constituency, including Chesham, stayed in the Aylesbury seat, while the Amersham and Beaconsfield end of the seat formed the major part of the new South Buckinghamshire constituency. With Stanley Reed choosing to retire, both seats were open.

The revised Aylesbury seat proved to be rather more marginal than the old one. For the 1950 election the Conservatives selected Spencer Summers, who came from a North Wales steelworking family and had been the MP for Northampton from 1940 until losing his seat in 1945; Summers had been a junior trade minister in the caretaker government going into that election. The Labour candidate was Tony Harman, a farmer from Chesham who, many years later, became a *Guardian* columnist and wrote a bestselling memoir *Seventy Summers* which was televised by the BBC. Summers beat Harman with a majority of 3,361, which increased at rematches in 1951 and 1955; after that he was only seriously threatened in 1966 when Labour got within 3,907 votes. Away from politics, Spencer Summers had suffered tragedy in 1961 when his son Shane Summers, a promising young racing driver, was killed in a practice session at Brands Hatch at the age of 24.

Summers retired as MP for Aylesbury in 1970 after twenty years and passed the seat on without fuss to the new Conservative candidate Timothy Raison, a journalist who went on to represent the seat for 22 years. Both Summers and Raison were, however, outdone in the length-of-service stakes by Sir Ronald Bell, who was elected as the Conservative candidate for South Buckinghamshire in 1950 and was still an MP in 1982, when he suffered a fatal heart attack in his Commons office. As well as 32 years as MP for South Buckinghamshire (being the only MP to represent that seat) and then Beaconsfield, we can add four weeks as MP for Newport after Bell won the last of the 219 by-elections to the wartime 1935–45 parliament*. A barrister by career and a prominent member of the Monday Club, Bell came to public notice in the 1970 Parliament as an implacable opponent

* *Andrew's Previews 2019*, page 77.

of Edward Heath's leadership, to the point where Heath unsuccessfully tried to get Bell deselected in favour of Michael Heseltine. Heseltine needed a new political home, as his Tavistock constituency was disappearing in the forthcoming boundary changes.

Those boundary changes granted a sixth MP to Buckinghamshire from the February 1974 election, and the new seat was given the name Chesham and Amersham. Amersham and the Chalfonts came in from the old South Buckinghamshire seat (the remainder of which was renamed as Beaconsfield), with the Chesham area and Great Missenden transferred from the Aylesbury constituency. The new seat had exactly the same boundaries as the Chesham and Amersham seat of today, although different boundaries were in force from 1983 to 2010.

Heath's attempt to deselect Ronald Bell came to nothing, and Michael Heseltine ended up with the Conservative nomination for the Henley seat. Bell sought re-election in Beaconsfield and Timothy Raison stayed in Aylesbury, so the new Chesham and Amersham seat was open. It proved to be a nice Parliamentary berth for the outgoing Defence Secretary Ian Gilmour, whose career to date had included service in the Grenadier Guards and the editorship of *The Spectator*. Gilmour had been elected in a 1962 by-election for the Central Norfolk constituency, which disappeared in the 1974 boundary changes. He was a junior minister for most of the Heath administration, being appointed as Secretary of State for Defence and joining Cabinet in January 1974. Gilmour won the new constituency with a majority of 10,416 over the Liberals.

Sir Ian Gilmour, as he became in 1977 after inheriting a baronetcy, went on to serve for 18 years as MP for Chesham and Amersham. He returned to Cabinet in 1979 as Lord Privy Seal, but was very much on a different political wavelength to Margaret Thatcher and was on the backbenches from 1981 onwards.

Gilmour retired to the Lords in 1992, although he didn't end his career on the Conservative red benches: he was thrown out of the Tories in 1999 for supporting the Pro-Euro Conservative Party, of which more later. He passed the Chesham and Amersham seat on to the first female MP for this corner of Buckinghamshire, Cheryl Gillan. A former member of the LSO chorus, Gillan had spent her career to date in marketing although she had served in 1987–88 as chair of the Bow Group think-tank. In the 1989 European Parliament elections she had contested the safe Labour constituency of Greater Manchester Central.

Cheryl Gillan saw off a number of future Labour MPs in her 29 years as MP for Chesham and Amersham: Candy Atherton (Falmouth and Camborne 1997–2005) stood here in 1992, Paul Farrelly (Newcastle-under-Lyme 2001–19) in 1997, Rupa Huq (Ealing Central and Acton 2015–) in 2005. She got on the government ladder in 1995 as a junior education minister. Gillan made Shadow Cabinet rank in 2005 as shadow Welsh secretary, and served as Welsh secretary for the first half of the Coalition government.

Gillan left the frontbenches in 2012 amid a huge local controversy in her constituency. Chesham and Amersham lies on a straight line between London and Birmingham, and the High Speed 2 railway line was planned to run through the constituency from end to end. This did not go down well among the voters of Chesham and Amersham, but High Speed 2 duly passed its Parliamentary stages. Construction began last month on a 9.9-mile tunnel to take the new railway underneath this constituency.

This is not the only local controversy here. In a constituency with a census district (in Little Chalfont) where the median property price in 2018 was £1.3 million, there is significant local opposition to moves to try and make housing affordable by the simple expedient of building more of it. To make things more complicated, almost all of the constituency is within the London Green Belt. Cheryl Gillan was working to get the Chilterns designed as a National Park, which would have provided a further brake on development.

Cheryl Gillan was appointed DBE, becoming a Dame, in 2018. She died from cancer in April 2021 at the age of 68, prompting this third by-election of the 2019 Parliament. In December 2019 Gillan had been re-elected for an eighth term of office with a 55–26 lead over the Liberal Democrats, a majority of 16,223 votes.

By length of service Dame Cheryl Gillan was the most senior female Conservative MP, a title which is now shared by the Deputy Speaker Eleanor Laing and the former Prime Minister Theresa May who were both first elected in 1997. Only seven Conservative MPs (Sir Peter Bottomley, Sir Edward Leigh, Sir David Amess, Sir Roger Gale, Sir Bill Cash, Sir John Redwood and arguably David Davis) have longer continuous service in the Commons than Gillan.

From 2010 to 2020 this seat had the same boundaries as the Chiltern district of Buckinghamshire, whose last local elections in 2015 returned 35 Conservative councillors, 3 Lib Dems and 2 independents. Chiltern district council was abolished in May 2020 in favour of a single Buckinghamshire council, which at its first elections last month returned a large Conservative majority. Across the nine Buckinghamshire wards which cover this constituency, the Tories polled 43% of the vote in May against 25% for the Lib Dems and 16% for the Greens, with the Conservatives carrying all nine wards and winning 26 councillors out of a possible 27; a Lib Dem seat in Chiltern Ridges ward (covering a number of villages to the north-west of Chesham plus part of Chesham town) was the one that got away. In a parliamentary by-election, this sort of Conservative lead is not

Figure 30: Wards of the Chesham and Amersham constituency

foolproof: the last by-election where the Conservatives held all but one council seat within the constituency took place in Richmond Park in 2016*. They lost that one.

Chesham and Amersham may superficially share some similarities with Richmond Park (Remain-voting, lots of London commuters, sky-high property prices, that sort of thing) but this is an area which the Conservatives have represented continuously since 1924. This was one of the two-dozen or so seats which were over 50% Conservative even against the Labour landslide of 1997.

* *Andrew's Previews 2016*, page 311.

Buckinghamshire council wards: Amersham and Chesham Bois, Chalfont St Giles, Chalfont St Peter, Chesham, Chess Valley, Chiltern Ridges, Great Missenden, Little Chalfont and Amersham Common, Penn Wood and Old Amersham
December 2019 result C 30850 LD 14627 Lab 7166 Grn 3042
June 2017 result C 33514 Lab 11374 LD 7179 Grn 1660 UKIP 1525
May 2015 result C 31138 UKIP 7218 Lab 6712 LD 4761 Grn 2902
May 2010 result C 31658 LD 14948 Lab 2942 UKIP 2129 Grn 767
(1983–2005 elections on different boundaries)
May 1979 result C 32924 Lib 12328 Lab 7645 NF 697
October 1974 result C 25078 Lib 14091 Lab 10325
February 1974 result C 27035 Lib 16619 Lab 9700

Figure 31: House of Commons, Chesham and Amersham

Both of the previous MPs for the current seat have served in Conservative or Conservative-led cabinets. There is a lot of Tory pedigree here.

Defending for the Conservatives is Peter Fleet, whose only previous parliamentary campaign was in that 1997 landslide where he contested Southampton Itchen. Fleet has spent much of the intervening 24 years living and working in the Far East as a senior executive with Ford Motors; now back in the UK, he is the current chairman of the Retail Automotive Alliance. If he is elected, with a height reported as 6 feet and 9 inches he would probably be the tallest MP of all time.

Fleet gives an address in this constituency as does the Liberal Democrat candidate Sarah Green, who runs a communications firm. Again, this is not her first parliamentary contest: in 2010 she was the Lib Dem candidate for Arfon in North Wales.

Third here in December 2019 with 13% of the vote were Labour, who have selected Natasa Pantelic. Pantelic is a Slough councillor, sitting on the council's cabinet with the social care and public health portfolios.

The only other party to stand here in 2019 were the Greens, who narrowly saved their deposit. Their candidate is Carolyne Culver, a former Labour councillor in Hampshire who now leads the Green group on West Berkshire council; she is running on an explicitly anti-High Speed 2 ticket. And there was me thinking the Greens were in favour of improving public transport on environmental grounds.

Four other candidates have come forward, and I shall take them in ballot paper order. Brendan Donnelly has come to the notice of this column again: he was elected as a Conservative MEP for Sussex in 1994, unsuccessfully sought re-election in 1999 as co-leader of the Pro-Euro Conservative Party, and has since popped up at a number of elections under a wide variety of pro-EU labels with (to date) a total lack of success. Last month Donnelly was fifth on the Rejoin EU list which came sixth with 1.9% of the vote in the London Assembly elections, and for this by-election he again has the nomination of Rejoin EU, whose political programme is left as an exercise for the reader. Fighting its first election campaign is the Breakthrough Party, which describes itself as a "democratic socialist party, led by the younger generations set to inherit a world in crisis"; they have selected local resident Carla Gregory to try to make their breakthrough. Finally we come to two candidates who appear to be going for the political space to the right of the Conservatives: Adrian Oliver (a former Green Party candidate for Camden council, now based in High Wycombe) is the candidate of the anti-lockdown Freedom Alliance, while Alex Wilson has the nomination of Reform UK.*

Sewell

Norfolk county council; and

Sewell

Norwich council, Norfolk; both postponed from 6th May following the death of Conservative candidate Eve Collishaw at the age of 76.

The parliamentary by-election in Chesham and Amersham is not the only electoral action taking place today. We also have seven local elections to consider, four of which comprise unfinished business from the main local elections in May. These are cases where a candidate died after close of nominations, and the election had to be postponed in consequence.

Two of these arise in Norwich following the death in April of Eve Collishaw, who was a Conservative candidate for both Norfolk county council and Norwich city council. She had served on both councils before: Collishaw was a county councillor for 12 years (1997–2009) and a city councillor for 7 years (2004–11), serving in 2010–11 as the 100th Lord Mayor of Norwich.

Collishaw had continued to do her bit for the local Conservative cause by standing for election nearly every year. This year she was contesting Sewell, a ward to the north of Norwich city centre. Norwich has a tradition of naming some of its wards after local worthies: the Norwich School artist John Crome and the half-blind Norfolk admiral Viscount Nelson are commemorated in ward names here, as are the Sewell family who gave the city the open space of Sewell

* *House of Commons, Chesham and Amersham*: LD 21517 C 13489 Grn 1480 Lab 622 Reform UK 414 Breakthrough 197 Freedom Alliance 134 Rejoin EU 101 [LD gain from C]

Parliamentary constituency: Norwich North
May 2017 result Lab 1591 C 466 Grn 300 LD 197 UKIP 118
May 2013 result Lab 805 Grn 631 UKIP 368 C 322 LD 64
June 2009 result Grn 826 Lab 676 C 553 LD 477
May 2005 result Lab 1632 LD 797 C 643 Grn 487 Norwich over the Water 423

Figure 32: Norfolk CC, Sewell

Park in 1908. This is the same family that gave us Anna Sewell, the author of the perennially popular novel *Black Beauty*; a horse trough has been placed in the park in Anna's memory.

The Sewell ward has a relatively young population, and makes the top 60 wards in England and Wales for people of no religion (45.3%). The city ward was created in 2004, and the county division has had the same boundaries since 2005. Norfolk county council was due to get new division boundaries this year, but the Local Government Boundary Commission's review was knocked off course by the pandemic and couldn't report in time. The city ward was left unchanged by a separate boundary review which was implemented in 2019; accordingly, two years ago all three of the Norwich city councillors for Sewell ward were up for election.

On its current boundaries Sewell has voted Labour on every occasion except the 2009 county council elections, when the Green Party won here. In the May 2017 Norfolk county elections Labour led the Conservatives here 60–17; the city council election here in May 2019 was a bit closer with the Labour slate enjoying a 53–28 lead over the Green Party. Norwich city council has a Labour majority, while Norfolk county council is run by the Conservatives. Sewell is part of the Norwich North constituency represented by the Conservative minister Chloe Smith, who has spent much of the last few months being treated for breast cancer: this column sends our best wishes to her for a full and swift return to health.

Both outgoing Labour councillors for Sewell are seeking re-election. Defending the county council seat is Julie Brociek-Coulton, who has represented the area on the county council since 2013 and is seeking a third term in office. The replacement Conservative candidate is Simon Jones, a financial consultant and chairman of the party's Norwich branch. Also standing in the county by-election are Adrian Holmes for the Green Party and Helen Arundell for the Lib Dems.*

For the city council the defending Labour candidate is Laura McCartney-Gray, who was elected in third place two years and accordingly was due for re-election this year; she is seeking a second term of office. The Green Party have selected Gary Champion, a teacher who stood here two years ago. Simon Jones is

* *Norfolk CC, Sewell*: Lab 1132 Grn 1005 C 320 LD 40

Parliamentary constituency: Norwich North
May 2019 result Lab 1451/1152/1143 Grn 779/750/581 C 318/276/252 LD 212/191/139 May 2018 result Lab 1652 C 431 Grn 325 LD 155
May 2016 result Lab 1257 Grn 402 C 321 UKIP 254 LD 160
May 2015 double vacancy Lab 2018/1454 Grn 1058/1015 C 1046/1031 UKIP 628 LD 383/205
May 2014 result Lab 983 Grn 712 UKIP 446 C 343 LD 121 Left Unity 52
May 2012 result Lab 990 Grn 770 C 332 LD 123
May 2011 result Lab 1187 Grn 720 C 573 LD 243 UKIP 160
September 2010 result Lab 792 Grn 604 C 333 LD 168 UKIP 103
May 2008 result Lab 687 Grn 579 C 425 Norwich over the Water 354 LD 290
May 2007 result Lab 931 Grn 573 C 453 LD 428
May 2006 result Lab 674 Norwich over the Water 463 LD 416 Grn 401 C 317
June 2004 result Lab 748/693/639 Norwich over the Water 561/499/424 LD 405/369/366 C 350/332/294 Grn 328/313/278 Legalise Cannabis Alliance 94

Figure 33: Norwich, Sewell

again the replacement Conservative candidate, and he and the Lib Dems' Helen Arundell complete the city by-election ballot paper.*

Elham Valley

Kent county council; postponed from 6th May following the death of Chris Deane, who had been nominated as the Labour candidate.

We continue our unfinished business with a trip to the frontline of Brexit. Part of the Folkestone terminal of the Channel Tunnel can be found within the Elham Valley division of Kent county council; this is named after the village of Elham ("Eel-ham"), lying in the North Downs a few miles north of Folkestone and Hythe. The river here is the Nailbourne, which flows north to meet the River Stour at Thanet. Elham was the birthplace of the Kent and England wicketkeeper of yesteryear Les Ames, while other notable people associated with the village include the actresses Audrey Hepburn (who spent some of her schooldays here) and Pam Ferris.

Elham is just one of fourteen parishes which make up this division. The largest of these is Hawkinge, a village just to the north of Folkestone which has greatly expanded in population in recent years. Hawkinge was the location of the closest RAF airfield to France, and consequently it saw much action during the Battle of Britain. Some of the RAF Hawkinge site is now occupied by the Kent Battle of Britain Museum, but most of it has been given over to housing.

* *Norwich, Sewell*: Grn 1154 Lab 995 C 316 LD 39 [Grn gain from Lab]

Parliamentary constituency: Folkestone and Hythe
Folkestone and Hythe district wards: North Downs East, North Downs West
May 2017 result C 2706 UKIP 639 Grn 616 LD 515 Lab 513

Figure 34: Kent CC, Elham Valley

This division was last redrawn for the Kent county council elections in 2017, when it elected the Conservatives' Susan Carey with 54% against evenly-split opposition: 13% for UKIP, 12% for the Greens, 10% each for the Lib Dems and Labour. In the May 2019 elections to Folkestone and Hythe district council the Tories won all five seats in the North Downs East and North Downs West wards which cover this division; Susan Carey was one of them, finishing top of the poll in North Downs West.

Susan Carey has represented Elham Valley on the county council since 2005, and she is seeking re-election for a fifth term of office as part of the majority Conservative group. UKIP have not returned. The Green Party, who have a significant group on Folkestone and Hythe council now, have selected Douglas Wade: he is a district councillor for Hythe Rural ward, which is not in this division. Labour have changed their candidate to Gordon Cowan, and independent Joe Egerton (who was on the ballot paper in May for a by-election to Canterbury council, polling 24 votes in Swalecliffe ward[*]) completes the ballot paper.[†]

Felbridge

Tandridge council, Surrey; caused by the death of Conservative councillor Ken Harwood, and postponed from 6th May following the death of Christopher Kelly, who had been nominated as the Labour candidate.

Our last piece of unfinished business from 6th May is rather unusual, in that this is a by-election to fill the longest-standing vacancy in British local government. Ken Harwood, a Tandridge councillor for Felbridge ward who had served since winning a by-election in 2004, died from cancer in May 2020. Because of the pandemic, the by-election could not be held before May 2021. Tandridge is one of those districts which renews a third of its councillors at each election, but Felbridge ward is only large enough for one councillor and Harwood wasn't due for re-election until 2023, so this is a by-election rather than an ordinary election. The by-election subsequently had to be postponed again to give Labour time to nominate a replacement for their original candidate, the late Christopher Kelly.

The village of Felbridge is now essentially a suburb of the neighbouring

[*] See page 152. [†] *Kent CC, Elham Valley*: C 1809 Grn 1335 Lab 247 Ind 221

Parliamentary constituency: East Surrey
Surrey county council division: Lingfield
May 2019 result C 489 Ind 175 Grn 88
May 2015 result C 1151 Lab 145
May 2011 result C 709 LD 91 UKIP 68
May 2007 result C 611 LD 95 UKIP 37
June 2004 by-election C 601 LD 135 UKIP 61
May 2003 result C 379 LD 155

Figure 35: Tandridge, Felbridge

town of East Grinstead; but East Grinstead itself is over the county boundary in West Sussex. Accordingly, Felbridge continues to get its services from Surrey county council and from Tandridge council, which is based in Oxted. This is very much a middle-class area—in 2011 46% of Felbridge's population were in the ONS' professional and managerial occupational groups—but following May's elections Tandridge council is no longer run by the Conservatives. They are still the largest group on 14 seats and they are defending this by-election, but the council is controlled by a minority coalition of 10 independents and 8 councillors from the localist and anti-development Oxted and Limpsfield Residents Group. The remaining 9 seats on the council are held by the Lib Dems, who are strong in the North Downs commuter towns of Caterham and Warlingham.

Here at the other end of Tandridge district, Ken Harwood enjoyed very large majorities in his almost 16 years on the council. In 2015 he polled 89% of the vote in a straight fight with Labour; at his last re-election in 2019 Harwood defeated an independent candidate by 65–23.

This by-election has a larger field. The defending Conservatives have turned to the next generation by selecting Harry Baker-Smith. Local resident Judy Moore, who has recently been made redundant after 34 years working for Mid Sussex council, is standing as an independent candidate as is Mark Taylor. Completing the ballot paper are Richard Fowler of the Lib Dems and the replacement Labour candidate Emba Jones.*

Old Cleeve and District

Somerset West and Taunton council; caused by the resignation of Liberal Democrat councillor Peter Pilkington.

For our final two English by-elections today we travel to the West Country, starting on the Somerset coast. The Old Cleeve and District ward covers eight

* *Tandridge, Felbridge*: Moore 264 Taylor 159 C 128 Lab 18 LD 12 [Ind gain from C]

parishes to the west and south of Watchet, including the eastern end of the Exmoor National Park. This is an area of steep hills as the name Old Cleeve ("Old Cliff") suggests; the Old in the name distinguishes the village from the site of Cleeve Abbey, a nearby Cistercian foundation from 1198. Over the six centuries since its dissolution the Cleeve Abbey church has disappeared, but the rest of its buildings are well-preserved and can be visited under the auspices of English Heritage.

Another old building here, often pressed into service as a polling station, is the 14th-century tithe barn at the ward's other main population centre of Dunster. Lying on the edge of the National Park, Dunster is a major tourist centre on the road and railway line to Minehead as I described in *Andrew's Previews 2017*, page 87. At this time of year, it should be buzzing.

Until 2019 this area was part of the West Somerset district, which had a tiny and ageing population and which relied heavily on business rates from the Hinkley Point nuclear power station. The Age of Austerity led to financial difficulties for West Somerset council, forcing a merger with the larger and (as it was thought two years ago) more secure district of Taunton Deane. The resulting local government district of Somerset West and Taunton may well end up having an extremely short lifespan, because further local government reform for Somerset is clearly in the works: the 2021 Somerset county council elections were postponed for a year to see how things work out.

Both Taunton Deane and West Somerset councils had Conservative majorities going into the 2019 election, although in the past Taunton Deane had been Lib Dem-controlled and West Somerset could return large numbers of independent councillors. To general surprise the inaugural 2019 Somerset West and Taunton election returned a Liberal Democrat majority with 30 councillors, against 14 independents, 10 Conservatives, 3 Labour and 2 Greens. The Lib Dems bolstered their position with two by-election gains later that year, but have suffered a couple of defections and also have two vacancies in their group at the moment; they will need to hold this by-election and a further one next week to keep their majority on the council.

Old Cleeve and District was included in the Lib Dem majority in 2019: the party won the ward's two seats with 45% of the vote, against 31% for the Conservative slate and 24% for an independent candidate. The ward makes up the vast majority of the Dunster division of Somerset county council, which was Conservative in May 2017; as stated, the 2021 county elections didn't take place here. Peter Pilkington, whose resignation for family reasons has caused this by-election, served in the council's cabinet with the climate portfolio. The other Lib Dem councillor for the ward, Marcus Kravis, has since left the party and

Parliamentary constituency: Bridgwater and West Somerset
Somerset county council division: Dunster
May 2019 result LD 757/705 C 514/496 Ind 401

Figure 36: Somerset West and Taunton, Old Cleeve and District

gone independent but still sits on the council cabinet.

So, a difficult defence for the Lib Dem candidate Steve Griffiths, who lives outside the ward in Watchet; he served on West Oxfordshire council from 1991 to 1999 before relocating to Somerset. As well as doing community work, he volunteers on the preserved West Somerset railway as an assistant stationmaster and trainee signalman. The other two candidates were both elected in 2015 as Conservative councillors for the former Old Cleeve ward of West Somerset council, and both lost re-election here in 2019; Martin Dewdney, who was the runner-up two years ago, has the Conservative nomination, while Richard Lillis tries again as an independent candidate.*

Upper Culm

Mid Devon council; caused by the death of Conservative councillor Glanmor Hughes at the age of 90.

> Perlycombe, Perlycross and Perliton, are but as three pearls on one string, all in a line, and contiguous. The string is the stream; which arising at the eastern extermity of Perlycombe parish, passes through the village, then westward through Perlycross, and westward still through the much larger village of Perliton. At Perlycombe it is a noisy little brook, at Perlycross, a genial trout stream; while Perliton, by the time it gets there, entitles it "the River Perle" and keeps two boats upon it, which are not always more aground than landsmen should desire.
>
> — R D Blackmore, *Perlycross*

For our second by-election we travel to the Devon/Somerset border. The Culm valley is the major transport artery into Devon, being followed down to Exeter by the Great Western main line and the M 5 motorway; but its upper reaches are less well-connected. The river rises in Somerset in the Blackdown Hills, flowing west into Devon through the villages of Hemyock and Culmstock whose major access to the outside world is a dead-end B-road.

These villages—disguised as Perlycombe and Perlycross in the novel *Perlycross* by the Victorian novelist R D Blackmore, who lived in the area for some

* *Somerset West and Taunton, Old Cleeve and District*: LD 500 C 494 Ind 120

Parliamentary constituency: Tiverton and Honiton
Devon county council division: Willand and Uffculme
May 2019 result LD 666/464 C 486/452 Lab 185
May 2015 result C 1401 Ind 1066 UKIP 768
May 2011 result C 924 Ind 843 Lab 372
May 2007 result C/Ind unopposed
May 2003 result C 539/381 Ind 505/178 LD 299

Figure 37: Mid Devon, Upper Culm

years in his youth—form the core of Upper Culm ward of Mid Devon district, which covers four parishes a few miles south of Wellington. Hemyock is the major population centre in the Blackdown Hills, whose main industry is farming: until the 1990s the major employer here was the St Ivel factory which made dairy products such as “Utterly Butterly”.

Appropriately enough, every election in Upper Culm this century has resulted in the winning councillors covering a spread of political opinion. (Thomas) Glanmor Hughes was first elected in 2003, and represented the ward until 2019 in tandem with independent councillor Frank Rosamond. Hughes and Rosamond were elected without a contest in 2007, and enjoyed large majorities over Labour in 2011 and UKIP in 2015. Things changed for the 2019 election when Rosamond retired: the Lib Dems’ Simon Clist topped the poll, and Hughes saved his seat with a margin of just 22 votes over the second Lib Dem candidate Sean Ritchie. The vote shares were 50% for the Lib Dem slate and 36% for the Conservatives. Clist was the Lib Dem candidate here in the Devon county council elections last month, but the Conservatives easily held the local county division of Willand and Uffculme.

Elsewhere in the 2019 Mid Devon council elections, the Conservatives lost their majority. A coalition of independent, Lib Dem and Green councillors was formed, but following ructions in 2020 the Lib Dem councillors were sacked from the ruling coalition and replaced by the Conservative group. In May there were three by-elections to the council (page 123), with the Conservatives gaining two seats in Tiverton; they now hold 19 of the 42 seats against 11 Lib Dems, 9 independents, 2 Greens and this vacancy.

Defending for the Conservatives is James Bartlett, a dairy farmer from just over the county boundary in Sampford Arundel. The Lib Dems have reselected their runner-up from two years ago Sean Ritchie, who is the only candidate to live in the ward (in Hemyock). Also standing are Fiona Hutton for Labour and Adam Rich for the Green Party.*

* *Mid Devon, Upper Culm*: C 361 LD 346 Grn 74 Lab 31

East Garioch

Aberdeenshire council; caused by the death of Liberal Democrat councillor Fergus Hood at the age of 64.

We finish with something rather different as we travel to the north of Scotland. The Garioch (pronounced Geerie) is an agricultural area to the north-west of Aberdeen, centred on Inverurie. East Garioch ward lies between Aberdeen and Inverurie, immediately outside the Aberdeen city boundary.

The main population centre here is Kintore, which has been a Royal Burgh since the ninth century. Kintore lies on the main road and railway line from Aberdeen to Inverurie, and it gained a railway station in October last year as a part of major improvement works to the railway. The station was clearly needed: Aberdeen's economy has boomed as the home of the North Sea oil industry, and Kintore's population has nearly doubled since 2000.

The ward was created in 2007 when Scotland's local elections went over to proportional representation. In that year it elected two Lib Dems, Martin Ford and Nan Cullinane, and an SNP councillor, Fergie Hood. Ford subsequently defected from the Lib Dems to the Greens, being appalled at what Donald Trump was doing long before that became fashionable; he was re-elected in 2012 under his new colours.

Boundary changes for the 2017 election bumped the ward up from three councillors to four, reflecting the population growth, with a slight boundary extension to the west of Kintore. The outgoing SNP councillor, Fergus Hood, had by this time defected to the Liberal Democrats and he sought re-election under his new colours. The Conservatives surged into first place, polling 31% of the first preferences against 27% for the SNP and 19% each for the Greens and Lib Dems; those four parties all won one seat each. Had the count been for one seat, the Conservatives would have beaten the SNP by 57% to 43%.

Most of the ward is within the Gordon constituency at Westminster, and the Tories carried forward that good performance into the June 2017 general election to gain the seat from the then-SNP now-Alba figure Alex Salmond. The SNP took the Gordon constituency back in 2019, and new SNP MP Richard Thomson resigned from Aberdeenshire council; the Nationalists held the resulting council by-election in Ellon and District ward last October. In May the ward went to the polls for the Scottish Parliament election: the Aberdeenshire East constituency, which covers the Newmachar and Fintray part of the ward, was held by the SNP, while Kintore and Blackburn are covered by the Conservative-held constituency of Aberdeenshire West.

The fourth-placed Liberal Democrats are defending this by-election fol-

Westminster constituency: Gordon (most of ward), West Aberdeenshire and Kincardine (Blackburn)
Holyrood constituency: Aberdeenshire East (Newmachar and Fintray); Aberdeenshire West (Kintore and Blackburn)
May 2017 first preferences C 1429 SNP 1239 Grn 850 LD 842 Lab 179

Figure 38: Aberdeenshire, East Garioch

lowing the death of Fergie Hood, who had chaired the council's Garioch area committee since 2014. They will have to improve their position significantly to get into the final two, never mind win. The Lib Dems are part of the ruling coalition on Aberdeenshire council, which consists of 18 Conservatives, 13 Lib Dems plus this vacancy and 9 independents; in opposition are 17 SNP councillors plus a further vacancy, 5 independents, 3 councillors who have defected to Alba, 1 Labour councillor, 1 Green councillor and a Scottish Libertarian.

Defending for the Lib Dems is Trevor Mason, who finished a distant third in the Ellon and District by-election last October. I described him then* as the chair of Ellon community council, having lived in that town for 36 years. The Conservatives, who probably start as favourites, have selected David Keating who lives in Kintore and has worked in the oil industry for more than 40 years. The SNP's Dan Ritchie also lives in the ward, in Newmachar; he also worked in the oil industry before setting up a retail business. Standing for the Scottish Greens is Jamie Ogilvie, who is currently an NHS vaccination support worker. Completing a ballot paper of five candidates is Labour's Andy Brown, who was their Holyrood candidate for Aberdeenshire West last month. The usual Scottish disclaimers apply: it's Votes at 16 and please mark your ballot paper in order of preference.†

* *Andrew's Previews 2020*, page 108. † *Aberdeenshire, East Garioch*: first preferences C 1240 SNP 963 LD 281 Grn 130 Lab 111; final C 1394 SNP 1146 [C gain from LD]

24th June 2021

There are six local by-elections on 24th June 2021. In England, Labour and the Liberal Democrats defending one seat each, while the Conservatives attempt to defend one seat and recover a second which they lost to defection. There are also two independent defences in Wales and Scotland, with which we start:

Murdostoun

North Lanarkshire council, Scotland; caused by the death of independent councillor Robert McKendrick.

It's time for this column to return to North Lanarkshire for the third time in four months, following council by-elections in Fortissat and Thorniewood wards in March (page 12) and the Airdrie and Shotts parliamentary by-election in May (page 195). A small corner of the Airdrie and Shotts constituency, around the village of Newmains, lies in a ward named after the Murdostoun estate, centred on the fifteenth-century Murdostoun Castle.

Murdostoun Castle was in the hands of the aristocratic Inglis-Hamilton family until the 1850s, when it was bought by the Lord Provost of Glasgow Robert Stewart. Stewart was one of a number of industrialists who had cashed in on the discovery of extensive ironstone and coal reserves under this corner of Lanarkshire in the 1830s; by 1840 a number of ironworking factories were already in place at Newmains and Coltness, and the opening of a railway line to Coatbridge in 1841 secured the future of heavy industry in this corner of Scotland. The Coltness Iron Works made it into the 21st century, diversifying into brick and cement manufacture, but they were demolished in 2004.

Newmains is the largest standalone population centre in the modern Murdostoun ward, as Coltness (which saw large population growth after the Second World War with the building of new estates) is effectively now a suburb of Wishaw. The ward's railhead, however, is at the pit village of Cleland which lies on the recently-electrified line between Edinburgh and Glasgow via Shotts.

Westminster constituency: Motherwell and Wishaw (most of ward), Airdrie and Shotts (Newmains area)
Holyrood constituency: Motherwell and Wishaw
May 2017 first preferences SNP 1791 Ind 1765 Lab 1520 C 825 Ind 284 Ind 154 UKIP 67

Figure 39: North Lanarkshire, Murdostoun

Politically, Newmains was unusual in the 2003 North Lanarkshire elections in that it returned an independent councillor. In fact, both of the top two places in that ward were taken by independents, with David McKendrick narrowly beating his brother Robert McKendrick. If press reports from the time are anything to go by, they weren't exactly on good terms. David McKendrick stood down at the 2007 election, which was the first to be held for the modern Murdostoun ward under proportional representation: Labour won two seats, with the other two seats going to the SNP and to Robert McKendrick.

That's still the political balance in the ward today, following an extremely close result in the May 2017 election. On slightly revised boundaries Robert McKendrick topped the poll with 28% of the first preferences, and was re-elected on the first count; the SNP also polled 28%, Labour crashed to 24%, and the Conservatives polled 13%. The two Labour candidates were well-balanced, with outgoing councillor Nicky Shevlin and new candidate Louise Roarty starting on 12.2% and 11.5% each; by contrast, two-thirds of the SNP first preferences went to Cameron McManus, with his running-mate Anum Qaisar starting on just 9.1% of the vote. In Scotland's proportional representation system, piling most of your party's votes on your lead candidate tends not to be a winning strategy because it leaves your trailing candidates vulnerable to being knocked out before the final stages: sure enough, Qaisar was the last candidate to be eliminated. Her transfers were *just* enough to enable both Labour candidates to overtake the Conservatives in the final count: Roarty finished on 1,014 votes, Shevlin was re-elected to the final seat on 1,008 votes, and the Conservative candidate Cindy Mackenzie finished as the runner-up with 1,005 votes. Anum Qaisar-Javed, as she now is, has subsequently put that defeat behind her to go on to greater things: she won the Airdrie and Shotts parliamentary by-election last month.

Elsewhere in North Lanarkshire the Labour party lost their majority in 2017, but they still continue to govern as a minority. At the last count the council had 31 Labour members, 27 SNP, 8 Conservatives, 8 independents, 2 councillors who had defected to Alex Salmond's new party Alba, and this vacancy.

The usual Scottish disclaimers apply, with Votes at 16 and the Alternative Vote in effect. We saw in May 2017 that transfers can be absolutely crucial, and that might be the case this time round as well. If we re-count the votes cast in May 2017 for one seat, it goes to Robert McKendrick with a 59–41 margin over the SNP in the final count. There's a good chance we might see something like that happen again in this by-election, because Robert McKendrick's son—also called Robert McKendrick—is seeking to take over his late father's seat on North Lanarkshire council. Like his father, Robert junior is standing as an independent candidate. The SNP needed to find a new candidate after Qaisar's election to Westminster; they have selected Julia Stachurska, a local resident who is studying for a society, politics and policy degree at the University of the West of Scotland and who is the national convenor of SNP Students. Like the McKendricks and the SNP, Labour have also turned to the next generation by nominating Chris Roarty, the son of ward councillor Louise Roarty; Chris is a construction worker and drummer who sits on Cleland community council. The Conservatives have reselected Cindy Mackenzie after her very close near-miss in 2017. Completing the ballot paper are independent candidate Robert Arthur who also stood here in 2017, polling 2.4% and finishing eighth out of nine candidates; Nathaniel Hamilton of the Scottish Greens; Julie McAnulty, a former SNP North Lanarkshire councillor who is now the deputy leader of the Independence for Scotland Party which makes its electoral debut here; and Billy Ross, who is the first Scottish council by-election candidate for Reform UK.*

Harlech

Gwynedd council, Wales; caused by the resignation of independent councillor Freya Bentham.

For our Welsh by-election, it's time for something completely different. Welcome to the west coast of Wales, to the Snowdonia National Park, and to the tiny town of Harlech. This is a major location in Welsh and indeed British history thanks to the well-preserved Harlech Castle, which was built on a coastal location at the command of the English King Edward I in the 1280s. The castle saw action in the Glyndŵr rebellion of the 1400s, serving as Owain Glyndŵr's headquarters; two centuries later, it was the last Royalist castle to surrender in the English Civil War. In between, during the Wars of the Roses, the Yorkists besieged the castle for seven years; that siege inspired the military march and song *Men of Harlech*.

In the 1280s Harlech Castle lay on the shoreline and had a watergate; today it's set back a long way from the sea, overlooking a flat landscape of sand dunes, a golf course, the town's railway station (a passing-place on the Cambrian Coast

* *North Lanarkshire, Murdostoun*: first preferences McKendrick 1504 SNP 884 Lab 617 Arthur 293 C 264 Grn 61 Independence for Scotland 14 Reform UK 7; final McKendrick 1873 SNP 1060

line), and the Ysgol Ardudwy secondary school. Ysgol Ardudwy, whose former pupils include the novelist Sir Philip Pullman, serves the entire Ardudwy area from Barmouth in the south to Penrhyndeudraeth in the north; many pupils commute into the school on the railway.

The Ardudwy area contains a relatively large amount (by Meirionnydd standards) of flat, fertile land, but once the ground starts to rise it rises very quickly towards the impassible Rhinog mountains in the east. So quickly, indeed, that Ffordd Pen Llech (a single-track road climbing around the north side of the castle) was once considered the steepest street in the world. (Unfortunately, since a sign saying that was installed Guinness have reverted that title back to Baldwin Street in Dunedin, New Zealand.) The sign at the top end of Ffordd Pen Llech warns of a gradient of 40%, which is a slight overexaggeration, with the statement "Unsuitable for motors"; should you wish to ignore that warning, the street is one-way for motor traffic in the downhill direction only. Having walked up the street myself last year as a pedestrian, all I can say is that I wouldn't want to walk down it.

But unless you're prepared to walk, there is no way east from Harlech. All communication links follow the coast south towards Barmouth and Dolgellau, or north towards Porthmadog or Ffestiniog. The road and railway line north will take you through Talsarnau, which is part of the Harlech electoral division, and to the railway and road bridge of Pont Briwet which forms the link across the Traeth Bach estuary to Penrhyndeudraeth. The original Victorian wooden toll bridge, which despite its Grade II listing had become increasingly dilapidated, was demolished in 2014 and replaced by a modern structure for which no tolls are charged.

Harlech is part of Gwynedd council, which is controlled by the Welsh nationalist party Plaid Cymru. From 1999 to 2017 it was represented on the council by local sheep farmer Edmund Caerwyn Roberts of Plaid, who didn't face a contested election until 2012 when he despatched a candidate from Llais Gwynedd (an anti-Plaid localist party) without much trouble. However, in 2017 Roberts lost his seat to independent candidate Freya Bentham by just five votes, 297 to 292; Bentham and Roberts both polled 39% of the vote.

For this by-election two independent candidates have come forward to succeed Bentham. One is Lisa Birks, who describes herself as a working parent from Talsarnau. The other is Martin Hughes, who sits on Harlech community council and on the standards committee for the Snowdonia National Park; he is an energy broker who previously was finance director of Coleg Harlech, a now-defunct adult education college in Harlech. Plaid Cymru will want the seat back and they have selected Gwynfor Owen, a professional translator who has previously

Westminster and Senedd constituency: Dwyfor Meirionnydd
May 2017 result Ind 297 PC 292 C 70 Lab 70 UKIP 24
May 2012 result PC 471 Llais Gwynedd 187
May 2008 result PC unopposed
June 2004 result PC unopposed
May 1999 result PC unopposed
May 1995 result Ind 462 PC 360

Figure 40: Gwynedd, Harlech

served on Gwynedd council (Porthmadog East, 1995–99); Owen gives an address outside the division in Penrhyndeudraeth. Those are your three candidates: more information on all of them is available from the Local Democracy Reporting Service*. Don't forget that Wales has recently extended its local election franchise, so Votes at 16 apply in this by-election.†

North Curry and Ruishton

Somerset West and Taunton council; caused by the resignation of Liberal Democrat councillor Phil Stone.

As we move into England, it would be remiss of me not to talk about the Liberal Democrats following their important by-election win last week. No, not the one in Chesham and Amersham: I'm talking about the Old Cleeve and District ward of Somerset (page 226), one of two polls in consecutive weeks which the Liberal Democrats needed to win to preserve their overall majority on Somerset West and Taunton council. The Conservatives cut the majority in the seat to just six votes, but a win is a win and the Lib Dems can now move on to the second part of this two-part series.

So, for some spicy electoral action we come to the ward of North Curry and Ruishton. This is a diverse rural area, running from the eastern edge of Taunton at Ruishton down to the Somerset Levels at Burrowbridge. The excellence of the area's mediaeval churches demonstrates that this was a rich agricultural area in centuries gone by; indeed North Curry was the centre of its own Hundred. Stoke St Gregory, down on the Levels, is home to the Willows and Wetlands visitor centre; tennis fans can also travel there to visit the grave of Bunny Austin, the last Briton before Sir Andy Murray to reach the Wimbledon men's singles final, who lies at rest in the Stoke St Gregory churchyard. Part of the modern-day

* `https://tinyurl.com/2p8b4dpw` † *Gwynedd, Harlech*: PC 161 Birks 154 Hughes 153 [PC gain from Ind]

Parliamentary constituency: Taunton Deane
Somerset county council division: Monkton and North Curry (Burrowbridge, North Curry and Stoke St Gregory parishes); Blackdown and Neroche (Ruishton, Stoke St Mary and Thornfalcon parishes)
May 2019 result LD 1362/1090 C 455/443

Figure 41: Somerset West and Taunton, North Curry and Ruishton

village of Athelney lies within the ward, although the Isle of Athelney itself is over the boundary in Sedgemoor district.

This ward, like Somerset West and Taunton council itself, was created in 2019. Before then the area was covered by two wards of Taunton Deane council: North Curry and Stoke St Gregory ward was the political fiefdom of veteran Lib Dem councillor Phil Stone, while Ruishton and Creech ward was a Conservative-inclined marginal. The Conservatives did very badly in the inaugural Somerset West and Taunton elections in 2019, and the Lib Dems won both seats in the new ward with a large majority of 75–25.

The Lib Dems unexpectedly won a majority of one seat on the new council in those 2019 elections, and bolstered that by gaining two by-elections later that year. However, there appears to have been some infighting within the group. North Curry and Ruishton councillor Phil Stone resigned earlier this year, 34 years after his first election to Taunton Deane council, after falling out with the council leadership; and other defections mean that the party has to hold this resulting by-election to preserve its majority on the council. Following last week's by-election, the council composition stands at 29 Lib Dems plus this vacancy, 14 independents, 10 Conservatives, 3 Labour and 2 Greens.

That this may be a more difficult task than it looks is shown by the last Somerset county council elections, which were held in May 2017 at a better time for the Tories. The North Curry half of the ward is part of the safely Conservative county division of Monkton and North Curry, while the Ruishton half is covered by the Blackdown and Neroche county division which the Conservatives gained from the Lib Dems in 2017. There were no county council elections in Somerset in 2021, to allow for a consultation on further local government reform in the county.

Defending for the Liberal Democrats is Barrie Hall, a physics teacher at Richard Huish sixth-form college in Taunton. The Conservatives have selected Tom Linnell, who describes himself as a local businessman and resident. Completing the ballot paper is Cathy Parmenter for the Green Party.*

* *Somerset West and Taunton, North Curry and Ruishton*: LD 798 C 678 Grn 133

Priory Vale

Swindon council, Wiltshire; caused by the resignation of independent councillor Emma Faramarzi, who was elected as a Conservative.

For our other South West by-election we consider something completely different. The town of Swindon has seen large population growth in this century, and this has been achieved through the development of large housing estates. Such as the parish of Haydon Wick, once a rural area on the northern edge of Swindon, which has been almost entirely filled with houses over the last 25 years.

To some extent, the Local Government Boundary Commission saw this coming. In their review of Swindon's wards which was implemented in May 2000, they created a brand-new ward called Abbey Meads with three councillors and a 1998 electorate of 992 (in a year when the average three-member ward in Swindon would have had an electorate of 6,900). By May 2000 the electorate was up to 2,649 voters, who returned a Conservative slate including a recent Oxford Brookes graduate called Justin Tomlinson. Abbey Meads grew and grew and grew into a safe Conservative ward, and Tomlinson used it as a springboard into Parliament: since 2010 he has been the MP for the local seat of North Swindon, and he has joined the government ladder as a junior DWP minister.

We can paint a fairly accurate picture of the sort of people who were attracted to all these new houses from Abbey Meads' return in the 2011 census. It made the top 20 wards in England and Wales for full-time employment (59.8%) and the top 20 wards in England and Wales for the 30–44 age bracket (34.1%, which was the highest figure for any ward in the South West). The proportion of under-16s (26.4%) is the third-highest figure in the South West. High proportions of the workforce are in managerial and professional work, although the number with degrees is a bit lower than you might expect given that.

By 2010 Abbey Meads ward had grown far beyond the 1998 projections to 13,408 voters, a figure which was still rising strongly, in a year when the average three-member ward in Swindon would have had an electorate of 7,989. The ward was broken up for the 2012 election, with much of it going into a new ward called Priory Vale covering the western half of Haydon Wick parish. Priory Vale has continued as a safely Conservative area; in the ordinary Swindon elections last month the Tories beat Labour here 54–33. Excellent local election performances in 2019 and 2021 have given the Conservatives a strong majority on Swindon council: they hold 36 seats, Labour have 20 and the remaining seat is this vacancy left behind by former council cabinet member Emma Faramazi. She had left the Conservatives in 2020, some months before her recent resignation from the council.

Parliamentary constituency: North Swindon
May 2021 result C 1470 Lab 891 Grn 211 Ind 138
May 2019 result C 1260 Lab 860
May 2018 result C 1605 Lab 798 Grn 146 LD 118 UKIP 67
May 2016 result C 1131 Lab 505 UKIP 258 LD 88 Grn 83
May 2015 result C 3314 Lab 1213 UKIP 658 Grn 282
May 2014 result C 1232 UKIP 519 Lab 513 LD 158
May 2012 result C 1227/1161/1109 Lab 466/464/459 UKIP 308 LD 145

Figure 42: Swindon, Priory Vale

Defending for the Conservatives is Kate Tomlinson, the wife and constituency office manager of Justin Tomlinson MP. Labour have reselected Ian Edwards, who fought the ward in the ordinary election in May. Two other candidates returning from May are Stephen Litchfield of the Greens and independent candidate Elena Mari; together with Joseph Polson of the Lib Dems, they complete the ballot paper.*

Wolvey and Shilton

Rugby council, Warwickshire; caused by the resignation of Conservative councillor Chris Pacey-Day.

For our Midlands by-election this week it's back to the villages. In these football-mad weeks the name "Shilton" might bring to mind the great England goalkeeper of yesteryear, but the Shilton I'm talking about in this article is a village just to the north-east of Coventry. Together with the village of Wolvey to the north, Shilton is part of an electoral ward which runs from the edge of Coventry to the Roman Road of Watling Street.

Despite its location close to the city of Coventry and to the towns of Nuneaton and Hinckley, Wolvey and Shilton ward is administered as part of the Rugby local government district. Rugby council got new ward boundaries in 2012 which created this ward, and the Conservatives' Chris Pacey-Day had sat since then with very large majorities. He was last re-elected in 2018, defeating Labour in a straight fight by exactly 3 to 1 (561 votes to 187). The ward went to the polls in May as part of the Fosse division of Warwickshire county council, which had a wider choice of candidates but was also safely Conservative.

Defending for the Conservatives is Becky Maoudis, who lives in Shilton. Labour have selected Richard Harrington, who has contested a few local elections in the Rugby area in recent years with no success to date. Completing the ballot

* *Swindon, Priory Vale*: C 1139 Lab 508 LD 102 Grn 83 Ind 47

Parliamentary constituency: Rugby
Warwickshire county council division: Fosse
May 2018 result C 561 Lab 187
May 2014 result C 545 Lab 171 Grn 91
May 2012 result C 465 Lab 225

Figure 43: Rugby, Wolvey and Shilton

paper is the ward's first Liberal Democrat candidate, Sam Edwards.*

Chichester East

Chichester council, West Sussex; caused by the resignation of Labour councillor Kevin Hughes.

We finish for the week in the cathedral city of Chichester, the home of West Sussex county council and one of the oldest cities in the UK. The Romans knew the city as *Noviomagus Reginorum*, there are extensive Roman remains here, and Chichester was the southern end of the Roman Road of Stane Street which ran to a small town on the Thames estuary called *Londinium*. Stane Street started at the city's eastern gate and ran (now as the A 285 road) through the modern Chichester East ward, which has become extensively built up over the last two millennia.

This column may not be following in the footsteps of the Romans, but the ground I write about has definitely been trodden before by the great psephologist Robert Waller, whose magisterial *Almanac of British Politics* forms the benchmark against which all future electoral commentary is judged. Believe me, this previewing game is harder than it looks; there have been many occasions on which Andrew's Previews has been weighed in the balance of Waller's work and found wanting. Every edition of Waller's *Almanac* joked that "even after the revolution the workers' soviet for Chichester would be Tory"; well, like all good jokes, there's a grain of truth and a lot of exaggeration in that.

Chichester may be a city, but its city council is a parish-level body: this by-election is for Chichester district council, which covers a huge swathe of true-blue rural Sussex all the way up to the Surrey boundary. The forerunner to the future Chichester Workers' Soviet does normally have a Conservative majority, but the first election to the modern Chichester council in 1973 saw the Conservative group outnumbered by independent councillors, and at the Tory nadir of 1995 the Liberal Democrats were the largest party on a hung council. The May 2019 elections to the city also saw the Conservatives lose their majority

* *Rugby, Wolvey and Shilton*: C 370 Lab 60 LD 29 Grn 24

Parliamentary constituency: Chichester
West Sussex county council division: Chichester East
May 2019 result Lab 462/441 C 380/355 LD 283/246 Grn 279 UKIP 146

Figure 44: Chichester, Chichester East

on the council, crashing from 42 seats out of 48 to 18 seats out of 36; and there are signs that the long-awaited left-wing revolution may be cranking into life here. The Labour Party won two seats on Chichester council in 2019, both of them here in Chichester East ward: that's the first time Labour had won a seat on this council since 1995, and the first time ever that Chichester had returned more than one Labour councillor. Shares of the vote in Chichester East were 30% for Labour, 25% for the Conservatives and 18% each for the Lib Dems and Greens.

This Cicestrian red wave didn't translate through to the May 2021 West Sussex county elections, partly because Labour's performance last month was generally nothing to write home about and partly because the county division boundaries give the city four "rurban" divisions, with each of the four Chichester county divisions covering significant territory outside the city proper. The larger Chichester East county division remains safe Conservative.

The ruling Conservative group on Chichester council got their majority back in November 2019 by taking a by-election off the Lib Dems*, but they have suffered two defections since then to put them in a minority again. There are currently 17 Conservative councillors, 10 Lib Dems, 5 independents across two council groups, 2 Greens, and 1 Labour plus this vacancy. As can be seen, the Tories need to gain this by-election to get back to half of the seats, while Labour need to hold the seat to retain group status on the council.

Defending for Labour is Clare Walsh. The Conservatives have selected their constituency party chairman Jane Kilby, who was a councillor for the previous Chichester East ward from 2015 to 2019 and also sat on the district council before then from 1987 to 2003. The Liberal Democrat candidate is Bill Brisbane. The Green Party have not nominated a candidate, so that is your ballot paper.†

* *Andrew's Previews 2019*, page 374. † *Chichester, Chichester East*: LD 430 C 310 Lab 261 [LD gain from Lab]

1st July 2021: Parliamentary Special

There are eight by-elections taking place in England on 1st July 2021 with nine seats up for election. It's a balanced picture with three defences each for the Conservatives, Labour and independent councillors, and a nice spread between the North, the Midlands and the South. All the local by-elections are in the Midlands and the South, but we'll start with the Parliamentary Special in the sun-soaked north:

Batley and Spen

House of Commons; caused by the resignation of Labour MP Tracy Brabin, who is now the Mayor of the West Yorkshire Combined Authority.

Welcome to what this column determinedly calls the Wrong Side of the Pennines. To quote no less a figure than the Speaker of the House of Commons, there are only two good things that come out of Yorkshire: Yorkshire Tea (slightly too many cups of which have powered the writing of this column) and the M 62 taking you to Lancashire. Those intrepid souls who traverse the M 62 in the opposite direction, *into* the Land of the White Rose, will find themselves soon enough within the constituency known as Batley and Spen, which covers a series of small towns in the space between West Yorkshire's large urban centres: Leeds lies to the north-east, Bradford to the north-west, Wakefield to the east, Huddersfield to the south-west.

The largest town in the seat is Batley, which has come a long way since the days of the Batley Ladies Townswomen's Guild. This is a classic Pennine textile town, but the textiles here weren't wool or cotton but shoddy: that is, recycled rags and clothes. In order to staff the textile mills, Batley saw large amounts of immigration from the Indian subcontinent in the 1950s and 1960s, mostly from Gujarat and the Punjab.

A few generations on, we can see the effect of this in modern census returns. Batley East ward is majority Asian (54%) and majority Muslim (52%), and makes the top 30 wards in England and Wales for those looking after home or family (11.3% of the workforce). 17% of the ward's workforce have never worked or are long-term unemployed. There are also significant Asian populations in Batley West and Heckmondwike. With the demise of the textile industry, the major contributions to Batley's economy come from the Fox's Biscuits factory and The Mill, a factory outlet in a renovated textile mill.

But Batley is only a third of the seat. The Spen Valley towns, on the other hand, have a low non-white population and in places a commuter demographic, being within easy reach of both Leeds and Bradford (if the M 62 is playing nicely, and this is a notoriously congested stretch of it); while Leeds and Bradford come here to shop at the West Yorkshire IKEA store in Birstall. This is a land of small towns like Cleckheaton, Birstall, Liversedge and Birkenshaw: places that are little-known and little-visited outside by-election time. Meat and drink for this column.

In another timeline, Birstall could have been famous as the name of a parliamentary seat. The 1885 redistribution, which essentially created the single-member constituency system the UK has today, split up the old Eastern Division of the West Riding (plus the Knaresborough and Ripon borough constituencies, which were abolished) into six single-member constituencies, one of which—covering Liversedge, Cleckheaton and associated towns in a corner of the old Eastern Division—was identified in the accompanying map as "Birstal". (This is Yorkshire, we don't bother with unnecessary letters.) There was some debate over this name in Parliament, and the seat which eventually emerged had the same boundaries but a different name: "Spen Valley", after the river running through the area.

At this time the Spen Valley seat was dominated by the woollen industry and by nonconformism. This was a recipe for Liberal votes, and throughout the period 1885–1910 this was a Liberal constituency. Both of its MPs during this period were newspaper proprietors: Joseph Woodhead, who served from 1885, had been a co-founder of the *Huddersfield Examiner* newspaper, while Thomas Whitaker, who took over from Woodhead in 1892, had edited a number of periodicals. Whitaker's smallest majorities were 821 in the 1895 election and 496 in December 1910; otherwise, his seat was safe.

Batley was also part of a Liberal constituency throughout this period. It was part of the parliamentary borough of Dewsbury, which had been enfranchised in 1868 as part of the Second Reform Act: the boundaries of the Dewsbury seat during this period consisted of Dewsbury, Batley and the village of Soothill to the east of Batley.*

Dewsbury's first MP was Sir John Simon, who had been born into a Jewish family in Jamaica but had made his career in England, in the law. (He was not related to the twentieth-century Liberal MP also called Sir John Simon, of whom more later.) In 1864 Simon was created a serjeant-at-law, a barrister's position which fell into disuse shortly afterwards as Queen's Counsel outranked them. Simon had won the inaugural Dewsbury election in 1868, defeating future Bristol MP Handel Cossham in an all-Liberal contest; once he became the agreed Liberal candidate in 1885 he enjoyed very large majorities over the Conservatives.

Sir John Simon left the Commons in 1888 on health grounds. The resulting first Dewsbury by-election easily returned the Liberals' Mark Oldroyd, a local boy who owned a very successful textile firm in the Heavy Woollen District. Oldroyd's company owned four mills in Dewsbury which employed over 2,000 people, and was wealthy enough to have its own dedicated colliery to supply coal to power the looms. Like many Victorian Liberal entrepreneurs, Mark Oldroyd used some of the profits from this industry in philanthropic works in Dewsbury and Batley, and he had served as mayor of Dewsbury. In the 1888 by-election he easily defeated the Liberal Unionist H O Arnold-Forster, who would go on to serve as War Secretary in Arthur Balfour's cabinet.

Mark Oldroyd left the Commons in late 1901 to concentrate on his business. The resulting second Dewsbury by-election on 28th January 1902 provided a route back into Parliament for one of the Liberals' rising stars.

Walter Runciman, the son of a Tyneside shipping magnate of the same name†, had first been elected to Parliament in July 1899 in a double by-election for the two-seat Oldham constituency; his Liberal slate defeated a rather unconventional Conservative slate of James Mawdsley, a trade unionist (in the Amalgamation, a politically-moderate cotton-spinners' union) and Winston Churchill, a 24-year-old war correspondent with the *Morning Post* who was fighting his first election campaign. The 1899 Oldham double by-election returned Runciman in second place, with a majority of 1,293 over Churchill, but Churchill had defeated Runciman by 222 votes in the rematch at the following year's general election.

The 1902 Dewsbury by-election duly returned Runciman to Parliament,

* The originally-published version of this column stated that Batley was part of the Morley constituency during the period 1885–1918. While this is technically true, in practice most people from Batley who were eligible to vote at this time would have been eligible to vote for the Dewsbury borough; only the small minority who were not qualified as Dewsbury voters would have cast votes for the Morley county division. The paragraphs relating to Morley have been removed, and the next page or so covering the Dewsbury constituency in 1885–1918 has been specially written for this book. † For more on Walter Runciman senior see page 159.

although he was pushed hard by the Conservative candidate Joe Haley, a former mayor of Dewsbury who owned a blanket and rug-making mill in the town. Haley's total of 4,512 votes was the Conservatives' best-ever total in the constituency, although Runciman eventually prevailed with a majority of 1,148. Some left-wing votes undoubtedly went to the noted Marxist Harry Quelch, standing for the Social Democratic Federation as the first socialist candidate in Dewsbury.

Runciman made Dewsbury safe again in the 1906 and both 1910 elections, by which time he had started to ascend the greasy pole of government. He joined Asquith's Cabinet in 1908 as President of the Board of Education; under the rules at the time, that meant he had to seek re-election from his constituents. He was duly re-elected in the third Dewsbury by-election, held on 23rd April 1908, with a reduced majority of 1,516 over the Conservatives.

Walter Runciman went on to serve in Cabinet for over eight years, becoming President of the Board of Agriculture in 1911 and President of the Board of Trade on the outbreak of the First World War in 1914. He left the frontbenches when the Asquith coalition fell in December 1916, and he did not serve under Lloyd George.

The 1918 redistribution made major changes in this area. The Dewsbury constituency was cut back to cover just the county borough of Dewsbury, and Batley transferred into a redrawn Morley division of the West Riding which was renamed as Batley and Morley. Runciman sought re-election in the revised Dewsbury seat (which he lost), and the Liberal nomination in Batley and Morley went to the previous Morley MP Gerald France. France was a businessman and temperance campaigner (like Thomas Whitaker in the Spen Valley) who had represented the seat since January 1910.

Whitaker and France were both re-elected in 1918 as Coalition Liberals, in straight fights with Labour. Spen Valley was safe enough for Whitaker, but Gerald France held Batley and Morley with a majority of just 1,468 votes.

Thomas Whitaker died in November 1919 at the age of 69. The resulting Spen Valley by-election, held five days before Christmas but not declared until 3rd January, broke the mould of British politics. At the time the Liberal Party was split over whether to continue in the coalition government, and two Liberal candidates contested the by-election: Colonel Bryan Fairfax with the coupon, and the former Home Secretary and Attorney-General Sir John Simon (who had lost his seat in 1918) without. Fairfax polled 8,134 votes, Simon beat him with 10,244; but both of them lost the Spen Valley by-election to the Labour candidate Tom Myers, a Dewsbury councillor who had previously fought the seat in 1918. Myers polled 11,962 votes, or 39%, winning with a majority over Simon of 1,718. The Labour Party had arrived, and shown themselves as a political force to be reckoned with.

Sir John Simon won the rematch against Myers in 1922 by 787 votes, regaining the Spen Valley seat for the Liberals. Batley and Morley, however, went the other way with a big win for the Labour candidate Ben Turner, a Batley councillor and general president of the newly-formed National Union of Textile Workers. Turner had previously contested the Dewsbury constituency in 1906 and the 1908 by-election, on both of those occasions as a Labour Representation Committee candidate.

The Liberals made ground in both seats in 1923 and 1924. By 1924 Sir John Simon's majority in Spen Valley was over 4,000 votes, and the Liberal candidate Walter Forrest defeated Ben Turner that year in Batley and Morley by 16,369 votes to 15,966, a majority of 403. A former West Riding county councillor and Mayor of Pudsey, Forrest had previously served in parliament after winning the 1919 Pontefract by-election, but had lost his seat there in 1922.

Both seats swung back to Labour in 1929. Turner easily defeated Forrest in Batley and Morley (no Liberal has represented Batley since), while Sir John Simon's majority in Spen Valley was cut to 1,739. Simon's re-election was helped by a deal with the Conservatives, as he had agreed to chair the so-called Simon Commission on constitutional reform in India on condition that the Conservatives did not stand against him in 1929.

During the 1929 parliament Simon became the leader of the faction of the Liberals which opposed Lloyd George's maintenance in office of the second Ramsay Macdonald Labour government. Matters came to a head in June 1931 when Sir John Simon resigned the Liberal whip, precipitating a split in the party: he became the leader of the Liberal National Party, or the "Simonites".* Simon contested the October general election of that year under the new Liberal National label, was re-elected in Spen Valley by a landside, and following the election he returned to Cabinet as Foreign Secretary.

The 1931 general election was a notorious disaster for Labour, and one of the seats they lost was Batley and Morley. Wilfred Wills, from the Wills tobacco family, became the first Conservative candidate and the only Conservative MP for that seat, defeating Ben Turner in a landslide.

Labour made a recovery in 1935, regaining Batley and Morley with a majority of 2,828 on a 15% swing. The seat's new MP was Willie Brooke, a Bradford city councillor who had served from 1929 to 1931 as MP for Dunbartonshire. After a torrid time as Foreign Secretary, Sir John Simon held Spen Valley by 21,671 votes to 21,029 for Labour, a majority of just 642. Following the election, Stanley

* As opposed to the Simmonites, who were based on the other side of Huddersfield in Holmfirth and were best known for riding down hillsides in bathtubs.

Baldwin reshuffled Simon to Home Secretary; he became Chancellor of the Exchequer in Neville Chamberlain's first government.

Neither Brooke nor Simon made it to the end of the 1935–45 Commons term. Willie Brooke's health failed in 1938, and he died in January 1939 at the age of just 43. After some speculation that J B Priestley might contest the resulting Batley and Morley by-election as an Independent Progressive candidate (*plus ça change, plus c'est la même chose*), the candidate list settled down to Labour versus Conservative as in 1935. Wilfred Wills tried to get his old seat back, but was defeated by the new Labour candidate Hubert Beaumont who was elected to Parliament at his fourth attempt. Beaumont increased the Labour majority to 3,896. Sir John Simon was appointed Lord Chancellor in 1940 and accordingly elevated to the Lords as the first Viscount Simon; the resulting Spen Valley by-election was held during the wartime political truce, and the new Liberal National candidate William Woolley was returned unopposed.

The Attlee landslide of 1945 swept Woolley away. Labour won the Spen Valley seat rather easily with their new candidate Granville Sharp, who had spent the Second World War as a senior Army officer, mostly serving on the Allied staff; by polling day he had the rank of lieutenant-colonel. The Batley and Morley MP Hubert Beaumont was also re-elected, and following the election he was appointed as a Deputy Speaker.

Hubert Beaumont died in December 1948 at the age of 65, and the resulting Batley and Morley by-election of February 1949 returned Labour's Alfred Broughton without fuss. Broughton was a doctor and (at the time) a Batley councillor.

The 1950 redistribution abolished the Spen Valley seat and cut the Batley and Morley seat down to just the two towns of the same name, with Ossett being transferred into the Dewsbury constituency. The Dewsbury seat also took in Mirfield and Heckmondwike from the Spen Valley constituency, with the remaining towns (by now merged into the Spenborough urban district) joining with three towns to the west: Brighouse, Queensbury and Shelf, all of which had previously been in the Elland constituency. The Spen Valley MP Granville Sharp elected to retire, and Brighouse and Spenborough was won in the February 1950 general election by the outgoing Labour MP for Elland, Frederick Cobb. Cobb had been a radio engineer before entering politics, having worked on radios for the Merchant Navy, 2LO and the Indian Broadcasting Company. He defeated the former Spen Valley Liberal National MP William Woolley (now standing as a National Liberal and Conservative) by 25,588 votes to 23,456, a majority of 2,132.

Frederick Cobb died just five weeks later at the age of 49, cutting the Attlee government's overall majority to just three seats. The resulting first Brighouse and Spenborough by-election, held in May 1950, was narrowly held by the Labour candidate John Edwards who had lost his seat in Blackburn at the general election. Edwards had been general secretary of the Post Office Engineering Union before being elected in Blackburn in 1945, and he was a junior minister from 1947 in the Ministry of Health and the Board of Trade. He beat William Woolley by 24,004 votes to 23,567, a reduced majority of 437.

The 1950 Parliament was short-lived, but there was time for Edwards to get back on the ministerial ladder as a junior Treasury minister. He held his seat in 1951 with a majority of 2,277 over Woolley. With Labour now in opposition, Edwards became chairman of the Commons Public Accounts Committee and some years later, the first British president of the Parliamentary Assembly of the Council of Europe. Boundary changes for the 1959 election, which restored Heckmondwike to the seat with Queensberry and Shelf transferred to Bradford South, shored up his marginal seat but only a little. Edwards held Brighouse and Spenborough in 1955 by 1,626 votes, and he was re-elected in 1959 by 23,290 votes to 23,243, a majority over the Conservative and National Liberal candidate Michael Shaw of just 47 votes.

Just a month after the 1959 election John Edwards died suddenly at the age of 55, while in Strasbourg on Council of Europe business. The resulting second Brighouse and Spenborough by-election, which didn't take place until March 1960, has entered British electoral folklore as one of only five (arguably six) occasions since the Second World War in which the governing party has taken a seat off the opposition at a by-election. (The other four or five are Sunderland South in 1953, arguably Bristol South East in 1961, Mitcham and Morden in 1982, Copeland in 2017, and Hartlepool two months ago.) With the Macmillan government at the height of its power, on a swing of under 1% the National Liberal and Conservative candidate Michael Shaw overturned a Labour majority of 47 to win by 22,472 votes to 21,806, a majority of 666 votes.

Michael Shaw, who died in January this year at the age of 100, went on to have a long Parliamentary career, but not from Brighouse and Spenborough as he lost re-election here in 1964. He served from 1966 to 1992 as Conservative MP for Scarborough (or its successor seat, Scarborough and Whitby), and was subsequently elevated to the Lords in 1994.

Shaw was defeated in Brighouse and Spenborough in 1964 by Labour's Colin Jackson, who had lost the by-election four yours previously; Jackson won with a majority of 922 after losing less support than Shaw to a Liberal intervention. The first Liberal (as opposed to National Liberal) candidate for the Spen Valley since 1929 was James Pickles, a barrister and former Labour Brighouse councillor who at the time was best known as a nephew of the actor Wilfred Pickles; James, who saved his deposit in the election in the days when you needed 12½% to do that, subsequently became a somewhat controversial judge and writer.

The 1970 election in Brighouse and Spenborough resulted in yet another photofinish. Colin Jackson polled 22,894 votes, but lost his seat to the Conservatives' Wilf Proudfoot who polled 22,953 votes and won with a majority of 59. Proudfoot was an entrepreneur with a growing chain of Yorkshire supermarkets and a number of sidelines, including politics. He had been elected in 1950 as the youngest member of Scarborough council, and this was his second stint in the Commons after serving from 1959 to 1964 as Conservative MP for Cleveland. Since then, in 1966–67 Proudfoot had been the managing director and main financial backer for Radio 270, a pirate station broadcasting from a ship off Scarborough. One of Radio 270's DJs, Sir Roger Gale, is now a long-serving Conservative MP; another of Proudfoot's employees, Christine Holman, who worked as a secretary during his spell as MP for Brighouse and Spenborough, later became famous under her married name of Christine Hamilton.

Colin Jackson got his seat back in February 1974, defeating Wilf Proudfoot by 1,546 votes; a rematch between them in October 1974 resulted in Jackson increasing his majority to 2,177. That was the last Parliamentary campaign for both of them, as Jackson didn't seek re-election in 1979.

While all this action was going on Brighouse and Spenborough, Batley and Morley was re-electing Dr Alf Broughton as its Labour MP with large majorities on each occasion. By the late 1970s Sir Alfred (as he now was) was in his tenth and final term of office, he was in his mid-70s, and he was in poor health. With the Labour government having lost its majority, his hospital treatment in Yorkshire was constantly being interrupted by trips to London so that he could be counted in important parliamentary votes. Matters came to a head on 28th March 1979, with Broughton close to death and the government facing a confidence motion on the floor of the Commons; the Prime Minister James Callaghan declined to ask him to come to London to vote, and the Labour government was no-confidenced by 311 votes to 310. Sir Alfred died five days later, aged 76. He had served as MP for Batley and Morley for just over 30 years.

Broughton's death left the Batley and Morley seat open going into the 1979 general election, and it was held for Labour without fuss by Kenneth Woolmer who had won the Labour selection for the seat back in 1976. A university lecturer, Woolmer was at the time the leader of West Yorkshire county council. Brighouse and Spenborough, meanwhile, was gained by the Conservatives; Gary Waller became the new MP, defeating the Labour candidate Michael McGowan (who would later serve three terms as MEP for Leeds) by 1,734 votes.

The redistribution of 1983 created the current seat of Batley and Spen, reflecting the creation of the Kirklees metropolitan borough in 1974. Both the previous seats crossed the new boundary. Batley and Morley was broken up, with Morley (now part of the city of Leeds) joining the new seat of Morley and Leeds South; while the Brighouse half of Brighouse and Spenborough (now part of the Calderdale borough) joined the new Calder Valley constituency. The remaining halves were fused together into a new seat covering six wards at the northern end of the Kirklees metropolitan district: namely, Batley East, Batley West, Birstall and Birkenshaw, Cleckheaton, Heckmondwike and Spen. These are basically the boundaries we have today, although Spen ward was redrawn in 2004 as Liversedge and Gomersal, and Heckmondwike was absent from the constituency from 1997 to 2010.

The new seat was projected to be friendly to the Conservatives, although not friendly enough for the Brighouse and Spenborough MP Gary Waller to go for the Conservative nomination. Instead he transferred to the Keighley constituency.* The Batley and Morley MP Kenneth Woolmer did stand here, but he lost to North Yorkshire county councillor Elizabeth Peacock, who was the Conservative candidate and won by 21,433 votes to 20,563, a majority of 870. She was the first female MP for the area. A rematch between Peacock and Woolmer in 1987 saw Peacock increase her majority to 1,362, and there was no swing in the 1992 election at which Peacock's majority was 1,408.

Batley and Spen grew a reputation for being a seat with relatively low swings. Even when Peacock was one of the MPs to fall in the Labour landslide of 1997, the swing to Labour was quite low at 7.7% allowing for boundary changes, and a rematch in 2001 between Peacock and the new Labour MP again resulted in almost no swing. Peacock is still with us, now aged 83.

The Labour MP who defeated Peacock was Mike Wood. He was a former deputy leader of the local Kirklees council, had represented Cleckheaton as a councillor, and had fought the safe Tory seat of Hexham in 1987. He had worked as a probation officer and social worker. Wood was on the left of the Labour party, and he managed John McDonnell's abortive campaign for the Labour leadership in 2007. Like Peacock before him, his time in the Commons was spent on the backbenches.

Mike Wood stood down in 2015 and passed his seat on to Jo Cox, the head of policy for Oxfam GB and a campaigner for Syrian refugees. In an election with a relatively high swing of 1.7% to Labour, Cox won with an increased majority of 6,057. As an MP, she continued her campaigning and founded the all-party Parliamentary Friends of Syria group.

* After losing Keighley in 1997, Waller subsequently served on Epping Forest council in Essex from 2011 until his death in 2017: *Andrew's Previews 2017*, page 296.

In June 2016, a week before what would have been her 42nd birthday, Jo Cox turned up for a constituency surgery at Birstall Library, and was murdered in the street by a right-wing extremist who I won't bother to name here; I will simply note that he is serving a whole-life order.

The resulting first Batley and Spen by-election didn't take place until October 2016, with none of the major parties standing against Labour as a mark of respect to Jo Cox. The nine candidates opposing Labour were all independents or representing fringe parties, mostly on the right or far-right of British politics, and they all lost their deposits. Labour's Tracy Brabin won with 86% of the vote on a turnout of just 26%.

With normal political service resumed for the June 2017 election, Brabin beat the Conservatives by 8,961 votes, a majority which was cut to 3,525 votes in December 2019. On that occasion Brabin polled 43% to 36% for the Conservative candidate Mark Brooks. Third place, with 12% of the vote, went to Paul Halloran of the Heavy Woollen District Independents, a localist party active in Batley, Spen and Dewsbury which holds one seat on Kirklees council. That seat is in Dewsbury East ward, which is not in this constituency.

Like Jo Cox before her, Tracy Brabin was born in Batley. Before entering politics she was best known as an actress and TV screenwriter: she played Tricia Armstrong in *Coronation Street* for three years in the 1990s. In Parliament she briefly served in the Shadow Cabinet at the tail-end of the Corbyn leadership, shadowing the digital, culture, media and sport portfolio from January to April 2020.

Tracy Brabin has left the Commons for a job with more power and responsibility than being an opposition MP can provide. She was elected in May as the first Mayor of the West Yorkshire Combined Authority, with control over regional transport, adult skills, housing and West Yorkshire Police. In the first round Brabin led with 43% of the vote, to 29% for the Conservatives and 10% for the regionalist Yorkshire Party; her win in the runoff came with a 60–40 margin, by 310,923 votes to 208,957.

The mayoral election was combined with the most recent elections to Kirklees council*. For many years the six wards which make up the constituency have been stuck in a rut: at every election from 2007 onwards Labour have won the two Batley wards and Heckmondwike (which was a BNP hotspot in the mid-Noughties), the Conservatives have won Birstall and Birkenshaw, and Liversedge and Gomersal, and the Liberal Democrats have won Cleckheaton. The only exception to this pattern came in a 2013 by-election in which Labour won Liversedge and Gomersal. The Conservatives performed well in this constituency

* See the Local Elections Archive Project: `andrewteale.me.uk/1f66`

Figure 45: Wards of the Batley and Spen constituency

in May 2021, narrowly coming out on top in votes cast across the seat and coming close to gaining Heckmondwike ward; shares of the vote were 40% each for the Conservatives and Labour and 12% for the Liberal Democrats, nearly all of which came out of Cleckheaton. Kirklees is the only one of the five West Yorkshire boroughs not to have a Labour majority: Labour currently run the council as a minority with 33 councillors, against 19 Conservatives, 9 Lib Dems, 3 Greens and 5 independents (one of whom is the aforementioned Heavy Woollen District independent).

As you can hopefully tell from the above paragraphs and from an excellent piece which the *Britain Elects* co-founder Ben Walker has written on Batley and Spen for the *New Statesman*[*], this constituency is not Hartlepool. It's not anything like Hartlepool. (In fact, there are very few places which are anything like Hartlepool, with the possible exception of Grimsby; more on that story later.) Recall from the beginning of this piece that the Batley and Spen seat has a significant commuter demographic in the Spen Valley, and a large Muslim population in Batley; neither of these can be found to any significant extent in Hartlepool, which is a very white and unusually self-contained town. This is a seat which will need different techniques to win from those which were successful in Hartlepool.

[*] tinyurl.com/42xbz7wn

As we can see from various rows which have characterised this discordant by-election campaign, such as the furore over a teacher at Batley Grammar School showing *Charlie Hebdo* cartoons to his pupils, or the planning controversy over Amazon proposing to put a warehouse next to the Chain Bar roundabout on the M 62 (in Cleckheaton ward). You wouldn't have seen either of those happen in the Pool.

Defending for Labour is Kim Leadbeater, sister of the late Jo Cox. She is a personal trainer and, until this campaign started, she was an ambassador for the Jo Cox Foundation and chair of More in Common Batley and Spen, two charities which are trying to build something positive out of her sister's death. Leadbeater was appointed MBE in the 2021 New Year honours for services to social cohesion, to the community in Batley and to combatting loneliness during Covid-19. She lives in Liversedge, and is the only one of the sixteen candidates in this by-election to give an address in this constituency.

Second here in December 2019 were the Conservatives. Their candidate is Ryan Stephenson, who is a Leeds city councillor representing the rural and affluent Harewood ward (although he lives just outside the Leeds city boundary, and accordingly his nomination papers list an address in the Selby and Ainsty constituency).

The Heavy Woollen District Independents, who finished third in 2019, have not returned for this by-election. They hadn't contested any of the constituency's wards in May either.

There were three other parties standing in 2019, none of whom saved their deposits. The Lib Dems had to reselect after their original candidate for this by-election stood down on health grounds; their replacement candidate is Tom Gordon, a Wakefield councillor for Knottingley ward who was their parliamentary candidate for Normanton, Pontefract and Castleford in 2019. His record in Knottingley, which you can look up on the Local Elections Archive Project*, speaks for itself; but this may be a tougher nut to crack. The Brexit Party were fifth last time: their successors, Reform UK, have endorsed the Conservative candidate. There's no candidate from the Greens either: they had selected Ross Peltier, a professional rugby league player, but dropped him at the last moment after finding out that he had sent offensive tweets when he was 19 years old, 10 years ago. The Greens didn't have a substitute candidate in place and there wasn't time for them to find one before nominations closed.

Of the other thirteen candidates, one stands out for his impact on the campaign. TV and radio presenter and failed *Celebrity Big Brother* contestant George Galloway is currently the leader of two political parties, the left-wing Workers

* andrewteale.me.uk/iklb

Kirklees council wards: Batley East, Batley West, Birstall and Birkenshaw, Cleckheaton, Heckmondwike, Liversedge and Gomersal
December 2019 result Lab 22594 C 19069 Heavy Woollen District Ind 6432 LD 2462 Brexit Party 1678 Grn 692
June 2017 result Lab 29844 C 20883 LD 1224 Ind 1076 Grn 695 Ind 58
October 2016 by-election Lab 17506 EDP 969 BNP 548 Ind 517 English Independence 241 Liberty GB 220 Ind 153 Ind 118 NF 87 One Love 34
May 2015 result Lab 21826 C 15769 UKIP 9080 LD 2396 Grn 1232 TUSC 123 Patriotic Socialist 53
May 2010 result Lab 21565 C 17159 LD 8925 BNP 3685 Grn 605

Figure 46: House of Commons, Batley and Spen

Party of Great Britain and the anti-Scottish independence All for Unity. In May's Scottish Parliament election he was top of the All for Unity list for the South of Scotland region, which polled 1.5% of the vote and finished in sixth place. For this by-election he has the Workers Party nomination. Galloway has won a Yorkshire by-election before (Bradford South in 2012) so it would be foolish to count him out.

To take the remaining candidates in ballot paper order: Paul Bickerdike, a foster carer from Tingley near Wakefield, is standing for the Christian Peoples Alliance. Mike Davies has the nomination of the Alliance for Green Socialism, a left-wing group based in Leeds which has been contesting Leeds city council elections for years and whose candidates have been known to reach the dizzy heights of 100 votes. (The AGS were originally on the party register with the name "Left Alliance", and for many years one of their registered logos was the Highway Code "No Right Turn" sign, but I see they have dropped that now. A pity.) Immediately above George Galloway on the ballot is another candidate who comes hotfoot from May's Scottish Parliament election, but there the similarities end: independent candidate Jayda Fransen, the former deputy leader of the far-right Britain First, finished eighth and last in the Glasgow Southside constituency two months ago with 0.1% of the vote, less than a third of the total amassed by somebody who had changed his name for the election to "Greg Energy Adviser". Fransen, who gives an address in Northern Ireland, is currently disqualified from being a local councillor on account of a 36-week prison sentence she picked up in 2018 for religiously aggravated harassment. Answers on a postcard to the usual address as to why that disqualifies her from being a councillor but not from being an MP. Thérèse Hirst is back on the campaign trail for the English Democrats: she was the runner-up in the 2016 by-election after Cox' death, and she finished seventh and last in May's West Yorkshire mayoral election with 1.5% of the vote. The Official Monster Raving Loony Party leader Howling Laud Hope is back for his umpteenth election campaign. Susan Laird is the candidate of the Heritage Party, a socially conservative group led by the former UKIP London Assembly member David Kurten. Oliver Purser, from County Durham, stands for the Social Democratic Party. The Yorkshire Party, a serious regionalist movement as can be seen from their 10% score in the West Yorkshire mayoral election, have selected Corey Robinson; he is a senior medical research engineer. Andrew Smith, who gives an address in Oxfordshire, stands for Rejoin EU whose central policy is left as an exercise for the reader. The official UKIP candidate is Jack Thomson, who gives an address on Tyneside. Jonathan Tilt is having a tilt at this by-election as candidate of the Freedom Alliance, an anti-lockdown party. Completing the ballot paper is Anne Marie Waters, leader of the far-right For Britain Movement.

At the time of writing one opinion poll has been conducted for this by-election, carried out by Survation for the *Daily Mail* and showing the Conservatives leading on 47%, Labour on 41% and Galloway on 6%. Fieldwork was conducted from 9th to 17th June with a sample size of 510. There is, of course, plenty of time for things to change from that in any direction.

Looking forward, this seat is unlikely to survive the forthcoming boundary changes unaltered. The current draft proposal from the Boundary Commission is for the Heckmondwike ward to move back into the Dewsbury constituency, to be replaced by the Hipperholme and Lightcliffe ward from over the border in Calderdale, and with a name change to "Batley and Hipperholme". The Spen Valley, which forms half of the electorate of the new proposed seat, doesn't get a mention. The Boundary Commission are consulting on these proposals until the start of August, so there is time for you to make representations should you so wish.

We can safely say that this Batley and Spen by-election won't be like the one that Tracy Brabin won five years ago. Will it be like the 1960 poll in the predecessor seat of Brighouse and Spenborough: a government gain? Will it be like both Brighouse and Spenborough by-elections: a photo-finish? Will it be like the Spen Valley by-election of 1919, showing the emergence of a new political force to be reckoned with? We'll know when the votes come out of the ballot boxes on Thursday night and Friday morning.*

Until then, we turn to the local by-elections which are also taking place on 1st July...

* *House of Commons, Batley and Spen*: Lab 13296 C 12973 Workers Party of Britain 8264 LD 1254 Yorkshire Party 816 EDP 207 UKIP 151 Loony 107 Alliance for Green Socialism 104 CPA 102 Freedom Alliance 100 For Britain Movement 97 Rejoin EU 75 SDP 66 Ind 50 Heritage Party 33

Heneage

North East Lincolnshire council; caused by the resignation of Labour councillor Chris Nichols.

I promised you more on Grimsby, and here we are as we turn to the seven local council by-elections taking place on 1st July. First on the bill is the Heneage ward of Grimsby, an utterly working-class ward located south-east of the town centre. As well as the grid of Victorian terraces along Heneage Road, the ward runs to the south and east to take in the newer housing at Weelsby and Old Clee.

One of the Conservative gains in 2019, the Great Grimsby constituency has since 1995 anchored the local government district of North East Lincolnshire. This has a more complicated history than you might expect, because North East Lincolnshire is not just Grimsby: the district also covers the seaside resort of Cleethorpes, the hive of industry that is Immingham and a large rural hinterland. A couple of years back your columnist travelled to Waltham, just south of Grimsby, which struck me as an extraordinarily nice place to live. Waltham ward last went to the polls in May 2019, and voted Conservative. It wasn't up for election last month, when Heneage ward also voted Conservative.

There the similarities between Waltham and Heneage end. Heneage ward's current boundaries date from the election in 2003, when the Labour administration of North East Lincolnshire was unpopular and the Tories and Lib Dems put together an electoral pact to oust Labour. It worked very well: despite polling the most votes across the district Labour won just 7 seats out of a possible 40, with the Conservatives on 16 and the Lib Dems on 13. Heneage ward was a straight fight between Labour and the Lib Dems, the Lib Dem slate winning very comfortably. It took the advent of Coalition for Labour to defeat the last Lib Dem councillor here.

In the simultaneous local and European elections of 2014 North East Lincolnshire put in one of the best performances for the UK Independence Party, which topped the poll across the district and won 7 of the 15 seats up for election, including Heneage ward. UKIP weren't far off taking a second seat in 2015, but then their vote faded away and Labour recovered the seat in 2018. In May 2019 Labour polled 43% of the vote here against 29% for the Conservatives and 27% for UKIP.

That was generally a bad year for Labour locally, as they lost a number of seats and the Conservatives won an overall majority on the council. 2021 was far worse in that regard: Labour went into last month's polls defending seven of the twelve wards up for election in North East Lincolnshire, and lost the lot. The Lib Dems held East Marsh ward, and the Conservatives won everything else

Parliamentary constituency: Great Grimsby
May 2021 result C 931 Lab 734 LD 73 TUSC 64 Freedom Alliance 57
May 2019 result Lab 800 C 595 UKIP 552
May 2018 result Lab 996 C 681 UKIP 322 TUSC 46
May 2016 result Lab 948 UKIP 500 C 345 LD 158 TUSC 51
May 2015 result Lab 1730 UKIP 1335 C 917 LD 289 TUSC 105
May 2014 result UKIP 918 Lab 779 C 408 LD 108 Grn 97 TUSC 43
May 2012 result Lab 1039 LD 366 UKIP 304 C 244 Ind 103
May 2011 result Lab 1089 LD 585 C 525 UKIP 299
May 2010 result Lab 1357 LD 1212 C 1175 UKIP 575
May 2008 result LD 865 C 666 Lab 484
May 2007 result LD 861 Lab 676 C 453
May 2006 result LD 1229 Lab 758
June 2004 result LD 1507 Lab 1002
May 2003 result LD 1308/1214/1198 Lab 793/662/610

Figure 47: North East Lincolnshire, Heneage

including, for the first time this century, Heneage. Shares of the vote were 50% for the Conservatives and 39% for Labour.

Suddenly this by-election is looking rather difficult for Labour to defend, particularly given that the local Labour party appears to have issues. The outgoing councillor Chris Nichols resigned after falling out with the group leadership, citing particular disappointment over the deselection of his former ward colleague Ros James for the 2021 election. She was replaced as Labour candidate by Emma Clough, who lost the seat in last month's ordinary election and now has the task of defending this by-election. The Conservatives have also selected a losing candidate from May, Catherine Hogan (who stood in East Marsh ward, the only ward the Conservatives didn't win). Completing the ballot paper are Les Bonner for the Lib Dems and David Bolton, a former North East Lincolnshire cabinet member who finished fourth here in May for the Trade Unionist and Socialist Coalition.*

Penkhull and Stoke

Stoke-on-Trent council, Staffordshire; caused by the resignation of City Independents councillor Randy Conteh.

We travel to another place where the local Labour party has issues. Welcome to Stoke-upon-Trent, one of the six towns in northern Staffordshire that were fused together in the pottery kiln of local government to create a single borough

* *North East Lincolnshire, Heneage*: C 507 Lab 344 LD 336 TUSC 24 [C gain from Lab]

in 1910. Although Hanley is the main commercial centre in the area, the borough took the name of Stoke (which is the main railhead for the Potteries) and the city council has been based in Stoke-upon-Trent since federation.

Despite this fame, Stoke-upon-Trent itself is a rather small place in the scheme of things. Its tiny town centre is located in a corner of this ward, which stretches west through the districts of Hartshill and Penkhull to the Royal Stoke University Hospital. The presence of the hospital means that almost a quarter of the ward's population were employed (at the time of the 2011 census) in human health and social work, a figure which is in the top 15 wards in England and Wales and the second-highest figure for any ward in the West Midlands.

Stoke-on-Trent city council has had unitary status since the 1990s, and its first elections as a unitary council returned 60 Labour councillors out of a possible 60. That didn't last: the 2002 elections, on new ward boundaries, returned a majority of independent councillors. One of them was Randolph Conteh, who won one of the three seats in Hartshill and Penkhull ward, the other two going to Labour.

The independents and Labour ebbed and flowed on the council, and not just at elections. Stoke council became notorious among local government watchers for the frequency of defections between its council groups. Eventually central government lost patience with this political dysfunctionality, and the usual medicine was applied: a move to all-out elections with a cut in the number of councillors, which came in for the 2011 election. This has, to a large extent, stopped the merry-go-round of independent groups, but it hasn't knocked out the independent councillors who coalesced into a single group with the name of "City Independents". Labour lost control of Stoke council in 2015, and a coalition of the Conservatives and City Independents has governed the city since then.*

That coalition included Randy Conteh, who had represented Penkhull and Stoke ward since its creation in 2011. He made it onto the council's cabinet for a time, stepping down from the communities and safer cities portfolio in June 2020. That followed a rather narrow re-election in May 2019, when he held Penkhull and Stoke with a 44–41 lead over Labour, a majority of 59 votes. Conteh was one of 12 City Independents councillors; also elected in May 2019 were 16 Labour members, 15 Conservatives (who, as stated, are part of the ruling coalition with the City Independents) and a standalone independent. The Conservatives are now the largest party by some distance with 20 councillors, mostly due to a collapse among the City Independents who have just five left in their group; a by-

* After writing this piece, I was informed that the Conservatives have recently dumped their coalition partners and are now governing the city alone.

Parliamentary constituency: Stoke-on-Trent Central
May 2019 result City Ind 679 Lab 620 Grn 129 C 99
May 2015 result City Ind 1209 Lab 745 C 521 Grn 279 LD 79
May 2011 result Ind 727 Lab 567 C 156 LD 128 UKIP 120 Community Voice 50

Figure 48: Stoke-on-Trent, Penkhull and Stoke

election gain in a safe Labour ward last month counts towards that Conservative total as well. The ward is part of the Stoke-on-Trent Central constituency which, like the other two Stoke seats, was a Conservative gain in December 2019.

This by-election has come about because Randy Conteh resigned from the council after being charged with rape. The offences are alleged to have taken place in 1995–97, before he became a councillor, and to involve a girl aged under 16. Conteh appeared before Cannock magistrates last month and was bailed to appear at Stoke-on-Trent crown court later this month.*

Defending for the City Independents is Hazel Lyth, a former Stoke councillor. She was elected in 2007 as a Conservative councillor for the East Valley ward and served on the council's cabinet with the health portfolio, but lost her seat in 2011 and had not sought election to the council since. The Labour candidate is Lee Polshaw, whose nomination papers were signed by the former Stoke Central MP Gareth Snell; she is described as having lived in the ward for over a decade. Also standing are Adam Colclough for the Green Party (who was an unsuccessful candidate for Staffordshire county council in May) and Dean Richardson for the Conservatives.†

Bridge

Newark and Sherwood council, Nottinghamshire; a double by-election caused by the resignations of independent councillors Irene Brown and Gill Dawn.

Our other independent defences of the week come further down the River Trent in the town of Newark-on-Trent. The Bridge ward of Newark is one of those wards where successive boundary reviews have removed the feature that originally gave it its name: the Trent Bridge, where the original Great North Road crossed the river, is now part of Castle ward. There are, however, bridges within the ward boundary, including a large viaduct which takes the A 46 bypass over the river and the East Coast main line. Adjacent to this viaduct is the Newark flat crossing, at which that railway crosses the Nottingham-Lincoln railway line on the same level—a major bottleneck on the main line. Express trains to London

* As of the end of 2021, Conteh was still awaiting trial. † *Stoke-on-Trent, Penkhull and Stoke*: C 582 Lab 572 City Ind 171 Grn 109 [C gain from City Ind]

Parliamentary constituency: Newark
Nottinghamshire county council division: Collingham (most of ward), Newark East (south-west corner)
May 2019 result Ind 671/647 Lab 300 C 269/230
May 2015 result Ind 920/794 C 461 Lab 411 UKIP 404

Figure 49: Newark and Sherwood, Bridge

and the north depart from Northgate station within the ward; while the slower A 1 trunk road, with its poorly laid-out junction at Winthorpe, lies on Bridge ward's eastern boundary.

This is the northern of the four wards covering Newark town, and for many years it has been the fiefdom of independent councillors Gill Dawn and Irene Brown. Dawn was originally elected, with the Labour nomination, at a by-election in May 1989; her 33 years' service included spells as both leader and chairman of the council. Irene Brown, who recently completed two years as mayor of Newark, had continuous service since winning a by-election in January 2002.

The Boundary Commission had cut Bridge ward from three councillors to two in 2003, and Brown and Dawn had been the two councillors for the ward continuously since then with large majorities. In May 2019 they polled 54% of the vote against 24% for a single Labour candidate and 22% for the Conservative slate.

Going up to county council level doesn't really help in determining how this ward might vote without Brown and Dawn on the ballot; this is because most of Bridge ward is covered by the Collingham county division which returned an independent candidate, Maureen Dobson, to Nottinghamshire county council last month.

So, this rare double by-election could be quite unpredictable. Brown and Dawn have endorsed two new independent candidates to succeed them: they are Ryan Bickerton and Debbie "Deb's" Darby, both of whom are voluntary workers and charity fundraisers in the area. Bickerton is the manager of Newark's Bridge Community Centre, and Darby and him both support Gill and Irene's Food Pantry, a foodbank opened by Brown and Dawn last autumn. The Labour Party have nominated Lisa Geary, who took over from Brown last month as mayor of Newark, and Mark Palmer. Two new candidates have also come forward for the Conservatives, who run Newark and Sherwood council: Simon Haynes lost his seat in 2019 in the town's Devon ward and is seeking to come back, while Jack Kellas has recently represented Newark in the Youth Parliament. Also standing are Ryan Cullen and Keith Melton for the Liberal Democrats, and Steve Platt

Parliamentary constituency: Saffron Walden
Essex county council division: Broomfield and Writtle
May 2019 result C 829/662 LD 537/410
May 2015 result C 1592/1344 LD 883/720 UKIP 551
May 2011 result C 1269/1237 Lab 424/413 LD 267/242
May 2007 result C 992/983 LD 632/598 Lab 136/135
May 2003 result C 692/690 LD 661/644 Lab 191/167 Ind 171 Grn 68

Figure 50: Chelmsford, Writtle

and Mike Poyzer for the Green Party.*

Writtle

Chelmsford council, Essex; caused by the death of Conservative councillor Malcolm Watson.

For our only rural by-election of the week we come to a place which was described in 1909 as "one of the loveliest villages in England, with a ravishing variety of ancient cottages". Hopefully it's just a nice a century later. Lying just to the west of Chelmsford, the large village of Writtle was held in mediaeval times by the de Brus family, whose most famous member—the future Scottish king Robert the Bruce—married his second wife Elizabeth de Burgh here in 1302.

In modern times employment here is provided by Writtle University College, a higher education institution specialising in agriculture and horticulture; while from 1996 to 2017 Writtle hosted the southern leg of the V Festival, with tens of thousands of people turning up each August for a good time. We didn't know that was so precious then. The festival was held in the grounds of Hylands House, a neoclassical stately home which is now in the hands of Chelmsford council.

Chelmsford city council was one of a number of councils in the London commuter belt taken over by the Liberal Democrats in 2019. The Lib Dem majority is concentrated in the Chelmsford urban area, and Writtle ward remains safe for the Conservatives. In May 2019 the Tory slate beat the Lib Dems here by 61–39, and the local Essex county council seat (Broomfield and Writtle) and parliamentary seat (Saffron Walden) are also safely Conservative. The late councillor Malcolm Watson was first elected in 2011 for Chelmsford's Waterhouse Farm ward, moving to safer pastures here in 2019.

* *Newark and Sherwood, Bridge*: C 310 (Kellas)/267 (Haynes) Ind 236 (Bickerington)/181 (Darby) Lab 177 (Geary)/162 (Palmer) LD 104 (Cullen)/59 (Melton) Grn 81 (Platt)/57 (Poyzer) [2 C gains from Ind]

Defending for the Conservatives is Andrew Thorpe-Apps, a local solicitor. The Liberal Democrat candidate is Lynne Foster. Also standing are Ronnie Bartlett for the Green Party and Edward Massey for Labour.*

Bush Hill Park

Enfield council, London; caused by the resignation of Will Coleshill, who was elected for the Conservatives.

We cross into North London for two contrasting by-elections, starting with the one further out from the centre. Since 1880 Bush Hill Park has been the last stop for branch line trains (London Overground trains, these days) going to Enfield Town; the station was opened to serve a housing estate built on the grounds of a country house of the same name. We're a fair way from central London here and the estate was rather slow to grow, a process not helped by its developer going bankrupt in 1887; but the growth of the firearms industry in Enfield to supply the Boer War caused demand to pick up, and by the outbreak of the First World War Bush Hill Park was fully developed. Many of those Edwardian houses are still with us today thanks to a conservation area being created in the mid-1980s; only the northern end of the ward, around Enfield cricket club, has seen significant redevelopment.

For parliamentary purposes Bush Hill Park is within the Edmonton constituency and is by far the least-deprived ward within it. That gives a right-wing slant to its politics which would have pleased one of the ward's most famous residents: Ross McWhirter, the sports journalist and *Guinness Book of Records* co-founder, lived in this ward on Village Road and was murdered there by the IRA in 1975. McWhirter had been the Conservative candidate for Edmonton in the 1964 general election, doing rather poorly in what had five years earlier been a very close seat.

In fact the Edmonton constituency was often a key marginal until quite recent times. The Conservatives gained it at the 1987 election and held it in 1992; but since then the Tory vote across Enfield has fallen off a cliff and by June 2017 the Conservatives had just 23% of the vote across this constituency, a 12-point swing against them since the Coalition was formed. A large proportion of those Tory votes will have come out of Bush Hill Park, which is the only ward within the seat to reliably return Conservative councillors. Until the 2010s, that is: Labour came from a long way back to gain one of the ward's three seats in 2014, and while the Tories got that seat back in May 2018 it was only with a majority

* *Chelmsford, Writtle*: C 716 LD 572 Grn 78 Lab 67

of 64 votes. Vote shares were 39% for the Conservatives, 37% for Labour and 11% for the Green Party.

The Conservative slate elected here in May 2018 included Will Coleshill and Jon Daniels. Coleshill had the Conservative whip suspended shortly afterwards for making racist comments in a council meeting, and it appears that he was never readmitted to the group. Daniels resigned after a few months, finding himself unable to balance his democratic duties with his family and work commitments: the resulting by-election in November 2018* saw a big swing to the Conservatives, with their candidate James Hockney (a former South Cambridgeshire councillor, and the Tory candidate in the 2011 Barnsley East parliamentary by-election) defeating Labour by 52% to 28%. Hockney went on to be the Conservatives' parliamentary candidate for Edmonton in December 2019, putting together a 4% swing to the Tories but still finishing nearly 40 points behind the Labour MP Kate Osamor. Coleshill, who has since picked up a fixed penalty notice for breaching lockdown restrictions, has now resigned provoking this further Bush Hill Park by-election.

This column was last in London three weeks ago, previewing two by-elections in Waltham Forest borough (page 207). Those were the first standalone by-elections in Greater London since the Mayor and Assembly elections in May, and this column quoted the results from two of the three votes which took place in those elections: the Mayoral ballot, and the London Members list vote. Your columnist has been doing this as standard practice in almost eleven years of previewing council by-elections.

Following the 10th June Previews there were some comments raised on the Twitter as to whether the London Assembly constituency ballot might be a better comparator for council by-elections. There are arguments for doing this. The London Members ballot traditionally attracts a galaxy of parties competing for your vote, whereas Assembly constituencies and council by-elections tend to have a much more restricted choice. In May there were 18 parties seeking list votes, while this Bush Hill Park by-election has six candidates.

To answer this, I would point out that in an Additional Member system, like those in London, Scotland, Wales, Germany and New Zealand, the constituency vote and the list vote are two separate things posing two separate questions. The constituency ballot is asking "who do you want to be your MP", but the list vote is asking "who do you want to run the country/assembly"? For most voters, the answer to those two questions will be the same; but some might want a local MP or AM or equivalent from a different political tradition to the one they want to run the government. We saw this in the 2012 Assembly election in

* *Andrew's Previews 2018*, page 411.

which Brian Coleman, who had attracted a lot of controversy as the Conservative AM for Barnet and Camden, massively underperformed his party's list and lost re-election as a result.

The list vote (in this case, the London Members ballot) is also the more powerful of the two votes. A constituency vote only elects one AM; in London, the list vote can contribute to the election of eleven AMs. Partly for that reason, in a number of polities which use the Additional Member system of PR only the list vote is the subject of opinion polls. This is the case in, for example, Germany; and published German opinion polls (which election watchers will see a lot of in the run-up to the next Bundestag election in September) refer only to what is known there as the "second vote" (*Zweitstimme*). The constituency vote (*Erststimme* or "first vote") is simply ignored by the pollsters.

In this column's opinion—and I accept that some psephologists may disagree with me on this—the GLA list vote does a better job than the GLA constituency vote of stripping out local factors and giving us something close to the ward's underlying political persuasion. This column has plenty of space to discuss the local factors for readers' consideration, as long as I'm aware of them. So, I'm not going to change my practice going forward.

However, on this occasion as a one-off I will quote the GLA constituency vote for Bush Hill Park last month: it was 44% for the Conservatives, 36% for Labour and 11% for the Green Party. The London mayoral ballot in May was more decisive, with Shaun Bailey defeating Sadiq Khan in the ward's ballot boxes by 46–32; the London Members list vote was narrower, with 40% for the Conservatives, 33% for Labour and 10% for the Greens.

Those results came against the backdrop of a mini-revival for the Conservatives in Enfield, continuing the swing we saw in the Edmonton constituency in December 2019. In three council by-elections held in May (page 61), simultaneously with the GLA elections, the Tories gained the semi-rural Chase ward from Labour and gained vote share in the more urban wards of Jubilee and Southbury, although those two wards remained safe for Labour.

Defending for the Conservatives is Peter Fallart, whose policies include greening the ward's streets by restoring weekly bin collections, planting more trees, installing pollution monitors and opposing Low Traffic Neighbourhoods. The Labour candidate is Nia Stevens. Also standing are Ade Adetula for the Lib Dems, Benjamin Maydon for the Green Party, John Dolan for the Trade Unionist and Socialist Coalition and former Enfield Labour councillor Clive Morrison for the recently-founded Taking The Initiative Party.*

* *Enfield, Bush Hill Park*: C 1694 Lab 875 Grn 233 LD 225 TUSC 27 Taking the Initiative 15

Parliamentary constituency: Edmonton
London Assembly constituency: Enfield and Haringey
November 2018 by-election C 1540 Lab 828 LD 313 Grn 127 Women's Equality 79 Ind 50
May 2018 result C 1976/1959/1926 Lab 1862/1831/1681 Grn 539 LD 484 UKIP 144
May 2014 result C 1679/1521/1334 Lab 1522/1277/1223 UKIP 897 Grn 621 LD 453
July 2011 by-election C 1108 Lab 668 Ind 230 LD 177 Grn 100 UKIP 70 BNP 61 Christian Party 45 EDP 29
May 2010 result C 3451/3225/3224 Lab 2230/2077/2049 LD 1747 Grn 942 UKIP 618
January 2009 by-election C 1320 Lab 413 LD 129 UKIP 123 Grn 97
May 2006 result C 2248/2178/1827 Save Chase Farm 1442 Lab 780/683/649 Grn 604 LD 547/533 UKIP 298
May 2002 result C 2400/2276/2272 Lab 974/867/830 LD 565/433/421 UKIP 187/144
May 2021 GLA results (excludes postal voters)
Mayor: C 1423 Lab 983 Grn 203 LD 99 Omilana 73 Reclaim 61 London Real Party 40 Count Binface 30 Women's Equality 24 Rejoin EU 23 Obunge 19 UKIP 16 SDP 15 Let London Live 14 Heritage Party 14 Animal Welfare 13 Farah London 13 Renew 10 Burning Pink 3 Fosh 3
Constituency: C 1401 Lab 1141 Grn 343 LD 234 Reform UK 59 Ind 22
London Members: C 1285 Lab 1044 Grn 329 LD 160 Women's Equality 63 Animal Welfare 60 Rejoin EU 48 CPA 35 Reform UK 32 London Real 30 UKIP 23 Let London Live 20 Comm 17 Heritage 17 SDP 15 TUSC 8 Londonpendence 7 Nat Lib 5

Figure 51: Enfield, Bush Hill Park

Tollington

Islington council, London; caused by the resignation of the Leader of the Council, Labour councillor Richard Watts.

We travel south from Enfield towards a ward with an old name. *Tolentone* was mentioned in the Domesday Book as a manor within the ancient parish of Islington, but the manor fell into the hands of Clerkenwell Priory in the thirteenth century and the name of Tollington rather fell out of use after that. There is still a road called Tollington Park along the south-east boundary of this ward, but that's about it. To outsiders the main feature of the ward is probably the railway station at Crouch Hill, on the recently-electrified Gospel Oak to Barking line.

In the 2011 census return, Tollington just crept into the top 100 wards in England and Wales for mixed-race population (6.75%) and was just outside the top 20 for those born in the Republic of Ireland (3.35%). The ward has high levels of social renting.

Islington council is a Labour fiefdom these days. The last two elections to the council in 2014 and 2018 both returned 47 Labour councillors out of a

Parliamentary constituency: Islington North
London Assembly constituency: North East
May 2018 result Lab 2764/2727/2707 Grn 674/456/380 LD 328/322/278 C 216/212/200
May 2014 result Lab 2355/2320/2302 Grn 1006/951/752 LD 400/393/313
May 2010 result Lab 2476/2350/2263 LD 1604/1466/1425 Grn 1199/1044/883 C 732/642/547
May 2006 result Lab 1338/1312/1270 LD 827/790/757 Grn 531/429/406 C 226/222/183
May 2002 result Lab 1185/1176/1168 Save Arthur Simpson Library 437 Grn 364/319/245 LD 356/325/304 Socialist Alliance 191
May 2021 GLA results (excludes postal voters)
Mayor: Lab 1940 Grn 475 C 422 LD 83 Omilana 61 Count Binface 54 Women's Equality 52 Reclaim 42 Let London Live 34 London Real 33 Animal Welfare 20 Heritage Party 17 Rejoin EU 15 Burning Pink 14 Farah London 10 Fosh 8 Renew 6 SDP 6 Obunge 6 UKIP 5
London Members: Lab 1801 Grn 721 C 278 LD 165 Women's Equality 140 Animal Welfare 57 Rejoin EU 35 Reform UK 31 CPA 26 TUSC 24 London Real 20 Let London Live 19 Heritage Party 17 Londonpendence 14 UKIP 13 Comm 11 SDP 8 National Liberal 2

Figure 52: Islington, Tollington

possible 48, with a Green councillor in Highbury East being the one that got away. Tollington has returned a full Labour slate at every election this century: in 2018 Labour polled 69% of the vote here, with the Greens in second in 17%.

Labour and the Greens were also the top 2 here in the London Mayor and Assembly elections last month. In the ward's ballot boxes Sadiq Khan beat Siân Berry 59–14, while the list vote had a closer but still comfortable Labour lead at 53–21. There wasn't much love for anti-lockdown campaigner Piers Corbyn, who placed ninth here in the mayoral ballot and whose list finished twelfth in the London Members vote; the voters of Tollington have, however, taken a liking to his brother Jeremy who has represented the area in Parliament for 38 years and counting. Only four current MPs (Dame Margaret Beckett, Sir Peter Bottomley, Barry Sheerman and Harriet Harman) have longer service on the green benches.

All those people are notable enough for Wikipedia as, apparently, is the outgoing councillor Richard Watts. Watts had represented this ward since 2006, and had served since 2013 as Leader of the Council. He has joined Sadiq Khan's team at City Hall as Khan's deputy chief of staff, a role which is politically restricted.

Defending for Labour is Mick Gilgunn, a Unite activist who works in a maintenance department at a London university. The Green candidate is Jonathan Ward, who is described by the local party as an "expert sustainability engineer" (whatever that is) and local resident. Also standing are Jane Nicolov for the Lib Dems, who also stood here in 2018, and Vanessa Carson for the Conservatives.*

* *Islington, Tollington*: Lab 1243 Grn 730 C 127 LD 94

Cobham and Downside

Elmbridge council, Surrey; caused by the death of Conservative councillor Dorothy Mitchell.

We finish this week outside Greater London, but still (mostly) within the M 25. Cobham is the sort of place that confirms any stereotypes you might have about Surrey: it's a village full of middle-class commuters to London and a place with a lot of money. The census return bears out the middle-class commuter demographic (just over 50% of the workforce are in managerial and professional work) but the money doesn't necessarily follow from that: the training ground for Chelsea FC is just over the ward boundary in Stoke d'Abernon, and consequently a number of Chelsea players live here. Hopefully those players who are still involved in Euro 2020 have sorted out absent votes.

To the south of Cobham, over the River Mole, is the small village of Downside, next to the M 25 motorway whose recently-completed Cobham service area is here. In between is the country estate of Cobham Park, home in the eighteenth century of John Ligonier who was commander-in-chief of the Army during the Seven Years' War; the present country house, built in the 1870s after the previous one was destroyed by fire, was divided into apartments in 2001.

Further confirming any stereotypes you might have about Surrey, Cobham and Downside forms a safe Conservative ward of Elmbridge council. At the first election on the current boundaries, in 2016, it returned the Conservative slate of Mike Bennison, James Browne and Dorothy Mitchell. Browne was re-elected in 2018, and he became leader of the Conservative group and Leader of the Council in January 2019. James Browne's leadership of the council may have felt good at the time but proved to be a short one: although his ward colleague Mitchell was re-elected in May 2019, the Conservative council administration was defeated that year and a coalition of the Residents Associations and Lib Dems took over. In September 2019 Mike Bennison defected to the Brexit Party. Bennison's term was subsequently extended to 2021 because of COVID, but he failed to finish it; he was kicked off Elmbridge council in June 2020 under the six-month non-attendance rule.

Once the May 2021 elections rolled around, these shenanigans didn't have much effect on the Conservative vote. The Tories beat the Lib Dems here by 65% to 22%, a swing in their favour since May 2019. Mike Bennison, trying to get his old seat back as a Reform UK candidate, finished fifth and last with 3% of the vote. The Residents/Lib Dem coalition running Elmbridge council was re-elected. The Conservatives held the Cobham division of Surrey county council, which covers nearly all of this ward, by a similar margin.

Parliamentary constituency: Esher and Walton
Surrey county council division: Cobham (almost all), Hersham (small part)
May 2021 result C 1416 LD 475 Lab 185 UKIP 63 Reform UK 56
May 2019 result C 902 LD 598 UKIP 238 Lab 166
May 2018 result C 1280 LD 268 Lab 253 UKIP 128
May 2016 result C 1157/1155/1041 LD 593 UKIP 378 Lab 370

Figure 53: Elmbridge, Cobham and Downside

Curiously, the parliamentary seat covering Cobham is much more marginal. This is part of the Esher and Walton constituency, where the Foreign Secretary Dominic Raab was nearly unseated by the Liberal Democrats in December 2019. The Boundary Commission's draft proposals for the new parliamentary map move Cobham and Downside ward out of the Esher and Walton constituency into a new seat called Weybridge and Chertsey, which may have the effect of notionally wiping out Raab's majority.

This by-election has come about because of the death of veteran Conservative councillor Dorothy Mitchell, who was first elected as a councillor for the Cobham area in 1983 and had served continuously since then. She was Mayor of Elmbridge in 1991–92, and after that she was the Surrey county councillor for Cobham from 2001 to 2009. It'll be hard for her successor to match that length of service.

Defending for the Conservatives is Corinne Sterry, a local businesswoman. The Liberal Democrats have selected Robin Stephens, an entrepreneur in the software sector. Also standing are Irene Threlkeld for Labour (who stood here for the county council in May), Elaine Kingston for Reform UK and Laura Harmour for the Green Party.*

* *Elmbridge, Cobham and Downside*: LD 890 C 778 Grn 54 Lab 47 Reform UK 19 [LD gain from C]

8th July 2021

The political editor of the *New Statesman* Stephen Bush, a kind patron of the Local Elections Archive Project, remarked last week that he was surprised how few errors I make in researching Andrew's Previews. Inevitably, he's put the mockers on me, and before we start this week there are some entries to note for Correction Corner.

First, I regret that there was an error in the Batley and Spen preview last week regarding the seat which included Batley in the period 1885–1918. Although Batley was *technically* part of the Morley division of the West Riding at this point in time as I stated, it was also within the area covered by the parliamentary borough of Dewsbury, and most of the people in Batley who were eligible to vote would have voted for the MP for Dewsbury rather than Morley. My apologies for referring you to the wrong seat there.*

Second, a rather lost and exhausted-looking carrier pigeon has arrived from the Potteries with news that the Stoke-on-Trent Conservatives had dumped the City Independents some time ago and are ruling the city on their own as a minority. The former City Independents councillor, Randy Conteh, had also left the group some time before his resignation from the council which provoked last week's by-election there. Hopefully that's clear.

With that now out of the way there are six local by-elections, for seven seats, on 8th July 2021. All of today's polls are in the south of England, but there's a wide variety of areas up for election with something for everyone to enjoy. As you will hopefully discover if you read on…

Aldeburgh and Leiston

East Suffolk council; a double by-election following the resignations of Conservative councillors Jocelyn Bond and T-J Haworth-Culf.

* The relevant part of the Batley and Spen preview has been rewritten: see footnote on page 244.

We start our discussion of today's by-elections with a "venal little borough" on the Suffolk coast. The name "Aldeburgh" comes from Old English words for an "old fortification", which—along with a number of other places along the rapidly-eroding Suffolk coast—no longer exists today. We are left with an old fishing port and minor seaside resort with a notable electoral record.

The town of Aldeburgh was enfranchised in 1571, giving its freemen the right to send two members to Parliament. It was one of the rotten boroughs swept away by the first Reform Act in 1832, but its most striking electoral feature came in local government. Elizabeth Garrett Anderson, the first British woman to qualify as a doctor and as a surgeon, retired to Aldeburgh in the early 1900s. As we shall see, she had family in the area, and in 1908 she followed in the footsteps of her father Newson Garrett by being elected as Mayor of Aldeburgh. She was the first woman to serve as a mayor in England.

Given that big leap for equality, it's a bit of a shame that it's not Garrett Anderson's name which immediately comes to mind when the name "Aldeburgh" is mentioned. She's not even the only twentieth-century mayor of Aldeburgh notable enough for Wikipedia: in the 1970s Gerry Fiennes, some years on from trying to run a railway, served a year as the town's first citizen. But they have been upstaged.

In 1942 an up-and-coming composer called Benjamin Britten moved to the town, shortly after reading *The Borough*, a poetry collection by the nineteenth-century Aldeburgh poet George Crabbe. Britten turned one of Crabbe's poems, *Peter Grimes*, into an opera which premiered in June 1945 at Sadler's Wells: Britten's partner Peter Pears played the title role opposite Joan Cross, manager of the Sadler's Wells company, in the lead female role of Ellen Orford. Britten, Pears and Cross are still in Aldeburgh today, lying in eternal rest in the town's churchyard.

Peter Grimes was a huge success, firmly establishing Britten as a composer of the first rank. Its prologue scene is set in Aldeburgh's Moot Hall, a timber-framed Tudor building where Garrett Anderson, Fiennes and all the other mayors of Aldeburgh over the centuries have presided over council meetings. Aldeburgh town council is still based in the Moot Hall to this day.

Having given Aldeburgh to the world of music, Britten and Pears then brought the world of music to Aldeburgh with the founding of the annual Aldeburgh Festival, attracting some of the world's greatest musicians to this corner of Suffolk each June. Since 1967 the Aldeburgh Festival has had a permanent home, although not in Aldeburgh itself. Elizabeth Garrett Anderson's father, Newson Garrett, was an entrepreneur who had built a factory in Snape, a few miles up the Alde estuary, which turned Suffolk barley into malt for export down the river to breweries in London and on the Continent. The Snape Maltings complex went out of business in the early 1960s, and was quickly turned into an arts centre under Britten's direction. The largest malthouse in the complex became an 832-seat concert hall, opened by the Queen in 1967 and re-opened by her in 1970 after burning down the previous year.

Snape Maltings wasn't the only industrial centre of note in the Aldeburgh area. Elizabeth Garrett Anderson's great-grandfather, Richard Garrett, founded a company in the nearby town of Leiston in 1778 making agricultural machinery. By the late 19th century Richard Garrett and Sons, under the management of Newson Garrett's brother Richard Garrett III, was the largest employer in Leiston. As I wrote in *Andrew's Previews 2018*, page 179, they had one of the world's first industrial assembly lines going, with parts going in at one end of the "Long Shop" building and traction engines and other steam-powered vehicles coming out of the other end. Garrett's works went out of business in the 1980s and were mostly redeveloped, but the Long Shop was saved from the demolition men and turned into a museum. For one day only, it's also a polling station for this by-election.

But for all this art and industry, it's energy which is Aldeburgh and Leiston's most important export. To the east of Leiston, next to the North Sea, can be found two rather large buildings: the Sizewell A and B nuclear power stations. Sizewell A is now being slowly decommissioned after generating electricity from 1967 to 2006; Sizewell B, with its distinctive white dome, came online in 1995 as the UK's only commercial Pressurised Water Reactor plant. I wrote three years ago that construction of the next nuclear plant on the site, Sizewell C, seemed "several years off at best"; there has been some progress to report since, as last year EDF Energy put the planning application in to East Suffolk council and applied for the relevant nuclear power licences, but ground is yet to be broken on the scheme.

All this adds up to a fascinating electoral ward, which was created in 2019 for the first elections to the brand-new East Suffolk council. The Conservatives did well in those elections, winning 39 seats out of a possible 55 and generally sweeping the rural wards: but they didn't have it all their own way here. Top of the poll in Aldeburgh and Leiston were two of the three Conservative candidates, Terry-Jill "T-J" Haworth-Culf (who had previously represented Aldeburgh on the predecessor Suffolk Coastal council) and Jocelyn Bond, but the third seat went to independent candidate Tony Cooper who had previously been an independent Suffolk Coastal councillor for Leiston. He won with a majority of three votes over the third Conservative candidate, 1154 to 1151. Shares of the vote were 29% for the Conservatives, 26% for Cooper, 19% for Labour (who can often poll

Parliamentary constituency: Suffolk Coastal
Suffolk county council division: Aldeburgh and Leiston (Aldeburgh, Aldringham cum Thorpe, Knodishall and Leiston parishes), Blything (Middleton and Theberton parishes), Wilford (Benhall, Friston, Snape and Sternfield parishes)
May 2019 result C 1265/1179/1151 Ind 1154/1051 Lab 835/779/612 Grn 717/577/504 LD 429

Figure 54: East Suffolk, Aldeburgh and Leiston

respectably in Leiston, although not usually respectably enough to finish first) and 16% for the Greens.

T-J Haworth-Culf was subsequently elected in May 2021 as the Suffolk county councillor for Aldeburgh and Leiston, defeating Labour in a straight fight by almost two to one. Unusually, the county division of that name is actually smaller than this district ward: it doesn't cover the Snape area or a couple of rural parishes to the north-west of Leiston, which are in different safe-Conservative divisions. Haworth-Culf and her Conservative ward colleague Jocelyn Bond promptly handed in their resignations as East Suffolk councillors; Haworth-Culf is concentrating on her new elected office, while Bond has expressed dissatisfaction with the Sizewell C project.

Defending this double by-election for the Conservatives are Russ Rainger and Andrew Reid. Rainger retired in May as the county councillor for Aldeburgh and Leiston, while Reid was re-elected in May as the county councillor for the Wilford division which includes the Snape area. There are no independent candidates this time, so it will be interesting to see where their votes go. The Labour slate consists of two losing candidates from May, Ian Ilett (the unsuccessful candidate in the Aldeburgh and Leiston county division) and Mark Turner. Matt Oakley, the lead Green candidate for this ward in 2019, returns and is joined by Thomas Daly. who lost to Reid in May's county elections. Completing a ballot paper of seven candidates is Steve Marsling, who has the nomination of the Communist Party of Britain.*

St Neots East

Huntingdonshire council, Cambridgeshire; caused by the election of Labour councillor Nik Johnson as Mayor of Cambridgeshire and Peterborough.

Not all of East Anglia is rural and full of nice-looking old buildings, as we now demonstrate by turning to two wards which were entirely developed in the last seventy-five years. One of these is in a New Town; the other is much newer

* *East Suffolk, Aldeburgh and Leiston*: Grn 1110 (Daly)/1101 (Oakley) C 1103 (Rainger)/1006 (Reid) Lab 355 (Ilett)/311 (Turner) Comm 61 [1 Grn gain from C]

than that.

The population of Cambridgeshire has rocketed in recent decades, but (with the notable exception of Cambourne) this growth hasn't been achieved by building entirely new settlements. Instead housing estates have been tacked on to the sides of existing towns and villages. One of the largest of these is the Love's Farm development, started in the last ten years and still growing, which took the town of St Neots over to the east side of the East Coast main line for the first time.

Love's Farm became a ward of its own in 2018, under the name of St Neots East. The development is so new that statistics on it are rather hard to come by. Figures from the 2021 census are not yet available; at the time of the 2011 census the area was part of a larger St Neots ward, Priory Park, but that was really before the development got going. The current ward was drawn with a very low 2015 electorate, to allow room for future growth.

This area was only incorporated into St Neots in 2010. Before then it was part of the now-abolished St Neots Rural parish and the rural ward of Gransden and the Offords.* Love's Farm and other developments have turned St Neots into the largest town in Cambridgeshire without city status, overtaking Huntingdon; and the draft Boundary Commission proposals for the new parliamentary map create a completely new parliamentary seat based on St Neots and the surrounding area.

Huntingdonshire district last went to the polls in 2018, which was a year when the Conservatives did pretty badly in St Neots town. A localist slate swept two of the town's other wards, while East ward surprisingly saw Labour candidate and local children's doctor Nik Johnson top the poll with 40% of the vote, a long way ahead of his running-mate. Johnson had previously been the Labour parliamentary candidate for the local Huntingdon seat in 2017, putting in a decent performance. The Conservatives polled 32% and won the ward's other seat, with the Lib Dems close behind on 28%. Johnson and Tory councillor David Wells' vote totals of 345 and 273 in this two-seat ward were the lowest scores for any winning candidate in Huntingdonshire that year, including those in the district's single-member wards; as indicated above, this isn't an unusually low turnout but a symptom of the ward having an unusually low electorate. If the growth forecasts are any good, the population should be a lot larger now than it was three years ago.

Johnson was one of four Labour councillors elected in Huntingdonshire in

* It's still shown as part of Gransden and the Offords in the Huntingdonshire maps for 2010–16 on the Local Elections Archive Project, as I hadn't appreciated before writing this Preview just how extensive the interim Huntingdonshire boundary changes in the early 2010s were. Apologies for anyone who might have been confused by that.

Parliamentary constituency: Huntingdon
Cambridgeshire county council division: St Neots East and Gransden
May 2018 result Lab 345/186 C 273/193 LD 235

Figure 55: Huntingdonshire, St Neots East

2018, and the only one outside Huntingdon town. He was selected as the Labour candidate for the May 2021 Cambridgeshire and Peterborough mayoral election, campaigning on a ticket to introduce bus franchising to the county and to cancel an ambitious (bordering on crazy) plan from the incumbent Conservative mayor, James Palmer, for an "autonomous metro" for Cambridge. In the first round Palmer topped the poll but only with 41% of the vote, against 33% for Labour's Johnson and 27% for the Lib Dem candidate. In the runoff an unusually-high 73% of the Lib Dem transfers went to Labour, ensuring that Johnson won in the final reckoning by 113,994 votes to 108,195 (51.3% to 48.7%). He promptly delivered on part of his manifesto, cancelling the "autonomous metro" project in his first week in office.

The Cambridgeshire county council elections were held on the same day. This ward is part of the St Neots East and Gransden county division, which the Conservatives lost to an independent candidate by just 9 votes; that was one of the losses which cost them control of the county council, which is now run by a Lib Dem-led coalition of all the other groups. The Tories remain in control of Huntingdonshire council.

We saw in Batley and Spen last week that Labour are capable of defending marginal by-elections caused by their elected representatives becoming metro mayors. They will have to repeat that trick here, because Johnson's seat on Huntingdonshire council was vacated as a result of his election to the mayoralty.

Defending for Labour is Helen Stroud. The Tories have selected Sam Collins, who was on the wrong end of that 9-vote defeat in the county division two months ago. The Lib Dem candidate is Geoff Seeff, a party veteran who has recently relocated to Love's Farm from Waltham Forest: Seeff has stood for Parliament six times, most recently in Chingford and Woodford Green in 2019, and he was the party's candidate for Havering and Redbridge at the first London Assembly elections in 2000. Also standing are Lara Davenport-Ray for the Greens (who also stood here in the county elections in May) and independent candidate Ben Pitt, who represents the area on St Neots town council.* The Love's Farm Community Association has interviewed all the candidates, and you can find out more from their website†.

* *Huntingdonshire, St Neots East*: Ind 249 Grn 196 LD 68 C 47 Lab 26 [Ind gain from Lab]
† `tinyurl.com/4smz85wh`

Mark Hall

Harlow council, Essex; caused by the death of Labour councillor Danny Purton.

As we have seen, Cambridgeshire's approach to population growth has mostly been to tack bits onto existing towns and villages. The neighbouring county of Essex has historically taken a different tack.

Harlow is unambiguously a New Town. In fact, it was one of the first New Towns, built in the early 1950s to house families which had been bombed out of London; one legacy of that history is that the town has the third-highest proportion of social housing of any district in England. Harlow became an urban district in 1955, and now forms a local government district of its own.

Mark Hall was the first part of the New Town to be completed. It consists of two separate residential areas either side of First Avenue, which are imaginatively named Mark Hall North and Mark Hall South. In Mark Hall North can be found The Lawn, built in 1951 as the UK's first modern residential tower block. Many of the tower blocks which came later have bitten the dust over the years, but The Lawn has survived and it is now a listed building. To the north of Mark Hall North is Temple Fields, a large industrial area next to the River Stort which includes the ward's railway station, Harlow Mill on the West Anglia main line.

This ward has a very strange electoral history, although those who remember the Heneage preview from Grimsby last week may start to feel a sense of *déjà vu*. It was generally Liberal Democrat until 2008, then developed into a Labour ward. The last Lib Dem councillor for the ward died just before his term was due to end in 2012, and Labour picked the seat up easily. In 2014 one of the Labour councillors resigned for work reasons, resulting in two of the ward's seats being up for election, and UKIP came from nowhere to win both of them. One of the UKIP councillors resigned shortly afterwards on health grounds; Labour's Danny Purton won the resulting by-election in February 2015, and Labour gained the other UKIP seat in May 2015.

Towards the end of the last decade Harlow was in a rather unusual electoral position. Since 2010 it has had a Conservative MP, Robert Halfon, whose position was bolstered by the fact that the town isn't quite big enough to form a parliamentary seat on its own and the Harlow constituency consequently includes a significant amount of rural territory outside the town. Since 2017 the Harlow borough has had a full slate of four Conservatives on Essex county council. But, despite all that, the borough council had a consistent Labour majority. This was partly due to boundary effects, as the Conservative vote in Harlow was not well-distributed. Most of the party's voters were packed into four safe wards, which meant that in a nationally-even year Labour would generally win the ward count 7–4; and the district council election years in 2015–19 were all nationally-even years. In May 2019, despite some well-publicised left-wing infighting among the ruling group, Labour polled 43% of the vote in Mark Hall ward, to 25% for UKIP and 23% for the Conservatives.

So the 2021 Harlow borough elections must have come as a shock. The Tories won ten of the town's eleven wards in May, some of them for the first time this century, and suddenly found themselves in control of the council with a large majority: they now have 20 councillors, while Labour have 12 left plus this vacancy. The result in Mark Hall ward in particular was something to behold: 61% for the Conservatives against just 32% for Labour, a swing since 2019 of nearly 25%.

Danny Purton, who had been a senior manager at the council before his election in 2015, passed away a few days before the May election. The by-election to replace him is looking like a difficult defence for the Labour candidate Kay Morrison, who will have to call on all of her extensive previous local government experience. Before she relocated to Harlow from Scotland, Morrison was a member of Fife council from 1999 to 2017, representing wards in another New Town (Glenrothes) and serving as depute provost of Fife. She was also the Labour candidate for Mid Fife and Glenrothes in the 2016 Scottish Parliament election. The Conservative candidate is John Steer. The ward's regular Lib Dem candidate Lesley Rideout, who lost her council seat here in 2011 and has tried to get it back at every election from 2014 onwards, is having another go; she completes the ballot paper along with Jamie Gilbert of the Green Party.*

Ardingly and Balcombe

Mid Sussex council; caused by the death of Conservative councillor Andrew Macnaughton.

We travel south of London to the High Weald of Sussex. The Ardingly and Balcombe ward is a landscape of woods and hills to the south of Crawley; not easy territory through which to thread a railway, and the builders of the Brighton Line had to construct a long tunnel to the north of Balcombe and a long viaduct over the River Ouse to the south of it. In between is Balcombe railway station, which has brought the area within the range of London commuters.

If Balcombe has a commuter dependence, as do the villages of Pease Pottage and Handcross on the main road from Crawley to Brighton, Ardingly (pronounced "Ardinglye", apparently) has an economic base of its own. This is partly

* *Harlow, Mark Hall*: C 549 Lab 493 Grn 86 LD 55 [C gain from Lab]

Parliamentary constituency: Harlow
Essex county council division: Harlow North
May 2021 result C 1033 Lab 539 LD 120
May 2019 result Lab 613 UKIP 354 C 335 LD 139
May 2018 result Lab 761 C 503 UKIP 140 LD 121
May 2016 result Lab 751 UKIP 449 C 390 LD 104
May 2015 result Lab 1296 C 1060 UKIP 731 LD 175
February 2015 by-election Lab 586 UKIP 353 C 334 Grn 55 LD 47
May 2014 double vacancy UKIP 662/646 Lab 602/599 C 346/346 LD 137/124
May 2012 result Lab 849 C 440 LD 312
May 2011 result Lab 913 LD 555 C 542
May 2010 result Lab 1145 LD 1114 C 961
May 2008 result LD 744 C 681 Lab 599
May 2007 result LD 752 Lab 740 C 570
May 2006 result LD 761 Lab 735 C 562
June 2004 result Lab 800 LD 584 C 381 Ind 290
May 2003 result LD 598 Lab 510 C 179 Socialist Alliance 48
May 2002 result LD 1098/1091/1075 Lab 791/782/772 C 276/269/255

Figure 56: Harlow, Mark Hall

due to the presence of Ardingly College, a boarding school which propels the ward into the top 100 in England and Wales for the 16–17 age group. A number of future Conservative MPs have passed through Ardingly over the years, and other Old Ardinians include the *Private Eye* editor Ian Hislop, the author Neil Gaiman and the upper-class twit Tim Nice-But-Dim. To the north of the village is Wakehurst, a sixteenth-century stately home whose grounds have been taken over by Kew Gardens. Also here is the South of England Showground, an excellent venue for the sort of events which—oh.

The late councillor Andrew Macnaughton had served this ward as a councillor continuously since 1987. At the time of his death he was Mid Sussex council's cabinet member for housing and planning. He had a safe ward, notwithstanding a rather large fall in the Tory vote here in 2019: the Conservative slate polled 39% against 27% for the Liberal Democrats and 23% for the single Green candidate. In May's election to West Sussex county council the local Worth Forest county division was much safer for the Tories.

Defending for the Conservatives is Lorraine Nunes-Carvalho, who lives in the Balcombe area: she is a finance director for a company providing services to the hotel and leisure industry. The Lib Dem candidate is Ben Jerrit, a teacher at Ardingly College who has previously worked behind the camera in the TV and film industry; his credits include a number of episodes of *The Bill* and *EastEnders* and a *Harry Potter* film. The Greens have selected Jenny Edwards, a

Parliamentary constituency: Horsham
West Sussex county council division: Worth Forest
May 2019 result C 684/642 LD 470/404 Grn 409 Lab 192
May 2015 result C 1620/1596 Grn 692 Ind 594 Lab 543
May 2011 result C 1233/1104 LD 556
May 2007 result C 934/879 Grn 396 LD 387
May 2003 result C 868/706 LD 328/222

Figure 57: Mid Sussex, Ardingly and Balcombe

business coach and West Hoathly parish councillor. Completing the by-election is independent candidate Carole Steggles, a parish councillor in Turners Hill (not part of this ward) who also stood here in the county elections two weeks ago.* The *Mid Sussex Times* has interviewed all the candidates, and you can find out more from their website†.

Feniton; and Honiton St Michael's

East Devon council; caused respectively by the resignations of independent councillor Susie Bond and Liberal Democrat councillor Luke Jeffery.

We finish in the West Country with a trip to the East Devon district. This is one of the larger second-tier districts, covering nearly everything in Devon to the east of Exeter. Exmouth is the major town in the district, with other towns including Sidmouth on the coast and, inland, Honiton.

Honiton is an old market town, located on the Fosse Way and the A 30 London–Exeter road and known for its Georgian architecture and its traditional lace-making industry. The Georgian buildings are a byproduct of the town having been mostly destroyed by fire in the mid-eighteenth century; and heat is also a feature of the town's annual Hot Pennies ceremony, dating from the Anarchy, in which warm pennies are thrown from balconies in the High Street to crowds of local people each of July. The Hot Pennies organisers are hoping for a particularly special event this year on 27th July, to mark the 800th anniversary of Honiton's market charter. The town is divided into two wards, of which St Michael's is the south-western one.

Immediately to the south-west of Honiton lies the Feniton ward, covering three parishes in the Devon countryside. Feniton village was greatly expanded by the coming of the railways, to the extent that it's actually two separate settlements:

* *Mid Sussex, Ardingly and Balcombe*: Grn 452 C 409 LD 340 Ind 23 [Grn gain from C]
† `tinyurl.com/mr2cje47`

the original Feniton around the parish church, and the larger "New Feniton" around the railway station. There was a junction here on the Waterloo–Exeter main line for branch line trains to Sidmouth, and until the 1960s Feniton station had the name "Sidmouth Junction". The station then fell victim to the Beeching cuts, but this closure was quickly reversed in 1971.

The Conservatives had badly underperformed in this corner of Devon in recent years. In the 2019 elections they crashed to 20 out of 60 seats, and the administration was taken over by an independent-led coalition which includes the Lib Dems and Green Party. The Tories did, however, stop the rot in the 2021 Devon county elections, holding all their seats in the district and gaining a seat from the independents on both the county council and in a district council by-election. Both of today's by-elections take place within the Feniton and Honiton county division, which swung strongly to Labour but was still safe Conservative. Given that, what chance of two more Tory gains here?

Well, Honiton St Michael's could be a distinct possibility. The Conservatives have topped the poll in every election here since 2007, including a by-election in July 2016[*]. On slightly adjusted boundaries, in 2019 the Conservative slate were opposed only by Lib Dem councillor Luke Jeffery who was elected in third place; shares of the vote were 53% for the Conservatives and 47% for the Lib Dems.

For Feniton, however, your guess is as good as mine. Independent councillor Susie Bond won the ward (then known as "Feniton and Buckerell") at a by-election in May 2013, and she has been re-elected twice since with extremely large shares of the vote. In 2019 she polled 83% against Conservative and Labour opposition.

No independent candidate has come forward to succeed Bond in Feniton, so that's a lot of votes up for grabs. The Conservatives have picked a candidate with local government experience: Alasdair Bruce, a beekeeper, was a Thanet councillor from 2007 to 2015 and sat on that council's cabinet. The Labour candidate is local resident Linda Baden. Finally, the Liberal Democrats contest Feniton ward for the first time since 2011; their candidate is Todd Olive, a Warwick University postgraduate student who is fighting his second East Devon council by-election in three months, as he was the losing candidate in the Whimple and Rockbeare by-election last May.[†]

For Honiton St Michael's the defending Liberal Democrat candidate is Jules Hoyles, a former chairman of the party's Tiverton and Honiton branch. He fought Axminster in May's county elections. Returning for the Conservatives is the winner of the 2016 by-election, Jenny Brown; in 2019 she attempted to trans-

[*] *Andrew's Previews 2016*, page 130. [†] *East Devon, Feniton*: C 239 Lab 126 LD 82 [C gain from Ind]

Parliamentary constituency: Tiverton and Honiton
Devon county council division: Feniton and Honiton
May 2019 result Ind 638 C 97 Lab 37
(Previous results as "Feniton and Buckerell")
May 2015 result Ind 1048 C 288
May 2013 by-election Ind 772 C 113
May 2011 result C 512 LD 394
May 2007 result C 401 LD 391
May 2003 result C 420 LD 258 Lab 61

Figure 58: East Devon, Feniton

Parliamentary constituency: Tiverton and Honiton
Devon county council division: Feniton and Honiton
May 2019 result C 790/763/530 LD 700

Figure 59: East Devon, Honiton St Michael's

fer to the town's other ward, Honiton St Paul's, but lost to her running-mate by one vote. Due to what appears to be an error in filling out her nomination papers, she will appear on the ballot as "Brown Jenny". Completing the Honiton St Michael's ballot paper is Labour's Jake Bonetta, who put in a creditable performance here in the county council elections in May.*

* *East Devon, Honiton St Michael's*: Lab 807 C 522 LD 63 [Lab gain from LD]

15th July 2021

One by-election on 15th July 2021:

Tividale

Sandwell council, West Midlands; caused by the death of Labour councillor Sandra Hevican.

After the excitement of recent weeks this will be a short edition of Andrew's Previews with just one local by-election taking place today. We have come to the heart of the industrial Black Country, the upper slopes of the Rowley Hills. Rising to over 200 metres above sea level, the Rowley Hills divide Dudley from the Birmingham area and the Severn basin from the Trent catchment. Their northern slopes look down towards lower ground in Oldbury, beyond the Wolverhampton Road and the Birmingham Canal.

The A 4123 Wolverhampton Road, built in the 1920s as an unemployment relief project, forms the northern boundary of Tividale ward. This is based on a number of housing estates of both private and council origin; the Tividale Hall and Grace Mary estates were started in the 1930s, but most of the houses here are postwar. The 2011 census return found a rather low White British population (82%); there are significant black and Asian minority groups in the ward, the Asian community here being mostly Sikhs of Punjabi heritage. In 2019 Tividale was assessed as one of the least-deprived wards of the Metropolitan Borough of Sandwell.

Sandwell council's elections had got very boring in the last few years. Since the fall of the Labour government in May 2010 Labour had won every ward at every Sandwell election, with just two exceptions: in 2011 the Conservatives held Charlemont with Grove Wale ward, and Princes End ward returned a UKIP councillor in 2014. UKIP also came close to winning Tividale that year, and Tividale has been fertile ground for the radical right in the past: the British National Party, in the days when they were a significant electoral force, won here in the 2006 local elections by the narrow margin of 33 votes. The BNP leader Nick Griffin himself had stood here in the 2000 Parliamentary by-election for the local seat of West Bromwich West, following the retirement of Speaker Boothroyd: he finished in fourth place and lost his deposit.

Since December 2019 West Bromwich West has been a Conservative parliamentary seat for the first time, in what must go down as a revolution in the politics of the Black Country. The Conservatives now control two-and-a-half of the three-and-a-half parliamentary seats in Sandwell, those being the two West Bromwich seats and the Rowley Regis part of Halesowen and Rowley Regis. They managed this despite the fact that Sandwell council had, at the time, 72 Labour councillors out of a possible 72.

The Conservatives followed up on their parliamentary gains by carrying six wards in the May 2021 Sandwell council election, by far their best performance in the borough since 2008. There was a very large number of casual vacancies filled in Sandwell in May, so this translated into 9 seats for the Conservatives; Labour continue to run the council with 59 seats plus this vacancy, and the remaining three councillors are independents who were elected on the Labour ticket. Tividale ward remained in the Labour column this May, but only narrowly so: the ward was a straight between Labour and the Conservatives, with Labour winning by 53–47.

Tividale councillor Sandra Hevican died from COVID-19 in late March, at the age of 55. Her death came just before the legal notices for the May elections were due to be published, and the by-election wasn't called in time to schedule this vacancy for May. Hevican had served as a councillor for Tividale ward since 2014; away from her democratic duties, she worked for Wolverhampton council as a housing benefits officer.

Defending for Labour is Sandra Hevican's widower, Robert Hevican. The Conservatives have reselected their candidate from May Emma Henlan, an MP's office manager who also works in the family aquarium business. There is a wider choice for the electors of Tividale in this by-election, as also standing are Nicholas Bradley for the Liberal Democrats, Richard Gingell for the Trade Unionist and Socialist Coalition, and independent candidate Energy Kutebura.*

Catchup

Since it's a slow by-elections week, we've time to bring you some other election-related news. One piece of good news is that the Cabinet Office minister respon-

* *Sandwell, Tividale*: C 986 Lab 810 Ind 40 LD 30 TUSC 9 [C gain from Lab]

Parliamentary constituency: West Bromwich West
ONS Travel to Work Area: Dudley
May 2021 result Lab 1323 C 1173
May 2019 result Lab 1051 C 446 Grn 437
May 2018 result Lab 1137 C 637 Grn 226
May 2016 result Lab 1489 C 434 Grn 189
May 2015 result Lab 2447 UKIP 1445 C 1052 Grn 142
May 2014 result Lab 1085 UKIP 968 Grn 342 C 280
May 2012 result Lab 1637 C 390
May 2011 result Lab 1884 C 840 LD 189
May 2010 result Lab 2166 C 1571 LD 793 BNP 761
May 2008 result Lab 1485 C 1155
May 2007 result Lab 1309 BNP 938 C 567 LD 333
May 2006 result BNP 1191 Lab 1158 C 562 LD 308
June 2004 reuslt Lab 1735/1539/1438 BNP 1174

Figure 60: Sandwell, Tividale

sible for elections, Chloe Smith, has successfully completed her treatment for breast cancer and been given the all-clear. This column sends its congratulations.

Last week Miss Smith introduced into the Commons her major project for the new Parliamentary session, as the Elections Bill was given its first reading. The headline provisions in the bill relating to photographic ID being required for voting have generated some controversy, but there's a lot of other things going on in the Bill as well, including: allowing British citizens living overseas to vote in UK elections regardless of how long they have been away from the country; new rules on EU citizens' eligibility to vote and stand in English and Northern Irish local elections (Scotland and Wales have already made their own rules on this); changes to the role of the Electoral Commission; and requirements for digital campaign material to carry imprints. At the time of writing, a date for the second reading is yet to be set. As usual, the Parliament website has the text of the Bill and some explanatory notes[*].

The Association of Electoral Administrators, whose members will have the job of actually delivering these changes for your benefit, have published their report on May's giant local elections[†] together with their *Blueprint for a Modern Electoral Landscape*, a list of process changes which they want making or least considering. Top of their wishlist is a rationalisation and extension of the election timetable together with a new consolidation of election law. As your columnist wrote last year in my piece on issues around postponing elections in a pandemic, the last consolidation (the Representation of the People Act 1983)

[*] tinyurl.com/fkpvujcp [†] tinyurl.com/bde7n3jn

> was passed into law at a much simpler time when there were only elections to Parliament, local councils and that newfangled thing called the European Parliament. Since then we have had all sorts of constitutional innovations: devolution to Wales and London, the establishment of the Electoral Commission, mayors of districts and boroughs, regional and metro mayors, police and crime commissioners, newfangled electoral systems, extensions to the franchise, you name it. All of that has to be bolted onto the 1983 Act which now has so many extensions that the structure is starting to sag under its own weight.*

Yes, I forgot the elections to Scottish Parliament and the Inner London Education Authority, although to be fair not many people remember the Inner London Education Authority over thirty years after it was abolished. To give you a flavour of just how heavily the 1983 Act has been amended and how difficult it now is to follow, let's look at the sections of it relating to electoral registration. My printed copy of the Act has four A4 pages of text under the heading "Registration of parliamentary and local government electors", divided into six sections numbered 8 to 13. A Herculean effort from the team at `legislation.gov.uk`, who really shouldn't have had to do this, has finally managed to bring the 1983 Act completely up to date with all the hundreds (possibly thousands) of amendments which have been made by scores of later Acts in the following thirty-eight years. According to them†, the relevant part of the table of contents now reads:

> *Registration of parliamentary and local government electors*
>
> 8. Registration officers.
>
> 9. Registers of electors..
>
> 9A. Registration officers: duty to take necessary steps.
>
> 9B. Anonymous registration.
>
> 9C. Removal of anonymous entry.
>
> 9D. Maintenance of registers: duty to conduct canvass in Great Britain.
>
> 9E. Maintenance of registers: invitations to register in Great Britain.
>
> 10. Maintenance of registers: duty to conduct canvass in Northern Ireland.
>
> 10ZA. Northern Ireland: timing of canvass.
>
> 10ZB. The relevant registration objectives (Northern Ireland).
>
> 10ZC. Registration of electors in Great Britain.
>
> 10ZD. Registration of electors in Great Britain: alterations.

* *Andrew's Previews 2020*, page 70. † `tinyurl.com/bdffekyp`

10ZE. Removal of electors in Great Britain from register.

10ZF. Digital registration and canvass in Northern Ireland.

10A. Maintenance of the registers: registration of electors in Northern Ireland..

10B. Register of electors in Northern Ireland: digital registration number.

11. Correction of registers..

12. Right to be registered..

13. Publication of registers..

13A. Alteration of registers..

13AB. Alteration of registers: interim publication dates.

13B. Alteration of registers: pending elections..

13BA. Alteration of registers in Northern Ireland: pending elections.

13BB. Election falling within canvass period.

13BC. Alteration of registers: recall petition.

13C. Electoral identity card: Northern Ireland.

13CZA. Provision of false information: application for electoral identity card.

13CA. Scottish local government elections: false information in connection with applications for absent voting.

13D. Provision of false information

I wish I was making this up. That's 29 sections and God knows how many sides of A4. I'm not trying to say all this isn't needed, but the thicket of suffix letters is a barrier to understanding not just for the average voter but for the election professionals in our local town halls. The AEA point out in section 3 of their post-poll report that this fragmentation of our electoral law caused problems in drafting last year's emergency legislation to deal with the current public health situation. So does the Elections Bill clean up this alphabet soup? No. In fact it *adds* two more sections relating to electoral registration (13BD and 13BE) among pages and pages of further amendments.

And this is just one example of how the state of the UK's electoral law got beyond a joke many years ago. The AEA are completely right to call for a single Electoral Administration Act, and hopefully they won't be repeating that call for much longer.

One welcome change in the Elections Bill is a restating of the electoral offence of undue influence, which dates from 1883 and whose definition—written in very Victorian and increasingly archaic language—hasn't significantly changed since. This change will hopefully help the Election Court in the future, although it won't be relevant to the three pending legal cases which this column is aware of arising from the May elections.

Of those three cases, the most straightforward would appear to be the one in the Banbury Ruscote division of Oxfordshire county council, which Labour are challenging on the basis that the result was declared for the Conservatives incorrectly following an administrative error at the count.* In Coldhurst ward, Oldham, an independent candidate has lodged a case making various allegations about the conduct of the poll†. Finally, the Liberal Democrats have launched a case in the Totteridge and Bowerdean ward of High Wycombe‡, where they lost in the Buckinghamshire county elections to an independent slate. As this column has pointed out in the past§ Totteridge and Bowerdean is a ward where elections before 2021 have led to electoral fraud allegations, so this could be a fun one for the Election Court to sort out. Andrew's Previews will of course keep an eye on what's going on with those cases, and once an update comes to my attention I will pass it on.

* For the outcome of this petition see page 334. † Report from the *Manchester Evening News*: `tinyurl.com/yc2fvbhd`. As of the end of 2021 this petition had not yet reached trial. ‡ Report from the *Bucks Free Press*: `tinyurl.com/2p9xtm82`. As of the end of 2021 this petition had not yet reached trial. § *Andrew's Previews 2019*, pages 29 and 33.

22nd July 2021

It's 22/7, and Andrew's Previews wishes a happy Pi Approximation Day to all readers. To celebrate in this heatwave, let's take a tour of the eight by-elections today in England and Wales. We have some hot electoral action to match this hot weather, with Labour defending three seats, two Conservative defences in Kent, a Lib Dem defence in London and, unusually, rather a focus on the Green Party. They have one defence and a good chance of a gain in an open seat which we start with:

Congresbury and Puxton

North Somerset council; caused by the resignation of Liberal Democrat councillor Stuart Treadaway.

Environmentalism has become a feature of our politics over the last few decades. The work which has already been done in this country is impressive. Within living memory there were times when the air we breathe was so polluted it could be impossible to see across a London street in choking fog, and the UK's rivers were, in many cases, lifeless drains for industrial and agricultural chemicals.

How times have changed. Smoke no longer fills the air from every industrial or domestic chimney, and (unless it's raining) the hills on the far horizons tempt the eye to look outwards for many miles from high viewpoints. Our coal-fired power stations now lie for the most part idle, superseded by wind turbines that rotate out to sea. Wheelie bins multiply and bring colour to our back yards, stopping our rubbish from going to waste. Our post-industrial landscapes have gone back to nature, which has taken up the task enthusiastically. The talk for the future is all of electric cars and environmental friendliness.

That doesn't mean everything is well in the garden. There's a lot to do to consolidate these gains and preserve them for the next generation. As usual, some of this will end up getting political; and in this argument there is one party whose *raison d'être* is environmentalism.

The Green Party has done very well at the ballot box in recent years. The most recent local elections cycle was their best ever: the party now has over 400 local councillors and is represented on more councils than ever before. The Greens run Brighton and Hove council as a minority, a Green-led administration has recently taken over in Lancaster, and the party participates in a number of ruling coalitions in other councils including North Somerset council. The Greens are now tied with Labour for the most council seats in Bristol, and are the official opposition in Mid Suffolk, Norwich and Solihull. Proportional representation has ensured that the Green Party has been consistently represented in the Scottish Parliament and the London Assembly since their formation over two decades ago, and the Greens' single MP Caroline Lucas was re-elected in December 2019 for her fourth term of office.

Not bad work for a minor party whose core vote is not geographically concentrated, and which accordingly struggles with England's first-past-the-post electoral system. Forty years ago, there were no Green councillors at all (indeed, the party was still known then by its previous name, the Ecology Party). Their breakthrough came in local government in the 1986 local elections in which the party won its first two council seats. One was won by John Marjoram, who was elected by the Trinity ward of Stroud council in Gloucestershire and was still a councillor there until he retired in May this year. The other was won by Richard Lawson. He was a GP from the village of Congresbury, located a few miles to the east of Weston-super-Mare in what was then the county of Avon, and he defeated an independent councillor to win the Congresbury ward of Woodspring council.

Once the Green Party get a foothold in a ward they have proven hard for other parties to shift. Congresbury continued to elect Dr Lawson and his Green successors continuously from 1986 until 2019. In that time, Woodspring council became a unitary council in 1995 under the name of North Somerset, and Congresbury ward was redrawn in 2015 and renamed as Congresbury and Puxton.

In 2019 the Green councillor Thomas Leimdorfer retired and the party didn't nominate a candidate to succeed him. Into this political vacuum stepped the Liberal Democrats' Stuart Treadaway, who defeated Labour by the score of 54–32. The Conservatives had been in second place last time, but fell to a poor third: they generally did badly in North Somerset in 2019, losing control of the council to an independent-led rainbow coalition.

This by-election is caused by Stuart Treadaway's resignation. The Lib Dems have not nominated a candidate to succeed him, so we have a free-for-all! Second last time were Labour who have selected Dawn Parry, a former Conservative figure: she was a North Somerset councillor for Weston-super-Mare West ward from 2007 to 2011 and fought Newport East as the Conservative candidate in

Parliamentary constituency: Weston-super-Mare
May 2019 result LD 664 Lab 391 C 166
May 2015 result Grn 1269 C 787 Lab 222

Figure 61: North Somerset, Congresbury and Puxton

the 2010 general election. Today Parry is a parish councillor in Banwell, just to the south, and runs a film production company. The Conservatives have reselected their usual candidate for this ward Samantha Pepperall, who runs a stables in the village of Wick St Lawrence to the west. However, given the ward's previous history the candidate to beat here is probably Phil Neve of the Green Party, whose LinkedIn profile describes him as "allegedly retired but not often unbusy". Neve has recently retired (allegedly) from a career in designing and building energy-efficient and sustainable houses; he is the chairman of Wrington parish council to the east, and was the Green candidate for North Somerset in the December 2019 general election. Those are your three candidates.*

Tyn-y-nant

Rhondda Cynon Taf council, Glamorgan; caused by the death of Labour councillor Clayton Willis.

We cross the Bristol Channel for our Welsh by-election today. The village of Tynant, to give it the Anglicised name it's usually known by in the area, lies around 4 miles south of Pontypridd; it has effectively merged with the neighbouring village of Beddau to the west to form a single urban area, although Beddau and Tynant are still separate wards of Rhondda Cynon Taf council. As with many villages in south Wales, Tynant is a former pit village which was dependent on its colliery: specifically Cwm Colliery, which was sunk in 1909 to provide coal for the Great Western Railway's locomotives. Cwm Colliery closed in 1986, but the associated coking plant stayed in production all the way to 2002 and is still there today, lying derelict while arguments are made over its redevelopment.

Like many pit villages, the area's best-known local heroes are sportsmen and women. A number of pupils at the secondary school for Beddau and Tynant, Bryn Celynnog, have gone on to play top-level sport: recent pupils here include the Paralympic table tennis player Sara Head and the legendary Wales prop of recent years Gethin Jenkins.

Welsh local government was reorganised in 1995 creating the present Rhondda Cynon Taf council, and local man Clayton Willis had represented Tyn-y-nant

* *North Somerset, Congresbury and Puxton*: Grn 594 C 270 Lab 57 [Grn gain from LD]

Parliamentary and Senedd constituency: Pontypridd
May 2017 result Lab 557 C 215
May 2012 result Lab 791 PC 116
May 2008 result Lab 700 PC 223
June 2004 result Lab 675 PC 219
May 1999 result Lab 890 PC 285
May 1995 result Lab 1018 PC 165

Figure 62: Rhondda Cynon Taf, Tyn-y-nant

continuously from then until his death last month at the age of 80. He had served on Rhondda Cynon Taf's cabinet from 2004 to 2014. Willis enjoyed very large majorities in his ward: his final re-election in 2017 was with the unusually close lead of 72–28 over the Conservatives, who had stood here for the first time. The Conservatives only have a handful of seats on Rhondda Cynon Taf council, which has a large Labour majority: Plaid Cymru are the largest opposition party. Tyn-y-nant is part of the Pontypridd constituency, which comfortably re-elected Labour MS Mick Antoniw in May.

A quick note on boundaries. The present boundaries of Tyn-y-nant ward were modified in 2017 following changes to the boundary between the Llantrisant Town and Llantwit Fardre communities; in particular, the Cwm Colliery site was transferred into this division from Llantwit Fardre division. The map of the 2017 election results available from the Local Elections Archive Project has not been updated to reflect these changes and shows the *previous* boundaries of the ward. Apologies for any confusion.

Defending for Labour is Julie Barton, a media consultant who sits on Llantrisant community council for the neighbouring Beddau ward. The Conservatives have selected Rob Green, who gives an address in Church Village to the east of the ward. Completing the ballot paper is Ioan Bellin for Plaid Cymru.*

Liscard

Wirral council, Merseyside; caused the resignation of Labour councillor Sarah Spoor.

From the land of Wales we come to the island of the Welsh, as "Wallasey" literally means. Liscard (which, appropriately enough, is a Celtic name) is the middle of three extensively built-up wards on the Mersey side of the Wirral peninsula, lying in between the docks of Seacombe to the south and the sands

* *Rhondda Cynon Taf, Tyn-y-nant*: Lab 411 C 62 PC 35. All the candidates have been interviewed by Wales Online, and you can find out more here at `tinyurl.com/2knpuh69`.

of New Brighton to the north. The pedestrianised Egremont Promenade gives excellent views over the river to the Liverpool docks, while inland the Cherry Tree shopping centre acts as a focal point for the ward. All of the ward is in the bottom half of the deprivation indices (most of it in the most deprived 20%), and just 23% of the population are educated to degree level.

This is a good point to pick up an article which this column's genial host Ben Walker contributed to the *New Statesman* last month entitled "Which of the Conservatives' 'Blue Wall' seats are most vulnerable?"*. Walker identified a number of deprived and/or Leave-voting areas in the Midlands and South, such as Shropshire and Worthing, which the Conservatives hold but where they are struggling in local elections. He goes on to say:

> Here, again, are constituencies that have become more competitive despite supposedly favourable demographics for the Tories. This phenomenon, as also seen in areas such as Sunderland and the Wirral, could be attributed to parties being in power for prolonged periods of time without any effective opposition. In the instance of Sunderland and the Wirral, those establishments were Labour, but in the case of Worthing and Shropshire, they happened to be Conservative.

This column would have no difficulty agreeing with that assessment in the case of Sunderland, which has had a continuous Labour majority for decades; but with due respect to my host the Wirral is a bit of a different case. It's not all Birkenhead. There are some seriously attractive areas on the peninsula like West Kirby and Hoylake which give the Conservatives a secure base on the council even in their worst years, and which returned a Conservative MP solidly until 1997. Wirral council had a Conservative majority from its creation in 1974 until 1986, and since then it has alternated between Labour majorities and hung councils. As recently as 2008–11 the Conservatives were the largest party, with Labour then in majority control from 2012 to 2021 when the council became hung again. The latest composition is 29 Labour councillors (plus this vacancy) forming a minority administration, against 23 Conservatives, 6 Lib Dems, 5 Greens and 2 independents, of whom one is ex-Labour and the other is ex-Green.

Conservative majorities in the Land of Plastic have historically always included Liscard ward, which had a full slate of Conservative councillors until 1984 and again from 2008 to 2010. The ward has swung strongly to the left since 2010 in line with most of Merseyside, and interestingly the Labour vote has held up a lot better in the Wallasey wards than it has in Birkenhead where the Greens are doing very well at the moment. The Green Party were a very distant third in Liscard in May, with Labour beating the Conservatives here 57–26.

* tinyurl.com/yc2vjr8z

Parliamentary constituency: Wallasey
May 2021 result Lab 1898 C 875 Grn 271 LD 221 Reform UK 71
May 2019 result Lab 1733 C 609 UKIP 374 Grn 360 LD 319
May 2018 result Lab 2241 C 756 LD 337 Grn 190
May 2016 double vacancy Lab 2240/1672 C 690/427 UKIP 504 Grn 338 LD 280
May 2015 result Lab 4397 UKIP 1352 LD 578 Grn 542 TUSC 118
May 2014 result Lab 1619 UKIP 815 C 649 Grn 273 LD 94
May 2012 result Lab 1882 C 1261 UKIP 400 Grn 230
May 2011 result Lab 2523 C 1673 UKIP 204 Grn 146 LD 121
May 2010 result Lab 3220 C 2474 LD 718 UKIP 238 Grn 231
May 2008 result C 2122 Lab 1369 UKIP 304 LD 195 Grn 159
May 2007 result C 2116 Lab 1609 LD 244 UKIP 149 Grn 143
May 2006 result C 2047 Lab 1396 LD 286 Grn 209 UKIP 166
June 2004 result Lab 1908/1789/1776 C 1760/1516/1450 LD 653/630/590

Figure 63: Wirral, Liscard

Sarah Spoor has resigned as a Labour councillor just over two years into her first term, indicating that she had been unable to juggle her work, family and democratic commitments. Defending the by-election to replace her is Labour candidate Daisy Kenny, a business support co-ordinator. The Conservatives have reselected their candidate from May Jane Owens, who was appointed MBE in 2016 for services to education on the Wirral; she is the chair of governors at a number of local schools. Also standing are Edward Lamb for the Green Party, Sue Arrowsmith (who has fought the ward at the last three elections) for the Liberal Democrats, Gary Bergin for the For Britain Movement* and independent candidate Lynda Williams, who finished second here in 2014 and 2015 as the UKIP candidate.†

Humberstone and Hamilton

Leicester council; caused by the death of councillor John Thomas, who was elected for Labour but had been sitting as an independent.

For our final Labour defence this week we come to the north-east corner of the city of Leicester. As the compound name suggests, Humberstone and Hamilton ward covers a number of different areas of the city: Humberstone itself is an old village which has been absorbed by Leicester's growth, Humberstone Garden is a garden city-style development from the turn of the 20th century,

* The originally-published version of this column incorrectly stated that Bergin was standing for Reform UK. My apologies to Reform UK for th error. † *Wirral, Liscard*: Lab 1137 C 582 LD 201 Grn 109 Ind 68 For Britain Movement 26

Parliamentary constituency: Leicester East
May 2019 result Lab 2095/1905/1895 C 1128/958/903 Grn 650 LD 421
May 2015 result Lab 3035/2759/2620 C 1983/1813/1624 UKIP 1021/9218/898 Grn 676 TUSC 368/320 Ind 205

Figure 64: Leicester, Humberstone and Hamilton

while Hamilton is a modern estate on the edge of the city. The ward is majority non-white and makes the top 40 wards in England and Wales for Hinduism (21% of the population).

This ward is part of the Leicester East constituency, which has been on the potential parliamentary by-election watchlist for some considerable time due to the behaviour of its MPs. From 1987 to 2019 it was represented by someone whose whose parliamentary career was not exactly a quiet one, the Labour MP Keith Vaz.* Vaz was replaced in 2019 by Islington Labour councillor Claudia Webbe, who was subsequently charged with harassment: she was due to stand trial in March this year, but the trial had to be adjourned after her defence barrister was taken ill and had to be sent to hospital. Also in March Webbe resigned her previous elected role on Islington council in London, and the by-election to replace her there was duly held in May (page 60).

The selection process that produced Webbe had been controversial, and was one factor in the resignation from the Labour party of Humberstone and Hamilton ward councillor John Thomas, a former Lord Mayor of Leicester who had been chair of the party's Leicester East branch. He was first elected to the city council in 1993 and had continuous service since 1999. In 2019 Thomas transferred to Humberstone and Hamilton ward which is, like most of the city, a safe Labour area: the Labour slate polled 49% of the vote that May against 26% for the Conservatives and 15% for the Green Party. John Thomas died in May after a long illness, aged 77.

Thomas' resignation from Labour made no difference to the running of Leicester council, which has a directly-elected Labour mayor (Sir Peter Soulsby), and where the 2019 elections returned 53 Labour council seats out of a possible 54. The one that got away is a Liberal Democrat seat in Aylestone ward, at the other end of the city.

Defending for Labour is Abdul Abdul Ghafoor. The Conservatives have selected Daniel Crewe, a local builder. The Green candidate is Pam Bellinger, who appears to be linked to the local branch of Extinction Rebellion. Also standing are Bicram Athwal for the Liberal Democrats, David Haslett for the

* Apologies to any readers who may have been playing the Keith Vaz game.

For Britain Movement and Raj Solanki for Reform UK.*

Fortune Green

Camden council, London; caused by the resignation of Liberal Democrat councillor Flick Rea.

We start the second half of this week's Previews with two polls in what was once Middlesex. The county of Middlesex, of course, no longer exists except in the anachronistic dreams of the Association of British Counties, having been almost entirely swallowed up by the growth of London. One of the first parts of it to disappear, becoming part of the County of London in the 1880s, was Fortune Green.

Fortune Green itself is an area of open space between Finchley Road and the Midland railway line, adjacent to Hampstead Cemetery. The ward of the name is often linked with West Hampstead to the south; there are no railway or Underground stations within the boundary, although Kilburn underground station is just off the southern corner. Fortune Green's census return from 2011 paints a picture of a generally middle-class area with very high levels of immigration from Ireland and other EU-15 countries: the ward was in the top 10 in England and Wales for those who did not answer the census' religion question (21.2%) and also made the top 100 for the White Other ethnic group (25.6%) and for those educated to degree level (57.8%).

Until the advent of Coalition Fortune Green was a safe Liberal Democrat ward and a secure base for one of the party's longest-serving councillors in London. Felicity "Flick" Rea had served as a councillor for this ward since 1986, and this by-election has come about because of her retirement after 35 years in office. It's clearly her personal vote which has enabled her to hold on for so long: Labour drew level with the Lib Dems here in 2014 and have held the ward's other two seats since then. The shares of the vote at the last Camden elections in 2018 were 36% each for the Lib Dems and Labour and 18% for the Conservatives. Camden council has a strong Labour majority, and Rea was one of only three Lib Dems elected to the council that year (the other two were in Belsize ward, a three-way marginal).

The Liberal Democrats generally do not perform well in London Assembly elections, and in May they placed fourth here in both the Mayoral and London Member ballots. The ward's ballot boxes gave 47% to Sadiq Khan, 23% to the Conservatives' Shaun Bailey and 10% to the Greens' Siân Berry, who represents

* *Leicester, Humberstone and Hamilton*: C 1062 Lab 790 LD 262 Grn 190 For Britain Movement 37 Reform UK 37 [C gain from Lab]

Parliamentary constituency: Hampstead and Kilburn
London Assembly constituency: Barnet and Camden
May 2018 result LD 1496/1209/1138 Lab 1468/1353/1326 C 758/663/659 Grn 378
May 2014 result LD 1151/950/865 Lab 1028/967/904 C 893/739/686 Grn 403/326/318
May 2010 result LD 2123/1898/1788 C 1342/1335/1326 Lab 1207/1190/1177 Grn 595/536/287
February 2008 by-election LD 1206 C 551 Lab 405 Grn 178
May 2006 result LD 1446/1187/1132 C 667/608/576 Lab 580/545/402 Grn 354/305/291
May 2002 result LD 1295/1121/1111 Lab 483/414/409 C 326/323/314 Grn 221/199/132
May 2021 GLA results (excludes postal voters)
Mayor: Lab 986 C 477 Grn 214 LD 209 Omilana 41 Reclaim 37 Count Binface 21 Rejoin EU 19 Women's Equality 19 Let London Live 17 London Real Party 16 UKIP 8 Animal Welfare 8 Obunge 8 Heritage Party 7 Farah London 6 Fosh 5 Renew 4 SDP 3 Burning Park 1
London Members: Lab 865 C 425 Grn 330 LD 291 Women's Equality 49 Animal Welfare 40 Rejoin EU 30 Reform UK 16 UKIP 13 CPA 12 Let London Live 9 Heritage Party 8 Comm 7 London Real Party 6 Londonpendence 5 SDP 4 TUSC 4 National Liberal 2

Figure 65: Camden, Fortune Green

Highgate on Camden council; she narrowly beat the Lib Dems for third place. The London Members ballot split 41% for Labour, 20% for the Conservatives, 16% for the Greens and 14% for the Lib Dems.

So this could be a difficult defence for the Lib Dems' Nancy Jirira, who won a by-election for this ward in February 2008 and served as a councillor for Fortune Green until losing her seat in 2014. (The Labour candidate she defeated in the 2008 by-election was Tulip Siddiq, who is now the MP for the local seat of Hampstead and Kilburn.) Jirira is a long-serving NHS nurse. Labour have selected Lorna Greenwood, who works in the arts and charity sector. Completing the ballot paper is a Conservative candidate whom the party intriguingly describe as "dry cleaner to the stars": he is Ian Cohen, who previously stood in this ward in 2014.*

Staines

Spelthorne council, Surrey; caused by the resignation of Green Party councillor Jan Doerful.

Big up da West Staines Massive. Yes, we have come to the home town of Ali G, a character of Sacha Baron Cohen who first hit our screens on *The Eleven O'Clock Show* more than two decades ago. (God, that makes me feel old.) For the

* *Camden, Fortune Green*: LD 1197 Lab 849 C 518. For a nice piece of improvisation by the presiding officer of one polling station in this by-election, see page 301.

benefit of those who are too young, too old or too uncool to remember Ali G, his shtick was to conduct a series of interviews with public figures and celebrities with the intention of getting them to say or do something stupid.

Ali G's home town was of course Staines, a town on the north bank of the River Thames which was one of the few parts of Middlesex to escape incorporation into Greater London; it was instead transferred to Surrey in 1965. Since 1974 the parts of Surrey north of the Thames, including Staines-upon-Thames (as it now is), have formed the Spelthorne local government district.

Although Staines is outside Greater London, it is still within the M 25 motorway and the town centre's railway station has very frequent trains to Waterloo station. Staines is also just a few miles to the south of Heathrow Airport, which has been badly hit by the current public health emergency.

This drastic downturn in Spelthorne's economy may spell bad news for the council. Spelthorne council's Conservative leadership had a cunning plan to offset the effect of cuts to local government by investing heavily in commercial property which could generate a solid rental income. Since 2016 the council has borrowed more than £1 billion from the Public Works Loans Board—equivalent to around 100 years' revenue—to buy a number of large office blocks and commercial developments in and around the district. While the developments are continuing to generate rent as intended, the council's auditors were reportedly not happy and the amount of debt involved could leave the council badly exposed in the event that the economy turns down—oh.

The Conservatives suffered large losses in the May 2019 Spelthorne elections, although they kept their majority in the council chamber at the time. However, the above scandal has led to a major split in the Conservative group which has left the council in a rather unstable state. The May 2021 AGM deposed the rump of the ruling Conservatives and elected a Liberal Democrat leader, who has formed a coalition with the Independent Spelthorne Group which controls just 9 of the 39 council seats. Following a by-election gain from the Lib Dems in May in the neighbouring Staines South ward, the Conservatives have 18 seats on the council, the Lib Dems have 7, Labour have 2, the Greens have 1 plus this vacancy, and the remaining ten seats are split between four different independent groups.

Staines ward was one of the Conservatives' losses in May 2019, with the Tories losing the three seats to a Green slate of two and a single Labour candidate. With the caveat that these partial slates make vote share calculations perhaps more unreliable than normal, the percentages were 39% for the Greens and 25% each for Labour and the Conservatives. The Staines division of Surrey county council (which is larger than this ward) was close in May between the Conservatives, an ex-UKIP independent candidate and the Greens. We have to go up to Parliamentary

Parliamentary constituency: Spelthorne
Surrey county council division: Staines
May 2019 result Grn 978/890 Lab 633 C 630/623/606 UKIP 297
May 2015 result C 1642/1610/1593 Lab 1144/673 Grn 1045 UKIP 905 Spelthorne Ind 699 TUSC 212
May 2011 result C 1179/1076/1069 LD 893/790/743
May 2007 result C 794/753/751 LD 520/439/432 Lab 260/223/210
May 2003 result C 686/681/667 LD 407/387/381 Lab 318

Figure 66: Spelthorne, Staines

level for the Tories to breathe more easily: Kwasi Kwarteng, the Business Secretary and a member of the Trinity College, Cambridge team which won *University Challenge* in 1995, has represented the Spelthorne constituency since 2010 with large majorities.

So, this by-election needs watching closely. Defending for the Greens is Malcolm Beecher, who stood in May's Surrey county elections in the Ashford division. The ward's Labour councillor left the party in May to join a new Independent Labour group on the council, and it would appear that Labour here are still in some disarray from that: there is no Labour candidate in this by-election. The Conservatives have guaranteed a place at the bottom of the alphabetical ballot paper by selecting local man Michael Zenonos, who runs a logistics company. Also standing are Paul Couchman for the Trade Unionist and Socialist Coalition, Gerald Gravett for Reform UK and independent candidate Paul West, who is a former UKIP figure.*

Cliftonville East

Thanet council, Kent; caused by the resignation of Conservative councillor Lesley Game.

Our final two by-elections next week come on the Kent coast. We start on the Isle of Thanet with Cliftonville East ward, the point where the north coast of Kent starts to curve southward towards the North Foreland. This ward is based on the Palm Bay estate, built in the 1930s overlooking the sandy beaches that turned Cliftonville into a seaside resort back in the day.

In the last section this column discussed the political instability and scandal surrounding Spelthorne council. Spelthorne have a lot to learn on both of those fronts from Thanet. The 2003 and 2007 Thanet elections returned a Conservative majority with a significant Labour opposition. Cliftonville East

* *Spelthorne, Staines*: Grn 651 C 486 Ind 275 TUSC 39 Reform UK 29

was a safe Conservative ward included in that majority, and from 2003 until 2010 ward councillor Sandy Ezekiel was leader of the council.

The Conservatives lost their majority in Thanet in 2011 against the national trend, and then the fun started. Initially they continued as a minority, but the independents who held the balance of power then deposed the Conservatives and installed a Labour minority administration. It then came out that Sandy Ezekiel had corruptly used the council's inside information to buy two properties in Margate via an intermediary: on 1st March 2013 a jury at Maidstone Crown Court found Ezekiel guilty of four charges of misconduct in public office, and Mr Justice Nicol sentenced him to eighteen months' imprisonment. A £2,000 confiscation order was added later.

Ezekiel did not resign from Thanet council following his conviction and sentence: instead he was disqualified as a councillor three weeks later, when the deadline to appeal against the conviction expired. Because of the timing of the disqualification, the resulting by-election had to be held a week after the 2013 Kent county council elections meaning that the voters of Cliftonville East were dragged out for elections on two consecutive weeks. On 2nd May 2013 UKIP won one of the two county council seats in Margate and Cliftonville division; on 9th May their candidate Rozanne Duncan won the Cliftonville East by-election.

Despite being on the north coast of the Isle of Thanet, Cliftonville East is included within the South Thanet parliamentary seat. This was the seat contested by the then UKIP leader Nigel Farage in the 2015 general election. He didn't win, but UKIP had the consolation prize of winning an overall majority on Thanet council. This majority included two of the three seats in Cliftonville East ward, although outgoing UKIP councillor Rozanne Duncan was not one of them: she sought re-election as an independent, and performed very poorly. The remaining seat went to new Conservative councillor Lesley Game.

The large UKIP group on Thanet council fell apart in a number of stages, and by the time of the May 2019 election they had been deposed and the Conservatives were back in minority control. That election returned another hung council with 25 Conservative councillors, 20 Labour, 7 Thanet Independents (the main remnant of the former UKIP group), 3 Greens and an independent. Cliftonville East ward reverted to safe Conservative status, with a 60–23 lead over Labour. The Conservative minority administration continued, but was deposed later that year with Labour taking control. The Labour leader resigned in April ahead of three by-elections in Thanet in May, in which Labour lost a seat to the Greens and a seat to the Conservatives, who also picked up a seat from the Thanet Independents (pages 151 and 193). A counter-coup at May's AGM resulted in the Conservatives taking back minority control of the council.

Parliamentary constituency: South Thanet
Kent county council division: Cliftonville
May 2019 result C 1076/951/870 Lab 410/375/349 Women's Equality Party 317
May 2015 result UKIP 1531/1354/1336 C 1349/1321/1261 Lab 614/611/603 Ind 228/201
May 2013 by-election UKIP 699 C 526 Lab 352 Ind 112 LD 32
May 2011 result C 1187/1165/1155 Ind 601/598 Lab 515/490/456 Grn 283
May 2007 result C 1381/1240/1225 Lab 574/522/452 Grn 352
May 2003 result C 1531/1400/1369 Lab 524/516/471

Figure 67: Thanet, Cliftonville East

The May elections in Thanet also re-elected Lesley Game as the Kent county councillor for Cliftonville division. She has decided to stand down from Thanet council to concentrate on her county council role, provoking this by-election.

Defending for the Conservatives is Charlie Leys, a former Broadstairs and St Peter's town councillor who was deputy mayor of that town in 2017–18 and 2018–19. He has recently completed a degree in international conflict analysis at the University of Kent. The Labour challenger is Don Challinger. Completing the ballot paper is the last-placed candidate from 2019, Kanndiss Riley of the Women's Equality Party.*

Alkham and Capel-le-Ferne

Dover council, Kent; caused by the resignation of Conservative councillor James Rose.

We finish on the south coast of Kent, atop the White Cliffs of Dover. On a clear day, the shore of France can be seen from here across the English Channel; in 1940 this put the village of Capel-le-Ferne, between Folkestone and Dover, on the front line of the Battle of Britain. In recent years this has been recognised by the Battle of Britain Memorial, opened in 1993 and expanded in 2015, which brings tourists to the cliffs south of Capel-le-Ferne. To the north of the village can be found the major transport arteries to Europe: the A 20 to Dover on the ground, and the Channel Tunnel below.

This ward at the terminus of the North Downs was created in 2019 as an expanded version of the former Capel-le-Ferne ward. Capel-le-Ferne ward was safe Conservative, and Alkham and Capel-le-Ferne has continued in that vein: its 2019 election, the only previous poll on the current boundaries, resulted in a 52–36 lead for the Conservatives over the Liberal Democrats. The ward is covered by the rural Dover West division of Kent county council, which is also safely

* *Thanet, Cliftonville East*: C 723 Lab 211 Women's Equality 37

Parliamentary constituency: Dover
Kent county council division: Dover West
May 2019 result C 455 LD 317 Lab 101

Figure 68: Dover, Alkham and Capel-le-Ferne

Conservative.

There was some controversy over the Dover parliamentary seat in 2019, as the then Conservative MP Charlie Elphicke was awaiting trial on sexual assault charges when the December general election was confirmed. The Conservatives effectively deselected him in favour of his wife Natalie, who increased the Conservative majority. Mr Elphicke was subsequently found guilty of sexual assault and is now serving a two-year prison sentence. As we can see from subsequent election results, this controversy hasn't had much effect on the electors of Dover.

Defending the Alkham and Capel-le-Ferne by-election for the Conservatives is Martin Hibbert, the vice-chairman of Alkham parish council; he is retired after a career as a manager at the Port of Dover and as a health and safety advisor. The Liberal Democrats have selected Roben Franklin, a politics student at Canterbury Christ Church University and chair of the party's Dover branch. Also standing are Gordon Cowan for Labour and Nick Shread for the Green Party.*

* *Dover, Alkham and Capel-le-Ferne*: C 315 LD 173 Lab 101 Grn 58

29th July 2021

Last week's heatwave also saw a nice piece of improvisation from one of the presiding officers in the Fortune Green by-election in Camden, who elected to set up a polling station in the open air of a school playground when the schoolroom booked proved to be too hot at 6:15am.

This may be a good time to remind readers that our polling stations do not run on electricity. The secret ballot is older than the domestic lightbulb. The Representation of the People Act is older than Windows and Macintosh. There is a long history of presiding officers using their own initiative to set up alternatives when the intended polling place is unexpectedly unavailable or, as on this occasion, unsuitable. Those who think that modern technology can improve our polling stations might wish to consider whether it would be feasible in the above situation.

There are five by-elections on 29th July 2021. The schools have broken up, so inevitably there is rain in the weather forecast; and we try to avoid this by concentrating this week on the drier side of Britain. The Conservatives and Labour have two seats each to defend in the eastern half of England, with the final by-election as an independent defence. We have our first two vacancies from the Class of 2021, and two of this week's polls have rather unusual features. Read on…

Pitsea North West

Basildon council, Essex; caused by the resignation of Labour councillor Gavin Callaghan.

For our first by-election we come to a New Town. Pitsea is one of the villages which was swallowed up to create the New Town of Basildon; the Pitsea North West ward covers the New Town development areas of Felmore (mostly residential) and Burnt Mills (mostly industrial, so hopefully the name is not literal). These can be found at the eastern end of Basildon's built-up area, with the area to the east being green space separating Basildon from the village of Bowes Gifford.

Pitsea North West's 2011 census return has an unusual feature. It makes the top 40 wards in England and Wales for households in shared ownership, which form 4.8% of the ward; within the Eastern region, the only ward with a higher figure on this statistic was Bourn ward in South Cambridgeshire, which at the time covered the very new quasi-New Town of Cambourne. 18 of the top 20 wards in England and Wales for shared ownership are in London, the South East or the Eastern region, with Milton Keynes accounting for 9 of them including all of the top 6. In modern times shared ownership is promoted as a way of getting onto the housing ladder without having to raise the money to buy the house outright, so this clustering in areas with a large number of newish houses and high property prices makes sense. In 2018 the median property within Pitsea North West ward went for around £190,000 to £230,000, and when we look at the ward's educational profile (it's in the top 20 for those educated to Level 1, ie 1–5 GCSE passes or equivalent) and socioeconomic profile (35% in routine occupations) we can see that those prices might not be affordable for a large proportion of the people who might want to live here. The New Town legacy can also be seen in the census return, with just over 1 in 3 households being socially rented.

This mix creates a fascinating marginal ward, which has had at least one Labour councillor consistently since the current boundaries were introduced in 2002 but which the Conservatives and UKIP have won on a number of occasions in the past. The last Conservative win here was in 2010, while the UKIP wins came in 2014 and 2015; the UKIP councillor elected on the second occasion sought re-election as a Conservative in 2019 and was defeated.

Gavin Callaghan was first elected as a councillor for this ward in 2012, gaining his seat from the Tories. He was the Labour parliamentary candidate for Basildon and Billericay in 2015, and in 2017 he was elected as leader of Basildon council at the age of just 28.

This May's elections saw the Conservatives take overall control of Basildon, which had previously been a hung council with a Labour-led administration. Following some defections the Tories now have 24 seats, Labour have 11 plus this vacancy, and the remaining 6 seats are split between two independent groups. Gavin Callaghan was re-elected for a third term in Pitsea North West with a 47–42 lead over the Conservatives, but lost the council leadership. He resigned from the council a month later, indicating that he was looking to pursue other interests. The ward is part of the very large Essex county council division of Basildon Pitsea, which since 2017 has split its two county councillors between

Parliamentary constituency: South Basildon and East Thurrock
Essex county council division: Basildon Pitsea
May 2021 result Lab 1101 C 987 Basildon Community Residents Party 213 LD 63
May 2019 result Lab 885 C 696 LD 246
May 2018 result Lab 956 C 655 UKIP 342 Democrats and Veterans 74
May 2016 result Lab 955 UKIP 720 C 480
May 2015 result UKIP 1731 Lab 1611 C 1424 LD 149
May 2014 result UKIP 1156 Lab 906 C 427 LD 73
May 2012 result Lab 932 C 564 UKIP 323 LD 97
May 2011 result Lab 1111 C 702 UKIP 391 LD 143
May 2010 result C 1654 Lab 1508 LD 770 BNP 460 UKIP 453
May 2008 result C 945 Lab 739 BNP 370 UKIP 266
May 2007 result Lab 734 C 714 BNP 362 UKIP 167 LD 162
May 2006 result C 1014 Lab 882 LD 388
June 2004 result C 838 Lab 789 LD 458
May 2003 result Lab 738 C 541 LD 248
May 2002 result Lab 997/893/856 C 543/491/456 LD 238/229

Figure 69: Basildon, Pitsea North West

the Conservatives and Labour.

The winning Labour county council candidate here in May was Aidan McGurran. Readers with long memories may recall that McGurran has appeared in this column before: he successfully defended a by-election to Basildon council in Vange ward in 2019*. At the time he was the managing editor of Mirror Group Newspapers; he now works for a PR agency. McGurran lost re-election to Basildon council in Vange ward in May, but he was elected to Essex county council for the first time: he defeating his Labour running-mate Patricia Reid in Basildon Pitsea division.

Aidan McGurran is the defending Labour candidate for this by-election, seeking a quick return to Basildon council. All three defeated candidates for Pitsea North West in May have returned for another go including the Conservatives' Stuart Terson, a local primary school governor and chairman of the Basildon and Pitsea carnival. Also back are Jake Hogg of the Basildon Community Residents Party and the ward's regular Lib Dem candidate Martin Howard, while Christopher Bateman of the For Britain Movement and Daniel Tooley of Reform UK (who stood here in the county elections in May) complete an all-male ballot paper.†

* *Andrew's Previews 2019*, page 60. † *Basildon, Pitsea North West*: C 794 Lab 430 Basildon Community Residents Party 82 LD 57 Reform UK 23 For Britain Movement 19 [C gain from Lab]

Gaywood South

Norfolk county council; caused by the resignation of Conservative county councillor Thomas Smith.

We travel north from Basildon to the town of King's Lynn. Once one of the most of the most important towns in England as a major port for agricultural East Anglia—a couple of Hanseatic League warehouses still exist here—King's Lynn has declined over the centuries into a provincial backwater. It now forms three-and-a-half divisions of Norfolk county council, of which Gaywood South is the eastern one.

The main feature of this division is the Queen Elizabeth Hospital, the main hospital serving western Norfolk and nearby parts of Cambridgeshire and Lincolnshire. It was named after Queen Elizabeth the Queen Mother who was treated here on a few occasions. Possibly the most famous person to come out of the Queen Elizabeth Hospital's maternity unit was Alan Partridge, who according to my notes entered the world here in 1955. The present hospital was built in 1980 with a projected lifetime for the building of thirty years; forty years on, that projected lifetime has unfortunately proven to be accurate.

Despite its rapidly-decaying state the Queen Elizabeth Hospital dominates the local economy: it is in the Springwood ward of King's Lynn and West Norfolk, which in the 2011 census was the number 1 ward in England and Wales for employment in human health and social work activities (31.5% of those in employment). The other two wards which covered this county division in 2011, Fairstead and Gaywood Chase, are strongly working-class areas: Fairstead made the top 100 wards in England and Wales for semi-routine occupations, and the census picked up a significant Lithuanian minority. We may be remote from the big city here, but Fairstead was originally built as a London overspill estate.

Further housebuilding in the last decade has left the division oversized, and its electorate is now over 20% above the average Norfolk county council division. The Local Government Boundary Commission were intending to redraw the boundaries in advance of this year's election, but their review was knocked off course by the pandemic; instead a new, smaller Gaywood South division will be contested at the Norfolk county elections in 2025.

Although the division stretches to the edge of the town centre, facilities here are few. The Fairstead estate in particular is a seriously deprived area with no surviving pub and where—as the BBC reported earlier this month*—the charity shop was recently threatened with closure. Instead it has transformed into the Fairstead Community Shop, although the green armchair inside is not for sale:

* `tinyurl.com/2p9c3bnp`

Parliamentary constituency: North West Norfolk
King's Lynn and West Norfolk district wards: Fairstead, Gaywood Chase (part), Gaywood Clock (part), St Margaret's with St Nicholas (part), Springwood (part)
May 2021 result C 980 Lab 724 LD 228 UKIP 99
May 2017 result C 857 Lab 758 LD 370 UKIP 230
May 2013 result Lab 835 UKIP 758 C 466 LD 173
June 2009 result C 865 Lab 551 LD 435 UKIP 376 BNP 273 Grn 196
May 2005 result Lab 2130 C 1765 LD 926

Figure 70: Norfolk CC, Gaywood South

this is the "worry chair", for visitors to share and halve their problems over tea and biscuits.

Gaywood South was once a safe Labour area but in this century it has often been marginal, and the voters here have elected both Conservative and Labour councillors since 2005. Thomas Smith gained the division from Labour in 2017, and was re-elected in May with an increased majority of 48–36. Shortly afterwards he was offered a job in London, as a journalist on trade magazines, which was too good to turn down. As a diehard Andrew's Previews fan, Smith is clearly a man of good judgment.

So we have a by-election. Defending for the Conservatives is Phil Trask, who as a football referee will be hoping for a fair and clean election. Again, all three defeated candidates from May have returned for another go including Labour's Micaela Bartrum, a 40-year-old mother of two. Also returning are the Lib Dems' Rob Colwell and UKIP's Michael Stone, who are both regular candidates here (Stone finished a close second to Labour in 2013, but has faded since then), while shopowner Robin Talbot completes the ballot paper as an independent candidate.*

East Retford South

Bassetlaw council, Nottinghamshire; caused by the resignation of Labour councillor Helen Richards, who is seeking re-election as an independent candidate.

We travel north to Retford, or East Retford as it's sometimes called. This is the smaller of the two major towns in the Bassetlaw district of Nottinghamshire, the other being Worksop. Worksop is a larger town, but Retford is better connected thanks to its location on the original Great North Road and the East Coast Main Line; these connections resulted in Retford having a market charter of unusually long standing.

* *Norfolk CC, Gaywood South*: LD 648 Lab 561 C 378 Ind 35 UKIP 28 [LD gain from C]

East Retford was one of the most notorious rotten boroughs of the eighteenth and early nineteenth century. In the eighteenth century it had been a pocket borough controlled by the Duke of Newcastle, who was the main landowner in the area, but by the 1820s East Retford was at the centre of a power struggle between Newcastle, Earl Fitzwilliam and the borough corporation's preferred candidates. This was good news for the town's freemen, who were paid large bribes for their votes by potential candidates; the going rate was around 20 guineas per vote. With the freemen trying to ensure that enough votes were bought to avoid the election being contested, campaigning here was an expensive business. Matters came to a head in the 1826 election which ended in a riot and with the result being voided by the House of Commons for corruption. After a number of unsuccessful attempts to disenfranchise the town, Parliament eventually extended the boundaries of the East Retford borough to cover the entire Wapentake of Bassetlaw, ensuring that the town's corrupt freemen could be comfortably outvoted in future.

Nearly 200 years down the line, the modern Bassetlaw constituency remains interesting for its politics. This was gained by the Conservatives in the December 2019 general election with an enormous majority on an enormous swing, and the Tories followed up on that in May by gaining two county seats from Labour here (Worksop North and Worksop South) and overall control of Nottinghamshire county council. Those gains involved enormous swings; but the swing in the local Retford East county division, a key marginal the Tories were defending, was under 3%. Mike Introna increased the Conservative majority from 37 votes to 212.

By contrast the last Bassetlaw district elections, in May 2019, were very poor for the Conservatives who only won one council seat within the constituency. East Retford South ward, covering the Ordsall area to the south of the railway lines, is a strongly working-class area which has returned Labour councillors on every occasion since 2002 with the exception of a Conservative win in 2008. In May 2019 Labour enjoyed a 68–17 win here over Introna, who on that occasion had the UKIP nomination.

Labour councillor Helen Richards had represented the ward since 2015, and was the losing Labour candidate in Retford East in May. She resigned from Bassetlaw council in June in protest at plans for a new development of 1,250 homes in East Retford South ward.

Having reviewed the situation, Helen Richards is now seeking re-election as an independent candidate, presumably on an anti-development ticket, in the by-election caused by her own resignation. Labour will want their seat back and have selected James Napier, who was a close runner-up in the other Retford

Parliamentary constituency: Bassetlaw
Nottinghamshire county council division: Retford East
May 2019 result Lab 897/679 UKIP 228 C 197/179
May 2015 result Lab 1194/1186 C 689 UKIP 488
May 2014 result Lab 642 UKIP 314 C 220
May 2012 result Lab 831 C 331
May 2010 result Lab 1287 C 730
May 2008 result C 526 Lab 459
May 2006 result Lab 618 C 468
June 2004 result Lab 746 C 575
May 2002 result Lab 591/527 C 283/261

Figure 71: Bassetlaw, East Retford South

county division in May. This may present an opening for Mike Introna, the runner-up here in May 2019, who is the Conservative candidate. That is your three-person ballot paper.*

Knaresborough Scriven Park

Harrogate council, North Yorkshire; caused by the resignation of Conservative councillor Samantha Mearns.

For our Yorkshire by-election today we come to Knaresborough, a market town on the River Nidd which grew up around a Norman castle. This was held in the mid-12th century by Hugh de Morville, one of the four knights who murdered Thomas Becket in Canterbury Cathedral in 1170; the assassins took refuge in Knaresborough Castle for a while before eventually being sent in disgrace to the Holy Land, from which they did not return. The Nidd runs through the town in a steep-sided and attractive gorge, and the town is photogenic enough that readers of a certain age might recognise it as the scene of the election in the opening episode of *The New Statesman*.

Knaresborough is one of the three major settlements in the Harrogate local government district, which extends into the Yorkshire Dales to take in Ripon, Masham and Pateley Bridge and whose acreage isn't far off that of Greater London. It appears that this isn't good enough for the government, who last week announced plans to sweep away all the district councils in North Yorkshire and replace them with a single unitary council for the whole county (except the city of York). That's one council for an area stretching from Settle to Selby to Scarborough and whose internal communications (with the exception of the A1 (M))

* *Bassetlaw, East Retford South*: C 493 Ind 488 Lab 247 [C gain from Lab]

Parliamentary constituency: Harrogate and Knaresborough
North Yorkshire county council division: Knaresborough
May 2018 result C 457 LD 441 Lab 291

Figure 72: Harrogate, Knaresborough Scriven Park

are generally poor. Another piece of work brought to you by the cabinet minister responsible for local government, Robert Jenrick.

Harrogate's ward boundaries were redrawn in 2018 and, in all probability, won't be used again for an ordinary election. Scriven Park is the northern of the four wards covering Knaresborough, stretching along the road towards Boroughbridge, and it was very close in 2018 between the Conservatives and Liberal Democrats: the Conservatives won with 38% of the vote to 37% for the Lib Dems and 24% for Labour, a majority of 16 votes. The Conservatives have a large majority on Harrogate council.

The Knaresborough division elects two members of North Yorkshire county council, and was a Conservative gain from the Lib Dems in May 2017. The 2021 county elections were cancelled in advance of the reorganisation and Harrogate council's next ordinary election isn't due until 2022, so the last local election here was a county council by-election in August 2018* in which the Lib Dems took back one of the Knaresborough seats they had lost the previous year.

This by-election comes after the resignation of Conservative councillor Samantha Mearns, who is stepping down following a number of health issues among her family members. Cllr Mearns had also come under scrutiny following the collapse of her husband's car dealership in 2019, with allegations that a number of Porsches had gone missing. She was in her first term on the council, having served since 2018.

Defending for the Conservatives is Jaqui Renton, a former pub landlady. The Liberal Democrats have selected Hannah Gostlow, a Knaresborough town councillor. The Labour candidate is Sharon Calvert, a special needs teacher. Completing the ballot paper is Harvey Alexander for UKIP. The Local Democracy Reporting Service has interviewed all the candidates, and you can find out more from the *Harrogate Advertiser*†.‡

Fellgate and Hedworth

South Tyneside council, Tyne and Wear; caused by the resignation of independent councillor John Robertson, who is seeking re-election.

* *Andrew's Previews 2018*, page 291. † `tinyurl.com/56jtwt4e` ‡ *Harrogate, Knaresborough Scriven Park*: LD 635 C 384 Lab 91 UKIP 11 [LD gain from C]

For our final by-election of the week we travel to the north-east. Fellgate and Hedworth can be found at the southern end of the town of Jarrow, on the edge of the Tyne and Wear built-up area. The ward's housing is concentrated in the northern corner, between the A 19 and A 194 dual carriageways as they approach the Tyne Tunnel; but the ward also includes a large open area to the south. Like most of the wards we have featured this week, this is a working-class area: Fellgate and Hedworth also makes the top 80 wards in England and Wales for those with Apprenticeship qualifications (7.1% of the workforce) and for those born in the UK (98.4%). Fellgate station, on the Tyne and Wear Metro, links the area to the centres of Gateshead and Newcastle.

While this has normally been a Labour-voting ward in recent years, Fellgate and Hedworth has shown that it can vote for independent candidates under the right circumstances. In the period 2006–08 it returned three independent councillors, Steven Harrison, George Waddle and Geraldine White. Waddle retired in 2011 and was replaced by Linda Hemmer; White lost re-election in 2012 as an independent candidate, and Harrison and Hemmer lost re-election in 2014 and 2015 respectively as UKIP candidates.

Since then Fellgate and Hedworth has generally been Labour-voting: in May Labour defeated independent candidate John Cullen here by 54–28. The exception to this pattern was 2019 when the ward returned independent candidate John Robertson. Robertson has previous with South Tyneside council: in 2011 he deliberately drove a lorry into a council office building following a row over contracts, causing over £160,000 worth of damage. For that he subsequently got 40 weeks in prison, suspended, and was declared bankrupt.

Robertson's bad behaviour did not stop when he was elected, nor when he became leader of the Independent Alliance opposition group on the council. He got straight into hot water over an offensive social media post aimed at one of his constituents, Michelle Potts, whose husband Jay's sister is divorced from Robertson[*]. In February 2021 he was sanctioned by the council's standards committee for bullying a Labour councillor on social media, and suspended from the Jarrow and Boldon Community Area Forum[†]. A month later the council sanctioned him *again*, this time for email and social media harassment of a senior officer at South Tyneside Clinical Commissioning Group; the council ordered that all Robertson's outgoing council emails be monitored by officers[‡].

In yet another apparent rush of blood to the head, Robertson sent in a resignation letter to the council in June and posted a copy of it to his Facebook[§]. He *then* had second thoughts, tried to retract his resignation and found out, as

[*] *Shields Gazette*: tinyurl.com/ycymm4r2 [†] BBC: tinyurl.com/k29tfarh [‡] *The Chronicle*: tinyurl.com/2p9frbfr [§] *Shields Gazette*: tinyurl.com/y2j7vjve

Parliamentary constituency: Jarrow
May 2021 result Lab 1264 Ind 643 C 290 Grn 69 Ind 61
May 2019 result Ind 1163 Lab 959 LD 199 C 108
May 2018 result Lab 1365 Ind 460 LD 325 C 140 Grn 61
May 2016 result Lab 1541 C 282 Grn 248
May 2015 result Lab 2042 UKIP 1075 C 329 Grn 131
May 2014 result Lab 1163 UKIP 981 C 132
May 2012 result Lab 1226 Ind 786 BNP 83 C 81 Lib 33
May 2011 result Ind 1234 Lab 1101 C 113 BNP 76
May 2010 result Ind 1492 Lab 1478 C 336 BNP 236
May 2008 result Ind 1212 Lab 1090 C 209
May 2007 result Ind 1169 Lab 855 C 150 Grn 139
May 2006 result Ind 1162 Lab 852 C 187
June 2004 result Lab 1116/1071/1011 C 647

Figure 73: South Tyneside, Fellgate and Hedworth

this column has previously discussed[*], that you can't do that.

Instead, John Robertson is seeking re-election in the by-election caused by his own resignation. To stand against him Labour have selected the aforementioned Jay Potts. Also standing are Chris Smith for the Conservatives, Kelly Hill for the Green Party (who stood here in May), and David Wilkinson for the Liberal Democrats.[†]

[*] *Andrew's Previews 2018*, pages 84 to 87. [†] *South Tyneside, Fellgate and Hedworth*: Lab 850 Ind 555 C 158 LD 125 Grn 44 [Lab gain from Ind]

5th August 2021

One by-election on 5th August 2021:

East Livingston and East Calder

West Lothian council; caused by the death of Labour councillor Dave King.

July's local by-elections were an exciting set: nineteen of the twenty-eight council seats up for election were gained from the incumbent party, confirming the sense that our politics is very much in flux at the moment. August is traditionally a slow month for by-elections before we hit the peak period of the autumn, but there are still eighteen polls for this column to bring to you over the next month. Just one of those takes place on 5th August, in the county of West Lothian.

The main population centre in West Lothian is the New Town of Livingston, which forms two-and-a-half of the nine electoral wards of the county. This is the half, covering the eastern end of the town around the Pumpherston area. Pumpherston was a pre-New Town mining and industrial village which sprang up at the end of the nineteenth century: the ground underneath what is now Livingston contained large reserves of shale oil, and Pumpherston became the location of a major refinery for Scottish Oils Ltd, a subsidiary of what is now BP. The Pumpherston retort, a vessel which refined the shale rock into oil and gas, is named after the village.

Much of Pumpherston is still given over to industry today, particularly the northern end of the ward approaching Uphall railway station (on the Bathgate line). To the south of Pumpherston lies Craigshill, one of the first parts of Livingston New Town to be developed. These areas lie to the east of the A 899 road which forms the western boundary of the ward; on that boundary can be found the Cousland Interchange, one of the UK's two remaining cloverleaf road junctions and the only surviving cloverleaf in Scotland.

On the southern side of the River Almond can be found the villages of Midcalder and East Calder and the ward's other railhead: the station at Kirknewton on the Shotts line. To the south-west of these is a large rural area running into the Pentland Hills as far as Cobbinshaw, a small hamlet at the summit of the Edinburgh-Carstairs railway line; the railway passes Cobbinshaw Reservoir, built in the 1810s to supply the Union Canal with water.

Since 1992 East Calder had been the electoral base of West Lothian councillor Dave King, who died in May at the age of 79 after 29 years' service on the council. King had been the Depute Provost of West Lothian since 2012, and served on the council's executive with the culture and leisure portfolio. Following his death, West Lothian council unanimously voted to rename the East Calder Partnership centre in King's honour.

From 2007 onwards King was one of four councillors for the East Livingston and East Calder ward. This ward returned two Labour and two SNP councillors in both 2007 and 2012, with the local pressure group "Action to Save St John's Hospital" finishing as runner-up on both occasions and coming close to winning a seat in 2007. In 2017 the Labour vote fell and they lost their second seat: the SNP polled 41% and won 2 seats, with the other two seats split between Labour (31%) and the Conservatives (22%).

This by-election is for one seat, and with the Alternative Vote in use Labour may need to rely on Unionist transfers from the Conservatives to hold it. Quite how many transfers they can expect is a matter of some debate. The indefatigable Allan Faulds of Ballot Box Scotland, who really should be on your reading list if you are not following his work already, has crunched the numbers and found that had the 2017 election in East Livingston and East Calder been for a single seat then King would have beaten the lead SNP candidate, Frank Anderson, by 3,255 votes to 2,928 (52.6% to 47.4%). That SNP score is actually lower than the 3,008 first preferences the three SNP candidates scored, reflecting the fact that some votes failed to transfer or leaked out of the SNP ticket when their other two candidates were eliminated. As Faulds points out in his article on this by-election:

> The SNP have a clear first preference lead, but oddly the rate of exhaustion is such that they end up with fewer votes at the finish line here. Even if they held onto all of their votes, Conservative preferences would have still pushed Labour out in front for a single seat election anyway.*

Faulds' analysis is normally excellent and, as I say, comes strongly recommended; but this appears to be a rare error in his arithmetic. By this column's

* `https://ballotbox.scot/by-election-preview-elec`

Westminster constituency: Livingston
Holyrood constituency: Almond Valley
May 2017 first preferences SNP 3006 Lab 2274 C 1620 Grn 265 LD 198
May 2012 first preferences SNP 2607 Lab 2596 Action to Save St John's Hospital 380 C 372
May 2007 first preferences Lab 3302 SNP 2713 Action to Save St John's Hospital 625 C 591 LD 421 SSP 133

Figure 74: West Lothian, East Livingston and East Calder

reckoning, if we take the votes cast in 2017 and redistribute the votes for the Conservatives and other parties, then in fact the three SNP candidates end up with 3,291 votes between them while the two Labour candidates have 3,219 between them (50.6% to 49.4%).

Mind, for all this talk of transfers Labour are not going to hold this by-election unless they can retain their vote share from May 2017. In this connection we should note that there was a by-election in March in the neighbouring ward of Livingston South, which saw the SNP hold a seat they were defending with a 7% swing in their favour.

That by-election hold meant that the SNP retained their position as the largest party on West Lothian council, with 13 out of 33 seats. However, the council has a Unionist majority and a minority Labour administration is in place: Labour have 11 seats plus this vacancy, with 7 Conservatives and an independent holding the balance of power.

Defending this by-election for Labour is Danny Logue, a former West Lothian councillor for Livingston South ward who lost his seat there in 2017. The SNP have selected Tom Ullathorne, an autism service manager and founder member of West Lothian Shinty. The Conservative candidate is David Philip, a former chair of the East Calder community council and founder of a mental health charity. Also standing are Neal Drummond for the Scottish Green Party who returns from the 2017 election, Hans Edgington for the Lib Dems and John Hannah for the Independence for Scotland Party.*

* *West Lothian, East Livingston and East Calder*: first preferences SNP 1890 C 1085 Lab 969 Grn 336 LD 118 Independence for Scotland Party 47; final SNP 2368 C 1425 [SNP gain from Lab]

12th August 2021

There's something for everyone in the 12th August 2021 edition of Andrew's Previews with six by-elections, three in England and three in Scotland. All of the four largest parties in Westminster are defending one seat each, but we start with two independent defences in the Scottish Highlands:

Inverness West; and Wick and East Caithness

Highland council, Scotland; caused respectively by the resignations of independent councillors Graham Ross and Nicola Sinclair.

Welcome to the far north. We start with two by-elections to the Highland council, which (using the standard European area metric) sprawls across 0.84 Belgiums at the northern end of Great Britain. This area is mountainous and extremely sparsely populated, with most of the Highland Council's 235,000 or so constituents concentrated in the city of Inverness and other towns.

Around a tenth of the Highland council's residents live in the historic county of Caithness, a generally low-lying area which includes one of Europe's largest boglands, the Flow Country. Most of Caithness' residents live in the two burghs of Thurso and Wick, leaving the rest of the county essentially empty. On the coast between Thurso and Wick can be found the traditional northeastern corner of Great Britain, the village of John o'Groats from where ferries go to the Orkney islands in summer.

161 railway miles from Wick, and a rather shorter distance along the A 9 trunk road, lies the city of Inverness, the commercial and administrative capital of the Highlands. The Inverness West ward covers the city's western residential suburbs: Balnafettach and Clachnaharry on the western side of the Caledonian Canal, and Ballifeary between the canal and the River Ness.

Politically, the Highlands are an area where the candidate often matters more than the party label. Political trends in the rest of the UK reverberate less strongly here when general elections come around; and local elections have traditionally been dominated by independent candidates to the point that they often went uncontested. The introduction of PR for Scottish local elections in 2007 put a stop to unopposed elections here, meaning that everybody had something to vote for, and it also broke the independent stranglehold on the council chamber in Inverness. At the last Scottish local elections in 2017 the Highlands' electors returned 28 independent councillors, 22 SNP, 10 Conservatives, 10 Lib Dems, 3 Labour and a Green. The main independent group still leads the council, but they rely on a coalition with the Lib Dems and Labour for overall control.

Inverness West ward dates from the introduction of PR in 2007 and was redrawn in 2017. Its three ordinary elections to date have all returned one independent, one Lib Dem and one SNP councillor. The Lib Dems won a by-election in April 2009 for a seat previously held by an independent councillor, but didn't defend their gain in 2012. In May 2017 the SNP topped the poll with 29% of the first preferences, the Lib Dems had 28%, independent councillor Graham Ross was re-elected with 21%, and the Conservatives finished as runner-up with 12%. If we recount the votes for one seat, the Lib Dems finish top with a convincing 61–39 lead over the SNP.

The 2017 boundary changes cut the size of Highland council from 80 councillors to 74, and the big loser in the redistribution was Caithness which went down from ten councillors to eight. Previously the burghs of Thurso and Wick had formed separate wards with a Landward Caithness ward covering all the rural villages; following the reduction the Landward Caithness ward was split up, with its southern and eastern parts being added to Wick ward to form a new ward called Wick and East Caithness.

The previous Landward Caithness ward was dominated by independent candidates, and going into the 2017 election it had a full slate of four independent councillors following a by-election gain from the SNP in November 2013: the SNP councillor had been forced to resign after it came out that he had gone over the expense limit in the 2012 election. Wick ward started off with independent dominance too, but an SNP gain in an April 2011 by-election broke the mould; the new SNP councillor, Gail Ross, was re-elected in 2012 at the top of the poll with 46% of the vote.

Ross didn't seek re-election in 2017, and the first election for the new Wick and East Caithness ward returned to independent dominance, with five independent candidates polling 62% of the vote between them. Top of the poll was Willie Mackay, outgoing councillor for Landward Caithness ward, who polled 22% of the vote and was elected on the first count. Also elected on the first count was

Parliamentary constituency: Inverness, Nairn, Badenoch and Strathspey
Scottish Parliament constituency: Inverness and Nairn
May 2017 first preferences SNP 1022 LD 964 Ind 849 C 416 Lab 235

Figure 75: Highland, Inverness West

new independent candidate Nicola Sinclair, who polled 21%. Another Sinclair on the ballot was Andrew Sinclair of the Conservatives, who polled 14% and won the third seat. Raymond Bremner of the SNP (12%) narrowly defeated Neil Macdonald (9%), the outgoing Labour councillor for Wick ward, for the fourth and final seat.

So, for the same council we have two very different wards over a hundred miles apart geographically and almost as far apart politically. The by-election in Wick and East Caithness has arisen due to the resignation of independent councillor Nicola Sinclair, the chair of Highland council's Caithness committee, who is going back to her previous career in local journalism. In this connection she has written an article[*] for the *Press and Journal* on the candidates to succeed her on the Highland council.

For the Wick and East Caithness poll you might fancy the independent candidate on previous form, and there is only one defending independent candidate here. He is Bill Fernie, who was a long-serving independent councillor for Wick West ward from 2003 to 2007 and then for Wick ward from 2007 to 2017. Fernie topped the poll in Wick in 2007 with 30% of the vote, but his star has fallen somewhat since then; he scraped in on the final count in 2012, and in 2017 he polled 7% in this ward and was eliminated in sixth place. The Conservative candidate Daniel Ross was given a large interview in the local paper[†], calling for devolution to Caithness in full "glumly pointing at potholes" mode. Most of Ross' fire was trained on the SNP, who have selected Michael Cameron. Also standing are Jill Tilt for the Liberal Democrats (who represent Caithness at Westminster) and Libertarian candidate Harry Christian.[‡]

The Inverness West by-election is also an independent defence following the resignation of Graham Ross, the deputy provost of Inverness. Ross had served since 2012, and is leaving the council for family reasons. Again, there is one independent candidate to replace him: Duncan McDonald, who is semi-retired after a 34-year Army career in the Royal Logistics Corps. McDonald has been firmly endorsed by the Highland council's ruling independent group. The SNP have selected Kate MacLean, who works for the NHS as a community development

[*] `tinyurl.com/mryfrew7` [†] `tinyurl.com/47sy4w9u` [‡] *Highland, Wick and East Caithness*: first preferences LD 657 Ind 622 SNP 593 C 523 Libertarian 16; final LD 986 Ind 963 [LD gain from Ind]

Parliamentary constituency: Caithness, Sutherland and Easter Ross
Scottish Parliament constituency: Caithness, Sutherland and Ross
May 2017 first preferences Ind 2902 C 649 SNP 549 Lab 404 LD 172

Figure 76: Highland, Wick and East Caithness

officer. The Lib Dem candidate is 25-year-old Colin Aitken, a native Canadian who moved to the Highlands in 2015. Another young candidate is the Conservatives' Max Bannerman. Completing a ballot paper of seven candidates are Iain Forsyth of the Independence for Scotland Party, Libertarian Calum Liptrot and Ryan Mackintosh of the Scottish Greens.* The usual Scottish disclaimers apply: Votes at 16 are in force and the Alternative Vote will be used, please fill out your ballot paper in order of preference.

Dalry and West Kilbride

North Ayrshire council, Scotland; caused by the resignation of Scottish National Party councillor Joy Brahim.

For our remaining Scottish by-election we move to a ward which covers a large chunk of rural Ayrshire. Dalry (pronounced Dal-RYE, for those who weren't aware) is an industrial town on the main railway line from Glasgow to Ayr and the A 737 road towards Paisley; a bypass road for Dalry has recently been opened. The main industry here back in the day was ironworking; today a large employer is the DSM chemical factory, improving the health of the nation by producing vitamins.

This would no doubt have pleased the 1st Lord Boyd-Orr, who grew up in the nearby small town of West Kilbride on the Firth of Clyde coast. He was briefly an MP, representing the Combined Scottish Universities from an April 1945 by-election to 1946. John Boyd Orr was the first Director-General of the UN Food and Agriculture Organisation, a position which followed on from a career doing important scientific research in nutrition. In 1949 he was awarded the Nobel Peace Prize. Boyd-Orr was one of eleven British winners of that prize, eight of whom have served in the House of Commons: the other three are the 1976 winners Mairead Corrigan (now Maguire) and Betty Williams, and the 1977 winner Amnesty International.

West Kilbride has also given us Nicola Benedetti, a classical violinist who was born here in 1987 and whose musical career has blossomed since she won the BBC Young Musician of the Year award in 2004. This column isn't always

* *Highland, Inverness West*: first preferences SNP 718 LD 678 C 293 Ind 230 Grn 159 Independence for Scotland 42 Libertarian 11; final LD 970 SNP 869 [LD gain from Ind]

appreciative of string players, but Benedetti can certainly play. You might have heard her at the Proms last Saturday, performing Prokofiev's *Violin Concerto No.2* with the National Youth Orchestra of Great Britain.

But this area's main export has traditionally been not music but energy of some form or another. Just up the coast from West Kilbride is Hunterston, home to two nuclear power stations (one closed 1990, the other about to cease generation) and a port through which raw materials were imported into the UK for the Ravenscraig steelworks and our coal-fired power stations. With Ravenscraig long gone and coal-fired power stations about to go the same way, the Hunterston terminal's coal-handling facilities are now being demolished.

Dalry and West Kilbride ward also has a large rural element, so it's not a strong left-wing area. Its first election, in 2007, returned independent councillor Elizabeth McLardy, Robert Barr for the Conservatives and John Reid for Labour. Barr successfully sought re-election as an independent candidate in 2012, when Reid lost his seat to the SNP's Catherine McMillan.

There was a clearout here in the 2017 election, as the SNP's McMillan stood down and independent McLardy lost her seat to the Conservatives after polling 8% and finishing in sixth place. The new SNP candidate Joy Brahim topped the poll with 24%, the Conservatives returned Todd Ferguson with 22%, and independent Robert Barr was re-elected with 19%. A second independent, Kay Hall, was runner-up with 12%, and Labour crashed to 8%. The five independent candidates polled 46% between them, and if we rerun the count for one seat then it goes to Robert Barr, who leads Brahim by 56% to 44%.

Across North Ayrshire council the SNP and Labour tied for first place on 11 seats each in the May 2017 election, despite the SNP polling 35% while Labour had just 26%. There is a Unionist majority on the council (the other 11 councillors are 7 Conservatives and 4 independents). Labour run the council as a minority, and they recently became the undisputed largest group after one of the SNP councillors walked off to join Alex Salmond's new Alba party.

The SNP's Joy Brahim is now working outwith Dalry, and she has resigned from the council. To replace her the Nationalists have selected Robyn Graham; she is the national secretary of the SNP's youth branch YSI. As with the two Highland by-elections above there is one independent candidate here: John Willis previously fought this ward in 2017, polling 27 first-preference votes and finishing in eighth and last place. Standing for the Conservatives is Ronnie Stalker, who runs a butchers shop in Dalry. The Labour candidate is Valerie Reid, who stood in 2017 as the second Labour candidate in Saltcoats ward. Completing the ballot paper are the Lib Dems' Ruby Kirkwood, who stood in the local seat of Cunninghame North in the Scottish Parliament elections three months ago; and

Parliamentary constituency: North Ayrshire and Arran
Scottish Parliament constituency: Cunninghame North
May 2017 first preferences Ind 2335 SNP 1219 C 1137 Lab 432

Figure 77: North Ayrshire, Dalry and West Kilbride

James McDaid of the Socialist Labour Party. Whoever wins may have to move fast to seek renomination for the 2022 North Ayrshire elections, when there will be new boundaries and this ward will be broken up.*

Grange

South Lakeland council, Cumbria; caused by the resignation of Liberal Democrat councillor Dave Khan.

We come down the coast into England to reach Lancashire over the Sands. The town of Grange-over-Sands lies on the west bank of the Kent estuary, as it flows into the flat and dangerous sandbanks and mudflats and saltmarshes of Morecambe Bay. This mini-Riviera is a Victorian seaside resort, with the railway line over the estuary and around the bay to Lancaster being the main link with the outside world. The railway runs along the coast next to a mile-long promenade, which is interrupted by the forlorn remains of the Grange Lido: this is an Art Deco open-air swimming pool which closed in 1992 and which the council may now be deciding to do something about. The Grange ward extends to the west, beyond the town boundary, to take in the village of Allithwaite.

Grange-over-Sands was included within Cumbria in 1974, and now forms part of the South Lakeland district and the Westmorland and Lonsdale parliamentary constituency. This is the last major holdout of Liberalism in north-west England: Westmorland and Lonsdale is the region's only Lib Dem parliamentary seat (held by the former party leader, Tim Farron), and South Lakeland is the only district in the region with a Liberal Democrat majority. For now, at least; Farron's seat is due to be broken up in the next parliamentary boundary changes, and local government in Cumbria is up for reorganisation as well. The current plan is for South Lakeland to merge with Eden and Barrow-in-Furness districts into a new council from 2023 onwards.

In advance of this plan the May 2021 county and district elections in South Lakeland were cancelled, but Grange ward went to the polls anyway in May (page 76) because a by-election was held alongside the election for Cumbria Police and Crime Commissioner. Grange-over-Sands is part of the Lib Dem majority in

* *North Ayrshire, Dalry and West Kilbride*: C 2016 SNP 1292 Lab 305 LD 58 Soc Lab 57 Ind 42 [C gain from SNP]

Parliamentary constituency: Westmorland and Lonsdale
Cumbria county council division: Grange (Grange-over-Sands parish), Cartmel (part of Lower Allithwaite parish)
May 2021 by-election LD 1427 C 627 Grn 163 Lab 155
May 2019 result LD 1366 C 665 Grn 202 Lab 134
May 2018 result LD 1215/1139/1121 C 1058/1016/975 Grn 272/115/75 Lab 189

Figure 78: South Lakeland, Grange

South Lakeland, and the Liberal Democrats held the by-election by the wide margin of 60–26 over the Conservatives. That was a swing to the Lib Dems since the May 2019 South Lakeland elections, when their lead was 58–28. The Grange division of Cumbria county council was safely Conservative when it was last contested in May 2017, but it has very different boundaries to this ward (the county division extends north as far as the eastern shore of Windermere).

This second Grange by-election of 2021 is the result of the resignation of Lib Dem councillor Dave Khan, who was their candidate for the county division in 2017. He was narrowly elected for the Grange ward in 2018 (when the current boundaries were drawn up) and easily re-elected in 2019.

Defending for the Lib Dems is Fiona Hanlon, a singer and guitarist from Grange. The Conservatives have selected Steve Chambers, who was runner-up here in 2018 just 63 votes behind Khan; Chambers is a businessman and former police officer from Allithwaite and a governor of Allithwaite primary school. Also standing are Robin le Mare for the Green Party (who returns from May's by-election) and Patricia Wright for Labour.*

Orwell and Villages

East Suffolk council; caused by the resignation of Conservative councillor Melissa Allen.

For our Conservative defence of the week we travel to rural Suffolk. The Orwell and Villages ward covers the countryside between Ipswich and Felixstowe, from the Orwell estuary in the south to the Deben estuary in the north. Anything coming in or out of Felixstowe—and there is a lot of traffic here, because Felixstowe is one of the UK's largest container ports—has to traverse this ward.

The largest population centres in the ward are the twin villages of Trimley St Martin and Trimley St Mary, named after two different churches which share the same churchyard. These are the last villages on the main road before Felixstowe, and they were bypassed in the 1970s.

* *South Lakeland, Grange*: LD 1336 C 541 Grn 85 Lab 56

Parliamentary constituency: Suffolk Coastal
Suffolk county council division: Martlesham (Bucklesham, Falkenham, Hemley, Kirton, Levington, Nacton, Newbourne, Stratton Hall and Waldringfield parishes); Felixstowe North and Trimley (Trimley St Martin and Trimley St Mary parishes)
May 2019 result C 1179/1141 Ind 1040/1017 Grn 694 Lab 459

Figure 79: East Suffolk, Orwell and Villages

This ward is the southern end of the East Suffolk district, which was established following a reorganisation in 2019; before then this area was the southern end of Suffolk Coastal district. The inaugural election for the current ward was close between the Conservatives and an independent slate led by Sherrie Green, a former Conservative councillor who had represented the Trimleys on Suffolk Coastal council. Shares of the vote were 35% for the Conservatives, 31% for the independent slate and 21% for the Green Party. The ward is split between two divisions of Suffolk county council, both of which were safe Conservative in May's election.

Defending for the Conservatives is Trimley St Mary resident and Felixstowe town councillor Mick Richardson, a former policeman and Police Federation rep who now runs a business flying drones. The independent slate and the Greens have not returned, so Richardson is opposed for the vacancy by Michael Ninnmey of the Lib Dems and Labour candidate David Rowe; Rowe returns from May's county council elections, in which he stood for Felixstowe North and Trimley.*

Weavers

Tower Hamlets council, London; caused by the death of Labour councillor John Pierce.

> What was too vile for Kate Street, Seven Dials, and Ratcliffe Highway in its worst day, what was too useless, incapable and corrupt—all that teemed on the Old Jago.
>
> — Arthur Morrison, *A Child of the Jago*

We finish for the week in the east end of London. This has always been a poor and industrial area, and in the eighteenth century the Spitalfields area became a major centre for silk-weaving. London was a melting-pot even then, and most of the weavers were immigrants: French Huguenots and Irish were the

* *East Suffolk, Orwell and Villages*: C 873 LD 800 Lab 230

main groups. The Huguenot and Irish weavers did not always see eye to eye, and there were major riots in Spitalfields in 1769.

As the population of Spitalfields grew, the weaving district expanded northwards into the west end of Bethnal Green, whose population trebled between 1801 and 1831. By the middle of the century, what is now Weavers ward was almost entirely built-up. This is the north-west corner of the modern borough of Tower Hamlets, located north of the Great Eastern railway line and west of Warner Place, Squires Street and Vallance Road. Shoreditch High Street railway station, on the East London line of the Overground, lies within the ward boundary.

This is not the sort of weaving industry those of us in the textile towns of the Pennines are used to. In Lancashire and Yorkshire the large industrial mills dominated, with their ranks of power looms producing miles of cloth on a daily basis. By contrast, the Bethnal Green textile industry harked back to an earlier time: weaving here was still the preserve of small family units living and working in specialised weaver's cottages. Some of these cottages (with their trademark large windows, allowing natural light to illuminate the looms) have escaped the predations of the wrecking ball and the London Blitz, and still stand today.

There aren't many of those cottages left though, and one reason for that is that Bethnal Green was, to put it mildly, a poor and deprived part of the city. The modern Weavers ward included Old Nichol Street, one of the most notorious slums in the whole of Victorian London, which inspired Arthur Morrison's 1896 novel *A Child of the Jago* quoted above. By the time that novel came out, Old Nichol Street was already being demolished; its replacement, the London County Council's Boundary Estate, has the distinction of being one of the UK's first council housing schemes. The estate is centred on Arnold Circus, a roundabout named after the chairman of the LCC Alderman Arnold, and much of it is Grade II listed. The superlative London vlogger Jago Hazzard has recently looked into the Boundary Estate in some detail, and his video on the subject is worth a watch.*

Despite further improvement schemes over the 120 years since the Boundary Estate was opened, this is still a rather poor area. The entire Weavers ward was in the more deprived half of the 2019 indices of multiple deprivation. The weaving industry here is long gone, and the Irish and Huguenots have generally moved on to be replaced by immigrants of a different kind. In the early twentieth century, the Boundary Estate had a large Jewish population fleeing from pogroms on the continent. Some decades later the 2011 census return, taken when Weavers ward had slightly different boundaries to those of today, found a significant population of Bengali heritage—appropriate for a ward which takes in the northern end of

* youtu.be/GAM6V1V44zI

Brick Lane. However, the same census placed Weavers ward in the top 50 wards in England and Wales for those employed in professional, scientific and technical activities, and in the top 100 for those born in the EU-15 countries. The reason for this is obvious: the ward borders the trendy Shoreditch area and (particularly in the south-west corner) is easily within walking distance of the City of London and the jobs located there.

If you thought that history and demographic mix was interesting, wait till I start talking about the local politics.

Weavers ward was created in 1978 and redrawn in 2002 and 2014. It was one of the last strongholds in Tower Hamlets of the Liberal Democrats, who had won a majority on the council in 1986 and 1990; Labour won the 1994 and 1998 elections here partly due to a split which saw rival Lib Dem slates standing, but the unified Lib Dems came back to win the ward in 2002.

The 2002–06 term of Tower Hamlets council saw politics here start to become racial. The area became the first stronghold of the Respect party, a far-left group with strong support among the Muslim community. Respect topped the poll in the 2004 European Parliament elections across Tower Hamlets and won its first ever council seat at a by-election the following month. In 2005 the expelled Labour MP George Galloway, whose Glasgow seat had disappeared in boundary changes, fought the Bethnal Green and Bow constituency and narrowly defeated the sitting Labour MP Oona King. That acrimonious campaign set the tone for what was to come.

The 2006 council elections resulted in a one-seat Labour majority, with Respect winning 12 council seats. The Respect party progressively fell apart after that and many of their councillors ended up in the Labour group, changing the balance of power within the group and leading to the election of Lutfur Rahman as group leader and Leader of the Council. Rahman's administration proved to be controversial and polarising. He was deposed as leader after the 2010 borough elections (which returned a large Labour majority, including three gains from the Lib Dems in Weavers ward).

What happened next has led to this column describing Tower Hamlets on a number of occasions as a "21st-century rotten borough". And, unfortunately, we do need to go through this all over again in some detail for reasons which will become apparent.

The 2010 borough elections were combined with a referendum at which the voters of Tower Hamlets voted in favour of an elected mayoralty for the borough. Lutfur Rahman sought the Labour nomination for the October 2010 mayoral election, was blocked from getting it, stood as an independent candidate and won in the first round. His election led to a number of Labour councillors leaving the party to rally round his banner, forming a Lutfurite ruling group on the council. In the spirit of placename localism, they called themselves "Tower Hamlets First".

The Mayor and council came up for re-election together in May 2014, with the council cut from 51 to 45 members on new ward boundaries. Weavers ward, on slightly smaller boundaries, lost a seat. Of the three Labour councillors elected here in 2010, Anna Lynch had resigned in 2012 and been replaced in a by-election by Labour's John Pierce. He and Abdul Mukit sought re-election as Labour candidates, and Kabir Ahmed stood for re-election on the Lutfurite ticket. At least one of them was going to lose out.

The resulting election in Weavers ward was extensively dissected by the Election Court. I quote here directly from paragraphs 322 to 327 of the judgment of the Commissioner, Richard Mawrey QC:

> Next we have Mr Kabir Ahmed. He is one of several brothers and is an active member of the Mayor's team. Mr Ahmed was a Labour Councillor in the previous administration and was one of those who had 'defected' to Mr Rahman and become an independent. He was 'selected' as a THF candidate for Weavers Ward in 2014 and stood unsuccessfully.
>
> For some time Mr Ahmed had given his address as 236a Bethnal Green Road E2, a flat above a shop. This was said to be a property with four double en-suite bedrooms and a shared living room. The other occupants were said to be: Mr Ahmed's wife Sibly Rahman, his brother Mohammed Ansar Hussein, a Mohammed Mokit and Ala Uddin, who was said to work in the shop on the ground floor. According to Councillor Mohammed Abdul Mukit MBE, who knew Mr Ahmed well, he was not actually resident at that address, although he undoubtedly used it as an address for receiving mail. Both Mr Mukit and Mr [Andrew] Gilligan stated that the room allegedly occupied by Mr Ahmed and his wife was completely bare except for one bed, one chair and one desk.
>
> Mr Ahmed's non-residence in the Borough was a matter of some notoriety. Councillor Peter Golds, an indefatigable letter-writer had written to various people to complain about this more than once and had raised it in open council. Councillor Mukit confirmed that Mr Ahmed actually lives at 52 Gants Hill Crescent, Ilford [in the London Borough of Redbridge]: he had attended his wedding, the invitation to which had given that property as Mr Ahmed's address. Mr Ahmed admitted in cross-examination that he paid no rent for 236a Bethnal Green Road and that he spent a lot of time in Gants Hill visiting his elderly parents.
>
> Mr Gilligan told the court that Tracesmart and credit records he had checked also showed Mr Ahmed and his wife as resident in Gants Hill.
>
> Applying the statutory test of residence..., I am quite satisfied that 236a Bethnal Green Road was not such a 'residence' as would entitle Mr

> Ahmed to be registered to vote from that address and I am equally satisfied that this was a mere accommodation address, used for administrative purposes. I did not accept that Mr Ahmed had any genuine belief that this was his residence: he quite clearly knew that the falsity of the residence was well-known to his political opponents and he continued to use that address.
>
> It follows that Mr Ahmed's registration was a false registration and that his votes were unlawful.*

The declared result in Weavers ward gave 1,237 votes to Abdul Mukit for Labour and 1,223 to Mukit's running-mate John Pierce, with the Lutfurite Kabir Ahmed finishing as a close runner-up with 1,214 votes and losing his seat. As Ahmed was not a councillor the Election Court took no further action against him, although his false registration was an electoral offence and it is noticeable that he was absent from the candidate list for the 2018 Tower Hamlets election.

Shocking enough. But there was more to come. Mawrey's judgment went on to conclude that postal voting fraud had taken place in Weavers ward. I quote from paragraphs 353 and 355 to 359:

> The principal evidence of the [postal vote] frauds was the testimony of Councillor Mukit and, to a smaller extent, Mr Gilligan, and the expert evidence of Mr Robert Radley. ...
>
> The reliability of Mr Mukit was put in issue. Unfortunately for Mr Rahman, Mr Mukit was cross-examined on his instructions about one episode (the Water Lily wedding event...) where it was suggested to Mr Mukit that his evidence was deliberately untruthful. Mr Mukit stuck to his guns. Subsequent evidence was turned up that completely vindicated Mr Mukit's account and, at the same time, established that the account of the same incident given by Mr Rahman had not been the truth.
>
> The court accepted Mr Mukit as a truthful and reliable witness.
>
> Mr Mukit knows the Weavers Ward well, having lived there for over thirty years. For the 2014 election he canvassed a large number of properties in the ward. He discovered a considerable quantity of addresses where there appeared to be no trace of the voter whose name appeared on the register. Though some of his evidence was admittedly hearsay, it painted a pattern of postal voters having been asked by supporters of Mr Rahman to hand over their postal votes and of voters having handed completed [Application to Vote] forms to Mr Kabir Ahmed and his brothers. Mr Mukit was astonished to discover several voters who told him that they had voted by post at a time when the postal votes had not yet been sent out. It turned out that these voters had been induced to hand over their completed ATV forms in the belief that they were actually voting. Mr Mukit discovered evidence that at one address, 7 Bacon Street

* *Erlam v Rahman*, [2015] EWHC 1215 QB.

E1, seven postal votes had been 'collected by Mr Rahman's men' which apparently meant that they had collected the completed [personal voting statements] but uncompleted accompanying ballot papers.

One of the voters mentioned was an elderly lady, Gulab Bibi. This lady gave evidence in response to a witness summons (properly using an interpreter). Other members of her family also gave evidence. Both she and her family were adamant that she had cast her postal vote herself. A chance question from the Bench, however, revealed that what she had done was to sign a document and hand it over (clearly the PVS) and she denied ever having put a cross on a piece of paper. On the face of it this was a further instance of the first of the two frauds having been perpetrated on this lady (and the electorate).

Mr Gilligan told the court:

> We also visited another address, 37 Cavell Street E1, a small block of about twelve flats reserved for elderly Bangladeshi people, where I was told that a number of the residents had had their blank ballot papers taken from them against their will by supporters of Lutfur Rahman and Tower Hamlets First. Through the translator, one resident told me that this had indeed occurred. She said: 'A woman came and said, we are here from Lutfur Rahman's party. Many people of your age have voted for him already, so I'm here to take your vote. They came to me and took my signature and then took the blank ballot paper from me. I normally go to the polling station. I told them I was used to doing it myself and didn't understand why it was different this year. I am a long-term Labour supporter and would never have supported Lutfur Rahman...'

The Election Court went on to consider the evidence of Mr Radley, a document expert, who reported on a number of postal ballot papers which had been admitted into the count and their associated paperwork. Mr Radley examined 134 ballot papers, of which 105 were from Weavers ward, and found a number of features which indicated that a large number of the ballots and documents had been completed by the same person. To return to the judgment (paragraphs 369 to 372):

> Many of the unusual features were present in groups of documents ostensibly emanating from the same household, a finding which is consistent with documents from several voters in one household coming into the hands of a third party who later completed them.
>
> It is not without significance that a large proportion of the questioned documents came from Weavers Ward where there was already the

> evidence of Councillor Mukit as to the activities of Mr Kabir Ahmed and his brothers and as to other voter irregularities within the ward.
>
> None of these pieces of evidence is necessarily conclusive in isolation. The question is whether, taking all the evidence of... voter fraud mentioned above, the court can be satisfied to the appropriate standard that voter fraud... had occurred. In my view it can and I am so satisfied.
>
> Furthermore the pattern and number of the irregularities, particularly in Weavers Ward is such that, in my judgment, it would be perverse to come to any conclusion other than that these frauds were organised by persons who meet the criteria of agent [of Lutfur Rahman].

The Election Court accordingly concluded that Lutfur Rahman was guilty by his agents of personation and postal vote fraud. It was one of a number of electoral offences which were committed by him or by his agents in the most corrupt British election campaign of modern times, and which resulted in his disqualification as Mayor of Tower Hamlets and the voiding of the 2014 mayoral election.

The resulting Mayoral by-election in June 2015 returned the Labour candidate John Biggs, then a member of the London Assembly, who defeated the continuity Lutfurite candidate Rabina Khan. Biggs was very easily re-elected for a second term in May 2018, by which time the Lutfurites had split into two parties: the moderate People's Alliance of Tower Hamlets and the more hardline Aspire. PATH returned a grand total of one councillor in the 2018 elections, the aforementioned Rabina Khan who has since wound the party up and joined the Lib Dems. Aspire came out of the 2018 elections empty-handed, despite finishing second in votes across the borough, but have since got back onto the council by winning a February 2019 by-election in Rabina Khan's Shadwell ward*. Abdul Mukit and John Pierce were re-elected as Labour councillors for Weavers ward with a big majority, the Labour slate polling 50% against 15% for Aspire and 10% for the Green Party.

For a look at what happens here in elections without a Lutfurite or two on the ballot, we can go up to London Assembly level. In May Weavers ward's ballot boxes gave a 56–16 lead to Sadiq Khan over the Conservatives' Shaun Bailey, while in the London Members ballot Labour polled 54% against 17% for the Greens and 12% for the Conservatives. Also in May, another referendum was held across Tower Hamlets which resulted in a strong vote in favour of retaining the mayoralty.

Mind, May's GLA results might not be too relevant for this by-election. The poll is to replace John Pierce, who died in June at the appallingly early age of 40.

---

* *Andrew's Previews 2019*, page 17.

Parliamentary constituency: Bethnal Green and Bow
London Assembly constituency: City and East
May 2018 result Lab 1773/1516 Aspire 533/517 Grn 342/316 LD 266/139 Peoples Alliance of Tower Hamlets 231/141 C 220/194 Renew 154
May 2014 result Lab 1237/1233 Tower Hamlets First 1214/1128 Grn 557/527 UKIP 316 C 254/197 LD 202 TUSC 113
May 2021 GLA results (excludes postal voters)
Mayor: Lab 1668 C 469 Grn 312 Omilana 106 LD 86 Count Binface 45 Reclaim 45 London Real 35 Women's Equality 34 Animal Welfare 32 Farah London 21 Let London Live 20 Burning Pink 13 Rejoin EU 13 Fosh 12 UKIP 12 Obunge 10 Heritage 9 Renew 7 SDP 5
London Members: Lab 1631 Grn 520 C 361 LD 139 Women's Equality 85 Animal Welfare 43 Rejoin EU 42 Reform UK 28 Comm 27 London Real 23 TUSC 20 UKIP 20 Let London Live 16 Heritage 12 SDP 10 CPA 9 Londonpendence 8 Nat Lib 4

Figure 80: Tower Hamlets, Weavers

Pierce was an Irishman who moved to London at the age of 19; he worked for the National Housing Association, an industry body for social housing providers, and he had served on Tower Hamlets council since winning a by-election in May 2012.

Defending for Labour is Nasrin Khan, who describes herself on Twitter as a would-be barrister and secretary of the party's Stepney Green branch. Fasten your seatbelts, as the Aspire candidate is former councillor Kabir Ahmed who has learned one lesson from his corrupt 2014 election campaign: the Statement of Persons Nominated gives his address as "in the London Borough of Redbridge". The Green Party have selected Nathalie Bienfait, who works in legal marketing and is studying for a master's degree at Birkbeck. Also standing in Weavers ward are Emanuel Andjelic for the Lib Dems, Elliott Weaver for the Conservatives (a nice bit of nominative determinism there, although it didn't help him much in 2018), and former UNISON general secretary candidate Hugo Pierre for the Trade Unionist and Socialist Coalition.*

* *Tower Hamlets, Weavers*: Aspire 1204 Lab 742 C 360 Grn 205 LD 50 TUSC 30 [Aspire gain from Lab]

19th August 2021: Police and Crime Commissioner Special

There are eight by-elections on 19th August 2021, with the Conservatives defending five seats, the Liberal Democrats two and the Scottish National Party one. Without further ado, we start with the big one:

Wiltshire Police and Crime Commissioner

Caused by the disqualification of Conservative PCC Jonathan Seed, who did not make his declaration of acceptance of office.

Welcome to the biggest by-election of 2021. You thought the recent parliamentary by-elections in Hartlepool, Chesham and Amersham, and Batley and Spen were big; well, this poll is more than twice as big as those three put together. We have a county-wide by-election for the Wiltshire Police and Crime Commissioner.

You might reasonably ask what the hell is going on here. We only had police and crime commissioner elections in May, and now there's a by-election less than three months later? Well, bad luck is not involved here. The electors of the whole of Wiltshire are being called to the polls in the middle of the summer holidays, at a cost of £1,500,000 to the local council taxpayers, because of a series of failures and unintended consequences.

The story starts 29 years ago on 11th July 1992, when there was an incident in the village of Netheravon in Wiltshire. There was a hit-and-run car crash on the High Street; nobody was hurt but some damage was caused. The police caught the driver responsible: he was 34-year-old Jonathon Seed, a Royal Artillery officer, and tests revealed him to be nearly three times over the alcohol limit. Seed was charged with three offences arising from this incident: drink-driving, failure to stop at the scene of an accident, and failure to leave his name and address following a crash.

In March 1993 Seed appeared before Kennet magistrates and pleaded guilty to the first two offences, with the third charge being dropped. The magistrates fined him a total of £500 and disqualified him from driving for 18 months. And in most circumstances that would have been the end of the matter.

This column normally talks about by-elections to local government, and as a result your columnist knows what sort of court sentence can get you disqualified from being a local councillor. £500 and an 18-month driving ban, incurred 28 years ago, is nowhere near that threshold. Disqualification from being a local councillor kicks in if you have been sentenced to a term of imprisonment of three months or more, including suspended sentences, within the last five years. There is one by-election coming up in the next few weeks where a councillor has fallen foul of this rule.

You can be far more of a crook than that and still be an MP, as we saw a couple of years ago with the case of Fiona Onasanya MP. She got four months in prison for perverting the course of justice, and had she still been a Cambridgeshire county councillor her political career would have ended then. However, it takes a *twelve*-month prison sentence to disqualify from Parliament, and the electors of Peterborough had to go through the hassle and expense of an election petition to force Onansanya off the green benches.*

Jonathon Seed's offences from 1993 are now spent convictions. This is thanks to the Rehabilitation of Offenders Act 1974, which (to quote from official Police advice) "aims to rehabilitate offenders by not making their past mistakes affect the rest of their lives if they have been on the right side of the law for some time". And indeed Seed went on to a successful and laudable career: he eventually left the Army with the rank of Major, went into business and became the master of a hunt. Seed also went into politics: he has been a Wiltshire councillor since 2013, served on the council's cabinet, had been an agent for a number of Conservative MPs, and had applied (unsuccessfully, as far as I can tell) to be a Conservative parliamentary candidate. In 2018 Seed was selected as the Conservative candidate for Wiltshire police and crime commissioner in succession to Angus Macpherson, who was intending to retire at the 2020 election (subsequently postponed to 2021 for obvious reasons) after two terms.

The police and crime commissionerships in England and Wales are one of the few surviving constitutional innovations of the 2010–15 Coalition government. The legislation and rules for their elections and eligibility were written by the Home Office, who don't normally have anything to do with elections. And it shows. For those who know and work with the eligibility and by-election timing rules for local government, what the Home Office came up with is ludicrous in a

* *Andrew's Previews 2019*, page 157.

number of aspects which directly affect this poll.

To start with eligibility: why are we having this by-election? The eligibility rules are set out in sections 64 to 69 of the Police Reform and Social Responsibility Act 2011. To quote from the relevant parts of section 66 (subsections (3)(c) and (4)(a)(i)):

> A person is disqualified from being elected as, or being, a police and crime commissioner if the person has been convicted in the United Kingdom, the Channel Islands, or the Isle of Man, of any imprisonable offence (whether or not sentenced to a term of imprisonment in respect of the offence).
>
> For [this purpose] "imprisonable offence" means an offence for which a person who has attained the age of 18 years may be sentenced to a term of imprisonment.

There's no time limit here. The Rehabilitation of Offenders Act doesn't apply. If you've *ever* been done over by the courts for something you could have been sent to prison for, *whether you were actually sentenced to imprisonment or not*, then you're not qualified to be a police and crime commissioner.

This rule caught out a number of intended candidates when the first police and crime commissioner elections rolled around in darkest November of 2012. The most high-profile case was that of Simon Weston, the Falklands War veteran and charity fundraiser, who had intended to seek election as the PCC for South Wales. At the age of 14 Weston had been caught as a passenger in a car which some older friends of his had stolen, and he received a police caution for that. Opinion was divided as to whether this disqualified him, and in the end Weston did not stand in the election.

Section 66(3)(c) clearly does apply to Jonathon Seed. He has been convicted of two historic driving offences, both of which are imprisonable (both now and in 1993). Under the current law, the maximum penalty for both drink-driving and failure to stop at the scene of an accident is six months' imprisonment and an unlimited fine.

Seed declared his previous convictions to the Conservative Party when he sought their nomination for the police and crime commissioner position, and it appears he was wrongly advised by the party that he was eligible to stand. His nomination papers for the election included signing a declaration that "to the best of my knowledge and belief I am not disqualified from election as Police and Crime Commissioner".

It took some fantastic work from the team of investigative journalists at ITV News, who deserve an award for this, to uncover the truth. Unfortunately, the story of Seed's disqualification broke after polling day on Thursday 6th May

2021, but before the votes in the election were counted on the following Monday. On first preferences, Seed polled 41% of the vote against 17% each for the Lib Dems and Labour and 15% for an independent candidate. The Lib Dems beat Labour for second place by 866 votes and went through to the runoff, which Seed won 63–37. Accordingly, the returning officer declared Seed elected as PCC in the full knowledge that he was disqualified from the office. Sometimes you just have to do these things.

Which brings us to the second question: why is this by-election being held now, in the middle of the summer holidays? Well, this is another case of the PCC elections legislation being ludicrous. The timing rules for by-elections, set out in section 51 of the 2011 Act, say that (unless the term is within its last six months) PCC by-elections must be held within 35 working days of the vacancy occurring. Given that notice of election has to be published 25 working days before the poll, and the nomination deadline is 19 working days before the poll, this gives almost no flexibility for the polling day. One of these days we will end up with a PCC by-election having to be scheduled over the Christmas and New Year period because of this.

There has already been one instance of a PCC by-election taking place in the summer holidays. That was the West Midlands PCC by-election of 21st August 2014, held after the death of the incumbent on 1st July. The turnout just about crawled over 10%.

For comparison, vacancies in Scottish local government, the Scottish Parliament and Senedd Cymru have to be filled within three months. There is no deadline for filling vacancies in Parliament or in English and Welsh local government, although it's considered bad form to leave seats vacant for months on end without a good reason.

Now, we are clearly more than 35 working days on from the May ordinary elections, so why hasn't this poll happened already? Well, in order to take up the office of PCC (and its salary and pension benefits), Seed had to make a declaration of acceptance of office under section 70 of the 2011 Act. He chose not to do so for the police and crime commissionership (although Seed had also been re-elected to Wiltshire county council, which he is not disqualified from, and he did accept *that* office). The deadline for making the declaration was 7th July, and the returning officer could not confirm that the position was vacant and start the timetable for election until that date had passed. Inevitably, this resulted in a polling date in the second half of August. Well done everyone.

It might take a high-profile mess-up like the one involving Seed for the Conservatives to lose this by-election. As stated, they had a 63–37 lead over the Lib Dems in May, and the two previous PCC elections (in November 2012 and

May 2016) were comfortable Conservative wins as well. Wiltshire is divided into seven parliamentary constituencies, which have returned a full slate of seven Conservative MPs since 2015. The Tories have had a majority of Wiltshire's MPs continuously since 1924, with only the seat or seats based on Swindon having ever returned Labour MPs; the rest of the county has been true blue for 97 years with the exception of 2010, when the Liberal Democrats won the newly-drawn Chippenham seat.

The May 2021 elections were combined with local elections in every one of Wiltshire's 118 electoral wards: the 98 wards of Wiltshire council were up for election in the ordinary course, the 2020 elections for one-third of Swindon council were postponed to this year for obvious reasons, and there was a by-election in the one ward of Swindon which was not scheduled to hold an ordinary election.

Adding up the votes cast across the county, the Conservatives polled 48%, the Liberal Democrats 22% and Labour 15% (the vast majority of which was from Swindon); the council seats split 77 to the Conservatives (including Jonathon Seed in Melksham Without West and Rural), 27 to the Lib Dems, 8 to Labour and 7 to independent candidates. The Conservatives have majorities on both councils. They lost seats in Wiltshire in May, but gained seats in Swindon.

Defending for the Conservatives is another ex-military officer. Like Jonathon Seed, Philip Wilkinson is ex-Royal Artillery; he has also served as a commando, as a Para and with the special forces in Northern Ireland. He was appointed MBE for his service in Northern Ireland, and promoted to OBE for writing the NATO manual on peace support operations. Since leaving the Army with the rank of Colonel, Wilkinson has worked on security with the Rwandan, Iraqi, Afghan (oh dear), Palestinian and most recently the Somali governments.

The Lib Dems have selected Brian Mathew, who is a Wiltshire county councillor for the Box and Colerne ward and also sits on the Wiltshire Police and Crime Panel. Mathew was the Lib Dem candidate for the North Wiltshire constituency in the last three general elections.

Standing again for Labour is Junab Ali, who finished third in May. Ali, who runs an electrical contracting business, is the chair of the Wiltshire Police and Crime Panel; he has sat on Swindon council since 2008, currently represents the town's Central ward, and was Mayor of Swindon in 2018–19. In the 2010 general election Ali was the Labour candidate for the Devizes constituency.

Also returning is independent candidate Mike Rees, who finished in fourth place in May with 15% of the vote. Rees is a former Wiltshire Police detective inspector, who had a 30-year career with the force; he now runs a cleaning business.

Parliamentary constituencies: Chippenham, Devizes, North Swindon, North Wiltshire, Salisbury, South Swindon, South West Wiltshire
May 2021 result C 84885 LD 35013 Lab 34147 Ind 31722 Grn 16606 Reform UK 4348; runoff C 100003 LD 58074
May 2016 result C 56605 Lab 28166 LD 19294 UKIP 18434; runoff C 68622 Lab 39365
November 2012 result C 28558 Lab 16198 Ind 11446 LD 10130 UKIP 7250 Ind 5212; runoff C 35319 Lab 21157

Figure 81: Wiltshire Police and Crime Commissioner

Completing the ballot paper is Julian Malins, who finished sixth and last in May with 2% of the vote. He is a former Alderman of the City of London and has been a Conservative parliamentary candidate in the past; his brother is the former Conservative MP Humfrey Malins. As in May, Julian is the candidate of Reform UK.

As with all police and crime commissioner elections the Supplementary Vote will be in use, and you can mark two preferences on your ballot paper. Polls will be open across Wiltshire from 7am to 10pm.*

Election Court Watch

The Election Court didn't need to get involved in the wrongful election of Jonathon Seed in Wiltshire, but they have disposed of one of the petitions before them arising from May's elections. This was the case of *Cherry v Strangwood* affecting the Banbury Ruscote division of Oxfordshire county council, in which the deputy returning officer for Cherwell had declared the Conservative candidate Jayne Strangwood to be elected with outgoing Labour county councillor Mark Cherry in second place. It was widely reported at the time that the vote totals for Cherry and Strangwood had been accidentally swapped around in the declaration, and at last week's hearing the Election Court accepted this evidence. They have accordingly quashed Strangwood's election and declared that Cherry was the rightful winner in Banbury Ruscote.

With this Cherry added on top the Labour group on Oxfordshire county council has now increased to 16 councillors, while the Conservatives fall to 21 and are now tied with the Lib Dems for the status of largest party on the council. This is an increase in the majority for the pretentiously-named Oxfordshire Fair Deal Alliance, a coalition of the Lib Dems, Labour and Greens which runs the county council.

* *Wiltshire PCC*: first preferences C 32564 Ind 25197 LD 17966 Lab 12971 Reform UK 1859; runoff C 37752 Ind 34815

Sandwich

Dover council, Kent; caused by the resignation of Conservative councillor MJ Holloway.

We now turn to the seven local by-elections today in England and Scotland, starting in Sandwich. This is a Cinque Port, originally located on the estuary of the River Stour, but changes in the Kent coastline over the centuries have left Sandwich several miles away from the sea.

Back in the the day Sandwich was the scene of a number of French invasions which they don't tell you about in GCSE history. In 1216 a French force under the future Louis VIII landed here, supporting the Barons' side in the First Barons' War against King John. The French were back in 1457 with a raiding party, burning much of Sandwich to the ground; one of the dead was the town's mayor, and the present Mayor of Sandwich wears a black robe in memory of this incident.

In the space between the town and the sea is one of the world's best-known links golf courses. Royal St George's is the only golf course in the south of England on the Open Championship rota, and last month it hosted the 149th Open Championship won by the American Colin Morikawa. Ian Fleming was a member of Royal St George's, and the course appears under an assumed name in the James Bond novel *Goldfinger*.

The town's largest employer for many years was the pharmaceutical company Pfizer, which has had a large base in Sandwich since 1954 concentrating on research and development. Pfizer scaled back its operations here in 2011, and their site is now operated as "Discovery Park" with other businesses having joined the site.

Sandwich is located at the northern end of the Dover local government district, and has consistently returned Conservative candidates at all levels of government in recent years. There were new boundaries in 2019 which reduced the number of councillors for the ward from three to two: the Conservative slate won with 34%, outgoing Conservative councillor Paul Carter polled 25% as an independent candidate, while the Lib Dems and Labour polled 14% each. The Sandwich division of Kent county council (which is larger than this ward) was safely Conservative in May, and the ward is part of the Conservative-held South Thanet constituency. This was the seat contested by the UKIP leader Nigel Farage in 2015, and UKIP ran riot in that year's local elections across much of the constituency but did comparatively poorly here.

Outgoing councillor Michael John "MJ" Holloway had represented the ward since 2015. Previously he had been a senior official in the Diplomatic Service: he

Parliamentary constituency: South Thanet
Kent county council division: Sandwich
May 2019 result C 883/872 Ind 639 LD 371 Lab 351/314 Grn 328

Figure 82: Dover, Sandwich

was the British Ambassador to Panama from 2011 to 2013, and before that from 2005 to 2010 he was the Foreign Office's director for consular services in Iberia, work for which he was appointed OBE in 2009. Holloway was deputy leader of Dover council from October 2019 until his resignation in June 2021.

Defending for the Conservatives is Dan Friend, a Sandwich town councillor who runs a group of IT businesses in the town. In a straight fight, Friend is opposed by fellow Sandwich town councillor Anne Fox, a retired environmental health officer, who is the Liberal Democrat candidate.*

Downs North

Ashford council, Kent; caused by the resignation of Conservative councillor Charles Dehnel.

We move inland within Kent to the North Downs. Or, as the ward name has it, Downs North. This ward covers four small parishes midway between Ashford and Canterbury, of which the largest is Chilham in the Great Stour valley. Chilham is a relatively unspoilt and very photogenic village which has appeared in several TV dramas, including the 2009 BBC adaptation of Jane Austen's *Emma* and editions of ITV's *Agatha Christie's Marple* and *Poirot*. That *Poirot* episode, set during a snowbound Christmas, heavily featured the village's oldest building: Chilham Castle, which dates from 1174 and is still in private occupation. Until his death last year the castle's occupier was Stuart Wheeler, the spread betting millionaire and former treasurer of the UK Independence Party.

Wheeler had previously been a significant donor to the Conservative party, and the Downs North ward was traditionally a strong area for them. It survived a boundary review in 2019 unchanged, re-electing Tory councillor and former Grenadier Guards officer Stephen Dehnel with a relatively-low score of 47% of the vote; the Greens came second on 24% and the Lib Dems were third with 19%.

Sadly, Stephen Dehnel died very shortly afterwards. The by-election to replace him took place in July 2019† and saw a large ballot paper—with seven candidates in total—and an unusually close result for the ward. The Conservative candidate Charles Dehnel won the by-election to succeed his father on the council

* *Dover, Sandwich*: C 721 LD 676 † *Andrew's Previews 2019*, page 212.

Parliamentary constituency: Ashford
Kent county council division: Ashford Rural East
July 2019 by-election C 229 Grn 190 LD 70 Ashford Ind 67 UKIP 22 Lab 17 Ind 17
May 2019 result C 375 Grn 186 LD 148 Lab 82
May 2015 result C 932 Lab 291 Grn 290
May 2011 result C 580 Ashford Ind 279 Grn 162
May 2007 result C 511 Grn 240 LD 102
May 2003 result C 599 LD 158

Figure 83: Ashford, Downs North

with a majority of just 39 votes, polling 37% of the vote against 31% for the Green Party and 11% for the Liberal Democrats.

Charles Dehnel has now stood down from Ashford council after two years in office, provoking the second Downs North by-election of this council term. Defending for the Conservatives is Sarah Williams, who was an independent candidate here in the July 2019 by-election; on that occasion she polled 17 votes and tied for last place with Labour. Williams is the chair of the parish council for Molash, one of the four parishes which make up this ward. The Green Party have reselected Geoff Meaden, who lives within the ward in the wonderfully-named village of Old Wives Lees and sits on Chilham parish council; he's a former geography lecturer who has been in the Greens since the days when they were called the Ecology Party. Meaden was the Greens' parliamentary candidate for Canterbury in 2010, was a close runner-up in the July 2019 by-election, and was also runner-up (although much further back) in May's elections to Kent county council, where he contested the local division of Ashford Rural East. The Liberal Democrat candidate is Carol Wilcox, who stood in Ashford's Bockhanger ward in the 2019 borough elections. Only the top three parties from the July 2019 by-election have returned, so that is your ballot paper.*

Oakham South

Rutland council; caused by the resignation of Conservative councillor Nick Woodley.

The quiz I was playing at the weekend contained the following question:

> In November 2020 McDonalds opened their first "restaurant" in England's smallest county. This was in which town, the county town?

The answer expected was Oakham. Now, as this column has pointed out in the past the definition of those crucial words "smallest" and "county" can be rather

* *Ashford, Downs North*: Grn 273 C 239 LD 15 [Grn gain from C]

troublesome; but Oakham is indeed the county town of Rutland which has claimed the title of England's smallest county for many years.

The Oakham McDonald's is on the northern edge of town, whereas today we are concentrating on Oakham South ward. This ward takes in part of the town centre but is mostly residential, covering a series of outlying estates on the southern edges of the town. It has only existed since 2019, having been created from the merger of two predecessor wards called Oakham South East and Oakham South West.

Both predecessor wards had by-elections which were described in this column in 2018. Oakham South East ward had elected an independent and a Conservative councillor in 2015, and the March 2018 by-election* resulted in the Conservatives losing their seat to another independent. The volatile Oakham South West ward had also elected an independent and a Conservative councillor in 2015, and the July 2018 by-election† also resulted in the Conservatives losing their seat to another independent.

In the case of South West, thereby hangs a tale. The defending Conservatives fell to third position in a close three-way result, independent candidate Richard Alderman tied for first place with the Lib Dems' Joanna Burrows on 177 votes each, and Alderman won the by-election on the returning officer's drawing of lots. Very shortly afterwards newly-elected Councillor Alderman was arrested over some very dubious stuff on his Facebook aimed at the then-Prime Minister Theresa May and other high-profile MPs; he subsequently pleaded guilty to four charges of making menacing or grossly offensive social media posts, and was sentenced by Birmingham magistrates to a six-month community order and a six-month night-time curfew. The terms of his curfew prevented Alderman from attending council meetings, and he was eventually kicked off Rutland council under the six-month non-attendance rule. By this time the May 2019 elections were imminent, so there was no further by-election to replace him.

The South West and South East wards were merged into a new Oakham South ward in 2019 as stated, with one fewer councillor than previously. Curiously, none of the four previous independent councillors sought re-election here, and the candidate list saw a Conservative slate of three opposed only by the Lib Dems' Joanna Burrows. She topped the poll with 58%, the Conservative slate polling 42% and winning the other two seats by default.

Conservative councillor Nick Woodley resigned at the end of June in protest at a planning decision, which saw the Rutland council planning committee approve a new development of 62 homes on a greenbelt site off Braunstone Road within the ward. The by-election to replace him will again be a straight fight

* *Andrew's Previews 2018*, page 102. † *Andrew's Previews 2018*, page 245.

Parliamentary constituency: Rutland and Melton
May 2019 result LD 856 C 620/551/435

Figure 84: Rutland, Oakham South

between the Conservatives and Lib Dems.

Defending for the Conservatives is Andy Burton, who has previous local government experience: he sat from 1999 to 2019 on East Riding council in Yorkshire (which we shall come to presently), representing Wolds Weighton ward, and held several portfolios in the council's cabinet. Burton, who has recently been co-opted onto Oakham town council, runs a business advising farmers on sustainable agriculture. Challenging for the Liberal Democrats is Paul Browne, a retired solicitor who previously ran a large practice in the town.* The local press reported that a number of fake ballot papers for this by-election were discovered in a public litter bin during the campaign†, but there are security measures to guard against this sort of thing and electors can rest assured that the returning officer will only admit genuine ballots into the count.

East Wolds and Coastal

East Riding council, East Yorkshire; caused by the death of Conservative councillor Paul Lisseter at the age of 58.

We move to the north of England, starting for once on the wrong side of the Pennines. The East Wolds and Coastal ward sprawls across an enormous area of the East Riding, covering twenty-one rural parishes between Bridlington to the east and Driffield to the west. With an area of 148 square miles this was at one point the second-largest electoral ward in England, although subsequent reorganisations have seen it fall a long way down the table.

Back in the day the most important settlement in the ward was Kilham, which was an important market town on the old Roman road from York to Bridlington and had a larger population than Driffield. In the eleventh and twelfth centuries there was also a major centre at Skipsea, whose Norman castle—built around 1086, the year of Domesday—defended the region against Danish invaders. Today, with just over 3,000 electors on the roll, the largest population centre in this ward is Nafferton; this is a village just off the main road and on the railway line between Driffield and Bridlington.

East Wolds and Coastal is a safe Conservative ward. (William) Paul Lisseter had represented the area since winning a by-election in May 2016 and was re-

* *Rutland, Oakham South*: LD 886 C 420 [LD gain from C]

† `tinyurl.com/2p9au8s2` (*Leicester Mercury*)

Parliamentary constituency: East Yorkshire
May 2019 result C 2242/2072/1856 Grn 1222/928/757 Lab 522/522
May 2016 by-election C 1885 Lab 860 UKIP 835
May 2015 result C 4185/3788/3366 UKIP 2080 Lab 1527/1334 Grn 1393 LD 1040
May 2011 result C 2769/2595/2511 Grn 949 Lab 883/778/609 LD 470/431/418
May 2007 result C 2439/2347/2333 Grn 690 Ind 639 LD 568/533 Lab 477
May 2003 result C 2146/2055/2015 Lab 1046

Figure 85: East Riding, East Wolds and Coastal

elected for a second term in 2019. He ran a housing development company. Earlier this year Lisseter had been suspended from the Conservative group over comments he made to a public inquiry into housing plans for the East Riding: he denied any wrongdoing, but was still sitting as an independent at the time of his sudden death in June.

The May 2019 election here had only three parties on the ballot, with the Conservatives beating the Green Party slate 56–31 and Labour being the only other party to stand. As Humberside county council is long gone, the only elections here in May were for Humberside police and crime commissioner.

Defending for the Conservatives is Charlie Dewhirst, who has previous local government experience: he sat from 2010 to 2018 on Hammersmith and Fulham council in London, representing Ravenscourt Park ward. (One of his ward colleagues was the political journalist Harry Phibbs.) Dewhirst has now returned to his native East Yorkshire and works as an adviser to the British pig industry. The Green Party have reselected John Scullion who was on their slate here in 2019; he is the local coordinator for the National Cycle Network charity Sustrans. Also standing are Daniel Vulliamy for Labour (who returns from 2019), Peter Astell for the Liberal Democrats and Kim Thomas for the Yorkshire Party.*

Littlemoor; and Primrose

Ribble Valley council, Lancashire; caused respectively by the resignations of Liberal Democrat councillor Sue and Allan Knox.

We cross over the border to Lancashire for two Liberal Democrat defences in the town of Clitheroe. Located in the Ribble Valley some distance to the north of Blackburn, Clitheroe is based around Clitheroe Castle, a Norman building with one of the smallest keeps of any British castle. The town around it was a

* *East Riding, East Wolds and Coastal*: C 1190 Lab 447 Yorkshire Party 347 Grn 142 LD 79

textile centre like much of Lancashire.

In 1902 Clitheroe gained the distinction of being first parliamentary seat won by the Labour Party at a by-election. The previous Liberal MP Sir Ughtred Kay-Shuttleworth had been elevated to the peerage, and David Shackleton of the Labour Representation Committee won the resulting by-election unopposed. The key to understanding this result is that at the time Clitheroe was not typical of the seat named after it, which from 1885 to 1918 was based on the fast-growing textile towns of Nelson and Colne on the far side of Pendle Hill. The seat was called Clitheroe because it took in the previous parliamentary borough of Clitheroe, which had been disenfranchised by the 1885 redistribution.

In the 21st century Clitheroe has a very different political context because it is the main town in the Ribble Valley local government district and parliamentary seat. Those units have Conservative majorities and Labour representatives are nowhere to be seen. Deputy Speaker Nigel Evans has represented the Ribble Valley constituency since 1992, while the 2019 elections to Ribble Valley council returned 28 Conservative councillors, 10 Lib Dems and 2 independents. The Liberal Democrat vote is strongly concentrated in Clitheroe town, which returned nine Lib Dem councillors and one Conservative.

Littlemoor and Primrose are the two southern wards of Clitheroe. Primrose ward runs south along the railway line towards Blackburn from Clitheroe Castle and the Booths supermarket, which lie at the ward's northern end. (For the benefit of those who may be confused by this reference, Waitrose is the non-Lancashire equivalent of Booths.) Littlemoor ward lies immediately to the east between the Whalley Road and the Pendle Road, which goes straight up the hill towards the Nick o'Pendle pass. In between the two is the Primrose nature reserve, a mill lodge which has recently been restored and opened to the public.

Both of these are safe Liberal Democrat wards. The May 2019 elections, the only previous results on these boundaries, gave the Lib Dems leads of 58–24 over the Conservatives in Littlemoor and 60–24 over Labour in Primrose. Both wards are part of the Clitheroe division of Lancashire county council, which has the same boundaries as the town. This county division has consistently been a photofinish in recent years. The Lib Dems' Allan Knox held the seat by 23 votes over the Conservatives in 2009; he finished third in a close three-way result in 2013, the Conservatives gaining the seat with a 45-vote majority over an independent; in 2017 the Tories were re-elected with a majority of five votes over the Lib Dems, and they increased their majority to 12 votes in May this year.

Former Lib Dem county councillor Allan Knox was the leader of the opposition on Ribble Valley council, having sat for Primrose ward since 1997, and his wife Susan had served as one of the councillors for Littlemoor ward since 2011.

Parliamentary constituency: Ribble Valley
Lancashire county council division: Clitheroe
May 2019 result LD 474/411 C 193/151 Lab 151/150

Figure 86: Ribble Valley, Littlemoor

Parliamentary constituency: Ribble Valley
Lancashire county council division: Clitheroe
May 2019 result LD 418/403 Lab 166/151 C 109/98

Figure 87: Ribble Valley, Primrose

Both of them have previously served as Mayor of Clitheroe. They are relocating north of the border, where Sue has a new job in St Andrews.

Defending Littlemoor for the Lib Dems is Gaynor Hibbert. The Conservatives have selected Jimmy Newhouse, who runs a waste management company. Also standing in Littlemoor are Mandy Pollard for Labour and Anne Peplow for the Green Party.*

The same four parties are contesting the Primrose by-election. Here the defending Lib Dem candidate is Kerry Fletcher, wife of St Mary's ward councillor Stewart Fletcher. Labour have selected Michael Graveston, who was their county council candidate here in May. Katei Blezard for the Conservatives and Malcolm Peplow for the Greens complete the Primrose ballot paper.†

Mid Formartine

Aberdeenshire council, Scotland; caused by the resignation of Scottish National Party councillor Karen Adam.

We finish north of the border in Aberdeenshire. Formartine (a Gaelic name meaning "Martin's land") is an agricultural area to the north and north-west of Aberdeen. This area has boomed in population in recent years, and commuting to the big city and engineering (connected to the North Sea oil industry) have added to the area's economic mix in recent decades.

The main population centre in the Mid Formartine ward is Oldmeldrum, on the main road between Aberdeen and Banff. Oldmeldrum is home to one of Scotland's oldest distilleries: Glen Garioch whisky has been made here since 1797, trading on the area's reputation for producing Scotland's finest barley.

The Mid Formartine ward runs south-east from Oldmeldrum through Pitmedden (home to the Highland League football team Formartine United) to

* *Ribble Valley, Littlemoor*: LD 281 C 216 Lab 59 Grn 17

† *Ribble Valley, Primrose*: LD 200 C 119 Lab 109 Grn 28

Parliamentary constituency: Gordon (almost all)
Scottish Parliament constituency: Aberdeenshire East
May 2017 first preferences C 1797 SNP 1340 Ind 1070 LD 491 Ind 249 Lab 245

Figure 88: Aberdeenshire, Mid Formartine

the coast at Potterton and Balmedie. These lie just outside Aberdeen and as such are mostly commuter villages, although Balmedie does have some work of its own: part of the major sand-dune system here has been turned into the Trump International Golf Links, which have a Balmedie address but lie just outside the ward boundary.* Unlike Royal St George's which we discussed earlier, Trump International is yet to be added to the Open Championship rota.

This ward was created in 2007 and modified in 2012, losing some villages to the north to Turriff and District ward. In 2007 it elected two Lib Dems and one councillor each from the SNP and the Conservatives. For the 2012 election one of the Lib Dem councillors, Paul Johnston, was re-elected as an independent while the other lost his seat to the SNP.

The Conservatives moved into first place here in 2017, polling 35% against 26% for the SNP, 21% for Johnston and 9% for the Lib Dems. As with many Aberdeenshire wards the Conservatives could have won two seats here in 2017 if they had stood two candidates; instead their transfers gave the final seat to the Lib Dems who gained a seat back from the SNP. New face Karen Adam defeated outgoing councillor Cryle Shand for the SNP seat; the other elected councillors for the ward were Jim Gifford of the Conservatives, independent Paul Johnston and Andrew Hassan of the Lib Dems. Gifford subsequently became leader of the council at the head of a Unionist coalition, but left the leadership and the Conservative party last year.

If we re-run the 2017 count for one seat, the Conservatives beat Johnston 52.5–47.5; a Conservative-SNP final two is more of a blowout, with a 59–41 lead for the Tories against the two SNP candidates.

As we can see, the SNP face an uphill struggle to hold this by-election. Their councillor Karen Adam was elected to the Scottish Parliament in May as the MSP for Banffshire and Buchan Coast, holding the seat by the narrow majority of 772 votes over the Conservatives. She was the first MSP to take the oath of office in British Sign Language (her father is deaf). Adam has resigned from Aberdeenshire council to concentrate on her duties in Holyrood.

Defending for the Scottish National Party is Jenny Nicol, who manages the post office in Potterton. The Conservatives also have a Potterton-based candidate, Sheila Powell. Jeff Goodhall, who was an independent candidate here in 2017

* For more on Trump International see *Andrew's Previews 2020*, page 109.

(polling 5% and finishing as runner-up), returns with the Lib Dem nomination and the unlikely endorsement of Jim Gifford, the former Conservative leader of Aberdeenshire council; Goodhall completes a four-strong ballot paper along with Peter Kennedy of the Scottish Green Party.*

* *Aberdeenshire, Mid Formartine*: first preferences C 1480 SNP 1205 LD 412 Grn 144; final C 1645 SNP 1409 [C gain from SNP]

26th August 2021

Four by-elections on 26th August 2021:

Corby and Hayton

Cumbria county council; caused by the resignation of independent councillor William Graham.

We start the week in the north with our rural by-election. The Corby and Hayton division of Cumbria county council covers the northern end of the Pennines, as the 621-metre summit of Cold Fell—the most northerly mountain not just in the Pennines but also in Cumbria—lies within the division boundary. On the slopes running down from Cold Fell north to Hallbankgate and west to the River Eden lie seven-and-a-half rural parishes.

The half refers to Great Corby, which lies directly across the Eden from the village of Wetheral and is part of Wetheral parish. The river is crossed here by Corby Bridge, a very early railway viaduct: the bridge has carried the Newcastle–Carlisle railway line across the Eden since 1834. A footpath runs next to the line, giving Great Corby's residents easy access to the railway station in Wetheral. The Hayton element of the division name refers to the village of Hayton which is located midway between Great Corby and Brampton; there is another Hayton in Cumbria, near Aspatria, so it's important to get the location right here.

This area has a commuter profile, with Carlisle—the largest city for miles around—not that far away. However, its electoral history has been dominated for some years by William Graham, who has served on Hayton parish council for 40 years. Graham, who contested all of his elections as an independent candidate, won a by-election to Carlisle city council in 1995 and held Hayton ward on that council until his retirement in 2016. He failed in an attempt to return in 2019 (following boundary changes, he was the runner-up in the new Wetheral and Corby ward). Graham served as Mayor of Carlisle in 2009–10.

William Graham was first elected to Cumbria county council for this division

Parliamentary constituency: Penrith and The Border
Carlisle city wards: Brampton and Fellside (Carlatton, Castle Carrock, Cumrew, Cumwhitton, Farlam, Hayton and Midgeholme parishes), Wetheral and Corby (part of Wetheral parish)
May 2017 result Ind 830 C 608 LD 177 Grn 124
May 2013 result Ind 1083 C 390

Figure 89: Cumbria CC, Corby and Hayton

in 2013 and was re-elected for a second term in 2017, on that occasion defeating the Conservative candidate by 48–35. Now aged 80, he is standing down from the county council on health grounds. He might well have retired if the May 2021 Cumbria county council elections had gone ahead, but they were cancelled pending reorganisation of the county's local government.

That reorganisation meant that the 2021 Carlisle city elections were cancelled as well. The most recent city elections were held in 2019 with new ward boundaries: Great Corby is part of the Wetheral and Corby ward which returned a full slate of Conservative councillors, while the rest of the division is covered by Brampton and Fellside ward which split its three seats between two Conservatives and an independent. The whole division is covered by the Penrith and the Border constituency, which has been Conservative-held for many years.

No new independent candidate has come forward to replace Graham, so there are a lot of votes up for grabs. The Conservatives, who were runners-up last time and represented the area on the county council before Graham's win, have selected Tim Cheetham, who lives within the division in Hallbankgate. Cheetham is a former Army warrant officer, with service in Northern Ireland to his credit, who has organised the Royal British Legion Poppy Appeal in North Cumbria for some years. In a straight fight Cheetham is opposed only by Roger Dobson of the Liberal Democrats. A retired Human Resources professional, Dobson started his local government career some years ago as a community councillor in Anglesey; he was a Labour candidate for Anglesey county council in 2017 before joining the Lib Dems. Dobson also lives within the ward, and he is a parish councillor in Cumwhitton.*

Graig

Newport council; caused by the resignation of Conservative councillor Margaret Cornelious.

For our Welsh by-election this week we come to another area which is noted

* *Cumbria CC, Corby and Hayton*: LD 857 C 350 [LD gain from Ind]

for a very old railway viaduct. In fact the Bassaleg Viaduct, built in 1826 over the Ebbw River for the Rumney Railway, is claimed to be the oldest operational railway viaduct in the world. Unlike Corby Bridge, the Bassaleg Viaduct is no longer in passenger service: the line crossing the viaduct is a freight-only branch line serving a quarry in Machen.

The Graig division of Newport lies to the west of the city, outside the M 4 motorway bypass. It is based on Bassaleg, a middle-class suburb from which many professionals commute to Newport or Cardiff: in the 2011 census Graig division was in the top 20 divisions in Wales for people employed in the financial and insurance sector. However, the area is also known for its rugby players: the current Wales flanker Aaron Wainwright and the grand-slam winning Wales captain Ryan Jones head a long list of Welsh (or, in the case of Stuart Barnes, English) rugby players who attended Bassaleg School, the local secondary school. Bassaleg School also educated the present Monmouth MP and Welsh Office minister David TC Davies, the former Welsh secretary Ron Davies, the recently-retired Archbishop of Wales John Davies and the present Green Party deputy leader and leadership candidate Amelia Womack.

The Graig division extends to the west along the A 468 Newport–Caerphilly road to include the villages of Rhiwderin and Lower Machen. The Ebbw River forms the division's north-eastern boundary, and new housing developments in this century have caused the village of Rogerstone to spill over the river into this division. The resulting Afon Village development and the adjoining Rogerstone branch of Morrison's—built on the site previously occupied by Rogerstone power station—are cut off from the rest of this division by a hill and the A 467 road. Afon Village will be transferred out of this division at the next Welsh local elections in May 2022.

Although this area voted Labour at the height of their powers in the 1990s, Graig is essentially a Conservative area and has voted for that party at every election this century. Margaret Cornelious was first elected here in 1990 and has continuous service since 1999; she served as Mayor of Newport in 2011–12. She is stepping down on health grounds.

At the most recent Welsh local elections in May 2017 the Conservatives led Labour here 47–38. Since then we have had four elections for the marginal Newport West constituency, including an April 2019 parliamentary by-election following the death of long-serving Labour MP Paul Flynn.* Ruth Jones, the Labour winner of that by-election, was re-elected in December 2019 with a reduced majority of 902 votes over the Conservatives. In May the Newport West constituency of the Senedd re-elected Labour MS Jayne Bryant with a much

* *Andrew's Previews 2019*, page 72.

Westminster and Senedd constituency: Newport West
May 2017 result C 1026/976 Lab 825/758 LD 194 Grn 153
May 2012 result C 902/805 Lab 718/580 LD 169
May 2008 result C 1187/1070 Lab 589 LD 317/241
August 2005 by-election C 770 Lab 503 Grn 69
June 2004 result C 1030/798 Lab 626/577 LD 348

Figure 90: Newport, Graig

larger majority of 3,906, although there was a small swing to the Conservatives here.

So, a marginal division in a marginal constituency. We should watch this one closely. Defending for the Conservatives is John Jones, who runs a recruitment agency in Newport and has lived in the division for some years. The Labour candidate is John Harris, who represents Bassaleg on Graig community council; he has worked for the NHS for over 30 years. Completing the ballot paper is Jeff Evans for the Liberal Democrats.*

Princes Park; and Strood North

Medway council; caused respectively by the deaths of Tashi Bhutia and Steve Iles. Both were elected as Conservatives, although Iles was sitting as an Independent Conservative.

We finish for the week with two by-elections in the Medway towns. To start with Princes Park ward, which is based on the area around Princes Avenue in the southern part of Chatham. This area was mostly developed in the 1980s, partially as a council estate: social renting here is relatively low now, but despite the presence of a number of schools within the boundary educational attainment is not particularly high. In the 2011 census Princes Park ward was in the top 50 in England and Wales for those educated to Level 2 (5 or more GCSE passes or equivalent, but no further).

Down by the riverside we have the town of Strood, the only Medway Town on the western bank of the river. Strood has been a major crossing-point of the Medway since the days of the Romans, who built a bridge here on their route from the Channel Ports from London. Then known as Watling Street, now as the A 2 road, the Roman road now forms the southern boundary of Strood North ward.

* *Newport, Graig*: C 610 Lab 534 LD 71

In this week's Cumbrian and Welsh by-elections we saw some very old railway viaducts. Strood goes to the other extreme with a very old railway tunnel, which was opened in 1824 as a canal tunnel linking the Medway towns to Gravesend. The Thames and Medway Canal was not a success, and in 1845 it was sold to the South Eastern Railway who converted Strood Tunnel into a railway tunnel. Strood railway station now has regular trains to London via the high speed route to St Pancras, and is the junction for the Medway Valley branch line to Maidstone and Paddock Wood.

Strood North has often been a marginal ward, and in the elections of 2007, 2011 and 2019 it split its three seats between one Labour and two Conservative councillors. On each of those occasions the winning Labour candidate was Stephen Hubbard who clearly has something of a personal vote. The May 2019 election saw the Conservative and Labour slates poll 32% each, with UKIP on 15% and the Greens on 12%. Princes Park has been marginal on occasion in the past but swung strongly to the Conservatives in the last decade; in May 2019 the vote shares here were 48% for the Conservatives, 28% for Labour and 25% for UKIP. Medway council went down the unitary route in the 1990s, so the only elections here in May were for Kent police and crime commissioner.

Both by-elections are to replace councillors who have recently died. Tashi Bhutia, who passed away last month, came to the UK after service as a Gurkha; he met his wife, Vicky, in Hong Kong while they were both serving in the Forces, and they settled in Chatham after marrying in 1980. Bhutia was first elected to Medway council in 2009, winning a by-election in Luton and Wayfield ward for the Conservatives; he transferred to the neighbouring Princes Park ward in 2015.

Steve Iles, who died in June at the age of 65, was first elected in 2015 but already had some experience of public life by then: his wife, Josie, was Mayor of Medway in 2013–14. Iles himself served as mayor in 2018–19 and was twice deputy mayor: however, his second term as deputy mayor of Medway was cut short in 2019 by a controversy over Islamophobic social media posts, which also saw him thrown out of the Conservative party. From then until his death Iles sat on the council as an Independent Conservative.

Defending Princes Park for the Conservatives is Robbie Lammas, a Parliamentary researcher who contested Luton and Wayfield ward in 2019. Labour have selected John Strevens, who fought the neighbouring Lordswood and Capstone ward last time out. UKIP have not returned, so the ballot paper is completed by Lib Dem John Castle, independent candidate Matt Durcan (who fought Rainham Central ward in 2019 and finished as a strong runner-up; he is endorsed by a localist Medway Independents slate) and Sonia Hyner for the Green Party.*

* *Medway, Princes Park*: C 961 Lab 313 Grn 52 Ind 51 LD 49

Parliamentary constituency: Chatham and Aylesford
May 2019 result C 962/951 Lab 554/494 UKIP 497
May 2015 result C 1811/1633 UKIP 1144/907 Lab 1029/821 TUSC 60
May 2011 result C 1488/1317 Lab 1014/968 EDP 200 LD 119
May 2007 result C 1068/1029 Lab 975/832 EDP 252 Medway Ind Party 176/144 BNP 153
May 2003 result C 662/570 Lab 541/484 BNP 205 LD 205/203

Figure 91: Medway, Princes Park

Parliamentary constituency: Rochester and Strood
May 2019 result C 1331/1200/1055 Lab 1313/1118/1037 UKIP 604 Grn 499 Ind 410/349/264
May 2015 result C 2673/2230/2138 Lab 1841/1636/1500 UKIP 1791/1630/1513 Grn 630 TUSC 195
May 2011 result C 2016/1988/1699 Lab 1764/1480/1390 LD 318/228/198 EDP 282 TUSC 212
May 2007 result C 1771/1732/1593 Lab 1609/1402/1365 LD 477/445/340 UKIP 345
May 2003 result C 1604/1537/1531 Lab 1444/1355/1262 LD 347/276/251 UKIP 146

Figure 92: Medway, Strood North

The same five parties are contesting the Strood North by-election. Here the defending Conservative is Mark Joy, who was elected to Medway council in 2015 as a UKIP candidate from Strood South ward, but defected to the Conservatives in 2016. Joy contested Twydall ward in 2019, without success. The Labour candidate is Zöe van Dyke, who fought this ward in 2019; she has recently retired from a job as a mediator with UNISON. Again, there is no UKIP candidate this time. The Greens have selected Cat Jamieson, who fought Rochester West ward (where she lives) in 2019. Completing the ballot paper are independent Chris Spalding (who is also a Medway Independents candidate) and Alan Wells for the Liberal Democrats.*

Finally, a shoutout is in order for *Medway Elects*, a rather flashy website which aims to create "the most in-depth array of electoral history for Medway available online". The work already done is very impressive, and if you would like to see it for yourself their address is `medwayelects.co.uk`. Long may *Medway Elects* prosper.

* *Medway, Strood North*: Lab 913 C 728 Grn 565 Ind 216 LD 39 [Lab gain from C]

2nd September 2021

Three by-elections on 2nd September 2021, all in the North of England, with a Labour defence, a Residents defence and a free-for-all:

Park; and Ryburn

Calderdale council, West Yorkshire; caused respectively by the death of Labour councillor Mohammed Naeem and the resignation of independent councillor Robert Holden.

We start this week on the wrong side of the Pennines, although only just, and with a sight which will be familiar to anybody who drives from Lancashire to Yorkshire regularly. After a long climb up the motorway from Milnrow, the M 62 turns left then right into a cutting, passes a stone with a white rose marking the county boundary, runs under a footbridge carrying the Pennine Way, and suddenly the landscape opens out into wide and beautifully desolate moorland, sloping down to a reservoir on the left. The two carriageways separate, and travellers then pass one of the most famous landmarks in the north of England: the house in the middle of the M 62. Stott Hall Farm, to give it its proper name, was saved from the motorway demolition men by a geological fault, which meant that a route around the farm was easier to build.

To the north of the motorway, the county boundary runs along the escarpment of Blackstone Edge to meet the head of the Ryburn valley. The River Ryburn runs east from Blackstone Edge to meet the Calder at Sowerby Bridge, and the Ryburn ward of Calderdale covers virtually all of its valley. The A 58 Rochdale–Halifax road runs the length of the valley, whose main population centre is the village of Ripponden.

Calderdale's Park ward provides a complete contrast. Whereas Ryburn ward is full of wide open spaces, Park covers the tightly-packed Victorian terraces of western Halifax. In comparison to Ryburn, which is 96% White British and has something of a commuter demographic despite its relatively poor transport links (it is in the top 10 wards in Yorkshire for those employed in the financial and insurance sector, and has above-average education levels), Park ward is in the top 20 wards in England and Wales for those who have never worked or are long-term unemployed (23.1%), for those looking after home or family (12.8%), for Islam (64.7%), and for Asian ethnicity (68.0%, mostly of Punjabi heritage). It's also in the top 30 wards in England and Wales for population aged under 16 (29.6%). It's not too much of an exaggeration to say that Park ward is Halifax's Pakistani ghetto.

The Calderdale metropolitan borough has two parliamentary constituencies, both of which are rather marginal. Park ward is in the Halifax constituency which has been Labour-held since 1964 with the exception of the 1983–87 Parliament, but has delivered a series of close results in the last decade. Labour held the constituency by 1,472 votes in the 2010 election, and by 428 votes in 2015 when the previous Labour MP Linda Riordan stood down. Holly Lynch was re-elected for a third term in 2019 with a reduced majority of 2,569; unusually for a target seat, the Conservative vote fell here in December 2019.

The Calder Valley constituency (which includes Ryburn ward) was a Conservative gain with a large majority in 2010. This large majority was rather deceptive, as the opposition vote was evenly split that year between Labour and the Liberal Democrats. That didn't apply in 2017, when the opposition vote to a large extent lined up behind Labour and Craig Whittaker was re-elected for a third term with a majority of just 609 votes. In December 2019 Whittaker increased the Conservative vote share for the fourth election in a row and took the seat to the edge of safety, with a 5,774 majority over Labour.

One of the unsuccessful candidates for the Calder Valley seat in 2017 was Robert Holden, who stood as an independent candidate, polled 1,034 votes and lost his deposit. Holden had been elected in 2014 as a Conservative councillor for Ryburn ward, but left the party a couple of years later after blowing the whistle over irregularities in the local party's accounts. He sought re-election to Calderdale council in 2018 as an independent candidate, lost his seat by 149 votes, but convincingly got it back in 2019: the vote shares that year were 50% for Holden and just 28% for the Conservatives. That was a very unusual result in what is normally a safe Conservative ward. In May this year, without Holden on the ballot, the Conservatives held Ryburn with 47% against 22% for another independent candidate and 21% for Labour.

Park ward is normally safe Labour—it has returned Labour candidates at every election since 2004 with the exception of a Lib Dem win in 2008—but can also be electorally volatile. This is volatility of a different kind, depending rather less on the national scene and more on intangible variables like the ethnicity of the candidates and what's going on in the mosques at the time. You often see this sort of thing in strongly-Asian Pennine wards.

A look at the last three elections here serves to make the point. In 2018 Labour candidate Mohammed Naeem won Park ward with 57% of the vote, independent candidate Surraya Bibi (a former Labour figure who was reportedly unhappy with the party's selection process) coming in a strong second with 35%. The Conservatives, whose candidate here that year was serving ex-UKIP Yorkshire MEP Amjad Bashir, finished a poor third with just 5%. In 2019 Labour's Faizal Shoukat crushed the opposition, polling 87% of the vote as he was re-elected for a third term. In May this year Labour councillor Jenny Lynn was also re-elected for a third term, polling 61%; the second-placed Conservatives substantially improved to 33% with their candidate Shakir Saghir, who has made a number of attempts on this ward under a variety of political labels (normally Conservative, but he was the English Democrats candidate here in 2006).

Wild swings indeed. And if we go back long enough here, another source of electoral volatility comes into play. In the 1975 Calderdale local elections the area of the modern Park ward was covered by the former St John's ward, which was the scene of a howler by the counting team who accidentally overlooked one of the ballot boxes. Once the mistake was discovered the following day, the returning officer was upfront about the error: the votes in the missing box were counted, and it was found that they didn't change the winner of the election.

The Park by-election follows the death in July of Labour councillor Mohammed Naeem, who represented St John's ward from 1989 to 1992; after some decades away, he returned to the council in 2018. Much of his career was spent working for racial equality organisations in Halifax, Bradford and Rochdale.

Naeem was part of the Labour majority on Calderdale council. Labour gained overall control here in 2019 and currently hold 27 seats plus this vacancy, with the opposition consisting of 15 Conservatives, 5 Lib Dems, two independents and Holden's vacant seat.

Defending Park ward for Labour is Mohammed Shazad Fazal, who may be the same Mohammed Shazad Fazal who was the Liberal Democrat candidate for this ward in 2007, 2010 and 2011. We have another returning figure for the Conservatives: Naveed Khan fought this ward in 2011 and 2019, and stood in the neighbouring Town ward in May. Also standing are Jacquelyn Haigh for the Green Party and Javed Bashir for the Lib Dems. Whoever wins will not be off the campaign trail for long as they will be due for re-election in May.*

* *Calderdale, Park*: Lab 1980 C 212 Grn 137 LD 60

Parliamentary constituency: Halifax
May 2021 result Lab 2375 C 1297 Grn 124 LD 100
May 2019 result Lab 3518 C 268 Grn 160 LD 90
May 2018 result Lab 2800 Ind 1742 C 245 Grn 143
May 2016 result Lab 2734 Ind 637 C 252 Grn 104 LD 97
May 2015 result Lab 4183 C 980 LD 299 Grn 268
May 2014 result Lab 2762 C 1281 Grn 206 LD 135
May 2012 result Lab 2657 C 838 LD 651
May 2011 result Lab 2353 LD 1272 Ind 444 C 416
May 2010 result Lab 2381 LD 1856 C 1196
May 2008 result LD 1838 Lab 1678 C 489 Ind 442
May 2007 result Lab 1500 Respect 1147 LD 1022 EDP 567
May 2006 result Lab 1339 LD 971 Ind 668 C 510 Ind 273
June 2004 result Lab 2377/2346/2264 C 2035/1820/1701 LD 994/892/721 Ind 595 Red and Green 343/300/274

Figure 93: Calderdale, Park

The Ryburn by-election is to replace independent councillor Rob Holden. Holden has been suffering from depression for some years without seeking treatment for it, until in June he attempted to take his own life. He has stepped down from the council to seek a recovery away from the public eye. This column wishes Holden well for the future.

There is no independent candidate to succeed Holden, so we have a free-for-all in Ryburn ward! On paper his seat should revert to the Conservatives who have selected Felicity Issott; she is a Ripponden parish councillor, representing Barkisland ward, and works as a science teacher. Labour have reselected Leah Webster, who finished third here in May. Completing the ballot paper are two more returning candidates from May, Freda Davis for the Green Party and Pete Wilcock for the Lib Dems.*

Wilmslow Dean Row

Cheshire East council; caused by the resignation of Residents of Wilmslow councillor Toni Fox.

> In satellite towns
> There's no colour and no sound
>
> — Doves, *Black and White Town*

* *Calderdale, Ryburn*: C 1188 Lab 798 Grn 163 LD 66 [C gain from Ind]

Parliamentary constituency: Calder Valley
May 2021 result C 1785 Ind 848 Lab 798 Grn 207 LD 85 Reform UK 51
May 2019 result Ind 1852 C 1043 Lab 413 Grn 237 LD 144
May 2018 result C 1451 Ind 1302 Lab 805 LD 131 Grn 98
May 2016 result C 1258 Ind 1161 Lab 820 Grn 174 LD 131
May 2015 result C 3221 Lab 1382 UKIP 757 Grn 400 LD 380
May 2014 result C 1513 Lab 791 Grn 482 LD 186
May 2012 result C 1253 Lab 944 Grn 349 LD 229
May 2011 result C 1896 Lab 1089 Grn 300 LD 292
May 2010 result C 2687 Lab 1559 LD 1418 Grn 291
May 2008 result C 1667 LD 908 Lab 502
May 2007 result C 1570 LD 768 Lab 541 BNP 256
May 2006 result C 1338 LD 782 Lab 744
June 2004 result C 1800/1711/1457 LD 1137/991/876 Lab 1059/608/596

Figure 94: Calderdale, Ryburn

The Doves have a lot to answer for. If you hear their song *Black and White Town*, and particularly if you watch the song's video*, you might have trouble parsing that the satellite town they are actually from is Wilmslow.

Yes, that's the Wilmslow which is possibly the richest town in the north of England. Located at the southern end of Manchester's built-up area, Wilmslow is a classic commuter town from which the stockbrokers of Manchester go to work on the train while the Real Housewives of Cheshire buy designer clothes in the local charity shop. I'm not exaggerating much†. Almost the whole of the town is within the 10% least-deprived census areas in England, and Wilmslow has the busiest Aston Martin dealership in the UK and some of the most expensive housing in the north-west. The median property in Dean Row ward, the eastern end of the town north of the River Bollin, will set you back at least half a million pounds, and you'll be shelling out significantly more than that if you want to live in Dean Row itself.

You'll be shelling out even more if you want to buy 43 Adlington Road, a five-bedroom semi-detached house in Dean Row ward which was placed on the market earlier this year for £1.1 million. From 1949 this house was owned by the mathematician Alan Turing, who died here in 1954 from cyanide poisoning at the age of 41. Turing is possibly the most illustrious in a long list of rich and/or famous people who have lived in Wilmslow over the years; even the local MP, Tatton's Esther McVey, is a TV star. It says something that Wilmslow High School gave us not just the Doves but also The 1975, whose lead singer Matty Healy is the son of the actors Tim Healy and Denise Welch.

* `youtu.be/7sX4K0JRIDM` † *Knutsford Guardian*: `bit.ly/34oE01E`

Rather a contrast with the area immediately to the north of Wilmslow. Although this is outside the boundary of Dean Row ward and in that sense off-topic, we can't visit the Wilmslow area without mentioning the critically-acclaimed satirical drama* that is Handforth Parish Council Planning and Environment Committee. If by some mischance you have not yet seen this video, go get yourself a drink and some popcorn and settle down. If you have seen this video before, do the same thing.†

When your columnist first saw that video at the start of February it had under 2,000 views and was clearly going viral then. Seven months on, what has happened in Handforth since? Well, there has been a bit of a clearout on this notoriously dysfunctional council. Brian ("you have no authority") Tolver has been replaced as chairman by John ("the fact that there were no meetings held is irrelevant") Smith. Contrary to some press reports, Tolver is still a Handforth councillor, but Aled "read the standing orders" Brewerton and Barry ("where's the chairman gone") Burkhill have both resigned from that council. The vacancy discussed in the video, following the disqualification of Jean Thompson for not attending any meetings in six months ("the fact that there were no meetings held is irrelevant") was filled at a by-election in May by John Smith's wife Julie. No by-election was called to replace Burkhill and the council have co-opted another councillor allied to Smith, Kerry Sullivan, to replace him. A by-election to replace Brewerton took place in July in West ward and was won by Sam Milward. And Handforth Parish Council no longer exists under that name: the parish has rebranded itself as Handforth Town Council as of the end of July, and John Smith will become the Mayor of Handforth. It would appear that his faction has won the war.

Mind, Handforth Town Council may not last for very long in that form. Cheshire East council, which as the principal council for Wilmslow and Handforth ultimately has some responsibility for this mess, is in the middle of a review of its parish structure. One of their proposals is to abolish Handforth parish altogether with Wilmslow town council taking over the area's governance.

Handforth's two representatives on Cheshire East council are Barry Burkhill and Julie Smith. At the time of the video Burkhill was Mayor of Cheshire East. A number of complaints against his conduct as mayor were made on the strength of that video, but he was close enough to the end of his mayoral term that Cheshire East council were able to kick the matter into the long grass until it was too late to do anything.

One suspects that the arithmetic in Cheshire East may have had something to do with that inaction. Burkhill, who has represented the ward since 2011

* `imdb.com/title/tt14007878/` † `youtu.be/lgGmYeAm0jk`

Parliamentary constituency: Tatton
May 2019 result Residents of Wilmslow 930 C 409
May 2015 result Residents of Wilmslow 1189 C 1139
May 2011 result C 1072 Lab 262 LD 229

Figure 95: Cheshire East, Wilmslow Dean Row

for the Handforth Ratepayers Independent slate, sits in the main independent group on the council which takes in a number of other councillors elected on residents' tickets, including the Residents of Wilmslow party. (Julie Smith, who was elected as an independent, is non-aligned on Cheshire East council.) A controversial Conservative administration lost its majority in Cheshire East in 2019, and the Labour group are now running the council in coalition with the main independent group. That coalition has little or no majority, and in early 2021 they were a man down following the death of Crewe Labour councillor Brian Roberts and the COVID-enforced cancellation of the April 2020 by-election to replace him.*

The ruling coalition is also one down at the moment following the resignation of Toni Fox, who has represented Wilmslow Dean Row ward since 2015 for the Residents of Wilmslow. Fox, who was a Cheshire East cabinet member with the planning portfolio, is relocating to Shropshire. She gained her seat from the Conservatives in 2015 with a narrow majority of 50 votes, and was re-elected in 2019 by the much wider margin of 69% to 31% for the Conservatives.

Defending for the Residents of Wilmslow is Lata Anderson; she is a Wilmslow town councillor. The Conservatives have reselected Frank McCarthy who stood here in 2019; he is the vice-chairman of Wilmslow town council. The 2015 and 2019 elections here were straight fights; this time there is more choice for the local electors, thanks to the nominations of James Booth for the Green Party and Birgitta Hoffmann for the Liberal Democrats.†

* The by-election eventually took place in May 2021: page 83. † *Cheshire East, Wilmslow Dean Row*: Residents of Wilmslow 447 C 354 LD 46 Grn 34

9th September 2021

There are six local by-elections on 9th September 2021, with the Conservatives defending three seats, Labour and the Lib Dems one each, and one final case where it's complicated. Half of today's polls are in Derbyshire, including two locations this column has visited quite recently. The other half are in Tyne and Wear, which is where we start:

Cleadon and East Boldon

South Tyneside council, Tyne and Wear; caused by the disqualification of councillor Jeff Milburn.

Your columnist is going away for a few days. I was supposed to be travelling to a quiz in London, which has unfortunately fallen through; so rather than waste my leave instead I'm off to what will hopefully be the sunny and dry North East. (Please do the sun-dance on my behalf!) Putting this week's column together has certainly whetted my appetite for the trip.

We start this week's Previews in the green belt between South Shields and Sunderland. Put away any preconceptions you may have about Tyne and Wear; there'll be time for those later, but Cleadon is a rather nice suburban village in pleasant if unspectacular countryside. It is first recorded in the twelfth-century Boldon Book, a *Domesday*-style survey of the estates of the Prince-Bishop of Durham. One of the first entries in the Boldon Book was for the Bishop's manor at Boldon, to which a large number of later entries refer (customal dues "as at Boldon").

Modern-day Boldon has split into three villages: Boldon Colliery, West Boldon and East Boldon. The first two are in the Boldon Colliery ward of South Tyneside, leaving East Boldon in this ward. This is by far the most upmarket of the three Boldons thanks to its location on the railway line between Newcastle and Sunderland, resulting in quite a strong commuter demographic. In 2002 East Boldon station was transferred to the Tyne and Wear Metro, on which it forms part of the Sunderland and South Hylton branch.

We can see this commuter demographic in the census return. 91.3% of households in Cleadon and East Boldon are owner-occupied, which is in the top 80 wards in England and Wales and the second-highest figure for any ward in Tyne and Wear. 48% of the workforce are in managerial or professional occupations.

Cleadon and East Boldon forms part of the South Tyneside metropolitan borough which, it has to be said, has not been well-served by its elected representatives in recent years. The Labour group, which has had impregnable control of the council for decades, is prone to infighting. The opposition councillors don't always give off a good impression either, as this column covered at the end of July with the case of independent councillor John Robertson. To cut a long story short, after acting so badly on social media for so long that the council disciplined him twice, Robertson submitted his resignation to the council apparently by mistake, stood for re-election in the resulting by-election in Fellgate and Hedworth ward, and lost (page 308).

John Robertson was by no means the first opposition councillor in South Tyneside to turn out to be a controversy magnet. Unfortunately there has been a high concentration of these in Cleadon and East Boldon ward, which is the only ward of South Tyneside capable of electing Conservative councillors. The ward returned a full slate of Tories at the 2004 election, including a 21-year-old man called David Potts.

The then council leader Iain Malcolm exercised huge restraint in describing David Potts after his death as a "colourful but often controversial figure". Potts led the council's Conservative group for a while, but resigned from the party in 2011 after making an offensive tweet about David Miliband, who was the MP for South Shields at the time. His social media account also led to him being recognised as "Socialite of the Year 2012" by *Private Eye*, after he tweeted what looked like an invitation for people to join a sex party. More seriously, Potts was once cautioned by police for leaking confidential information to the local press. He eventually ended up in UKIP.

Sadly, underpinning all the controversies that attached themselves to David Potts was a horrific addiction to alcohol. By his own account, Potts would sometimes down a bottle of vodka in the morning, go to work as a financial investor, do his job while sipping from a hip-flask, and then wash his lunch down with up to eight gin and tonics. His alcohol intake reached, on occasion, 70 units a day. Eventually, it killed him. David Potts died in April 2013, aged just 30 years old.

The resulting by-election in June 2013 was a Labour gain and sparked a revival for the party in Cleadon and East Boldon. Following the 2016 council elections, when the last Tory councillor Jeffrey Milburn was defeated by 35 votes, Labour held all three seats in the ward for the first time. However, the Conservatives got one back in 2018, as Milburn returned to the council with a majority of 271.

Like John Robertson and the ill-fated David Potts, Jeff Milburn has trashed his reputation with his own destructive behaviour. He was elected to South Tyneside council in a September 2006 by-election as a Conservative candidate, and as stated lost his seat to Labour in 2016 but got it back in 2018. In 2019 he was thrown out of the Conservative party following claims—which he denied—that he had used racist language. From what happened next, it would appear that the party is well rid of him.

Some time later Milburn was stopped by police in Northumberland who suspected him of drink-driving. He was charged with failing to provide a specimen and the case was sent to South Tyneside magistrates, who imposed an 18-month driving ban and a 12-month community order. Milburn appealed against the sentence, and his driving licence was returned pending the outcome of his appeal. I haven't been able to find out the result of that appeal, but nothing turns on it.

While on his way into South Tyneside Magistrates' Court to answer the drink-driving charge in January 2020, Milburn was searched by the court's security team who found that he was carrying a lock knife. He was charged with possession of a bladed article, and at a subsequent hearing in July 2020 South Tyneside magistrates imposed a four-month suspended prison sentence and another community order, also ordering that the weapon be destroyed. Milburn appealed against that sentence, too.

In March 2020 Jeff Milburn went into a drunken meltdown during a family dinner, and the police were called to his home. A subsequent search found a number of swords, machetes and air weapons at Milburn's home along with two antique shotguns, in poor but working condition, which it was illegal for him to possess without a licence. At a hearing last month Milburn pleaded guilty to two firearms charges, and Newcastle Crown Court imposed a 20-month suspended prison sentence.

By this point Jeff Milburn had finally been kicked off South Tyneside council because of the knife conviction. The four-month suspended prison sentence for that offence disqualified him from being a councillor, but the disqualification could not kick in until Milburn's appeal against the sentence was disposed of. Which is why this by-election is only being held now, rather than having been combined with the ordinary council elections in May.

May's election in Cleadon and East Boldon was another Conservative gain, with a 48–37 lead over Labour. Labour had won the 2019 election here quite comfortably, so the seat count in the ward now stands at 1–1. If the Conservatives

Parliamentary constituency: Jarrow
May 2021 result C 1673 Lab 1300 Grn 450 Reform UK 63
May 2019 double vacancy Lab 1507/1076 C 839/594 Ind 386/359/284/152 Grn 363/354 LD 117
May 2018 result C 1601 Lab 1330 Grn 365
May 2016 result Lab 1503 C 1468 Grn 305
May 2015 result Lab 2631 C 2043 Grn 383
May 2014 result Lab 1249 C 1153 UKIP 713
May 2013 by-election Lab 991 C 899 UKIP 666
May 2012 result C 1692 Lab 1443
May 2011 result Lab 1931 C 1590 Progressive 238 Ind 88
May 2010 result C 2082 Lab 1978 Progressive 776 BNP 165
May 2008 result C 2224 Lab 1054 Lab 1054
May 2007 result C 1988 Lab 1080
September 2006 by-election C 1057 LD 669 Lab 601 Grn 124
May 2006 result C 1330 LD 700 Lab 660 Ind 546
June 2004 result C 1649/1569/1500 LD 1456/1177/1176 Lab 495/423/414

Figure 96: South Tyneside, Cleadon and East Boldon

hold this by-election, they will be able to form a group on South Tyneside council (which currently stands at 45 Labour councillors, 4 independents, 3 Greens, 1 Conservative and this vacancy).

Defending for the Conservatives is Stan Wildhirt, a local businessman who had interests in the sportswear industry. The Labour candidate is Philip Toulson. Since I've had a pop at the Tories here, it's only fair to mention that Toulson has one thing in common with Jeff Milburn: back in 2000 Northumbria Police caught him drink-driving. For extra embarrassment points, Toulson was a Northumbria Police Inspector at the time and had been responsible for a "Pubwatch" scheme to stop drunken behaviour*. Toulson, who has also served as an officer in the Royal Australian Air Force, now works as an associate tutor at Sunderland University. Completing the ballot paper is David Herbert for the Green Party, who returns from May's election. The *Shields Gazette* has interviewed all the candidates, and you can find out more from them†.‡

Castle

Newcastle upon Tyne council, Tyne and Wear; caused by the death of Liberal Democrat councillor Anita Lower.

We take the Metro from East Boldon and travel north of the Tyne, into

* *Northern Echo*: `tinyurl.com/yufhzk5a` † `tinyurl.com/33wk9nxk` ‡ *South Tyneside, Cleadon and East Boldon*: C 989 Grn 943 Lab 886

what was once Northumberland and into Castle ward. We're in the city of Newcastle upon Tyne here, and given that what's left of the eponymous New Castle (established in the 1080s) is in the city centre, you might expect this by-election to be in the city centre.

You'd be wrong there, and the reasons why you'd be wrong go back centuries to the days when local government in England was administered on the basis of counties and *hundreds*, which were ancient subdivisions of counties that in many cases predated the Norman conquest. The hundred system didn't entirely cover the whole of England: a number of counties in the former Danelaw, including the three ridings of Yorkshire, were divided into wapentakes instead.

In the four northernmost ancient counties of England, namely Cumberland, Durham, Northumberland and Westmorland, the name "hundred" wasn't used either. Instead, those counties had "wards". The old county of Northumberland had six wards: in modernised spelling they were Bamburgh, Coquetdale, Glendale (covering the north of the county around Wooler), Morpeth, Tynedale and Castle. The remit of Northumberland didn't run to Bedlingtonshire, Norhamshire (the south bank of the Tweed, including Norham and Cornhill but not Berwick) or Islandshire (Lindisfarne and associated parts of the mainland), all of which were detached parts of County Durham until well into the nineteenth century; and it would probably be better not to discuss here the historical can of worms which is Berwick upon Tweed.

The Castle Ward of Northumberland was the county's south-eastern corner, clearly based on the city of Newcastle. It took in basically all of the area of the current Newcastle and North Tyneside boroughs together with some areas which didn't make it into the 1970s metropolitan county, notably the modern towns of Cramlington and Ponteland.

By the time of the 1890s, when the system of hundreds was finally swept away in favour of a new system of boroughs, urban and rural districts, Newcastle upon Tyne had declared independence as a county borough and much of the rest of Castle Ward was already industrial enough that it could be covered by urban districts. The remaining rural parishes to the west of Newcastle were grouped together into a new Castle Ward Rural District, with its offices in Ponteland. The Castle Ward Rural District was dissolved in the big bang reorganisation of the 1970s, in which five of its parishes became part of the metropolitan county of Tyne and Wear and were annexed by Newcastle.

Three of those parishes—Brunswick, Dinnington and Hazlerigg—are covered by the modern Castle ward of Newcastle upon Tyne, which as can be seen takes its name from the old rural district (and the Ward of Northumberland before it). Dinnington is the most rural of these parishes, lying beyond the airport nine miles north of the city centre: this is an old pit village, and there were a number of collieries in the area back in the day. Brunswick Village (once called Dinnington Colliery) and Hazlerigg are rather better connected thanks to their location on the A 1, although some housebuilding and rather confusing boundaries have left both of those villages as part of a single urban area split between Newcastle and North Tyneside boroughs.

To the south of these parishes, along the western side of the A 1 bypass, can be found Newcastle Great Park. Partly built on the site previously occupied by Hazlerigg Colliery, Newcastle Great Park is described as the largest housing development in the North East, with thousands of homes either already built (construction has been ongoing since 2001) or in the planning stage. One of the estate's first occupiers was the technology company Sage, whose head office was here from 2004 until earlier this year. Most of the houses around the former Sage building have gone up in the last decade.

Some of the Newcastle Great Park estates form an add-on to the rather earlier development of Kingston Park, which dates from the 1970s and early 1980s. Located at the southern end of Castle ward, Kingston Park is connected to Newcastle city centre by the Tyne and Wear Metro: a station here on the Metro's Airport branch opened in 1985.

That's the Castle ward of Newcastle. Since 1983 this area has been part of the Newcastle upon Tyne North constituency, which as currently drawn is a safe Labour seat. (The present Newcastle North has little or nothing in common with the parliamentary seat of that name which existed before 1983: the pre-1983 constituency was based on the city centre, Heaton and Jesmond and consistently voted Conservative.) However, in local elections Castle ward votes for the Liberal Democrats, who form the major opposition to the Labour majority on Newcastle city council. The Liberal Democrats have lost this ward only once in the last twenty years (to Labour in 2015), and they improved their position here in May: the votes then were 41% for the Lib Dems, 28% for Labour and 20% for the Conservatives.

This by-election is to replace a veteran and high-profile Lib Dem councillor. Anita Lower, who died in July at the age of 64, had sat on Newcastle city council since 1994, originally representing Blakelaw ward before transferring to Castle ward in 2004. Lower had briefly served as deputy leader of the council in 2011 and was leader of the Liberal Democrat group from 2013 to 2020, and she was the party's parliamentary candidate for Newcastle upon Tyne North in the 2015 and 2017 general elections. Judging from the 2018 result, when all three seats in the ward were up following boundary changes, she had a significant personal vote.

Parliamentary constituency: Newcastle upon Tyne North
May 2021 result LD 1522 Lab 1026 C 731 Ind 230 Grn 197
May 2019 result LD 1085 Lab 945 C 394 UKIP 331 Ind 237 Grn 189
May 2018 result LD 1416/1118/1093 Lab 911/882/872 C 500/490/453 Ind 359/176/151 Grn 244

Figure 97: Newcastle upon Tyne, Castle

A hard act to follow for the defending Lib Dem candidate Thom Campion, who (then under the name of Thom Chapman) was the party's parliamentary candidate for Blyth Valley in December 2019. Since I've already had a pop at the Conservatives and Labour this week, it's only fair to mention that Campion—in a case analogous to that of the Middlesbrough footballer Marc Bola—hit the headlines during the campaign for sexist and abusive messages he put on Twitter in 2012 and 2013[*]. Like Bola, Campion is aged 23 and was under 16 at the time he tweeted that, so hopefully he has grown up a bit since. Labour have reselected Andrew Herridge who fought the ward in May. The Conservatives have nominated John Watts, the chairman of the party's Newcastle upon Tyne branch. Also standing are regular Green Party candidate Andrew Thorp and Brian Moore, who was an independent candidate for this ward in 2018; for this by-election Moore has the nomination of the North East Party, a serious regionalist movement who are part of the ruling anti-Labour coalition on Durham county council.[†]

Camperdown

North Tyneside council, Tyne and Wear; caused by the death of Labour councillor Raymond Glindon.

We finish our tour of Tyneside just a mile or two east of Newcastle's Castle ward, but in the borough and constituency of North Tyneside. The name of Camperdown recalls a battle of 1797, a major British naval victory over the Dutch. This may have been fresh in the mind when the village of Camperdown grew up in the 19th century, becoming yet another pit village on the Northumberland coalfield.

Although this may look like a small-town area (the villages of Burradon and Annitsford are also part of the ward), Camperdown ward is not in fact like that. The ward takes in the western half of Killingworth, a quasi-New Town built by Northumberland county council in the 1960s with rather a lot of high-rise buildings, many of which didn't make it into the 21st century. Among the people

[*] BBC: `tinyurl.com/47ubzawu`

[†] *Newcastle upon Tyne, Castle*: LD 1306 Lab 773 C 657 Grn 250 North East Party 89

Parliamentary constituency: North Tyneside
May 2021 result Lab 1575 C 746
May 2019 result Lab 1281 UKIP 485 C 388
May 2018 result Lab 1565 C 547
May 2016 result Lab 1457 Ind 790 C 240
May 2015 result Lab 2915 UKIP 842 C 790
May 2014 result Lab 1391 UKIP 696 C 268
May 2012 result Lab 1747 C 353
May 2011 result Lab 1946 C 621
May 2010 result Lab 2675 C 814 LD 746 BNP 313
May 2008 result Lab 1312 C 562 BNP 363 LD 231
May 2007 result Lab 1330 C 460 LD 328 BNP 308
May 2006 result Lab 1327 C 612 BNP 405
June 2004 result Lab 1551/1399/1131 LD 610 Ind 574 C 463/462/383 BNP 309

Figure 98: North Tyneside, Camperdown

who moved to Killingworth in its early days were Bob and Thelma Ferris in *Whatever Happened to the Likely Lads?*; one of the houses in this ward was used as the filming location for their home.

There's a fair amount of deprivation in western Killingworth and the villages, and Camperdown is a very safe Labour ward within a safe Labour parliamentary seat (North Tyneside). May's election here was a straight fight between Labour and the Conservatives, with Labour winning 68–32. North Tyneside council has an elected mayor, Labour's Norma Redfearn, who was re-elected in May almost as comfortably.

The Labour MP for the North Tyneside seat is Mary Glindon, whose husband Ray passed away in April at the age of 74. He had been diagnosed with prostate cancer five years ago. Mary and Ray Glindon had been elected to North Tyneside council in 2004, representing Battle Hill ward in Wallsend; Ray lost his seat there to the Liberal Democrats in 2006 before finding a safer berth here in 2007. Mr Glindon's association with the council went back a long way: he started working for the council in 1974 as an electrician, worked his way up to building manager until his retirement in 2001, and as the cabinet member for finance he presented his final budget to the council earlier this year.

Defending for Labour is Tracy Hallway. The Conservatives have selected David Lilly, who contested the safe-Labour Chirton ward in May. There is a wider choice for the electors this time, with the nomination of Martin Collins for the Green Party and Nathan Shone for the Lib Dems.*

* *North Tyneside, Camperdown*: Lab 957 C 352 Grn 78 LD 48

Barlow and Holmesfield; and Killamarsh East

North East Derbyshire council; caused respectively by the resignations of Conservative councillors Carol Huckerby and Nick Whitehead.

For the second half of this week's Previews we travel south to Derbyshire and to territory which this column has covered quite recently. We start with a journey from Killingworth to Killamarsh.

Killingworth and Killamarsh have a lot of history in common, as it was coalmining that made both towns. Killamarsh lies on the eastern side of the Rother valley on the northern edge of Derbyshire, looking across the river and the county boundary to the quasi-New Town of Mosborough on the edge of Sheffield.

The town of Killamarsh has also caught the eye of housing developers thanks to its proximity to the big city. Its population has increased by half in the last fifty years, and from looking at the census return one suspects that white flight is a major part of that. In the 2011 census Killamarsh East ward was 98.5% White British, which was the second-highest figure for any ward in the East Midlands and within in the top 60 wards in England and Wales.

The White British population in Barlow and Holmesfield isn't much lower, at 97.7%. However, this is a very different area: Barlow and Holmesfield is a rural ward based on a number of villages to the north-west of Chesterfield. The ward covers a large area, and much of its western half lies within the Peak District National Park.

Barlow and Holmesfield ward has had unchanged boundaries since North East Derbyshire council was set up in the 1970s, and Killamarsh East escaped a boundary review for the 2019 election unchanged. So we can compare results here over quite a long period of time. Not that there's much to report on in the case of Barlow and Holmesfield, which has been in Conservative hands since 1991. After standing here as an independent candidate in 1995, the Conservatives' Carol Huckerby had represented the ward continuously since 1999 without serious opposition: she was re-elected for a sixth term in 2019 with a 65–22 lead over Labour. She is standing down after 22 years' service.

Killamarsh used to be such a strong Labour town that its local elections would regularly go uncontested. Labour won Killamarsh East ward unopposed in 1987, 1991, 1995, 2003 and 2007, and the Conservatives didn't stand a candidate here between 1979 and 2011. As recently as May 2015 the Labour slate had a 68–32 lead in Killamarsh East.

Since then Killamarsh has swung a mile to the right. In May 2019 the Con-

Parliamentary constituency: North East Derbyshire
Derbyshire county council division: Dronfield West and Walton
May 2019 result C 370 Lab 122 LD 75
May 2015 result C 719 Lab 286 UKIP 208
May 2011 result C 553 Lab 208
May 2007 result C 524 Lab 131
May 2003 result C 398 Lab 126
May 1999 result C 406 Lab 183
May 1995 result C 369 Lab 264 Ind 189
May 1991 result C 500 Lab 253 Ind 165
May 1987 result Ind 422 C 321 Lab 121
May 1983 result C unopposed
May 1979 result C 787 Ind 233 Lab 151
May 1976 result Ind 695 Lab 164
May 1973 result Ind 594 Lab 194

Figure 99: North East Derbyshire, Barlow and Holmesfield

servative slate polled 53% to Labour's 47% and won both of the ward's seats, the second by a majority of one vote. Those two seat gains helped the Conservatives to gain control of North East Derbyshire council from Labour in the May 2019 elections, which returned 30 Conservative councillors against 18 Labour, 3 Lib Dems and two independents. A further Labour seat has since gone Conservative in a by-election.

The lead Conservative councillor in Killamarsh East, Kevin Bone, subsequently resigned from the council along with his wife Patricia (who was elected for Killamarsh West ward); both by-elections were held in May alongside the Derbyshire county council elections, and both of them were held by the Conservatives. The East ward by-election in May (page 96) had an increased Conservative lead of 56–39 over Labour.

It's not technically accurate to describe Killamarsh as part of the Red Wall. Killamarsh (like Barlow and Holmesfield) is part of the North East Derbyshire constituency, which had already been an against-the-trend Conservative gain in June 2017. However, you can see from that recent history that it does share many characteristics with Red Wall-type areas.

May's Derbyshire county council elections also saw the Conservatives convincingly gain the two-seat Eckington and Killamarsh county division from Labour, after a near-miss in May 2017. Barlow and Holmesfield ward is part of the Dronfield West and Walton division of the county council, which was close between the Tories and UKIP in 2013 but is now very safe for the Conservatives.

Killamarsh East's other Conservative councillor, Nick Whitehead, has now

Parliamentary constituency: North East Derbyshire
Derbyshire county council division: Eckington and Killamarsh
May 2021 by-election C 519 Lab 359 LD 42
May 2019 result C 395/354 Lab 353/348
May 2015 result Lab 1044/1017 C 502/496
May 2011 result Lab 743/652 C 282/206
May 2007 result 2 Lab unopposed
May 2003 result 2 Lab unopposed

Figure 100: North East Derbyshire, Killamarsh East

resigned in his turn provoking the ward's second by-election in four months. He was the councillor elected in May 2019 by one vote, polling 354 votes to 353 for the lead Labour candidate.

So, this one should be closely watched. Defending Killamarsh East for the Conservatives is Wendy Tinley, who represents the ward on Killamarsh parish council. The Labour candidate is Tony Lacey, who appears to be fighting his first election campaign. Completing the ballot paper is Mark Firth for the Lib Dems.*

The Conservatives should have an easier defence in Barlow and Holmesfield, where they have selected the wonderfully-named Bentley Strafford-Stephenson. He is described as actively involved in a number of local charitable and voluntary causes. Labour have selected Ross Griffin, who stood for the council in Tupton ward (on the far side of Chesterfield) in 2019. Again, the Lib Dems complete the ballot paper with their candidate John Wilcock.†

Seales

South Derbyshire council; caused by the resignation of independent councillor Amy Wheelton, who was elected as a Conservative. She is seeking re-election.

It's traditional for a performance to be ended by clapping, so let's finish this week's edition of Andrew's Previews by considering Seales. Not maritime ones though. The Seales ward of South Derbyshire includes the village of Coton in the Elms, which is recognised as the farthest point in the UK from the sea. We are 70 miles away from the Wash, the Dee Estuary or the Severn Estuary.

Despite that, you can almost get to Coton in the Elms by boat. The village is one of six rural parishes making up Seales ward, which lies to the south-west of Swadlincote and is the southernmost ward of Derbyshire. The ward's western

* *North East Derbyshire, Killamarsh East*: Lab 291 C 251 LD 41 [Lab gain from C]
† *North East Derbyshire, Barlow and Holmesfield*: C 294 Lab 90 LD 42

boundary is the River Trent, just beyond which (via the bridge at Walton on Trent) is the Derby–Birmingham railway line, the Roman Road of Ryknield Street (now the A 38), the Trent and Mersey Canal and a marina at Barton-under-Needwood. From here it is possible to float to the North Sea, via the Trent and Mersey Canal, the navigable River Trent and the Humber estuary. Or, if you go the other way along the Trent and Mersey Canal, you can float to the Irish Sea, or to the Severn Estuary via the West Midlands' canal network.

Seales ward (perhaps not surprisingly, given its location) is part of a local government district called South Derbyshire. The ward was created in 2003 with two councillors as a merger of three previous single-member wards (Netherseal, Overseal and Walton) which were undersized, and it survived a boundary review in 2011 unchanged. Although there was a Labour history in some of the previous wards, Seales has proven to be a safe Conservative ward with the exception of the 2011 election, when it returned one councillor each from the Tories and Labour.

In 2019 the Conservative slate of Amy Wheelton, a farmer from Walton-on-Trent, and Andrew Brady won Seales ward with an increased majority of 51–30 over Labour. Both of them were new candidates. May 2019 was the fourth election in a row that the Conservatives had won a majority on South Derbyshire, although they did lose two seats nett for a 22–14 lead. The South Derbyshire district has the same boundaries as the parliamentary seat of that name, which the Conservatives have held since 2010 and where they now enjoy a very large majority.

However, the Conservative group in South Derbyshire has fallen apart over the last year or so. Going into the 2021 Derbyshire county elections there were four vacant seats on the district council, all following the resignations of Conservative councillors; Seales councillor Amy Wheelton had been suspended from the Party; and a number of other Conservatives had walked off to form a splinter group. They removed the Conservative leadership of the council and installed a Labour minority administration, which remains in place.

The Conservatives held all four by-elections to South Derbyshire council in May, one of which was in Seales ward following the resignation of Councillor Brady. In a straight Tory-Labour fight, the Conservatives increased their majority to 67–33 (page 97). At the last count, the council was finely balanced with 15 Labour councillors, 15 Conservatives, 5 councillors in the splinter "Independent Group" and this vacancy.

Also in May Amy Wheelton fought the local Derbyshire county council division of Linton as an independent candidate. She finished a strong third with 23% of the vote, against 46% for the Conservatives and 31% for Labour—an against-the-grain swing to Labour compared with the 2017 Derbyshire election.

Parliamentary constituency: South Derbyshire
Derbyshire county council division: Linton
May 2021 by-election C 1070 Lab 527
May 2019 result C 667/657 Lab 400/303 SDP 251
May 2015 result C 1371/1359 Lab 1005/925 UKIP 650
May 2011 result C 1015/919 Lab 928/730
May 2007 result C 1048/989 Lab 582/458
May 2003 result C 895/785 Lab 523/495

Figure 101: South Derbyshire, Seales

Wheelton stood down from South Derbyshire council in June provoking the ward's second by-election in four months. Although the reason for this was not disclosed at the time, she had been diagnosed with breast cancer and was to undergo a mastectomy. It appears that this procedure was a complete success, and in her case chemotherapy was not required.

Following this better-than-expected medical news Amy Wheelton is seeking re-election, as an independent candidate, in the by-election caused by her own resignation. It will be the second contest in four months between her and Conservative candidate Stuart Swann, who was elected in May as the local Derbyshire county councillor. Swann has sat on South Derbyshire council before, representing Church Gresley ward from 2015 to 2019 when he lost his seat to a running-mate. The Labour candidate is Louise Mulgrew, who contested Swadlincote South division in May's county elections. Completing the ballot paper is Amanda Baker for the Green Party.*

* *South Derbyshire, Seales*: Ind 399 C 390 Lab 188 Grn 27

16th September 2021

Four by-elections on 16th September 2021, with two Labour defences, one Conservatives and one case where it's complicated:

Hobbayne

Ealing council, London; caused by the resignation of Labour councillor Lewis Cox.

We start the week in Outer London in the valley of the River Brent, which runs generally south-west from Hendon to join the Thames at Brentford. The Brent valley was a major obstacle to the builders of the Great Western Railway on their way out of London; the result was the Wharncliffe Viaduct, whose eight arches carry Brunel's billiard-table over the valley. The viaduct was completed in 1838 and bears the coat of arms of the 1st Lord Wharncliffe, who piloted the GWR's bill through Parliament.

The valley to the north of the Wharncliffe Viaduct is maintained as a country park, partly because of the risk of flooding from the river. It includes Hanwell Zoo, a small zoological garden with a variety of small mammals, reptiles and exotic birds to see.

Hanwell Zoo is part of the Hobbayne ward of Ealing, which lies between the river to the west and north, the Great Western railway line to the south and the Greenford branch railway line to the east. Hanwell and Drayton Green railway stations lie on the ward boundary, and Greenford Avenue links the ward together.

The ward's census return shows a high immigrant population here. Hobbayne ward makes the top 20 wards in England and Wales for those born in Ireland (3.4%), the top 60 for those born in the new EU states (11.6%) and the top 80 for the White Other ethnic group (23.7%). The new EU immigrants are overwhelmingly Polish, and we shouldn't be too surprised by this: Ealing borough is home to one of the UK's longest-established Polish communities.

Hobbayne ward has swung a mile to the left in the last decade after electing

Parliamentary constituency: Ealing North
London Assembly constituency: Ealing and Hillingdon
May 2021 by-election Lab 2345 C 1477 Grn 609 LD 366 TUSC 56
May 2018 result Lab 2595/2579/2479 C 1009/979/961 Grn 669 LD 344/327/284 Duma Polska 266/254 Ind 210
May 2014 result Lab 2854/2790/2707 C 1533/1189/1140 Grn 716 LD 309/256/164
May 2010 result Lab 2673/2580/2425 C 2447/2007/1855 LD 1187/861/838 Grn 598 Ind 245
May 2006 result C 1532/1319/1184 Lab 1298/1109/1039 LD 648/640/583 Grn 589
May 2002 result Lab 1501/1436/1374 C 879/824/776 LD 428/392/349 Grn 368
May 2021 GLA result (excludes postal voters)
Mayor: Lab 1009 C 756 Grn 222 LD 70 Omilana 63 Reclaim 45 London Real 39 Count Binface 30 Rejoin EU 26 Let London Live 20 Women's Equality 19 Animal Welfare 17 Renew 13 Farah London 13 SDP 11 UKIP 11 Heritage 10 Burning Pink 7 Fosh 7 Obunge 3
London Members: Lab 1050 C 684 Grn 335 LD 112 Women's Equality 52 Animal Welfare 51 Rejoin EU 41 CPA 25 London Real 24 Reform UK 24 UKIP 19 Heritage 14 Let London Live 11 TUSC 11 SDP 8 Comm 7 Londonpendence 6 Nat Lib 2

Figure 102: Ealing, Hobbayne

both Conservative and Labour councillors in 2006 and 2010. The most recent ordinary London borough elections were in 2018, when Labour won here with 51% against 20% for the Conservatives and 13% for the Greens.

One of the Labour councillors, Anna Tomlinson, died from cancer in June 2020. The resulting by-election, which couldn't be held until May 2021, saw a swing to the Conservatives with 48% for Labour, 30% for the Conservatives and 13% for the Green Party (page 62).

We can compare and contrast this by-election result with the votes in the London Mayor and Assembly elections which took place on the same day. The ward breakdowns for the GLA elections exclude postal votes, which are tallied separately; the on-the-day vote gave 42% to Sadiq Khan for Labour, 32% to Shaun Bailey for the Conservatives and 9% to Siân Berry of the Green Party. In the London Members ballot Labour also polled 42%, against 28% for the Conservatives and 14% for the Greens. Taking into account that the GLA election had much longer ballot papers, the differences from the council by-election are not that great.

The voters of Hobbayne are going back to the polls for the second time in four months following the resignation in May of Labour councillor Lewis Cox, who had first been elected in 2018 and was in his first term of office. He does not appear to be happy with the leadership of Ealing council's ruling Labour group.

Defending for Labour is Claire Tighe who is contesting her second Ealing by-election of the year; in May she stood in another poll for the Conservative-held

Ealing Broadway ward (page 62). Tighe is vice-chair of the Labour Party Irish Society, and currently works in Keir Starmer's office. The Conservatives have reselected David Castle who was runner-up here in May's by-election; he is a law student, and like Tighe has worked alongside MPs in Westminster. The Greens have changed candidate to Alan Anderson, an editor for a health and wellbeing website. Completing the ballot paper are two other returning candidates from May's by-election, Alastair Mitton for the Liberal Democrats and Tony Gill for the Trade Unionist and Socialist Coalition.*

Tenbury

Malvern Hills council, Worcestershire; caused by the resignation of Conservative councillor Tony Penn.

For our rural by-election this week we travel to the Teme Valley. The Teme starts off as a Welsh river, rising near Newtown, and flows east through Knighton and Ludlow to eventually merge with the Severn near Worcester.

This is an agricultural area with an unusual focus. The town of Tenbury Wells is well-known as the venue for the UK's only mistletoe market, which takes place in the run-up to Christmas each year. Outside the festive period, Tenbury has traditionally drawn an income from people coming to take the waters at the town's mineral springs: the architecturally-striking Pump Rooms are now in the hands of Tenbury town council, who have their offices and meetings here.

It's presumably the communication lines provided by the Teme valley that ensured Tenbury Wells ended up as part of Worcestershire. Tenbury, which has been a typical tiny Marches market town since the thirteenth century, is very much out on a limb within Worcestershire: this ward (consisting of five parishes, including Tenbury) forms a salient between Herefordshire to the south and Shropshire to the north. The main service centre and railhead for the town is Ludlow, further up the valley in Shropshire.

The Heath local government reform also took the view that the Herefordshire/Worcestershire county boundary was perhaps not the sanest. The 1974 big bang placed Tenbury Wells within the county of Hereford and Worcester and within the district of Leominster, which is a Herefordshire town but whose district took in much of north-western Worcestershire. This proved to be unpopular, and Hereford and Worcester were demerged in the 1990s. As a knock-on effect of this, Tenbury was transferred to the Malvern Hills district council in exchange for the Ledbury area, which returned to Herefordshire.

* *Ealing, Hobbayne*: Lab 1617 C 865 Grn 362 LD 207 TUSC 48

Parliamentary constituency: West Worcestershire
Worcestershire county council division: Tenbury
May 2019 result 2 C unopposed
May 2015 result C 1414/991 Lab 618
May 2011 result C 966/730 Ind 416
May 2007 result C 1042/834 LD 451/419 Ind 269
May 2003 result C 748/675 Ind 691/324

Figure 103: Malvern Hills, Tenbury

The present Malvern Hills council is hung after the Conservatives lost their majority in 2019. That year's elections returned 13 Conservative councillors, 10 independents, 9 Lib Dems, 5 Greens and (for the first time in many years) a Labour councillor. The present administration is a coalition of the independents, the Greens and the Lib Dems. The Malvern Hills Liberal Democrats have since fallen apart a bit and there are only four Lib Dem councillors left here; most of the defectors have joined the ruling independent group.

The voters of Tenbury didn't get to participate in this fun in 2019, because nobody stood against the Conservative slate of Tony Penn and Bridget Thomas who were therefore elected unopposed. Thomas was a new face; Penn was re-elected for his fourth term. The Conservatives have held both seats in the ward since 2007; in 2011 and 2015 they were opposed here only by Jonathan Morgan, who was an independent in 2011 and had the Labour nomination in 2015. On both of those occasions the scores were 70% for the Conservatives and 30% for Morgan. The Conservatives also polled 70% last May in the election for the Tenbury division of Worcestershire county council, which covers a larger area than this ward.

Tony Penn is a retired architect who grew up in Coventry during the Second World War, and he was in the city on the night of the Coventry Blitz in November 1940. With the passage of time, there are not many people left who can remember that night. Penn is now 87 years old, and he retired from the council in July to allow someone younger to take up his role.

Defending for the Conservatives is Liam Thompson, who was a candidate for the county council in May (he contested the Green-held Malvern Trinity division). Jonathan Morgan returns for his fifth attempt on Tenbury ward this century, again as the Labour candidate. The Tenbury town clerk Lesley Bruton is standing as an independent candidate, and she completes the ballot paper along with Jed Marson of the Liberal Democrats.*

* *Malvern Hills, Tenbury*: Ind 481 C 269 Lab 78 LD 32 [Ind gain from C]

Firth Park

Sheffield council, South Yorkshire; caused by the resignation of Labour councillor Alan Law on health grounds.

Our remaining two by-elections this week are at opposite ends of traditional Yorkshire. We start in the city of Sheffield with a ward whose name derives from a prominent steelmaking firm of days gone by. Thomas Firth and Sons was set up in the 1840s and quickly grew: in the 1850s they had the largest rolling mill in Sheffield and a major contract with the Samuel Colt firearms company, making them a big player in the armaments market. Following a series of mergers over the last two centuries, Firth's became one of the ancestors of the modern Sheffield Forgemasters.

Mark Firth, one of the eponymous Sons and a founder of the business, used much of his wealth in major philanthropic works in Sheffield. He was Master Cutler in 1867–9 and Mayor of Sheffield in 1874–5, founded the educational institution of Firth College (now part of Sheffield University), and in 1875 he presented 36 acres of land to Sheffield Corporation as a public park. Firth Park, located around four miles north-east of Sheffield city centre, was officially opened in August 1875 by the Prince of Wales, the future Edward VII.

Firth Park gave its name to a neighbouring council estate which was developed between the two world wars on what was then the northern edge of Sheffield. This remains a working-class area full of council houses (a massive 51% of households here are socially rented), but manufacturing here is not what it was. The major employer in Firth Park today is the Northern General Hospital, which lies just south of the ward boundary. At the 2011 census 22% of the ward's working adults were in human health and social work activities, which was the highest figure for any ward in Yorkshire and made the top 60 wards in England and Wales.

Sheffield city council fell into No Overall Control at the 2021 election, following controversy over the previous Labour administration's policy of felling a large number of the trees on the city's streets. The city is still Labour-led but the party now has to run Sheffield in coalition with the Green Party. There are currently 40 Labour (plus this vacancy) and 13 Green councillors opposed by 29 Lib Dems and a single Conservative. After a 15-year absence the Tories broke through onto Sheffield council in May, not in the middle-class areas of Hallam but in the isolated steelworking town of Stocksbridge.

One of Stocksbridge's former city councillors was Alan Law, who was elected there in 1991 but lost his seat to the Lib Dems the following year. In 1994 Law was elected as a councillor for Firth Park ward, which he had represented continuously

Parliamentary constituency: Sheffield Brightside and Hillsborough
May 2021 result Lab 1896 C 810 Grn 327 Ind 157 LD 153
May 2019 result Lab 1573 Grn 779 C 453 LD 270
May 2018 result Lab 1931 C 577 Grn 478 LD 287
May 2016 result Lab 2424/1916/1844 UKIP 752/622/577 Grn 443/305/246 C 302/239/198 LD 269/229/190

Figure 104: Sheffield, Firth Park

since then: he was re-elected in 1995, 1996, 2000, 2004, 2006, 2010, 2014 and 2016, winning his tenth term of office in May this year. Firth Park is a safe Labour ward, and four months ago Law enjoyed a 57–24 majority over the Conservatives. He subsequently stepped down in July on health grounds.

Defending for Labour is Fran Belbin, a community activist who fought Walkley ward in May and lost a seat which Labour were defending to the Green Party. That council seat had previously been held by Olivia Blake, who was elected in December 2019 as the Labour MP for Sheffield Hallam; Blake resigned from the council after her election to Westminster, and because of the cancellation of the 2020 local elections her seat was left vacant for more than a year. This should be safer territory for Belbin. The Conservatives have reselected Steve Toone who was runner-up here in May; he chairs a local brass band committee and is a wheelchair user. Also standing are two more returning candidates from May, Marieanne Elliot for the Greens and independent April Worrall, who complete the ballot paper along with Irshad Akbar for the Liberal Democrats.*

Ladgate

Middlesbrough council, North Yorkshire; caused by the death of councillor June Goodchild, who was elected for Labour but was sitting as an independent aligned to the town's mayor.

We finish for the week in Teesside. The Ladgate ward is one of Middlesbrough's outer estates, running along the western side of Stokesley Road and divided into two halves by Ladgate Lane. The two halves of the ward form a rather stark contrast. The northern half is the Easterside estate, a 1960s open-plan development with large amounts of green space. The southern half of the ward, around the Marton Manor primary school, is higher in both elevation and social class.

Teesside has been a disaster area for the Labour party in recent years, as can be seen from the re-election of the Conservative Tees Valley mayor Ben Houchen

* *Sheffield, Firth Park*: Lab 1091 LD 1050 C 258 Grn 162 Ind 155

in May by the thumping margin of 73–27 over the Labour candidate. On paper Middlesbrough is the strongest of the five Tees Valley boroughs for Labour, but the borough uses the elected mayoral system. The first Middlesbrough mayor was independent Ray "Robocop" Mallon, who served three terms before standing down in 2015. That year's mayoral election was a very narrow win for Labour over new independent candidate Andy Preston, who resoundingly won the rematch in 2019.

The 2019 Middlesbrough mayoral election was combined with the Middlesbrough council election, which returned 23 independent councillors, 20 Labour and 3 Conservatives. Labour have performed very poorly in two subsequent by-elections: the independents held Park End and Beckfield ward in July 2019[*], and the Conservatives resoundingly held a seat in Coulby Newham ward in February 2020 despite their previous councillor having been charged with seven historic child sex offences[†]. Having been charged in July 2019, his trial is now not due to begin until April 2022.

Coulby Newham, like most of Ladgate ward, is part of the Middlesbrough South and East Cleveland constituency which the Conservatives gained against the national trend in June 2017. That snap election was called by Theresa May the weekend after another excellent Conservative performance in a Coulby Newham by-election in April 2017[‡]; the winner of that by-election is now the Conservative MP for Redcar.

Ladgate ward has been won by Labour at every election this century. There were no independent candidates here in 2019, and the Labour slate won by 60–40 in a straight fight with the Conservatives. That Labour slate included June Goodchild, who had been appointed MBE in 2007 for her voluntary work on the Easterside estate. Goodchild was first elected for the ward in 2015; she subsequently left Labour in 2020 and joined the council's Middlesbrough Independent Group. It's quite difficult for an outsider to work out what is going on in the council, as there are three separate independent groups and the independent mayor all with their own agendas.

June Goodchild passed away in July, aged 79. The by-election to replace her has a long ballot paper. Labour, who won the last election here, have selected Mick Thompson, who was their losing candidate in the 2019 Middlesbrough mayoral election; Thompson is a former Middlesbrough councillor currently working for UNISON. There are three competing independent candidates. The Middlesbrough Independent Group, which Goodchild was a member of when she died, have endorsed Tony Grainge: he is a community worker from Easterside

[*] *Andrew's Previews 2019*, page 191. [†] *Andrew's Previews 2020*, page 42. [‡] *Andrew's Previews 2017*, page 99.

Parliamentary constituency: Middlesbrough South and East Cleveland (most), Middlesbrough (Buckthorn Grove area)
May 2019 result Lab 561/451 C 367/310
May 2015 result Lab 1070/946 C 516/399 UKIP 427

Figure 105: Middlesbrough, Ladgate

and a school governor at Easterside Academy. The rival Middlesbrough Independent Councillors Association have endorsed Sharon Platt, a former marketing chief who is hoping to join her husband Jim (the former Middlesbrough and Northern Ireland goalkeeper) as a councillor. The third independent candidate on the ballot is Vic Hoban, who is a full-time carer for her daughter. Hoping to come through the middle of all this are the Conservatives, who have selected Lee Holmes: he is an NHS Responder volunteer and runs a small property business in Middlesbrough. Completing the ballot paper is Paul Hamilton for the Liberal Democrats, who are contesting Ladgate ward for the first time this century.*

* *Middlesbrough, Ladgate*: Grainge 362 C 315 Lab 226 Platt 121 LD 14 Hoban 3 [Ind gain from Lab]

23rd September 2021

There are six by-elections in England on 23rd September 2021 with a good spread across the country and something for everyone. There is a Conservative defence in Leicestershire, a Labour defence in London and a Residents' seat up for election in Surrey, but this week is a bit of a Liberal Democrat special with the party defending three of the seats up for election. Including our first one:

Kendal North

South Lakeland council, Cumbria; caused by the resignation of Liberal Democrat councillor Jon Owen.

We start the week in the last bastion of Liberalism in the North of England. Welcome to Kendal, the once and possibly-future main town of Westmorland and the southern gateway to the Lake District: the main road and railway line to Windermere both pass by or through Kendal.

This is an old town with notably grey architecture, thanks to the local stone. Textiles were traditionally the main industry in Kendal, but the town is also known for an unusual food export, the energy snack known as Kendal Mint Cake. Eat this and your body will thank you for the energy boost, but (given its extremely high sugar content) your teeth might not be as happy. A number of rival mint cake factories still operate in Kendal today.

The town's proximity to the Lakes makes Kendal a favourite base for Kendal Mint Cake's largest market: mountaineers. Alfred Wainwright, whose *Pictorial Guides to the Lake District* are still the industry-standard guidebook for the Lakes' hikers more than sixty years after their first publication, wrote those books while he had a day job in Kendal Town Hall as the borough treasurer.

Kendal borough council has been succeeded by South Lakeland district council, which is still under the political spell cast by the former Liberal Democrat leader Tim Farron. Farron has been the MP for the local seat of Westmorland and Lonsdale since 2005, and he achieved that by persuading the former Labour vote in Kendal to defect to the Lib Dems *en masse*. Until 2000 there was some decently-sized Labour and Conservative support in Kendal, and in the 2002 local elections the town's 14 wards returned 7 Lib Dem councillors, 6 Labour and 1 Conservative. Four years later the Lib Dems won a clean sweep of all 14 wards, with their *worst* score in any ward being 58% of the vote in Highgate ward. That gave the party overall control of South Lakeland council, which they are yet to relinquish. Your columnist had seen nothing similar since until Jason Zadrozny got to work on Ashfield council in Nottinghamshire ahead of the 2019 local elections.

The reason that there were 14 wards for a town the size of Kendal is that South Lakeland had a rather unusual electoral cycle in those days, combining a predominantly single-member ward pattern with thirds elections. The Local Government Boundary Commission told them they had to drop one or the other ahead of a boundary review implemented for the 2018 local elections; the council decided to keep thirds elections, and the review reorganised Kendal (plus the parish of Natland to the south) into four wards returning three councillors each and a fifth ward of two councillors.

The two-seat ward is Kendal North, which is based on the former wards of Strickland and Underley. It covers the town's north-west corner, between the River Kent and the Windermere Road. The former Kendal Underley ward was based on Hallgarth, a council estate built just after the Second World War, and in the 2011 census Kendal Underley made the top 50 wards in England and Wales for part-time employment (18.9% of those of working age) and the top 70 wards for the ONS employment classification "Wholesale and retail trade; repair of motor vehicles and motor cycles", with 23.5% of the workforce in this rather broad category.

Underley ward was represented from 2014 to its abolition in 2018 by Matt Severn, one of *Andrew's Previews*' most ardent fans. Severn transferred to Kendal West ward in 2018, and Kendal North was won by the Lib Dem slate with a rather low vote share of 38%, against 27% for the Green Party and 21% for the Conservatives. That is the only previous result on the current boundaries: the ward was not up for election in 2019, and the 2021 South Lakeland and Cumbria county council elections were cancelled in advance of a reorganisation of Cumbria's local government. The ward forms part of the Kendal Strickland and Fell county division, which was safely Liberal Democrat when last contested in May 2017.

This by-election results from the resignation last month of Liberal Democrat councillor Jon Owen, who was first elected in 2018. Owen has also left the Liberal Democrats and switched his allegiance to the Green Party. He would have been up for election last May had those elections gone ahead; right now it's anyone's

Parliamentary constituency: Westmorland and Lonsdale
Cumbria county council division: Kendal Strickland and Fell
May 2018 result LD 667/543 Grn 468/270 C 372/324 Lab 238/183

Figure 106: South Lakeland, Kendal North

guess how long his successor will serve for.

Defending for the Liberal Democrats is Jonathan Cornthwaite, a manufacture technician and Kendal town councillor. The Green Party have selected Liz Hendry, a retired teacher. The Conservative candidate is Aron Taylor who, according to a local newspaper report, is concentrating on residents' issues "from stamping out dog fouling ('not literally, thankfully') through to ensuring 'council tax is kept as low as possible'". Completing the ballot paper is Virginia Branney for Labour.*

Shepshed West

Charnwood council, Leicestershire; caused by the resignation of Conservative councillor Joan Tassell.

For our Midlands by-election of the week we are very close to the centre of England, in the town of Shepshed. Located a few miles to the west of Loughborough, Shepshed was traditionally dominated by the mediaeval wool trade—the "shep" in the name refers to sheep—but in modern times its easy access to the M 1 motorway has turned it into a dormitory town for the cities of the East Midlands.

Until its recent promotion from a parish to a town Shepshed was a claimant for the title of England's largest village, with a population well in excess of 10,000. This is big enough for the town to return four members to Charnwood council, from two electoral wards.

West ward has traditionally been a key marginal ward in a key marginal Parliamentary seat (it's part of the Loughborough constituency). In this century the ward has generally voted Conservative with the exception of the 2003 election and a by-election in October 2013, but the Tory majority at the last Charnwood elections in 2019 was unusually large: 41% for the Conservatives, 26% for Labour and 14% for UKIP. Some of that Tory lead is clearly a personal vote for their councillor Christine Radford, who is also Shepshed's county councillor; Radford was re-elected to Leicestershire county council in May with a whopping 60–28 lead over Labour. The Labour candidate in May was Jane Lennie, the winner of the October 2013 West ward by-election.

---

* *South Lakeland, Kendal North*: LD 622 Grn 527 C 122 Lab 54

Parliamentary constituency: Loughborough
Leicestershire county council division: Shepshed
May 2019 result C 824/667 Lab 519/489 UKIP 269 Grn 227 LD 153/98
May 2015 result C 1712/1240 Lab 1156/1142 UKIP 849/632 LD 381
October 2013 by-election Lab 683 C 560 LD 178
May 2011 result C 1000/960 Lab 934/801 LD 481/396
May 2007 result C 722/677 Lab 626/560 BNP 540 LD 522/411
May 2003 result Lab 601/600 C 507/422 LD 239/179

Figure 107: Charnwood, Shepshed West

This by-election follows the resignation of the ward's other Conservative councillor, Joan Tassell. She had finished as runner-up to Lennie in the 2013 by-election but won the rematch in 2015, increasing her majority in 2019 against a much lower turnout.

Defending for the Conservatives is Ian Williams, an engineer and Shepshed town councillor. Labour have changed candidate to town councillor Myriam Roberts, who contested Shepshed East ward in the 2019 Charnwood elections; she is a school teaching assistant and, according to her declaration of interests, a "YouTube creator". UKIP have not returned, so completing the ballot paper are John Hounsome for the Green Party and Katy Brookes-Duncan for the Liberal Democrats.*

Soham North

East Cambridgeshire council; caused by the resignation of Liberal Democrat councillor Victoria Charlesworth.

We travel to East Anglia for a return visit to Soham, which has previously appeared in this column in *Andrew's Previews 2017* (page 167) and *2018* (page 345). As I recounted there, Soham is a town which never really fulfilled its potential: it had a cathedral in Anglo-Saxon times whose status didn't stick, was saved from being flattened in 1944 only by extreme bravery on the part of the crew of a goods train carrying ammunition which had caught fire; and the town is still probably best-known nationally for the 2002 murder of two ten-year-old girls by their school caretaker.

Really that's a bit unfair on Soham, which is a pleasant enough market town some miles to the north-east of Cambridge. Cambridge's hinterland has seem massive population growth in this century which has mostly been achieved by tacking housing estates onto existing towns and villages, and Soham has not

* *Charnwood, Shepshed West*: C 511 Lab 316 Grn 302 LD 44

Parliamentary constituency: South East Cambridgeshire
Cambridgeshire county council division: Soham North and Isleham
May 2019 result LD 599/558 C 528/465 Lab 124/107

Figure 108: East Cambridgeshire, Soham North

escaped this process: the electorate of Soham North ward grew by 40% between 2003 and the 2017 by-election. Following a boundary review implemented for the 2019 local elections, Soham's representation on East Cambridgeshire council changed from 5 councillors out of 40 to 4 councillors out of 28—an increase in percentage terms.

That population growth looked to have turned Soham into a safely Conservative area. Soham North was represented until 2017 by the Tory leader of East Cambridgeshire council, James Palmer; in that year Palmer won the inaugural election for Mayor of Cambridgeshire and Peterborough, and his council seat was automatically vacated. The resulting by-election in June 2017 was won easily by the new Conservative candidate Mark Goldsack, who also won a by-election to Cambridgeshire county council in October 2018 for the local division of Soham North and Isleham.

However, the Conservatives have been struggling in Cambridgeshire of late. The 2019 East Cambridgeshire district elections saw a strong challenge from the Liberal Democrats, who eventually came up just short: the final results were 15 Conservative councillors against 13 Lib Dems. Included in the Liberal Democrat column was the redrawn Soham North ward, which gave 48% to the Lib Dem slate and 42% to the Conservatives.

The Conservatives lost control of Cambridgeshire county council in May and also lost the county mayoralty to Labour, thanks to Lib Dem transfers. However, Mark Goldsack was re-elected in Soham North and Isleham division very comfortably, which will give the Tories some encouragement that they can win this by-election.

The by-election is to replace Lib Dem councillor Victoria Charlesworth, who was a distant runner-up to Goldsack in the 2018 county by-election but won the rematch in the 2019 district council elections. Charlesworth, who was in her first term in office, is relocating to the Midlands with her family.

Defending for the Liberal Democrats is Anne Pallett, a Soham town councillor. The Conservatives have reselected Mark Goldsack after he lost his district council seat in 2019. Also standing are Sam Mathieson for Labour and Andrew Cohen for the Green Party.*

* *East Cambridgeshire, Soham North*: C 484 LD 369 Lab 71 Grn 28 [C gain from LD]

Wormholt and White City

Hammersmith and Fulham council, London; caused by the death of Labour councillor Colin Aherne.

We travel to what was once one of the most iconic areas of West London. In 1908 the world came to London to attend the Franco-British Exhibition, a huge public fair which was the world's first exhibition sponsored by two countries. Attractions included an Irish village and a Senegalese village, displaying Irish industry and day-to-day life in Africa respectively. All the exhibition buildings were clad in white marble or painted white, and the site came to be known as "White City". It was a huge public success, with the local Underground railway companies opening new stations specially to serve the exhibition.

In that summer of 1908 White City was also the focus of the fourth modern Summer Olympic Games. The 1908 Olympics had originally been awarded to Rome, which subsequently pulled out after the Italian government diverted the necessary funds towards rebuilding efforts after the 1906 eruption of Mount Vesuvius. Stepping in at short notice, London built the White City Stadium as part of the exhibition site to host the Games. Although this depends on how you classify the Panathenaic Stadium in Athens, White City can reasonably claim to be the first purpose-built Olympic stadium.

The White City stadium had a huge influence on one modern Olympic event: the marathon. The 1908 Olympic marathon was run from Windsor Castle to the finishing line in the White City stadium, a distance of 26 miles and 385 yards. Now metricated as 42.195 kilometres, this has been the standard marathon distance ever since. Those last 385 yards inside the stadium took ten minutes for the leading marathon runner, Italy's Dorando Pietri, to cover. Pietri, who was suffering from fatigue and dehydration, did eventually make it over the finish line in first place but was subsequently disqualified because he had been helped onto his feet by the race umpires after a number of falls. Queen Alexandra, who had watched the whole thing from the royal box, gave him a gilded silver cup in lieu of a medal.

White City Stadium subsequently became primarily a greyhound stadium, but it hosted the British athletics championships from 1932 to 1970, the athletics events in the 1934 British Empire Games and one game in the 1966 FIFA World Cup. That was the group match between Uruguay and France, which was moved to White City because Wembley Stadium's owners refused to reschedule a greyhound-racing meeting.

The stadium was demolished in 1985 (its site is now occupied by BBC offices) and was one of the last parts of the original White City to disappear. The only remaining part of the exhibition site is Hammersmith Park, behind the former BBC Television Centre, which was originally part of the Japanese garden. Most of the exhibition grounds were redeveloped in the late 1930s into the White City Estate, a high-rise council estate which is one of the major parts of the modern Wormholt and White City ward. The roads within the estate—Commonwealth Road, South Africa Road and so on—are named after countries which took part in the Franco-British Exhibition.

To the west of Bloemfontein Road lie the Wormholt and Cleverly estates, which date from the 1920s—the era of "homes fit for heroes"—and were designed on garden-city principles. The name "Wormholt" goes back a long way, as it was a ward of the original Hammersmith metropolitan borough council.

Since the formation of the current Hammersmith and Fulham council in the 1960s this has been a Labour-voting area. White City is the only part of the borough to have never elected a Conservative councillor. Wormholt was also generally Labour, with the exception of the 1968 disaster and the 1982 election. In the latter year one of the seats in Wormholt ward was taken by the Conservatives' Bill Smith, the serving Mayor of Hammersmith and Fulham and a former leader of the council, who transferred here from a safer ward. Labour took that result to the Election Court, crying foul over an allocation of free tickets for a Queens Park Rangers home game which were distributed to local schools a week before polling; Smith was a director of QPR. The legal action failed and the Court upheld the election.

The current ward, combining Wormholt and White City, dates from 2002. The legacy of the White City estate can be seen in the fact that a majority of the ward's households are socially rented, and Wormholt and White City makes the top 40 wards in England and Wales for those born in the Republic of Ireland (3.0%) and is in the top 100 for both black (25.7%) and mixed-race (6.8%) ethnicity.

The late Colin Aherne, whose death at the age of 77 has caused this by-election, was first elected for Wormholt ward in 1986 and was the longest-serving member of Hammersmith and Fulham council. Born into a mining family in Tredegar in South Wales, Aherne had joined the Army at 15 and saw action in the Malayan emergency; he left the Army in 1968 with the rank of sergeant. He had come to elected office through the TGWU, which he joined in 1974 while working for Premier Foods in west London. Aherne had been the Hammersmith and Fulham Labour group's chief whip continuously since 1990. In death he achieved the highest honour a left-wing politician can be granted: an obituary in the *Grauniad*[*].

Aherne had been top of the Labour slate which crushed the opposition

[*] tinyurl.com/47ubzawu

Parliamentary constituency: Hammersmith
London Assembly constituency: West Central
May 2018 result Lab 2493/2396/2261 C 473/450/404 LD 242/187/172 Ind 89
May 2014 result Lab 2222/2014/1845 C 570/532/506 Grn 370 LD 171
February 2013 by-election Lab 1419 C 251 LD 209 UKIP 122 Ind 75 BNP 45
May 2010 result Lab 3052/2971/2813 C 1186/1152/1071 LD 843/727/723
May 2006 result Lab 1292/1278/1151 C 767/623/519 LD 442/404/382 Ind 184
May 2002 result Lab 1141/1084/1082 C 366/337/272 LD 289/279/242
May 2021 GLA results (excludes postal voters)
Mayor: Lab 1376 C 668 Grn 182 Omilana 73 LD 64 London Real 44 Reclaim 42 Let London Live 31 Count Binface 30 Rejoin EU 28 Animal Welfare 28 Women's Equality 16 Renew 12 Heritage 11 Farah London 10 Fosh 9 Obunge 9 UKIP 8 SDP 6 Burning Pink 2
London Members: Lab 1504 C 506 Grn 347 LD 108 Rejoin EU 56 Animal Welfare 51 CPA 38 Women's Equality 35 London Real 29 UKIP 22 Heritage 16 Let London Live 16 Reform UK 13 Comm 10 Londonpendence 7 SDP 7 TUSC 6 Nat Lib 4

Figure 109: Hammersmith and Fulham, Wormholt and White City

with 76% of the vote in Wormholt and White City at the last London borough elections in 2018. Since then we have had the GLA elections in May, which had a wider choice of parties and candidates; we can see that from the fact that the YouTuber Niko Omilana ran fourth here in the mayoral ballot (although with only 3%). The ward's ballot boxes gave a 52–25 lead to Labour's Sadiq Khan over the Conservatives' Shaun Bailey, while the London Members ballot had 54% for Labour, 18% for the Conservatives and 13% for the Green Party.

Defending for Labour is Frances Umeh, a school governor. She is opposed by three candidates: Constance Campbell for the Conservatives, Michael Illingworth for the Liberal Democrats and Naranee Ruthra-Rajan for the Green Party. Whoever wins may need to move fast to secure reselection for the 2022 elections, when this ward will be broken up.*

Cuddington

Epsom and Ewell council, Surrey; caused by the death of Residents Association of Cuddington councillor Rob Foote.

We stay within the London area and the M 25 but jump just over the Greater London boundary, although that's rather difficult to notice here on the ground. Cuddington was mentioned in the Domesday Book of 1086 with 28 households; but the village recorded by the Domesday surveyors was swept away after Henry VIII bought the manor in 1538. Henry had Cuddington demolished to make

* *Hammersmith and Fulham, Wormholt and White City*: Lab 1462 C 431 Grn 110 LD 86

way for the Great Park surrounding Nonsuch Palace, and presumably he had some good hunting around here.

The Great Park subsequently took the name of Edward Somerset, the fourth Earl of Worcester, who was an important figure in the court of James I. James appointed Worcester as Keeper of the Great Park in 1606, and the Earl promptly built Worcester Park House as a residence for himself. (Worcester was a distant ancestor of Daniel Boone, the American frontiersman.) The house was home successively to two major figures of the English Civil War, Thomas Pride (who died here in 1658) and Sir Robert Long, and Samuel Pepys visited Long at Worcester Park House in 1665. Because of the Great Plague, the Exchequer had been evacuated to Nonsuch at that time.

Worcester Park House was destroyed by fire in 1948, by which time the park had been filled with houses as another London suburb. The railways had come here in 1859 and Worcester Park railway station (just outside the ward's north-east corner) has regular trains to London Waterloo. The part of Worcester Park that lies in the Epsom and Ewell borough is a very affluent area, and it successfully fought off the threat of incorporation into Greater London in the 1960s.

Epsom and Ewell borough dates from the 1930s, when most of the houses in this ward were built. For the whole of its existence it has been controlled by Residents Association councillors, and Cuddington ward is part of the Residents' majority. At the last borough elections in May 2019 the Residents Association of Cuddington slate polled 65% of the vote, with the Lib Dems finishing as runner-up on 13% just ahead of the Conservatives.

May 2019 was a very poor election for the Surrey Conservatives in general. For Epsom in particular there may have been a national factor depressing their vote: since 2001 the MP for Epsom and Ewell has been international laughing stock Chris Grayling, who was at the height of his infamy as transport secretary in early 2019. Grayling proved to be so incompetent in a series of Cabinet posts that he failed to make the Johnson governments. Two years later in the May 2021 Surrey county elections, the Conservatives did recover second place in the Ewell Court, Auriol and Cuddington county division although they were still thrashed 66–14 by the Residents.

Rob Foote had served as a district councillor for Cuddington since 2003. He was Mayor of Epsom and Ewell in 2014–15. He spent 30 years working in the airline industry as an engineer, and also worked as an MoT tester and ran a car servicing business. His wife Rosemary, who passed away from breast cancer at the end of last year, had worked for many years with ITN and was a behind-the-scenes veteran of several ITV general election nights.

On 31st July Rob Foote was at the Brands Hatch racecourse in Kent, working

Parliamentary constituency: Epsom and Ewell
Surrey county council division: Ewell Court, Auriol and Cuddington
May 2019 result Res Assoc of Cuddington 977/969/962 LD 190 C 175/160/118 Lab 159/136/124
May 2015 result Res Assoc of Cuddington 1304/1228/1165 C 971/937/878 Lab 589/586/484 LD 314
May 2011 result Res Assoc of Cuddington 1257/1246/1204 C 347/329/282 Lab 219/208 LD 120/120
May 2007 result Res Assoc of Cuddington 830/804/786 C 537/493/448 Lab 94/83/76 LD 85/78/75
May 2003 result Res Assoc of Cuddington 881/837/801 Lab 181/119/113 LD 142

Figure 110: Epsom and Ewell, Cuddington

as a volunteer marshal at a motor racing event organised by the British Automobile Racing Club. A car spun off the track into Foote and another marshal, and Foote died of his injuries at the scene. He was 67 years old. Tributes to him were led by the Formula 1 world champion Lewis Hamilton, who described volunteer marshals like Foote as "heroes" who make racing possible. Kent Police identified no suspicious circumstances and were working with BARC to provide a report for the coroner.

This by-election is to fill the seat left by Foote following his tragic death. Defending for the Residents Association of Cuddington is Graham Jones, a professional musician with a glittering former career in the Corps of Army Music: he retired from the Army in 2011 as senior director of music for the Household Division, with the rank of lieutenant-colonel and a military MBE.* Standing against Jones are Dan Brown for the Liberal Democrats (no, not that one; this Dan Brown works in the HR world), George Bushati for the Conservatives (who was runner-up here in the county elections in May), and Kevin Davies for Labour (who fought this ward in 2019).†

Exe Valley

East Devon council; caused by the resignation of Liberal Democrat councillor Fabian King.

We finish in the West Country with this week's rural ward. The Exe Valley ward of East Devon consists of seven parishes lying immediately to the north of Exeter. The largest of these, with 524 electors on the roll, is Stoke Canon, which lies between the River Exe to the west and the River Culm to the east. The

* Footage of Jones in action, directing the Band of the Coldstream Guards at his farewell concert from the Army in November 2011, is available at `youtu.be/whWtNiItytY`. † *Epsom and Ewell, Cuddington*: Res Assoc of Cuddington 585 Lab 207 C 135 LD 117

Parliamentary constituency: Central Devon (part: Brampford Speke, Huxham, Nether Exe, Rewe, Stoke Canon and Upton Pyne parishes), East Devon (part: Politmore parish)
Devon county council division: Broadclyst
May 2019 result LD 378 C 289

Figure 111: East Devon, Exe Valley

Great Western railway line runs through Stoke Canon, and stray cinders from a steam locomotive were responsible for a devastating fire here in 1847. (In an interesting link with the previous section, Stoke Canon was the location where George Boone III, grandfather of the American frontiersman Daniel Boone, was baptised.) The Exe and the Culm are in wide valleys here and have changed their meanders over the years, but the parish boundaries haven't been updated to match resulting in a number of places where the ward includes territory which is now cut off on the far side of the Exe.

The Exe Valley ward is rather out on a limb in a corner of East Devon district, which is based in Honiton and whose main focus is the towns and countryside to the east of Exeter. East Devon council was run by the Conservatives until 2019, when they lost their majority and an independent-led coalition took over. That coalition includes the Liberal Democrats, which makes Exe Valley ward something of a bellwether: it was held by the Conservatives until 2015, then gained by the Lib Dems (on revised boundaries, with the parish of Poltimore added) in the 2019 election. That election was a straight fight here between the Conservatives and Lib Dems, who won 57–43. The ward is part of the Broadclyst division of Devon county council, which split its two seats in May between the Green Party and the Conservatives.

East Devon has been going through a rash of by-elections recently: this is the fourth poll in the district this year. All of the previous three polls resulted in a change of party: the Conservatives picked up Whimple and Rockbeare ward in May (page 124) and Feniton in July (page 278) from independent councillors, and the Lib Dems resoundingly lost a by-election in Honiton St Michael's ward to Labour in July (also page 278).

None of those by-elections had any independent candidates, and that pattern continues here in the Exe Valley by-election which follows the resignation of Liberal Democrat councillor Fabian King. He has stepped down to focus on his business interests.

Defending for the Liberal Democrats is Jamie Kemp, an environmentalist, beekeeper, tailor and stay-at-home dad who was the party's candidate here in the Devon county elections four months ago. The Conservatives have reselected Kevin Wraight who lost here in 2019: by his own account he lives in Stoke Canon and is recently retired. There will be more choice for the electors here, as Michael Daniell completes the ballot paper for Labour.*

Tynwald

A special mention is also due to the Isle of Man. Today is the day of the Manx general election, with all 24 members of the House of Keys—the lower house of Tynwald—up for election. Man has the population of a smallish English district council and an electoral system to match: the island is divided into twelve constituencies, which each return two MHKs using multi-member first-past-the-post. The Isle of Man was the first polity in the world to enfranchise women—female property-owners have been able to vote here since 1881—but women's representation on the island has been slower to take off, with the last Manx general election in September 2016 setting a new record of 5 female MHKs. In that election independent candidates won 21 of the 24 seats, with the other three going to the Liberal Vannin party and Manx Labour being wiped out. There will be a new head of government after the election, as the Chief Minister Howard Quayle is retiring. A continued independent majority looks the most likely outcome.

* *East Devon, Exe Valley*: LD 190 C 164 Lab 161

Tuesday 28th September 2021

There are two by-elections, for three seats, on Tuesday 28th September:

Brundall; and Old Catton and Sprowston West

Broadland council, Norfolk. The double by-election in Brundall ward is caused by the resignations of Conservative councillors Rebecca Grattan and Michael Snowling. The by-election in Old Catton and Sprowston West ward is caused by the resignation of Samuel Walker.

Autumn is normally peak time for local by-elections, and the week ending 1st October is the busiest week so far this autumn with nine seats up for election. Three of these are polling on a Tuesday, because why not? It's only tradition that by-elections have to be on a Thursday; any working day will do, and sometimes some other day of the week might be more convenient for everyone involved. In this particular case, Tuesday polls will allow the winners of these by-elections to be in place for Broadland's full council meeting on Thursday. Don't wait up all night for the results, as the counts will start at 1000 on Wednesday morning.

So it is that we travel on a Tuesday to two wards on the edge of the city of Norwich, although that description is not immediately obvious for the Brundall ward. Brundall itself is a large village (with 3,504 electors on the roll) on the north bank of the River Yare downstream of Norwich, and the ward named after it also includes three other parishes on the Yare. The Wherry Lines railway between Norwich and Lowestoft links the ward together, with stations at Brundall Gardens, Brundall, Buckenham and Cantley. There's no railway station at Postwick, which is the main eastern point of entry for the Norwich built-up area and has a park-and-ride site for the city centre; Postwick is also the eastern terminus of the Broadland Northway, a dual-carriageway road around the north of Norwich which opened in 2018. The ward's major employers include the British Sugar factory at Cantley, which has been processing sugar beet for more than a century.

Before the railway was built in the nineteenth century the River Yare was the main mode of transport here. This is one of the main waterways of the Norfolk Broads, and is navigable as far as Norwich. Much of the low-lying ground around the river is part of the Broads national park, and there is a boundary oddity here. For centuries the harbour authority for the Yare has been Norwich city council, which controls the river all the way down to the confluence with the River Chet at Hardley Cross, and one result of that is that the Norwich city boundary includes the River Yare upstream of Hardley Cross. Accordingly, the southern boundary of this ward is not with South Norfolk district on the far side of the river, but with the city of Norwich.

Boundary oddities of a different kind apply to the Old Catton and Sprowston West ward, which is to all intents and purposes part of the built-up area of Norwich but has never been formally incorporated into the city. Old Catton was once an agricultural area—Anna Sewell wrote her novel *Black Beauty* here in the 1870s—but became fashionable among the Norwich business classes following the laying-out of Catton Park in the late 18th century. This was the first major work of the landscape gardener Humphrey Repton, who was commissioned by two-time Mayor of Norwich Jeremiah Ives in 1788 after Ives had taken over the brand-new stately home of Catton Hall. Catton Hall still stands today but has been split up into apartments; much of Catton Park has been turned into housing estates, but some of it survives as a public park to this day. The area has seen strong population growth this century, thanks to the building of more housing in the Sprowston West part of the ward.

The Parliamentary boundaries in Norwich are rather saner than the Norwich city boundary, and Old Catton and Sprowston West ward is firmly part of the Norwich North parliamentary constituency. This traditionally-marginal seat has been represented since a 2009 by-election by Chloe Smith, who was the junior minister responsible for the Elections Bill which has passed its second reading in the Commons and is currently at the committee stage. However, Smith was transferred to the DWP in the recent reshuffle. Presumably a new minister will be taking the Elections Bill over.

One recent piece of news regarding the Elections Bill is a government proposal to amend the bill to change the electoral system for local and combined authority mayors, and for police and crime commissioners. The idea is to move from the supplementary vote (which has always been used to elect these positions, and has been legislated for by both Conservative and Labour governments) to first-past-the-post. This column is old enough to remember when electoral system changes were seen as important enough to require a public referendum, so it's disappointing that the current government couldn't even bother to have such a proposal ready for the second reading of the Elections Bill. It's not an urgently-required change and it deserves to be properly considered in a second-reading debate. Although elections offices around the country will shudder at the thought of yet more legislation landing on their desks, perhaps having a separate bill for this electoral system change would be a neater way of doing things.

The supplementary vote has never been applied to elections of local councillors in England, which have always been first-past-the-post. On the current ward boundaries (which were introduced in 2004), both Brundall ward and Old Catton and Sprowston West ward have always returned Conservative councillors, usually with lots of room to spare. At the last Broadland elections in May 2019 the Conservative slate won Old Catton and Sprowston West with 47% of the vote, against 20% for the Liberal Democrats and 18% for Labour. This ward has the same boundaries as the Old Catton division of Norwich county council, which in May this year had a 60–24 Conservative lead over Labour in second place. In 2019 the Conservatives carried Brundall ward with 41% of the vote, with Labour and the Greens disputing second place on 22% each; Brundall ward is part of another safely-Conservative county council division (Blofield and Brundall).

The Old Catton and Sprowston West by-election is to replace Samuel Walker, a young man who was in his first term on the council having been elected in May 2019. He is moving away from Norwich to take up a new job.

Similar considerations apply to the outgoing Brundall ward councillor Rebecca Grattan, who was also first elected in May 2019. In February 2020 Grattan relocated to Prague to take up a new job with Avast, the Czech cybersecurity firm. She was able to keep her position on the council because the recent public health emergency forced council meetings to take place virtually; there has been some controversy over this, mainly because Grattan was still drawing councillor allowances, but if *everybody*'s dialling into meetings then realistically it makes little difference whether you're dialling in from the Norfolk Broads or the Czech Republic. Once the provisions for remote council meetings expired in May this year Grattan's position on Broadland council was no longer tenable, and she resigned at the end of July 2021.

Once that vacancy opened up, Brundall ward's other councillor Michael Snowling also took the opportunity to leave the stage. Snowling had represented this ward since 1998, and he was appointed MBE in January 2009 for services to children and young people in Norfolk. No reason was given for Snowling's resignation, but he has recently been reported to have been in poor health.

Defending the Brundall double by-election for the Conservatives are Tim Catmull and Michael Phelps. Catmull, who runs a children's shoe shop in

Parliamentary constituency: Broadland
Norfolk county council division: Blofield and Brundall
May 2019 result C 814/720 Lab 441/385 Grn 427/295 LD 304
May 2015 result C 1672/1420 Lab 782 LD 692 UKIP 606
May 2011 result C 1314/1208 Lab 407/334 Grn 305 LD 286/236
May 2007 result C 1174/1111 LD 238/139 Grn 225/116 Lab 206/185
June 2004 result C 1214/1196 LD 508 Lab 434/348

Figure 112: Broadland, Brundall

Parliamentary constituency: Norwich North
Norfolk county council division: Old Catton (same boundaries)
May 2021 county council result C 1420 Lab 580 Grn 227 LD 153
May 2019 result C 1024/985/962 LD 433/425/236 Lab 401/398/351 Grn 344
May 2017 county council result C 1356 Lab 418 LD 310
May 2015 result C 2107/2020/1661 Lab 1256/1017/901 UKIP 904 LD 528/483/300
May 2013 county council result C 796 UKIP 497 Lab 389 LD 362 Grn 119
July 2011 county council by-election C 664 LD 414 Lab 337 UKIP 107 Grn 75
May 2011 result C 1688/1493/1398 Lab 849/691 LD 439/350 UKIP 306
June 2009 county council result C 1206 UKIP 402 LD 334 Lab 267 Grn 262
May 2007 result C 1357/1288/1248 LD 574/553/529 Lab 480
May 2005 county council result C 1790 Lab 1456 LD 1019 Grn 217
June 2004 result C 1060/1022/1006 LD 779/753/692 Lab 497/477/439

Figure 113: Broadland, Old Catton and Sprowston West

Norwich, had contested the Buxton ward of Broadland in the 2019 district elections, finishing two votes short of gaining the seat from the Lib Dems; Phelps, who appears to be standing for election for the first time, should not be confused with the serial Olympic gold medal-winning swimmer of the same name. The Labour slate consists of Alice Free and Glenn Springett: Free was the runner-up here in the Broadland elections two years ago, while Springett was the runner-up here in the Norfolk county elections four months ago. On those occasions Free and Springett both finished one position ahead of the Green Party's Jan Davis, who returns for another go and is joined by running-mate Eleanor Laming. The Liberal Democrats put in nomination papers for three different candidates, but one of them has withdrawn leaving their slate of Eleanor Mason and Victor Scrivens to complete the Brundall ballot paper.*

The same four parties contest the Old Catton and Sprowston West by-election. Defending this seat for the Conservatives is Richard Potter, a former

* *Broadland, Brundall*: Grn 594 (Davis)/530 (Laming) C 480 (Catmull)/453 (Phelps) LD 425 (Mason)/303 (Scrivens) Lab 161 (Free)/137 (Springett) [2 Grn gains from C]

military man with a prosthetic leg to show for his service. The Lib Dems have selected John Chettleburgh, a biker and automotive engineer according to his Twitter. Standing for Labour is Martin Booth, a retired osteopath who sat on Norfolk county council from 1989 to 2001; at the time he represented the very rural area of North Walsham, in one of the last gasps of the strong agricultural vote which Labour used to enjoy in Norfolk. Completing an all-male candidate list in Old Catton and Sprowston West is Ian Chapman for the Green Party.*

* *Broadland, Old Catton and Sprowston West*: C 721 Lab 332 LD 278 Grn 110

30th September 2021

We have six by-elections to cover today, Thursday 30th September. This may have been Labour conference week, but the party has few obvious targets today with one seat to defend. There are three Conservative defences and one free-for-all to be discussed later, but we start in Kent with a seat the Liberal Democrats will be trying to get back...

Priory

Swale council, Kent; caused by the resignation of councillor Benjamin A Martin, who was elected for the Liberal Democrats but sitting as an independent.

It's the last day of September, and the big ship sails on the alley-alley-o; so it's appropriate to end the month by starting in an old port. On a creek off the Swale, which separates the Isle of Sheppey from the Kent coast, can be found the town of Faversham which was quite an important port back in the day. In mediaeval times Faversham was a junior member of the Cinque Ports, as a limb of Dover, and before that it was an important stopping-point on the Roman road from the Channel and Canterbury to Londinium. Many pilgrims would have passed through here on the way to Canterbury and the shrine of Thomas Becket.

In England, important mediaeval towns often had a religious institution or two, founded by and enjoying the patronage of kings and nobles. Faversham was particularly favoured by King Stephen, who founded the Cluniac Faversham Abbey in 1148, during the Anarchy. Stephen's wife Queen Matilda, who was countess of Boulogne in her own right, was buried in Faversham Abbey in 1152 and Stephen himself was interred there two years later. Unfortunately they are not lying in eternal rest: their graves were disturbed when Faversham Abbey was demolished, and a 1964 excavation found their tomb to be empty.

One of King Stephen's last acts was to found another religious house in Faversham. Davington Priory was established in 1153 as a nunnery, under the

Benedictine rule. The priory became defunct when its last nun died at the time of the dissolution of the monasteries, but some of its buildings survive today. The priory church's nave is still in use as a parish church, and part of the cloister was converted into a house which was bought in 1982 by Bob Geldof. Geldof was reportedly still living in Davington Priory in 2013, and his many honours include the freedom of the Borough of Swale, which the council awarded him in 1986.

The grounds of the former Davington Priory have long been swallowed up into the town of Faversham. In more modern times this area was the centre of the British explosives industry, but the gunpowder factories were all closed in the 1930s as they were too close to the Continent. That left brewing as the town's longest-standing industry: Shepherd Neame claims to be the UK's oldest brewery still in production, with an official foundation date of 1698.

Faversham is divided into four electoral wards, of which Priory is the northern one. The present ward was created by a boundary review in 2015 but has effectively the same boundaries as the Davington Priory ward which existed before then. In the 2011 census Davington Priory's population was 96.5% White British, which is nothing special on the national level but was the second-highest figure for any ward in Kent; the ward also has high levels of social renting and a working-class demographic profile.

This doesn't translate to a Labour-voting ward. Swale council does have a decent-sized Labour group these days, but most of the party's councillors represent wards in Sittingbourne or Sheerness. Instead, Faversham is the district's Liberal Democrat hotspot. The Lib Dems' Michael Henderson gained Davington Priory ward from the Conservatives in 2008, was re-elected as a Lib Dem in 2011, and won a third term in the renamed Priory ward in 2015 as an independent candidate without Lib Dem opposition. Henderson stood down in 2019 and his seat went back to his old party; the new Lib Dem candidate Benjamin A Martin won with a 52–29 lead over the Conservatives. I have given Martin's full name and middle initial here because there were two Faversham Lib Dem councillors both called Ben Martin, and the other one (who represents Watling ward, and is the leader of the council's Lib Dem group) is still *in situ*.

The 2019 Swale elections saw the Conservatives lose their majority, and a Labour-led rainbow coalition was put together to run the council. That coalition currently controls 25 seats on the council (10 Labour, 10 Swale Independents, 3 Lib Dems and 2 Greens) plus this vacancy, with the opposition consisting of 17 Conservatives, three independents and a councillor who was elected as UKIP and is now in Reform UK. There was a by-election in May in Sheerness ward (page 151), which the Conservatives gained from Labour; also in May we had the

Parliamentary constituency: Faversham and Mid Kent
Kent county council division: Faversham
May 2019 result LD 382 C 215 Lab 86 Grn 55
May 2015 result Ind 610 C 356 Lab 196 Grn 61
(Previous results for Davington Priory ward)
May 2011 result LD 360 C 256 Lab 145 Grn 60
May 2008 result LD 495 C 235 Lab 121
June 2004 result C 429 Lab 224
May 2002 result C 414 Lab 254

Figure 114: Swale, Priory

Kent county council elections, in which the Lib Dems increased their majority over the Conservatives in Faversham division.

Defending this by-election for the Lib Dems is Michael Henderson, who has extensive electoral experience in this ward: he first stood here in 1988 for what was then the Social and Liberal Democrats, and he represented Davington Priory from 1992 to 2000 and again from 2008 to 2019. As stated above, Henderson's last re-election was as an independent, but he is now back in the Lib Dem fold. He is up against another candidate with a long history in the ward: the Tories' Andy Culham, who lost here in 2011, 2015 and 2019 and was also the unsuccessful Conservative candidate for Faversham in May's county elections. Completing the ballot paper are Frances Rehal for Labour and Viv Moore for the Green Party.*

Horndean Downs

East Hampshire council; caused by the resignation of Conservative councillor Tony Denton.

For our other by-election in the South East we come to an area of much more recent vintage than Faversham. The village of Horndean can be found at the northern end of the Portsmouth-Havant urban area, running along the A 3 dual carriageway towards Petersfield and London. Horndean has seen large population growth in the last few decades, and some of this has been concentrated in a large and rather isolated housing development to the west of the A 3, north of the original village and running seamlessly into the village of Clanfield to the north. The dual carriageway forms a hard eastern boundary to the estate and ward, and the open ground on the far side of the A 3 is now part of the South Downs national park.

* *Swale, Priory*: LD 215 C 173 Grn 128 Lab 49

Parliamentary constituency: Meon Valley
Hampshire county council division: Catherington
May 2019 result C 425 Ind 151 Grn 128 LD 103

Figure 115: East Hampshire, Horndean Downs

This area became a ward of its own in 2003 under the name of Horndean Downs, having previously been associated with the village of Catherington to the west. Horndean Downs was Liberal Democrat at its first election in 2003, but the Conservatives gained the ward in 2007 by a 9-vote majority and have now made it safe. In May 2019, on slightly revised boundaries, Horndean Downs gave 53% to the new Conservative candidate Tony Denton, 19% to independent candidate David Alexander (who had also finished second here in 2015, on that occasion with the UKIP nomination) and 16% to the Green Party. Horndean Downs is part of the Conservative majority on both East Hampshire council and Hampshire county council; the local county division (Catherington) was safe Conservative in May.

This by-election is caused by the resignation of Tony Denton from East Hampshire council for the second time in five years. He had been elected in 2015 as a Conservative councillor for the neighbouring Clanfield and Finchdean ward, but didn't last a year before resigning due to pressure of work; a by-election for his previous seat was held in May 2016. Denton returned to East Hampshire council in 2019, representing this ward. Then in May 2021 he was elected to the neighbouring Havant council, gaining his seat from UKIP, and subsequently joined that council's cabinet. He has presumably stood down from East Hampshire council to concentrate on his new elected role.

Defending for the Conservatives is Jonathan Whtifield. Independent candidate David Alexander is back for another go after two second-place finishes. The Green Party have selected Blossom Gottlieb, a writer, podcaster and Petersfield town councillor, who completes the ballot paper.*

The Rows

West Suffolk council; caused by the death of independent councillor John Smith.

Last week Andrew's Previews was in the Cambridgeshire town of Soham, describing a by-election in Soham North ward (page 382) which the Conservatives eventually gained from the Liberal Democrats. We now turn to one of Soham North's neighbouring wards, over the county boundary in Suffolk, to see if the

* *East Hampshire, Horndean Downs*: Grn 320 C 291 Ind 40 [Grn gain from C]

Conservatives can gain that one too.

The eponymous Rows here are three villages to the west of Mildenhall: Beck Row, Holywell Row and West Row. The ward also takes in the village of Kenny Hill and a large area of fenland to the west. West Row has gone down in history as the place where the Mildenhall Treasure was discovered by a local farmer; this collection of Roman silver masterpieces can now be seen in the British Museum.

At the time of the 2011 census this area was part of the Eriswell and the Rows ward of what was then Forest Heath district. This ward had a very unusual census return. In 2011 Eriswell and the Rows ranked number 1 in England and Wales for people with non-UK qualifications, number 5 in England and Wales for the proportion of households living rent-free, made the top 20 wards in England and Wales for people born outside the UK or an EU country and for the White Other ethnic group, made the top 40 wards in England and Wales for "intermediate" occupations, and had the highest mixed-race population of any ward in the Eastern region (6.7%). This is the sort of return you'd expect to see in London or another city with a large immigrant population, not in rural Suffolk.

Well, the reason for this is not hard to seek. In between the Rows villages lies RAF Mildenhall, which for over sixty years has been on the front line of the Cold War and subsequent conflicts as the United States Air Force's main base in Britain. Since 1959 Mildenhall has been the main point of entry to the UK for American service personnel. Among its most recent arrivals was President Biden, who landed here in June on his way to the G7 summit in Cornwall and addressed US troops here.

RAF Mildenhall is a major local employer and its population dwarfs that of the Rows, but very few if any of the military personnel there will have the right to vote in this by-election. Instead it's the villagers who will decide this election in an area whose administrative boundaries have been subject to some flux in recent years. The whole of this ward was part of Mildenhall parish (hence the name "Mildenhall Treasure") until 1999, when Beck Row, Holywell Row and Kenny Hill declared independence. West Row also subsequently became a parish of its own, as recently as May 2019.

That May 2019 reorganisation also extended to the district council. From the 1970s the local authority had been Forest Heath, a district with a rather low population based on Mildenhall and Newmarket. Forest Heath district was effectively taken over by the neighbouring St Edmundsbury district in 2019, the two fusing into a new district with the name West Suffolk.

This merger went down pretty badly in the former Forest Heath area, which had been strongly Conservative: the wards covering that area returned a majority of independent councillors in May 2019. The Rows ward voted for an

Parliamentary constituency: West Suffolk
Suffolk county council division: Row Heath
May 2019 result Ind 636/467 C 402/306

Figure 116: West Suffolk, The Rows

independent slate of John Smith and Donald Waldron, who beat the Conservative slate 61–39 in a straight fight. Smith had contested the former Eriswell and the Rows ward in previous elections, with both the Lib Dem and West Suffolk Independent nominations (although not both at the same time).

Subsequent election results suggest that the Conservatives are well on the way to recovery here. They have performed well in a number of subsequent by-elections to West Suffolk council, including a gain from an independent in the neighbouring Lakenheath ward in May. This ward is covered by the Row Heath division of Suffolk county council, where the Conservatives had a big lead in May. Mind, the less said about the local Tory MP (Matt Hancock) the better.

This by-election arises from the death of John Smith, who passed away in June after a short but difficult illness. Smith was one of the major advocates of the new parish council for West Row, and he had hit the headlines in March last year with a campaign for the Mildenhall Treasure to be renamed as the West Row Treasure.

There is no independent candidate to replace John Smith, so we have a free-for-all! On paper the Conservatives look best-placed to gain The Rows ward, and their defending candidate has extensive local government experience. Matt Hancock's election agent Lance Stanbury served from 1995 to 2004 on Welwyn Hatfield council in Hertfordshire, and was leader of that council for two years; more recently he had sat on Forest Heath council from 2015 to 2019 for Red Lodge ward, serving in that council's cabinet until its abolition. Stanbury now lives in West Row and was on the defeated Conservative slate here in 2019. He is opposed by two candidates, Theresa Chipulina for Labour (who was a distant runner-up here in May's county council elections) and Robert Pinsker for the Liberal Democrats.*

Tutbury and Outwoods

East Staffordshire council; caused by the resignation of Conservative councillor Gary Raybould.

For our Midlands by-election we come to the valley of the River Dove. This forms an obvious communication link between the high ground of the Peak

* *West Suffolk, The Rows*: C 428 Lab 126 LD 102 [C gain from Ind]

District to the north and Needwood Forest to the south, and the main road and railway line from Stoke-on-Trent to Derby run through the Dove valley. However, the Dove is also a county and regional boundary: Derbyshire and the village of Hatton are located on the left bank, Staffordshire and the village of Tutbury on the right.

Overlooking the right bank of the Dove is what's left of Tutbury Castle, which in its original form dates back to the Norman Conquest. The first Tutbury Castle belonged to Henry de Ferrers, one of the Conqueror's leading Norman magnates who was rewarded with large amounts of land in Staffordshire and Derbyshire. His descendants became the first line of the Earls of Derby. As well as the castle, Henry also founded a Benedictine priory in Tutbury, part of whose church survives as the parish church; its west door retains a well-preserved Norman archway.

Tutbury Castle came into the hands of the Crown centuries ago and is still owned by the Duchy of Lancaster to this day. It was largely destroyed in the Civil War and never rebuilt. However, the damage to Tutbury Castle doesn't come close to what happened during the Second World War at RAF Fauld, a couple of miles to the west. Located just outside the present ward boundary, RAF Fauld was an underground depot used for storing munitions. At 11:11 on 27th November 1944 at least 3,500 metric tons of high explosive went up in the largest explosion ever on UK soil. The resulting crater, which obliterated a farm and a reservoir, is still visible today. The explosion and flooding are thought to have killed around 70 people, some of whom now lie in eternal rest in the churchyard at Tutbury.

The ward containing Tutbury extends to the south into the higher ground of Needwood Forest. The Outwoods part of the ward name refers to the parish of Outwoods, or more specifically to what's left of that parish after some of it was annexed by Burton upon Trent many years ago. Some recent development on the edge of Burton has spilled over into this ward.

This area is covered by East Staffordshire council, which is based in Burton but stretches west to take in the town of Uttoxeter and some associated countryside. Burton is traditionally quite a Labour town, but it's outvoted at local elections by Tory-voting Uttoxeter and the villages. Tutbury and Outwoods ward is part of the Tory majority on the council; at the most recent elections in May 2019 they had a 58–42 lead over Labour in a straight fight. The local county council division (Dove) is also safe Conservative.

District councillor Garry Raybould stood down in August, midway through his first term of office. Defending for the Conservatives in the resulting by-election is Russell Lock, the chair of Tutbury parish council; he is a lecturer in

Parliamentary constituency: Burton
Staffordshire county council division: Dove
May 2019 result C 935/856 Lab 683/627
May 2015 result C 1774/1502 Lab 963/782 UKIP 732 Grn 292
May 2011 result C 1266/1238 Lab 752/671
May 2007 result C 1275/1183 Lab 485/470
May 2003 result C 1207/1132 Lab 718/658 LD 292/270

Figure 117: East Staffordshire, Tutbury and Outwoods

computer science at Loughborough University. The opposition appears to have split: John Anderson, who was the Labour runner-up here in the 2015 and 2019 elections, is this time standing as an independent candidate while the official Labour candidate is Dale Barr. Completing the ballot paper is Lynn Furber for the Green Party.*

Penrith West

Eden council, Cumbria; caused by the resignation of Conservative councillor John Thompson.

We want the finest by-elections known to humanity, we want them here and we want them now. Let me oblige. Welcome to Penrith, the main town in the very sparsely-populated Eden district of Cumbria. This is the point where all the main communication links in eastern Cumbria meet: the main road and railway line between Carlisle to the north and Lancaster to the south cross the main road going west to Keswick and Workington and east to Scotch Corner.

All those roads lead to Penrith, a small but perfectly-formed market town which is the largest population centre for a long way in any direction. The Penrith West ward covers most of the town centre together with the railway station and points west along the road to Greystoke, including the industrial estate at Gilwilly.

In the 2011 census, Penrith West ward was in the top 100 in England and Wales for those employed in the wholesale and retail sector (23%) and for those with 5+ GCSE passes or equivalent but no higher qualification (19.9%, the highest figure for any ward in Cumbria).

Eden's ward map is one of the oldest in England, having been unchanged since the 1999 local elections. All of Penrith West's six ordinary elections since then have resulted in split representation. In 1999 the ward returned an independent councillor and a Labour representative; Labour gave up their seat in

* *East Staffordshire, Tutbury and Outwoods*: C 549 Ind 464 Lab 186 Grn 39

Parliamentary constituency: Penrith and the Border
Cumbria county council division: Penrith West
May 2019 result LD 283 C 159 Lab 154/108 UKIP 100
May 2015 result LD 571 C 545 Lab 475
May 2011 result LD 488 C 318 BNP 94
October 2009 by-election LD 387 C 157 BNP 102 Ind 58 Lab 26 Grn 18
May 2007 result Ind 324 C 276 Lab 116
May 2003 result Ind/C unopposed
May 1999 result Ind 264 Lab 147/121

Figure 118: Eden, Penrith West

2003 and it went to the Conservatives' John Thompson, who won without a contest. The ward's independent councillor Colin Nineham, who was leader of the council at the time, resigned in 2009 after being arrested on suspicion of fraud at a recycling company he ran, and the resulting by-election was won by the Liberal Democrats.

Since then the ward has had one Lib Dem and one Conservative councillor, with both parties seemingly content not to challenge the other for a full slate. May 2019 was a poor election for the Eden Conservatives, and John Thompson kept his seat with a majority of just five votes over Labour; shares of the vote were 41% for the Lib Dems, 23% for the Conservatives and 22% for Labour. Eden council has been run since 2019 by a rainbow anti-Conservative coalition, with Penrith West ward's Lib Dem councillor Virginia Taylor serving as leader of the council. The Penrith West county council division, which also takes in the Penrith South district ward, is Conservative-held; however, the 2021 Cumbria county council elections were cancelled pending a reorganisation of the county's local government.

This by-election is defended by the Conservatives following the retirement of John Thompson after 18 years' service. With the party starting from second place in the ward this may be an uphill struggle for their defending candidate Dale Normington. The Lib Dems have selected Roger Burgin, an accountant and Penrith town councillor. Labour's Dave Knaggs, who lost out here by five votes in 2019, is standing again; he is also a Penrith town councillor. Also standing are Jonathan Davies for the localist slate Putting Cumbria First, Richard O'Brien for the Green Party and independent candidate Jeff Thomson, a PR copywriter and campaigner against smells from an animal byproducts processing plant in the ward.*

* *Eden, Penrith West*: LD 173 C 87 Ind 51 Lab 40 Putting Cumbria First 28 Grn 19 [LD gain from C]

Hetton

Sunderland council, Tyne and Wear; caused by the death of Labour councillor Doris Turner.

We finish for the week in the north-east with our Labour defence, on the Durham coalfield. The village of Hetton-le-Hole was described as "a close-knit community where coal was king and football was religion" by the great Liverpool manager Bob Paisley, who was born here in 1919. Deep mining in Hetton had started here a century before that with the sinking of Hetton Colliery's first shaft.

Hetton has an unusual distinction in transport history. The colliery owners decided to export their coal by building a waggonway to cover the eight miles from Hetton to the River Wear. To build it they commissioned George Stephenson, who had already done something similar for the colliery at Killingworth in Northumberland. Stephenson's resulting railway, opened in 1822, was the first in the world that used no animal power; the wagons were hauled by locomotives on the level stretches and by gravity down the inclines. His locomotives, as on the Killingworth waggonway, had wheels 4 feet 8 inches apart, which (with the addition of an extra half-inch) remains to this day the standard gauge for most of the world's railways.

Football might still be the religion in Hetton-le-Hole (Steph Houghton, the England and Manchester City women's team captain, went to school here), but coal is no longer king. The last pit here, Eppleton Colliery, closed in 1986 and most of the spoil tips have been landscaped. The legacy of coal has left its mark on the census return, with Hetton ward just creeping into the top 100 wards in England and Wales for those born in the UK (98.3%), but this is now for the most part a post-industrial landscape.

Hetton ward is the southernmost ward in the county of Tyne and Wear, and has been part of Sunderland city council since the 1970s. Its current boundaries were introduced in 2004, and the ward has voted Labour at every election since. This record has been maintained despite a number of strong challenges from UKIP, who came close to winning in 2012, 2014 and 2019 when the anti-Labour vote was split a number of ways. Labour councillor Doris Turner was lucky to be re-elected that year for a second term on just 33% of the vote.

Labour put in some appalling election results generally in Sunderland in 2019 and 2021, and their majority is now down to 41 seats out of 75, plus this vacancy; there are 19 Conservatives, 12 Lib Dems and 2 Wearside Independent councillors, who were originally elected on the UKIP ticket. Mind, in Hetton ward Labour's May 2021 result was a lot better than two years previously: they improved their vote share to 45%, against 20% for independent candidate David

Parliamentary constituency: Houghton and Sunderland South
May 2021 result Lab 1258 Ind 554 C 545 UKIP 313 Grn 81 LD 63
May 2019 result Lab 990 UKIP 854 Ind 642 Democrats and Veterans 208 C 168 Grn 111
May 2018 result Lab 1480 Ind 799 C 358 Grn 74 LD 54
May 2016 result Lab 1531 UKIP 1037 C 159 Ind 135 LD 92
May 2015 result Lab 2544 UKIP 1617 C 435 LD 154
May 2014 result Lab 1470 UKIP 1351 C 188 LD 75
May 2012 result Lab 1628 UKIP 1363 LD 154
May 2011 result Lab 1940 UKIP 956 C 239 LD 167
May 2010 result Lab 2465 LD 966 C 575 BNP 389
May 2008 result Lab 1843 C 821
May 2007 result Lab 1506 LD 489 BNP 402 C 328
May 2006 result Lab 1364 BNP 544 C 494
June 2004 result Lab 1670/1663/1413 LD 920 C 676 BNP 442

Figure 119: Sunderland, Hetton

Geddis and 19% for the Conservatives.

This by-election follows the death of councillor Doris Turner at the age of 81. Turner had served on Sunderland city council since 2015, and had also been Mayor of Hetton. Away from politics she was a Sunderland FC fan, and could often be seen at the Eppleton Colliery Welfare Ground in Hetton selling raffle tickets at Sunderland Reserves matches.

Defending for Labour is Iain Scott, a Hetton town councillor. Independent town councillor David Geddis is having another go after finishing as runner-up in 2018 and in May this year. The Conservatives have selected Adelle Burnicle, a primary school teacher. Also standing are Justine Merton-Scott for the Green Party, John Lennox for the Lib Dems and Maurice Allen junior, who is standing as an independent candidate.*

* *Sunderland, Hetton*: Lab 661 LD 634 Geddis 386 C 303 Allen 67 Grn 41

7th October 2021

There are seven by-elections on 7th October 2021. It's Tory conference week, and that party is on the front foot in the sense that they are not defending in any of the polls today. There are four Lib Dem seats up for election in Taunton, Surrey and greater Nottingham, in at least some of which the Conservatives might fancy their chances, and there is a wildcard Independent versus Labour contest in north Wales. But we start in England, in Nottingham proper, with two safe Labour defences...

St Ann's; and Sherwood

Nottingham council; caused respectively by the resignations of Labour councillors Chantal Lee and Lauren O'Grady.

Welcome to Nottingham, one of the three cities that vie for primacy over the East Midlands. Like many places north of the Trent, Nottingham boomed during the industrial revolution as a textile centre, specialising in the manufacture of lace. Also like many places north of the Trent, this led to rather a lot of poor-quality housing being built, much of which has now been redeveloped.

The patron saint of lace makers is St Anne, and a district of nineteenth-century housing north-east of the city centre for the working poor of Nottingham was named after her. St Ann's has always been a poor area of Nottingham, and in the postwar period this led to a large number of Caribbean immigrants to Nottingham being housed here. There were race riots in St Ann's in August 1958.

There has been a lot of redevelopment here as you might have seen from the acclaimed 2006 film *This Is England*, much of which was filmed in St Ann's. The slum terraces have been replaced by new council estates, but the area is still at the wrong end of the deprivation indices and the demographic profile remains highly multicultural more than six decades after the St Ann's riots. In the 2011 census St Ann's ward (which then had slightly different boundaries) was number 2 of all the wards in England and Wales for mixed-race population, at 9.9%.* St Ann's also had the highest black population (13.9%) of any ward in the East Midlands. Nearly half of all the ward's households are socially rented. As well as St Ann's itself, the current ward boundaries take in part of the city centre including the Victoria Centre, a 1970s shopping mall built on the site of the former Nottingham Victoria railway station.

Nottingham's Sherwood ward lies a mile or two north of the city centre, along the main road towards Mansfield. This ward takes in Nottingham City Hospital, a teaching hospital run by Nottingham University which is a major centre for cancer care and shoulder surgery.

Both of these wards form part of the Nottingham East parliamentary constituency, which is currently represented by the Baby of the House Nadia Whittome. Whittome was born in Nottingham in August 1996, which makes her now 25 years old, and is of mixed immigrant stock herself: her father is a Punjabi Sikh, her mother an Anglo-Indian Catholic. She was elected in December 2019 with a large majority in what is currently a safe Labour seat: the previous Labour MP Chris Leslie, who had defected to Change UK, lost his deposit seeking re-election under his new banner.

In local elections, the city of Nottingham (which, as we shall see, only covers a fraction of the city's urban area) has swung a long way to the left over the last decade. Sherwood ward split its seats betwen two Labour and one Conservative councillor in 2003, but the Tories lost that seat in a by-election later that year. It's now as safe as St Ann's, whose vote shares change little from year to year.

Both outgoing councillors were first elected in 2019 and resigned just over halfway through their first terms of office. Councillor O'Grady of Sherwood ward was one of a number of Nottingham councillors who formed the board of Robin Hood Energy, a not-for-profit energy supplier which the council had set up in 2015. Robin Hood Energy inspired a number of other copycat municipal utility firms, all of which—given the cash-starved state of our local government—ran into financial trouble well before the current headwinds in the energy supply market. Nottingham council was eventually forced to close Robin Hood Energy down in September 2020, with the company's customer accounts being sold to British Gas.

On revised boundaries at the May 2019 election, both St Ann's and Sherwood wards gave 65% to the Labour slate and 14% to their nearest challengers—an independent in St Ann's, the Conservatives in Sherwood. Labour won a clean

* Number 1 was Princes Park ward in Liverpool, or in other words Toxteth: see *Andrew's Previews 2019*, page 321.

sweep of all 50 Nottingham city council seats north of the Trent, with the five councillors for the isolated Clifton estate splitting three to an independent slate and two to the Conservatives.

Before turning to the candidate lists, we should pay tribute to one candidate who is not standing this time. David Bishop has been entertaining the returning officers of Nottingham and other areas for many years as a perennial election candidate, being one of those people who are prepared to fill out the paperwork and (in the case of a Parliamentary election) hand over £500 in order to get their picture on the TV from an election count while wearing fancy dress. The name of Bishop's registration with the Electoral Commission—"Church of the Militant Elvis Party"—gives you an idea of what his fancy dress costume is. Time waits for none of us, and if you are old enough to remember Elvis Presley performing live you are now in a dwindling minority of the UK's population. Bishop has recently passed the age of 75, and after a number of entertaining by-election campaigns over the last 24 years it would appear that he has finally decided to hang up his blue suede shoes. He never came anywhere near winning any of those contests, although he did notoriously once finish ahead of the Lib Dems in a by-election to Nottingham city council.*

With Elvis having left the ballot, the voters in the St Ann's and Sherwood by-elections will both have six candidates to choose from. In St Ann's the defending Labour candidate is former Nottingham city councillor Corall Jenkins, who represented Clifton South ward from 2015 to 2019; Clifton South was abolished in boundary changes that year, and Jenkins lost re-election in the new Clifton East ward to the Nottingham Independents slate. That party have selected Franceso Lari to stand against Jenkins; Lari is a parish councillor for St Albans parish, just outside the Nottingham city limits on the northern edge of the built-up area, and he runs an IT company. Also standing are Ngoc Thanh Tran for the Conservatives, James Housley for the Lib Dems, Florence Chadwick for the Trade Unionist and Socialist Coalition, and Barbara Coulson for the Green Party.†

The defending Labour candidate in Sherwood ward also has previous experience in local elections. Nayab Patel has recently moved to the city from Redditch in Worcestershire, and she was a Labour candidate for Redditch council in 2016, 2018 (losing a seat Labour were defending) and 2019. The Conservatives start second here and they have selected Alfie Pryor, who is described as having a wide background of experience in catering, the care sector and community work. The

---

* Elvis subsequently got in touch with this column, indicating that he is ready for a Comeback Special if this is necessary in the national interest. You heard it here first.

† *Nottingham, St Ann's*: Lab 1048 Nottingham Ind 204 C 193 Grn 92 LD 40 TUSC 24

Parliamentary constituency: Nottingham East
May 2019 result Lab 1990/1900/1838 Ind 434 C 335/329/252 LD 322

Figure 120: Nottingham, St Ann's

Parliamentary constituency: Nottingham East
May 2019 result Lab 2773/2715/2634 C 599/556/481 LD 529/490/406 UKIP 372/365/357

Figure 121: Nottingham, Sherwood

other four candidates are Alison Rouse for the Lib Dems, Colin Barratt for the Nottingham Independents, Catriona Sibert for the Green Party and Geraint Thomas for the Trade Unionist and Socialist Coalition.*

Musters

Rushcliffe council, Nottinghamshire; caused by the resignation of Liberal Democrat councillor Annie Major.

We now travel over the Trent to the southern end of Nottingham's built-up area. Despite being the home of Nottingham Forest FC and Nottinghamshire county cricket club, West Bridgford—on the south side of the Trent Bridge—has never been incorporated into Nottingham and has always remained an independent town. This is a strongly middle-class area favoured by Nottingham's professional classes, and in the 2011 census all of the top three wards in the East Midlands for people with degree-level qualifications were in West Bridgford. One of them is Musters ward.

Located in the south of the town, Musters ward is named after the Musters family, who owned much of the town—including the Trent Bridge cricket ground—until the First World War. The family placed strict restrictions on the housing along Musters Road when it was built, with tree-lined streets, minimum bedroom numbers and constraints on housing density. You can see why this has become a middle-class enclave. A majority of the ward's workforce are in managerial or professional occupations, and Musters is in the top 75 in England and Wales (and number 2 in the East Midlands) for the ONS' higher managerial and professional employment category.

The fact that the local secondary school is rather good helps this image too. The Rushcliffe Spencer Academy (recently renamed from "Rushcliffe School") regularly comes near the top of the annual league tables for comprehensive schools, and its former pupils include one current MP (the South Yorkshire

* *Nottingham, Sherwood*: Lab 1174 Nottingham Ind 629 C 320 Grn 195 TUSC 76 LD 63

Parliamentary constituency: Rushcliffe
Nottinghamshire county council division: West Bridgford West (part west of Musters Road), West Bridgford South (part east of Musters Road)
May 2019 result LD 917/873 C 379/311 Lab 320/278
May 2015 result LD 1209/1158 C 814/723 Lab 596/586

Figure 122: Rushcliffe, Musters

mayor Dan Jarvis), the *Sun* editor Victoria Newton (whose father served as deputy headmaster of the school), and a number of recent Olympic gymnasts.

This ward has been in Liberal Democrat hands since 2007. At the most recent elections to Rushcliffe council in May 2019 the Liberal Democrat slate had 57% of the vote, well ahead of the second-placed Conservatives on 23%. The ward is split between two divisions of Nottinghamshire county council, both of which remained in Conservative hands after May's county elections. The Labour candidate for West Bridgford West in the May 2017 county elections was Nadia Whittome, in her first election campaign; four years on, her successor got a swing towards Labour which has turned the division marginal. None of Musters ward is in a marginal Parliamentary seat, though: Ken Clarke represented West Bridgford, as part of the Rushcliffe constituency, in the Tory interest for 49 years and his successor Ruth Edwards has a safe enough seat for now. Rushcliffe council also has a Conservative majority.

The Musters ward by-election follows the resignation of Lib Dem councillor Annie Majors, who had served since 2019 and was in her first term of office. She is relocating with her family to Switzerland.

Defending for the Liberal Democrats is Vicky Price, who runs an IT consultancy business: as a cricket fan, it's appropriate that she contested her home Trent Bridge ward in May 2019. The Conservatives' Paul Coe, a retired chemist, has also previously contested Trent Bridge ward, in 2003 and 2015; he is looking to return to Rushcliffe council after many years away, having previously represented the town's Lady Bay ward between 1983 and 1991. Completing the ballot paper is Julie Chaplain for Labour.*

Penyffordd

Flintshire council, North Wales; caused by the death of independent councillor Dave Williams.

For our wildcard this week we travel to north Wales, a few miles to the southwest of Chester. Penyffordd—"the summit of the road"—is a largish village on

* *Rushcliffe, Musters*: LD 557 Lab 353 C 320

the road between Wrexham and Queensferry, in the Alyn valley. The valley forms an obvious communication link given the high ground of the Clwydian range to the west, and Penyffordd retains a railway station on the Borderlands line between Wrexham and the Wirral.

The Penyffordd ward runs along the main road to the north to take in the villages of Penymynydd and Dobs Hill, the latter lying on the busy A 55 road through North Wales. The ward is in the top 10 wards in Wales for Apprenticeship qualifications, which is almost certainly driven by the nearby presence of the Airbus factory at Broughton. This employs 6,000 people making wings for Airbus commercial aircraft, and underpins the economy of this part of Flintshire.

This by-election could be crucial for control of Flintshire council. This has been hung since 2008, but the 2017 elections left Labour close to a majority with 34 seats; they run the council as a minority against 24 independents (plus this vacancy), six Conservatives and five Lib Dems. A gain in this by-election would give Labour half of the seats on the council.

Penyffordd's local elections tend not to be exciting ones. Flintshire's ward boundaries were last reviewed for the 1999 local elections, and ever since then the ward has returned one Labour councillor and one independent. No party other than Labour has stood here in that timeframe. The late Dave Williams had served since 2008, when he gained his seat from independent councillor Colin Bithell by 7 votes; the result that year gave 630 votes to new Labour councillor Cindy Hinds, 629 to Williams and 622 to Bithell. Williams increased his majority over Bithell to 201 votes in 2012, and that was the last contested election here. Nobody opposed Hinds and Williams at the last Welsh local elections in 2017, at which Penyffordd division's boundaries were realigned to match changes to the community boundaries in the area. The Flintshire 2017 map available from the Local Elections Archive Project hasn't been updated for this, and continues to show the old lines.

That electoral history is rather unusual, given this ward's presence in a marginal Parliamentary seat. Alyn and Deeside has had only three MPs, all Labour, since it was created in 1950 under the name of East Flintshire; but Mark Tami, the last remaining Labour MP in North Wales, won his sixth term of office in December 2019 with a majority of just 213 votes over Conservative candidate Sanjoy Sen. (Your columnist has since had the pleasure of playing quiz against Sen: he knows his stuff.) This column extensively previewed Alyn and Deeside for the Senedd by-election there in February 2018*: Jack Sergeant, who held that by-election for Labour following the suicide of his father, was re-elected as the constituency's MS in May by the convincing margin of 4,378.

* *Andrew's Previews 2018*, pages 38 to 46.

Parliamentary and Senedd constituency: Alyn and Deeside
May 2017 result Lab/Ind unopposed
May 2012 result Lab 812 Ind 563/362
May 2008 result Lab 630 Ind 629/622
June 2004 result Ind 694 Lab 693/446
May 1999 result Ind 758/607 Lab 696/451

Figure 123: Flintshire, Penyffordd

However, yet again we have a Penyffordd contest which is entirely Labour versus Independent. There are three competing independent candidates seeking to take over Williams' seat, all of whom are Penyffordd community councillors. To take them in ballot paper order, Pat Ransome has been on the community council on and off since the 1990s and she is a school governor at Ysgol Penyffordd; Steve Saxon is a former professional wrestler who works as a wrestling promoter and as general manager of the Red Lion in Penyffordd; and Roy Wakelam is the vice-chairman of the community council for 2021–22. Hoping to come through the middle of all this is community councillor Alasdair Ibbotson, who already has a parliamentary campaign under his belt: Ibbotson was the Green candidate for Alyn and Deeside in the 2015 general election, when he was 20 years old, but six years on he is now firmly in the Labour camp.*

Cranleigh East

Waverley council, Surrey; caused by the resignation of Liberal Democrat councillor Richard Cole.

We now move to the Home Counties to consider one claimant for the hotly-contested title of "largest village in England". Located around seven miles south of Guildford, Cranleigh parish contains around 11,000 souls most of whom live in Cranleigh itself. The ward is a centre for the local area but has few major industries: agriculture (in the form of plant nurseries) and the independent Cranleigh School form large parts of the local economy. Cranleigh is one of Surrey's more remote areas, lying away from the main roads and with Beeching having closed the local railway station many years ago.

The Cranleigh East ward contains most of the village and returns three members of Waverley council, which is named after Waverley Abbey and covers the towns to the west and south of Guildford. Farnham and Godalming are its main population centres. This district and the neighbouring Guildford district saw extraordinarily high Conservative losses in tha May 2019 local elections. In

* *Flintshire, Penyffordd*: Lab 437 Saxon 286 Ransome 283 Wakelam 163 [Lab gain from Ind]

2015 the Conservatives had won 53 seats on Waverley council out of a possible 57; four years later they crashed to 23 seats, with 15 going to the Farnham Residents slate, 14 to the Liberal Democrats, 2 each to Labour and the Green Party and one to an independent. The independent councillor died shortly afterwards and the resulting by-election in February 2020 returned another independent candidate*. All the non-Conservative councillors have formed a coalition to run the council.

Cranleigh East ward had a bit of a Lib Dem tradition from when that party had a majority on this council back in the Noughties. In 2003 the ward returned split representation of two Lib Dem councillors and one Conservative; the Lib Dems held their seat at a by-election in July 2004 and gained the Conservative seat in 2007. The Tories subsequently won a full slate in 2011 and 2015, on the latter occasion with a 45–25 lead over the Liberal Democrats (an independent finished third with 16%). So the 2019 result was a bit of a turnaround: the Lib Dem slate polled 45% and gained two seats from the Conservatives, who polled 39% and held one seat.

Subsequent results have shown that this was not a flash in the pan. Cranleigh is part of the Guildford parliamentary seat, which saw a large swing to the Liberal Democrats in December 2019 and is now firmly in the marginal column. Matters on the Tory side were not helped by the outgoing Conservative MP for Guildford Anne Milton being thrown out of the party for voting in Parliament against a no-deal Brexit; Milton stood for re-election as an independent, and saved her deposit. Then, in the Surrey county council elections five months ago the Liberal Democrats narrowly gained the Cranleigh and Ewhurst division from the Conservatives. That seat had previously been safe Tory, and from 2009 to 2011 its county councillor was Jonathan Lord who is now the MP for Woking.

This by-election follows the resignation of Lib Dem district councillor Richard Cole, who had been the losing runner-up here in the 2017 county council elections. Cole has reportedly relocated to Devon. Like nearly all the ruling councillors in Waverley, he was in his first term on the council.

The candidate list for the by-election reveals a straight fight. Defending in the yellow corner is Philip Townsend, who runs a gardening firm and is the husband of the ward's newly-elected county councillor Liz Townsend. Challenging from the blue corner is Rosemary Burbridge, a teacher who represents the ward on Cranleigh parish council.†

I can't leave Cranleigh without mentioning some music. One of the most prolific composers you've never heard of, Derek Bourgeois (1941–2017), attended Cranleigh School and later became a music teacher there. For his first wedding in 1965 Bourgeois composed his *Serenade*, a lovely piece of music which was

* *Andrew's Previews 2020*, page 37. † *Waverley, Cranleigh East*: LD 903 C 686

Parliamentary constituency: Guildford
Surrey county council division: Cranleigh and Ewhurst
May 2019 result LD 779/702/664 C 678/648/610 Lab 280
May 2015 result C 1652/1600/1570 LD 901/879/831 Ind 600 Lab 509/490
May 2011 result C 1219/1201/970 LD 850/804/745 Lab 394/387
May 2007 result LD 1237/1173/1170 C 1121/1093/1031
July 2004 by-election LD 936 C 855 Lab 156
May 2003 result LD 1029/975/884 C 915/836/803 Lab 228/210/189

Figure 124: Waverley, Cranleigh East

designed to be impossible to march to and therefore is rather a test for a military band. Bourgeois's *Serenade* is on the programme for your columnist's military band in our first concert back this weekend: if you can get to All Saints Church, Hindley, Wigan on Saturday night for 7:30pm, we'd love to see you in the audience.

Comeytrowe and Trull

Somerset county council; and

Wilton and Sherford

Somerset West and Taunton council; both caused by the death of Liberal Democrat councillor Alan Wedderkopp.

We finish the week with yet another visit to the district of Somerset West and Taunton. This is getting beyond a joke, now. Somerset West and Taunton council has only existed for two-and-a-half-years, and this is the sixth by-election that has been held to it and the fourth this year. There are some councils out there that haven't yet got to six by-elections so far this century. Sort it out, please.

Anyway, we're in the Somerset county council division of Comeytrowe and Trull. Trull parish covers the rural area immediately to the south of Taunton, but most of the division's electors live in 1970s and 1980s estates on the southern fringe of Taunton. Although this is an integral part of the Taunton urban area, only the area of Wilton and Sherford ward (the north-east corner of the division) is actually part of Taunton proper. Instead the majority of the electors live in the parish of Comeytrowe, which was created in 1986 from an area previously included in Trull parish.

At the time of the 2011 census, this area was covered by two-and-a-half wards of what was then Taunton Deane district: Comeytrowe, Trull, and the southern half of Taunton Manor and Wilton. Both Comeytrowe, and Manor and Wilton wards made the top 50 wards in England and Wales for those employed in human health and social work activities: many of those will work at Musgrove Park Hospital, the largest acute hospital in Somerset, which is just outside the boundary. Manor and Wilton ward also made the top 60 wards in England and Wales for population aged 85 or over, which is surprising to say the least given that it included much of the town centre; presumably the boundaries took in an unusually large number of nursing homes.

In Taunton Deane district elections this century Comeytrowe ward was consistently Lib Dem, Manor and Wilton was consistently Conservative (although not all of it was in this division), and Trull was strongly Conservative but had a small electorate. The Comeytrowe and Trull county division was created in 2013 as a cut-down version of the former Taunton and Trull division, which was a rather curiously drawn Conservative-held marginal; by contrast, in its two elections to date Comeytrowe and Trull has been a Lib Dem-held marginal. Alan Wedderkopp was re-elected for a second term in May 2017 with a 48–40 lead over the Conservatives; the May 2021 county elections were cancelled pending another reorganisation of Somerset's local government.

That reorganisation may mean that the 2019 Somerset West and Taunton election proves to be the only ordinary election to that council. The 2017 and 2019 results for this area form quite a contrast. In May 2019 the Liberal Democrats rather unexpectedly won a majority, with 30 seats against 14 independents, just 10 Conservatives, 3 Labour and 2 Greens. Comeytrowe parish was included in a ward with Bishop's Hull, which returned an independent and two Lib Dems; Trull parish was included in a large rural ward with Pitminster and Corfe, which surprisingly returned two Lib Dems; and the brand-new ward of Wilton and Sherford returned the Lib Dems' Alan Wedderkopp with a 68–32 majority over the Tories in a straight fight. The Lib Dems subsequently gained two seats in by-elections[*], and also held Trull, Pitminster and Corfe ward in a by-election held on 6th May this year[†]. However, they have also suffered from defections, and if the Wilton and Sherford by-election is lost their overall majority will be gone.

Frederick Alan Wedderkopp died in July at the age of 89. He had a long and varied life. Wedderkopp was brought up in North Shields where his father was a docker, served in the Korean War (although he never saw action), and spent most of his career in the oil industry, ending up supervising the running of entire rigs in the North Sea. After leaving the rigs he ended up in Taunton as a taxi driver, got into politics and served as a Lib Dem councillor for a total of eighteen years.

[*] *Andrew's Previews 2019*, pages 284 and 311. [†] Page 119.

Parliamentary constituency: Taunton Deane
Somerset and West and Taunton wards: Wilton and Sherford; Comeytrowe and Bishop's Hull (part); Trull, Pitminster and Corfe (part); Vivary (part)
May 2017 result LD 1790 C 1496 Lab 219 Grn 132 UKIP 128
May 2013 result LD 1498 C 1164 UKIP 713 Lab 243 Grn 139

Figure 125: Somerset CC, Comeytrowe and Trull

Parliamentary constituency: Taunton Deane
Somerset county council division: Comeytrowe and Trull
May 2019 result LD 692 C 320

Figure 126: Somerset West and Taunton, Wilton and Sherford

Defending Wedderkopp's county council seat is Dawn Johnson, who won the district by-election for Trull, Pitminster and Corfe ward in May and now has the chance to double up at district and county council level. For how long, who knows? Ruth Harmon also has the chance to double up as she is the Conservative candidate for both the county and district by-elections; she is involved with the Wilton and Sherford Community Association. Completing the county ballot paper is Michael McGuffie for Labour.*

A different set of three parties contest the Wilton and Sherford by-election for the district council. Here the defending Lib Dem candidate is Tom Deakin, a digital consultant who has recently moved to Taunton from Exeter. As stated Ruth Harmon is the Conservative candidate, and also standing for the district ward is Fran Hicks for the Green Party.†

Croydon governance referendum

This column omitted to preview it at the time, but a referendum was held in Croydon on 7th October on whether the council should move to the directly-elected mayoral system. Croydon council has been effectively bankrupted by underwriting a town centre redevelopment which fell through, leaving the council responsible for huge amounts of office and shopping space in the town centre which is lying empty (because all the tenants were moved out in advance of the redevelopment) and consequently isn't generating the rent that was budgeted for.

The result showed a huge vote in favour of changing to the mayoral system: 47,165 in favour versus 11,519 against, a clear mark of popular disgust with the

* *Somerset CC, Comeytrowe and Trull*: LD 1677 C 886 Lab 92 † *Somerset West and Taunton, Wilton and Sherford*: LD 489 C 314 Grn 57

present Labour administration. This may have implications for control of the council, as Croydon is often close in vote terms between Labour and the Conservatives but is a polarised borough with very few marginal wards. The 2018 election gave Labour a 41–29 seat lead on a vote lead of 43.9–39.5, and previous Croydon elections (most recently in 2002) have seen wrong-winner results. A mayoral election here would give many more Croydon voters a chance of affecting the outcome.

The first Croydon mayoral election will be held in May 2022, alongside the next London borough elections.

14th October 2021

There are four by-elections on 14th October 2021, with something for everyone. There is one defence for each of the three main English parties, and a Labour seat up for election in Scotland. That will come last in this week's Previews; instead we start by discussing a Conservative seat in outer London. Read on...

Pinner South

Harrow council, London; caused by the death of Conservative councillor Chris Mote.

We start the week in Greater London by taking a trip along the Metropolitan Line to Pinner. This is the heart of Metroland, that quadrant of north-west London which was aggressively developed by the Metropolitan Railway in the inter-war era and which provided the railway with a secure commuter base. Most of the housing in Pinner South ward dates from the 1930s, and the area is no longer the Middlesex village it once was but instead part of the urban sprawl, although the green belt is not so far away.

These nice suburban houses remain sought-after nearly a century after they were built. Pinner South's census return shows nearly half of the ward's workforce in professional or managerial occupations, and all of the ward's census districts are in the 20% least-deprived in England and Wales. The list of famous people who were born in Pinner includes the astronomer Patrick Moore, the children's author Michael Rosen and the global pop star Sir Elton John; but the long list of local worthies also attests to the fact that this is a place celebrities tend to come to as well as come from.

In recent years inner Metroland has come a major centre for London's Indian community, by which I mean here people of specifically Indian heritage rather than subcontinental heritage in general. Pinner is on the edge of this area, and Pinner South ward is not dominated by residents born in India or speaking Indian languages. However, this ward is in the top 50 in England and Wales for

Hinduism (19.0%) and miscellaneous other religions (1.8%) and was also in the top 90 for Judaism (4.7%) at the time of the 2011 census.

The present Pinner South ward was created in 2002 and has similar boundaries to the Pinner West ward which existed from 1978 to 2002. With the exception of a Liberal Democrat victory in 1994, the Conservatives have won every election here since 1978 and usually quite comfortably so. At the last London borough elections in May 2018 the Conservatives had a 57–26 lead over Labour, who have run second here since 2010. The ward is included within the parliamentary seat of Ruislip, Northwood and Pinner, which is safely Conservative too.

The recent London Mayor and Assembly elections don't suggest that anything has changed in that respect. In May the Conservative mayoral candidate Shaun Bailey beat Sadiq Khan 50–29 in the ward's ballot boxes, and the London Members ballot for the Assembly gave 49% to the Conservatives, 25% to Labour and 11% to the Green Party.

Harrow council as a whole is rather more left-wing than this ward, and it has returned Labour majorities at every election since 2010. It hasn't been Labour-controlled throughout that period, though: there was a bizarre episode in advance of the 2014 borough elections when a small Labour splinter group briefly held the leadership before collapsing under the weight of numbers.

The last time the Conservatives held a majority on Harrow council was after the 2006 election, when Pinner South ward councillor (Charles) Chris Mote became leader of the council. Mote had first been elected in 1982 as a councillor for Rayners Lane ward, standing down in 1986 after one term.* Mote returned to Harrow council representing this ward in 1998, and his two years (2006–08) as leader of the council were the high point of his local government career. He subsequently served as Deputy Mayor of Harrow in 2009–10. Chris Mote passed away at the end of July after a short illness, having served his constituents here for 23 years.

Defending this by-election for the Conservatives is Hitesh Karia, who is described as a local resident and businessman (although the address he gave on his nomination papers is in Hatch End). The Labour candidate Brahma Mohanty, who went into a career in finance after studying at both Oxford and Cambridge, already has a parliamentary campaign to his credit: he faced off in December 2019 against Michael Gove in the Surrey Heath constituency. More on that story later. Completing an all-BAME ballot paper are Sanjay Karia for

* In that year Rayners Lane was gained by the Liberals, one of whose slate—James Bartrick—was subsequently forced to resign after it was revealed that he was underage at the time of the election. Bartrick was re-elected in the resulting by-election, held after his 21st birthday.

Parliamentary constituency: Ruislip, Northwood and Pinner
May 2018 result C 2156/2024/2019 Lab 965/941/910 LD 653/487
May 2014 result C 1889/1751/1659 Lab 1062/1007/949 UKIP 511
May 2010 result C 3400/3002/2801 Lab 1740/1535/1343 LD 1527
May 2006 result C 2226/2068/1886 LD 670/612/549 Lab 609/591/537
May 2002 result C 1812/1766/1734 Lab 897/818/795
May 2021 GLA results (excludes postal voters)
Mayor: C 1243 Lab 705 Grn 176 LD 110 Omilana 52 Reclaim 35 Count Binface 29 Rejoin EU 18 Animal Welfare 15 Let London Live 12 UKIP 11 London Real 11 Obunge 10 SDP 8 Farah London 8 Heritage Party 7 Renew 6 Fosh 6 Women's Equality 5 Burning Pink 3
London Members: C 1223 Lab 634 Grn 272 LD 178 Animal Welfare 43 Rejoin EU 35 Reform UK 25 Women's Equality 25 Heritage 12 Let London Live 10 CPA 9 London Real 9 Nat Lib 7 Comm 6 UKIP 6 Londonpendence 4 TUSC 4 SDP 3

Figure 127: Harrow, Pinner South

the Liberal Democrats and Alex Lee for the Green Party.*

Frimley Green

Surrey Heath council; caused by the resignation of Liberal Democrat councillor Benjamin Leach.

I promised you more on Surrey Heath, so we now travel outside London to the western edge of Surrey. Frimley Green lies on the eastern side of the Blackwater valley, which is home to a surprisingly large urban area: the towns of Camberley, Farnborough, Aldershot, Sandhurst and Frimley have effectively merged together into a single conurbation. Because of the location of this urban sprawl on the borders of Surrey, Hampshire and Berkshire, our local government structures rather disguise this. Camberley and Frimley, the Surrey towns in this conurbation, are included in the Surrey Heath local government district.

Frimley Green still has a bit of a village feel to it even though it's now part of this urban area. The Blackwater valley towns have traditionally had an economy dominated by the Army and aerospace, but the largest single employer in Frimley Green is a large factory making SC Johnson cleaning products; and the town is best known for flying projectiles which, while sharp, are distinctly not military. Frimley Green is home to the Lakeside Country Club, which from 1986 until 2019 advertised itself as the "Home of World Darts", being the venue for the BDO World Darts Championship.

The BDO moved from here to the madhouse of the O2 in London in January 2020, for a tournament which fell short of financial expectations. As all darts

* *Harrow, Pinner South*: C 1392 LD 390 Lab 331 Grn 188

players know, if you go for madhouse and fall short with your first shot then you go bust, and that's what subsequently happened to the BDO.

Full disclosure: Your columnist once aimed three darts at a dartboard on the stage of the Lakeside in Frimley Green, and missed the scoring area of the board with every one. This game is harder than it looks on the telly.

Surrey Heath's council elections have consistently returned a Conservative majority this century, the party's fortunes peaking in 2015 when they polled 58% across the district and won 36 seats out of a possible 39. Previous elections were closer, and Frimley Green ward returned a full slate of Liberal Democrats in 2003 and 2007. The ward was redrawn for the 2019 elections, gaining part of Frimley ward to the north.

As I mentioned last week the May 2019 local elections saw enormous Conservative losses in western Surrey, with the party losing control of Guildford and Waverley districts. They came very close to losing control of Surrey Heath district as well, finishing with 18 councillors out of 35 and a majority of one. Frimley Green swung a long way to the Lib Dems who gained the ward with 49% of the vote, against just 29% for the Conservatives and 13% for UKIP. The ward was also contested by the Pirate Party in a rare foray for them into UK local elections: the Pirates finished last with a creditable 9%.

The Conservatives have since lost their majority on Surrey Heath council after two of their councillors formed a new "Camberley Independent" group. The current council composition stands at 17 Conservatives, 8 Lib Dems plus this vacancy, 6 independents (including the two Camberley Independents) and two Greens.

However, subsequent elections here have been more encouraging for the Tories. Michael Gove was re-elected as the MP for Surrey Heath very comfortably in December 2019, and following the recent reshuffle he is now the Cabinet minister responsible for local government. In May 2021 the Conservatives held all six of the district's Surrey county council divisions and gained a district council by-election from the Lib Dems in Bagshot ward (page 145). That by-election followed the sad death of Sam Kay, whose short but luckless life is remembered in *Andrew's Previews 2020*, page 90.

Frimley Green has a larger Lib Dem lead than Bagshot, but the party will still need to be on their guard in this by-election. The poll follows the resignation of Ben Leach, who stood down from the council last month on health grounds.

Defending for the Lib Dems is Jacques Olmo, who gives an address in Deepcut and sits on the committee of the Mytchett, Frimley Green and Deepcut Society. The Conservatives will regain an overall majority on the council if they win this by-election, and their candidate is Stuart Black who has lived in Frimley

Parliamentary constituency: Surrey Heath
Surrey county council division: Frimley Green and Mytchett
May 2019 result LD 1019/1012/889 C 601/568/519 UKIP 269 Pirate Party 190

Figure 128: Surrey Heath, Frimley Green

Green for 20 years and has "a background in industries from defence to healthcare, delivering innovation and change". UKIP have not returned, so Labour's Christine Richards completes the ballot paper.*

Leigh West

Wigan council, Greater Manchester; caused by the death of Labour councillor Lord Smith of Leigh.

For our English Labour defence this week we come to a place which is emblematic of the so-called "Red Wall". Until 2019, the Leigh parliamentary constituency had never returned a Conservative MP: it had been Liberal from its 1885 creation until 1922, and then Labour continuously from 1922 to 2019.

That included the catastrophe of 1931, when the Labour MP for Leigh Joe Tinker—one of the most vocal advocates of better working conditions for coalminers—survived with a majority of just over 2,000 against the Conservative candidate, a Leigh lad made good called Peter Eckersley. Eckersley was a star cricket player who had captained Lancashire to the County Championship the year before. He eventually got into Parliament in 1935 as the Tory MP for Manchester Exchange, but was then killed in a plane crash while serving in the Second World War.

The Conservatives had never come so close to winning Leigh in Parliament since 1931. Even in 2015, when Andy Burnham (now the Mayor of Greater Manchester) won his final term in the Commons, he enjoyed a majority of 14,096 in Leigh and the Conservative vote was under 23%. His successor, Jo Platt, won by over 9,500 votes in June 2017.

We can see the seeds for the Conservative gain of Leigh in what happened next. Platt promptly resigned from Wigan council, and a by-election was held for her seat in Astley Mosley Common ward in October 2017† which saw a sharp swing to the Conservatives.

This fitted into a wider pattern. Like many ex-coalfield areas, Leigh is changing. The town of Leigh itself is notoriously one of the largest towns in England without a railway station, but the A 580 East Lancashire Road and the M 6 mo-

* *Surrey Heath, Frimley Green*: C 896 LD 877 Lab 76 [C gain from LD] † *Andrew's Previews 2017*, page 302.

torway together give the area excellent road connections to the major urban centres around it—Manchester, Warrington, Liverpool. Astley Mosley Common ward borders the strongly middle-class commuter area of Boothstown in Salford, Golborne and Lowton in particular are transforming into a commuter centre on the quiet, and many years of solid, hard work by the local Conservatives have turned the pit ward of Lowton East into a Conservative stronghold. The Conservative candidate for Leigh in December 2019, Lowton East ward councillor James Grundy, was one of the prime movers behind that hard work and he can take a lot of personal credit for his result. A generic Tory candidate might not have done so well.

If Leigh were a town in the Midlands then it and the mining district around it would probably be a local government district of its own, as we see in Derbyshire and Nottinghamshire. However, we're in Greater Manchester here and the Leigh area is instead administered as part of the Metropolitan Borough of Wigan, whose council has an almost impregnable Labour majority.

For many years Wigan council was led by Peter Smith, an Old Boltonian and LSE economics graduate who was first elected to Wigan council in 1978. In 1982 Smith became chairman of the council's finance committee; in 1991 he was elected as Leader of the Council, a post he went on to hold for 27 years until retiring in 2018. During this time Smith was elevated to the House of Lords in 1999, taking the title Lord Smith of Leigh. He died in August, aged 76.

Lord Smith was Leigh born and bred and his ward was Leigh West, based on the Westleigh area and taking in the Bickershaw Country Park and Pennington Wharf. The collieries have left their mark on the landscape with a number of large lakes—"flashes"—which owe their origins to mining subsidence. Just to the south of the ward is the largest of these, Pennington Flash, which for some years now has been the starting point for the Ironman UK triathlon. This isn't the only sport associated with Leigh: Leigh Sports Village includes a 12,000-seat stadium which hosts Leigh Centurions rugby league club and Manchester United reserves, and it was due to be the venue for three group games in the Rugby League World Cup this autumn before that tournament's postponement.

Leigh West is a safe Labour ward where the party has not been seriously threatened for many years. In May's Wigan council elections Labour led the Conservatives here 57–26; that was the first time the Tories had finished second here since 2008 and 2014, when the ward was a straight Labour–Tory fight. In 2019 UKIP were runners-up here with third place going to a new localist party, "Leigh, Atherton and Tyldesley Together". Lord Smith was last re-elected in 2018, so the winner of this by-election will have to go back to the polls next May to seek re-election.

Parliamentary constituency: Leigh
May 2021 result Lab 1582 C 714 Leigh, Atherton and Tyldesley Together 394 LD 104
May 2019 result Lab 1049 UKIP 613 Leigh, Atherton and Tyldesley Together 412 C 196 LD 161
May 2018 result Lab 1308 Ind 578 C 374 LD 158
May 2016 result Lab 1610 UKIP 738 C 205 Grn 129
May 2015 result Lab 3066 UKIP 1418 C 645 Grn 278
May 2014 result Lab 2005 C 658
May 2012 result Lab 1761 Ind 650 C 195
May 2011 result Lab 1844 Ind 430 C 334 BNP 239
May 2010 result Lab 2509 LD 828 BNP 693 C 557 Ind 280 Ind 255 UKIP 247
May 2008 result Lab 1543 C 817
May 2007 result Lab 1380 Ind 600 C 289 Community Action 280
May 2006 result Lab 1377 LD 721 C 410
June 2004 result Lab 1708/1624/1503 Community Action 669/549/508 BNP 513

Figure 129: Wigan, Leigh West

Defending this seat for Labour is Samantha Brown, who gives an address in the ward and works at Leigh Sports Village. The Conservatives have selected James Geddes, who works in prisoner rehabilitation: he stood in Leigh East ward in May. Completing the ballot paper are Jayson Hargreaves, standing again for the Leigh and Atherton Independents (as Leigh, Atherton and Tyldesley Together now appear to be called); and Sharron Honey who returns for the Lib Dems after contesting May's election.*

Falkirk South

Falkirk council, Scotland; caused by the resignation of Labour councillor Pat Reid.

We finish north of the border in Scotland's most beautiful town, according to a 2011 poll for the STV television station. Falkirk might not have seemed so beautiful back in the day to the Romans: in the second century AD this was the northern frontier of the Roman empire, with the Antonine Wall guarding the high ground overlooking the Forth estuary.

The Romans recorded the site as *Varia Capella*; this, the Celtic *Ecclesbrith*, the Gaelic *An Eaglais Bhreac* and the Scots *Fawkirk* all refer to a "speckled" church on the site of the present Falkirk Trinity Church. Falkirk's location next to the Forth and with easy access to local ironstone resulted in it becoming an early centre of the Industrial Revolution, with communication links to match. The Forth and Clyde Canal opened in 1790, the Union Canal in 1822 and the

* *Wigan, Leigh West*: Lab 1004 C 432 Leigh and Atherton Ind 257 LD 103

Figure 130: The Falkirk Wheel

railways came in the 1830s, giving easy access to Edinburgh and Glasgow. All of them run through this ward. The two canals were rejoined in the twenty-first century by the Falkirk Wheel, a unique rotating boat lift which draws large numbers of tourists to the area. Including your columnist, who came here in April 2019 (Figure 130).

The Falkirk Wheel lies on the boundary of Falkirk South ward, which takes in the town centre and points south of it including a small rural hinterland. Both of the town's main railway stations (High and Grahamston) are here, as is the mansion of Callendar House which serves as the main museum and heritage centre for Falkirk.

This ward was originally drawn up for the May 2007 elections when Scotland introduced proportional representation to its local elections. In both 2007 and 2012 Labour won two seats, the SNP and Conservatives one each.

Boundary changes for the 2017 cut the ward down from four councillors to three, and it was Labour who lost out from this. The SNP took over first place with 36% of the first preferences, the Conservatives were second with 32% and Labour fell to third on 27%. All three of those parties won one seat each; in fact, all of the winning candidates (Lorna Binnie for the SNP, John Patrick for the

Conservatives and Pat Reid for Labour) got over the 25% required for election on first preferences alone, so there was no need to go to transfers.

That was back in May 2017, since when we have had two general elections to Westminster and one to Holyrood. The ward is part of the Falkirk constituency at Westminster (where an awful Labour performance in 2019 was exacerbated by their candidate being disendorsed for anti-Semitism), while in Holyrood the vast majority of the ward is in Falkirk West with the rural hinterland included in Falkirk East. All of these are SNP units with large majorities.

There is not too long to go now before the next Scottish local elections in May 2022, and the six-month rule cutoff point is fast approaching. Currently this column is aware of three Scottish vacancies: this one, a Tory seat in the Highlands which will go to a by-election at the start of December, and a very messy situation involving independent Renfrewshire councillor Paul Mack. That story is too long to explain here without digressing too far from Falkirk: suffice to say it's one for the Councillors Behaving Badly file. In short, the Standards Commission for Scotland has disqualified Mack from office (again) for bad behaviour (again); Mack has appealed against the decision (again); and the by-election is on hold (again) while the appeal is sorted out (again).*

If we don't get a final resolution to the Paul Mack saga soon, and no other Scottish vacancies arise in the next month, then this will be the last Scottish by-election in the central belt during this council term. So, everyone will be looking to make a good impression.

This by-election arises from the resignation of Labour councillor Pat Reid, who is retiring from public life at the age of 79. Reid's connection with Falkirk council lasted for more than six decades, as he started working for the council in 1959 while still a boy; he retired from its employment in 2002 as head of administration, won a by-election to the council in 2004 and ended up serving for ten years (2007–17) as Provost of Falkirk. During those years Reid represented Falkirk North ward; he transferred here in 2017 after that ward lost its fourth councillor.

Following the May 2017 local elections the Scottish National Party were the largest group on Falkirk council with 12 councillors, and they have formed a minority administration with the support of two independent councillors. Labour (9) and the Conservatives (7) are in opposition. An SNP gain in this by-election would give the SNP/Independent administration half of the seats on the council.

If we re-run the 2017 count in Falkirk south for one seat it goes to transfers, with the SNP winning by the narrow margin of 2,868 to 2,727 over the Conser-

* For more on Paul Mack see page 601.

Parliamentary constituency: Falkirk
Scottish Parliament constituency: Falkirk West (most), Falkirk East (rural part)
May 2017 first preferences SNP 2216 C 1993 Lab 1686 Grn 315

Figure 131: Falkirk, Falkirk South

vatives. Labour would have more comfortably beaten either the Conservatives or the SNP in a head-to-head, but to do that they need to get into the top two. And they're starting from third place.

Defending this difficult seat for Labour is James Marshall, a former community councillor in Denny who has retired after a 30-year career in waste management and recycling. The SNP candidate is Emma Russell, who is studying for a masters degree in Human Resources and is a former vice-chair of a dementia services charity. Standing for the Conservatives is Sarah Patrick; the daughter of the present Conservative ward councillor John Patrick, Sarah is a solicitor and an elder with the Falkirk Trinity Church. Completing the ballot paper, as they did in 2017, are the Scottish Green Party who have selected Stuart Duffin.*

* *Falkirk, Falkirk South*: first preferences SNP 1691 C 1676 Lab 679 Grn 267; final SNP 2019 C 1903 [SNP gain from Lab]

21st October 2021

Three by-elections on 21st October 2021, Trafalgar Day, as we replace three councillors who had 83 years of local government service between them. There is something for everyone to enjoy as we consider villages, a city and a town, with Labour defending one seat and the Lib Dems two. Let's start with the Labour defence which, for reasons which will become clear, is the village ward...

Rainworth South and Blidworth

Newark and Sherwood council, Nottinghamshire; caused by the death of Labour councillor Kathleen Arnold.

We start this week with our Labour defence in the heart of Sherwood Forest. Indeed the village of Blidworth, around five miles to the south-east of Mansfield, is sometimes cited as the burial place of Will Scarlet, one of Robin Hood's Merrie Men. However, there is no documentary evidence to support this or the claim that Maid Marian was born here.

We're on safer ground when considering the area's recent history. Blidworth was a small rural village until the 1920s, when Blidworth Colliery was sunk as the latest development of the Nottinghamshire coalfield. The colliery remained in operation until 1989, leaving behind a village of around 4,500 souls.

The village of Rainworth—or at least the part of it which hasn't been incorporated into Mansfield—has a similar history. Rainworth's mine was Rufford Colliery, which closed in 1993 and whose site is now being returned to nature, after the locals fought off an attempt by the county council in 2008–12 to site an incinerator there.

There used to be rather a lot of nature round this corner of Nottinghamshire thanks to the efforts of Joseph Whitaker, a noted naturalist of the early 20th century. Whitaker lived in Rainworth for most of his life, and his animal and bird collections included his own deer park here with 21 acres of land. He died in Rainworth in 1932, having lived long enough to see the collieries begin operation

Parliamentary constituency: Sherwood
Nottinghamshire county council division: Blidworth
May 2019 result Lab 450/401 Ind 345/334 C 341/292
May 2015 result Lab 1401/1361 C 792/732 Ind 304

Figure 132: Newark and Sherwood, Rainworth South and Blidworth

in the local villages.

With the local landscape now being decidedly post-industrial, the local politics is following suit. It's only in the last decade that the Conservatives have started contesting this area in local elections, and for much of this century Blidworth's local elections were instead contests between Labour and an independent candidate, Geoff Merry. Merry represented Blidworth on both Newark and Sherwood council and Nottinghamshire county council, eventually retiring in 2015 and 2017 respectively.

With Merry off the scene, the 2015 local election—the first contest for this ward, which was created in boundary changes that year—was an easy win for the Labour slate of Yvonne Woodhead and Kathleen Arnold. Councillors Woodhead and Arnold were re-elected in 2019 with rather more narrow margins: Labour polled 40% that year while an independent slate and the Conservatives had 30% each.

Subsequent results will give the opposition to Labour grounds for optimism. This ward is part of the Sherwood constituency, where the Government Chief Whip Mark Spencer now has a very large majority over Labour. In the May 2021 Nottinghamshire county council elections Yvonne Woodhead lost her seat in the Blidworth division, finishing a poor third: the Conservatives gained the division, but only with a majority of 54 votes over independent candidate Tina Thompson.

That result introduces some unpredictability into this by-election, which follows the death of veteran Labour councillor Kathleen Arnold. She had first been elected for Blidworth ward in 1991, and served on Newark and Sherwood council for a total of 22 years (excluding 2007–15).

Defending this seat for Labour is Callum Walsh, on whom I have no information. Independent candidate and Blidworth resident Tina Thompson returns to the campaign trail after her near-miss in May's county elections. Completing the ballot is another candidate who gives an address in Blidworth: she is Sheila Jackson for the Conservatives.*

* *Newark and Sherwood, Rainworth South and Blidworth*: Ind 650 C 168 Lab 164 [Ind gain from Lab]

Yardley East

Birmingham council, West Midlands; caused by the death of Liberal Democrat councillor Neil Eustace.

We stay within the Midlands for our big city by-election, which takes place in the city of Birmingham. If you start in Birmingham city centre and travel east, you will pass through a heavily Muslim area in Bordesley Green and Sparkhill before coming to outer and whiter areas on the way to the airport. This is the core of Yardley, which was a part of Worcestershire until it was incorporated into Birmingham in the 1910s.

Although the Asian population here is increasing, Yardley is still best characterised as a white working-class area. But it doesn't have the sort of electoral history you would expect for a white working-class area. For decades now this has been Birmingham's Liberal Democrat hotspot. Yardley was the political home of John Hemming, who was the only third-party MP elected for a Birmingham seat in the last fifty years: Hemming represented the Yardley constituency from 2005 to 2015 and came close to winning on a number of other occasions.

Hemming's election agent was Neil Eustace, who was one of the longest-serving members of Birmingham city council. Eustace was first elected as a city councillor for the former Yardley ward in 1986, gaining the seat from the Conservatives. The hard work of Eustace and his ward colleagues quickly turned Yardley and a number of neighbouring wards into Liberal and then Liberal Democrat strongholds, providing the base for their parliamentary campaigns. Eustace' seat was redrawn in 2004 with the name Stechford and Yardley North, but—with the exception of a narrow Labour win in 2015—remained in the Lib Dem column.

Times change, of course. The Lib Dems ran a very poor third in the Yardley seat in December 2019, with future Labour leadership candidate Jess Phillips winning a third term in the Commons very easily. By contrast, the last Birmingham city council election was in 2018 on radical new ward boundaries; Stechford and Yardley North ward was split up, with about half of it forming the new ward of Yardley East. Neil Eustace stood for re-election here and was returned by the wide margin of 65–30 over Labour.

Eustace passed away last month at the age of 65, having served the residents of Yardley for 35 years. Hoping to step into his shoes is the defending Lib Dem candidate Deborah Harries, who has worked for Birmingham council and for central government in senior communications roles. The Labour candidate is Carmel Corrigan, who contested Longbridge and West Heath ward in the 2018 city council elections; she is a caseworker for Jess Phillips MP. Completing the

Parliamentary constituency: Birmingham Yardley
May 2018 result LD 1856 Lab 863 C 140

Figure 133: Birmingham, Yardley East

ballot paper is Pervez Akhtar, a retired railwayman, for the Conservatives.*

Forest

Horsham council, West Sussex; caused by the resignation of Liberal Democrat councillor Godfrey Newman.

We finish for the week back in what is nominally a forest, but really one in name only. The Forest ward of Horsham is the eastern ward of Horsham town, and actual forested territory is confined to the ward's eastern fringe. This marks the edge of St Leonards Forest, which covers much of the area between Horsham and Crawley.

Horsham was the major town of inland western Sussex before the New Town of Crawley got going, and its history is mainly as a market town for the surrounding agricultural villages. The area was a major centre for iron smelting back in the day, but this industry had died out long before the Industrial Revolution got going and modern Horsham is not politically left-wing. Major industries in the town these days include brickmaking and brewing, while RSA Insurance and the RSPCA (whose head office is located just outside the town) are important local employers.

Forest ward was extensively redrawn for the 2019 local elections, taking in a large chunk of the abolished Horsham Park ward around Horsham railway station and going up from one councillor to three. It would probably be more accurate to say that Horsham Park ward was the main predecessor: this was rather more downmarket than the old Forest ward and included Horsham's most deprived census district, although that's not really saying much. Both Horsham Park and the old Forest ward had been closely fought between the Lib Dems and Conservatives in the period 2003–15, and the 2015 elections in the two wards had returned two councillors from each party.

May 2019 was a good election for the Horsham Lib Dems, who won the new Forest ward comfortably with 39%. Surprisingly, the Conservatives finished in third place with 21% of the vote, behind the Labour slate on 22%. The ward is split between all three Horsham divisions of West Sussex county council, all of which voted Liberal Democrat in May's county elections (the party held Hurst

* *Birmingham, Yardley East*: LD 1312 Lab 609 C 89

Parliamentary constituency: Horsham
West Sussex county council divisions: Horsham East (part), Horsham Hurst (part), Horsham Riverside (part)
May 2019 result LD 1305/1224/1120 Lab 742/719/613 C 703/623/567 Peace Party 314 UKIP 243

Figure 134: Horsham, Forest

and Riverside, and gained East from the Conservatives). The Tories do, however, still have a large majority on Horsham council and in the Horsham constituency.

As with our two other polls this week, the voters of Horsham will be replacing a long-serving councillor. (David) Godfrey Newman was first elected for Forest ward in 1991, gaining his seat from the Conservatives; he lost his seat in the 2007 election by just 13 votes, but returned in 2011 with a convincing majority. Newman was also the Liberal Democrats' parliamentary candidate for Horsham in 2010. He is standing down from the council due to ongoing health issues, having served his constituents for 26 years.

Defending this by-election for the Lib Dems is Jon Olson, who sits on a local residents' group and volunteers at a primary school in the area. The Labour candidate is David Hide, who works as a technical manager at a plant nursery and was a candidate in May's county elections. The Conservatives' Ross Dye has a point to prove after losing the Horsham East county division in May: he is recently retired from an IT career and is a parish councillor in Southwater, just to the south of the town. Completing the ballot paper is Jon Campbell for the Green Party.*

* *Horsham, Forest*: LD 921 Lab 517 C 410 Grn 97

28th October 2021

There are eight by-elections in England and Wales on 28th October 2021, with the Conservatives defending six seats (two of them to replace council leaders who have recently died), Labour defending one and a crucial free-for-all to finish off. We have a nice geographic and demographic spread this week, but there's only really one place to start. Welcome to the Greatest Town in the Known Universe...

Bromley Cross

Bolton council, Greater Manchester; caused by the death of the Leader of the Council, Conservative councillor David Greenhalgh.

The Dunscar Conservative Club is a very well-appointed venue. Its entrance hall proudly proclaims that the building was opened in 1974 by Enoch Powell, and above that plaque can be found portraits of the Queen, the Duke of Edinburgh and the present party leader. Mind, the last time your columnist was there for some quiz, in late 2019, the wall had a prominent gap where you might expect Boris Johnson to appear. A lot of money has been spent on the place since Enoch's day, and with its large performance space, decent-sized breakout room (from which a bust of Churchill looks disapprovingly at your quiz answers), and good food and drink offerings it's always a bustling place.

Which is appropriate for the area it's located in. We're in Bromley Cross, a prosperous northern suburb of Bolton on the railway line towards Blackburn. With its attractive location in the Pennine hills and regular trains to the big city, Bromley Cross is an excellent location for the well-heeled Manchester commuter who might not be sufficiently well-heeled to afford a mansion in Cheshire. In 2011 the place was ranked by an investment and savings firm as the fifth-best place for a family to live in England and Wales. You can see why Theresa May, in her ill-fated 2017 general election campaign, made Bromley Cross her first stop.

Mind, one of Bromley Cross' greatest claims to fame is not all that salubrious.

This was the home of the Greenhalgh family, who raised hundreds of thousands of pounds over the years as one of the most diverse art forgery teams ever caught. A number of artworks forged in Bromley Cross by Shaun Greenhalgh were exhibited as the real thing by several museums and galleries, most notoriously Bolton Museum which was successfully fooled by— and paid £440,000 for—an ancient Egyptian-style statue, the *Amarna Princess* (Figure 135). Shaun's parents George and Olive Greenhalgh, the public-facing part of the frauds, have now passed on; Shaun, after some years in prison, has gone straight and now produces art under his own name, with occasional TV work on the side.

The present Bromley Cross ward extends north-west to Egerton, a large village on the A 666 Bolton–Blackburn road (and yes, the road number is appropriate given its dire accident record), and also runs south to Bradshaw Brow and Canon Slade School. Canon Slade has a strong academic reputation, and its former pupils include one current MP (Lilian Greenwood, the opposition Deputy Chief Whip and Labour MP for Nottingham South), the current England cricketer Matt Parkinson, the noted actress Maxine Peake and the Radio 2 drivetime presenter Sara Cox.

The Bromley Cross area wasn't incorporated into Bolton until the big bang of the 1970s, having previously been the major part of the Turton urban district. There has been a ward on roughly these lines since the modern Bolton borough was created, and it has voted Conservative on every occasion over the last half-century, normally with large majorities. This is one of the safest Conservative wards in Greater Manchester.

That may surprise, given that we are in a very marginal parliamentary seat here. The Bolton North East constituency was a Conservative gain in December 2019 with a majority of just 378 votes. However, Bolton North East is an extremely socially-divided constituency, with three prosperous middle-class Conservative-voting wards (this one, Astley Bridge and Bradshaw) counterbalanced by three deprived and Labour-voting wards (Halliwell, Crompton and Tonge with the Haulgh). Only one of the constituency's seven wards, the working-class estates of Breightmet on the eastern edge of the town, can be described as marginal. That's one reason why swings in this constituency don't tend to be huge. The swing from June 2017 to December 2019 in Bolton North East was 4.6% Labour to Conservative, almost exactly in line with the national average. Bromley Cross is not Red Wall territory in the slightest, and anybody who describes it as such should be pointed to this Preview until they see the error of their ways.

Bolton council elections (outside Bromley Cross) are a different matter. A discredited Labour administration of the borough has crashed and burned over the last electoral cycle, and following the 2019 election Bolton became the

Figure 135: The *Amarna Princess*

only Conservative-run metropolitan borough in the north of England. David Greenhalgh (no relation of the art forgers), who had represented Bromley Cross ward on the council since 2006 and had led the Conservative group since 2013, became leader of a minority Conservative administration propped up in office by the Liberal Democrats, UKIP and a gaggle of localist parties for the small towns outside Bolton proper.

Greenhalgh's time as leader was generally not a happy one, and that wasn't his fault. Almost nowhere in England has been worse hit by COVID and lockdown than Bolton. For those who moan on Twitter that the government were slow to lock down in autumn 2020, all I can say is that you did not have the same experience I did as a Bolton resident. And if you had had it, you wouldn't have enjoyed it. Household visiting was banned here from the end of *July* 2020, a decision announced by the Health Secretary on Twitter with 2½ hours' notice; the town's pubs and restaurants were closed down in the first week of September 2020, with no notice whatsoever. Other measures changed so many times that I lost track, at a time when losing track of what was permitted, where it was permitted and who it was permitted for could lead to a criminal offence. It might not surprise to learn that these measures had little discernible effect on the spread of the virus.

Despite this, the Conservative administration led by David Greenhalgh became the largest party on Bolton council after the May 2021 elections. Bromley Cross ward had a 62–28 Conservative lead over Labour, representing almost no swing since 2016, but the gains came elsewhere. The latest council composition is 20 Conservatives plus this vacancy, 18 Labour, 5 Lib Dems, 5 Farnworth and Kearsley First, 3 Horwich and Blackrod Independents, 2 Bolton Independent Group (both elected as Conservative), 2 Crompton Independents (both elected as Labour), 2 other independents (1 elected as Conservative, 1 as Labour), a "One Kearsley" councillor (elected as Farnworth and Kearsley First) and a UKIP councillor (elected as UKIP, twice). The Lib Dems have withdrawn support for the Conservative administration, but there are enough localist and ex-Conservative councillors in the chamber for this not to matter too much.

Immediately after the May 2021 local elections, Bolton—and specifically the Great Lever, Harper Green and Farnworth wards—became the first part of the UK to be hit by the Delta variant of COVID in a big way. Rather than bring in yet more local lockdowns, this time the local health leaders thought outside the box and organised more effective ways to damp down the outbreak, by bringing vaccination to the heart of the communities and areas affected and damn the people in Whitehall telling them not to do that. The Vaccine Bus became a regular feature in the Greatest Town, and the people who hopped onto

Parliamentary constituency: Bolton North East
May 2021 result C 2748 Lab 1261 Grn 282 LD 164
May 2019 result C 2566 Lab 658 UKIP 342 Grn 296 LD 241
May 2018 double vacancy C 2928/2257 Lab 1023/910 Grn 374 LD 303/196
May 2016 result C 2443 Lab 1022 UKIP 460 LD 196 Grn 183
May 2015 result C 4340 Lab 1589 UKIP 1057 Grn 424 LD 368
May 2014 result C 2312 Lab 957 UKIP 878 LD 169
May 2012 result C 2207 Lab 1215 LD 317
May 2011 result C 2821 Lab 1244 Grn 336 LD 327
May 2010 result C 4236 Lab 1774 LD 1456 Grn 303
May 2008 result C 2933 Lab 705 LD 331 Grn 147 You Party 141
May 2007 result C 2784 Lab 677 LD 362 Grn 350
May 2006 result C 2725 Lab 712 LD 462 Grn 292
June 2004 result C 3315/3286/3257 Lab 1043/997/890 LD 938/782/614

Figure 136: Bolton, Bromley Cross

it included your columnist: I got my second vaccine dose from the bus in Moses Gate Country Park on a wet Saturday morning in July.

In the event that you haven't been vaccinated yet, it's still not too late to board the Vaccine Bus yourself. It will be parked in Victoria Square in Bolton town centre between 1000 and 1600 hours on Saturday. Pfizer, first and second doses available.

It's a shame that David Greenhalgh never lived to see the ultimate success of the vaccine programme. He passed away at the end of June, only a couple of weeks after badgering Nicola Sturgeon to lift a travel ban between Scotland and Greater Manchester. Greenhalgh's health had never been particularly good, as a moving obituary published by Bolton council made clear. His early career performing in musicals on the West End stage was cut short by his first kidney failure, and he ended up under the surgeon's knife at various points for two kidney transplants, a heart valve replacement and a broken spine. But even given all that, 53 is no age at all. Rest in peace, David.

Those are big shoes to fill for David Greenhalgh's successor as councillor for Bromley Cross. Defending this by-election for the Conservatives is Amy Cowen, who chairs a community group in Egerton where she lives. Labour have reselected Emily Mort, who stood here in May. Also standing are the ward's regular Green candidate Liz Spencer, James Haslam for the Lib Dems and Laura Armstrong for "Bolton for Change", another new localist group which failed to establish itself in May.*

* *Bolton, Bromley Cross*: C 1732 Lab 409 Grn 165 Bolton for Change 99 LD 68. For an update and some reaction to this result, see page 451.

Gresford East and West

Wrexham council, North Wales; caused by the resignation of Conservative councillor Andrew Atkinson.

We travel south-west from Bolton into the Welsh Marches. Gresford is close enough to the border to have been listed in the *Domesday Book* as part of Cheshire, but is now most definitely part of Wales. The village of Gresford lies over coal measures just to the north of Wrexham, and has a handy location on the main road and railway line between Wrexham and Chester.

Gresford boomed in the early 20th century with the sinking of Gresford Colliery, one of the deepest mines in the Denbighshire coalfield. This came at a cost: the mine proved to be working coal seams containing high levels of gas. At 2:08am on 22nd September 1934 Gresford Colliery was the scene of one of Britain's worst coalmining disasters, with 266 men killed by an underground explosion and fire; only eleven of the bodies were recovered. The disaster was commemorated in music with the composition of the so-called "Miner's Hymn", appropriately named *Gresford*, which remains a favourite of ex-colliery brass bands.*

Gresford Colliery finally closed in 1973, and its site has been redeveloped as an industrial estate. The mining heritage has left its mark: Gresford East and West ward has a much more working-class demographic profile than the village-based wards around it.

With the death of mining in Gresford, the Labour stranglehold on this ward has been well and truly broken. The ward became marginal in 2004 and has voted for three different parties in its last three elections: Liberal Democrat in 2008, Labour in 2012, Conservative in May 2017.

The Tory win was a very convincing one, with a 73–16 lead over Labour for new councillor Andrew Atkinson. Atkinson had a high local profile at the time, as he was the Conservatives' parliamentary candidate for the Wrexham constituency at the general election five weeks later. On that occasion he finished 1,832 votes behind Labour, having lost by 1,831 votes two years previously. Atkinson had also contested the Wrexham seat in the 2016 Welsh Assembly election.

The Wrexham constituency was eventually gained by the Conservatives in the December 2019 general election (without Atkinson as the candidate), but it stayed with Labour in the May 2021 Senedd election. Wrexham council had been hung at every ordinary election this century, but the May 2017 election here gave independent councillors half of the council: 26 seats, against 12 Labour, 9 Conservatives, 3 Plaid Cymru and two Lib Dems. Two by-elections since then

* For a recording of *Gresford* by the Black Dyke Band, see `youtu.be/2BjdaMGaVLs`.

Parliamentary constituency: Wrexham
May 2017 result C 917 Lab 204 LD 125 UKIP 11
May 2012 result Lab 314 LD 311 C 248
May 2008 result LD 386 C 347 Lab 286
June 2004 result Lab 401 C 343 LD 181
May 1999 result Lab 470 PC 278
May 1995 result Lab 695 C 268

Figure 137: Wrexham, Gresford East and West

have resulted in gains for Plaid Cymru: one from an independent in Gwersyllt North in February 2020*. and one from Labour in March†.

Continuing this mixed political picture, the Wrexham council cabinet consists of independent and Conservative councillors. It included Andrew Atkinson as cabinet member for children's services. Atkinson attracted controversy in July this year after it emerged that he was on a working holiday to Panama ahead of a planned emigration, and that he was carrying out his council duties remotely from there. He was eventually forced to announce his resignation from the cabinet and council, effective from the end of August.

Defending this seat for the Conservatives is Jeremy Kent, who was the losing Conservative candidate for Wrexham in May's Senedd election and in the 2020 Gwersyllt North by-election. Kent is a former restaurant manager who now works with the Air Cadets. Labour have selected Aled Canter, who gives an address in Llay on the far side of the River Alyn. Also standing are the ward's former Lib Dem councillor (2004–08) Beryl Blackmore, Alan Butterworth for the Green Party, Charles Dodman in a rare local election outing for Reform UK, and Aimi Waters for Plaid Cymru who have not contested this ward since 1999.‡

Kinver; and Wombourne South East

South Staffordshire council; caused respectively by the deaths of Conservative councillors Brian Edwards (who was Leader of the Council) and Reginald Williams.

We cross back over the border into England for the rest of this week's column, considering two wards which lie just off the western edge of the Black Country. Not all of southern Staffordshire ended up in the West Midlands metropolitan county at the 1970s reorganisation: a small rural fringe, sandwiched between the Black Country and Shropshire, remains part of Staffordshire. And that's where

* *Andrew's Previews 2020*, page 57 † Page 26). ‡ *Wrexham, Gresford East and West*: C 351 LD 165 PC 163 Lab 132 Reform UK 6 Grn 5

we are today.

The South Staffordshire district is effectively everything in south-western Staffordshire which didn't get incorporated into Stafford, Cannock, Wolverhampton or anywhere else in the Black Country. A number of its settlements are clearly part of somewhere else: Great Wyrley is part of the Cannock urban area, Perton is effectively a part of Wolverhampton which has escaped over the border. The district contains no large towns of its own and Wombourne, a settlement south-west of Wolverhampton which readers may reasonably have never heard of despite its population of around 14,000, is its largest independent urban area.

As this column has previously discussed*, Wombourne is in effect a Black Country industrial town which managed to escape the urban sprawl. Its traditional nailmaking industry has been effectively supplanted by commuting to Wolverhampton and the other Black Country towns.

Kinver, located at the southern end of the district a few miles to the west of Stourbridge, has a rather older history than that of Wombourne. The name is first recorded in AD 736 as *Cynibre*, the second half of the name referring to a steep hill: this is most likely Kinver Edge, which was home to a hillfort in prehistoric times. Kinver Edge is a local beauty spot which deserves to be better known, and a tourism industry here was established here in the 20th century thanks to the opening of the Kinver Light Railway, a tram line from the village to Amblecote. The steep sandstone rock of Kinver Edge provided a base for England's last troglodyte dwellings: the Rock Houses on Holy Austin Rock were inhabited into the 1960s, and some of them have been restored by the National Trust. A visit is strongly recommended, although you can surely do better than the photograph in Figure 138 which I took earlier this year.

Kinver has left its mark on our elections in an unusual way, following the death on 2nd May 2005 of Josephine Harrison. This was three days before the 2005 general and local elections, in which Harrison was the Liberal Democrat candidate for the South Staffordshire constituency and for the Kinver division of Staffordshire county council. Both elections were postponed to allow nominations to be reopened, eventually taking place on 23rd June 2005; the postponed polls eventually re-elected county councillor Brian Edwards, who in the interim had been elected as leader of South Staffordshire council, and the long-serving MP Sir Patrick Cormack. This was the first time for many years that a general election had been postponed following the death of a candidate. Cormack was unhappy with the experience, and he sponsored an amendment to the Representation of the People Act to allow parliamentary elections to proceed to polling if an independent candidate dies during an election campaign. The Cormack

* *Andrew's Previews 2019*, page 170.

Figure 138: Rock Houses, Kinver, Staffordshire

amendment doesn't apply to local elections in England and Wales, but one Scottish council by-election and at least one parliamentary general election (following the death of former Eurovision contestant Ronnie Carroll) have since proceeded to polling with a deceased candidate on the ballot paper.

Sir Patrick Cormack retired to the Lords in 2010, after successfully fighting off a deselection attempt from his local party, and was replaced as MP for

South Staffordshire by Gavin Williamson who remains *in situ* eleven years later. Williamson's times in Cabinet have been notably ill-judged: he was dismissed as defence secretary on 1st May 2019 by Prime Minister May for leaking confidential information, and a subsequent appointment as education secretary in the Johnson government did not reflect well on anyone involved.

Brian Edwards proved to have rather more staying power at the top. He was first elected to South Staffordshire council in 1983 and to Staffordshire county council in 1989, and as stated he became leader of South Staffordshire council in 2005. Edwards was still holding that office when he passed away in August 2021 at the age of 81, after 38 years as a district councillor and 16 years as council leader. He had been appointed MBE in 2015 for his work to local government and communities.

Edwards' death came a week after the passing of another long-serving district councillor, Reg Williams, at the age of 90. Williams had sat on Wombourne parish council for 25 years, and also represented the town's South East ward on South Staffordshire council. He had a reputation as a planning expert, but suffered a reverse in 2013 with an abortive plan to erect a wooden replica of Stonehenge in Wombourne; South Staffordshire council asked Williams to carry out a public consultation, which revealed concerns from locals that the structure would become an "arena for alcohol". A shame.

Williams had won his district council seat in 2003 in a close fight in Wombourne South East ward, but he was not remotely threatened at later elections. The ward was uncontested in 2015, and in May 2019 the Tory slate beat Labour here 73–27.

Kinver ward, which is more rural in nature and covers a number of hamlets outside Kinver itself, split its three seats in 2003 and 2007 between Brian Edwards for the Conservatives, an independent and a Lib Dem candidate. In 2011 the Lib Dem councillor stood down and the independent was narrowly defeated, and since then this ward has been safely Conservative. The 2019 election saw the Conservative slate of three candidates opposed only by a single Green and a single Lib Dem candidate; shares of the vote were 45% for the Conservatives, 29% for the Green and 26% for the Lib Dem.

Which brings me to a point I've seen discussed on the Twitter recently: there have been a number of good Green Party performances in recent local by-elections. Since normal service resumed in June the party has gained six by-elections, mostly from the Conservatives in unlikely-looking places, and come close to winning a few other contests. For a party which historically tends not to have a lot of luck in local by-elections, this is notable. With environmentalism and the forthcoming climate summit in Glasgow high on the political agenda,

Parliamentary constituency: South Staffordshire
Staffordshire county council division: Kinver
May 2019 result C 1022/1004/889 Grn 665 LD 598
May 2015 result C 2903/2760/2521 Lab 1055
May 2011 result C 1659/1655/1122 Ind 1071 Lab 644
May 2007 result C 1305/977/976 Ind 1096 LD 1002
May 2003 result C 972/765/600 Ind 947 LD 941/743

Figure 139: South Staffordshire, Kinver

Parliamentary constituency: South Staffordshire
Staffordshire county council division: Wombourne
May 2019 result C 677/585 Lab 250/172
May 2015 result 2 C unopposed
May 2011 result C 873/860 UKIP 501
May 2007 result C 784/636 UKIP 432
May 2003 result C 556/545 LD 494 Ind 458

Figure 140: South Staffordshire, Wombourne South East

and with hard work by local Green Party activists having given the party representation on an increasing number of councils over the last electoral cycle, we might reasonably expect this trend to continue in the near future. In this context I note that the Greens won three seats on South Staffordshire council at the last district elections in 2019; one of their councillors is long-serving activist Ian Sadler, who was a close runner-up in Wombourne South East back in 2003 as a Liberal Democrat candidate.*

Something to think about, perhaps, as we turn to the candidate lists, although the fact that the Tory vote share was over 70% in May's county elections in both Kinver and Wombourne may dampen grounds for opposition optimism.

Defending Kinver for the Conservatives is parish councillor Geoff Sisley. The Greens have reselected Bernadette McGourty, who was runner-up in the 2019 district elections and a much more distant runner-up in May's county elections in Kinver. The Lib Dems have not returned, so Labour's Michael Vaughan completes the ballot paper.†

In Wombourne South East the defending Conservative candidate is Mark Evans, who gives an address in the neighbouring Wombourne South West ward. The other two candidates on the ballot both contested Wombourne in May's county elections: Denis Beaumont stands for Labour, Claire McIlvenna for the

* Green Party district councillor Ian Sadler should not be confused with Conservative Kinver parish councillor Ian Sadler. They are different people. † *South Staffordshire, Kinver*: C 865 Lab 154 Grn 149

Green Party.[*]

South

Luton council, Bedfordshire; caused by the death of Labour councillor Paul Castleman.

Our Labour defence this week is in our southernmost by-election, taking place in the aptly-named South ward. We have been wafted from paradise to the centre of Luton, the largest town in Bedfordshire and rather different from the rest of the county. This is quite an industrial town, having grown during the Industrial Revolution on hat manufacturing and then in the twentieth century on vehicle manufacturing. The Vauxhall Motors factory here was in operation from 1907 to 2002, and Luton Airport was opened in 1938.

Luton Airport has always been owned by the borough council, and over the last couple of years this has proved to be bad news. The council had been funding a number of its services using its income from the airport's dividend; when this dried up overnight as the pandemic hit, the council suddenly found itself unable to balance its budget. Despite passing an emergency budget in July 2020 with £22 million of cuts, central government still had to step in with a bailout of £35 million to stabilise the council's finances.

Luton councillors have faced the full wrath of their public before. On 19th July 1919, a bank holiday known as "Peace Day" marking the end of the First World War, Luton town hall was burned to the ground by rioters who were unhappy with the town's high unemployment rate. The replacement town hall, an Art Deco building opened in 1936, is located on the same site in the town centre.

Luton's town centre is contained in the town's South ward, which runs south to take in the New Town and Park Town areas and the business park at Capability Green. Luton railway station and Luton Airport Parkway railway station lie on the ward boundary, providing fast links to London and the East Midlands. The ward includes a number of buildings belonging to the University of Bedfordshire, together with a large number of students.

That gives South ward's census return a very different look from your average ward in the East of England. The ward is in the top 30 wards in England and Wales for people born in the EU 2004–07 accession countries, is in the top 40 for those born in the Republic of Ireland, and is in the top 70 for private renting and full-time students.

---

[*] *South Staffordshire, Wombourne South East*: C 370 Grn 323 Lab 42

Parliamentary constituency: Luton South
May 2019 result Lab 938/813/710 Grn 445 C 373/316 UKIP 339 Ind 259
May 2015 result Lab 1898/1787/1655 C 1075/1061/773 Grn 649
May 2011 result Lab 994/957/930 C 653/528/518 UKIP 196 Grn 161/150/108 LD 149/142/114
May 2010 by-election Lab 1493 C 1015 LD 616 UKIP 201 Grn 155
May 2007 result Lab 840/734/657 C 619/610/447 Grn 266 LD 249/221/162
May 2003 result Lab 681/681/678 C 354/289/250 LD 261/234/221 Ind 242/120

Figure 141: Luton, South

South ward has voted Labour at every election this century, usually quite comfortably. At the most recent poll, in May 2019, the Labour slate had 40% of the vote against 19% for the Greens, 16% for the Conservatives and 14% for UKIP.

The ward is part of the Luton South parliamentary seat, which was a Conservative seat until the 1997 Labour landslide but is now safe Labour. Its 2010–19 MP Gavin Shuker was one of the Labour MPs who defected to Change UK; he sought re-election in 2019 as an independent candidate, saving his deposit. The seat's new Labour MP Rachael Hopkins was a Luton councillor for the neighbouring ward of High Town; she resigned her council seat after being elected to Parliament, and the resulting High Town ward by-election took place in May 2021[*].

Councillor Paul Castleman, who passed away in August, was a lifelong Lutonian who was first elected in a March 2014 by-election in the neighbouring Farley ward. He transferred to this ward in 2015. Until a reshuffle in May, he had been the council's cabinet member for planning and transport.

Defending the South ward by-election for Labour is Fatima Begum, a "lover of all things good" according to her Twitter. Marc Scheimann, who had been the ward's regular Green Party candidate and has contested general and European elections under the Green banner, is standing this time as an independent candidate without Green opposition. The Conservatives have selected Abid Aziz, a businessman and former special constable. UKIP have not returned, so completing the ballot paper are Markus Kearney for the Communist Party of Britain and Nigel Marshall for the Liberal Democrats.[†]

Grantham Arnoldfield; and Stamford All Saints

South Kesteven council, Lincolnshire; caused respectively by the resignation of Helen Goral and the death of Mike Exton, both of whom were Conservative council-

[*] See page 137. [†] *Luton, South*: Lab 547 LD 332 C 198 Ind 134 Comm 28

lors.

We travel to the East Midlands for contests in two towns off the A 1 Great North Road. The town of Stamford, located at the point were Lincolnshire, Cambridgeshire, Northamptonshire and Rutland all meet, was as important as the great cities of the East Midlands in the time of the Danelaw, but Stamford never really grew into a major city. Some miles to the north lies Grantham, the birthplace of Margaret Thatcher. Grantham is home to the headquarters of South Kesteven district, which also covers Stamford and a large rural area in south-western Lincolnshire.

The Arnoldfield ward of Grantham is the town's north-western corner. It covers two disconnected urban areas either side of the railway line towards Nottingham: the larger of these is Gonerby Hill Foot, on what was once the Great North Road. The ward was drawn up for the 2015 election and includes a small amount of overspill beyond the town boundary: this is still part of the Sleaford and North Hykeham constituency, leaving the ward split between two seats at parliamentary level. The Boundary Commission should sort this out for the 2024 general election.

Further south the Great North Road entered Stamford, whose narrow town-centre streets ensured that this was one of the first towns on the A 1 to be bypassed, in 1960. Stamford's four wards are all named after ecclesiastical parishes: All Saints is the town's north ward, covering housing around the Little Casterton Road.

All Saints ward suffered from a lack of opposition candidates in the 2019 election: the two-person Tory slate was opposed only by a single Labour candidate, who lost 62–38. The ward returned an independent councillor in 2007 and 2011 and also elected a Lib Dem in 2007. Arnoldfield ward was brand new for 2015: the predecessor wards, Green Hill and Greyfriars, had consistently returned Conservative councillors this century. Arnoldfield is split between two divisions of Lincolnshire county council which both voted Conservative in May; All Saints ward is split between the two Stamford county divisions, with East voting Conservative and West gained in May by an independent candidate, Richard Cleaver.

So, on this evidence the Stamford All Saints by-election looks the more interesting of these two contests to South Kesteven council. It follows the death of Conservative councillor Mike Exton, who passed away in August at the age of 80. A double kidney transplant recipient and passionate supporter of opening up the organ donor register, Exton had served on South Kesteven council since winning a by-election in 2005; he had also previously sat on Lincolnshire county council, and he was Mayor of Stamford in 2003–04.

Parliamentary constituency: Grantham and Stamford (almost all), Sleaford and North Hykeham (small part)
Lincolnshire county council division: Grantham North (part), Grantham West (part)
May 2019 result C 655/612 Lab 232/225
May 2015 result C 1203/886 UKIP 516/483 Lab 382/349 Ind 335

Figure 142: South Kesteven, Grantham Arnoldfield

Parliamentary constituency: Grantham and Stamford
Lincolnshire county council division: Stamford East (part), Stamford West (part)
May 2019 result C 562/533 Lab 343
May 2015 result C 1100/826 Stamford Group of Inds 646/609 UKIP 603 Lab 529

Figure 143: South Kesteven, Stamford All Saints

The Grantham Arnoldfield by-election is caused by the resignation of Helen Goral, who is concentrating on her other roles as a mother of two children and with the housing and planning PR company which she works for. Goral had stood down from the council cabinet last year for the same reason.

Defending Grantham Arnoldfield for the Conservatives is Kaffy Rice-Oxley. A cousin of the Keane songwriter and keyboardist Tim Rice-Oxley, Kaffy is a singer and music teacher and she has recently been appointed as secretary of the Conservatives' Grantham and Stamford branch. The Labour candidate is Stuart Fawcett, who trains horses for carriage driving. Also standing is Mike Turner for the Green Party.*

In Stamford All Saints the defending Tory candidate is Amanda Schonhut who is a freelance photographer, director of fundraising at Grantham Museum and founder of a charity for domestic and workplace abuse victims. She is opposed by three independent candidates. Richard Cleaver, as already stated, was elected in May as Lincolnshire county councillor for Stamford West; Maxwell Sawyer contested this ward in 2011 and 2015 on a Stamford localist slate; and Tony Story is a former Mayor of Stamford.†

Currock and Upperby

Carlisle council, Cumbria; caused by the death of UKIP councillor John Denholm.

We finish in the north with our city by-election of the week. The city here is Carlisle, which for the moment is the capital of Cumbria and is home to both Cumbria county council and Carlisle city council.

* *South Kesteven, Grantham Arnoldfield*: C 460 Lab 136 Grn 112 † *South Kesteven, Stamford All Saints*: Cleaver 496 C 214 Story 114 Sawyer 46 [Ind gain from C]

The Currock and Upperby ward is on the southern edge of the city, lying in between the West Coast railway line and the Maryport railway line. Drawn for the 2019 local elections, it takes in the majority of two previous wards. The former Upperby ward, on the southern edge of the city, was an utterly working-class area: at the 2011 census 27.1% of the workforce were in semi-routine occupations, which was the highest figure for any ward in the North West region and the seventh-highest figure in England. (Four of the six wards with higher figures were in Boston, for what that is worth.) Currock ward, which extended into part of the city centre around Citadel railway station, was in the top 100 wards in England and Wales for those with 1–5 GCSE passes or equivalent (19.6%), part-time employment (18.4%) and, again, semi-routine occupations (18.9%).

With that sort of profile, you'd expect this to be a Labour area; but stranger things have happened in elections. When this ward was contested for the first time in May 2019 Labour did indeed top the poll, but only with 37% of the vote; and the ward's third and final seat went to UKIP candidate John Denholm. Denholm had contested both predecessor wards in the past without much success; but this time his tally was enough to beat Labour's third candidate Robert Rynn by a margin of one vote, 556 to 555. Don't let anybody tell you your vote never changed anything.

Having won the ward's third and final seat, John Denholm would have been due for re-election in May 2020 when Carlisle council went back to elections by thirds. However, the May 2020 elections were postponed to May 2021 because of the pandemic; and then the May 2021 Carlisle elections were postponed to May 2022 in advance of local government reorganisation. The same thing happened to the May 2021 Cumbria county elections. This ward covers the whole of the Upperby county division and most of the Currock county division, both of which were safe Labour at the last Cumbria elections in May 2017.

John Denholm suddenly passed away in July 2021, 27 months into his 12-month term of office. He was 73 years old. His death leaves the UK Independence Party (who recently elected Neil Hamilton as their leader, for those who are keeping track or want to win *Pointless*) with nine councillors remaining: two in Folkestone and Hythe, and one each in Bolton; Bournemouth, Christchurch and Poole; Great Yarmouth; Pembrokeshire; South Staffordshire; Tamworth; and Tendring. Councillor Dowson in Pembrokeshire (who was elected as an independent and subsequently joined UKIP) is due for re-election next year, with all the rest being up in May 2023. The Bolton UKIP councillor represents my ward and might have enough name recognition to get re-elected, but faced with this evidence even your columnist has had to accept that UKIP are no longer a major national party.

Parliamentary constituency: Carlisle
Cumbria county council division: Upperby, Currock (part)
May 2019 result Lab 798/667/555 UKIP 556 C 326/293/283 Grn 251 LD 237

Figure 144: Carlisle, Currock and Upperby

The UK Independence Party are not defending this by-election. We have a free-for-all, I repeat we have a free-for-all! And this could have a major impact on the council composition. Labour lost control of the council in 2019 with the Conservatives becoming the largest party on the council, and the Tories formed a minority administration. In May the Tories took two by-elections off Labour (page 72) in working-class city wards not dissimilar to Currock and Upperby, and that has left them with 19 seats on the council to 13 Labour, 4 independents, 1 Green, 1 Lib Dem and this vacancy. If the Conservatives can gain this by-election from UKIP, they will win overall control of Carlisle city council.

With Labour holding the other two seats in this ward they should start as favourites here. Their candidate is Chris Wills, who lives in this ward and works for the National Trust; in May he fought a county council by-election on less-promising territory in Brampton (page 72), coming third. The Conservatives, who are reportedly giving this by-election some serious hard work, have selected Geoff Mitchell who gives an address in the village of Scotby; he fought Dalston and Burgh ward in 2019, and his wife Linda won one of the May by-elections to Carlisle council. The Greens have selected Tom Adams, who gives an address some distance away in Brampton; he completes a ballot paper of three candidates.*

* *Carlisle, Currock and Upperby*: Lab 636 C 412 Grn 59 [Lab gain from UKIP]

4th November 2021

A quick update to last week's item from Bromley Cross in Bolton. First, having been there on Tuesday night for a quiz league match I can report that the Dunscar Conservative Club have now found a picture of Boris Johnson, looking uncharacteristically serious, for their entrance hall. The late Duke of Edinburgh is still there, too.

I had thought that the concept of a safe Conservative ward in Bolton might be too much for some people to handle, and my goodness social media delivered last week. Some of the Twitter commentary on the Bromley Cross result was absolutely hilarious. All I can say is, you either need to get out more or read the Previews—at least then you won't be making elementary mistakes. Hopefully.

Welcome to what is shaping up to be a busy November. Your columnist is currently aware of thirty-three local by-elections taking place this month, with the first six of them on 4th November 2021. The Conservatives defend three, Labour and the Lib Dems defend one each, and there is a free-for-all! This week we'll travel from south to north, starting with the first Conservative defence on the south coast...

Bourne

West Sussex county council; caused by the resignation of Conservative councillor Mike Magill.

As stated, we begin in the south-western corner of West Sussex, just off the edge of the Portsmouth and Havant urban area. The Bourne electoral division bears no relation to a well-known film franchise of the same name: this area takes its name from the villages of Southbourne, Westbourne and Nutbourne, which lie on the north bank of Chichester Harbour roughly halfway between Portsmouth and Chichester. Southbourne is the largest population centre in the ward, and has a railway station linking it to the outside world. To the north are a number of smaller parishes within the South Downs National Park, including the country estate of Stansted Park with its Edwardian country house, where generations of Royals have been entertained.

The southern end of the ward is rather more bleak. Thorney Island (now linked to the mainland by seawalls) has been a military base for many years thanks to its isolated position in Chichester Harbour. It was on the front line of the Second World War as an RAF Coastal Command airfield; the Air Force moved out in the late 1970s and were replaced by the Army in the mid-1980s. In between Thorney Island provided a temporary home to hundreds of Vietnamese refugee families, before they were properly resettled in the UK.

The psephologist Robert Waller wrote in every edition of his magisterial and much-missed *Almanac of British Politics* that "even after the revolution the workers' soviet for Chichester would be Tory". Like all good jokes, there's a grain of truth and a lot of exaggeration in that. The forerunner to the future Chichester Workers' Soviet does normally have a Conservative majority, but the first election to the modern Chichester council in 1973 saw the Conservative group outnumbered by independent councillors, and at the Tory nadir of 1995 the Liberal Democrats were the largest party on a hung council.

It's a mark of the volatile political times in which we live that the May 2019 election to Chichester council delivered no overall control: the Tories crashed from 42 seats out of 48 to 18 out of 36. They did return to a majority six months later by taking a by-election off the Lib Dems[*], but some defections mean that the ruling Conservative group is now in a minority again with 17 seats. The opposition is made up of 11 Lib Dems (who took a by-election off Labour in June[†]), 3 independents, 2 Green Party councillors, 2 Selsey localists and one remaining Labour councillor. This county division is mostly covered by the Southbourne ward (which voted Lib Dem in May 2019) and the smaller Westbourne ward (which voted Conservative on that occasion).

The Tories do still retain a strong majority on West Sussex county council. The Bourne division, thanks to its position in a corner of the county, has survived a number of boundary reviews to remain unchanged since at least 2005. In that timescale it has normally been Conservative, but did vote for UKIP in 2013. The Tories recovered the seat in May 2017, but then their county councillor Viral Parikh defected to the Brexit Party.

Parikh subsequently relocated to Sunderland, and he was the Brexit Party's parliamentary candidate for Sunderland Central in the December 2019 general election. He resigned from West Sussex county council in advance of that, and a by-election was held for Bourne division in November 2019[‡]. The Brexit Party

---

[*] *Andrew's Previews 2019*, page 374 (Loxwood). [†] Page 240. [‡] *Andrew's Previews 2019*, page 374 (Bourne).

Parliamentary constituency: Chichester
Chichester council wards: Southbourne, Westbourne, Harbour Villages (part: Chidham and Hambrook parish)
May 2021 result C 1869 LD 1064 Grn 400 Lab 336
November 2019 by-election C 1368 LD 1009 Grn 250 Lab 161 Patria 12
May 2017 result C 1357 UKIP 865 LD 659 Lab 264 Grn 234
May 2013 result UKIP 1241 C 1158 LD 360 Lab 295
June 2009 result C 1948 LD 1382 Lab 127
May 2005 result C 2377 LD 1922 Lab 841 Ind 375 UKIP 347

Figure 145: West Sussex CC, Bourne

Parliamentary constituency: Huntingdon
Cambridgeshire county council division: Huntingdon North and Hartford (part), Godmanchester and Huntingdon South (part)
May 2018 result LD 896/749 C 744/626 Lab 264/256

Figure 146: Huntingdonshire, Huntingdon East

didn't defend their defection gain, and the Conservatives' Mike Magill won the by-election with a 49–36 lead over the Lib Dems.

Magill was re-elected in May this year with an increased majority over the Lib Dems of 51–29. He stepped down from the county council three months later, prompting this by-election.

Defending this second Bourne by-election in as many years is Conservative candidate Bob Hayes, who is a Southbourne parish councillor: he represented Southbourne on Chichester council from 2007 until 2019, when he lost his seat to the Lib Dems. The Lib Dems have re-selected Andrew Kerry-Bedell, who was their candidate here in May and in the 2019 by-election. Also standing are Ann Stewart for the Green Party and Alan Butcher for Labour.*

Huntingdon East

Huntingdonshire council, Cambridgeshire; caused by the death of Liberal Democrat councillor Trish Shrapnel.

For our Liberal Democrat defence of the week we come to a relatively-recent hotspot for the party: the county of Cambridgeshire. Following May's elections this is one of two English county councils with a Lib Dem-led administration: the other is Oxfordshire, and the party is also the junior partner in the coalition running Cumbria county council.

* *West Sussex CC, Bourne*: LD 1180 C 893 Grn 178 Lab 25 [LD gain from C]

In recent years the Liberal Democrats have had less luck in Cambridgeshire's district councils. They hold a majority only in South Cambridgeshire district: the city of Cambridge itself is strongly Labour these days, and Peterborough has a minority Conservative administration. Cambridgeshire's other three local government districts, including Huntingdonshire, have Conservative majorities. The elected Mayor of Cambridgeshire and Peterborough is a representative of the Labour Party, elected in May thanks to Lib Dem transfers.

The Huntingdon East ward is based on Hartford, an old village on the north bank of the River Great Ouse which has been swallowed up by the town's growth. Hartford is located north-east of Huntingdon town centre, on the main road towards Wisbech.

This has traditionally been a marginal ward of Huntingdon council which has returned councillors from the Conservatives, the Liberal Democrats and (on one occasion) UKIP in the last decade. Going into the 2018 election here Huntingdon East ward had two Liberal Democrat councillors and one Conservative; boundary changes cut the ward down to two councillors so someone was going to miss out, and in the end it was the Conservatives who lost as the ward voted Lib Dem by a 47–39 margin.

There have been no ordinary elections to Huntingdonshire council since 2018, although there has still been a lot of electoral action as this is the ninth by-election of the current council's term. The score in the previous seven by-elections stands at 5 Conservative holds, 1 Lib Dem hold, 1 Labour hold and 1 independent gain from Labour.*

Some weird boundaries mean that the part of this ward closest to Huntingdon town centre is part of the Godmanchester and Huntingdon South county division, which is Lib Dem-held. However, most of the Huntingdon East ward forms part of the Huntingdon North and Hartford division of the county council, which was an against-the-trend Conservative gain in May. Huntingdon North is traditionally the strongest Labour part of the district, and Labour fielded their district councillor Patrick Kadewere, who finished in second place; the Lib Dems, who were defending the seat, fell to third and the Conservatives came through the middle to win.

That will not happen in this by-election, as there is a straight fight. Defending for the Liberal Democrats is Michael Shellens, who represented the former Huntingdon East ward from 2008 to 2018 and also sat on Cambridgeshire county council from 2013 until May this year; on both occasions, he retired. Challenging for the Conservatives is Jonas King, a local resident who took over from Shellens

* *Andrew's Previews 2019*, pages 241 and 404; *2020*, page 33; this book, pages 130 and 272. This paragraph has been rewritten as I had omitted the 2020 by-election in error.

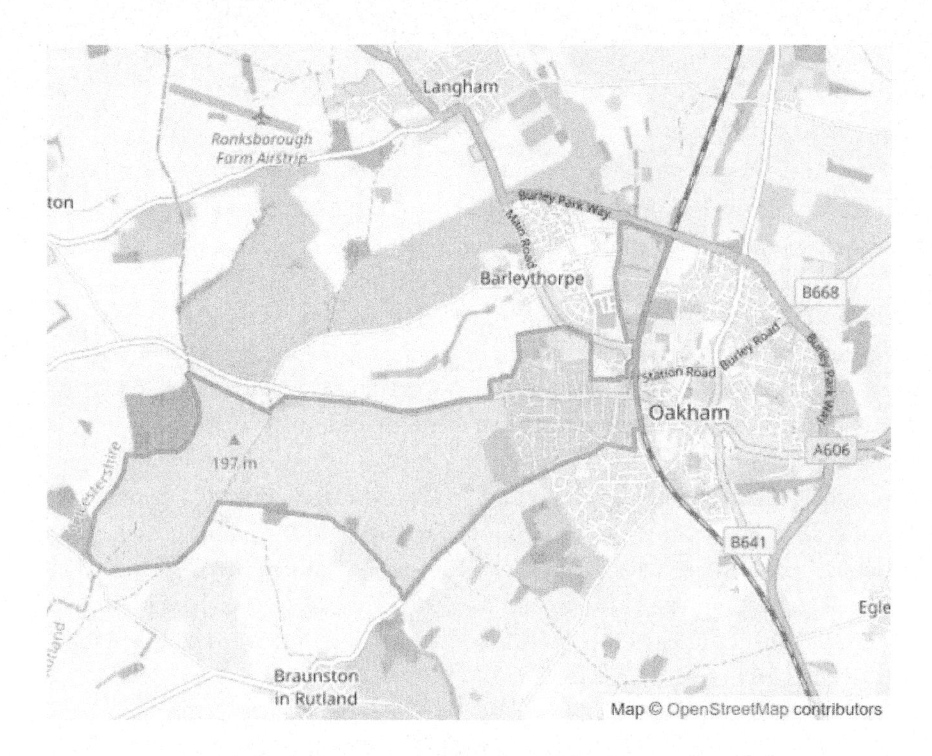

Figure 147: Oakham North West

in May as county councillor for Huntingdon North and Hartford.*

Oakham North West

Rutland council; caused by the resignation of independent councillor Adam Lowe.

We stay in the east for our second trip this year to England's "smallest" "county", as we consider what must rank among the most bizarrely-shaped wards this column has seen in a long time. Your columnist's first reaction on seeing Figure 147 was to wonder what the Local Government Boundary Commission had been smoking. The Commission, of course, has far more integrity than that and there is an explanation for this bizarre shape.

The explanation is to do with Barleythorpe, which used to be a small village just out of Oakham on the road towards Melton Mowbray and which until 2019 was covered by Oakham North West ward. Barleythorpe's Wikipedia entry quotes a population, from the 2001 census, of 178.

No longer is that the case. There is a lot of new housing going up in Bar-

* *Huntingdonshire, Huntingdon East*: LD 813 C 656

Parliamentary constituency: Rutland and Melton
May 2019 result C/Ind unopposed

Figure 148: Rutland, Oakham North West

leythorpe at the moment, and the village's population is booming out of all recognition. Barleythorpe declared independence from Oakham in 2016 by becoming a parish of its own, and for the 2019 election the Boundary Commission drew a brand-new Barleythorpe ward based on that parish, with two Rutland councillors to allow room for further population growth in the next few years.

The shape we see here is basically what was left of Oakham North West ward after Barleythorpe was taken out. The ward doesn't include the first Rutland branch of McDonald's (which recently opened, to some local controversy, just outside the parish and ward boundary in Barleythorpe), but the salient to the north takes in an industrial area on Pillings Road and the Lands' End factory outlet shop. However, the ward's electors live in the southern part along the Cold Overton and Braunston Roads; landmarks here include the Oakham Memorial Hospital, the secondary school Catmose College, and the town's railway station which lies on the ward boundary.

The 2003–19 Oakham North West ward had two seats. One was held throughout this period by independent councillor Richard Gale, while the other seat was won by four different candidates (two independents, two Conservatives) at the four elections in this period. On the revised boundaries in 2019 only two candidates were nominated, Paul Ainsley for the Conservatives and independent Adam Lowe; since two seats were available in the ward, Ainsley and Lowe were both declared elected unopposed. The only elections here in May were for Leicestershire police and crime commissioner, so there is a distinct lack of information to go on in predicting this by-election.

Adam Lowe handed in his resignation as a Rutland councillor in September, explaining that he was seeking a better work:life balance. Lowe also sits on Oakham town council, and away from politics he works 12-hour shifts for the Probation Service and does all sorts of other worthy and time-consuming things. When push came to shove, there weren't enough hours in his week and something had to give. Lowe chose to give up his county council role.

No new independent candidate has come forward to replace Lowe, so we have a free-for-all! It's a straight fight. In the blue corner is Daniel Bottomley, a former Oakham town councillor. In the red corner is Leah Toseland, who is a mother of two children with special needs; she is described as a community campaigner.*

* *Rutland, Oakham North West*: Lab 293 C 175 [Lab gain from Ind]

Parliamentary constituency: Tewkesbury
Gloucestershire county council division: Longlevens
May 2021 result C 1645/1312/1129 LD 1523/1250/1147 Libertarian 204
November 2016 by-election C 1066 LD 852 Lab 223 UKIP 167
May 2016 result C 1657/1636/1410 Lab 696 UKIP 541 LD 515 Grn 494
May 2015 result C 2870 Lab 955 UKIP 815 LD 548 Grn 262
May 2014 result C 1545 UKIP 683 Lab 463 LD 282 Grn 135
May 2012 result C 1425 LD 1111 Lab 372 Grn 127
May 2011 result C 2005 LD 821 Lab 695
May 2010 result C 2958 LD 1686 Lab 863
May 2008 result C 1819 LD 1537 Lab 172
May 2007 result C 1884 LD 822 Lab 272 UKIP 158
May 2006 result C 1962 LD 1256 Lab 215
June 2004 result LD 1704 C 1650 Lab 247
May 2003 result C 1506 LD 1287 Lab 269
May 2002 result C 1511/1465/1367 LD 1246/1118/1001 Lab 386/329/307

Figure 149: Gloucester, Longlevens

Longlevens

Gloucester council; caused by the resignation of Conservative councillor Clive Walford.

We move to the western half of England for the three remaining by-elections this week, starting in the south-west with the city of Gloucester. The Longlevens ward is the north-eastern corner of the city's built-up area, between the Tewkesbury and Cheltenham roads, and consists entirely of privately-developed lower-middle-class housing from the twentieth century, with very high levels of owner-occupation. This area was not fully incorporated into Gloucester until 1967, and it is still not fully linked with the city even now: since 2010, this ward has been part of the Tewkesbury parliamentary constituency.

Longlevens ward was left unchanged by a boundary review implemented in 2016, the year in which Gloucester came off the thirds electoral cycle and moved to whole-council elections. In this century it has mostly voted Conservative, although the Lib Dems won the ward in 2004 and came close on a number of other occasions. The ward became safe Conservative during the coalition years, but turned back into a marginal at a by-election in November 2016* at which the Conservative majority was cut to 46–37.

That by-election returned Conservative councillor Clive Walford, who was fairly well-known in the city having played on the back row for Gloucester Rugby in the mid-1970s. Walford was re-elected quite narrowly in May 2021, with a

* *Andrew's Previews 2016*, page 276.

majority of 62 votes over the Lib Dem runner-up Sarah Sawyer: overall the Conservatives polled 49% of the vote and won two seats, while the Lib Dem slate polled 45% and won one seat. The city council ballot paper only had Conservative, Lib Dem and Libertarian candidates: the Longlevens division of the county council, which takes in part of the Lib Dem-held Elmbridge ward, had a Labour candidate in addition and a much larger Conservative lead on the same day.

Clive Walford became deputy mayor and Sheriff of Gloucester for 2021–22, but he resigned in September partway through his term. Defending the resulting by-election for the Conservatives is Julie Evans, who was the losing Conservative candidate here in May. The Lib Dems have reselected Sarah Sawyer, who as stated was runner-up here in May. Also standing are Claire Carter for the Green Party and Alfie Harrison for Labour.*

Blackfriars and Trinity

Salford council; caused by the death of Labour councillor Raymond Walker.

If anywhere can be described as being the heart of Salford, this is it. The Blackfriars and Trinity ward lies in a bend of the River Irwell, immediately across the river from That Other City on the far bank. Salford is the only locality in this area mentioned in the Domesday Book—indeed, it was the centre of its own hundred—but the presence of That Other City means that it never really fulfilled its potential. Of the two main thoroughfares of original Salford, Chapel Street never became the major commercial destination that Deansgate turned into; while Greengate has all but disappeared under railway viaducts and relief roads. To add insult to injury, the railway station built on top of Greengate—Exchange station, which closed in the 1960s—bore the name of That Other City rather than Salford.

Mind, it's not all bad. There is a five-star hotel within this ward: the Lowry, with its landmark footbridge over the Irwell to That Other City. Employment is provided by (among others) HMRC, who occupy a large tower block next to the Lowry. Salford Cathedral, further along Chapel Street, will administer to your soul if you happen to be a Catholic. And a couple of blocks up from Salford Cathedral can be found the imposing building once occupied by Salford Royal Hospital, now turned into flats.

The 1885 constituency map for Salford, which divided the borough into three parliamentary constituencies, shows that the modern area of this ward was covered by four of the twelve wards of Salford county borough at the time:

* *Gloucester, Longlevens*: LD 1520 C 781 Lab 135 Grn 86 [LD gain from C]

Greengate, St Matthias, St Stephens, and Trinity. This area had enough population then to be a constituency in its own right (although in the event it was divided between Salford North and Salford South).

But waves of slum clearance have swept away nearly all of old Salford. The Cathedral and the Royal Hospital are rare survivors of old buildings in Blackfriars and Trinity ward. There's not much of the old Victorian housing left here now. The area outside Trinity Way is characterised by low-rise residential areas, of much lower density than the terraces they replaced, while inside the inner relief road an orgy of modern tower blocks is going up—apartments for contemporary city living. Whether it's Salford or That Other City.

We can see one effect of this just outside the ward boundary. Immediately opposite the old Salford Royal Hospital can be found Transport House, which was built in 2005 on a site which used to be offices for the Transport and General Workers Union and whose flats were sold as housing for key workers. A number of its apartments are in shared ownership. Transport House is a five-storey apartment block which has proved, in a post-Grenfell survey, to be unsafe in its current form thanks to flammable insulation; however, it is not tall enough to qualify for a government assistance fund for fire safety improvements. Instead, the occupiers have been presented by the freeholder with a bill for £3 million—more than the block cost to build in the first place—to remove the unsafe insulation from the building's walls. Lewis Goodall, the policy editor of the BBC's *Newsnight* programme, has covered the plight of Transport House's leaseholders on a number of occasions this year.

Despite the experience of Transport House, the population projections for inner-city Salford are through the roof as more and more of these apartment blocks are built. The 2004–21 Ordsall ward, which covered the Chapel Street area along with Salford Quays, was becoming seriously out of shape. The Boundary Commission's response was a new ward map for Salford, introduced in May this year, which effectively created a new ward in the inner city. The three previous wards of Irwell Riverside, Langworthy and Ordsall were reorganised into four new wards: this one, a cut-down Ordsall, Pendleton and Charlestown, and Quays. Apart from Pendleton and Charlestown, all of these were drawn with low headcounts (in the case of Quays ward, a spectacularly low headcount) to allow for population growth. Blackfriars and Trinity ward's electorate was projected to grow by 80% between 2018 and 2024.

There has only been one previous contest on these boundaries, in May 2021. On that occasion the Labour slate won all three seats in Blackfriars and Trinity with a 54–27 lead over the Greens. There was wide variation between the candidates on the Labour and Green slates, partly because the lead Green

Parliamentary constituency: Salford and Eccles
May 2021 result Lab 1226/1205/946 Grn 606/349/276 C 177/137 LD 142/96/61 Ind 118

Figure 150: Salford, Blackfriars and Trinity

candidate Wendy Olsen was also the Green candidate in the simultaneous Mayor of Salford election. (She finished third in that contest, polling 9%). In Blackfriars and Trinity Olsen polled twice as many votes as her running-mates, mostly at the expense of Labour's Ray Walker for no obvious reason other than the fact that Walker's name is at the wrong end of the alphabet.

Walker had been a council servant for decades, although he had only recently made it into the council chamber up in Swinton. He was employed by Salford council for 31 years as a librarian and on reception at the civic centre, and he got into politics through the trade union route. Walker had once been on the executive of the Communist Party of Britain, but he later joined the Labour Party. He was first elected in 2019 for Irwell Riverside ward, which then covered the Blackfriars area, and transferred here in 2021 when that ward was broken up. Sadly, Ray Walker passed away in August after a sudden illness, aged 57. No age at all.

Because he was the third-placed candidate in May 2021 Walker was due for re-election next May, so the winner of this by-election will not be able to rest for long. Defending for Labour is Roseanna Wain, who stood in May on the Labour slate for Kersal and Broughton Park ward and got thrashed by the Conservatives in the most Jewish ward in the UK. Wendy Olsen is no longer on the scene in Salford so the Green Party needed a new candidate: they have selected David Jones, who stood in Broughton ward (over the river to the north) in May: Jones was the Green candidate for Blackley and Broughton in the 2019 general election. Also standing are Christopher Bates for the Conservatives and Joseph Allen for the Lib Dems.*

North Meols

West Lancashire council; caused by the death of Conservative councillor Tom Blane.

We finish the week as we began: by the seaside. The word "meols" (here pronounced "meals") is a Norse-derived word for sand-dunes which appears in a number of places on the Lancashire and Cheshire coasts, but the landscape of North Meols ward is utterly flat and dominated by saltmarsh and worse.

* *Salford, Blackfriars and Trinity*: Lab 408 Grn 160 LD 152 C 68

Parliamentary constituency: South Ribble
Lancashire county council division: West Lancashire North
May 2019 result C 595 Lab 459 UKIP 152
May 2018 result Lab 625 C 503
May 2015 result C 1026 Lab 586 UKIP 420
May 2014 result C 439 UKIP 364 Lab 277
May 2011 result C 785 Lab 422
May 2010 result C 1192 Lab 638
May 2007 result C 567 LD 254 Lab 137
May 2006 result C 620 Ind 243 Lab 126 Grn 108
May 2003 result C 386 Ind 286 Lab 117
May 2002 result C 549/548 Ind 383 Lab 304

Figure 151: West Lancashire, North Meols

Don't set off walking towards the bright lights of Lytham to the north: that way lies the Ribble estuary, which is impassable unless you have a hovercraft handy. Even more of this area was under water until Martin Mere was drained in the nineteenth century, and the result of this land reclamation is utterly flat and very rich agricultural land.

While the ward's arable landscape may look similar to somewhere in Lincolnshire or the Dutch polders, this is Lancashire. The largest population centre is the village of Banks, just to the east of Southport off the main road towards Preston. Although Southport is the main service centre for the area, it is part of Merseyside whereas North Meols has remained part of Lancashire. So for the moment the ward is part of the South Ribble parliamentary seat, based on Leyland and southern suburbs of Preston, while its council services are administered from Ormskirk by West Lancashire council.

West Lancashire went into No Overall Control at May's council elections after many years of Labour majority. The main reason for this is the OWLs, who are not what they seem. OWL here is Our West Lancashire, a localist group which now holds seven seats on the council. There is also one independent, 19 Conservatives plus this vacancy and 26 Labour councillors, two short of a majority. Labour continue to run West Lancashire as a minority administration, and if they gain this by-election they will hold half the seats on the council.

What are the chances of that? Well, West Lancashire district tends to have very few marginal wards but this can now be counted as one of them. North Meols voted Labour in 2018 for the first time this century, the party winning 55–45 in a straight fight having never come particularly close in previous years. The ward last went to the polls in 2019, when Tom Blane was re-elected for a second term of office by a 49–38 margin over Labour. The Conservatives enjoyed a much larger majority in May's Lancashire county council elections, at which North Meols ward was part of the West Lancashire North division.

Tom Blane passed away in September at the age of 78, leaving an intriguing by-election which is a straight fight. Defending for the Conservatives is John Howard, a North Meols parish councillor. Challenging for Labour is Liz Savage, who is a former West Lancashire councillor (for Ashurst ward in Skem, 2011–19) and has three very creditable parliamentary campaigns under her belt: Savage was the Labour candidate for the neighbouring Southport constituency in 2015, 2017 and 2019, taking her party's share of the vote in Southport from 9% in 2010 to 39% in 2019. This could be one to watch.*

* *West Lancashire, North Meols*: C 634 Lab 343

11th November 2021

There are eight by-elections on Armistice Day, 11th November 2021, and this is a very interesting set. We have two seats defended by the Lincolnshire Independents, one defence each for the Conservatives, the Green Party and Plaid Cymru, together with three free-for-alls! With hung councils galore, two councillors having left the country and a wide mix of places and issues to talk about, there really is something for everyone this week. Let's start this week's edition of Andrew's Previews by talking turnout, in the UK's most millennial ward…

University and Scotforth Rural

Lancaster council; caused by the resignation of Jack O'Dwyer-Henry.

Last week this column discussed a by-election in inner-city Salford, a place where there is a lot of building of new apartments going on. New apartment blocks in city centres can be very difficult places for political campaigns: they are often impossible to access or leaflet for people who don't live there, and the people who do live there in many cases don't stay for long before moving on. Those were some of the excuses given for the turnout in last week's Blackfriars and Trinity by-election (page 458), which was a pathetic 10.06% of the electorate. Salford Council reckon this is the lowest ever turnout for an election in the city, and I'm not going to contradict that.

It's not a record low turnout for the UK, though. The last by-election before the pandemic hit, in Coventry in March 2020[*], had a turnout of 9%—but that was with the public health emergency at its height. That's a one-off factor (at least we hope so). For a turnout that's really difficult to beat you need a highly transient population—preferably somewhere where the electorate completely turns over every year, perhaps have little connection to the area, and are largely absent for a large chunk of the year…

[*] *Andrew's Previews 2020*, page 79.

Welcome to Lancaster University. This is one of the 1960s "plate-glass" universities located on its own separate campus just to the south of Lancaster. The university is known for the high quality of its teaching: its alumni include the Opposition Chief Whip, Sir Alan Campbell, and the present Labour MP for Lancaster and Fleetwood Cat Smith, while the former Labour cabinet minister Alan Milburn is the present Chancellor of the university. The University is on a growth spurt and has expanded beyond the original campus in recent years.

From 2003 to 2015 Lancaster council had a University ward, which covered the original Lancaster University campus and nothing else. Its 2011 census return is unique. 94% of the population were full-time students, 94% were aged between 18 and 29, 68% were educated to A-level but not (yet) further: all of these were by a long way the highest figures for any ward in England and Wales. University ward also made the top 100 in England and Wales for households living rent-free, which appears to be an artefact of the census enumerators recognising the university's colleges as one household each—only 62 households were counted in the ward for 3,384 residents.

It probably shouldn't come as a surprise that the most millennial ward in the UK turned out to be politically left-wing. University ward voted Lib Dem on its creation in 2003, then Green in 2007, was won by Labour in 2011 and went back to the Greens at a by-election in 2014.

The University's expansion has made a mess of the administrative boundaries in the area. The building of the original campus left Scotforth parish divided into two parts, while the new south-west campus forms part of Ellel parish. For the 2015 Lancaster elections an expanded University and Scotforth Rural ward was drawn up, taking in all of these areas. Scotforth parish covers some lovely but sparsely-populated countryside, so this expansion hasn't had much effect on the ward's unique demographic. The University and Scotforth Rural ward has not proven to be particularly workable in practice, and draft proposals from the Local Government Boundary Commission will break it up for the 2023 Lancaster elections. That change would create something similar to (but smaller than) the local county council division of Lancaster South East, which is safely Labour but has a permanent population to give the demographic profile a more conventional look.*

The LGBCE faces an extra difficulty in its current work which it didn't have in the last review of Lancaster: Individual Electoral Registration. When this was brought in for the December 2015 register the enrolment of University and

* These proposals did not survive the public consultation. The LGBCE's final recommendations retain a separate University ward, but this time without Scotforth Rural parish and with a drop to two councillors.

Scotforth Rural ward dropped like a stone, because the University administration was no longer able to process applications to vote and send them to Lancaster electoral services *en bloc*. For the following academic year the University brought electoral registration back in-house with an opt-out for those students who for whatever reason don't want to register: but this hasn't brought the ward's register back up to scratch in the long term. The December 2020 register, which the Commission are using for their current review, gives University and Scotforth Rural an entitlement of just 1.77 Lancaster councillors, a figure which is not projected to change significantly in the near future. The ward simply doesn't have the electorate to justify its three councillors.

As to why the ward has proven difficult in practice: remember that the vast majority of electors here are students. University students generally don't vote in local elections. This may seem like a heretical question for a psephological piece to ask, but: why *should* they? Most students won't hang around for a full electoral cycle. Student housing is let on contracts of one year or less: students will often move in and out of halls of residence, finding themselves in different wards or even different council areas from one year to the next. Student residences are exempt from council tax. And campus-based universities like Lancaster are very much their own bubble, with those inside the bubble taking very little notice of what is going on in the city next door. In May 2002 your columnist was a poll clerk at the campus polling station for another "bubble" campus university, Warwick, in the Coventry city council elections: we recorded an on-the-day turnout of 8.4%.

The first election for the present ward was in 2015, and it returned two Labour councillors (Lucy Atkinson and Matt Mann) and a Green (Sam Armstrong). The Tory slate, despite including a candidate with the name Ice Dong, finished in third place. Mann resigned from the council in late 2016, having taken up a new job outside Lancaster, and the resulting by-election featured a campaign visit from none other than Jeremy Corbyn.

This did help the new Labour candidate Nathan Burns hold the December 2016 University and Scotforth Rural by-election* with 98, to 79 for the Greens and 68 for the Conservatives. Those figures are not percentages: they are *votes*. Nathan Burns holds the dubious distinction of being the only English district councillor this century (outside the City of London and the Isles of Scilly) to be elected with fewer than 100 votes at a contested election. The final turnout was around 7%, which this column suspects to be the record low turnout for a UK local election. It's going to be very difficult to beat.

The other two ward councillors, Lucy Atkinson for Labour and Sam Arm-

* *Andrew's Previews 2016*, page 328.

strong for the Greens, both stood down in early 2018. The resulting double by-election in May 2018[*] returned the Labour slate of Amara Betts-Patel and Oliver Robinson quite comfortably with a much higher turnout: they polled 518 and 423 votes respectively. Labour held the ward at the May 2019 Lancaster city council elections with 41% of the vote, against 30% for the Green Party and 17% for the Conservatives: Robinson was re-elected, with Katie Whearty and Jack O'Dwyer-Henry joining the Labour slate.

Lancaster has been a hung council for many years. Labour came close to winning a majority here in 2015, but fell back in 2019 largely thanks to a resurgence from the Morecambe Bay Independents, a long-standing Morecambe localist party. The 2019 election returned 21 Labour councillors, 14 Morecambe Bay Independents, 12 Conservatives, 10 Greens and 3 Lib Dems. A by-election in the rural Kellet ward in May 2021 saw the Conservatives recover a seat they had lost to the Lib Dems in 2019.

The Labour group on the council has since split, with a number of councillors elected on their ticket forming a new "Eco-Socialist Independent" group. At the 2021 AGM the Eco-Socialist Independents deposed the Labour council leader and installed a new leader from the Green Party, who have formed a minority coalition with the Eco-Socialist Independents to run the council. The Greens have 10 councillors and the Eco-Socialist Independents have 4: the opposition now consists of 14 Labour councillors plus one vacant seat, 11 Conservatives plus two vacant seats, 9 Morecambe Bay Independents, 2 Lib Dems, 6 other councillors and this vacancy. Three different dates over the next few weeks have been set for the four pending by-elections, so this is the first in a three-part series of Previews covering Lancaster city council.[†]

The 2021 University and Scotforth Rural by-election is to replace Councillor Jack O'Dwyer-Henry, who was one of the Labour councillors who defected to the Eco-Socialist Independents. O'Dwyer-Henry has now graduated from Lancaster University, and he has returned to his native Belfast to take up a new job with the Green Party of Northern Ireland.

This by-election has no defending Eco-Socialist Independent candidate, so we have a free-for-all! You need four people to make up a *University Challenge* team, and four people is what we have here. Labour will want their seat back: their candidate is (Sayeda) Fabiha Askari, who is described as a Lancaster lass and student. The Greens, whose policies are rather high on the news agenda at the moment with the ongoing COP26 climate change conference in Glasgow, will presumably want to pick up the seat previously held by their Eco-Socialist

[*] *Andrew's Previews 2018*, page 173. [†] For the other parts of the trilogy see pages 515 and 550.

Parliamentary constituency: Lancaster and Fleetwood
Lancashire county council division: Lancaster South East
May 2019 result Lab 295/278/267 Grn 217/175/142 C 119/113/112 LD 88/83/72
May 2018 double by-election Lab 518/423 Grn 264/235 C 184/184 LD 120/114
December 2016 result Lab 98 Grn 79 C 68 LD 36
May 2015 result Lab 605/500/480 Grn 555/440/417 C 405/391/339 LD 143/79/66

Figure 152: Lancaster, University and Scotforth Rural

Independent partners: their candidate is Jamie Payne, who is a final-year student reading politics and international relations. The Conservatives have broken with the trend and not selected a student for this by-election: their candidate is Matthew Maxwell-Scott, who represents the neighbouring Lancaster Rural East division on the county council. Completing the ballot paper is Zanna Ashton for the Lib Dems.*

Melton Dorian

Melton council, Leicestershire; caused by the disqualification of Conservative councillor Alan Pearson, who failed to attend any meetings of the council in six months.

For our first East Midlands by-election this week we have come to what is, in population terms, the smallest remaining non-metropolitan district in England. Melton district council covers a population of just over 50,000, according to the latest ONS estimates; only Rutland (which this column visited last week), the City of London and the Isles of Scilly have smaller headcounts. Should the current proposals for reorganisation in North Yorkshire and Cumbria go through, Melton would be one of only three shire districts with a population under 60,000, along with West Devon and another Leicestershire council, Oadby and Wigston.

Slightly more than half of Melton district's electors live in the town of Melton Mowbray, which has given us not only the famous pork pie but also Stilton cheese: the Tuxford and Tebbutt creamery is one of only six dairies in the UK permitted to produce the real thing. The town is surprisingly industrial for its size, and Dorian ward (covering the south-west corner of the town) is in the top 100 wards in England and Wales for those employed in manufacturing. Within the ward boundary is the Melton Foods factory, the world's largest supplier of genuine Melton Mowbray pork pies.

Despite the presence of all that pork the Conservatives have a large majority on Melton council, and even with this manufacturing profile the Labour Party

* *Lancaster, University and Scotforth Rural*: Lab 216 Grn 193 C 44 LD 16

Parliamentary constituency: Rutland and Melton
Leicestershire county council division: Melton West
May 2019 result C 477/429/385 Grn 438
May 2015 result C 1221/1146/1039 Lab 797/646/579 Ind 642
May 2011 result C 649/540/524 Lab 642/563
May 2007 result C 581/484/439 Ind 352 Lab 313
August 2004 by-election C 397 Lab 140 Ind 125
May 2003 result C 367/302 Ind 297 Lab 268/239/237 Melton Borough Progressive Alliance 188

Figure 153: Melton, Melton Dorian

have won just two seats in Dorian ward this century, both in the 2011 election. At the first contest on the current boundaries in 2003 Dorian elected two Conservative councillors and an independent, Patricia Cumbers, who subsequently joined the party and has topped the poll at each ordinary election since. The ward returned a full slate of Conservatives in 2007 and 2015, but not in 2019 when the Tory slate was opposed only by Philip Wood as a Green Party candidate. Wood polled 48% and was elected in second place, with the Tory slate polling 52% and winning the other two seats. At other levels of government Dorian ward is part of safe Conservative units: the Melton West division of Leicestershire county council, and the Rutland and Melton parliamentary seat.

Alan Pearson had represented this ward on Melton council since 2015 and was also the ward's county councillor from 2013 until this May, when he didn't seek re-election. Pearson is currently in Western Australia, having gone there before Christmas to see family and to get a second opinion following recent surgery on his shoulder. It appears that the second opinion was not a good one. Pearson has not returned to Leicestershire, and as a result he has now been thrown off Melton council under the six-month non-attendance rule.

The by-election to replace him has a curious candidate list, given the 2019 result. Defending for the Conservatives is Timothy Webster, a former manager of the town's livestock market who is a trustee of the Melton Mowbray Town Estate. One of the longest-running forms of town government in England, the Town Estate has been doing good work in Melton since the sixteenth century and still runs the town's parks, sports grounds and market. The curious bit is that there is no Green Party candidate, so the opposition to Webster comes from Sarah Cox. A local resident, Cox is a former police chief inspector who also plays a leading role in local charities, and she has been nominated by the Labour Party. It's a straight fight: seconds out!*

* *Melton, Melton Dorian*: C 362 Lab 284

Parliamentary constituency: Sleaford and North Hykeham
Lincolnshire county council division: Metheringham Rural (part: Blankney, Dunston and Metheringham parishes), Potterhanworth and Coleby (part: Nocton parish)
May 2019 result Lincs Ind 814/807 C 544/489
May 2015 result C 1641/1340 Lincs Ind 1336
May 2011 result 2 C unopposed
May 2007 result Ind 1054/949/585

Figure 154: North Kesteven, Metheringham

Metheringham; and Sleaford Castle

North Kesteven council, Lincolnshire. The Metheringham poll is a double by-election following the resignations of Lincolnshire Independents councillors Nick Byatt and Laura Pearson. The Sleaford Castle by-election follows the resignation of a third Lincolnshire Independents councillor, Cara Sandy.

In a change to some advertised listings, our other East Midlands by-elections this week take place in North Kesteven council, which covers a large rural area immediately to the south of Lincoln. They were notified to this column very late; and by "very late" here I mean "two-and-a-half hours before polls closed", which was the time I had to research and write this section. As such, take this piece with even more salt than usual.

The main town in the North Kesteven district is Sleaford, which has an important location at a place where the River Slea breaks through the ridge of high ground which runs south from Lincoln. The town had a castle to go with it: Sleaford Castle, located rather curiously on flat fenland, was constructed during the early twelfth century by the Bishop of Lincoln. Little remains of the castle today, and its site is a green space just to the west of the present-day town centre. Sleaford Castle is the central of the five wards for Sleaford town, and covers housing either side of the railway line to the west together with a small part of the town centre (the western side of South Gate).

Sleaford's main focus has always been as an agricultural town servicing the rich fenland of Lincolnshire. Some of the fenland villages are covered by the Metheringham ward, which covers four long and thin parishes about halfway between Sleaford and Lincoln. The shape of the parish boundaries show that these are spring-line villages, located at places on a ridge slope where streams rise before flowing down to the fens. Metheringham itself has a railway station, linking the village to Lincoln and Sleaford.

The North Kesteven district forms the basis for the Sleaford and North

Hykeham parliamentary seat, which (with slightly different boundaries) returned the largest Conservative vote total and largest Conservative vote percentage in the 2017 general election. Less than two years later, the Conservatives lost overall control of the council: the 2019 election returned 22 independent and 20 Conservative councillors, with one vacancy due to insufficient nominations. The Conservatives won the resulting by-election* and they have managed to stay in power on North Kesteven council—but only by peeling off some of the independent councillors to form a coalition administration.

A number of the opposition councillors were returned with the nomination of the Lincolnshire Independents, who at one point had a sizeable group on the county council but have been down to one county councillor since 2017. The Lincolnshire Independents are defending all three seats today, so there is a chance for the Conservative-led administration to increase its majority here. Both wards are in divisions which voted Conservative in May's county elections by large margins.

Metheringham ward has only previously been contested by independent and Conservative candidates this century. In 2003 and 2007 all the candidates were independents; the Conservative slate gained the ward in 2011 without a contest, and held both seats in 2015 against a challenge from a single Lincolnshire Independent, Nick Byatt, who lost out by just four votes. The Lincolnshire Independents won both seats in 2019 rather convincingly, with a 60–40 margin.

Sleaford Castle ward has been in independent hands since 2011 when Keith Dolby gained the ward from the Conservatives. Dolby stood down in 2019 and his seat went to the Lincolnshire Independents in a close three-way result: Cara Sandy won with 194 votes, while the Labour candidate Linda Edwards-Shea and the Conservatives' Steve Fields (a former Lincolnshire Independents councillor) tied for second place on 172 votes each. In percentage terms that's 36–32–32, and it's the closest Labour have come to winning a seat on North Kesteven council since they were wiped out in 2007.

The Sleaford Castle by-election is a free-for-all, with no defending Lincolnshire Independents candidate. There are, however, two independents on the ballot. Ken Fernandes is a Sleaford town councillor, while Steve Mason was an independent candidate in May's Lincolnshire county elections (for Sleaford Rural division, which doesn't cover this ward). Labour's runner-up from last time Linda Edwards-Shea, the deputy mayor of Sleaford, is back for another go. The Conservatives' offer to the electors is Malcolm Offer, who is also seeking election to the town council in a different by-election. Completing the Castle

* *Andrew's Previews 2019*, page 175.

Parliamentary constituency: Sleaford and North Hykeham
Lincolnshire county council division: Sleaford
May 2019 result Lincs Ind 194 Lab 172 C 172
May 2015 result Ind 678 C 451
May 2011 result Ind 492 C 225
May 2007 result C 271 LD 187 Lab 146

Figure 155: North Kesteven, Sleaford Castle

ballot paper is Susan Hislop for the Lib Dems.*

We have seven candidates chasing the two available seats in Metheringham. The Lincolnshire Independents have put up a slate of Amelia Bailey and Mark Williams; Bailey runs a tearoom in Metheringham, while Williams is a qualified FA coach who works in IT for the county council. The Conservatives will be looking to recover their 2019 loss with their slate of Dave Parry and Fran Pembury; Parry is a Metheringham parish councillor, while Pembury runs a hairdressers' in the village. For the first time this century other parties are getting in on the act here: Labour have nominated Paul Edwards-Shea and Calvin Rodgerson, while Diana Catton stands for the Liberal Democrats.†

Llandrillo

Denbighshire council, North Wales; caused by the resignation of Plaid Cymru councillor Mabon ab Gwynfor.

We have reached the second week of November, which as long-term readers of Andrew's Previews know can mean only one thing: it is now time for your columnist to mount the pulpit and read out the following notice.

The six-month rule has now come into effect as we approach the next ordinary local elections on Thursday 5th May 2022. What this means is that from now on, if a councillor who was due for re-election in May 2022 dies, resigns or gets disqualified, then there will be no by-election to replace them and their seat will be left vacant.

The May 2022 local elections will see all local councillors in Greater London, Scotland, Wales, Birmingham, Huntingdonshire, Newcastle-under-Lyme, St Helens and South Cambridgeshire up for election, together with one-third or one-half of those councils which hold elections by thirds or halves (generally, these are boroughs and districts in urban England outside London). If the

* *North Kesteven, Sleaford Castle*: C 135 Lab 93 Mason 49 Fernandes 22 LD 21 [C gain from Lincs Ind] † *North Kesteven, Metheringham*: C 424 (Pembery)/404 (Parry) Lincs Ind 404 (Bailey)/369 (Williams) Lab 85 (Edwards-Shea)/69 (Rodgerson) LD 29 [Bailey elected on drawing of lots; 1 C gain from Lincs Ind]

government gets its act together, we may also have some form of elections to a new local government structure in Cumbria, North Yorkshire and Somerset.

My list of council vacancies currently has two entries in London (not counting the parliamentary vacancy in Old Bexley and Sidcup), four in Scotland and six in Wales (one of which, in Torfaen, has been left vacant for over six months now and nobody appears to be in any hurry to call it). Once those are cleared, this column will take its leave of London, Scotland and Wales until the summer of 2022 at the earliest. The first half of next year is looking likely to be an England-only diet for council by-elections.

So, savour today's two Welsh polls while you can. We start in the north with a ward in the Dee valley at the southern end of Denbighshire. Llandrillo yn Edeirnion is a small village to the south of Corwen, in the shadow of the high Berwyn mountains. This is very much rural Wales. Llandrillo ward's census return has an unusual feature: 27 of its 489 households were living rent-free, which is the highest proportion for any ward in Wales and in the top 50 for England and Wales.

Cadair Berwyn, on the ward boundary, rises to an altitude of 832 metres and dominates the horizon for a large swathe of western England: on the clearest of days, views from the summit of Cadair Berwyn extend north to the Lake District, over 100 miles away. The Berwyn range forms an impassable ward boundary to the east: that's something which Henry II, in one of his invasions of Wales, failed to appreciate until it was too late. His 1165 campaign made the mistake of starting from Oswestry, struck west over the Berwyns, and quickly ground to a halt against guerilla military action and terrible weather. The mountains were also the scene of an obscure incident in January 1974 which has been claimed to be a UFO crash; the MoD investigation ascribed the loud noise and bright lights on the Berwyns to a combination of a small earthquake, a meteor and poachers.

The modern Denbighshire district is based on the Vale of Clwyd, with its main towns being Rhyl and Prestatyn on the north coast. However, Llandrillo yn Edeirnion and its sister village of Cynwyd, further down the valley, are in the Dee valley rather than the Clwyd valley and form a rather remote corner of the district. Indeed, until its transfer to Clwyd in the 1974 reorganisation, this ward was a part of Merionethshire. So from February 1974 until the parliamentary boundaries caught up in 1983, Llandrillo was represented by the Plaid Cymru MP Dafydd Elis Thomas.

Thomas was the Baby of the Commons between the two 1974 elections (he was aged 27 when first elected), and his long career in politics didn't finally come to an end until May this year when he retired from the Senedd. He was the leader of Plaid Cymru from 1984 to 1991, has been a member of the House of Lords (as

Lord Elis-Thomas) since 1992, was Presiding Officer of the Welsh Assembly (as the post was then known) from 1999 to 2011, and he finished his political career from 2017 to 2021 as an independent MS and as a junior minister in the Welsh Government.

Lord Elis-Thomas sat in the Senedd until 2021 for Dwyfor Meirionnydd, the successor to the Merioneth constituency he had first won 47 years earlier. Upon his retirement that seat was recovered for Plaid Cymru by Mabon ap Gwynfor. A grandson of the first Plaid Cymru MP Gwynfor Evans, Mabon started his political career in 2004 by being elected to Aberystwyth town council; he made the step up to principal council level in May 2017 by winning the Llandrillo division of Denbighshire without a contest. His new Senedd constituency borders his old ward.

The Welsh Government have recently tightened up the rules on "double-jobbing" by elected representatives. Local councillors who are elected to the Senedd are now required to resign their council seat unless they are in or entering the final year of their council term. As the next Welsh council elections are due in May 2022 this exception applied to Mabon ap Gwynfor, who was eligible to finish his term on Denbighshire council but would need to stand down from either the Senedd or the council in May next year. Mabon was not required to resign his council seat before May, but he has chosen to do so.

Mabon ap Gwynfor had previously stood in the 2011 Senedd election and the 2015 Westminster election as the Plaid Cymru candidate for the Clwyd South constituency, which has covered Llandrillo since the 1997 election. (In that year the Conservative candidate for Clwyd South was one Boris Johnson; answers on a postcard to the usual address as to what happened to him.) Clwyd South was a Conservative gain from Labour in December 2019 making this area technically part of the Red Wall, but the seat re-elected its Labour MS Ken Skates quite comfortably in May.

These figures are unlikely to be replicated in this by-election, not least because there is no Labour candidate. Mabon ap Gwynfor's predecessor as ward councillor was Plaid's Cefyn Williams, who was re-elected for his penultimate term of office in 2008 with 78% of the vote. After that experience, nobody bothered to oppose Plaid here in either 2012 or 2017.

The 2017 election left Denbighshire council very evenly balanced, with 16 Conservative councillors, 13 Labour (mostly from Rhyl), 9 Plaid, 8 independents and a Lib Dem. All the parties except Labour are represented in the ruling administration.

So this by-election is the first contested local election for Llandrillo in 13 years. Defending for Plaid Cymru is Gwyneth Ellis, a community councillor in

Parliamentary and Senedd constituency: Clwyd South
May 2017 result PC unopposed
May 2012 result PC unopposed
May 2008 result PC 405 Ind 93 C 19
June 2004 result PC 391 Ind 158

Figure 156: Denbighshire, Llandrillo

Cynwyd. The other two candidates both give addresses in Llandrillo: they are independent candidate David Robinson, who was a distant runner-up here in 2008, and Julian Sampson for the Conservatives.*

Heath

Cardiff council, Glamorgan; caused by the resignation of Heath and Birchgrove Independent councillor Fenella Bowden.

Our other Welsh by-election of the week is quite the contrast, as we travel from Wild Wales to suburban Cardiff. Heath ward is a leafy area a few miles to the north of Cardiff city centre: much of the heath was built on in the inter-war years with spacious houses and large gardens located on tree-lined roads.

Some of the open space survives as Heath Park and Cathays Cemetery, but in 1960s more of the heath disappeared with the construction of the University Hospital of Wales. Run by the NHS and Cardiff University, UHW is the largest hospital in Wales, and its presence propels Heath ward into the top 100 wards in England and Wales for those working in health or social work (21.1% of the workforce, according to the 2011 census).

Heath ward extends west across the Caerphilly Road to take in the Birchgrove area. This is rather lower down the social scale, with terraces rather than semis or detached houses dominating. Famous former Birchgrove residents include the Tour de France champion Geraint Thomas and the athlete Colin Jackson.

Heath ward has spectacularly volatile voting patterns and has returned councillors from all three main parties this century. In 2004 it was safely Liberal Democrat, but the Conservatives took two of the ward's seats off the Lib Dems in 2008. The remaining Lib Dem seat went to newly-elected Fenella Bowden, who subsequently left the party in late 2010: she then formed her own localist party, the Heath and Birchgrove Independents. The 2012 and 2017 elections here both returned a three-way split between Fenella Bowden, the Conservatives and Labour. Shares of the vote in May 2017 were 31% for Labour, 28% for the Conservatives and 27% for the Heath and Birchgrove Independents.

* *Denbighshire, Llandrillo*: PC 179 Ind 140 C 88

Parliamentary and Assembly constituency: Cardiff North
May 2017 result Lab 2010/1704/1667 C 1830/1602/1477 Heath and Birchgrove Ind 1737/1143/930 PC 410 Grn 251 LD 244/163/119
May 2012 result Heath and Birchgrove Ind 1500/1151/888 Lab 1416/1240/1116 C 1277/1242/1101 LD 349/175/140 PC 325 Ind 262 Grn 253
May 2008 result C 2205/2135/1819 LD 1877/1642/1545 Lab 896/656/575 PC 468 Grn 435
June 2004 result LD 2380/2305/1929 C 1040/1026/992 Lab 920/634/612 Cardiff Citizens 502/367/288 PC 265/248 Grn 244

Figure 157: Cardiff, Heath

Again, this is rather different from the local parliamentary seat. Heath ward is part of the Cardiff North constituency, a traditional marginal seat which has been trending to Labour in recent years. Cardiff North was gained by Labour in 2011 for the Senedd and in June 2017 for Westminster, and the Conservatives lost ground here in the last Westminster and Senedd elections.

Fenella Bowden has had some serious health problems over the last couple of years, and she has stood down on health grounds after 13 years in office,. There is just time to squeeze in a by-election for her seat before the next Cardiff city council elections in May 2022. To add extra excitement, there is no defending Heath and Birchgrove Independents candidate. It's a free-for-all! Labour, who topped the poll here in 2017 and will increase their very small majority on the council if they gain this by-election, have selected Julie Sangani: she is a healthcare volunteer and school governor at Ton yr Ywen primary school. The Conservatives have selected Peter Hudson, the husband of their current ward councillor Lyn Hudson. Also standing are Gwennol Haf for Plaid Cymru and Kathryn Lock for the Lib Dems.*

Thanet Villages

Thanet council, Kent; caused by the resignation of Green Party councillor Trevor Roper.

And now for something completely different as we finish the week at the eastern end of Kent. The Thanet Villages ward covers the relatively undeveloped southern and western ends of the Isle of Thanet, together with the low-lying ground which was once under water and made Thanet a genuine island back in the day. The ward's largest population centre, the village and railway junction of Minster-in-Thanet, is a long way from the sea now; but in AD 597 it was the location where St Augustine of Canterbury landed on English soil on a mission

* *Cardiff, Heath*: Lab 1729 C 1128 LD 561 PC 250 [Lab gain from Heath and Birchgrove Ind]

from God and the Pope. *Non Angli, sed angeli.*

Much of the acreage of Thanet Villages is taken up by the apron and very wide runway of Manston Airport. Opened in the winter of 1915–16 by the Royal Flying Corps, Manston has the UK's eleventh-longest and widest runway—wide enough for three planes to land simultaneously—and its location close to the Continent placed it on the front line during the Battle of Britain. Manston was heavily bombed, and often became the final destination for damaged RAF planes limping home to the UK. After use by the US Air Force in the early part of the Cold War, Manston from 1960 became a joint civilian and RAF airport with the occasional charter and scheduled flight. It was renamed Kent International Airport in 1989, but efforts to attract budget airlines were derailed by the collapse of EUjet—which had bought Manston—in 2005 and by the financial crash of 2008. Manston saw its final scheduled flight on 9th April 2014, a KLM departure to Amsterdam, and officially closed on 15th May 2014 with the loss of 144 jobs. Possibly the widest prominence for the airport came in 2001, when it featured as a North Korean airbase in the James Bond film *Die Another Day*.

The fate of Marston Airport has been a political open sore for many years. This column has covered some of the history before*. Thanet council elected a UKIP majority in 2015 with a manifesto pledge to reopen the airport to traffic, mainly air freight. A plan by the landowners to redevelop the airport site for housing, business and leisure now appears to have fallen through in favour of an eventual reopening. The transport secretary Grant Shapps granted a development consent order for the reopening in July 2020, but the High Court subsequently threw this out in February this year; and further assessments have questioned the long-term need for another air freight hub in the UK.

In the meantime, Manston hit the headlines last December for all the wrong reasons. The Government has for some years hired the airport for use as an emergency lorry park in the event of disruption at the Channel ports. In late December 2020, this actually happened: thousands of lorries and their drivers were trapped at Manston in December, spending Christmas in their cabs, thanks to chaos at Dover and Calais.

Thanet council's politics has been just as turbulent over the years. Since the last election in 2019 alone a Conservative minority administration has been deposed in favour of a Labour minority administration, which was then deposed in a counter-coup at June's AGM in favour of another Conservative minority administration. The latest available composition gives 26 Conservative councillors, three short of a majority, against 17 Labour, 6 Thanet Independents (the main remnant of the UKIP group which won a majority here in 2015), 3 other

* *Andrew's Previews 2018*, page 17.

Parliamentary constituency: North Thanet
Kent county council division: Birchington and Rural
May 2019 result C 638/602/460 Grn 599 LD 567 UKIP 551 C 460 LD 416 Lab 223
January 2018 by-election C 620 LD 313 Lab 206 Grn 66 Ind 52
May 2015 result Ind 1326/335 C 1273/1083 UKIP 1197/1033/916 Grn 601 Lab 515
May 2011 result Ind 1209/523 C 1011/837/720 Lab 516/472
June 2009 by-election Ind 937 C 596 LD 316 Lab 133
May 2007 result Ind 793 C 670/625/434 Lab 368/359
May 2003 result C 687/574/572 Ind 627/424/419 Lab 499/380/284

Figure 158: Thanet, Thanet Villages

independents, 3 Green Party councillors and this vacancy.

Thanet Villages ward has been politically split at every election this century. From 2003 to 2015 it was represented by two Conservatives and an independent councillor; in 2015 UKIP took one of the Conservative seats. In 2019 the Conservatives defeated the UKIP councillor, while independent councillor Bob Grove stood down. His seat went to the Green Party candidate Trevor Roper in a close fight for the final seat: Roper polled 599 votes, the Lib Dem candidate had 567 and the outgoing UKIP councillor ended on 551. Shares of the vote were 25% for the Conservatives, 23% for the Greens, 22% for the Lib Dems and 21% for UKIP.

Thanet Villages ward forms part of the large Birchington and Rural county division, which returns two Kent county councillors and is safely Conservative. Following May's county elections one of the Conservative county councillors for Birchington and Rural is Derek Crow-Brown, the former UKIP councillor for Thanet Villages.

So this could be a difficult seat for the Green Party to hold, particularly given the circumstances of the vacancy. Trevor Roper travelled to France last year with the intention of buying a home he and his wife could retire to, and then found himself unable to return to the UK. He resigned from the council after his situation was exposed by a local blogger.

Defending this by-election for the Green Party is Abi Smith, who lives in Westgate-on-Sea and has previously worked for Thanet's library service. The Conservatives have selected their unsuccessful candidate from 2019 Guy Wilson, who ran rather a long way behind his running-mates last time: he is a Manston parish councillor. The Lib Dem candidate Jeremy de Rose runs a railway service company and a bicycle business, and like Smith he was on the Kent county council ballot here in May. Thanet UKIP now appear to be defunct, so those are your three candidates.*

* *Thanet, Thanet Villages*: Grn 638 C 358 LD 67

18th November 2021

There are nine by-elections on 18th November 2021, and this week is very much a left-wing special with six of today's polls being Labour defence; the other three seats were previously independent, Liberal Democrat and continuing Liberal. There's a wide variety of wards up this week and we should have something for everyone. Without further ado, let's go to our Labour defence in the south of England…

Gorrell

Canterbury council, Kent; caused by the resignation of Labour councillor George Caffery. A former firefighter, Caffery was first elected in 2019.

> 'The time has come,' the Walrus said,
> 'To talk of many things:
> Of shoes — and ships — and sealing wax —
> Of cabbages — and kings —
> And why the sea is boiling hot —
> And whether pigs have wings.'

Oysters anyone? We start this week as we finished the previous week: in north Kent, this time visiting the seaside town of Whitstable. Whitstable has been known for its oysters since Roman times, but the modern town really got going in the mid-eighteenth century when a ferry service to London and a turnpike road to Canterbury were introduced.

From here on the town became a minor port and seaside resort, something which was enhanced in 1830 with the opening of the Canterbury and Whitstable Railway. Known from its initials as the "Crab and Winkle", the C&WR was one of the UK's first railways and was the first railway in the world to issue passenger season tickets (in 1834). Its original locomotive, *Invicta*, is now on display in the town. The railway terminated at Whitstable harbour, providing a port for the city of Canterbury.

Parliamentary constituency: Canterbury
Kent county council division: Whitstable West
May 2019 result Lab 1418/1416/1307 Grn 1298/894/638 C 889/707/690 LD 262
May 2015 result C 1977/1848/1427 Lab 1844/1658/1638 UKIP 1102 Grn 903/808/801 LD 531/476/451 Ind 412 TUSC 116/110/99

Figure 159: Canterbury, Gorrell

The present Gorrell ward, named after a local stream, was created in 2015 as a merger of two previous wards: a smaller Gorrell ward plus the former Harbour ward which covered the town centre. In the period 2003–11 Harbour ward was safely Labour while Gorrell was marginal; the new ward has also proven to be marginal. In 2015 Gorrell split its representation between two Conservatives and one Labour councillor. Labour won all three seats in 2019 as the Conservatives fell to third place, the Green Party surging into a close second: the lead Green candidate finished just nine votes behind the third Labour candidate. Shares of the vote were 37% for Labour, 34% for the Greens and 23% for the Conservatives.

Gorrell ward also forms part of a marginal division of Kent county council: Whitstable West, which swung strongly to Labour in May. It's also part of a marginal Parliamentary seat. The Canterbury constituency was possibly the most unexpected of the Labour gains in the 2017 general election, with Rosie Duffield becoming the city's first-ever Labour MP with a majority of 187 votes; despite some travails with her local party, she was re-elected in 2019 with an increased majority.

> But four young Oysters hurried up.
> All eager for the treat:
> Their coats were brushed, their faces washed,
> Their shoes were clean and neat —
> And this was odd, because, you know,
> They hadn't any feet.

The Labour selection produced as their defending candidate Dane Buckman, a self-employed gardener. Standing for the Greens is Clare Turnbull, who works in educational research. The Conservative candidate is Stephen Spencer. Completing the ballot paper is our fourth candidate Colin Gardner, standing for the Workers Party of Britain.*

> 'O Oysters,' said the Carpenter,
> 'You've had a pleasant run!

* *Canterbury, Gorrell*: Grn 1149 Lab 803 C 608 Workers Party of Britain 58 [Grn gain from Lab]

> Shall we be trotting home again?'
> But answer came there none —
> And this was scarcely odd, because
> They'd eaten every one.

Bere Ferrers

West Devon council; caused by the resignation of Liberal Democrat councillor Robin Musgrave.

For our Liberal Democrat defence of the week we have come to the West Country, for a ward on the Devon side of the Tamar Estuary. The Bere peninsula lies at the head of the estuary between the Tamar to the west and the Tavy to the east; its main population centre is the village of Bere Alston.

The city of Plymouth is only a few miles away, but the road connections to it are so poor (thanks to the Tavy estuary) that the railway line from Plymouth to Bere Alston managed to survive the Beeching cuts which had recommended it for closure. Bere Alston and Bere Ferrers were once on the second main line from Plymouth to Exeter via Okehampton, and trains now reverse at Bere Alston to take the former branch line to Gunnislake. The section of line between Okehampton and Exeter is due to reopen to passengers this weekend, but reopening of Okehampton to Bere Ferrers is a rather more distant prospect.

Bere Alston was one of most notorious of the rotten boroughs which were swept away by the 1832 Reform Act. Sir George Beaumont, the artist and art patron who was one of the founders of the National Gallery in London, was an MP for Bere Alston from 1790 to 1796. By the 1830s elections here were controlled by the Duke of Northumberland, with the freehold tenants of around 30 houses (out of 112 in the borough) having the right to vote. A vivid account of the 1830 general election here was published in *The Times*:

> Dr Butler [the Portreeve, who was Returning Officer for the borough]... met the voters under a great tree, the place usually chosen for the purpose of election. During the time the Portreeve was reading the acts of Parliament usually read on such occasions, one of the voters handed in to him a card containing the names of two candidates, proposed by himself and seconded by his friend. He was told... this was too early. Before the reading was completed, the voter on the other side handed in a card corresponding with the former, which he was told was too late. The meeting broke up. The Portreeve and assistants adjourned to a public house in the neighbourhood, and then and there made a return of Lord Lovaine and Mr Blackett, which was not signed by a single person having a vote.

The "voting tree" still stands in Bere Alston. Mr Christopher Blackett here was a colliery owner from Northumberland, while Lord Lovaine came from a cadet branch of the Percy family who were Dukes of Northumberland. Good local candidates both. Lovaine entered the Lords the following year after succeeding to the title of Earl of Beverley (he ended up as the 5th Duke of Northumberland), and the resulting by-election in January 1831 was contested: the Tory candidate won it by seven votes to nil. In the general election four months later the Conservative slate defeated the Whig slate by nine votes to nil.

Modern-day by-elections in Bere Ferrers are rather more democratic than that, although the returning officer did play a crucial role here again in the 2011 election. The outgoing Lib Dem councillor (Charles) Robin Musgrave tied for second place with the Conservatives' Andrew Sadleir on 486 votes each; but only one of them could be elected. Lots were drawn, and the returning officer's casting vote fell on Musgrave.

The Bere Ferrers ward was expanded in 2015 to take in the parish of Gulworthy to the north. Its two outgoing councillors Robin Musgrave and Mike Benson were re-elected that year, although Musgrave had by then left the Liberal Democrats and gone independent. Benson died in 2017, and the Conservatives held his seat in the resulting by-election*.

Musgrave, by now back in the Lib Dem fold, topped the poll again here in May 2019, with the Conservatives holding the other seat. Vote shares are a bit difficult to interpret here because of personal votes and partial slates, but for what it's worth the topline figures were 31% for the Lib Dems, 30% for the Conservatives, 20% for Labour and 18% for UKIP.

The ward is split between two divisions of Devon county council (Yelverton Rural and Tavistock), which were both safely Conservative in May's county elections. It is part of the Torridge and West Devon constituency represented by the former Conservative cabinet minister Geoffrey Cox, who has been in the news a bit recently.

Robin Musgrave is standing down on health grounds after many years of service as councillor for Bere Ferrers. He was first elected in 1991, and had continuous service from 2007. Musgrave served in 2012–13 as Mayor of West Devon.

Defending for the Liberal Democrats is their losing candidate from 2019 Graham Reed, who works as a craftsman in glass; Reed is a former Plymouth city councillor and has contested Plymouth constituencies in the last three general elections. The Conservatives have selected Angela Blackman, while Labour have changed candidate to Isabel Saxby. UKIP have not returned, so completing the ballot paper is a former European Parliament and London Assembly candidate:

* *Andrew's Previews 2017*, page 123.

Parliamentary constituency: Torridge and West Devon
Devon county council division: Yelverton Rural (Bere Ferrers parish), Tavistock (Gulworthy parish)
May 2019 result LD 491/258 C 473 Lab 320/149 UKIP 291
May 2017 by-election C 639 Lab 421 UKIP 164
May 2015 result Ind 738 C 681/630 UKIP 504 Grn 445 Lab 430

Figure 160: West Devon, Bere Ferrers

that's local resident Judy Maciejowska of the Green Party.*

Brockworth East

Tewkesbury council, Gloucestershire; caused by the resignation of independent councillor Sara Stevens.

For our remaining southern by-election we consider a strong contender for the most dangerous Quaint British Tradition. Every Spring Bank Holiday, a number of people who really should know better race 3 or 4 kilograms of the best Double Gloucester cheese down Cooper's Hill, above Brockworth in Gloucestershire. With the hillside having a 1-in-3 slope, and with the cheese travelling fast enough to injure anyone who gets in its way, someone always gets hurt at the Cooper's Hill Cheese Rolling. Councillor Sara Stevens, one of the organisers, was herself hurt by the cheese when the event was last held in 2019; she ended up in A&E with an internal crush injury.

Cheese-rolling here has been going on for centuries by and for the people of Brockworth, a village on the arrow-straight road going east out of Gloucester. This was once the Roman road of Ermine Street running towards Cirencester, and just outside the ward boundary are the remains of a Roman villa at Great Witcombe. In modern times Brockworth was the home of the Gloster aircraft factory, which closed in the 1960s and whose site has now been redeveloped.

Despite being much closer to Gloucester and Cheltenham, the parish of Brockworth is part of the local government district and parliamentary seat of Tewkesbury. Brockworth's location just outside Gloucester, with good road links, has led to strong population growth in recent years. Tewkesbury council got new ward boundaries in 2019 as a result of which Brockworth parish went up from three councillors to four; the Local Government Boundary Commission for England don't like drawing wards with more than three councillors, so this meant that the parish had to be divided into two new wards. Accordingly Brockworth East ward came into being.

* *West Devon, Bere Ferrers*: C 362 Lab 361 LD 216 Grn 176 [C gain from LD]

Parliamentary constituency: Tewkesbury
Gloucestershire county council division: Brockworth
May 2019 result Ind 352/324 C 227/184 UKIP 140 LD 120/70 Grn 89

Figure 161: Tewkesbury, Brockworth East

The old Brockworth ward had four by-elections in the period 2003–19, with one going to a now-defunct residents' party, two to the Liberal Democrats and the last one, in May 2014, to the Conservatives. The Conservatives followed up by winning all three seats in Brockworth in 2015. In May 2019 both Brockworth wards returned two independent candidates, with shares of the vote in East ward being 38% for the independents, 24% for the Conservatives, 15% for UKIP and 13% for the Liberal Democrats. However, the Conservatives held the Brockworth county division in May's Gloucestershire elections with a swing in their favour.

Sara Stevens stood down from Tewkesbury council in June, so there has been plenty of time for prospective candidates in this by-election to get their act together. Despite this, independent candidate Gareth Evans had his nomination papers rejected by the returning officer on the grounds that the two electors who had signed it do not in fact live within the ward. Evans will not be on the ballot. This leaves one defending independent candidate, Brockworth parish councillor Charlotte Mills (who is listed on the parish council website under her previous surname of Parry). The Conservatives have reselected Ronald Furolo who regularly contests local elections here; Furolo was a councillor for the former Brockworth ward from 2015 to 2019. UKIP have not returned. The Lib Dem candidate is Gilbert Yates, who stood in 2019 in the ward of Churchdown Brookfield with Hucclecote, closer to Gloucester. Completing the ballot paper is Joseph Ambrose for Labour.*

Anfield; Clubmoor; and Kirkdale

Liverpool council, Merseyside; caused respectively by the deaths of Ros Groves and Tim Jeeves and the resignation of Malcolm Kennedy, all of whom were Labour councillors.

We now travel to north-west England for three by-elections in adjoining wards in north Liverpool. Let's start with Clubmoor ward, which is a residential area of inter-war housing straddling Queens Drive, the inner ring road, about

* *Tewkesbury, Brockworth East*: Ind 499 C 110 LD 87 Lab 35

four miles north-east of the city centre. In the 2011 census Clubmoor made the top 100 wards in England and Wales for long-term sickness or disability (11.3%) and the top 80 wards for Christianity (80.4%).

To the west of Clubmoor ward lies Anfield ward, which is famous the world over as the home of Liverpool FC. The ward boundaries take in Anfield Stadium as well as the whole of Stanley Park. Its electors live in some very deprived Victorian and Edwardian terraces to the east and south-east of the park. According to the 2019 indices of multiple deprivation, two of the fifteen most-deprived census districts in England are in Anfield ward. Anfield Stadium itself shows up in the 2011 census return, with the output area covering the stadium reporting that almost half of the people who *work* there are in the "arts, entertainment or recreation" sector.

The western of the three polls today takes place in Kirkdale ward, which covers the Mersey waterfront north of the city centre. All of the waterfront here is dockland, and Liverpool's docks aren't nearly as busy as they used to be: a trip along Regent Road, with its buried railway tracks crossing at regular intervals, can give the impression that this is a land which time forgot. It's a reflection of how many jobs the docks once provided, and the scale of Liverpool's depopulation. that the boundaries of the modern Kirkdale ward aren't too dissimilar to those of the old Liverpool Scotland parliamentary seat. That constituency famously returned an Irish Nationalist MP, T P O'Connor, to Parliament from 1885 until his death in 1929. All the main transport links going north from the city centre pass through here: the main roads towards Bootle and Preston, the Northern line of Merseyrail (Bank Hall, Kirkdale and Sandhills stations are within the boundary), and the Leeds and Liverpool Canal, while the Wallasey Tunnel also surfaces here. Kirkdale ward is in the top 50 wards in the UK for long-term sickness or disability (12.6%) and has very high levels of social renting. All three wards have very low levels of car use for a location outside London, with corresponding high rates of bus travel and (in Kirkdale, which goes up to the edge of the city centre) walking to work.

One of the docks within Kirkdale ward is Bramley Moore Dock, which Everton FC have their eye on as the site of their new stadium. This hasn't impressed UNESCO, who earlier this year took the rare step of revoking the status of Liverpool's waterfront as a World Heritage Site in response to this and other developments.

But that is a long way from being the worst controversy which has attached itself to Liverpool council. For a couple of years now Merseyside Police have been conducting Operation Aloft, an investigation which has resulted in a number of arrests on suspicion of fraud, bribery, corruption and misconduct in public office. In December 2020 Inspector Knacker arrested the then Liverpool mayor, Joe Anderson, on suspicion of conspiracy to commit bribery and witness intimidation.

Although Operation Aloft is yet to reach its conclusion this arrest was something central government really couldn't ignore, and they sent in Max Caller to look into Liverpool's governance and see what was going on. Caller, who had previously done something similar in Northamptonshire, produced a report which detailed a number of failings by the council relating to highways, regeneration, property management, audit and governance arrangements. He recommended that the government send the Commissioners in to run those things and change the electoral cycle for the city to all-out whole council elections. Accordingly, the May 2022 elections to Liverpool city council have been cancelled, with the Mayor's and councillors' terms varied to end in May 2023 when a whole council election will be held.

What was the effect of this on the electors of north Liverpool? Well, it certainly cut through. Big Joe was forced to announce his retirement, and Labour selected Joanne Anderson to succeed him in the 2021 mayoral election. This column covered Joanne's first election to Liverpool city council at a by-election in October 2019*; as I made clear at the time, Joanne Anderson is not related to Big Joe Anderson. (Big Joe does have a daughter called Joanne, but she sits on the council under her married name of Joanne Calvert.)

Joanne Anderson did eventually become Mayor of Liverpool, but her performance in May was very poor compared to Big Joe, and indeed compared to the Labour candidates for Mayor of the Liverpool City Region and for Merseyside Police and Crime Commissioner, both of whom won in the first round on the same day. By contrast Ms Anderson was taken to transfers after polling just 39% of the first preferences, with independent candidate Stephen Yip on 22%, the Lib Dems on 17% and the Greens on 9%. In the runoff Anderson beat Yip by a 59–41 margin.

This Labour underperformance also fed through to the party's results in the three wards holding by-elections today. In recent years all of these have been places where the Labour vote is weighed rather than counted, where the party's dominance has been so great that it's difficult to find a non-Labour voter. Although Anfield ward voted Lib Dem until 2007, it is now dominated by the red team. The runner-up position there has been filled by six different parties in the seven elections since 2012 (in order, Lib Dem, National Health Action, UKIP, continuing Liberal, Conservative, Green and Liberal again). Kirkdale ward voted 90% Labour in a by-election on general election day in 2017†; second place there

* *Andrew's Previews 2019*, page 321. † *Andrew's Previews 2017*, page 151.

has been taken on a number of occasions by far-left candidate Roger Bannister, who has also stood in the past to be general secretary of UNISON. (Bannister should not be confused with the legendary athlete of the same name.) Clubmoor ward turned in a Labour vote of 86% at a by-election on general election day in December 2019*.

That Clubmoor by-election returned Tim Jeeves, who was re-elected for a full term in May with a 62–19 lead over the continuing Liberals. Sadly, Jeeves passed away in September at the appallingly early age of 42. To quote from his death notice in the *Liverpool Echo*, he was "taken too soon from his adopted city which he loved so much".

Jeeves' passing came a month after the death of Anfield ward councillor Ros Groves, who had served since 2016 and had also just been re-elected in May; her final score six months ago was 67%, with second place again going to the continuing Liberals on 11%.

The Kirkdale by-election has been the result of some local controversy. Malcolm Kennedy had represented this ward and the predecessor Vauxhall ward since 1998, and had served as Lord Mayor of Liverpool. He moved to Madrid in March 2020 and has been doing his council work remotely from Spain since then. Once remote council meetings were phased out from May, as the pandemic eases, this became an untenable position for Kennedy. He was due for re-election next year, but the cancellation of next year's Liverpool elections means that his successor will now serve an extended term until 2023. In May Kirkdale ward had the lowest Labour percentage of the three Liverpool wards up for election today, the party beating the second-placed Greens by 59–12.

Shoutouts are due to some previous unsuccessful candidates here. David Jeffery, a lecturer in British politics at Liverpool University who published the Important Piece of Research in Figure 162 this week, has had the thankless task of being the Conservative candidate in Kirkdale on a few occasions. The Lib Dem candidate for Clubmoor in 2016 was former city councillor Paula Keaveney who, like your columnist, is a former *Mastermind* semi-finalist. Finally, commiserations are due to George Edwards who was the continuing Liberal candidate for Kirkdale ward in 2006 and was declared as polling zero votes. Legend has it that the Liverpool Liberal leader and talisman Steve Radford demanded a recount after the declaration, by which time it was of course too late to change the result.

In wards like this the Labour selection is often more important than the actual poll. With the Labour party in Liverpool being in special measures following the recent scandals, the NEC has had rather more control of the selection

* *Andrew's Previews 2019*, page 396.

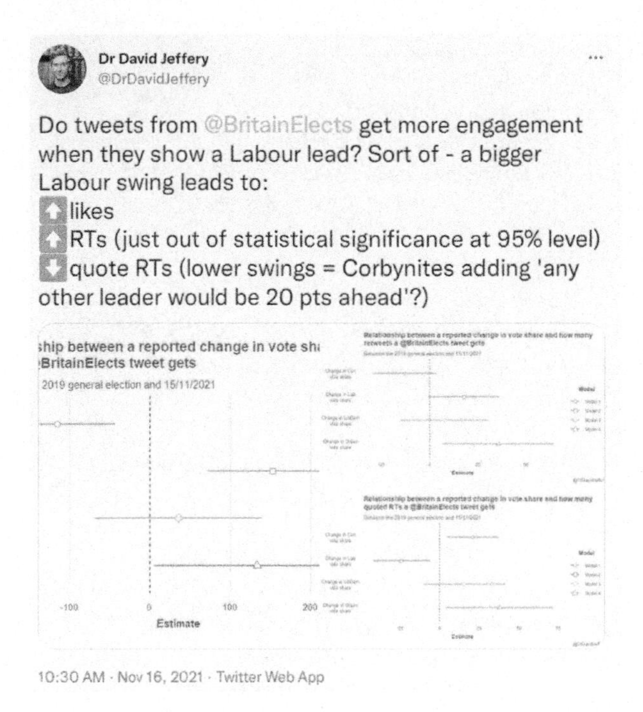

Figure 162: Important Research

process than some local members might like. The Labour party's branch for the Liverpool Walton constituency, which covers Anfield and Clubmoor, went so far as to put out a statement saying they weren't particularly happy. There are certainly some interesting choices there.

Defending Anfield for Labour is Tricia O'Brien, who had been the chair of the council's planning committee until she lost her seat to the Lib Dems in Cressington ward this May. It may not be unfair to suggest that she has taken the flak for a number of the committee's more controversial decisions. The Liberal candidate is Jimmy Richardson, who returns after his second-place finish in May. Also standing are Daryl Hodge for the Green Party, Alma McGing for the Conservatives, Wiebke Rueterjans for the Lib Dems and independent candidate Adam Heatherington, who has previously stood for election in Liverpool on the tickets of UKIP (he was the UKIP mayoral candidate in 2012), Five Star Direct Democracy and the Brexit Party.*

In Clubmoor the defending Labour candidate is Matthew Smyth, who is in his late twenties and works in a call centre. Smyth has done a lot of campaigning about Universal Credit, having been the victim of an error a few years ago which

* *Liverpool, Anfield*: Lab 604 Lib 281 LD 73 Grn 72 C 42 Ind 9

Parliamentary constituency: Liverpool Walton
May 2021 result Lab 1520 Lib 247 Grn 171 C 120 LD 104 Ind 94
May 2019 result Lab 1448 Grn 193 Lib 141 LD 97 C 97
May 2018 result Lab 1777 C 140 LD 134 Grn 114 Lib 56
May 2016 result Lab 1601 Lib 132 Grn 120 LD 120 C 89 TUSC 65
May 2015 result Lab 4276 UKIP 568 Lib 281 Grn 261 C 126 TUSC 68
May 2014 result Lab 1850 National Health Action 245 Lib 146 Grn 145 C 97
May 2012 result Lab 2312 LD 193 Grn 116 Lib 95 C 88
May 2011 result Lab 2223 LD 643 BNP 105 C 94 Lib 83 Grn 50
May 2010 result Lab 2817 LD 1526 BNP 278 Lib 274 C 185 Grn 88
May 2008 result Lab 1521 LD 1077 Lib 133 C 97 Grn 96 Ind 27
May 2007 result LD 1324 Lab 935 Lib 237 Grn 96 C 76
May 2006 result LD 1101 Lab 824 Lib 448 Grn 133 C 95
June 2004 result LD 1586/1500/1328 Lab 836/719/680 Lib 688/519 Ind 335 Socialist Alliance 108/55

Figure 163: Liverpool, Anfield

left him unable to claim a free prescription. The Liberals rather give the game away as to the secret of their success in Liverpool with their ballot paper description "Steve Radford's Candidate": Steve Radford's candidate for Clubmoor ward is again Liam Buckley, who was second here in May and lives and works in the ward. Also standing here are former Green Party European Parliament and leadership candidate Peter Cranie, Steve Fitzsimmons (the last Conservative to sit on Liverpool city council, after holding Woolton ward by seven votes in 1994) for the Lib Dems, Wendy Hine for the Conservatives, Ann Walsh for the Trade Unionist and Socialist Coalition, and independent candidate Laura-Jayne Wharton who appears to be standing after being disillusioned by the Labour selection process.*

Finally we come to Kirkdale where the Labour selection has produced another ex-councillor. Dave Hanratty represented Fazakerley ward from 1992 to 2018, when he stood down apparently under threat of deselection; for some years he was chair of the Merseyside Fire and Rescue Authority. The Greens ran second here in May, but their candidate from that election Peter Cranie is, as stated, contesting the Clubmoor by-election; for the Kirkdale by-election the Green candidate is instead local resident Maria Coughlan. Also standing are the aforementioned Roger Bannister for the Trade Unionist and Socialist Coalition, Jenny Turner for the Lib Dems, Kate Burgess for the Conservatives and Peter Furmedge, who is associated with a new party called Beacon Liverpool; the paperwork for the party wasn't filed with the Electoral Commission in time,

* *Liverpool, Clubmoor*: Lab 787 Lib 324 Ind 167 TUSC 54 Grn 45 LD 34 C 33

Parliamentary constituency: Liverpool Walton
May 2021 result Lab 1647 Lib 510 Grn 207 LD 147 C 139
December 2019 by-election Lab 6276 Lib 420 Grn 328 LD 243
May 2019 result Lab 1770 Lib 203 Grn 195 LD 118 C 98
May 2018 result Lab 2136 Lib 129 C 127 Grn 104 LD 75
May 2016 result Lab 2072 Grn 244 LD 204 Lib 200 C 105
May 2015 result Lab 5493 UKIP 711 Grn 260 Lib 221 C 184 LD 157
May 2014 result Lab 2201 UKIP 686 Lib 130 Grn 117 C 75
May 2012 result Lab 2587 UKIP 215 Lib 124 LD 106 TUSC 97 Grn 85 C 81 British Freedom Party 26
May 2011 result Lab 2904 LD 232 C 184 Lib 166 Grn 125
May 2010 result Lab 4245 Lib 1073 BNP 364 C 281 Grn 148
May 2008 result Lab 1341 Lib 859 BNP 358 C 150 Grn 68 Ind 18
May 2007 result Lab 1366 Lib 999 BNP 210 C 147 Grn 99
May 2006 result Lab 1440 Lib 791 LD 410 C 132 Grn 120 Soc Lab 71
June 2004 result Lab 1844/1626/1624 LD 1542/1445/1230 Lib 466/432/377 Soc Lab 72

Figure 164: Liverpool, Clubmoor

Parliamentary constituency: Liverpool Riverside
May 2021 result Lab 1703 Grn 334 TUSC 324 LD 231 C 168 Lib 107
May 2019 result Lab 1935 UKIP 182 Grn 149 LD 95 Socalist Alternative 69 C 31
May 2018 result Lab 2094 TUSC 149 Grn 104 C 103 LD 76 Lib 23
June 2017 by-election Lab 6416 C 346 Grn 177 LD 154
May 2016 result Lab 2166 TUSC 276 Grn 181 C 105
May 2015 result Lab 5280 UKIP 442 Grn 318 TUSC 236 C 210 Ind 70
May 2014 result Lab 2303 TUSC 206 Grn 177 Lib 140 C 100
May 2012 result Lab 2771 TUSC 143 Grn 89 Ind 76 C 59 LD 38 Lib 13
May 2011 result Lab 3001 TUSC 162 C 128 Grn 106 Lib 78
May 2010 result Lab 4284 BNP 403 Lib 336 C 246 Grn 133 Ind 86
May 2008 double vacancy Lab 1971/1737 BNP 389 Ind 146 LD 144/107 Grn 96/95 C 95/61 Lib 46
May 2007 result Lab 1927 BNP 169 LD 147 UKIP 109 Grn 84 C 66 Ind 47 Lib 37
May 2006 result Lab 1958 LD 232 UKIP 182 C 69 Grn 64 Lib 0
June 2004 result Lab 2378/2315/2145 Liverpool Labour Community Party 365/258/243 LD 274/260/250 Lib 125/125/105 Grn 125/121/115

Figure 165: Liverpool, Kirkdale

so Furmedge is on the ballot paper without a party description. As per the usual practice this column follows for undescribed candidates, Furmedge is listed in the footnote below as an independent.*

* *Liverpool, Kirkdale*: Lab 852 Ind 171 Grn 160 TUSC 84 C 57 LD 57

Chorlton

Manchester council; caused by the resignation of Labour councillor Matt Strong.

We now move east up the Mersey to the major city of north-west England. Chorlton-cum-Hardy was historically a village on the north bank of the Mersey, three miles from the growing industrial town of Manchester. The village grew rapidly in the late Victorian era as a middle-class suburb within easy striking distance of the city, and Chorlton was incorporated into Manchester in 1904. Chorlton tram stop, on the Airport and East Didsbury lines, has linked the ward to the city centre since 2011.

For those of a certain age, it's impossible to talk about Chorlton without mentioning some of the classic pieces of children's television. Chorlton was the home of the Cosgrove Hall animation studios, which gave us such great artistic works as *Chorlton and the Wheelies*, *Danger Mouse* and *Count Duckula*, together with feature-length versions of *The Wind in the Willows* and Roald Dahl's *BFG*. Cosgrove Hall's employees included a very young Bernard Sumner, before he found fame in the bands Joy Division and New Order. The studio ended up as part of ITV, which wound it up in 2009.

Modern-day Chorlton still has that middle-class vibe, with urban professionals dominating its current demographic. In the 2011 census Chorlton (which then had slightly different boundaries) was in the top 50 wards in England and Wales for those educated to degree level (60.6%), and 30.8% of its population was aged between 30 and 44: that was the highest figure for any ward in north-west England and in the top 100 wards in England and Wales. A majority of the workforce are in middle-class occupations and full-time employment is very high. Less salubriously, Chorlton's M21 postcode was reported in 2014 to be the most burgled postcode district in the UK.

Manchester is a monolithically Labour council these days: the latest composition has 93 Labour councillors plus this vacancy, opposed by one Liberal Democrat (John Leech, who represented Chorlton from 2005 to 2015 as the MP for Manchester Withington) and one Green (for the unlikely-looking Green ward of Woodhouse Park, which is in Wythenshawe). Chorlton ward last failed to vote Labour in 2010, when the Liberal Democrats won. In May this year Labour won with a 68–17 lead over the Green Party, and the Lib Dems fell to fourth place. Matt Strong had represented Chorlton since 2011, gaining his seat from the Lib Dems.

Defending this by-election for Labour is Mathew Benham, who describes himself on his Twitter as a "Volunteer, Allotmenteer and Leafleting Specialist". The Green candidate is Simon Milner-Edwards, who describes himself as a

Parliamentary constituency: Manchester Withington (most), Manchester Gorton (small part)
May 2021 result Lab 3656 Grn 917 C 368 LD 291 Women's Equality 141
May 2019 result Lab 2574 Grn 950 LD 575 C 212 Women's Equality 146 Ind 59
May 2018 result Lab 3175/3165/2974 Grn 731/728/653 LD 614/507/463 Women's Equality 465 C 301/242/221 Ind 145

Figure 166: Manchester, Chorlton

single-issue candidate: the single issue being stopping development on Ryebank Fields, an open space in the ward. Also standing are Kathleen Fitzgibbon for the Conservatives, Rosie Hughes for the Liberal Democrats, regular candidate Jo Heathcote for the Women's Equality Party, and independent candidate Paul Harnett.*

Bamber Bridge East

South Ribble council, Lancashire; caused by the death of Labour councillor Christine Melia at the age of 72. She had served as a councillor since 2019.

For the last of the five Labour defences this week in north-west England we travel north to the edge of Preston. Bamber Bridge lies a few miles to the south-east of Preston, forming another link in the chain of towns which connects Preston to Chorley. This a major location on the motorway network: the ward includes the original southern terminus of the UK's first motorway, the M 6 Preston Bypass, while the later M 61 and M 65 motorways also pass through the ward. Also here is the unnumbered Walton Summit motorway, a spur road which is one of the few places in the UK where you can legally do 70mph on a single-carriageway road.

There's nothing out of the ordinary about the ethnic profile of this ward, but Bamber Bridge has gone down in history as the unlikely location of an American race riot. The so-called Battle of Bamber Bridge occurred in June 1943, starting at a pub in the modern-day Bamber Bridge East ward called Ye Old Hob Inn. At the time the 1511th Quartermaster Truck regiment, a logistics unit of the US Air Force with almost entirely black GIs commanded by almost entirely white officers, was stationed in Bamber Bridge. Its soldiers often socialised in Ye Old Hob with the locals, in a way they couldn't do back home in segregated America. News had come through of race riots in Detroit earlier in the week, and the author Anthony Burgess—who lived in Bamber Bridge for a time—recounted that the

* *Manchester, Chorlton*: Lab 1581 LD 657 Grn 608 C 93 Women's Equality 66 Ind 27

Parliamentary constituency: Ribble Valley
Lancashire county council division: South Ribble East (most), Lostock Hall and Bamber Bridge (part)
May 2019 result Lab 474/433 C 303/269 UKIP 241
May 2015 result Lab 1127/1021 C 752/736

Figure 167: South Ribble, Bamber Bridge East

US authorities demanded a colour bar in Bamber Bridge's pubs in response. The landlords promptly put up signs saying "Black Troops Only".

Then a cack-handed attempt by white US military police to arrest a black soldier in Ye Old Hob, for not wearing the proper uniform, was thwarted by British servicewomen and local civilians. The military police subsequently came back in numbers for another go, and there was a firefight which lasted most of the night. One GI died. All the other soldiers involved were back to normal duties within thirteen months, which was a very light punishment considering that this was a mutiny in wartime; the Eighth Air Force commander, General Ira C Eaker, preferred to put most of the blame for the incident on the behaviour of the MPs.

These days the East ward of Bamber Bridge has a lot of industry, and it has been Labour-voting throughout this century. In the May 2019 elections to South Ribble council Labour polled 47% here, the Conservatives 30% and UKIP 24%; that election led to the Conservatives losing control of the council, and South Ribble is now run by a minority Labour administration with Lib Dem support. Until the death of ward councillor Christine Melia in September, the Labour and Conservative groups were tied on 22 seats each; accordingly, if the Conservatives gain this by-election they will become the largest party on the council.

The Tories may take heart from the fact that they represent this area at other levels of government. Most of Bamber Bridge East ward is covered by the South Ribble East division of Lancashire county council, which is safe Conservative; however, part of it is in the Lostock Hall and Bamber Bridge division which is a Conservative-held marginal. The ward is part of the Ribble Valley parliamentary seat held by Tory MP Nigel Evans, who returned to his former role as a Deputy Speaker after the 2019 general election.

Defending for Labour is local resident Clare Hunter. The Conservative candidate is Matthew Forshaw, a maintenance manager for a hospitality company. UKIP have not returned, but we will still have a three-way contest with the intervention of Rachel Knowles for the Green Party.*

* *South Ribble, Bamber Bridge East*: Lab 376 C 275 Grn 49

Cropton

Ryedale council, North Yorkshire; caused by the death of Liberal Party councillor John Clark.

As a warmup for next week's North Yorkshire Police and Crime Commissioner election, we finish the week by coming to, well, North Yorkshire. Yes, this means that the voters of Cropton are going to have to turn out for by-elections on two successive Thursdays. Blame the PCC by-election rules for that one.

The Cropton ward of Ryedale covers eight tiny parishes wrapping around the western and northern side of Pickering. Much of its acreage is within the North York Moors National Park, and those who have travelled the preserved North Yorkshire Moors railway—which runs along the valley of Pickering Beck which forms the ward's eastern boundary—will attest that this is beautiful countryside. It's not highly populated countryside even in the more lowland parishes, in the fertile Vale of Pickering: Middleton, located on the main road running west from Pickering, is the largest parish in the ward but has just 343 electors on the roll. There may well have been a larger population at the end of the 1st century, when the Romans had a camp at Cawthorne, just outside Cropton, which is thought to have been used by them as a training camp.

A look at the election results for Cropton ward reinforces the sense of historical throwback. Since the ward was created in 2003 it has had only one councillor: John Clark, one of the few remaining councillors for the continuing Liberal Party. Clark went through a number of very close elections—in 2011 he was re-elected with a majority of just six votes over the Conservatives—and it wasn't until his final re-election in 2019 that he achieved safety in Cropton ward. On that occasion he won with a 55–25 lead over an independent candidate.

Clark had also served on North Yorkshire county council, representing the local Pickering division from 2009 to 2017. Again, all those elections were photofinishes: Clark won by 58 votes in 2009, was re-elected by 50 votes in 2013, and lost his seat to the Conservatives by eight votes in 2017.

The May 2021 North Yorkshire county elections were cancelled due to possible local government reorganisation in the county. Ryedale council, which is based on the Vale of Pickering and whose largest towns are Pickering, Malton and Norton, may well be one of the main reasons for this reorganisation. Although it is a coherent economic unit—the ONS recognises a Malton Travel to Work Area with very similar boundaries—the district has a very low headcount and is one of the smallest remaining shire districts in England by population. Part of the reason for that is that Ryedale came off badly from the creation of a unitary York council in the 1990s: the new York city council expanded to cover the whole

Parliamentary constituency: Thirsk and Malton
North Yorkshire county council division: Pickering
May 2019 result Lib 362 Ind 167 C 128
May 2015 result Lib 526 C 471
May 2011 result Lib 359 C 353 LD 57
May 2007 result Lib 342 C 301 LD 86
May 2003 result Lib 368 C 306

Figure 168: Ryedale, Cropton

of the city's urban area and a rural hinterland, and that boundary change robbed Ryedale of a large chunk of its population and council tax base.

Ryedale council is too small to sustain a leader and cabinet system of governance, and John Clark's position as chairman of the council's policy and resources committee meant that he was in effect the council leader. The council chamber is hung, with currently 12 independent councillors (in at least three different groups), 11 Conservatives, 4 continuing Liberals plus this vacancy, and two new-style Liberal Democrats.

Defending this by-election for the Liberal Party is Alasdair Clark, John Clark's son. The independent from last time has not returned, so opposing Clark junior are Greg White for the Conservatives (who is the local county councillor), Richard McLane for the Green Party and Jill Wells for Labour.*

* *Ryedale, Cropton*: Lib 202 C 155 Grn 121 Lab 32

25th November 2021: Police and Crime Commissioner Special

It's Super Thursday today, with thirteen by-elections taking place today in England in the biggest test of public opinion remaining this year. There are six Labour defences, four Conservatives, two independent seats and a Lib Dem up for election in England. There are lots of stories to tell and there will be something for everyone to enjoy here. Without further ado, let's start with the big one:

North Yorkshire Police and Crime Commissioner; and Raskelf and White Horse

The by-election for North Yorkshire PCC follows the resignation of Conservative PCC Philip Allott. The by-election for Raskelf and White Horse ward, Hambleton council, follows the resignation of Conservative councillor Jill Mortimer.

> Are you going to Scarborough Fair?
> —parsley, sage, rosemary and thyme

Your columnist has a regular habit of doing a lot of Christmas shopping in the tiny city of Ripon. "Stay awhile amid its ancient charms", say the signs leading into the city, and Ripon is certainly a charming place which the Industrial Revolution essentially passed by. The market square was described by Daniel Defoe as "the finest and most beautiful square that is to be seen of its kind in England", and a few centuries on from Defoe's time that's still a fair assessment. Every evening at 9pm a hornblower turns up in the market square, providing a timecheck for the locals. The city's impressive cathedral dates from the twelfth century, and includes a tiny crypt from a previous Anglo-Saxon monastery constructed by the seventh-century St Wilfrid.

Just to the west of Ripon is the only UNESCO World Heritage Site in North Yorkshire. Studley Royal Park is a romantic landscape garden dating to the eighteenth century. You're probably a bit too late in the autumn now to get the full effect of the tree colours, but the Studley Royal Park also contains the impressive ruins of Fountains Abbey. Fountains controlled extensive lands in the Yorkshire Dales back in the day, making it one of the largest and richest monasteries in England up until the time of dissolution.

The preservation of Fountains' ruins owes a lot to the taste of John Aislabie, who was MP for Ripon for much of the early 18th century and owned the Studley Royal estate. Aislabie had been mayor of Ripon in 1702–03, and he erected the obelisk in the market square which still stands. He was appointed as Chancellor of the Exchequer in 1718, and in that capacity he negotiated a notorious deal whereby the UK national debt was taken over by the South Sea Company in return for government bonds. The South Sea Company subsequently collapsed in 1720 with huge losses for much of the UK's upper classes. Parliament set up an inquiry, which reported that the government's support for the scheme was a result of massive levels of corruption. Aislabie himself had received £20,000 in South Sea stock. He was expelled from the House of Commons and the Privy Council, which left him free to concentrate on the development of the Studley Royal garden once he was eventually released from the Tower of London.

The Industrial Revolution may have passed Ripon by, but it has had an effect on other locations in North Yorkshire. Most notably, Skipton, which is a classic Pennine textile town and also, these days, a commuter centre for the cities of west Yorkshire.

Skipton is also a major tourist draw, thanks to its proximity to the countryside of the Yorkshire Dales National Park. Within striking distance of Skipton can be found the village of Malham, where generations of northern schoolchildren have been sent to learn geology; while for hikers there is the attraction of the Three Peaks of Whernside, Ingleborough and Penyghent. The countryside around Skipton and the Dales was brought to a wider audience in 2014, when the first two stages of the Tour de France were routed through Yorkshire.

The Dales give way in the east to the Vale of York, a low-lying area in the north of the county through which the main communication links to north-east England pass. Major towns here include Northallerton (the home of North Yorkshire county council), Thirsk and Richmond, together with the enormous Army garrison at Catterick. The military have an extensive presence in North Yorkshire. As well as Catterick, there are a number of RAF airbases in the Vale of

York and two large intelligence stations: the "golf balls" at Menwith Hill which the US authorities use for surveillance, and the radar station on the coast at RAF Fylingdales watching for incoming missiles.

The Fylingdales radar station lies in North Yorkshire's second national park, the North York Moors. This rugged (although not particularly high) moorland extends over a wide area in the north-east of the county, and takes in the port of Whitby. That town is a tourist trap for all sorts of reasons—Captain Cook, Dracula, goth culture, superlative fish and chips—but it should also be well known for an event which took place here in 664. The Synod of Whitby, hosted here in that year by St Hilda, led to a decision by King Oswiu that the kingdom of Northumbria should come into line with the Roman Catholic church in customs including the calculation of Easter. St Wilfred, builder of the tiny crypt under Ripon Cathedral, led the argument in favour of the Roman practice at the Synod.

Whitby is not the major town on the Yorkshire coast. This is the resort town of Scarborough, located either side of a promontory in the North Sea. Scarborough has a long history and a fishing industry, but it was made what it is today by the Victorians. The Grand Hotel in Scarborough, at the time of its opening in 1867, was the largest hotel in Europe. Unfortunately, it has fallen into the hands of the Britannia group.

The Victorians also made the largest and most expensive population centre covered by North Yorkshire county council. This is Harrogate, a spa town which has given us Yorkshire Tea (which, according to no less an authority than the Speaker of the House of Commons, is one of only two good things to come out of Yorkshire), Betty's tearooms, a thriving conference industry and the 1982 Eurovision Song Contest. The Liberal Democrats have held a number of party conferences in Harrogate over the years.

The south of the county has an economy dominated by energy. Kellingley Colliery, which closed in December 2015, was the last deep coal mine in the UK. It was part of the Selby coalfield, which provided the fuel for three large coal-fired power stations at the southern end of North Yorkshire. The cooling towers at Eggborough power station were demolished last month, but some of Ferrybridge's towers are still standing for reuse in a future gas-fired plant. And then there is Drax. Now fully converted to biomass operation, Drax is the largest power station in the UK and provides 6% of the country's electricity.

In the centre of all this is an ancient city which was known as *Eboracom* to the Romans, *Eoforwīc* to the Anglo-Saxons and *Jórvík* to the Vikings. York, as centuries of smoothing of unnecessary letters have turned *Jórvík* into, was for centuries the most important urban centre in the north of England. The

Industrial Revolution has put paid to that status, but York is still by far the largest city in the North Yorkshire police area. Major employers here have traditionally included the Rowntree chocolate factory and the railways. The National Railway Museum, one of the UK's largest and most-visited museums, has been located here since 1975. The University of York was founded in 1963, on a duck-infested campus at Heslington to the south-east of the city; it has educated a number of our most prominent politicians, including the Mother of the House Harriet Harman.

York may be the largest city in North Yorkshire but only about a quarter of the county's population lives there (and this includes a significant rural hinterland which lies within the city boundary). Much of the acreage of North Yorkshire is agricultural, with prime farming land in the Vale of York complemented by upland sheep farming in the Dales. Those of a certain age might remember the books of the Yorkshire vet James Herriot, turned into the successful TV series *All Creatures Great and Small*; Herriot was the pseudonym of Alfred Wight, who worked as a vet in Thirsk for fifty years.

It's this rural area, and the Conservatism which dominates it, that sets the tone for North Yorkshire's elections. This is the most Conservative part of Yorkshire: even in the disaster year of 1997, the Tories still held four of the county's eight parliamentary constituencies (three went to Labour and one to the Lib Dems). The Richmond constituency, which has voted Conservative at every election since 1886 with the exception of the 1906 Liberal landslide, has since 1983 been represented successively by three titans of modern Conservatism: the European Commissioner Leon Brittan, the party leader William Hague, and the current Chancellor of the Exchequer Rishi Sunak.

Since 2010 North Yorkshire has been represented by 7 Conservative MPs against 1 Labour (from the York Central constituency). The December 2019 general election gave the Conservatives 54% of the vote across the county, with Labour coming in second on 26%.

The last ordinary local elections in North Yorkshire were in May 2019, with the exception of Harrogate (which last polled in 2018) and some wards in Craven (2018 or 2016). These elections reveal a more diverse picture than the recent parliamentary results. The Conservatives control the district councils in Harrogate (which includes Ripon and a large rural area), Hambleton (covering the Vale of York) and Selby, and also have half of the seats in Craven district (based on Skipton and Settle) which they run in coalition with independents. The other four districts covering the county have anti-Conservative coalitions: York is run by the Lib Dems and Greens and is the weakest Conservative area of the county, the politically-volatile Scarborough district (which takes in all of the coast, including Whitby) is run by Labour and independent councillors, Ryedale (based on the agricultural Vale of Pickering) is run by Lib Dem and independent councillors, and Richmondshire council has an independent-led coalition with the Lib Dems and Greens.

Not for much longer though, probably. Local government reorganisation is in the works, and the likelihood is that all of these councils (except for York, which has unitary status) will probably be swept away in a takeover by North Yorkshire county council, which has a Conservative majority. Mind, anybody who thinks that Bentham is local to Scarborough or Selby, despite their being in the same county, probably hasn't grasped the concept of *local* in local government. All of those locations are over an hour (in some cases, well over an hour) by road from Northallerton, where the new North Yorkshire council will likely be administered from.

The three elections to date for North Yorkshire Police and Crime Commissioner have resulted in Conservative wins, although they have all gone to runoffs with the exception of the 2012 election (which only had two candidates). The Conservative majority over Labour has steadily increased, from 58–42 at the comedy elections of November 2012 to 61–39 at the last PCC elections in May this year. The Tories weren't far off winning six months ago on first preferences alone: the first count gave 47% to the Conservatives, 26% to Labour and 14% to independent candidate Keith Tordoff.

That was the first major election win for Philip Allott, a former leader of the Conservative group on Harrogate council who had been elected as Mayor of Knaresborough when he was just 25 years old. Allott had previously stood for parliament four times, losing three contests in marginal seats: in Bolton West in 2005, and in Halifax in 2010 and 2015. On the last occasion, he finished just 428 votes behind the new Labour candidate. He finally got his chance at high office after the previous Conservative PCC Julia Mulligan, who had served since 2012, was deselected.

Philip Allott served for just five months as North Yorkshire Police and Crime Commissioner. His downfall came as the result of an interview he made to BBC Radio York following the sentencing of a police officer for the murder of Sarah Everard in London. Allott's remarks that women should be "streetwise" caused sustained outrage, and he resigned as commissioner two weeks later after losing the confidence of the North Yorkshire Police, Fire and Crime Panel.

This kicks into action the police and crime commissioner by-election rules, which have been criticised in this column on a number of previous occasions. Suffice to say that the timing of Commissioner Allott's resignation meant that the by-election would have to take place either this week or next week. It's a ridiculously short time to organise a by-election across such a large area for such an important post.

Anyway, we are here now. Defending for the Conservatives is Zoë Metcalfe, a project manager for a property asset management company, who sits on North Yorkshire county council and on Harrogate council. She represents the town of Knaresborough on the county council and Claro ward, which covers a number of villages to the north and east of Knaresborough, on the district council. Metcalfe has stood for Parliament twice, on both occasions in safe Labour seats (Doncaster Central in 2015, Leeds West in 2017).

Labour have gone for youth in selecting Emma Scott-Spivey, a 23-year-old student paramedic. Scott-Spivey lives in Thirsk and is the daughter of two police officers.

There are three other candidates on the ballot, headed by independent candidate Keith Tordoff who returns after his third-place finish in May. Tordoff served as a police officer in Leeds for 20 years, working on the Yorkshire Ripper investigation, and went on to work for the Bank of Scotland; for 20 years he has run the sweetshop at Pateley Bridge, in Nidderdale, and in the 2018 Birthday Honours he was appointed MBE for services to the community. Also returning from May's election is the Lib Dems' James Barker, a veteran of Iraq and Afghanistan who represents the Rural West York ward on York city council. Completing the ballot paper is Hannah Barham-Brown, a junior doctor who sits on the council of the British Medical Association; Barham-Brown is the candidate for and deputy leader of the Women's Equality Party.*

There is one local by-election taking place in North Yorkshire to help drive up turnout for the PCC by-election. The *Raskelf and White Horse* ward, part of Hambleton council, covers seventeen parishes in the countryside between Thirsk and Easingwold. Part of the ward is within the North York Moors National Park, including the eponymous White Horse at Kilburn: thought to be England's most northerly hill figure, the White Horse dates from the nineteenth century and dominates the horizon of the southern Vale of York. As well as the White Horse tourists can visit Shandy Hall, the former home of the *Tristram Shandy* writer Laurence Sterne, which is now a museum in the village of Coxwold. The ward runs downhill through Raskelf, which is the largest population centre in the ward with 443 electors on the roll, and its western boundary is the River Swale at Helperby and Myton-on-Swale. Myton-on-Swale was the location of a battle in 1319 when an army of locals, led by the Archbishop of York William Melton, were defeated by Scottish raiders.

* *North Yorkshire PCC*: first preferences C 34385 Lab 18094 Ind 14988 LD 9499 Women's Equality 8837; runoff C 41760 Lab 26895

Parliamentary constituencies: Harrogate and Knaresborough, Richmond (Yorks), Scarborough and Whitby, Selby and Ainsty, Skipton and Ripon, Thirsk and Malton, York Central, York Outer
May 2021 first preferences C 73657 Lab 40803 Ind 22338 LD 19773; final C 84737 Lab 53442
May 2016 first preferences C 53078 Lab 34351 Ind 30984 LD 13856; final C 65018 Lab 44759
November 2012 result C 47885 Lab 34328

Figure 169: North Yorkshire Police and Crime Commissioner

Parliamentary constituency: Thirsk and Malton
North Yorkshire county council division: Easingwold (part: Birdforth, Brafferton and Helperby, Fawdington, Myton-on-Swale, Raskelf, Tholthorpe and Thormanby parishes), Stillington (part: Angram Grange, Carlton Husthwaite, Coxwold, Husthwaite, Kilburn High and Low, Newburgh, Oulston, Thirkleby High and Low with Osgodby, Thornton-on-the-Hill and Wildon Grange parishes)
May 2019 result C 560 Grn 396
May 2015 result C unopposed

Figure 170: Hambleton, Raskelf and White Horse

This ward was created in 2015 as a merger of the former Helperby ward with most of the former White Horse ward. Neither of those wards had been contested in the 2003, 2007 or 2011 Hambleton elections. The new ward was also Conservative unopposed in 2015, but the Greens stood a candidate in 2019 after the previous Conservative councillor Caroline Patmore stood down: new face Jillian Mortimer won a straight fight by 59–41. Patmore remains the county councillor for Stillington, which covers the former White Horse ward; this was one of only two county council seats in the whole of England to go uncontested in the May 2017 local elections. We can see that contested local elections in this corner of the Vale of York are relative novelties.

Jill Mortimer is now an MP, having gained the Hartlepool parliamentary seat in May's by-election (page 153), and she has taken the opportunity to stand down from Hambleton council to concentrate on her duties in Westminster. To succeed her the Conservatives have selected Philippa James. The Greens have returned with new candidate Adam Harper, who gives an address in the ward in the village of Helperby, and the ballot is completed by the ward's first Liberal Democrat candidate Neil Beckwith.*

Don't wait up for these two results: although all the other by-elections today are overnight counts, the PCC and Raskelf by-election votes won't start being counted until Friday morning.

* *Hambleton, Raskelf and White Horse*: C 288 LD 127 Grn 102

Speldhurst and Bidborough

Tunbridge Wells council, Kent; caused by the death of Conservative councillor Julian Stanyer.

For our discussion of the remaining local by-elections this week we will start in the south and work our way back north. The Speldhurst and Bidborough ward covers the rural villages to the west of Tunbridge Wells which are part of the Tunbridge Wells district. As well as the two eponymous villages, the ward extends along the A 264 road towards East Grinstead as far as Ashurst, which is the ward's railhead (Ashurst station is on the Uckfield branch line). Also here is the village of Langton Green, which for many years was home to the factory which made Subbuteo figures.

For many years Speldhurst and Bidborough has been won by the team playing in blue, as you would expect for a leafy middle-class area in west Kent. A majority of the workforce in this ward are in managerial or professional occupations. However, Tunbridge Wells council has courted controversy in recent years with a now-abandoned plan for a new civic centre in the town which went down with the locals with, for want of a better word, disgust. The Conservatives performed appallingly here in the May 2019 local elections, with Speldhurst and Bidborough ward being won by the anti-civic centre Tunbridge Wells Alliance group, and there was enough residual disquiet that the ruling Conservatives lost their majority on the council this year. The Tories currently have 23 seats plus this vacancy, against 13 Lib Dems, 5 seats each for Labour and the Tunbridge Wells Alliance, and an independent; the Conservatives need to hold this by-election in order to retain control via the Mayor's casting vote.

Both of the remaining Conservative seats in Speldhurst and Bidborough came up for election this May following the resignation of councillor Julia Soyke. After the disaster of 2019 the Tories recovered to hold both seats quite comfortably: shares of the vote were 42% for the Conservatives, 22% for the Tunbridge Wells Alliance and 14% for the Green Party. Julian Stanyer, a chartered surveyor who had represented the ward since 2008 and was Mayor of Tunbridge Wells in 2014–15, was re-elected in second place; that meant that he would need to finish Soyke's term and seek re-election next May. As will the winner of this by-election. The Tories also won with 42% in May in the local county division of Tunbridge Wells West, where the Lib Dems ran second; this is not the strong Lib Dem part of the division.

Defending for the Conservatives is Rowena Stanyer, who will be hoping to take over the seat previously held by her late father. Rowena works as a communications specialist. The Tunbridge Wells Alliance have reselected their

Parliamentary constituency: Tunbridge Wells
Kent county council division: Tunbridge Wells West
May 2021 double vacancy C 912/860 Tunbridge Wells Alliance 486 Grn 311 LD 290/246 Lab 176/174
May 2019 result Tunbridge Wells Alliance 1007 C 613 LD 351
May 2018 result C 1186 LD 361 Lab 251
May 2016 result C 1139 Lab 283 UKIP 212
May 2015 result C 2289 LD 491 UKIP 446 Lab 366
May 2014 result C 1255 UKIP 396 LD 201 Lab 198
May 2012 result C 1011 UKIP 221 Lab 212 Lab 164
May 2011 result C 1613 LD 517 UKIP 265
May 2010 result C 2272 LD 921 UKIP 249
May 2008 result C 1345 LD 331 UKIP 152
May 2007 result C 1302 LD 457
May 2006 result C 1400 LD 451
June 2004 result C 1373 LD 568
May 2003 result C 1011 LD 333 Grn 89
May 2002 result C 1128/1126/1096 LD 420/415

Figure 171: Tunbridge Wells, Speldhurst and Bidborough

runner-up from May Matthew Sankey, who is a restaurateur. The Greens have not returned, so the ballot paper is completed by Labour candidate Aleksander Klimanski.*

Bedford

Wandsworth council, London; caused by the resignation of former Labour councillor Hannah Stanislaus.

We move into Greater London for what may be the last local by-election before all the London borough councillors are due for re-election next year. This is one of only two council vacancies in the capital at the moment which occurred before the six-month rule came into effect: the other is in the Kenton West ward of Harrow, which will have one fewer councillor once boundary changes kick in next year, and accordingly nobody seems to be in any hurry to call a by-election there for a seat which will shortly disappear anyway. However, this column will return to Greater London next week for the Parliamentary Special in Old Bexley and Sidcup.

Before then, we discuss a borough which will be the subject of a lot of column inches in the run-up to next year's elections: the borough of Wandsworth. This

* *Tunbridge Wells, Speldhurst and Bidborough*: Tunbridge Wells Alliance 788 C 730 Lab 65 [Tunbridge Wells Alliance gain from C]

district now has three Labour MPs following the gain of Putney, against the national trend, in the 2019 general election. However, the Conservatives have run Wandsworth council for decades with an aggressive low-council-tax policy, which has found favour with many local residents who would normally vote Labour for other levels of government.

Despite this, Wandsworth council has been trending to the left in recent years. The 2006 borough elections returned 51 Conservatives and just 9 Labour councillors; but by 2018 the Tory lead was down to 33–26, with one independent councillor. Labour actually topped the poll in the 2018 Wandsworth elections, polling 38.6% against 38.1% for the Conservatives, but their vote was not well distributed.

We can see this leftward shift in the electoral history of Bedford ward. If Balham is the Gateway to the South, then Bedford ward is the area immediately beyond the Gateway. The ward is named after Bedford Hill and takes in most of Tooting Common; Tooting Bec underground station, on the Northern Line, lies on the ward boundary. Unsurprisingly, the area is part of the Tooting constituency.

This is another middle-class ward, but it's very different in character to Speldhurst and Bidborough. In the 2011 census Bedford ward made the top 40 wards in England and Wales for full-time employment (57.0%) and for residents with degree-level qualifications (61.1%), was in the top 50 for those employed in professional, scientific and technical activities (19.1%), and was in the top 60 for lower managerial, administrative and professional occupations (33.0%) and for the 30–44 age bracket (31.7%).

Up until the 2014 borough elections Bedford ward had a full slate of Conservative councillors. In May 2014 Labour gained two seats in the ward, and both of their elected candidates that year went on to become MPs. Rosena Allin-Khan made it to the green benches just a couple of years later by winning the June 2016 Tooting by-election after Sadiq Khan's election as Mayor of London, while Fleur Anderson was the Labour candidate who gained the Putney constituency in December 2019.

Allin-Khan saw out her term on Wandsworth council, retiring at the 2018 election at which Labour won all three seats in Bedford ward with a large majority of 50–34 over the Conservatives. Anderson resigned from the council earlier this year to allow a by-election to be held alongside the 2021 London mayor and assembly election: that by-election (page 64) gave 48% to the defending Labour candidate Hannah Stanislaus, 32% to the Conservatives and 15% to the Green Party.

We can contrast these results with the Mayor and Assembly elections held

Parliamentary constituency: Tooting
London Assembly constituency: Merton and Wandsworth
May 2021 by-election Lab 2714 C 1778 Grn 815 LD 310
May 2018 result Lab 2835/2719/2376 C 1955/1889/1794 Grn 525 LD 354/317/295
May 2014 result Lab 1935/1843/1716 C 1895/1828/1826 Grn 673 LD 329/288 UKIP 243
May 2010 result C 3351/3068/3023 Lab 2673/2299/2025 LD 1458/1310/1309 Grn 710/525
May 2006 result C 1960/1929/1836 Lab 1093/1093/1062 Grn 750 LD 521/464 Ind 95
May 2002 result C 1394/1366/1276 Lab 1254/1057/1019 Grn 533 LD 468
May 2021 GLA results (excludes postal voters)
Mayor: Lab 2272 C 1055 Grn 405 LD 156 Count Binface 61 Reclaim 57 Omilana 42 Women's Equality 40 London Real 31 Rejoin EU 20 Animal Welfare 17 Farah London 15 Let London Live 14 Fosh 14 Heritage 10 SDP 9 Obunge 9 Burning Pink 6 UKIP 6 Renew 3
London Members: Lab 1936 C 1102 Grn 640 LD 235 Women's Equality 115 Rejoin EU 50 Animal Welfare 45 CPA 24 Reform UK 24 London Real 16 Comm 14 Let London Live 14 Heritage 13 TUSC 11 SDP 8 UKIP 7 Londonpendence 3 Nat Lib 2

Figure 172: Wandsworth, Bedford

on the same day, although some caution as required as the ward breakdowns for those elections do not include postal votes (which were tallied at borough level). The on-the-day vote in Bedford ward gave the former local MP and Labour candidate Sadiq Khan a 54–25 lead over the Conservatives' Shaun Bailey, while in the London Members ballot Labour led with 45% to 26% for the Conservatives and 15% for the Greens.

Hannah Stanislaus' time on Wandsworth council proved to be brief. Stanislaus left the Labour party at the end of August, citing bullying allegations, and subsequently resigned from the council in October after a couple of months sitting as an independent councillor.

As such the voters of Bedford ward are being called out for the second by-election here in six months. Defending for Labour this time is former Wandsworth councillor Sheila Boswell, who was the Labour parliamentary candidate for Putney in the 2015 general election and is now chair of the party's Tooting branch. The Conservatives have reselected Thomas Mytton, who will be hoping for a result which improves on what he got in May's by-election. The Greens' Roy Vickery returns after standing here in 2014 and 2018; Vickery worked for over 40 years as a botanist at the Natural History Museum in central London, and he still helps out with the museum's lichen collection as well as lecturing on plant folklore and studying the flora on Tooting Common. Completing the ballot is Paul Tibbles for the Lib Dems.*

* *Wandsworth, Bedford*: Lab 906 C 905 Grn 306 LD 135

Parliamentary constituency: Basildon and Billericay
Essex county council division: Basildon Laindon Park and Fryerns
May 2021 result Lab 966 C 921 Basildon Community Residents Party 354 Reform UK 123 LD 113
May 2019 result Lab 870 C 437 LD 348
June 2018 by-election Lab 612 C 267 UKIP 145 BNP 42
May 2018 result Lab 1160 C 552 UKIP 369
May 2016 result Lab 1003 UKIP 814 C 363 Ind 26
May 2015 result Lab 1895 UKIP 1825 C 1131 LD 215
May 2014 double vacancy UKIP 983/924 Lab 922/919 C 329/263 LD 99/91 National Front 80
May 2012 result Lab 1048 UKIP 359 C 343 National Front 107 LD 85
May 2011 result Lab 1408 C 740 National Front 244 LD 173
May 2010 result Lab 1818 C 1649 LD 855 BNP 536
May 2008 result Lab 972 C 604 BNP 358 LD 160 Grn 126
May 2007 result Lab 875 C 628 BNP 361 LD 218 Grn 134
May 2006 result Lab 1009 C 610 BNP 560 LD 212 Grn 153
June 2004 result Lab 996 C 604 BNP 519 LD 261 Grn 145 Respect 57
May 2003 result Lab 766 C 434 BNP 285 LD 207 Grn 114 Ind 80
May 2002 result Lab 1165/1159/1085 C 530/518/515 LD 241/229/214 Socialist Alliance 93

Figure 173: Basildon, Lee Chapel North

Lee Chapel North

Basildon council, Essex; caused by the resignation of Labour councillor Kayode Adeniran.

We travel out of London to one of the first New Towns, built to take overspill from London in the post-war era. This is Basildon, which now forms another link in the chain of towns on the north side of the Thames Estuary running from London to Southend.

Lee Chapel North ward is one of the New Town-type developments in Basildon. It covers the area between Laindon in the west and Basildon town centre in the east, and Laindon railway station lies on the ward boundary. The New Town origins are betrayed by Lee Chapel North's census return: it is in the top 20 wards in England and Wales for adults with "Level 1" qualifications (in real money, 1–5 GCSE passes or equivalent) and despite a few decades of Right to Buy over 40% of the households are still socially rented.

This makes Lee Chapel North one of the safest Labour wards in a town noted for its electoral volatility. Basildon was of course the constituency whose Conservative hold in April 1992, by the late and much-missed David Amess, symbolised the re-election of the Major government that year. In the local elections a month later the Conservatives won every ward in Basildon; two years later, they lost every ward in Basildon.

Since the current ward boundaries were introduced in 2002 Labour have only lost Lee Chapel North ward once. That was in 2014 when the winners were the UK Independence Party, who ran riot across Basildon that year in a result never repeated before or since. Labour regained the UKIP seats here in 2016 and 2018.

The May 2021 elections in Basildon were good for the Conservatives, who gained two seats from what was left of Basildon UKIP and two seats from Labour to regain overall control of the district, two years after losing control to a Labour-led hung council. The Conservatives scored a big swing in Lee Chapel North to take their best result yet on the current boundaries, although it wasn't quite enough to win here: shares of the vote were 39% for Labour, 37% for the Conservatives and 14% to the Basildon Community Residents Party. However, there was relatively little swing in the simultaneous Essex county council election: this ward is part of the large county division of Basildon Laindon Park and Fryerns, which continued to split its representation between a Conservative and a Labour county councillor.

So this is a marginal seat for Labour to defend following the resignation of Kayode Adeniran. He had won the last by-election here in June 2018* and was re-elected for a full four-year term in 2019, so the winner of this by-election will serve until 2023.

Defending this marginal seat for Labour is Terry Webb. The Conservatives have reselected Deepak Shukla after his near-miss in May. Also returning from May's election is Kay Quested of the Basildon Community Residents Party, which was formed in opposition to extensive redevelopment proposals by Basildon council for the town centre. Completing the ballot paper are former UKIP county councillor Frank Ferguson for Reform UK, and Michael Chandler for the Lib Dems.†

Horringer

West Suffolk council; caused by the resignation of Conservative councillor Terry Clements.

This is getting beyond a joke. West Suffolk district has only existed for two and a half years, but this is already the ninth by-election which has been held to the council. Some councils haven't had nine by-elections so far this century. Now,

* *Andrew's Previews 2018*, page 221. † *Basildon, Lee Chapel North*: Lab 451 C 395 Basildon Community Residents Party 135 Reform UK 98 LD 55

Parliamentary constituency: Bury St Edmunds (part: Great Whelnetham, Horringer, Ickworth, Little Whelnetham and Nowton parishes), West Suffolk (part: Hawstead parish)
Suffolk county council division: Thingoe South
May 2019 result C 524 Lab 237

Figure 174: West Suffolk, Horringer

West Suffolk is on the large side for a shire district council with 64 members, but even so that's already a vacancy rate of 14% with eighteen months of the council term still to go. We shouldn't necessarily read too much into this: while high numbers of by-elections can sometimes reflect a dysfunctional political culture, other times it can just be the result of random chance.

The latest West Suffolk by-election occurs in Horringer ward, which covers six parishes immediately to the south of Bury St Edmunds. Horringer is the largest of these parishes with 799 electors on the roll; it is located on the main road from Bury St Edmunds to Haverhill. Just to the west of Horringer is the neoclassical stately home of Ickworth House, until recently home to the Marquess of Bristol and now in the hands of the National Trust.

The retirement of Terry Clements brings to an end a long political career. Clements had served continuously as a councillor for this area since 1983, when he was elected to the former St Edmundsbury council. He was Mayor of St Edmundsbury in 2017–18, and also served on Suffolk county council from 2005 to 2017.

Clements had won his final term in Horringer ward in 2019, defeating Labour by a 69–31 margin. The area is just as safe Conservative at other levels of government: it is part of the wonderfully-named county division of Thingoe South, and is split between the Bury St Edmunds and West Suffolk constituencies.

Defending for the Conservatives is Nick Wiseman, a landscape gardener and fencing contractor. Labour have gone for youth in selecting Aaron McIntyre, who has only just turned 18; McIntyre is president of the students union at Abbeygate sixth-form college in Bury St Edmunds. Completing the ballot is Daniel Linehan of the Liberal Democrats.*

Bar Pool

Nuneaton and Bedworth council, Warwickshire; caused by the resignation of Labour councillor Patricia Elliott.

* *West Suffolk, Horringer*: C 257 Lab 204 LD 78

We now travel west for two difficult Labour defences in the West Midlands, starting in Nuneaton, a place this column hasn't profiled in detail since 2015 (and then only for the county council). There is a lot to catch up on.

The Bar Pool ward lies in western Nuneaton, taking its name from a local brook which opens out into a series of ponds on the ward's northern boundary. The ward takes in the eastern part of the Stockingford area along the Arbury Road; its eastern boundary is the Coventry Canal, while the ward extends south to take in St Thomas More secondary school. Nuneaton is an industrial town and this is a strongly working-class area of it, with over 41% of the workforce in routine or semi-routine occupations. The ward also includes a lot of council housing and takes in Nuneaton's most deprived census district.

Nuneaton and Bedworth is one of the few councils which re-elects half of its members every two years. Until this year, Bar Pool ward had voted Labour in every Nuneaton and Bedworth election since the current boundaries came into force in 2002, with one exception. That was 2008, when the British National Party came through the middle of a tight race between Labour and the Conservatives: the winning BNP candidate that year polled 663 votes, the Conservatives 650 and Labour 624. There has often been a strong Conservative vote here, but they could never break through until this year.

The May 2021 Nuneaton and Bedworth election was a stunning victory for the Conservatives, and its impact was all the greater because this was one of the few councils this year which counted its results overnight after polls closed. Going into the election Nuneaton and Bedworth had been a hung council with Labour holding 17 seats, half of the total; in opposition to them were 13 Conservatives, 3 councillors from a Tory splinter group and a Green. In a result well out of kilter with what had gone before, the Conservatives won 15 seats this year, out of a possible 17, to take overall control with a strong majority.

That total included ten gains from Labour, one of which was Bar Pool ward where the Conservatives suddenly ran out winners by the score of 56–33. Let me again stress, this is a ward which had not previously voted Conservative this century. On the same day the Stockingford division of Warwickshire county council, which has very similar boundaries, turned in a very similar result.

Following the May elections there were just seven Labour councillors left in Nuneaton and Bedworth, with six of them due for re-election next year. One of those was Patricia Elliott, who has represented Bar Pool ward since 2014. Elliott handed in her resignation last month, and there is just time to squeeze in a by-election before her term finishes.

The difficult task of defending this ward for Labour falls to Abi Olaifa, who is described by the party as a career-driven professional. Oliafa stood in

Parliamentary constituency: Nuneaton
Warwickshire county council division: Stockingford
May 2021 result C 917 Lab 536 Grn 135 Ind 54
May 2018 result Lab 744 C 607 Grn 135
May 2016 result Lab 677 C 429 UKIP 254 Grn 73
May 2014 result Lab 695 UKIP 402 C 382 BNP 71 TUSC 40
May 2012 result Lab 815 Ind 281 C 235 BNP 121
May 2011 by-election Lab 1034 C 519 BNP 204 LD 142 UKIP 65 TUSC 38
May 2010 result Lab 1513 C 907 LD 517 BNP 394 Socialist Alternative 40
May 2008 result BNP 663 C 650 Lab 624
May 2006 result Lab 762 C 632
May 2005 by-election Lab 1507 C 846 LD 615
June 2004 result Lab 622 Lib 377 C 371
May 2002 result Lab 620/570 C 380 Lib 273/227

Figure 175: Nuneaton and Bedworth, Bar Pool

May in the St Nicolas ward of Nuneaton and Bedworth and in the Coleshill North and Water Orton division of the county council, both of which are more traditionally weak Labour areas. The Conservatives have gone for youth in selecting Jamie Hartshorn, who works in COVID testing. Completing the ballot paper is Andrew Heritage for the Green Party.*

Knutton

Newcastle-under-Lyme council, Staffordshire; caused by the resignation of Labour councillor Brian Johnson.

For our other Midlands by-election this week we come to another district where Labour have been under pressure in recent years. The village of Knutton lies on the edge of the urban sprawl of the Potteries, about a mile to the north-west of Newcastle-under-Lyme town centre. Knutton lies on the North Staffordshire coalfield, which was still operating into the 1990s, and it remains a strongly working-class village. The present ward is a cut-down version of the Knutton and Silverdale ward which existed until 2018, and that ward made the top 100 in England and Wales for routine occupations at the 2011 census.

The collieries may have gone, but the site of the mines have now been put to other uses. Just to the south of the Knutton ward boundary lies Walleys Quarry, a landfill site which has been the scene of one of the most pungent political controversies in recent years. And when I say pungent, I mean pungent: the place stinks, and has stunk the borough out for years with high levels of

* *Nuneaton and Bedworth, Bar Pool*: C 508 Lab 215 Grn 196 [C gain from Lab]

hydrogen sulphide emissions. In September the High Court ruled that the Environment Agency's enforcement action against the landfill site operator had been inadequate, and ordered that action be taken to bring the emissions to safe levels by January next year. The Environment Agency have come up with a new plan to do this, and we wait to see whether that will work.

Before then, there's an election to talk about. Newcastle-under-Lyme council last went to the polls in May 2018, and the only previous result on these boundaries is from that year with Labour beating the Conservatives 75–25. As will become clear, there's more to this area's local elections results than that.

The previous ward of Knutton and Silverdale was generally Labour but rather complicated. Its first two elections, in 2002 and 2003, saw the runner-up spot go to Derrick Huckfield, standing for the "Caring Party". Huckfield then joined UKIP, came close to winning in 2006 and gained the ward in 2007.

Without Huckfield as their candidate UKIP struggled to make headway here in 2010, and in that year the ward went to new Labour candidate Gareth Snell who later had a brief term as MP for Stoke-on-Trent Central. Huckfield then lost his seat to Labour in 2011 by 30 votes.

In 2014 Snell moved to contest Chesterton ward (which he lost), and Labour selected as their candidate for Knutton and Silverdale Baroness Golding, who had been the Labour MP for Newcastle-under-Lyme from 1986 to 2001. Golding resoundingly lost the ward to Derrick Huckfield, who returned as a UKIP councillor. Huckfield left UKIP the following year, and he has ended up in the Conservatives.

The 2018 Newcastle-under-Lyme elections were held in the wake of a damning report into the running of the 2017 general election here[*]. That report led to the resignation of the Labour leader of the council and the installation of a Conservative-led administration. The 2018 borough elections returned a hung council, with the Conservatives polling more votes than Labour but winning fewer seats: 20 Labour councillors were returned, 18 Conservatives, 3 independents and 3 Lib Dems. Huckfield sought re-election in the new Silverdale ward, this time with the Conservative nomination, and lost. The Tory-led administration continued.

Since 2018 Labour have lost a by-election in Holditch and Chesterton ward to an independent candidate[†]. All four independent councillors joined the Conservative group earlier this month: together with a previous defection from the Lib Dems, that means that the Tories now have a majority on Newcastle-under-Lyme council.

This builds on excellent Conservative results at other levels of government.

---

[*] *Andrew's Previews 2017*, page 374. [†] *Andrew's Previews 2019*, page 64.

Parliamentary constituency: Newcastle-under-Lyme
Staffordshire county council division: Keele, Knutton and Silverdale
May 2018 result Lab 355 C 120

Figure 176: Newcastle-under-Lyme, Knutton

The Newcastle-under-Lyme constituency (which is rather more urban than the district) was a gain for the former *Krypton Factor* superperson Aaron Bell in December 2019, and the Conservatives won a full slate of Staffordshire county council seats in the district in May. That full slate included an excellent performance for Derrick Huckfield, who convincingly gained the Keele, Knutton and Silverdale county division from Labour. Huckfield had previously won the division in 2013 for UKIP, defeating Labour's Gareth Snell by two votes.

This by-election is a straight fight. Defending for Labour is Steph Talbot, who stood in May's county council elections for Newcastle South division; she runs Alice, a charity supporting disadvantaged and vulnerable families in Newcastle and Stoke. Challenging for the Conservatives is county councillor Derrick Huckfield. Despite the 3 to 1 margin in favour of Labour three years ago, this column would rate Huckfield as favourite.*

Halton Castle

Halton council, Cheshire; caused by the death of Labour councillor Harry Howard.

Now Runcorn lay over on one side of stream,
And Widnes on t'other side stood,
And, as nobody wanted to go either place,
Well, the trade wasn't any too good.

One evening, to Ted's superlative surprise,
Three customers came into view:
A Mr and Mrs Ramsbottom it were,
And Albert, their little son, too.

'How much for the three?' Mr Ramsbottom asked,
As his hand to his pocket did dip.
Ted said: 'Same for three as it would be for one,
Per tuppence per person per trip.'

— Mariott Edgar, *The Runcorn Ferry*

We now come to two by-elections on the south side of the Mersey, within the Liverpool City Region. The first of these lies not in Merseyside but in Runcorn,

* *Newcastle-under-Lyme, Knutton*: C 188 Lab 180 [C gain from Lab]

Parliamentary constituency: Halton (almost all), Weaver Vale (small parts)
May 2021 result Lab 669/635/560 Ind 234 C 229 LD 144

Figure 177: Halton, Halton Castle

as we come to our second New Town by-election of the week. Halton Castle ward is definitely one of the New Town areas, taking in the Castlefields and Halton Village residential areas away from the river and the industrial units of Astmoor down by the Ship Canal bank.

Astmoor has had a swathe cut into it in recent years thanks to the construction of the Mersey Gateway Bridge. Opened to traffic in 2017 to replace the ageing and congested Silver Jubilee Bridge (which replaced the Runcorn–Widnes Transporter Bridge, which replaced the ferry), the Mersey Gateway Bridge has an impressive cable-stayed design with three supporting towers. Unlike the former Silver Jubilee Bridge, there is a toll for crossings of £2. Stanley Holloway's "tuppence per part of a person per part of a trip" is clearly some years of inflation in the past.

At the time of the 2011 census Halton Castle ward was called Castlefields, after its main New Town development, and had slightly different boundaries. It is a seriously deprived area, with 13% of the workforce being long-term sick or disabled and 51% of the households being socially rented—both figures are in the top 100 wards in England and Wales. As this column has previously set out*, this ward was closely fought between Labour and the Lib Dems until the Coalition era, when the Lib Dem vote disappeared in line with the regional swing in Merseyside. Halton council got new ward boundaries in May this year meaning that all three seats in this ward came up for election; the Labour slate was re-elected with 52% of the vote, with left-wing independent candidate Darrin Whyte and the Conservatives polling 18% each.

This by-election is to replace councillor Harry Howard, who passed away in September at the age of 75. Howard was part of the council's majority Labour group, and he had sat on Halton council since winning a by-election for this ward in 2006. He had beat the alphabet to top the poll in May, so the winner of this by-election will be due to serve until 2024.

Defending for Labour is Sharon Thornton, a café owner and community volunteer. Darrin Whyte, who has contested this ward in every election since 2014 (originally for the Trade Unionist and Socialist Coalition, since 2016 as an independent candidate) is back for another go; he has been runner-up in the last four elections here. The Conservatives' Danny Clarke has also had a few goes at standing for Halton council, and he hit the headlines in 2019 with an attack on

* *Andrew's Previews 2018*, page 69.

the number of takeaways in Runcorn. Also standing are Anthony Dalton for the Lib Dems and Iain Ferguson for the Green Party.*

Oxton

Wirral council, Merseyside; caused by the death of Liberal Democrat councillor Andy Corkhill.

For our Liberal Democrat defence of the week we are well and truly in the Land of the Plastic Scouser. The Birkenhead suburb of Oxton, located south-west of the town centre and well away from the riverfront, has for well over a century been the sort of place where people who work in Liverpool and have money prefer to live and to commute from. The 2011 census showed Oxton to be the most middle-class ward in the Birkenhead constituency, and the ward's fine Victorian houses show that this status has been maintained for generations.

This being Merseyside, that doesn't translate to Oxton being a Conservative-voting area. Instead this has been a Liberal Democrat ward, with one exception, throughout this century. Oxton was safely Lib Dem until the advent of the Coalition, and then turned into a Lib Dem–Labour marginal in line with Merseyside's lurch to the left. However, Labour were only able to break through once, in 2015. In recent years the Lib Dems have pulled away again and the ward has reverted to safety: May's result gave the Liberal Democrats 57% against just 26% for Labour.

That rise provided an opportunity for Lib Dem rising star Andy Corkhill, who was elected in May 2019 and recovered the seat his party had lost to Labour four years earlier. Corkhill went on to be the Lib Dem candidate for the Wirral West constituency in the December 2019 general election, and he had been selected as the party's candidate for the recent Liverpool City Region mayoral election.

Unfortunately, Andy Corkhill had to give that up after being diagnosed with cancer. His health continued to decline after surgery in February, and he passed away in October at the appallingly early age of 36.

The resulting by-election is unlikely to affect control of Wirral council. This has swung in recent years between Labour majorities and hung councils; the 2021 election brought in another hung phase. Currently, 30 Labour councillors form a minority administration against 23 Conservatives, 5 Lib Dems plus this vacancy, 5 Greens and two independents.

Defending for the Liberal Democrats is Orod Osanlou, a consultant physician in clinical pharmacology and therapeutics. He was one of the doctors

* *Halton, Halton Castle*: Lab 373 Grn 117 Ind 69 C 45 LD 15

Parliamentary constituency: Birkenhead
May 2021 result LD 2311 Lab 1050 C 328 Grn 306 Reform UK 58
May 2019 result LD 2627 Lab 1298 UKIP 245 C 220
May 2018 result LD 2073 Lab 1700 C 376 Grn 205
May 2016 result LD 2381 Lab 1568 C 275 Grn 183
May 2015 result Lab 3085 LD 2788 C 854 UKIP 615 Grn 424
May 2014 result LD 1620 Lab 1483 UKIP 563 C 310 Grn 250
May 2012 result LD 2026 Lab 1763 UKIP 258 C 232 Grn 149
May 2011 result LD 1918 Lab 1792 C 655 UKIP 234 Grn 222
May 2010 result LD 2941 Lab 2310 C 1425 UKIP 301 Grn 276
May 2008 result LD 1910 C 748 Lab 614 UKIP 179 Grn 139
May 2007 result LD 2007 Lab 693 C 611 Grn 193 UKIP 158
May 2006 result LD 2067 Lab 646 C 565 UKIP 267 Grn 185
June 2004 result LD 3295/3074/2924 Lab 999/997/985 C 843/663/661 Grn 489

Figure 178: Wirral, Oxton

working on the clinical trial of the Novavax COVID vaccine, which at the time of writing is awaiting approval from the UK medical regulator. Labour have selected Sue Mahoney, who stood in May in the neighbouring ward of Birkenhead and Tranmere: she resoundingly lost to the Green Party a seat which Labour were defending. Also standing are Philip Merry for the Conservatives and Mary Heydon for the Green Party.*

Carnforth and Millhead

Lancaster council; caused by the resignation of John Reynolds, who was elected for Labour but sitting as an independent.

We'll divert north for the first of our Lancashire by-elections today. Carnforth is the most northerly town in Lancashire, and is a major railway junction. The Cumbrian Coast Line and a branch line towards Skipton both leave the West Coast main line here, at a station which is famous as the filming location for the acclaimed 1945 film *Brief Encounter*.

Carnforth station has been sympathetically restored and is a place of pilgrimage for fans of the film. Mind, on the occasion your columnist had a brew in the station's refreshment room the nuclear flask train turned up from Sellafield, and then stopped at the end of the platform waiting for its slot on the main line. Suddenly the place was swarming with armed police. Not exactly the sort of image that the tourist board like to tell you about.

Legend has it that a teenage Cecil Parkinson was an extra in *Brief Encounter*:

* *Wirral, Oxton*: LD 1666 Lab 460 C 168 Grn 147

Parkinson was from Carnforth, and his father was the stationmaster at the time. There is a large railway depot behind the station, maintaining and overhauling steam locomotives for excursion trains; and that continued railway influence has meant that Carnforth is historically a Labour-inclined town. However, it's not quite large enough for three Lancaster councillors of its own, so the neighbouring village of Millhead was added to the ward in 2015 to make up the numbers. This has made the Conservatives competitive.

The Tories won the first contest for Carnforth and Millhead ward in May 2015 fairly easily. One of the Conservative councillors, Christopher Leadbetter, passed away shortly afterwards while on holiday in Croatia; the Tories held the resulting by-election in November 2015. The by-election winner was George Askew, a former Pendle councillor who had been the election agent for Pendle's Conservative MP Andrew Stephenson; Askew had also been a regional director for the Vote Leave campaign.

George Askew didn't live to see the eventual success of that campaign. In February 2016 he was found dead by his fiancée at their home, aged just 32. The coroner heard that his death was the result of alcohol and drug abuse. The resulting by-election in May 2016 was narrowly gained by the Labour candidate John Reynolds.

All three outgoing councillors—Reynolds for Labour, Peter Yates and Mel Guilding for the Conservatives—were re-elected in 2019, with Reynolds polling almost twice as many votes as his Labour running-mates. He topped the poll with 37%, against 32% for the Conservatives and 19% for an independent slate. The ward is Conservative-held at other levels of government; it is the most Labour part of the safe Tory county division of Lancaster Rural North, and it is covered by the Morecambe and Lunesdale constituency.

John Reynolds has now stood down from the council for personal reasons, having previously left the Labour group last year. So we have the second episode in our current three-part series on Lancaster council, which kicked off with the Labour hold in University and Scotforth Rural ward two weeks ago (page 463).[*] This will be a tougher defence for Labour, who have given the job of holding this seat to Luke Taylor. Taylor sat on Blackpool council from 2014 to 2019, representing Clifton ward[†]; he was on the Labour slate for this ward in 2019 and stood here for Lancaster county council in May. The Conservatives have selected former Lancaster councillor Stuart Bateson, who lost his seat in Heysham South ward in 2019. The independents from last time have not returned, so the ballot

[*] For the concluding part of the trilogy see page 550. [†] The preview I wrote for the 2014 by-election Taylor won in Clifton ward was the only one I ever wrote in verse. I intended it as a parody of *Albert and the Lion*. It was godawful.

Parliamentary constituency: Morecambe and Lunesdale
Lancaster county council division: Lancaster Rural North
May 2019 result Lab 680/395/356 C 588/499/440 Ind 354/332 Grn 199/142/108
May 2016 by-election Lab 702 C 671 UKIP 134 LD 74 Grn 49
November 2015 by-election C 545 Lab 320 Grn 52 LD 38 UKIP 37
May 2015 result C 1405/1238/1184 Lab 1027/981/921

Figure 179: Lancaster, Carnforth and Millhead

paper is completed by Patrick McMurray for the Green Party and Tony Saville for the Liberal Democrats.*

Bryn

Wigan council, Greater Manchester; caused by the resignation of independent councillor Steve Jones.

It's now time for this column to consider an important question. When is a resignation not a resignation?

Our other by-election today in what was once Lancashire takes place in the town of Ashton-in-Makerfield. Located halfway between Wigan and Warrington, Ashton was once one of the main towns of the Lancashire coalfield; but the pits are now replaced by the industrial estates and the spoil heaps have been landscaped into the Three Sisters Recreation Area, a nature reserve of woodlands and ponds. Bryn, the northern ward of Ashton-in-Makerfield, has excellent connections to the main towns and cities of north-west England via the M 6 motorway, while Bryn railway station links the area to Wigan, St Helens and Liverpool.

In the 2011 census the Bryn ward had the 74th highest return of any ward in England and Wales for Christianity, at 80.4%. This is a common feature of the census results for north-west England: of the 73 wards with higher Christian results, 71 are in the north-west. For whatever reason, lapsed Christians—particularly lapsed Catholics—living in the north-west are more likely to list their old religion on the census form than lapsed Christians elsewhere in the country.

Bryn may be an ex-mining area, but that doesn't mean it's a Labour ward. The 2004 election returned a full slate of councillors for the now-defunct Community Action party, which at the time was the official opposition on Wigan council. Labour have only won here on current boundaries in 2010, 2014 and 2015; all the rest of the elections in Bryn since 2007 have returned independent councillors. With one exception.

* *Lancaster, Carnforth and Millhead*: Lab 538 C 315 Grn 54 LD 25

The 2016 election here returned independent candidate Steve Jones, standing with the nomination of the Wigan Independent Network, for his first term of office with a narrow majority of 77 votes over Labour. Jones got into a number of controversies the following year: he was prosecuted for drink-driving, and at the end of 2017 he accepted a police caution for common assault. The then leader of Wigan council, Lord Smith of Leigh, branded Jones as "unfit for office" and advised him to "seek professional help".

As the year ticked over to 2018, and as his assault arrest became public, Jones decided that he wanted to tender his resignation as a councillor, but he wasn't in a good enough financial position to leave the council immediately. So Jones emailed the council's chief executive on 5th January 2018, to advise that he would be stepping down on 20th February 2018.

At which point somebody at Wigan council decided to look in their copy of the Local Government Act 1972. Section 84 subsection (1) of that Act relates to resignation of councillors and, so far as is relevant, reads as follows:

> A person elected to any office under this Act... may at any time resign his office by written notice delivered... to the proper officer of the council;... and his resignation shall take effect upon the receipt of the notice by the person... to whom it is required to be delivered.

Wigan council's interpretation of this was that councillor resignations could not be postdated ("shall take effect upon the receipt of the notice"), and that Jones had delivered a written notice within the meaning of the section. Accordingly, they promptly declared Jones' seat to be vacant and a by-election was quickly called for 22nd February 2018.

Steve Jones withdrew his resignation notice three days later. He tried to sit in a full council meeting on 10th January, but was thrown out of the chamber.

For the by-election polling stations were booked, ballot papers were printed and postal votes were issued and returned, causing significant expenditure for Wigan council. Your columnist put time into researching and drafting a preview, which wasn't published at the time (for reasons which will become clear) but has been rescued from my archives: it appears in *Andrew's Previews 2018*, page 84. Candidates were nominated by Labour, the Conservatives and the Lib Dems. Steve Jones also stood in the by-election to seek re-election.

Jones had also taken Lord Smith's advice by seeking professional help—from lawyers. He took Wigan council to judicial review over its decision to declare his seat vacant. On 21st February 2018—the day before polling day in the Bryn by-election—the High Court heard the judicial review at the Manchester Civil

Justice Centre[*]. The judge, Mr Justice Martin Spencer, ruled that Steve Jones' email of 5th January was not a resignation letter within the meaning of the Act but merely a notice of an intention to resign on some future date; as the notice had subsequently been withdrawn, it followed that Jones' seat was *not* vacant. He found in favour of Jones and issued an injunction against the Returning Officer of Wigan to stop the by-election going ahead[†].

All this appears, in the end, to have had a positive effect on how Steve Jones' electors saw him. Jones was re-elected in May this year for a second term of office with a stonking majority of 67–23 over Labour.

Jones has now sent his resignation in to Wigan council again, and it's just as messy as the last time. I quote Wigan council's statement on the matter, published on 24th September, in full:

> **Joint statement from Wigan Council and Councillor Steve Jones:**
>
> "Wigan Council has developed a culture of kindness and compassion among its workforce and elected members. At the time of his resignation [in July 2021], Councillor Steve Jones was under a lot of pressure, which is why the resignation was not accepted immediately to give time for reflection and proper consideration.
>
> "Unfortunately, this decision has been challenged by an individual who is threatening legal action against the council. Therefore, in the interest of taxpayers and in agreement with Councillor Jones we have no choice but to accept the resignation."
>
> Councillor Steve Jones, independent member for Bryn ward, added: "I have thoroughly enjoyed my role as a local councillor and have been involved in some great community projects. I'd like to thank my constituents for voting me into office and my colleagues at the council for all their support over the last five years. I'd like to thank the council for all the help and support they've given me, especially Alison who has always shown me and other members nothing but kindness."
>
> Councillor David Molyneux, leader of Wigan Council, said: "I'd like to thank Councillor Jones for his hard work and commitment to his constituents during his time as a councillor. I'd like to wish him and his family all the best."

This column would submit that Wigan council and Steve Jones *both* need to get a grip on reality. After the fiasco of Wigan council accepting an invalid resignation, and incurring substantial legal and administrative costs for Wigan's

[*] *Stephen Jones v Wigan Council* [2018] EWHC 528 (Admin). [†] *Andrew's Previews 2018*, page 86.

council tax payers as a result, it appears that this time round they were prepared to *reject* a *valid* resignation. That's not something the council has the power to do either, and the High Court would likely have dressed them down a second time had it gone that far. As for Jones, meanwhile, while this column wishes him well for future I really don't want to have to write about him again.

Anyway, he's finally gone.

Three independent candidates put nomination papers in to replace Steve Jones in Bryn ward, but one of them has withdrawn. Jones has signed the nomination papers for independent Gareth Fairhurst, who has his own history with Wigan council. The Fairhurst family are from Standish on the other side of Wigan; Gareth's father George Fairhurst, who passed away earlier this year, had served as a Conservative member of the council before falling out with the party and forming his own localist group. He actually managed to get the party name "Wigan Independent Conservatives" registered with the Electoral Commission, in one of that Commission's more questionable decisions. The new group proved locally popular and at one point all three councillors for Standish with Langtree ward were Fairhursts. Gareth sat for that ward from 2012 to 2016 and got into a number of his own disputes with the council: in 2017 Wigan council took the unusual step of distributing a leaflet to Standish residents to remind them who their councillors are, following complaints that Gareth was continuing to hold surgeries and act as an elected member despite having lost his seat the previous year. The other independent candidate is James Richardson, who lives in the ward and whose nomination papers have been signed by one of Bryn ward's two remaining independent councillors. Labour have selected Sam Flemming, a politics and international relations student. Completing the ballot are Paul Martin for the Conservatives and David Burley for the Lib Dems.*

Maryport South

Allerdale council, Cumbria; caused by the disqualification of independent councillor Peter Little.

If you thought Bryn ward was bad for elected representatives saying and doing stupid things, you ain't seen nothing yet. It's time to finish this week's column with a bang.

There has been a harbour for centuries on the coast of West Cumbria, at the point where the River Ellen flows into the sea. The first record of Maryport is in AD 122, under the name of *Alauna*, when it was a Roman port: part of the

* *Wigan, Bryn*: Lab 429 Richardson 412 Fairhurst 353 C 142 LD 38 [Lab gain from Ind]

Parliamentary constituency: Makerfield
May 2021 result Ind 2047 Lab 703 C 252 LD 51
May 2019 result Ind 1147 Lab 1072 UKIP 284 C 131 LD 84
May 2018 result Ind 1065 Lab 973 C 198 UKIP 133 LD 67
February 2018 by-election cancelled
May 2016 result Wigan Ind Network 1200 Lab 1123 UKIP 438 C 161
May 2015 result Lab 2245 Wigan Ind Network 1717 UKIP 948 C 378 Ind 267 Community Action 141
May 2014 result Lab 1190 UKIP 724 Ind 625 Community Action 289 C 131
May 2012 result Ind 1516 Lab 1352 C 146
May 2011 result Ind 1955 Lab 1363 C 274
May 2010 result Lab 2274 Ind 1697 Community Action 609 BNP 531 C 525
May 2008 result Ind 1606 Lab 765 Community Action 394 BNP 284 C 204
May 2007 result Ind 1667 Lab 1030 BNP 307 C 179
May 2006 result Community Action 1429 Lab 1050 BNP 457 C 171 New Party 45
June 2004 result Community Action 2370/2297/2239 Lab 1233/1183/986 C 326

Figure 180: Wigan, Bryn

coastal defences on the Solway Firth which were developed at the same time as Hadrian's Wall.

Similar to Whitehaven further down the coast, modern Maryport is a planned settlement dating from the eighteenth century. Its developer was Humphrey Senhouse, who obtained an Act of Parliament in 1749 to construct the town at a location then known as Ellenfoot; Senhouse renamed the settlement as Maryport, after his wife.

The town became a major port for the Cumberland coalfield, and there were a number of pits in the area. In the 1840s Maryport was linked to the railway network with the opening of the highly-profitable Maryport and Carlisle Railway.

Maryport is part of the Allerdale district of Cumbria, which also takes in Workington, Keswick and a large agricultural area between the mountains and the Solway coast. Allerdale council got new wards at its last election in 2019, and Maryport South is an expanded version of the previous Ewanrigg ward. The 2011 census placed Ewanrigg in the top 80 wards in England and Wales for adults with no qualifications (42.2%) and for those working in construction (13.4%), and in the top 30 for those in routine (25.6%) and semi-routine (25.0%) occupations. There are few wards more working-class than this.

As well as the southern half of Maryport, this ward takes in the village of Broughton Moor. This was historically a pit village, but the mine here closed in the 1930s; after that, the colliery site was reused by the Royal Navy as an armaments depot. RNAD Broughton Moor was subsequently used by the West German and American forces under the auspices of NATO, before closing in 1992 upon the end of the Cold War. The extensive depot site is only now starting to be redeveloped, with the Derwent Forest Development Consortium having ambitious plans for lots of new houses there.

Although Workington has a Tory MP these days, Maryport is Labour at other levels of government. The last Cumbria county council elections, in May 2017, returned a Labour councillor for the Maryport South division (which is larger than this ward) with a big majority. In its previous contests this century Ewanrigg ward had been safe Labour, and nobody bothered to stand against the Labour slate in 2003.

Things changed in the 2019 Allerdale elections, when Labour lost a seat in the new Maryport South ward to independent candidate Peter Little. Shares of the vote were 43% for the Labour slate, with long-serving councillor Carni McCarron-Holmes re-elected at the top of the poll, and 39% for Little who won the ward's second seat with a majority of 23 votes over the second Labour candidate.

Peter Little has a bulging record in the Councillors Behaving Badly file. In May this year he got into a parking dispute with his neighbours while extremely drunk; the police were called and Little was arrested after his behaviour got worse. He was taken to Workington police station where he insulted and homophobically abused police officers, and that bad behaviour continued even after he had spent a night in the cells sobering up. Little subsequently pleaded guilty to three public order offences; in August the magistrates' court sentenced him to 12 weeks in prison, suspended. He was kicked out of the independent group on Allerdale council, but kept his position as a councillor. The threshold at which councillors are disqualified for convictions is 13 weeks' imprisonment, and Little's sentence was one week short of that.

A month later Little was back before the magistrates *again*, having sent an email on 9th September to the chief executive of Allerdale council in offensive terms, making threats against him and Mark Jenkinson, the Conservative MP for Workington. Little pleaded guilty to sending an email that was grossly offensive or of an indecent, obscene or menacing character, and the case was adjourned for pre-sentence reports. His sentencing hearing was scheduled for 18th October.

On that day, the news was dominated by the killing of the Conservative MP Sir David Amess, which had happened three days earlier. Workington magistrates, no doubt seeking to send a message loud and clear that abuse of public servants and elected representatives will result in consequences, sentenced Peter Little to six weeks in prison for the threatening communication *and* activated the

Parliamentary constituency: Workington
Cumbria county council division: Maryport South
May 2019 result Lab 377/324 Ind 347 For Britain Movement 98 C 60/55

Figure 181: Allerdale, Maryport South

12-week suspended sentence for the public order offences, the two sentences to run consecutively.

You can't really blame the Allerdale council staff for wanting to get Little off their council as soon as possible. The council added 6 weeks and 12 weeks together, noticed that the sum came to more than the 13-week threshold, and promptly pronounced him to be disqualified. A by-election was just as promptly called to replace him.

The by-election comes with Allerdale council rather evenly balanced between the three main groups. The Conservatives are in minority control but only hold 18 of the 49 seats; opposing them are 17 independents (plus this vacancy) and 13 Labour councillors.

One new independent candidate has come forward: he is Eric Galletly, a retired electrician who has been endorsed by the council's independent group. Labour have selected Bill Pegram, who is a Maryport town councillor and former Mayor of Maryport; he contested Maryport North in the 2019 Allerdale elections. The Conservatives' Steve Newton completes the ballot paper.*

* *Allerdale, Maryport South*: Lab 273 Ind 149 C 94 [Lab gain from Ind]

Tuesday 30th November 2021

One by-election on Tuesday 30th November 2021:

Franche and Habberley North

Wyre Forest council, Worcestershire; caused by the resignation of Health Concern councillor Susie Griffiths.

For a rare Tuesday by-election we travel to the Worcestershire town of Kidderminster. The Franche and Habberley North ward is the north-western of Kidderminster's six electoral wards. Franche, an old village which has been swallowed up by Kidderminster's growth, lies on the main road towards Bridgnorth, while the Habberley area can be found on the western edge of the town.

Kidderminster is the main town in the Wyre Forest district, where politics has never been quite the same since the rise of the Health Concern party at the start of this century in protest at the removal of A&E facilities at Kidderminster Hospital. Health Concern's fortunes have ebbed and flowed a bit over the two decades since then. They were on a high tide in 2019, winning eight seats across Wyre Forest including all three seats in this ward; but that was in a rather fragmented political scene. Health Concern's winning score in Franche and Habberley North was just 30%; the lead Conservative and Labour candidates tied for the runner-up spot on 20% each; UKIP had 11% and the Greens scored 10%.

From 2015 to 2019 Franche and Habberley North ward had split its representation between two Conservative councillors and one Labour; Franche, the main predecessor ward, had elected councillors on the Conservative, Health Concern, Labour and UKIP tickets between 2004 and 2015. From this you might conclude that this is a politically volatile area.

You might also conclude that from the makeup of Wyre Forest council, which is hung. The Conservatives are the largest party on 12 seats, but the administration is made up of a coalition of Health Concern (9 plus this vacancy), the Liberal Democrats (3) and the Greens (1). The Health Concern group includes two

Parliamentary constituency: Wyre Forest
Worcestershire county council division: St Barnabas (same boundaries)
May 2021 county council result C 1114 Lab 586 Health Concern 493 Grn 158 LD 76
May 2019 result Health Concern 956/890/651 C 628/536 Lab 628/502 UKIP 338 Grn 318 LD 311
May 2018 result C 993 Lab 696 Health Concern 452 LD 110 UKIP 81 Grn 40
May 2017 county council result C 1405 Lab 898 UKIP 165 LD 89 Grn 55
May 2016 result Lab 867 C 695 Health Concern 436 UKIP 385 Grn 62
May 2015 result C 2006/1930/1347 Lab 1443/1113 UKIP 1039/809/742 Grn 437 TUSC 155/112
May 2013 county council result C 735 Lab 626 Health Concern 431 UKIP 416 TUSC 44 LD 39
June 2009 county council result C 1134 Health Concern 902 Lab 668 Lib 127 Grn 101
May 2005 county council result Lab 2013 C 1534 Health Concern 1531

Figure 182: Wyre Forest, Franche and Habberley North

councillors who have defected from the Conservatives since 2019, but the ruling coalition is still in a minority; five independents and two Labour councillors hold the balance of power.

However, the county elections here tell a different story. Franche and Habberley North ward only dates from 2015, but it has the same boundaries as the St Barnabas division of Worcestershire county council which was last redrawn in 2005. This county division has been in Conservative hands since 2009, and in May this year the Conservatives had a strong lead: 46%, against 24% for Labour and 20% for Health Concern. Rather the contrast with what happened here in May 2019.

The Health Concern candidate here in the county elections was Susie Griffiths, who had served as a district councillor for this ward since 2019; she is the daughter of Health Concern's party leader Graham Ballinger. Griffiths stood down in October, choosing to focus on her mental health and wellbeing.

There is no Health Concern candidate in the resulting by-election. We have a free-for-all, I repeat we have a free-for-all! Susie Griffiths has signed the nomination papers for independent candidate Doug Hine, who has previously contested Wyre Forest elections on the Green Party ticket. On paper the Conservatives may be best placed for a pickup, and they have selected David Ross: Ross was elected in May as the Conservative county councillor for St Barnabas, and he is the leader of Kidderminster town council and a former mayor of Kidderminster. Standing for Labour is local government veteran Nigel Knowles, who has represented this area at town, district and county level and served in all the major civic offices (mayor of Kidderminster, chair of Wyre Forest council, and chair of Worcestershire county council); Knowles' first local election win came in London all the way back in 1982, and he was a Labour parliamentary candidate at every general election from 1979 to 2017, usually contesting seats he had little or no chance of winning. UKIP have not returned and the Greens do not seem to be opposing Hine, so the ballot paper is completed by the Lib Dem candidate Oliver Walker.*

* *Wyre Forest, Franche and Habberley North*: C 564 Lab 372 LD 245 Ind 198 [C gain from Health Concern]

2nd December 2021: Parliamentary Special

Eleven by-elections on Super Thursday, 2nd December 2021, and we start with the Parliamentary Special:

Old Bexley and Sidcup

House of Commons; caused by the death of Conservative MP James Brokenshire.

We come into a frenetic final month of 2021. After the excitement* of the North Yorkshire Police and Crime Commissioner by-election last week, it's time to consider the fifth parliamentary by-election of the year. Welcome to Old Bexley and Sidcup.

These are two towns which are administratively part of Greater London, and to all intents and purposes part of the London urban sprawl, but socially and demographically are very different to it. Old Bexley and Sidcup still are, to a large extent, Kentish towns which have been swallowed up by the capital.

Of the two towns in the constituency name Bexley is the outermost, lying 13 miles from Charing Cross on the River Cray as it flows north towards the Thames estuary. A couple of miles further in is Sidcup, which has a hilltop location on what was once the main road from London to Maidstone.

That road has been replaced by the A 20, an arterial road which bypasses Sidcup to the south. The Sidcup bypass forms the southern boundary of the constituency, while to a large extent the seat's northern boundary is defined by another arterial road: the A 2 Rochester Way, which relieves the Roman road passing though Welling and Bexleyheath. However, part of the constituency extends over the A 2, to take in the areas of Welling, Falconwood and East Wickham to the north.

This area was relatively undeveloped into the twentieth century, with all the places named still being independent countryside towns and villages. The railways came here quite late: the Dartford Loop line through Sidcup and Bexley opened in 1866, the Bexleyheath line through Welling wasn't completed until 1895. It wasn't until the Great War, when the expansion of the Woolwich Arsenal led to major housing developments at East Wickham, that housebuilding in this area really started to get going.

We can see this in the area's parliamentary history. This column's practice in writing Parliamentary Specials is to start from the year 1885, when a redistribution of seats led to single-member constituencies (as we have today) becoming the norm rather than the exception. Before 1885 the area now covered by this constituency had been part of the large two-seat West Kent constituency, which was broken up into single-member seats. From 1885 to 1918 the modern-day London Borough of Bexley was covered by the Dartford constituency, with the exception of the parish of Foots Cray which formed part of the Sevenoaks constituency.

Sevenoaks was safely Conservative throughout this period, returning two MPs. Charles Mills, who represented the seat from 1885 to 1892 and also sat in the Lords from 1898 to 1919 as the second Lord Hillingdon, is recorded by Hansard as speaking only once in Parliament: he asked a question in 1889 on the Delagoa Bay railway in South Africa. Henry Forster, who was MP for Sevenoaks from 1892 to 1918, was rather more active in politics: he was a junior Treasury minister under Balfour and Financial Secretary to the War Office in the wartime coalition government, before leaving these shores in 1920 to become Governor-General of Australia. Forster was also a noted cricketer, having played at first-class level for Oxford University and Hampshire and serving as president of the Marylebone Cricket Club.

The first MP for Dartford was even more active in politics, being one of the major figures of the Conservative Party in the 1870s and 1880s. A former world rackets champion, Sir William Hart Dyke had first been elected in 1865 for West Kent and was one of the two MPs for Mid Kent in the previous parliament. Hart Dyke had been the chief whip in Disraeli's second government from 1874 to 1880, and going into the 1885 election he was part of Lord Salisbury's cabinet as Chief Secretary for Ireland. The Liberals won the 1885 election, but Hart Dyke won the new Dartford constituency safely enough: he defeated the Liberal candidate James Saunders (one of the architects of the London Pavilion on Piccadilly Circus) by 482 votes in the 1885 election, increasing his majority to 1,233 votes the following year.

The 1886 election returned the Conservatives to power. Following a government reshuffle in early 1887 Sir William Hart Dyke returned to the Cabinet as vice-president of the Committee of the Council on Education, roughly equivalent to the modern-day post of Education Secretary. Under the rules at the time, this required him to seek re-election in a by-election (as this was an office of profit under the Crown). Ministerial by-elections were common in those days, and were often left uncontested: the 1886–92 Parliament had 34 ministerial by-elections, of which only two went to a poll. This was not one of them. The first Dartford by-election, in February 1887, duly re-elected Sir William Hart Dyke unopposed.

The Conservatives lost power in the 1892 general election, and that was the end of Hart Dyke's ministerial career. However, he stayed in the Commons until 1906 when he was swept away in the Liberal landslide while seeking a twelfth term of office. Hart Dyke had served for 41 unbroken years, and if he had held his seat that year he would likely have become Father of the House.

The new MP for Dartford was James Rowlands, who had been an MP before: he had represented Finsbury East from 1886 to 1895. A watch-case maker by trade, Rowlands was a freeman of the Goldsmiths' Company. Most of his work as an MP was on the subject of property law and housing: he ended up as secretary of the Land Law Reform Association, and he had also been associated with the Gas Consumers' Protection League and the Leaseholds Enfranchisement Association.

Rowlands was defeated in January 1910 by the Conservative candidate William Foot Mitchell, who had recently become the first managing director of Royal Dutch Shell. Much of Mitchell's previous career had been spent in the Far East: he chaired the Yokohama Foreign Chamber of Commerce for two years, and had been appointed to the Order of the Sacred Treasure by the Meiji Emperor of Japan.

Mitchell was Royal Dutch Shell's managing director for 35 years, but he only served as MP for Dartford between the two 1910 elections. James Rowlands won the rematch in the December general election of that year, overturning Mitchell's majority of 817 to win by 234 votes.

Rowlands had a much easier time at his final re-election in 1918, in which he had the Coalition's coupon and was not opposed by the Conservatives. This time Labour stood a candidate against him, but they didn't get very far.

By this time the Dartford constituency was the largest seat in Kent by electorate, and it stayed that way even after boundary changes for the 1918 election. That redistribution created a new constituency of Chislehurst, which took in Foots Cray urban district. That district covered Sidcup, which in predevelopment days was a smaller and less important settlement than Foots Cray; the urban district was, however, renamed as Sidcup in the 1920s. A subsequent reorganisation in 1934 saw Sidcup urban district abolished, replaced by a new urban district of Chislehurst and Sidcup.

James Rowlands died in 1920, aged 68. He was the last Liberal MP for Dartford, as the resulting Dartford by-election of 27th March 1920 marked a seachange in the constituency's politics. The coalition government gave its coupon to the Conservative candidate Richard Meller, a Surrey county councillor and the official lecturer on National Insurance. He would later serve for 17 years as MP for Mitcham. Judging from the candidate list, this selection appears to have offended quite a lot of people. The Dartford Liberal association nominated their own candidate, the former Grimsby and Houghton-le-Spring MP Thomas Wing. Meller was also opposed from the right by the Boer War and Great War veteran and machine-gun pioneer Lt-Col Reginald Applin, standing for the short-lived National Party; and by an independent Unionist candidate, Frank Fehr. Coming through the middle of all this mess was the Labour candidate John Mills, an Australian engineer who had become the senior union rep at the Woolwich Arsenal. Mills won the by-election with just over 50% of the vote against 17% for the Liberals and 16% for the Conservatives, Applin and Fehr losing their deposits; he enjoyed a majority of 9,048.

That was the first of three non-consecutive terms for Mills as MP for Dartford. He was defeated at the 1922 general election by George Jarrett, who stood as a National Liberal candidate without Conservative opposition: in contrast to the by-election two years earlier, this time the left-wing vote was split with the Liberals selecting the suffragist Alison Garland. Garland, the first woman to seek election as MP for this area, polled 2,175 votes and lost her deposit; Jarrett defeated Mills by 1,918 votes.

Lloyd George folded the National Liberals back into the Liberal Party after the 1922 election, but George Jarrett didn't join them. Instead, he became a "Constitutionalist" MP, a label which came to be used by a number of independent right-wingers at this point including Winston Churchill. It didn't do Jarrett much good. Although he was supported by the Conservatives in his re-election bid as a Constitutionalist candidate in 1923, this time the left-wing vote was unified behind Mills who returned as MP for Dartford with a majority of 2,829. Jarrett never returned to the green benches.

For the 1924 general election the Conservatives selected their own candidate, Angus McDonnell. A son of the 6th Earl of Antrim, McDonnell had spent much of his time up to this point in the USA where he worked in the railway business. He put this experience to good use in the Great War, serving with a Canadian unit which built railways behind the front lines of the Western Front. McDonnell defeated John Mills by 20,108 votes to 19,352, a majority of just 756.

Angus McDonnell stood down after one term in the Commons to concentrate on his business interests. John Mills returned as Labour MP for Dartford in

1929 with a large majority thanks to the intervention of the Liberals, who saved their deposit. However, he was swept away in the 1931 disaster by the Conservative candidate Frank Clarke, who won by 34,095 votes to 27,349. In 1935 Clarke became the first MP for Dartford to be re-elected in seventeen years, defeating the new Labour candidate Jennie Adamson.

Frank Clarke died in 1938 at the early age of 51. For the resulting third Dartford by-election, held on 7th November 1938, the Conservatives selected Godfrey Mitchell. A veteran of the Great War where he had served in the Royal Engineers, Mitchell had taken over the construction company George Wimpey in 1919; he had already built the company up into a major player in the housebuilding business, with a pre-war peak of 1,370 homes completed in 1934. A seat like Dartford, which by now had become grossly oversized thanks to housebuilding and the growth of London, must have seemed appropriate. On the left-wing side Labour reselected their 1935 candidate Jennie Adamson, a member and former chair of the party's National Executive Committee. Adamson had also previously served on the London County Council (as a councillor for Lambeth North), and she was married to William Adamson who was the Labour MP for Cannock. When the votes came out of the ballot boxes Adamson had won by 46,514 votes to 42,276, a majority of 4,238 on a turnout of 68%. Adamson ascribed her victory to the Munich Agreement, which had been concluded a few weeks earlier.

By contrast to this rapid turnover of MPs for Dartford, the Chislehurst constituency was safely Conservative throughout this period. Its first MP was Alfred Smithers, a businessman in the railway industry: Smithers was chairman of the Grand Trunk Pacific Railway in Canada, and the town of Smithers in British Columbia was named after him. He was knighted in 1919. Smithers stood down in 1922 and was replaced by Robert Nesbitt, a London solicitor. From 1924 to 1945 the MP for Chislehurst was Sir Waldron Smithers, the son of Sir Alfred Smithers, who remained on the backbenches throughout this period.

The scale of housebuilding in this corner of Kent meant that by the Second World War both the Chislehurst and the Dartford constituencies were grossly oversized: Chislehurst had a 1939 electorate of almost 115,000, Dartford almost 135,000. In 1918 the figures had been 27,000 and 46,000 respectively, although this isn't a like-for-like comparison because women under 30 didn't have the vote in 1918. The emergency redistribution of 1945 reorganised this area into four new parliamentary constituencies called Bexley, Chislehurst, Dartford and Orpington.

The new Dartford and Orpington seats contained no part of the modern Old Bexley and Sidcup, which means that Sir Waldron Smithers (who sought and won re-election in the new Orpington seat) now leaves our story. And a good thing too from his point of view, as the revised Chislehurst fell to Labour in the 1945 landslide. The Conservatives and Labour both put up candidates who were straight from war service: the Tories' Major Nigel Fisher, who earlier in the year had been awarded a Military Cross on the field, lost to Labour's Sergeant George Wallace, RAF. Wallace enjoyed a majority of 6,279.

George Wallace was defeated in 1950 by just 167 votes by the Conservatives' Patricia Hornsby-Smith. A former civil servant who had sat on Barnes borough council in Surrey from 1945 to 1949, Hornsby-Smith went on to increase her majority over Wallace at two rematches, winning by 980 votes in 1951 (Hornsby-Smith 31,679, Wallace 30,699) and by nearly 4,000 votes in 1955. She served as a junior minister in the Home Office from 1957 to 1959, and was sworn of the Privy Council in 1959.

Hornsby-Smith continued to serve as MP for Chislehurst until 1974 with the exception of the 1966–70 Labour government. During this time Chislehurst was a Labour seat represented by Alistair Macdonald, a bank clerk and officer of the National Union of Bank Employees. Macdonald had previously been a Chislehurst and Sidcup urban district councillor, and he was elected as an alderman of Bromley council on its creation in 1964.

The Bexley constituency of 1945–74 had the same boundaries as the pre-1964 Borough of Bexley, which covered Old Bexley, Bexleyheath, East Wickham and Welling. Dartford's Labour MP Jennie Adamson sought and won re-election here in 1945. Adamson's reward for this was to get a junior ministerial post in the Attlee government, in the Ministry of Pensions.

However, Adamson's time as MP for Bexley was a brief one. She resigned from Parliament in 1946 to become deputy chair of the Unemployment Assistance Board. The resulting Bexley by-election of 22nd July 1946 resulted in a sharp swing to the Conservatives, and the Labour candidate Ashley Bramall held the seat by just 1,851 votes.

This was the start of a long political career for Ashley Bramall, who had previously chaired the Labour club at Oxford University and served as treasurer of the Oxford Union, where he had often faced off in debate against the president of the Union, a young man called Edward Heath. Bramall had served in the Second World War in the Reconnaissance Corps and at the time of the by-election he had the rank of Major and was part of the Allied administration in Germany. (His younger brother Edwin did rather better in the military, winning an MC in the Normandy landings and ending up as Chief of the Defence Staff with the rank of Field Marshal.)

Ashley Bramall made his political career not on the national stage but on the municipal stage. He was elected as an alderman of Westminster city council in 1959, joined the London County Council in 1961 and transferred to the new Greater London Council in 1964. Bramall was one of eight councillors who served for the entire period of the GLC's existence (1964–86), chairing the council in 1982–83, and from 1970 to 1981 he was leader of the Inner London Education Authority. During this period he was a contestant on *Mastermind*, appearing on the 1976 series with the specialist subject "British politics since 1918". (In the Magnus Magnusson era of *Mastermind* specialist rounds on British politics were generally written by the psephologist David Butler, who is still with us today at the age of 97.)

All that lay in the future when Bramall lost the Bexley seat in 1950 to his old university sparring partner Edward Heath. Heath polled 25,854 votes to Bramall's 25,721, a majority of 133. A rematch in 1951 resulted in an increased majority of 1,639 for Heath. On both occasions a young Conservative candidate for the neighbouring Dartford seat, Margaret Roberts (later Thatcher), lost.

After graduating from Oxford, Heath had served in the Second World War as a Royal Artillery officer, taking part in the Normandy landings as an adjutant; he was mentioned in despatches for his service in France, and awarded a military MBE. After that he became a civil servant, but resigned from that to seek the Conservative nomination for Bexley. In Parliament he rose up the greasy pole via the Whips office, joining Cabinet in 1955 as Chief Whip. Following the Conservative loss of the 1964 general election Heath won the Conservative leadership contest of 1965, polling 150 votes against 133 for Reginald Maudling and 15 for Enoch Powell. He became Leader of the Opposition.

Party leaders usually get a boost in their constituencies at general election time, and that might well have saved Heath in 1966; he held his seat by just 2,333 votes. He did rather better in 1970, increasing his majority in Bexley to 8,058 despite the presence of an independent spoiler candidate who had changed his name to Edward Heath for the election. The Conservatives unexpectedly won the 1970 general election, and Heath became Prime Minister.

Heath's three-and-a-half years as Prime Minister reshaped the country. They certainly reshaped the local government map: the two-tier system of county and district councils dates from the Heath administration and in many areas of England remains almost unaltered today. Heath saw his greatest achievement as Britain's accession to the European Economic Community, which took effect on 1st January 1973. The decimalisation of Britain's coinage was completed. Against this, Heath's government came at the height of the Troubles in Northern Ireland, and his power-sharing deal to bring peace—the Sunningdale Agreement—quickly fell apart in the face of Unionist opposition. The Ulster Unionist MPs resigned the Conservative whip, and Northern Ireland's party system has been divorced from Great Britain's ever since. The Barber economic boom quickly turned into a Barber economic bust, inflation soared, and the winter of 1973–74 saw the introduction of a three-day week in the face of industrial action from the National Union of Mineworkers. On 7th February 1974, Heath asked the Queen for a dissolution on the question of "Who governs Britain?" As the Queen was in New Zealand at the time for the Commonwealth Games in Christchurch, the dissolution was granted by the Queen Mother and Princess Margaret acting as Counsellors of State.

The February 1974 election was fought on new boundaries, reflecting the reorganisation of London government in the previous decade. The new London Borough of Bexley was allocated three parliamentary seats, which meant that the Chislehurst constituency—which straddled the boundary between Bexley and Bromley—would have to be broken up. The Sidcup part of the Chislehurst seat was added to Old Bexley to create a new Sidcup constituency, while the rest of the Bexley constituency was renamed as Bexleyheath to reflect the boundary change. The boundary changes effectively forced the Chislehurst MP Dame Patricia Hornsby-Smith out of Parliament; she had intended to seek the Conservative nomination for Sidcup, but found herself unable to challenge her party leader. Hornsby-Smith instead contested the Aldridge-Brownhills seat in the West Midlands, which she lost.

"Who governs Britain?" Well, not Edward Heath as it turned out. The result of the February 1974 general election was inconclusive, with a hung parliament being returned for the first time since 1929. Heath's Conservatives had won the most votes, but Labour had won the most seats. After an attempt to seek Liberal support for a Conservative minority government failed, Heath tendered his resignation as Prime Minister. Harold Wilson, returning for a third term as Labour Prime Minister, called a new election for October 1974 at which his administration won a bare majority.

That was the end of Edward Heath's government career. He was challenged for the Conservative leadership in 1975 by Margaret Thatcher, resigned after finishing behind Thatcher in the first round, and went to the backbenches. There he remained until finally retiring from the Commons in 2001, after more than 50 years' continuous service as an MP. In 1992 Heath became a Knight of the Garter and (following the retirement of Sir Bernard Braine) the Father of the House.

Sir Edward Heath's Sidcup constituency was renamed as Old Bexley and Sidcup in 1983, with no change to its boundaries. The current seat of that name contains the Welling and East Wickham areas, which as previously stated were in the Bexleyheath constituency from 1974 to 1997. Bexleyheath was a more marginal Conservative seat than Old Bexley and Sidcup, but it only returned one MP during this period. Sir Cyril Townsend had been an officer in the Durham Light Infantry for ten years before entering politics, serving in Cyprus and Malaya and as ADC to the governor of Hong Kong. Townsend remained on the backbenches throughout his 23 years in the Commons; his lasting legacy is the private member's bill he introduced in 1977, which became the Protection of Children Act 1978.

The constituencies in Bexley borough were redrawn for the 1997 election, with the number of seats in Bexley and Greenwich reducing from six to five. The Old Bexley and Sidcup seat was expanded to take in Welling and East Wickham from the former Bexleyheath seat, together with a small area around Falconwood railway station which had been transferred into Bexley borough from Greenwich in the early 1990s. The new boundaries produced a Conservative seat which was strong enough to withstand the Labour landslde of 1997: Heath, by now in his seventies, held the redrawn seat with a majority of 3,569.

Sir Edward Heath's successor as MP for Old Bexley and Sidcup had also started his political career young. Derek Conway had been elected to Gateshead council in 1974 at the age of 21, and he became leader of the Conservative group on Tyne and Wear county council at 26. After contesting Labour seats in the north-east in October 1974 and 1979, in 1983 Conway was elected to Parliament as MP for Shrewsbury and Atcham. He served three terms as MP for that seat, and was a government whip from 1993 until 1997 when he was swept away by the Labour landslide. Old Bexley and Sidcup, which Conway represented from 2001 to 2010, was a safer berth for him.

Derek Conway's fall from grace was spectacular. In January 2008 the Commons Standards and Privileges committee reported that he had paid a large salary to his son Freddie for work as a part-time researcher, while Freddie was a full-time student at Newcastle University. The committee concluded that there was no record of what work Freddie had done and his salary was too high to represent a good use of Commons money. Conway was ordered to repay £13,000, was suspended for ten sitting days, and had the Conservative whip withdrawn. A further report by the standards committee the following year resulted in Conway being ordered to repay a further £3,758 which he had overpaid to his other son Henry.

The disgrace of Derek Conway provided an opportunity for another Conservative MP. James Brokenshire, a former corporate lawyer, had entered the Commons in 2005 by gaining the Hornchurch constituency, in the London Borough of Havering, from Labour. The Hornchurch seat was due to be abolished at the 2010 general election, and Brokenshire had unsuccessfully applied for the Conservative nomination in a string of safe seats before he finally won the selection for Old Bexley and Sidcup in 2008. Old Bexley and Sidcup's boundary changes in 2010 were minor, with the Danson Park area transferred out of the seat into the Bexleyheath and Crayford constituency.

James Brokenshire served as a Home Office minister throughout the Coalition government, piloting the Modern Slavery Act 2013 through Parliament. He was sworn of the Privy Council in 2015. In 2016 he was appointed to Theresa May's first Cabinet with the traditionally-difficult role of Northern Ireland secretary, in which role he called snap elections to the Stormont Assembly in 2017 following the Renewable Heat Incentive scandal.

In December 2017, Brokenshire started coughing up blood. He sought medical advice, and tests revealed early-stage lung cancer. He had never smoked. Brokenshire resigned as Northern Ireland secretary on his 50th birthday to put his health first, and in January 2018 he had part of his lung removed. Three months later he was back in the Cabinet with the job of Housing, Communities and Local Government secretary. He brought in legislation restricting landlords' rights to evict their tenants and capping most tenancy fees and deposits.

James Brokenshire was not included in the Johnson cabinet, but did go back to being a junior Home Office minister in 2020 in recognition of his effectiveness and competence as a minister. Unfortunately, his cancer returned. He took leave of absence in January 2021 in advance of another lung operation, and resigned from government in July after failing to recover. He passed away on 7th October 2021, at the appallingly early age of 53.

The by-election to replace James Brokenshire will take place in a seat which, as already stated, is part of Greater London in practice but very unlike it in character. The 2011 census here was taken based on ward boundaries which have since been replaced, but the returns from the eight wards which then made up Old Bexley and Sidcup are very consistent. Six of the eight wards make the top 100 in the UK for "intermediate" occupations, three are in the top 10 wards in London for level 2 qualifications (5+ GCSE passes or equivalent), two are in the top 10 wards in London for level 1 qualifications (1–4 GCSE passes or equivalent), two are in the top 10 wards in London for owner-occupation, two are in the top 10 wards in London for population born in the UK, two are in the top 10 wards in London for White British ethnicity. This is an area which has been relatively unaffected by the transformation of London into a world city. Detached and semi-detached housing, much of it built on garden-city principles, predominates.

Bexley council got new ward boundaries in 2014, as a result of which this seat is now covered by seven wards as shown in Figure 183. Two of these wards are mostly within Old Bexley and Sidcup, but straddle the boundary with Bexley-

Figure 183: Wards of the Old Bexley and Sidcup constituency

heath and Crayford. With the caveat that some of these votes were cast outside the constituency, those seven wards voted 54% Conservative and 25% Labour at the last Bexley local elections in May 2018. The Conservatives topped the poll in all 7 wards and won all 20 council seats; overall the 2018 Bexley elections returned 34 Conservative and 11 Labour councillors, so we can see that over half of the council's majority group represent wards in this constituency.

The London Mayor and Assembly elections from May are even more difficult to interpret than the most recent Bexley council elections, partly because of the boundary mismatch and partly because the ward breakdowns published for the London elections only include on-the-day votes (postal votes in GLA elections are tallied at borough level). For what it's worth, the aggregate of the seven ward tallies gives a 63–17 lead for the Conservative mayoral candidate Shaun Bailey over Sadiq Khan, with a slightly lower Conservative lead of 58–18 in the London Members ballot.

The constituency is part of the Bexley and Bromley seat which is the safest Conservative constituency in the London Assembly. All three of Bexley and Bromley's former AMs have gone on to serve in the Commons: Sir Bob Neill (2000–08) won the Bromley and Chislehurst by-election in 2006 and is now chair of the Commons Justice Select Committee, James Cleverley (2008–16) was elected in 2015 as MP for Braintree in Essex and is now a junior Foreign Office minister, and Gareth Bacon (2016–21) was elected in December 2019 as MP for Orpington. Bacon had been a Bexley councillor since 1998, and he stood down from Bexley council to allow a by-election in Longlands ward in May which was a safe Conservative hold (page 66).

These results are certainly not out of line with the result of the 2019 general election here, which re-elected James Brokenshire for a fourth term in the seat with 65% of the vote, against 23% for Labour.

The Boundary Commission are, of course, beavering away on a new constituency map for the currently-scheduled general election in May 2024. Their draft proposals leave this seat largely unchanged apart from realignment to Bexley's current ward boundaries, which would mean that the Danson Park area is transferred into the seat from Bexleyheath and Crayford. Possibly more controversial is that the Commission propose to drop Old Bexley from the name of the constituency, which would become "Sidcup and Welling".

Defending for the Conservatives is Louie French, the deputy leader of Bexley council. French represents Falconwood and Welling ward, which is partly in this constituency. In December 2019 he was the Conservative candidate for the neighbouring constituency of Eltham. He works in financial services in the City, specialising in sustainable investing and research.

The Labour candidate for the by-election is also a Bexley councillor. Daniel Francis, who represents Belvedere ward although he gives an address in this constituency, has sat on Bexley council for 17 of the last 21 years and was until recently the leader of the Labour group on the council.

The only other party to save their deposit here in 2019 were the Lib Dems, who polled 8.3%. They have reselected their candidate from last time, Simone Reynolds, who has appeared in this column before: Reynolds was the Lib Dem candidate for a by-election in the St Michael's ward of Bexley in the week after

Bexley council wards: Blackfen and Lamorbey, Blendon and Penhill, Longlands, St Mary's and St James, Sidcup, East Wickham (part: in this ward before 2014), Falconwood and Welling (part: in this ward before 2014)
London Assembly constituency: Bexley and Bromley
December 2019 result C 29786 Lab 10834 LD 3822 Grn 1477 CPA 226
June 2017 result C 29545 Lab 14079 UKIP 1619 LD 1572 Grn 820 BNP 324 CPA 83
May 2015 result C 24682 Lab 8879 UKIP 8528 LD 1644 Grn 1336 National Health Action 1216 Chr 245 BNP 218
May 2010 result C 24625 Lab 8768 LD 6996 BNP 2132 UKIP 1532 EDP 520 Ind to Save Queen Mary's Hospital 393 Grn 371 Loony 155

Figure 184: House of Commons, Old Bexley and Sidcup

the EU membership referendum in 2016*. She has since contested Bexleyheath and Crayford in the 2017 general election, and stood in Sidcup ward in the 2018 Bexley council elections. Reynolds works in social care for a local authority in south-east London.

The Greens were fourth here in 2019 with 3.2%. Their candidate for this by-election is Jonathan Rooks, who is a challenge for any stereotypes you may hold regarding Green Party candidates: Rooks is a lecturer in accounting at South Bank University. He was the Green candidate for Bexley and Bromley in the 2012 London Assembly elections. The 2019 ballot paper was completed by Carol Valinejad, who polled 0.5% for the Christian Peoples Alliance; Valinejad is standing again.

Six other candidates complete the ballot, and I shall take them in alphabetical order. Top of the ballot paper is Elaine Cheeseman for the English Democrats, who fought this seat in 2010 and finished sixth with 1.1%. Cheeseman was on the English Democrats' list for London in the 2009 European Parliament elections. Richard Hewison was the mayoral candidate and top of the list in May's GLA elections for the Rejoin EU party, whose signature policy is left as an exercise for the reader. David Kurten was elected as a UKIP member of the London Assembly in 2016, and was the UKIP candidate for his home constituency of Bognor Regis and Littlehampton in 2019; he subsequently set up the Heritage Party, and was their candidate for Mayor of London and top of their London Assembly list in May (failing to hold his seat). The official UKIP candidate is John Poynton, who fought Ealing Southall in the 2015 general election. Our third party leader on the ballot (after Hewison and Kurten) is Richard Tice of Reform UK; Tice was a Brexit Party MEP from 2019 to 2020, and in May's GLA elections he stood in the Havering and Redbridge constituency and was top of the Reform UK list. Completing the ballot paper is Mad Mike Young of the

* *Andrew's Previews 2016*, page 104.

Official Monster Raving Loony Party, who is hoping for a Loony mudslide in the election.*

Hartfield

Wealden council, East Sussex; caused by the death of Conservative councillor Chris Hardy.

Old Bexley and Sidcup is not the only poll taking place today. After last week's Super Thursday, it's time for another one: there are ten local by-elections today in what is proving to be a very busy end to the year. Unlike last week's diet, Conservative defences predominate today: there are seven Conservative local seats up for election. Three of them are in Sussex.

The Hartfield ward lies on the northern boundary of East Sussex, covering a large chunk of the High Weald between East Grinstead and Crowborough. Much of this hilly area was once part of the Ashdown Forest, which was used for hunting by mediaeval kings; the word "forest" here denotes hunting territory rather than woodland, and to this day much of the Ashdown Forest is open heathland.

The forest fell out of favour for hunting during the Tudor monarchy, instead turning into a minor industrial centre. Within this ward can be found the remains of England's first modern ironworks and blast furnace, established at Newbridge in 1496 to supply iron for Henry VII's military campaigns. There's a lot of ironstone under the High Weald, and the Newbridge Furnace was the seed from which Britain's iron and steel industry grew. But by the time the Industrial Revolution got going the Weald's ironworking industry had already died out, and this area remained rural.

In the twentieth century the Ashdown Forest came to a new audience thanks to an author who lived locally. Alan Alexander Milne, who lived on a farm near Hartfield (which, many years later, was also the home of Brian Jones of the Rolling Stones), composed two best-selling books in the 1920s about a boy called Christopher Robin, based on his own son, and a number of animal companions. A A Milne and his illustrator E L Shephard both took inspiration from the countryside of Ashdown Forest in *Winnie-the-Pooh* and *The House at Pooh Corner*: the [Five] Hundred Acre Wood is entirely within this ward, as is the bridge on which the game of Poohsticks was invented. The bridge was rebuilt in 1999 by East Sussex county council, with the Disney company donating much of the necessary funds; bring your own sticks.

* *House of Commons, Old Bexley and Sidcup*: C 11189 Lab 6711 Reform UK 1432 Grn 830 LD 647 EDP 271 UKIP 184 Rejoin EU 151 Heritage Party 116 CPA 108 Loony 94

Parliamentary constituency: Wealden
East Sussex county council division: Forest Row and Groombridge
May 2019 result C 566 Grn 428

Figure 185: Wealden, Hartfield

The Hartfield ward of Wealden district has been Conservative-held at every election this century, and was uncontested in 2003. There were major boundary changes for the 2019 election, which re-elected the Conservative ward councillor Chris Hardy for a third term; he was opposed only by the Green Party, who put up a decent showing in a 57–43 defeat. The Greens made an effort at the 2019 Wealden council elections, finishing in second place in vote terms with 21% across the district; this only got them two seats, in Forest Row and Withyham wards which are both adjacent to Hartfield. In May this year the Green Party built on that to gain the local county council seat (Forest Row and Groomsbridge) from the Conservatives.

The Hartfield by-election is to replace Conservative councillor Chris Hardy, who passed away in September after developing cancer. Hardy was retired from a long career as a loss adjuster—he was a Liveryman of the Worshipful Company of Insurers—and he had also dabbled in racehorse ownership, with 25 winners to his name. He was chairman of Wealden council from 2016 to 2019.

Like the county elections here in May, this by-election is a straight fight. Defending this by-election from the blue corner is Bruce Rainbow, a retired accountant who lives in the ward. Challenging from the green corner is Rachel Millward, who has a background in the arts and film sector; she is described as a local resident and environmental campaigner.*

Hillside

Adur council, West Sussex; caused by the death of Conservative councillor David Simmons.

Our other two by-elections in Sussex take place on the coastal strip. The Hillside ward of Adur is aptly named: the hill here is Southwick Hill, which is part of the South Downs National Park overlooking the town of Southwick and the sea. As there was no other way of improving the area's road network for through traffic, two tunnels were bored under Southwick Hill in the 1990s which now carry the A 27 Shoreham Bypass.

Southwick is a suburb of Brighton and Hove which has never been incorporated into the city, even though it's clearly part of the same urban area. The

* *Wealden, Hartfield*: Grn 589 C 467 [Grn gain from C]

Parliamentary constituency: East Worthing and Shoreham
West Sussex county council division: Southwick
May 2021 result C 702 Lab 338 Grn 89
May 2018 result C 652 Lab 290 Grn 69 LD 33
May 2016 result C 551 Lab 253 UKIP 186 Grn 40 LD 37
May 2014 result C 529 UKIP 402 Lab 214 Grn 65 LD 59
May 2012 result C 499 Lab 268 UKIP 150 LD 61
May 2010 result C 1008 LD 667 UKIP 294 Grn 141
May 2008 result C 611 Lab 165 UKIP 149 LD 119
September 2006 by-election C 445 LD 184 Lab 124
May 2006 result C 684 LD 250 Lab 219
June 2004 result C 793/657 LD 429 Lab 353

Figure 186: Adur, Hillside

Hillside ward lies immediately outside the Brighton city boundary; it is a lower-middle-class area with a very similar demographic profile to neighbouring Portslade.

However, its political profile is very different. Portslade generally votes Labour in local elections, but Hillside is a longstanding Conservative ward which forms part of the Tory majority on Adur council. In May this year Hillside gave the Conservatives a 62–30 lead over Labour, which was a slight swing to Labour from 2018. The Southwick division of West Sussex county council is also safe Conservative.

Until May this year Southwick was represented on the county council by David Simmons, a retired senior police officer. He was first elected to Adur council in 2006, transferring to this ward in 2014. Sadly, Simmons passed away in September.

Whoever wins this by-election will need to seek re-election again in May, so they won't be able to rest for long. Defending for the Conservatives is Leila Williams, who is a senior manager in the NHS. The Labour candidate is Rebecca Allinson, whose late father Les Alden was the leader of the Labour group on Adur council. Completing the ballot paper is Russell Whiting for the Greens.*

Marine

Worthing council, West Sussex; caused by the resignation of Conservative councillor Tim Wills.

The last of our three Sussex polls today is in a very interesting ward which this column has covered before. Although we do have to double-check we have

* *Adur, Hillside*: C 414 Grn 175 Lab 148

the right Marine ward here: there are three Marine wards in West Sussex, of which this is the middle one. The other two are in Bognor and Shoreham.

This Marine ward is in western Worthing, taking its name from Marine Gardens on the seafront. The ward runs north from there, through 1930s housing along Grand Avenue and George V Avenue, to the West Coastway railway line (between West Worthing and Durrington-on-Sea stations).

Worthing has a very long history: in the fourth millennium BC this was Britain's largest flint-mining area, and archaeologists have had a lot of fun excavating the local prehistoric hill forts. The town as we know it started up as a seaside resort in the eighteenth century.

But there's more to Worthing than the beach. The town has managed to escape the fate of many seaside resorts by successfully diversifying its economy. The local water company Southern Water, the pharmaceutical giant Glaxo SmithKline and a large HM Revenue and Customs office provide year-round employment. And the town has changed demographically in recent years: it has become a popular place to live for people of working age who have been priced out of London and Brighton. A number of the seaside resorts in Sussex are forgotten towns, elephants' graveyards or both: Worthing is neither.

The Marine ward has had unchanged boundaries since at least 1983. There were were 22 elections here between that year and 2010, all of which resulted in a Conservative win (usually very comfortably) over the Lib Dems or their predecessors in second place. Then from 2011 onwards this demographic change and the formation of the Coalition combined in unexpected ways. Labour took over second place in 2011 and 2012, UKIP were runners-up in 2014 and 2015, Labour again in 2016.

In 2017 one of Marine ward's Conservative councillors, Joan Bradley, resigned on health grounds. Unfortunately, she died before the resulting by-election took place in August 2017.

Looking back at what this column wrote then*, I did not see what was coming. The Labour candidate Beccy Cooper, fresh from contesting the local parliamentary seat of Worthing West in the general election two months previously, pulled off a stunning swing of 17% from the Conservatives to win the by-election by a 47–39 margin. Let's put this result into context: Labour had never polled over 20% in this ward before, never mind over 40%, and the last time a Labour councillor had been elected in Worthing was in 1973.

The 2017 Marine by-election broke the mould of Worthing politics. Suddenly, Labour became the main challengers in a number of the town's wards. In the May 2018 election they won 4 seats; they won 5 more seats in 2019, the same

* *Andrew's Previews 2017*, page 211.

Parliamentary constituency: Worthing West
West Sussex county council division: Worthing West
May 2021 result Lab 1456 C 1324 Grn 181 LD 140
May 2019 result C 1140 Lab 907 Grn 267 UKIP 234 LD 232
May 2018 result C 1460 Lab 1136 LD 194 UKIP 94
August 2017 by-election Lab 1032 C 846 LD 246 Grn 55
May 2016 result C 961 Lab 415 UKIP 348 LD 217 Grn 185
May 2015 result C 2296 UKIP 741 Lab 663 LD 472 Grn 455
May 2014 result C 1114 UKIP 692 Lab 298 Grn 264 LD 189
May 2012 result C 959 Lab 357 UKIP 349 LD 260
May 2011 result C 1614 Lab 465 LD 448 UKIP 312
May 2010 double vacancy C 2339/1981 LD 1467/1339 UKIP 510
May 2008 result C 1351 LD 508 UKIP 278
May 2007 result C 1511 LD 344 Grn 201 UKIP 171 Lab 155
May 2006 result C 1489 LD 383 Grn 271 Lab 173 UKIP 166
June 2004 result C 1713/1640/1637 LD 586/499/469 Grn 488 Lab 290
May 2003 result C 1282 LD 373 Lab 222 Grn 140
May 2002 result C 1235 LD 388 Lab 230 Grn 182
May 2000 double vacancy C 1207/1162 LD 562/544 Grn 182/169
May 1999 double vacancy C 1357/1267 LD 510/444 Lab 245 Grn 176
May 1998 result C 1174 LD 521 Lab 216 Grn 76
May 1996 result C 1263 LD 630 Lab 291 Grn 79
May 1995 result C 1316 LD 1132 Lab 310 Grn 69
May 1994 result C 1212 LD 1121 Lab 283 Grn 106
May 1992 result C 1619 LD 584 Lab 102 Grn 80
May 1991 result C 1580 LD 611 Grn 239
May 1990 result C 1802 SLD 582 Lab 479
May 1988 result C 1571 SLD 358 Lab 226
May 1987 result C 2054 Alliance 654 Lab 181
May 1986 result C 1545 Alliance 894 Lab 181
May 1984 result C 1642 Alliance 626 Lab 141
May 1983 result C 1866/1828/1764 Alliance 630/601/586 Residents 558/445

Figure 187: Worthing, Marine

figure as the Conservatives. All of those were gains.

That red wave also extended to West Sussex county council in May's elections. Three of the town's county councillors are now Labour, including Beccy Cooper who gained Worthing West division (which includes this ward) from the Conservatives.

The May 2021 elections for Worthing council saw the Labour party gain five more seats from the Conservatives, while Beccy Cooper was also re-elected for a second term in Marine ward. All of those Labour gains were on small majorities, and Marine was no exception: Cooper's majority fell to 47–43. The Conservatives lost their majority in Worthing as a result, and they now run the town as a minority with 17 seats plus this vacancy, against 16 councillors for Labour (who have recently picked up a defector from the Lib Dems), 2 Lib Dems and one ex-Conservative independent. If Labour can win this by-election they will draw level with the Conservatives to become the largest party; if Labour can win this by-election *and* repeat May's result next year, they will take overall control of Worthing council for the first time ever. It's incredible to write that sentence, given that just over four years ago there had not been a Labour councillor in Worthing for over forty years.

It has to be said that the circumstances of this by-election are not propitious for the Conservatives. The outgoing councillor is Tim Wills, who was first elected in 2019. Last month an investigation by Hope Not Hate, an anti-fascist group, revealed that Wills was a supporter of a far-right white nationalist group called Patriotic Alternative. After the council's monitoring officer had taken a look at the story, Wills was given an ultimatum by the Conservative leader of the council: deny the allegations or resign. He chose to resign.

Defending this by-election for the Conservatives is Syed Ahmed, a businessman who runs a restaurant in the town. The Labour candidate is Vicki Wells, a former BBC science producer who works at the Worthing Theatres and Museum. Also standing are Sonya Mallin for the Green Party and Emma Norton for the Liberal Democrats.*

Stalham

North Norfolk council; caused by the resignation of Liberal Democrat councillor Marion Millership.

We now move to two local by-elections in Norfolk, starting at the northern end of the Broads. The Museum of the Broads, containing a collection of boats and material on history of this landscape, can be found fifteen miles north-east of Norwich in the small market town of Stalham. The ward named after Stalham takes in two further parishes to the south, as far as Catfield. Catfield parish has some bizarre boundaries, leading to this ward taking in part but not all of the Broads' largest body of open water, Hickling Broad.

Stalham is part of the North Norfolk district and parliamentary seat, which swung in opposite directions in the 2019 local and general elections: North Norfolk now has a Conservative MP, but the council had gained a Liberal Democrat

* *Worthing, Marine*: Lab 1239 C 972 Grn 145 LD 112 [Lab gain from C]

Parliamentary constituency: North Norfolk
Norfolk county council division: Hoveton and Stalham (part: Stalham and Sutton parishes), South Smallburgh (part: Catfield parish)
May 2019 result LD 762/733 C 464/397 Grn 232 Lab 127

Figure 188: North Norfolk, Stalham

majority at the local elections seven months earlier. Before boundary changes in 2019 most of this area was covered by the former Stalham and Sutton ward, which split its representation between the Conservatives and the Liberal Democrats at every election from 2003 to 2015; however, the new and larger Sutton ward returned the Lib Dem slate quite comfortably in May 2019, with 48% of the vote against 29% for the Conservative slate and 15% for the Green Party candidate. However, the Hoveton and Stalham county division (which covers most of this ward) was very safely Conservative in May's Norfolk county council elections; Catfield parish is part of the South Smallburgh division, a longstanding Conservative-Lib Dem marginal which swung to the Tories in May.

Marion Millership had first been elected to North Norfolk council in a 2017 by-election for Waterside ward, which at the time covered Catfield[*]; she transferred here in 2019 following boundary changes. She has stepped down from the council for personal reasons.

Defending for the Liberal Democrats is Barbara McGoun, a former North Norfolk councillor who was chairman of the council in 2007–08: she represented the St Benet ward from a 2005 by-election until 2019, when she stood down to care for her late husband. McGoun has had a varied working life, having worked for British Airways as a stewardess and in a number of broadcasting roles, including behind-the-scenes work on Radio 4's news and current affairs programmes in the 1980s. The Tories have selected a candidate a couple of generations younger than McGoun: Matthew Taylor is only 22 but is already a Stalham town councillor. The Greens have not returned, so Labour's Richard Stowe completes the ballot paper.[†]

Hermitage

Breckland council, Norfolk; caused by the resignation of Conservative councillor Trevor Carter.

For our other Norfolk by-election we move west to higher ground at the northern end of the large Breckland district. Hermitage is a ward of seven parishes

[*] *Andrew's Previews 2017*, page 29. [†] *North Norfolk, Stalham*: C 559 LD 375 Lab 79 [C gain from LD]

Parliamentary constituency: Mid Norfolk
Norfolk county council division: Necton and Launditch
May 2019 result C 561 Lab 226
May 2015 result C 1016 UKIP 472

Figure 189: Breckland, Hermitage

in the countryside roughly halfway between Norwich and King's Lynn. The largest of these is Mileham, with 515 electors on the roll: this village is at the summit of the original road between Norwich and Lynn, with the Wensum (flowing east) and the Yar (flowing west) both rising nearby. A couple of miles to the north of Mileham can be found the site of Godwick, a village which had been abandoned by the 17th century; only the ruins of the church tower remain above ground. The ward extends north to the village of Colkirk, a couple of miles south of Fakenham. This is a strongly agricultural area, and in the 2011 census Breckland had four of the top ten wards in the Eastern region for those employed in agriculture, forestry or fishing: Hermitage ward, at just under 10% of the workforce, was one of them.

The ward boundaries changed in 2015 with the addition of Mileham parish. This brought Mileham within the remit of Trevor Carter, a former Army officer and retired teacher who had represented Hermitage ward since 2011. Carter enjoyed large majorities at the 2015 election (when he was challenged only by UKIP) and in May 2019, when he defeated Labour 71–29 in a straight fight. The local county council division (Necton and Launditch) was also strongly Conservative in May.

Carter has stood down for personal reasons after ten years in office, resulting in a by-election with four candidates. Defending for the Conservatives is Robert Hambidge, a former mayor of Dereham who farms sugar beet. The Labour candidate is Paul Siegert, who was a candidate for Norfolk county council in May (he contested Yare and All Saints division, which does not cover this ward). Also standing are Graeme Briggs-White for the Workers Party of Britain, and James Minto for the Liberal Democrats.*

Victoria

Newport council, Gwent; caused by the resignation of Labour councillor Majid Rahman.

For our Welsh by-election we come to a place with happy memories for your columnist. In June 2006 I travelled down to Newport in South Wales for the

* *Breckland, Hermitage*: C 243 LD 221 Lab 66 Workers Party 10

British leg of the World Quizzing Championships, held at the Newport Gwent Dragons (as they were then) stadium in Rodney Parade, Newport. The great and the good of the British quiz world were all there. Kevin Ashman off *Eggheads* won the main event.

While the scores in the main event were being totted up a giant game of *Fifteen-to-One* broke out, in which all the great and the good of the British quiz world concentrated on knocking each other out and some random twentysomething from Bolton came through the middle of all this to win from nowhere. Winning "Last Man Standing" against that field remains one of my greatest quiz achievements. The question that secured me the win asked for the name of the band which released the 1999 album *The Man Who*—the answer appears on page 556.

Happy memories indeed as we consider the Victoria division of Newport, which takes in Rodney Parade. This division is on the east bank of the Usk, immediately opposite the city centre, and takes in much of the Maindee area. It is one of the most ethnically-diverse wards in Wales. In the 2011 census Victoria returned an Asian population of 24.2%, mostly of Pakistani Muslim heritage, which was the highest figure for any ward in Wales. Victoria's black population of 4.2% was also in the top 10 wards in Wales, and it returned the third-highest Muslim population in Wales.

Appropriately enough, Victoria was the first place in Wales to elect a Muslim local councillor. That was Mohammad Asghar, who topped the poll here in 2004 to become the only Plaid Cymru member of Newport council. Asghar quickly got a leg-up the greasy pole and was elected to the Senedd in 2007 as a Plaid Cymru regional member for South Wales East. In 2009 he crossed the floor to the Conservatives and was re-elected on their ticket in the 2011 and 2016 elections. He died in office last year at the age of 74, but there is still an Asghar in the Senedd after his daughter Natasha was elected as a Conservative MS in May.

Mohammed Asghar stepped down from Newport council at the 2008 election, at which Victoria ward was gained by the Liberal Democrats. In 2012 the Lib Dems lost the ward to the Labour slate of Christine Jenkins and Majid Rahman, who were easily re-elected in 2017: shares of the vote were 48% for Labour, 21% for the Conservatives and 20% for the Liberal Democrats.

Christine Jenkins resigned from Newport council on health grounds in March 2020. A by-election was scheduled for April 2020 to replace her but had to be called off due to the pandemic, resulting in her seat being vacant for over a year. When the by-election eventually took place in May 2021 (page 55) it resulted in a Labour hold with an increased majority of 58–20 over the Liberal Democrats. On the same day Labour easily held the local Senedd constituency of Newport

Parliamentary constituency: Newport East
May 2021 by-election Lab 1138 LD 402 C 259 Grn 167
May 2017 result Lab 840/795 C 371/336 LD 344/333 PC 123 Grn 84
May 2012 result Lab 769/674 LD 418/345 C 224/174 PC 156/108
May 2008 result LD 618/604 Lab 486/450 PC 413/197 C 231
June 2004 result PC 571/459 Lab 561/511 LD 286/282

Figure 190: Newport, Victoria

East, with that seat's MS John Griffiths becoming one of only four members who have continuous service since the advent of devolution in 1999. (The other three are Jane Hutt and Lynne Neagle of Labour, and Elin Jones of Plaid Cymru.)

Majid Rahman has now resigned, and there is just time to squeeze in a by-election before the next Newport council elections in May 2022. Defending for Labour is Gavin Horton, who spent twenty years working in the Newport steelworks before setting up his own independent coffee shop, Horton's Lounge. The Lib Dem candidate is John Miller, who was their parliamentary candidate for Torfaen in 2019; Miller has spent most of his career in the steel trade. Completing the ballot paper is Muhammad Tariq for the Conservatives, who returns for another go after contesting May's by-election.*

Whitnash

Warwick council; caused by the death of Whitnash Residents Association councillor Tony Heath.

We now turn to the West Midlands, where the Conservatives—as flagged in advance by this column—performed very well in last week's council by-elections. This will be a tougher nut for them to crack.

To all intents and purposes, Whitnash is a suburb of Leamington Spa—although this column is probably going to get into trouble for saying that. There was originally a small village here, but it has long been swallowed up by the growth of the town.

Leam is not like other towns in Warwickshire. It looks grand and Georgian, but those nice-looking terraces hide a lot of deprivation, a significant number of Warwick University students and an ethnically-diverse population. Whitnash has mostly escaped the deprivation and the students, but it has a significant Asian minority of Punjabi Sikh heritage: this ward is in the top 50 wards in England and Wales for Sikhism, at 12% of the population.

Interestingly, Whitnash ward has gone for localism in its local elections: since

* *Newport, Victoria*: Lab 641 LD 258 C 93

Parliamentary constituency: Warwick and Leamington
Warwickshire county council division: Whitnash
May 2019 result Whitnash Residents Association 1487/1376/1260 Lab 661/536 Grn 317/202/200 C 198/157/142 UKIP 194 LD 150

Figure 191: Warwick, Whitnash

the 1980s its councillors have all come from the Whitnash Residents Association. In the May 2019 election the Residents won here with 49% of the vote, against 22% for Labour and 11% for the Green Party. The 2019 Warwick elections resulted in a hung council with 19 Conservatives, 9 Liberal Democrats, 8 Greens, 5 Labour and 3 Whitnash Residents; the Residents are the junior partner in a coalition with the Conservatives which controls half of the seats on the council. The ward has the same boundaries as the Whitnash division of Warwickshire county council, which in May's elections gave 46% to the Residents, 26% to Labour and 16% to the Conservatives.

This by-election is to replace Tony Heath, a veteran of local government who sat on Whitnash town council and the parish council before it for over 40 years until his death in September, including four years as Mayor of Whitnash or chair of the parish council. Heath had also sat on Warwick district council for over 20 years. He will be a hard act to follow.

Defending for the Whitnash Residents Association is Adrian Barton, another former Mayor of Whitnash. Labour have selected Lucy Phillips, a secondary school English teacher. The Green candidate is Sarah Richards, a hydrologist looking after the country's canals. Also standing are John Kane for the Conservatives and Trevor Barr for the Liberal Democrats.*

Bare; and Upper Lune Valley

Lancaster council; caused respectively by the deaths of Conservative councillors Stephie Barber and Stewart Scothern.

We now come to the final part of our current three-part series of Lancaster by-elections. Over the last month (pages 463 and 515) Labour have recovered seats from two Labour councillors who went independent. This time the focus turns to the Conservatives who have two seats to defend today, one urban, one rural.

The rural parts of the district may be looking bare at the moment with the leaves now almost all off the trees, but Bare is in fact our urban ward this week.

* *Warwick, Whitnash*: Whitnash Res Assoc 835 Lab 431 C 127 Grn 88 LD 32

This is the eastern end of Morecambe, served by Bare Lane railway station, and it's very much a retirement centre. At the last census 8% of the ward's population was aged over 85, which was in the top 40 wards in the UK and the second-highest figure for any ward in the north-west. Boundary changes for the 2015 election expanded the ward south of the railway line, into an area which was previously part of Torrisholme ward, and added a third councillor.

Upper Lune Valley ward is a very different area. This is the northernmost ward in modern-day Lancashire, covering ten rural parishes to the south and east of Kirkby Lonsdale (which is over the border in Cumbria). Here can be found the highest point of Lancashire, the 628-metre summit of Green Hill. The largest centre of population here is Hornby, located in lovely countryside on the main road between Lancaster and Skipton.

Until 2007 Upper Lune Valley ward was represented by James Airey, who subsequently transferred to Cumbria: he came very close to unseating the Lib Dem MP Tim Farron in the 2017 and 2019 general elections. Airey and his successor Peter Williamson enjoyed large majorities, but things suddenly changed at Stewart Scothern's first election in 2019: he saw the Conservative lead here slashed to 46–44 over the Liberal Democrats, a majority of 17 votes.

Bare ward has been closely fought in this century between the Conservatives and the Morecambe Bay Independents, a Morecambe localist group which once—many years ago—ran Lancaster council as a whole. Three of the ward's five elections during that period have returned split representation, including both contests on the current boundaries. In May 2019 the Morecambe Bay Independents topped the poll with 35% and won two seats (gaining one from the Conservatives), the Conservatives polled 31% and won one seat, and Labour came third with 17%.

The Morecambe Bay Independents didn't stand in May's county council elections, in which Bare ward was part of the Morecambe North division. As this column has pointed out before*, this is a rather misleading name for an electoral unit of which a large chunk is Bolton-le-Sands. This and Lancaster Rural East division (which includes Upper Lune Valley) were both safe Conservative in May's Lancashire county elections.

Following the two by-elections held over the last three weeks the administration of Lancaster council consists of 10 Green councillors and 4 Eco-Socialist Independents. The opposition is now made up of 16 Labour councillors, 11 Conservatives plus these two vacancies, 9 Morecambe Bay Independents, 6 other independent councillors and 2 Liberal Democrats.

Both of today's polls are to replace councillors who have passed away. Stewart

* *Andrew's Previews 2018*, page 71.

Parliamentary constituency: Morecambe and Lunesdale
Lancashire county council division: Morecambe North
May 2019 result Morecambe Bay Ind 827/800/597 C 721/708/598 Lab 406/396/178 LD 282/167/131 Ind 97
May 2015 result C 1288/1179 Morecambe Bay Ind 1098/1021/932 Lab 794/782/734 UKIP 603 Grn 384/298 LD 372

Figure 192: Lancaster, Bare

Scothern, who had represented Upper Lune Valley since 2019, died in October at the age of 73. Stephie Barber entered politics in 2019 after retiring from a 44-year career in the transport industry, finishing as a director of the bus giant Stagecoach, and quickly rose to become leader of the Conservative group. Barber passed away in May at the age of 68 after battling cancer for several years.

Defending Bare for the Conservatives is Jane Cottam, who contested Torrisholme ward in the last Lancaster elections and Skerton division (which covers Torrisholme) in May's county council elections. The Morecambe Bay Independents, who will have a full set of councillors if they gain this seat, have selected June Ashworth who has previously represented this ward from 2007 to 2019; she was Mayor of Lancaster in 2013–14. The Labour candidate is Valerie Rogerson, who fought the neighbouring ward of Bolton and Slyne in 2019. Completing the Bare ballot paper are Gerry Blaikie for the Liberal Democrats and James Sommerville for the Green Party.*

In Upper Lune Valley the Tory defence is led by Iain Harbinson, a registered nurse who is a parish councillor in Yealand Redmayne; in 2019 he fought Silverdale ward, which covers that parish. The Lib Dems have reselected Ross Hunter who stood here in 2019; Hunter had less luck earlier this year when he failed to defend a Lib Dem seat at a by-election in the neighbouring Kellet ward (page 80). Also standing are Faith Kenrick for Labour and Nicky Sharkey for the Green Party.†

Fort William and Ardnamurchan

Highland council, Scotland; caused by the death of Conservative councillor Ian Ramon.

> [*Train leaves Corrour station, leaving the gang from* Trainspotting *on the platform*]

---

* *Lancaster, Bare*: LD 428 Grn 301 Morecambe Bay Ind 243 C 215 Lab 107 [LD gain from C]
† *Lancaster, Upper Lune Valley*: LD 390 C 183 Grn 24 Lab 21 [LD gain from C]

Parliamentary constituency: Morecambe and Lunesdale
Lancashire county council division: Lancaster Rural East
May 2019 result C 419 LD 402 Lab 92
May 2015 result C 1103 Lab 221 Grn 187
May 2011 result C 829 Grn 277
May 2007 result C 776 Grn 210
May 2003 result C 653 LD 279

Figure 193: Lancaster, Upper Lune Valley

SICK BOY: Now what?

TOMMY: We go for a walk.

SPUD: What?

TOMMY: A walk!

SPUD: But where?

TOMMY: There! [*pointing at a mountain*]

SICK BOY: Are you serious?

[*The gang crosses a railway track.*]

TOMMY: Well, what are you waiting for?

SPUD: Tommy... this is not natural, man.

TOMMY: It's the great outdoors! It's fresh air!

SICK BOY: Look, Tommy, we know you're getting a hard time off Lizzy, but there's really no need to take it out on us.

TOMMY: Doesn't it make you proud to be Scottish?

RENTON: It's sh—e being Scottish! We're the lowest of the low, the scum of the f—g earth, the most wretched, miserable, servile, pathetic trash that was ever sh—t into civilization! Some people hate the English, I don't: they're just w—s! We, on the other hand, are colonized by w—s! We can't even find a decent culture to be colonized by! We are ruled by effete a—s! It's a sh—e state of affairs to be in, Tommy, and all the fresh air in the world won't make any f—g difference!

VOICEOVER: At or around this time, Spud, Sick Boy and I made a healthy, informed, democratic decision to get back on heroin as soon as possible. It took about twelve hours.

It's time for the voters of Corrour (if there are any people who live here year-round) to make a healthy, informed, democratic decision—hopefully one not involving heroin. Corrour is part of the Fort William and Ardnamurchan ward of Highland council, which sprawls across a thousand square miles of the Scottish Highlands. To put this into some sort of context, 1,000 square miles is almost exactly equal to one Luxembourg. This large area is very sparsely populated, with 8,939 electors on the roll.

Around a third of those people live in Fort William, at the head of Loch Linnhe. Fort William is the major settlement in the western Highlands and, together with its suburbs of Caol and Corpach which are not part of this ward, has a larger population than anywhere in the Highland council area except Inverness. The town itself dates from the seventeenth century, having originally been a military fort built by Cromwell's army. It has had a number of names over the years, with the current name commemorating the Butcher himself: Prince William, Duke of Cumberland.

Fort William's location at the foot of the UK's highest point Ben Nevis makes it a major tourist trap, but it also has a lot of industry. The town is home to the UK's only remaining aluminium smelting plant, which is presently recovering from the collapse of its main lender Greensill Capital. Aluminium smelting involves a huge amount of electricity, which the Fort William plant derives sustainably from the Lochaber hydroelectric scheme.

To the south of Fort William lies Ballachulish, where an impressive bridge carries the main road to Glasgow over Loch Leven. The south side of Loch Leven was once part of Argyll and is known for the valley of Glencoe, which has gone down in infamy as the site of a 1692 massacre of members of the Clan MacDonald by UK government forces.

There's no bridge over Loch Linnhe, so a rickety ferry crossing at Corran or a long detour out of the ward via Glenfinnan are the only way to Ardnamurchan. Also once part of Argyll, the peninsula of Ardnamurchan leads to Corrachadh Mòr, which at 6° 13′ West is the most westerly point of the British mainland. Just to the north of Corrachadh Mòr is the lighthouse at Ardnamurchan Point, which gets a namecheck just before 1am every morning in the Shipping Forecast on Radio 4.

"Ardnamurchan" in this ward name refers to the pre-1975 Ardnamurchan district of Argyll, which covered not just the peninsula itself but the whole area south of Glenfinnan and Loch Shiel. The main population centres here are Acharacle at the foot of Loch Shiel, and Strontian which is the location of the Ardnamurchan High School. Before the high school was built in 2002, Ardnamurchan's secondary school students had to travel from here to Fort William, to Mallaig, or over the water to Tobermory on Mull.

Strontian was a lead-mining centre from the 18th century, and it has given its name to the chemical element of strontium. Strontium is one of the alkaline earth metals, and used to be in major demand for making cathode ray tubes for colour TVs; these are rather out of fashion now, but strontium salts are also popular in the fireworks industry because they burn with a deep red colour.

That's the Fort William and Ardnamurchan ward, whose boundaries have been unchanged since PR came in for Scottish local elections in 2007. The main benefit of PR in places like the Highlands was to ensure contested elections, and we certainly had that in 2007 when eleven candidates stood for the four seats in this ward. The seats went to the Lib Dems, an independent (Donald Cameron), the SNP and Labour, with Labour having a 55-vote majority over independent Patricia Jordon in the final count. Jordon had done well to get that far, having started in eighth place and overtaken two other independents and the Conservative candidate.

That Conservative candidate was Andrew Baxter, who subsequently stood in the 2012 election as an independent and topped the poll. He repeated the trick again at the last Highland elections in May 2017, being elected on the first count with 37% of the first preferences. The SNP polled 33% and won two seats, while the Conservatives polled 13% and won a seat here for the first time. At the decisive count the second SNP candidate Niall McLean finished 120 votes ahead of Labour, with a Conservative surplus of 9 still to distribute. If we re-run the votes cast here in 2017 for a single vacancy then Andrew Baxter wins very comfortably. Since 2017 Baxter has been kicked out of the independent group which leads the coalition running Highland council, and he has rejoined the Conservatives.

This ward is represented by the SNP in the Westminster and Holyrood parliaments, and is part of the Ross, Skye and Lochaber constituency which returns the SNP's Westminster group leader Ian Blackford.

Ian Ramon, who had been a lighthouse keeper and tour guide on the Ardnamurchan peninsula, passed away in September. There is just time for a by-election to take place before the next Scottish local elections in May 2022.

Defending this difficult seat for the Conservatives is Ruraidh Stewart, who has appeared in this column before: he fought last year's by-election in Eilean a' Cheò ward, covering the Isle of Skye*. Stewart, who has recently graduated from St Andrews, has previously represented Skye in the Scottish Youth Parliament. You cannot count out independents here, and there are three of them on the ballot paper. Joanne Matheson, who is from Acharacle, stood here in 2017 and finished last with 4.3% of the vote, and has reportedly given up on her campaign after concluding that she doesn't have the spare time to be a councillor; Mark Drayton is on the Fort William community council; and Andy McKenna is a photographer working in the tourist sector in Fort William. The SNP candidate

* *Andrew's Previews 2020*, page 64.

Parliamentary constituency: Ross, Skye and Lochaber
Scottish Parliament constituency: Skye, Lochaber and Badenoch
May 2017 first preferences Ind 1550 SNP 1369 C 530 Lab 344 LD 192 Ind 177
May 2012 first preferences SNP 980 Ind 647 Lab 574 Ind 468 Ind 448 LD 180 C 175
May 2007 first preferences LD 1059 Ind 939 SNP 778 Lab 501 C 372 Ind 322 Ind 317 Ind 271 Ind 241 Ind 195 Ind 194

Figure 194: Highland, Fort William and Ardnamurchan

is French-born Sarah Fanet, who lives in Kinlochleven and also works in the tourism sector. Completing the ballot are Roger Liley for the Liberal Democrats and the ward's first Scottish Green Party candidate, Kate Willis. The standard Scottish reminders apply: Votes at 16 are in use as is the Alternative Vote, and transfers could end up being very important. Please mark your ballot paper in order of preference.*

And the answer to the quiz question on page 548: the 1999 album *The Man Who* was, of course, by Travis.

* *Highland, Fort William and Ardnamurchan*: first preferences SNP 905 C 485 Grn 328 LD 231 McKenna 194 Matheson 88 Drayton 56; final SNP 1182 C 688 [SNP gain from C]

9th December 2021

There are seven by-elections on 9th December 2021, with the Conservatives defending six seats and the remaining one having previously been independent. We start with the six Conservative defences:

Anston and Woodsetts; and Aughton and Swallownest

Rotherham council, South Yorkshire; caused respectively by the resignations of Conservative councillors Emma McClure and Jack Austin.

It's been a while since this column has talked about Rotherham. The last local by-elections in this district were nearly five years ago, when two polls were held in February 2017*; on that occasion Labour gained a seat in Dinnington ward from UKIP but lost Brinsworth and Catcliffe ward to an unexpected Liberal Democrat surge.

At that time, Rotherham council was being run by government Commissioners in the wake of an appalling scandal over child sexual exploitation. The scandal had already had huge effects on the town's politics. It forced the resignation of the then South Yorkshire Police and Crime Commissioner Shaun Wright, the abuses having happened while he was the Rotherham council cabinet member responsible for children's services. The resulting by-election in October 2014, with the appalling turnout we normally see for Police and Crime Commissioner elections, saw the UK Independence Party surge into second place.

This was not a flash in the pan. Five months previously, UKIP had won the 2014 Rotherham council election in vote terms. From virtually nowhere, they polled 44.3% of the vote across the district against Labour's 40.9%, and won 10 wards to Labour's 11. The party never really climbed those heights again: they only gained a further three seats in 2015, and won one further seat in 2016.

---

* *Andrew's Previews 2017*, page 20.

One permanent effect of the Rotherham scandal is that the council's electoral cycle has been changed. The entire council membership was placed up for re-election in 2016, with Labour winning 48 seats, UKIP 14 and an independent candidate one—almost no change on the previous council. From that year on Rotherham ceased electing its councillors by thirds and was converted to whole-council elections. Due to that and the pandemic there were no ordinary local elections in the borough between 2016 and 2021, something which is very unusual for a metropolitan borough.

That doesn't mean other elections weren't taking place here, particularly general elections. The borough covers the whole of the Rother Valley and Rotherham constituencies and most of the Wentworth and Dearne constituency, all of which saw huge swings to the right in December 2019. The Rotherham, and Wentworth and Dearne constituencies are now marginal, while Rother Valley was a convincing Conservative gain.

And it's in the Rother Valley seat, covering a series of small towns and villages to the east of Sheffield, that today's two local by-elections take place. The Tories gained Rother Valley in 2019 without having a single local councillor in the constituency (or indeed in Rotherham borough as a whole), which makes their parliamentary majority all the more impressive. The party followed up on that in convincing style at the Rotherham council elections in May, winning 20 seats from nowhere to become the official opposition on the council. Most of those gains came from wards in the Rother Valley constituency. Labour retained their majority with 32 seats, the Lib Dems won three, the former UKIP group—rechristened as the Rotherham Democratic Party—fell to three seats, and the remaining seat went to an independent.

Three of the new Conservative councillors—Timothy Baum-Dixon, Tracey Wilson and Emma McClure—came from Anston and Woodsetts ward, which is based on the twin villages of North Anston and South Anston. The two Anstons now form a single urban area with Dinnington to the north, and they are pit villages only in the sense that Dinnington was dominated by a large colliery until the 1990s; the Anstons are clearly less deprived than Dinnington itself. Mind, the area's geology continues to attract interest and there have been recent proposals for fracking under Woodsetts. These days the villages are commuter centres for Sheffield and Worksop, with the A 57 road and Kiveton Park railway station providing quick links between the two. In the 2011 census the ward (which then had slightly different boundaries, as we shall come to) had the second-highest population born in the UK of any ward in Yorkshire (98.2%), and had high levels of owner-occupation.

Boundary changes for the 2021 election added the tiny parish of Thorpe

Salvin and a small part of Dinnington to Anston and Woodsetts ward. The previous Anston and Woodsetts ward had been one of the stronger Conservative parts of Rotherham in this century, but the Tories only won it in 2008; their councillor Darren Hughes subsequently defected to Labour and sought re-election in 2012 on the Labour ticket, but lost his seat to independent candidate Clive Jepson. UKIP were within a handful of votes of winning seats here in 2014, 2015 and 2016.

I have already noted that the Tories won a full slate here in May, but there's a bit more to it than that. Their share of the vote was only 33%, and their third seat was won by Emma McClure just fifteen votes ahead of the Liberal Democrat slate which polled 22%. This in a ward where the Lib Dems hadn't previously stood a candidate in fifteen years. Labour fell to third with 20%, and independent councillor Clive Jepson finished in seventh place with 16% of the vote and lost his seat. There were a lot of ticket-splitters here, with wide variations in the shares of the vote between different candidates of the same party.

The boundary review for this year's Rotherham election created the new ward of Aughton and Swallownest, covering territory which had previously been part of Holderness and Rother Vale wards. Aughton and Swallownest are both part of the parish of Aston cum Aughton, which covers three large villages which are just outside the Sheffield city boundary and function as Sheffield suburbs. The ward also includes the tiny parish of Ulley to the north-east and what's left of the parish of Orgreave to the west. Don't be confused by the presence of that name: this ward doesn't cover the former Orgreave colliery site, which is being extensively redeveloped for housing and industry and has declared independence as the new parish of Waverley.

In the case of Aughton and Swallownest the extensive boundary changes make comparisons with previous years difficult, but for what it's worth both predecessor wards voted Labour at every election since 2004 with the exception of UKIP wins in Rother Vale (in 2014) and Holderness (one out of three seats in 2016). In May the new Aughton and Swallownest ward split its representation. Labour topped the poll with 40% of the vote, and former Holderness ward councillor Lyndsay Pitchley was re-elected a long way ahead of her running-mate. That allowed the Conservatives, who polled 32%, to win the ward's other seat; third place went to the Rotherham Democratic Party, whose outgoing councillor Mick Elliot finished on 16% and lost his seat.

The two outgoing Conservative councillors only served for five months before handing in their resignations in October. Emma McClure of Anston and Woodsetts ward cites changes in her family circumstances, while Jack Austin of Aughton and Swallownest ward is concentrating on running his engineering

Parliamentary constituency: Rother Valley
May 2021 result C 1491/1341/1020 LD 1005/786/522 Lab 906/744/461 Ind 737/535 Grn 375 Workers Party 47

Figure 195: Rotherham, Anston and Woodsetts

Parliamentary constituency: Rother Valley
May 2021 result Lab 817/503 C 666/625 Rotherham Democratic Party 341 Workers Party 136 LD 107

Figure 196: Rotherham, Aughton and Swallownest

business. The two by-elections to replace them have attracted a lot of interest, with fifteen candidates standing for the two vacancies.

Defending Anston and Woodsetts for the Conservatives is Adrian Knight, who lives in Woodsetts and is a former manager of Dinnington Town FC's junior side. The Lib Dems' Drew Tarmey is having another go after his near-miss in May; Tarmey is the vice-chairman of Anston parish council, and his day job is teaching medical students at the University of Manchester. The Labour candidate is Simon Tweed, who was a Rotherham councillor (representing Dinnington ward) from 2008 until May when he fought this ward and lost his seat. Another former Rotherham councillor who wants to get back is independent candidate Clive Jepson, who lost his seat here in May. Independent candidate (and former Labour councillor) Jonathan Ireland and David Foulstone for the Green Party also stood here in May, and they complete the Anston and Woodsetts ballot paper together with Allen Cowles for the Rotherham Democratic Party and the former Yorkshire Party leader Chris Whitwood.*

On paper Aughton and Swallownest looks like a more difficult Conservative defence. The party have given that job to Julia Mitchell, who lives in Swallownest and works part-time in a dental practice. The Labour candidate is former Rotherham councillor Robert Taylor, who represented Anston and Woodsetts ward from 2015 to 2016 and Holderness ward from 2016 to 2021. The Rotherham Democratic Party have changed candidate to Gavin Shawcroft, who contested Sitwell ward in May. Also standing are Mark Lambert for the Liberal Democrats, Dennis Bannan for the Yorkshire Party, Louisa Barker for the Green Party and Paul Marshall for the Trade Unionist and Socialist Coalition.†

* *Rotherham, Anston and Woodsetts*: LD 1016 C 686 Lab 533 Jepson 189 Ireland 118 Grn 63 Yorkshire Party 20 Rotherham Democratic Party 6 [LD gain from C] † *Rotherham, Aughton and Swallownest*: Lab 645 C 496 Grn 59 Yorkshire Party 35 TUSC 32 Rotherham Democratic Party 15 LD 14 [Lab gain from C]

Parliamentary constituency: Bracknell
May 2019 result C 626/569 Lab 493/485 LD 180
May 2015 result C 1191/1087 Lab 819/797 UKIP 461/406 TUSC 68/62
May 2011 result C 824/784 Lab 774/736
May 2007 result Lab 782/668 C 600/598 LD 171
May 2003 result Lab 628/624 C 565/534 LD 126 Grn 79

Figure 197: Bracknell Forest, Old Bracknell

Old Bracknell

Bracknell Forest council, Berkshire; caused by the resignation of Conservative councillor Malcolm Tullett.

All our remaining by-elections today are in the south of England, and we start our tour of the south with what might at first appear to be an oxymoron. There is very little that is old about Old Bracknell ward, but the ward does include much of Easthampstead.

Back in the day, Easthampstead was important enough to have a Rural District of Berkshire named after it. In fact Easthampstead Rural District is one of the very few pre-1974 districts to have survived unchanged to the present day: it's now called Bracknell Forest, after the New Town which has swallowed Easthampstead in its urban sprawl.

Bracknell is one of the most consistently right-wing of England's New Towns, and the Conservatives hold 38 seats on Bracknell Forest council out of a possible 42 following the 2019 elections. That was actually their worst performance here since 2003, when Old Bracknell ward voted Labour. The Conservatives gained this ward in 2011 and held it in 2019 with a 48–38 lead over the Labour slate.

Malcolm Tullett had first been elected to Bracknell Forest council in 2015, at the time representing Hanworth ward; he moved here in 2019. He had left the council's ruling Conservative group in July this year but remains a member of the Conservative group on Bracknell town council, a move which has reportedly led to some infighting among the local Conservative councillors. Tullett eventually submitted his resignation from Bracknell Forest council in October.

The by-election to replace Tullett is a straight fight. Defending from the blue corner is Iain McCracken, a former Conservative councillor who represented this ward from 2011 to 2019 when he stood down. Challenging from the red corner is Paul Bidwell, a Bracknell town councillor who works in the security industry; he was the Labour parliamentary candidate for Bracknell in 2017 and 2019.*

* *Bracknell Forest, Old Bracknell*: Lab 434 C 276 [Lab gain from C]

Castle;
Kings Hill; and
West Malling and Leybourne

Tonbridge and Malling council, Kent; caused respectively by the resignation of Jack Austin, the disqualification of Millie Langridge for non-attendance and the resignation of Liam O'Toole. All were Conservative councillors, and all had been first elected in 2019.

We now come to Kent for a Magical Mystery Tour around three wards within the Tonbridge and Malling district and parliamentary constituency.

To start with the first half of that name, Tonbridge itself is a market town which grew up at a crossing of the River Medway. To guard this crossing, the Norman invader Richard fitz Gilbert erected the first Tonbridge Castle, a motte-and-bailey structure typical of eleventh-century Norman castles.

It didn't stay that way for long. Fitz Gilbert's descendants, the de Clares, rebelled against King William Rufus, who besieged the castle in 1088; after a two-day siege Tonbridge Castle fell to William, who reportedly had both the castle and the town of Tonbridge burnt in revenge. This didn't put off the de Clares, and by the end of the thirteenth century Tonbridge Castle was a rather impressive stone structure. A few centuries of decay have taken their toll, but the gatehouse is now adjoined by an eighteenth-century mansion. This mansion was bought in 1900 by Tonbridge urban district council, and their successors Tonbridge and Malling council use it as offices.

However, Tonbridge Castle is no longer the head office of Tonbridge and Malling council. This is now located in the Malling area of the district, in the village of Kings Hill. It would certainly be accurate to describe Kings Hill as a new village. Until 1989 the area now occupied by Kings Hill was an airfield, which operated from 1940 to 1969 as RAF West Malling; in the 1970s it was a temporary home for thousands of Ugandan Asians expelled by Idi Amin. The officers' mess at RAF West Malling still stands and now serves as the council offices; it has been renamed as the Gibson Building after Wing Commander Guy Gibson VC, who was stationed here with 29 Squadron.

To the north of Kings Hill lie the town of West Malling and the village of Leybourne. West Malling is a market town on the old road and railway line from London to Maidstone, which gives its name to the Malling area. It is the site of Malling Abbey, which was founded in the eleventh century by Gundulf, bishop of Rochester. The abbey was dissolved in 1538, but refounded at the end of the 19th century. Despite its name Malling Abbey was always a nunnery, and there is still a Benedictine community of nuns here to this day.

Kings Hill has a reputation as one of the richest villages in the country, and the 2011 census bears this out to some extent: over half of the ward's workforce are in managerial or professional occupations, and the proportion of adults with no qualifications (10.0%) is extremely low. Its development led to West Malling being bypassed quite recently (the bypass, linking Kings Hill with the M 20 motorway and West Malling railway station, opened in 2007). In common with some other quasi-New Towns developed in the last decade or two, Kings Hill also makes the top 20 wards in England and Wales for under-16 population (31.3%); a more unusual feature is that it is in the top 100 wards for shared property ownership. Tonbridge Castle ward also has an unusual age distribution, making the top 40 wards in England and Wales for 16- and 17-year-olds: this is due to the presence here of Tonbridge School, a boys' public school with a significant number of boarders.

These three wards returned a full slate of eight Conservative councillors in 2015, when the current ward boundaries came in (although none of these wards were changed to any significant extent in 2015). The seat count changed in 2019 when the Liberal Democrats gained one of the three seats in West Malling and Leybourne ward: shares of the vote there were 36% and 2 seats for the Conservatives, 32% and 1 seat for the Liberal Democrats, and 26% for an independent slate. Kings Hill voted 47% Conservative, 35% for an independent slate and 18% Lib Dem; Castle ward had shares of 44% Conservatives, 24% Lib Dem and 23% Green Party.

Castle ward is part of the two-seat Tonbridge division of Kent county council, which now has two Green councillors who gained their seats from the Conservatives in May. Kings Hill is part of the Malling Rural East county division which is strongly Conservative; West Malling and Leybourne is split between the Malling North division (safe Conservative) and Malling Central (safe Lib Dem). An administrative error led to Labour nominating two candidates for Malling Central in May's county elections; they polled 4.5% and 1.0%, so this didn't cost the party a seat.

The Tonbridge Castle by-election arises following the resignation of Karen King, who has moved away from the area. Defending for the Conservatives is Johurul Islam, who works for Royal Mail and also runs an Indian restaurant in Kings Hill. Despite their second-place finish last time there is no Liberal Democrat candidate, so Islam's main competition may well come from the Green Party's Anna Cope, who teaches English at a secondary school in Tonbridge. Completing the Castle ballot paper is Julian Wilson for Labour.*

* *Tonbridge and Malling, Castle*: Grn 731 C 454 Lab 48 [Grn gain from C]

Parliamentary constituency: Tonbridge and Malling
Kent county council division: Tonbridge
May 2019 result C 640/623 LD 342 Grn 338/323 Lab 129/92
May 2015 result C 1485/1392 Grn 787 LD 751

Figure 198: Tonbridge and Malling, Castle

Parliamentary constituency: Tonbridge and Malling
Kent county council division: Malling Rural East
May 2019 result C 887/770/672 Ind 651/474 LD 344/269
May 2015 result C 2719/2044/1855 UKIP 843 Ind 747 Lab 673

Figure 199: Tonbridge and Malling, Kings Hill

Parliamentary constituency: Tonbridge and Malling
Kent county council division: Malling Central (West Malling parish), Malling North (Leybourne parish)
May 2019 result C 833/743/715 LD 739/661/608 Ind 613/393 Lab 138
May 2015 result C 1608/1524/1468 UKIP 761 LD 671/612/578 Ind 552/377/334 Lab 395 Grn 335

Figure 200: Tonbridge and Malling, West Malling and Leybourne

There are also three candidates for Kings Hill, where voters will elect a successor to Millie Langridge who was kicked off the council under the six-month non-attendance rule. Here the defending Conservative candidate is Dan Harman, who grew up in this area but has recently returned to the UK after a spell in New Zealand. There is a new independent candidate: local resident Louis Westlake is a 19-year-old student reading law and philosophy at the New College of Humanities in London, and he is standing on an anti-development ticket. The Lib Dem candidate is Raja Zahidi, a solicitor and Kings Hill parish councillor.*

Finally we come to West Malling and Leybourne, where Liam O'Toole has resigned for personal reasons. The Conservatives have selected West Malling parish councillor David Thompson to replace him. Standing for the Lib Dems is Leybourne resident Paul Boxall, who currently works in London for a watch company but has also worked in theatre production and in the Middle East. There's no independent in West Malling and Leybourne this time, so Robin Potter for Labour and Jordan Mahoney for the Green Party complete the ballot paper.†

* *Tonbridge and Malling, Kings Hill*: C 740 Ind 316 LD 191 † *Tonbridge and Malling, West Malling and Leybourne*: LD 776 C 624 Grn 137 Lab 29 [LD gain from C]

Northam

Torridge council, Devon; caused by the disqualification of independent councillor Giuseppe Rossi for non-attendance.

For our final poll this week we return to an occasional series in this column with the general title of "post-1066 invasions of England which they don't tell you about in GCSE history".

The scene here is shortly after the Norman conquest, with William in the ascendant after defeating King Harold Godwinson at Hastings, and with the Saxon nobles having settled on Edgar the Atheling as their claimant to the English throne. It might be guessed that these events didn't go down particularly well with Harold's family. His queen, Gytha Thorkelsdóttir, had holed herself up in Exeter from where she was causing trouble for the Norman conquerors. William himself turned up in Exeter at the start of 1068 and laid siege to the city; Exeter fell after 18 days of fighting, and Gytha fled.

Attention now turns to Harold's sons (and Gytha's stepsons) Godwin and Edmund, who shortly afterwards turned up at the court of Diarmait, the High King of Ireland. Diarmait fitted them out with some ships and soldiers, and Godwin and Edmund started raiding the coasts of Devon and Cornwall. The following June they came back with an invasion force and landed at Appledore on the north coast of Devon. Unfortunately Norman troops arrived quickly and beat the raiders back to their ships, which had become stranded on the beach by a low tide.

In the resulting Battle of Northam the Saxon army managed to hold the line until the tide came in and they were able to get away. They had taken heavy casualties. High King Diarmait appears to have been less than happy with the result of his investment, and that was pretty much the end of Godwin and Edmund's attempts to claim the English throne: their later attempts to persuade the king of Denmark to fund and supply another invasion attempt fell on stony ground.

Appledore is part of Northam parish, but it is not covered by the Northam ward. Northam parish is rather large, and following major boundary changes here in 2019 it is divided into three wards: one for Appledore, one for Westward Ho!, and this one. The present Northam ward takes in most of Northam town plus the former Orchard Hill ward, which is effectively a northern suburb of Bideford.

Goodness knows what's going to happen here. In the 2015 Torridge elections the previous Northam ward had split its seats between the Conservatives and UKIP, while Orchard Hill ward voted Conservative. However, the 2019

Parliamentary constituency: Torridge and West Devon
Devon county council division: Northam
May 2019 result Ind 783/602/539 C 381/372/296 UKIP 305 LD 255 Lab 214/209/175

Figure 201: Torridge, Northam

election (the only previous poll on these boundaries) comfortably returned an independent slate: shares of the vote were 40% for the independents, 20% for the Conservatives, 16% for UKIP and 13% for the Liberal Democrats. Top of the independent slate was Chris Leather, a former UKIP figure, with Giuseppe Rossi elected in third place with a comfortable majority. The larger Northam division of Devon county council was safely Conservative in May, but the Tory share of the vote was quite low against evenly-divided opposition from an independent and the Lib Dems. The local MP is the Conservatives' Geoffrey Cox, whom you'd think might have a spare bob or two to put towards his party's campaign here.

This by-election could be important for control of Torridge council. This is run by an independent administration which controls 17 seats, plus this vacancy: that adds up to 18, plus the chairman's casting vote. In opposition are the Conservatives on 10, Labour on 3, the Lib Dems and Greens on 2 each and a non-aligned councillor: that also adds up to 18. An independent loss here would tip their administration into a minority.

The Northam by-election arises from the disqualification of independent councillor Giuseppe Rossi under the six-month non-attendance rule. One independent candidate has come forward to succeed him: Timothy Tennant is an artist, doing paintings in the impressionist style which look rather nice on his Instagram. Standing for the Conservatives is Carrie Woodhouse, who contested Westward Ho! ward in the 2019 Torridge elections. UKIP have not returned. The Lib Dem candidate Sam Newman-McKie has previous local government experience, having sat on Winchester council in Hampshire from 2011 to 2016; she is now a Northam town councillor. Completing the ballot paper are Jen Radford for Labour and Wendy Lo-Vel for the Green Party (which won a seat in the former Northam ward, way back in 2007).*

* *Torridge, Northam*: C 386 LD 230 Grn 224 Lab 103 Ind 54 [C gain from Ind]

16th December 2021: Parliamentary Special

Thirteen by-elections on Super Thursday, 16th December 2021, and we start with the big one—the Parliamentary Special:

North Shropshire

House of Commons; caused by the resignation of Conservative MP Owen Paterson.

Have I mentioned that the Welsh Marches are beautiful? Well, the landscape of North Shropshire does test that proposition a bit. Here we don't have the grandeur of the Beacons, the spectacle of the Wye Valley or even the rolling moorland of southern Shropshire. North Shropshire is based on relatively high ground, with the boundary between the Dee and the Severn catchments running the length of the constituency; but this is generally a flattish landscape of prime agricultural land. You don't have to go far in North Shropshire to find fields full of crops or cows.

The Marches don't just specialise in beauty: they also contain a large number of small but attractive market towns, and we have five of these in North Shropshire. The easternmost of them is Market Drayton, located midway between Shrewsbury and Stoke-on-Trent. Market Drayton gave us Robert Clive, the man without whose work and dubious legacy India might never have become British; Clive was born nearby and attended the former Market Drayton Grammar School.

Market Drayton lies on the Shropshire Union Canal, the last great work of Thomas Telford, which runs south to the Black Country and north to the Mersey estuary. Our next town also lies on major north-south routes: the A 41 road between Chester and the Black Country, the A 49 road between Shrewsbury and Warrington, and the railway line between Shrewsbury and Crewe. Whitchurch advertises itself as the home of tower clocks: from 1790 to 2012 it was the location of the works for J B Joyce, whose public clocks have been installed all over the world. Joyce built what is reputed to be the second most-photographed clock in England, the Eastgate Clock on the Chester city walls; other Joyce clocks appear at locations as diverse as Birmingham University, Carnforth railway station, and the Shanghai Custom House.

Some miles to the south of Whitchurch lies Wem, on the old road and railway line from Whitchurch to Shrewsbury. Wem is centrally-located within the North Shropshire seat, and it was the home of North Shropshire district council until that council's abolition in 2009. William Hazlitt, the Georgian essayist, grew up here.

The main road west from Whitchurch crosses straight over the border into the English Maelor, which is part of Wales, and comes out of the other side of the Maelor into Ellesmere, which is part of England. Here the landscape starts to become hilly, and Ellesmere is surrounded by a number of lakes which have been left behind by the most recent Ice Age. Ellesmere stands on the Llangollen Canal, which was originally called the Ellesmere Canal and ran northwards to the Mersey estuary. The town which developed around the other end of the canal took the name of this small Shropshire town, and to this day it is called Ellesmere Port.

We continue west from Ellesmere, passing the ruined castle at Whittington, to the largest population centre in North Shropshire. Oswestry is a border town which has changed hands between England and Wales many times, but it's on the English side of Offa's Dyke and has ended up as part of Shropshire. Nevertheless this is one of the most Welsh parts of England. Oswestry lies on the main road from Wrexham into Powys, and a number of its streets and nearby villages bear Welsh-language names. The town is home to the Welsh Guards Museum and to The New Saints FC.

The New Saints are the most successful team in the history of the Cymru Premier, the top football league in Wales. They have won the league thirteen times, including eight seasons in a row from 2011–12 to 2018–19, and they are currently top of the Cymru Premier table. The New Saints have brought European football to Oswestry every autumn since 2009, with the exception of 2013–14 Champions League qualifying when their home tie against Legia Warsaw was switched to Wrexham; however, they are yet to qualify for the group stage of any UEFA competition. They went out in the third round of qualifying for this season's Europa Conference League, losing on penalties to Viktoria Plzeň.

The town's name in both English and Welsh (*Croesoswallt*) refers to a tree or cross associated with Oswald, a name often identified with King Oswald of Northumbria. That Oswald died in 641 or 642 at the Battle of Maserfield, whose location is the subject of debate but is often placed here by historians.

Oswestry differs from the other towns in North Shropshire in that it was a railway centre. This town was the headquarters of the Cambrian Railways, the major railway company in mid-Wales; the Cambrian's main lines ran from here to Wrexham, Whitchurch, Aberystwyth, Pwllheli and Brecon, with a few other branches. Much of the Cambrian network survives today, but the Welshpool to Whitchurch section has gone. That has left Oswestry with no mainline railway station today (the town's railhead is at Gobowen, some miles away on the Shrewsbury–Chester line), and the Cambrian Railways complex is now a museum.

The list of famous Oswestrians is a long one. It includes the First World War poet Wilfred Owen, who was born here in 1893; and the composer Sir Walford Davies, who was born here in 1869 and sung as a boy in the choir of Christ Church, a Congregational church in Oswestry. Davies became the first director of music for the Royal Air Force, composing its March Past, and succeeded Edward Elgar in 1934 as Master of the King's Music. For an example of Walford Davies' work which is appropriate for the time of the year, this column recommends his beautiful setting of the Christmas carol *O Little Town of Bethlehem*.

Another famous Oswestrian was the Welsh golfer Ian Woosnam, who learned to play the game at the Llanymynech golf club which straddles the English–Welsh border. Woosnam grew up in the village of St Martin's north of Oswestry, which along with the nearby village of Weston Rhyn forms a very unusual corner of this seat. St Martin's and Weston Rhyn were pit villages, lying at the southern end of the Denbighshire coalfield; Ifton Colliery, near St Martin's, was the largest coal mine in Shropshire until its eventual closure in 1968.

With the exception of Oswestry and the St Martin's area, agriculture is and remains the traditional mainstay of North Shropshire's economy. But that doesn't just mean farming. For example, Market Drayton's largest employers are the Müller yoghurt plant and the Pork Farms factory, which makes sausages and other meat products for well-known retailers. Whitchurch and Ellesmere both have a history of cheesemaking, and Whitchurch (thanks to its relatively good road links) is home to a large logistics firm which transports food from North Shropshire to your plate.

This reliance on agriculture and its associated industries has left its mark on the politics of the area. As we shall see, a large number of North Shropshire's MPs—including Owen Paterson—have owned and farmed estates in the area. The Conservative selection for North Shropshire has long been unofficially controlled by the local branch of the National Farmers' Union. The NFU have certainly done well out of that, because this is one of the longest-standing

Conservative seats in the UK.

As usual in these Parliamentary Specials I'll start discussing the parliamentary history of this area with the election of 1885, the year in which single-member constituencies became the norm in parliamentary elections. Shropshire did badly out of the 1885 redistribution, going down from ten MPs to just five: one for the borough of Shrewsbury, and four MPs for county divisions called Ludlow, Newport, Oswestry and Wellington.

The Newport (Shropshire) constituency of 1885–1918 covered the north-eastern corner of the county, including Whitchurch, Wem and Market Drayton as well as the eponymous town. Appropriately enough, the first Conservative candidate for the seat was George Bridgeman, Viscount Newport, who had been one of the two MPs for North Shropshire from 1867 to 1885. Newport, however, lost his seat to the Liberals' Robert Bickersteth by 4,694 votes to 4,333, a majority of 361. Newport eventually returned to Parliament, but not in the Commons: he succeeded to his father's titles and became the fourth Earl of Bradford in 1898. One of his granddaughters married into the Royal Family in 1935: Princess Alice, Duchess of Gloucester died in 2004 at the age of 102.

Robert Bickersteth was from an ecclesiastical family: his father, also called Robert Bickersteth, had served from 1857 to 1884 as Bishop of Ripon. Robert junior had got into Liberal politics as a protégé of the Earl of Kimberley, who was Secretary of State for India going into the 1885 election.

That general election returned a hung parliament, with the Liberals being the largest party and the Irish Nationalists holding the balance of power. This led to a split in the Liberals over the issue of Irish Home Rule, and Robert Bickersteth joined the breakaway Liberal Unionists. The split precipitated another general election in 1886, which the Conservatives won; Bickersteth sought re-election in Leicester as a Liberal Unionist candidate, without success.

With Bickersteth off the scene in Shropshire the Newport seat became safely Conservative. Its second MP was William Kenyon-Slaney, who holds an unusual sporting distinction. Kenyon-Slaney has gone down in the record books as the first player ever to score a goal in an international football match. He did so inside the first two minutes of the England v Scotland match at the Oval in March 1873. To quote from a match report:

> Scotland had the throw in, but threw the ball too far into the field, where Chenery got the ball and kicked straight for goal, and the goal keeper while stooping to lift the ball and kick it, slipped, and was at once charged by Slaney, who sent the ball under the tape.

The tradition of embarrassing performances from the Scotland football team has clearly been going for longer than you might have thought. Kenyon-Slaney went on to get a second goal as England ran out 4–2 winners. Three weeks later he was on the Wanderers team which won the second FA Cup final, beating Oxford University 2–0. (That wasn't the only loss for Oxford that day, as they went on to lose the Boat Race later that afternoon.)

As well as all this, William Kenyon-Slaney was a Grenadier Guards officer. He fought in 1882 at the Battle of Tel el-Kebir, the decisive British victory in the Anglo-Egyptian war. Four years later he was in Parliament, gaining Newport (Shropshire) from the Liberals with a large majority. In 1887 he married Lady Mabel Bridgman, Viscount Newport's sister.

Kenyon-Slaney was elected five times as MP for Newport, with nobody opposing him in 1895 or 1900. His final re-election came in 1906, when he managed to withstand the Liberal landslide by just 176 votes; he polled 4,853 against 4,677 for the Liberal candidate Francis Neilson.

William Kenyon-Slaney died in 1908, aged 60, after suffering an attack of gout. For the resulting Newport by-election of 14th May 1908 the Liberals again put up Francis Neilson. Neilson went on to be elected in 1910 as MP for Hyde in what was then Cheshire, and the relevant *Times Guide to the House of Commons* described him as an author and journalist who had founded the *Democratic Monthly*. That source fails to mention his work as a stage director which had already taken him to Broadway and Bayreuth. Neilson had directed a 1900 production of *Tosca* at Covent Garden under the supervision of none other than Puccini himself, and he later turned down an invitation from Puccini to direct the La Scala opera in Milan.

Neilson's politics were on the Radical side, which was not going to help him win Newport. The 1908 by-election resulted in a swing to the Conservative candidate Beville Stanier, a Shropshire county councillor who farmed an estate at Peplow Hall in the constituency. Stanier was re-elected in both 1910 elections (without opposition in December), and he was made a baronet in 1917.

That was Newport (Shropshire). To the west of this lay the Oswestry constituency, which covered much of the western half of Shropshire. Oswestry started off as a safe Conservative seat, and its first MP was Stanley Leighton who had been the other MP for North Shropshire between 1876 and 1885. Leighton was a barrister and antiquarian who owned a large brickworks at Sweeney, just outside Oswestry. Earlier in 1885 he had been one of the organisers of the Wenlock Olympian Games, a forerunner of the modern Summer Olympics.

Stanley Leighton was elected five times as MP for Oswestry, with no-one opposing his re-election in 1886, 1892 or 1900. He died in 1901, aged 63, having developed pneumonia after rushing through the rain to a Commons vote on the Coal Duty Bill.

The resulting first Oswestry by-election, held on 24th May 1901, was held for the Conservatives by George Ormsby-Gore who defeated the Liberal candidate Allan Bright by the large margin of 1,088 votes. Bright, who had recently moved to Weston Rhyn after two unsuccessful Parliamentary campaigns in Exeter, blamed his defeat on "landlordism" and "shortness of time", and he might have had a point as far as the landlordism goes. Ormsby-Gore was the heir to Lord Harlech, who had an estate at Brogyntyn near Selattyn, north-west of Oswestry.

In 1904 George Ormsby-Gore succeeded to his father's titles and entered the Lords as the third Lord Harlech. The resulting second Oswestry by-election, held on 26th July 1904, came at a time when the Balfour Conservative government had become unpopular and with the question of tariff reform or free trade as a major political issue of the day. The young Oldham MP Winston Churchill, a free-trader who had recently defected to the Liberals, turned up on the campaign trail in support of Bright, giving speeches in Ellesmere and Oswestry. The Conservatives selected William Bridgeman, who was a cousin of the 4th Earl of Bradford and sat on the London School Board; he was a former cricketer who had played at first-class level for Cambridge University. Bridgeman already had experience of politics at the highest level, as a private secretary to the former Chancellor of the Exchequer Michael Hicks-Beach. To general surprise, the Liberals' Allan Bright defeated Bridgeman by 4,542 votes to 4,157, a majority of 385.

Allan Bright was the last Liberal MP—indeed, the last non-Conservative MP—for this part of Shropshire. A rematch against Bridgeman in the 1906 general election saw Bright fail to hold the by-election gain, and the Oswestry seat reverted to the Conservatives with a majority of 503. The 1906 election nationally was a landslide for the Liberals, so this was an against-the-trend gain. William Bridgeman was re-elected in both 1910 elections, increasing his majority to 624 and then to 746 votes.

The 1918 redistribution cut the number of Shropshire constituencies from five to four. The Newport constituency disappeared, with its area split between a new constituency of The Wrekin and a radically redrawn Oswestry constituency. The new Oswestry seat, stretching across the north rather than the west of the county, had exactly the same boundaries as the North Shropshire constituency we have today.

It has proven to be a very safe Conservative constituency. Since 1918 the Conservative majority in Oswestry or North Shropshire has fallen below 10 points on only two occasions. The first of those was in 1923, when William Bridgeman was elected for a sixth term of office with a majority of 1,815 votes over the Liberals. By this point Bridgeman was firmly on the Conservative frontbench, having joined Cabinet in 1920 as the first Secretary for Mines. He was a supporter of the Conservative revolt against the Lloyd George coalition government in 1922, and was rewarded for that by being appointed as Home Secretary in the Bonar Law government. Bridgeman was one of the more hardline Home Secretaries, and this may have contributed to his narrow majority in 1923 as the Conservatives lost their majority in Parliament.

A year later Baldwin's Conservatives and Bridgeman were back in government after winning the 1924 election. William Bridgeman served throughout that Parliament as First Lord of the Admiralty in what was his final frontbench position. He retired at the 1929 general election after 23 years as MP for Oswestry, and shortly afterwards entered the Lords as the first Viscount Bridgeman. From the Lords Bridgeman later served a year as President of the Marylebone Cricket Club, and he was briefly chairman of the BBC for a few months before his death in 1935.

Bridgeman passed his Commons seat on 1929 to Bertie Leighton, son of the former Oswestry MP Stanley Leighton. Bertie had previously pursued a military career, serving both in the Boer War and in the First World War; he was severely wounded in the latter conflict. Leighton thrashed the Labour candidate by 74–26 in the 1931 election, and nobody opposed his re-election in 1935.

Bertie Leighton retired at the 1945 election and passed the Oswestry constituency to Oliver Poole, who won without fuss against the Attlee landslide. A member of Lloyd's of London, Poole had joined the family firm of City insurance brokers. He was also a Warwickshire Yeomanry officer, and had served during the Second World War in a number of spheres around the world; by the end of the war he was on the staff of the 21st Army Group, with the rank of colonel and a military CBE.

Poole served only one term in the Commons, being succeeded as MP for Oswestry in 1950 by David Ormsby-Gore. He was the heir to the fourth Lord Harlech, the grandson of the previous Oswestry MP George Ormsby-Gore, and a great grandson of the former Prime Minister the Marquess of Salisbury. David was farming his father's land at the time of his election.

Ormsby-Gore slowly worked his way up the greasy pole, becoming a junior Foreign Office minister in the first Macmillan government in 1957. He was distantly related to and a good friend of John F Kennedy, a connection which made him very useful to the British government after Kennedy's election as President of the United States. In 1961 Macmillan appointed Ormsby-Gore as the British Ambassador to the USA, an appointment which meant he would have to leave these shores. He applied for the Chiltern Hundreds.

David Ormsby-Gore ended up spending four relatively successful years in

Washington, becoming such a close confidant of the Kennedys that he proposed to JFK's widow Jacqueline Kennedy in 1967. She turned him down. By this point David had succeeded to his father's titles, becoming the fifth Lord Harlech. He became a TV executive—the H in HTV, the former Welsh ITV franchise, stands for Lord Harlech—and he served as president of the British Board of Film Classification from 1965 until his death in a car crash in 1985. A number of Kennedy family members turned up for his funeral at Llanfihangel-y-traethau, just north of Harlech on the Welsh coast. His grandson Jasset Ormsby-Gore, the 7th Lord Harlech, won a hereditary peers' by-election in July this year, and at 35 years old he is currently the youngest member of the Upper House.

The third Oswestry by-election, to replace David Ormsby-Gore, took place on 9th November 1961. It was the first time that Oswestry had seen a parliamentary election with four candidates, although there wasn't much support for the Patriotic Front candidate who lost his deposit. For the by-election Labour selected the former Oxford Union president Brian Walden, who was 29 at the time; Walden's career as a Labour MP and political interviewer lay in the future at this point. He came third, very close behind the Liberal candidate John Buchanan.

The by-election was won easily by a Conservative whom Walden described, many years later, as the most honest politician he had interviewed. John Biffen was 31 years old when he won Oswestry in 1961, but he was already on his second election campaign after contesting Coventry East (against Richard Crossman) in 1959. He had previously worked for the engineering group Tube Investments.

Biffen went on to serve as MP for Oswestry, and for its successor North Shropshire, for over 35 years. He was one of the few MPs to vote for Enoch Powell in the 1965 Conservative leadership election, and he remained on the backbenches under the leadership of Edward Heath. His "dry" economic views were more to Margaret Thatcher's taste, and Biffen served in Cabinet throughout the first two Thatcher terms: as Chief Secretary to the Treasury, as Trade Secretary, and then for five years as Leader of the Commons.

The 1983 election saw the boundaries of the Oswestry seat change for the first time since 1918. The Wrekin constituency had become oversized as a result of the growth of the New Town of Telford, and to reduce its electorate the town of Newport was transferred to the Oswestry constituency. The seat also got a new name: North Shropshire, reflecting the larger of the two new local government districts entirely within the seat. The boundary change was reversed in 1997 when Telford got a constituency of its own, but the seat's name is still North Shropshire and hasn't reverted back to Oswestry.

Shropshire had undergone a local government reform in the late 1960s, which reduced the number of councils within the Oswestry constituency from nine to three: Market Drayton, North Shropshire and Oswestry rural districts. The big bang of 1974 merged the first two of these into a larger North Shropshire district, while Oswestry rural district was one of the handful of councils which survived the Heath reorganisation unchanged.

John Biffen retired at the 1997 election, in which his successor Owen Paterson was nearly swept away by the Blair landslide. The Labour candidate Ian Lucas (who would later serve for eighteen years as MP for Wrexham) surged into second place with 36% of the vote, and Paterson's majority was only 2,195.

Paterson got stuck in after this rocky start, and he has made the constituency safe again. He is a local, Whitchurch born and bred. Before entering politics Paterson worked in the tanning industry: that's tanning as in leather, and at the time of his election to Parliament he was managing director of the British Leather Company. North Shropshire was not his first election campaign: he had contested Wrexham in the 1992 general election.

After increasing his majority in 2001 Owen Paterson started to climb the greasy pole, joining the Conservative frontbench in 2003 as shadow agriculture minister. In 2007 he became the party's Northern Ireland spokesman, and he negotiated an electoral pact with the Ulster Unionist Party whereby the UUP and Conservatives would run joint candidates in Northern Ireland at the next Westminster general election. The UUP were already well on the downward slide by this point, with just one MP left: Sylvia, Lady Hermon, in North Down. Hermon walked out of the party in disgust at this deal and sought re-election to Parliament in 2010 as an independent candidate for her North Down constituency; she was resoundingly re-elected, and the Ulster Conservatives and Unionists won nothing. The pact was not renewed.

However, things had gone well enough for the Conservatives in Great Britain that Owen Paterson was included in the first Coalition cabinet, as Northern Ireland secretary. He was reshuffled to become environment secretary in 2013, a position in which he didn't prosper. Paterson is a climate-change sceptic and a supporter of genetically-modified food, and his tenure as environment secretary included an attempted badger cull which was widely seen to have been ineffective. When interviewed by the BBC on the disappointing results of the cull, Paterson memorably said that "the badgers have moved the goalposts".

Owen Paterson was dropped from Cabinet in 2014, and returned to the backbenches. This represented rather a drop in his salary, and he started to take on paid consultancy work. In 2015 he was taken on by Randox Laboratories, a clinical diagnostics company; and the following year he became a consultant to the meat processing company Lynn's Country Foods. Taken together, his remuneration from Randox and Lynn's amounted to nearly three times his MP's salary. This was properly declared in the Commons register of interests.

What Paterson did with that consultancy work was another matter. In 2019 media reports were published which alleged that he had improperly lobbied for those two companies. The Parliamentary Commissioner for Standards, Kathryn Stone, opened an investigation in October 2019.

Stone's investigation was subject to a number of delays, partly due to the December 2019 general election, partly due to the COVID lockdown and partly due to the sad death of Owen Paterson's wife Rose in June 2020. Rose Paterson, a sister of Viscount Ridley and the chairman of Aintree Racecourse, was found dead in woods near the family home in Ellesmere; the coroner recorded a verdict of suicide.

The eventual report by Commissioner Stone found that Owen Paterson had breached the Commons rules prohibiting paid advocacy on fourteen occasions, involving approaches to the Food Standards Agency and the Department for International Development; he had also failed to declare his interest as a consultant to Lynn's Country Foods in four emails to the Food Standards Agency; and he had also abused parliamentary facilities by using his Commons office for business meetings and using Commons headed notepaper for two business letters. With the exception of the headed notepaper use, Paterson denied the charges and went on the attack, making allegations against the integrity of the Commissioner and her team.

This did not impress the Commons Select Committee on Standards, which duly considered Stone's findings and concluded that

> Mr Paterson's actions were an egregious case of paid advocacy, that he repeatedly used his privileged position to benefit two companies for whom he was a paid consultant, and that this has brought the House into disrepute.

In their report, published in October 2021, the Standards Committee recommended a suspension of 30 sitting days, which would inevitably result in a recall petition being opened in North Shropshire against Paterson.

If Paterson's actions hadn't brought the House into disrepute (as he continued to maintain), what happened next certainly did. The relevant motion to suspend Paterson duly came before the House of Commons on 3rd November 2021 for its approval. In an unexpected move, the motion was amended on the floor of the House to instead raise concerns about "potential defects in the standards system" and to refer the whole matter (including the Paterson case) to a new select committee for recommendations. The government whipped its MPs to support this amendment, which passed the Commons by 250 votes to 232.

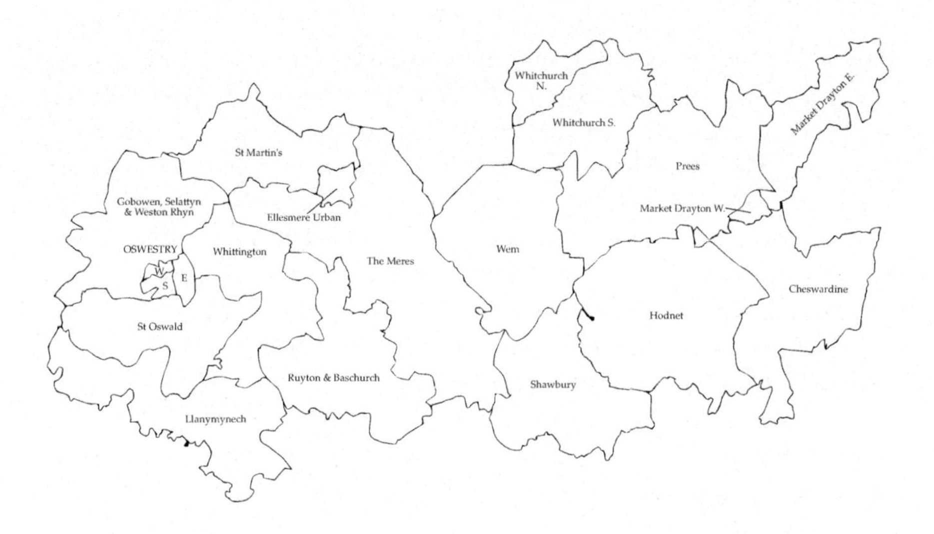

Figure 202: Divisions of the North Shropshire constituency

It quickly became clear that this was a major error. The opposition parties announced that they would boycott the new select committee, and the government came under heavy criticism for its decision to effectively let Paterson off the hook. A U-turn followed; the whole idea was abandoned, and it was announced the following day that the original motion to suspend Paterson for 30 days would instead go back before the House for ratification. The press declared open season on other MPs with high-paying jobs outside parliament, and the stench of sleaze started to hang around Westminster again. Owen Paterson concluded that his position as an MP was no longer tenable, and he applied for the Manor of Northstead, bringing a 24-year Parliamentary career to a sad end.

The resulting North Shropshire by-election takes place in a very safe Conservative seat. Paterson was re-elected for his seventh and final term of office in December 2019 with a majority of 22,949 votes over Labour; he polled 63% of the vote to Labour's 22%, a swing of nearly 6% in his favour compared with June 2017. When your columnist visited Whitchurch last summer the town centre was plastered with anti-Paterson stickers, but clearly that doesn't represent a critical mass of people who don't like him. As readers will have noted, Paterson was only the third MP to have represented this constituency since 1950, and the last time anywhere in this constituency returned a non-Conservative MP was the 1904 Oswestry by-election.

This large Conservative lead was mirrored in this May's elections to Shropshire council, which replaced the county council, North Shropshire council and

Oswestry council in 2009. The Shropshire divisions which make up this constituency (shown in Figure 202) gave 51% to the Conservatives in May, 21% to the Liberal Democrats and 10% to independent candidates; in councillor terms the Conservatives won 21 seats out of a possible 25, with two seats going to the Green Party (who are active in Oswestry town) and two to independent candidates. The Lib Dems have no councillors in this seat, and indeed in May they lost the one seat they were defending (in Wem). The only part of the constituency with a critical mass of Labour votes is the former coalfield villages of St Martin's and Weston Rhyn, but those villages have been placed in different divisions where they are outvoted by more right-wing territory.

So, despite the circumstances of the by-election, you'd think this should be a straightforward enough defence for the new Conservative candidate. Neil Shastri-Hurst, who lives in Birmingham, certainly has an interesting life story from his 38 years: he originally trained as a surgeon, served in the Royal Army Medical Corps, and now works as a barrister.

Labour ran second here in 2019, and they have selected Ben Wood. Aged 26, Wood is a political adviser to the party. He was born and grew up in Oswestry, and his first job was working in the tile department of an Oswestry hardware store. He gives an address in the constituency.

The only other party to save their deposit here in 2019 was the Liberal Democrats, who finished third with 10% of the vote. They have reselected their candidate from last time Helen Morgan, a chartered accountant who lives in the constituency. At the time of writing, she was the bookies' favourite.

Fourth in 2019 were the Green Party. Their candidate is Duncan Kerr, who has appeared in this column before. Kerr first came to my attention in 2011 when he became the first and, so far, the only Green Party member of Bolsover council in Derbyshire. He resigned from Bolsover council in 2013 and shortly afterwards turned up in Oswestry. Kerr was the Green candidate for North Shropshire in 2015, coming within a handful of votes of saving his deposit, and he then contested the Oswestry South by-election to Shropshire council in February 2016.* That by-election was vacated by the Shropshire council leader Keith Barrow after he became caught up in his own scandal over improper business interests; Kerr put the skills he had learnt in Bolsover to good use, and he won the Oswestry South by-election easily. He lost his seat on Shropshire council in 2017, but got it back in May's election.

Keith Barrow may be out of politics now, but his wife Joyce is still a Shropshire councillor (representing St Oswald division, to the south of Oswestry), and his daughter Kirsty Walmsley is standing in this by-election. Kirsty, who was

* *Andrew's Previews 2016*, page 24.

Shropshire council divisions: Cheswardine; Ellesmere Urban; Gobowen, Selattyn and Weston Rhyn; Hodnet; Llanymynech; Market Drayton East; Market Drayton West; The Meres; Oswestry East; Oswestry South; Oswestry West; Prees; Ruyton and Baschurch; St Martin's; St Oswald; Shawbury; Wem; Whitchurch North; Whitchurch South; Whittington
December 2019 result C 35444 Lab 12495 LD 5643 Grn 1790 Shropshire Party 1141
June 2017 result C 33642 Lab 17287 LD 2948 Grn 1722
May 2015 result C 27041 Lab 10457 UKIP 9262 LD 3184 Grn 2575
May 2010 result C 26692 LD 10864 Lab 9406 UKIP 2432 BNP 1667 Grn 808
May 2005 result C 23061 Lab 12041 LD 9175 UKIP 2233
June 2001 result C 22631 Lab 16390 LD 5945 UKIP 1165 Ind 389
May 1997 result C 20730 Lab 18535 LD 10489 Referendum Party 1764

Figure 203: House of Commons, North Shropshire

elected in 2003 as a Conservative member of the former Oswestry council at the age of just 21, now has the nomination of Reform UK.

The five candidates already named occupy the bottom five places on the ballot paper. For a change I'll take the other nine candidates in reverse alphabetical order, so we start with independent candidate Yolande Kenward who has contested Maidstone and the Weald in the last two general elections. The anti-lockdown Freedom Alliance group have nominated Earl Jesse, who gives an address in Berkshire. Howling Laud Hope is back for his umpteenth election campaign as leader of the Official Monster Raving Loony Party. The Heritage Party (a UKIP splinter group led by the former London Assembly member David Kurten) are represented by James Elliot from Preston. If the criterion for winning this election was how far away you live from North Shropshire, then Russell Dean would win hands down; Dean, standing for "The Party Party", lives and works in Monaco where he is a consultant for a yacht broker. Two London-based candidates appear next to each other on the ballot: Martin Daubney is deputy leader of the Reclaim Party led by the actor Laurence Fox; while Drew Galdron, who somehow manages to make money by being a Boris Johnson impersonator, has changed his name for this election to "Boris Been-Bunged" and has the nomination of the Rejoin EU group. Whitchurch parish councillor Andrea Allen, who contested this seat in the 2015 general election and fought the Eddisbury seat in 2019, is the UKIP candidate; and at the top of the ballot is independent candidate Suzie Akers Smith, who was elected in 2019 as an independent member of Cheshire East council.*

* *House of Commons, North Shropshire*: LD 17957 C 12032 Lab 3686 Grn 1738 Reform UK 1427 UKIP 378 Reclaim 375 Loony 118 Akers Smith 95 Heritage Party 79 Rejoin EU 58 Freedom Alliance 57 Party Party 19 Kenward 3 [LD gain from C]

Parliamentary constituency: Rochester and Strood
May 2019 result Lab 1332/1277 C 542/414 Grn 393 UKIP 329 LD 174
May 2015 result Lab 1861/1721 C 1406/1095 UKIP 1209/1039 Grn 560 TUSC 98
May 2011 result Lab 1570/1531 C 833/649 Grn 255 LD 180/98
May 2007 result Lab 1482/1460 C 673/652 Medway Ind 268 UKIP 232
May 2003 result Lab 1050/955 C 682/680 LD 241/209 UKIP 94

Figure 204: Medway, Rochester East

Oh, and just one more thing before I finish with North Shropshire...
...have I mentioned that the Welsh Marches are beautiful?

Rochester East

Medway council, Kent; caused by the death of Labour councillor Nick Bowler.

North Shropshire isn't the only by-election taking place today, as twelve vacancies on Great Britain's local councils will also be filled in polls on 16th December. The Conservatives are defending seven of these, Labour four and independents one.

We'll start with one of the Labour defences, by travelling to the Medway towns. These are all now towns, as a result of Rochester's loss of city status due to an administrative oversight in the 1990s. The Rochester East ward is rather misleadingly named, in that it runs south from the edge of the town centre along the old and new roads towards Maidstone. Your columnist used to go to Rochester every July to play quiz, and I have a rather vague and fuzzy memory of a resulting night out in the Man of Kent within this ward.

This ward is one of the strongest Labour areas in the Medway Towns, and it had returned the Labour slate of Nick Bowler and Teresa Murray at every election this century. Bowler had been first elected in 2000, for the predecessor ward of Troy Town; he also represented that ward from 1997 to 1998 when it was part of the former Rochester upon Medway city council. Nick Bowler was the Mayor of Medway in 2003–04. He was still only 59 when he passed away in October, after a long battle with lung fibrosis.

The last Medway council elections in 2019 gave Bowler's Labour slate 48% of the vote, with the Conservatives on 20% and the Green Party on 14%. There have been no local elections here since, but by-election results in nearby wards since 2019 have seen some good Labour performances.

Defending this seat for Labour is Lauren Edwards, who works as a financial regulator at the Bank of England and has extensive experience as a union rep. The Conservatives, who control Medway council, have selected local resident

Parliamentary constituency: Ashford
Kent county council division: Ashford East
May 2019 result C 290 Ashford Ind 201 Grn 132 LD 82

Figure 205: Ashford, Highfield

and former policeman Brian Griffin. The Green candidate is Bernard Hyde, who stood in 2019 in the neighbouring ward of Rochester South and Horsted. Completing the ballot paper is Sarah Manuel for the Liberal Democrats.*

Highfield

Ashford council, Kent; caused by the death of Conservative councillor Gerald White.

The Conservatives defend our other Kent by-election today, which is an urban ward in the town of Ashford. Highfield ward is the eastern end of Ashford's built-up area, next to the M 20 motorway and the end of the town's southern bypass. It takes in much of the Willesborough area together with an industrial and retail park to the south, which is still part of Sevington parish. The ward does not include one of the most visible dividends of Brexit: the Sevington Inland Border Facility, which has filled a very large field on the far side of the southern bypass. Following boundary changes in 2019, the High Speed 1 line is the southern boundary of Highfield ward.

On its pre-2019 boundaries Highfield ward was in the top 100 wards in England and Wales for those with Level 2 qualifications (5 or more GCSE passes, nothing higher). It had voted in 2003 for the Ashford Independents, for the Lib Dems in 2007, for the Ashford Independents again in 2011 and for the Conservatives in 2015. Gerald White was re-elected for a second term in 2019 on the ward's new boundaries, polling 41% against 29% for the Ashford Independents and 19% for the Green Party.

Looking up to county level only serves to confuse matters. This ward is part of the Ashford East division of Kent county council, which in 2017 voted Lib Dem with 41% of the vote, the Greens finishing last with 5.5%. However, in May this year Ashford East voted Green with 44.5% of the vote, the Lib Dems finishing last with 3%. Quite the turnaround.

Gerald White passed away in October, and if the Conservatives fail to hold the resulting Highfield by-election their majority on Ashford council will be down to one seat. Defending for the party is James Ransley, who runs a carpentry business and is the chairman of Kingsnorth parish council. The Ashford

* *Medway, Rochester East*: Lab 870 C 388 Grn 69 LD 48

Independents' Barry Ball, who runs a construction firm, tries again after his second-place finish two years ago. The Green Party will hope that everybody's talking about their candidate Dawnie Nilsson. Completing the ballot paper is Terry Pavlou, who is the ward's first Labour candidate this century.*

Roffey South

Horsham council, West Sussex; caused by the death of Conservative councillor Roy Cornell.

We make our second trip of the year to Horsham, following Andrew's Previews' visit to the Forest ward by-election in October. That was an easy Liberal Democrat hold; this will be a rather different proposition.

Roffey is a north-eastern suburb of Horsham, along the main road towards Crawley, which has now been absorbed into the town. The Roffey South ward runs in a generally north-easterly direction from the edge of the town centre, with Crawley Road generally being the northern boundary of the ward.

Roffey South ward was left almost untouched by boundary changes introduced for the 2019 election. It has swung rather wildly between the Conservatives and Lib Dems in this century: the ward voted Lib Dem in 2003, split its two seats in 2007, comfortably voted Conservative in 2011 and 2015, then split its two seats again in 2019. On that occasion the Conservatives and Lib Dems both polled 41% of the vote with the remaining 18% going to Labour. Roy Cornell had represented Roffey South in the Conservative interest continuously from 2007 until his death in September.

The ward is split between two divisions of West Sussex county council. Its eastern half is part of St Leonard's Forest division, which is based on the rural area east of Horsham town and is strongly Conservative. Its western half is part of the Horsham East county division, which was a Lib Dem gain from the Conservatives in May.

Defending for the Conservatives is Simon Torn, who was Roy Cornell's partner as councillor for this ward from 2011 until 2019. Torn didn't seek re-election that year. Standing for the Lib Dems is Sam Raby, who runs a small local business; he was the party's candidate for St Leonard's Forest in May's county elections. Labour have selected local resident Daniel Everett, who was also a candidate for West Sussex county council in May: he fought Imberdown division (in the East Grinstead area) on that occasion. Completing the ballot paper is Claire Adcock for the Green Party.†

* *Ashford, Highfield*: Grn 191 C 163 Ashford Ind 101 Lab 23 [Grn gain from C]

† *Horsham, Roffey South*: LD 462 C 335 Grn 222 Lab 95 [LD gain from C]

Parliamentary constituency: Horsham
West Sussex county council division: Horsham East (part), St Leonard's Forest (part)
May 2019 result C 561/532 LD 553/519 Lab 239/225

Figure 206: Horsham, Roffey South

Tilehurst South and Holybrook

West Berkshire council; caused by the death of Conservative councillor Peter Argyle.

For our final by-election in the South East we come to an area which is clearly a western suburb of Reading, and is part of the Reading West parliamentary seat, but has never been incorporated into the town. This is Calcot, located on the A 4—the old road from London to Bath—just outside the Reading borough boundary, but east of the M 4 motorway. The ward's southern boundary is the Berks and Hants railway line, to the north of which lies the Holy Brook: this is a channel of the River Kennet which gets its name from the fact that it was built or improved by the monks at Reading Abbey.

West Berkshire council got new ward boundaries in 2019, and this is a cut-down version of the former Calcot ward with one fewer councillor. Calcot was a safe Conservative ward and so is this one: in May 2019 the Tories enjoyed a 58–25 lead over Labour in Tilehurst South and Holybrook. There have been no local elections here since.

The area provided a secure electoral base for the late Conservative councillor Peter Argyle, who was first elected in 1997 for Theale ward, transferred to Calcot ward in 2003 and ended up here in 2019. He served two terms as chairman of West Berkshire council, in 2011–12 and 2015–16, and was part of the Conservative majority on the council.

The local MP since 2010 has been the Conservatives' Alok Sharma, who currently sits in Cabinet as President of COP26. Sharma may be a Cabinet minister but he has a marginal seat, with a majority over Labour of just over 4,000 votes in December 2019. While it's unlikely that the Conservatives will lose this by-election, the vote shares should be watched closely for an indication of how healthy the local political party branches are.

Defending for the Conservatives is local resident and Holybrook parish councillor Akinbiyi Oloko, a business turnaround specialist whose work has taken him all over the world; his political experience includes service as a special adviser to the governor of Oyo State in Nigeria. Labour have reselected Holybrook parish councillor Charles Croal who stood here in 2019: according to his Twitter he is a "proud Scot with 31 years in Berkshire". Completing the ballot paper is

Parliamentary constituency: Reading West
May 2019 result C 910/865 Lab 395/367 LD 266/206

Figure 207: West Berkshire, Tilehurst South and Holybrook

Steve Bown for the Liberal Democrats.*

Caerau

Bridgend council, Glamorgan; caused by the death of Labour councillor Phil White.

We now travel to the valleys of south Wales. Specifically the Llynfi valley, where the Caerau (or "Forts") ward of Bridgend can be found. This is the head of the Llynfi valley, and the Caerau division contains a number of villages in a mountainous landscape to the north of Maesteg. As with many South Wales valleys, there was very little here before the late nineteenth century: Caerau Colliery operated here from 1889 to 1977, and the villages in this ward were essentially developed to serve the mine and its workers.

The pithead is long gone and the spoil tips have been landscaped, but Caerau Colliery may well have a use yet. The mineworkings are now full of naturally-heated water, and a scheme looking to extract this heat for use by local homes is currently looking for sponsors.

If this idea can be made to work on a large scale—and latest indications are that the money to do that might not be forthcoming— then it could lead to a transformation of what is one of the most deprived parts of Wales. Over half of Caerau's workforce are in working-class occupations, and the figure for "routine" occupations (25.7%, mostly in manufacturing) is the third-highest for any ward in Wales and within the top 25 wards in England and Wales. 14.1% of the workforce are long-term sick or disabled, which is within the top 20 wards in England and Wales. 44.5% have no qualifications, which is in the top 40 wards in England and Wales. 98.8% were born in the UK, which is in the top 15 wards in England and Wales. 98.6% are White British, which is in the top 60 wards in England and Wales. All of these figures are quite typical of remote ex-coalfield areas in the Valleys.

And to this we can add a major and developing scandal over housing. Around 150 houses in Caerau have been badly affected by shoddy home insulation work undertaken in the last decade, which was funded by the Welsh Government's *Arbed* scheme or other energy-efficiency schemes administered by Bridgend

* *West Berkshire, Tilehurst South and Holybrook*: C 548 Lab 387 LD 359

Parliamentary and Senedd constituency: Ogmore
May 2017 result Lab 829/753/753 Ind 575/573/339 PC 319
May 2012 result Lab 1057/1028/764 Ind 756/751
May 2008 result Ind 992/936 Lab 895/822/648
June 2004 result Ind 911/809 Lab 760/633/622 LD 229/165

Figure 208: Bridgend, Caerau

council, the UK government and/or an alliance of energy companies. A survey of 36 homes in the ward which had been improved under those schemes found defects, caused by poor workmanship, in every single one. Nobody seems to want to stump up the money required to make good the damage. The main contractor involved—which has since gone out of business—had as one of its directors Phil White, who was also a Bridgend councillor for Caerau ward and sat on the council's cabinet for a number of years.

Which brings us to Caerau's politics. These are also quite typical of remote ex-coalfield areas in the Valleys, generally being Labour versus Independent contests at local election time. Labour have held all three seats in the ward since 2012, when independent councillors Steve Smith and Kenneth Hunt were defeated. At the last Bridgend council elections in May 2017 Labour polled 48% here, against 33% for independent candidates and 19% for Plaid Cymru. Outgoing Labour councillor Phil John, who is reportedly a victim of the cowboy builders himself, stood for re-election as an independent but lost his seat.

This was against the wider trend in Bridgend, where Labour lost their majority in the 2017 election. That election returned 26 Labour councillors, 13 independents, 11 Conservatives, 3 Plaid members and a Lib Dem. Following a defection Labour are currently running the council as a minority with 24 seats plus this vacancy, four votes short of a majority.

Phil White had served as a ward councillor for Caerau since 2008, and as stated for most of that time he sat on the Bridgend council cabinet. He passed away in October at the age of 67, having contracted COVID-19. His death came before the Adjudication Panel for Wales could finish an investigation into possible code of conduct breaches related to the Caerau housing scandal.

There was just time for a by-election to be held to replace White, which is rather awkward because this ward is due to lose a councillor in next year's elections. Whoever wins this by-election might not serve for very long at all. Defending for Labour is Robert Lewis, who represents Nantyffyllon (part of this ward) on Maesteg town council. There is one independent candidate standing, Chris Davies who lives down the valley in Maesteg; he is chair of the Caerau Men's Shed, a local community group. Kyle Duggan is back for Plaid Cymru after his last-place finish in 2017. Completing the ballot paper is the ward's first Conservative local election candidate, Thomas Dwyer.*

Dawley and Aqueduct

Telford and Wrekin council, Shropshire; caused by the resignation of Labour councillor Concepta Cassar who had served since 2019.

Our two remaining Labour defences of the week are both in the English Midlands. For one of these we are back in Shropshire, this time in the New Town of Telford. Or the New Town of Dawley, as it might have been before the decision was reached to honour Thomas Telford in the new town's name. Dawley was an old town which was mentioned in the Domesday survey, and whose major industry was mining and quarrying: there is coal and ironstone in the rocks below, and clay on top of that. Very little trace of the old industry exists, as the area was extensively landscaped when the New Town was built.

Famous locals associated with Dawley in the pre-New Town era include Matthew Webb, the first man to swim the English Channel, who has a school named after him in the ward; and Edith Pargeter, an author who wrote under a variety of pseudonyms. Her best-known work, published under the name "Ellis Peters", remains the Brother Cadfael murder mysteries set in twelfth-century Shrewsbury. A street in Aqueduct, a village south of Dawley towards Ironbridge, is called "Ellis Peters Close". Pargeter was one of the few people honoured in both the civil and military divisions of the Order of the British Empire, being awarded a civil OBE for services to literature and, half a century earlier, a military BEM for her Second World War service in the Wrens.

The current Dawley and Aqueduct ward dates from 2015 but has the same boundaries as the Dawley Magna ward which existed from 2003 to 2015. Whatever this ward is called, it has a rather high councillor attrition rate: this is the fourth by-election here in 18 years, and the last by-election was only seven months ago.

Dawley Magna voted strongly Labour in 2003, but a by-election at the end of 2006 was lost to the Telford and Wrekin Peoples Association, a now-defunct localist group. The TWPA followed up by gaining all three seats here in 2007, but lost them all back to Labour in 2011. A by-election in 2013 resulted in a strong Labour hold.

This proved to be illusory. The 2015 Telford and Wrekin local elections resulted in Dawley and Aqueduct ward splitting its three seats: Labour held 2,

* *Bridgend, Caerau*: Ind 515 Lab 441 PC 82 C 18 [Ind gain from Lab]

Parliamentary constituency: Telford
May 2021 by-election Lab 1310 C 1192 LD 72
May 2019 result Lab 1212/1157/1030 C 748/725/571
May 2015 result Lab 1820/1630/1492 C 1609/1232/1099 UKIP 1168
(Previous results for Dawley Magna ward)
February 2013 by-election Lab 957 C 379 UKIP 312 Ind 126
May 2011 result Lab 1315/1243/961 C 917 Telford and Wrekin Peoples Assoc 877/785/505
May 2007 result Telford and Wrekin Peoples Association 1220/1033/961 C 648/535/464 Lab 574/526/483
December 2006 by-election Telford and Wrekin Peoples Association 649 Lab 476 C 446
May 2003 result Lab 1522/1488/1268 C 878/844 Socialist Alliance 359/305

Figure 209: Telford and Wrekin, Dawley and Aqueduct

the Conservatives gained 1. Labour easily picked up the Tory seat in 2019, with a 62–38 lead, and the ward is part of the Labour majority on Telford and Wrekin council. However, the last by-election here in May 2021 (page 114) was close again: Labour held the seat, but their lead over the Conservatives was reduced to 51–46.

Can the Conservatives go one better now in what is clearly quite a volatile ward? We shall see. Defending for Labour this time is retired teacher Bob Wennington, who represents Aqueduct on Dawley Hamlets parish council. The Conservatives have reselected Kate Barnes, who was the runner-up in May's by-election; she is also a Dawley Hamlets parish councillor, and she is the assistant headteacher at Madeley Academy. Completing the ballot paper is Catherine Salter for the Lib Dems.*

Pleck

Walsall council, West Midlands; caused by the death of Labour councillor Harbans Singh Sarohi.

We now travel to the heart of the Black Country. The very word "Pleck", with its harsh consonants, suggests a harsh place to live and work. Which may be reasonable given Pleck's location at the heart of the industrial Black Country. Pleck is part of Walsall, which is traditionally the home of the English saddle-manufacturing industry: this hasn't died yet, and one business in Pleck ward (Huskissons) is still making and supplying saddles, harnesses and collars for horses. Ironically, their premises is next door to a large car dealership.

A few hundred metres up the road lies the Walsall Manor Hospital, where most people from Walsall begin and end their days. This is in the Alumwell

* *Telford and Wrekin, Dawley and Aqueduct*: Lab 996 C 735 LD 55

Parliamentary constituency: Walsall South
May 2021 result Lab 2310 C 778
May 2019 result Lab 2123 C 582
May 2018 result Lab 2453 C 609
May 2016 result Lab 2596 C 1062
May 2015 result Lab 3493 C 1436 Grn 547
May 2014 result Lab 1959 C 983 UKIP 590 LD 259 Ind 193
May 2012 result Lab 2137 C 878 Ind 220 LD 215
May 2011 result Lab 2449 C 767 Ind 475 LD 331 Democratic Labour 166
May 2010 result Lab 2340 C 1790 LD 810 UKIP 383 Ind 348
May 2008 result Lab 1241 C 1150 LD 709 Ind 203 UKIP 177
May 2007 result C 1533 Lab 1497 LD 452 UKIP 202 Democratic Labour 58
May 2006 result Lab 1324 C 1202 LD 555 Ind 488 Democratic Labour 92
June 2004 result Lab 1518/1308/1235 C 1338/1183/1101 Ind 800 Democratic Socialist Alliance 371

Figure 210: Walsall, Pleck

district west of Walsall town centre, whereas Pleck proper lies to the south of Alumwell over the Walsall Canal. Pleck's southern and western boundaries are defined by the Grand Junction railway line, the River Tame and the M 6 motorway, which here is on an elevated viaduct. Junction 9 of the M 6 lies at the southern end of Pleck ward, with junction 10 at its north-west corner.

In the 2011 census Pleck made the top 70 wards in England and Wales for those who have never worked or are long-term unemployed (17.7%) and for those who are looking after home or family (9.6%). This is a multi-cultural area, with 45% of the population being of Asian ethnicity and most of the major religions being well represented: in the 2011 census Pleck was 39% Christian, 31% Muslim, and 5.5% for both Hindus and Sikhs.

This adds up to a very safe Labour ward in current political circumstances. In May this year Pleck voted 75% Labour and 25% Conservative—and that was in a year when the Conservatives performed very well in Walsall generally. There is now a large Conservative majority on the council. The Tories did perform much better in Pleck ward during the last Labour government, winning one seat out of three in 2004 and holding it in 2007, but after 2010 their vote faded away here.

Harbans Singh Sarohi, who was in his 80s when he passed away in July after suffering a heart attack, had served continuously for this ward since his first election in 2000. He was the deputy mayor of Walsall at the time of his death, and was in line to become the borough's first Sikh mayor next year. Sarohi was due for re-election next year, so the winner of this by-election will need to get straight back on the campaign trail to seek re-election...

... or not, as the case may be. All Pleck local elections from 2016 onwards have been straight Labour–Conservative fights, and so is this by-election. Unfortunately, Labour have made a total hash of their candidate selection. It has emerged during the campaign that their defending candidate, Simran Kaur Cheema, is disqualified because she was an employee of the council on the day her nomination papers went in. She resigned her employment, but not until the following day. Should Cheema be elected, she will be unable to act as a councillor and the seat will remain vacant until May, because there isn't time to hold a further by-election now before Sarohi's term was due to end. Pleck residents who actually want a councillor to represent them are advised to vote for the only other candidate on the ballot paper, Mohammed Saghir of the Conservatives.*

Armitage with Handsacre

Lichfield council, Staffordshire; caused by the resignation of Conservative councillor Nicholas Binney.

Having discussed the two Labour defences in the Midlands we now turn to two Conservative defences in the Midlands. To start with we come to a ward covering two parishes on the south bank of the River Trent in Staffordshire. Armitage and Handsacre are two large villages located a few miles east of Rugeley, on the West Coast Main Line and the Trent and Mersey Canal.

The ward named after those villages extends east to take in the village of Kings Bromley, on the main road going north from Lichfield; and also runs west to take in some new developments on the edge of Rugeley. This includes part of the site of the former Rugeley B power station, which closed in 2016 and whose cooling towers were demolished earlier this year. For your columnist those cooling towers were always a landmark on a train journey to that London, signalling in my mind the transition point from North to South. I'll miss them.

With the power station gone, the main employer in this ward is now Armitage Shanks, the company which puts its signature on urinals and has made rather more money out of doing that than Marcel Duchamp ever did. Armitage Shanks has been making bathroom fixtures and plumbing supplies in Armitage since 1817.

Armitage with Handsacre is a safe Conservative ward, and at the last Lichfield council elections in 2019 the Conservatives were guaranteed one of its three seats before a vote was cast because only two opposition candidates had come forward. The Tory slate polled 47% against 28% for Labour and 25% for an independent

* *Walsall, Pleck*: Lab 698 C 382

Parliamentary constituency: Lichfield
Staffordshire county council division: Lichfield Rural West
May 2019 result C 850/799/663 Lab 508 Ind 457
May 2015 result C 2017/1917/1828 Lab 1127/1009/1003 Ind 516

Figure 211: Lichfield, Armitage with Handsacre

candidate.* That was a weak Tory performance compared to May's Staffordshire county elections, where the Conservatives led 74–17 in the county division of Lichfield Rural West.

Like Pleck, this by-election is a straight fight; unlike Pleck, we have two validly nominated and qualified candidates. Defending for the Conservatives is Richard Cross, who lives in Armitage. Challenging for Labour is Mark Pritchard, who was their candidate here in May's county elections.†

Nettleham

West Lindsey council, Lincolnshire; caused by the resignation of Conservative councillor Giles McNeill.

For our final Midlands by-election we travel to the wide open spaces of Lincolnshire. The Nettleham ward wraps around the north-east corner of the city of Lincoln, between the A 15 Roman road towards Scunthorpe and the Humber Bridge, and the A 158 running north-east towards Skegness. In between those arrow-straight roads is Nettleham, a large village which was the site of the palace of the Bishops of Lincoln, until the Lincolnshire Rising of 1536 trashed it. Today the ward's economy is based on rather more modern things, including an oil well which operates south of the village.

The ward takes in two other parishes to the west, one of which is Riseholme. This is the home of Riseholme College, an agricultural science college which is part of Lincoln University.

The present Nettleham ward was drawn up for the 2015 election and is a slightly cut-down version of the previous ward (which also included the parish of Greetwell to the east of Lincoln). This area was Liberal Democrat until the Conservatives broke through at a by-election in September 2012. Readers of Andrew's Previews who have extremely long memories will note that the winning Tory candidate was 30-year-old Giles McNeill, who had contested the seat three

* The independent candidate is missing from the 2019 election result shown on the Lichfield council website, and accordingly he was omitted from the original version of this preview. My apologies to him. This paragraph has been rewritten. † *Lichfield, Armitage with Handsacre*: C 458 Lab 301

times previously and had come within nine votes of winning in 2008. At the time he was the youngest member of West Lindsey council.

Ever since that by-election Nettleham has split its two seats between the Conservatives and the Lib Dems. Both the 2015 and the 2019 elections here returned Giles McNeill and Angela White respectively, and they were essentially tied in the 2019 election: McNeill polled 635 votes, White 632 for the Lib Dems.

Following the 2019 election McNeill became leader of West Lindsey council. He was a fan of Andrew's Previews and he has provided your columnist with information on some later by-elections in the West Lindsey district. In the interests of full disclosure, he has not been in touch with me about this one.

Unfortunately, it turns out that I should have been filing McNeill's occasional communications in the Councillors Behaving Badly file. The Gainsborough branch of the Conservative party appointed a new treasurer in 2019, and it quickly became clear that something was wrong. Quite a lot of money had disappeared. The police were called.

In September 2020 McNeill announced that he was stepping down as council leader, and also leaving the Conservative group on the council. Shortly afterwards, he was arrested on fraud charges: he faced six counts of fraud, one count of theft and one count of forging signatures on 93 cheques.

The case came before Lincoln magistrates in September 2021, with McNeill pleading guilty to all charges. The court heard that between 2014 and 2020 McNeill had defrauded the local Conservative associations and members to the tune of almost £30,000, and he had used the money to fund a gambling addiction. The case was sent to Lincoln crown court for sentencing, and McNeill is now serving a fourteen-month prison sentence. He submitted his resignation from the council in October, between the guilty plea and the sentencing hearing.

The 2019 election returned a Conservative majority of 2 on West Lindsey council, with 19 Tories, 12 Lib Dems and 5 independents. One of the Conservative councillors has since gone independent wiping out the party's majority, and if this by-election is lost the Tories will be in a minority on the council. However, there are enough Conservative-supporting independents that this is unlikely to make any practical difference. While the district by-election looks a difficult defence, the local Conservatives can take heart from the fact that they had a big lead in the local county division (Nettleham and Saxilby) in May, and by the fact that their income isn't being siphoned off to feed someone else's gambling habit any more.

Defending for the Conservatives is Maureen Palmer, who was McNeill's running-mate in the 2015 election here. Palmer has also appeared in this column before: she won a 2016 by-election in the neighbouring ward of Cherry Willing-

Parliamentary constituency: Gainsborough
Lincolnshire county council division: Nettleham and Saxilby
May 2019 result C 635/506 LD 632/580
May 2015 result C 1337/984 LD 1064/983

Figure 212: West Lindsey, Nettleham

ham*, but lost her seat in 2019. The Lib Dems have selected Jaime Oliver; she founded the Nettleham Community Hub in 2015. In a break to Nettleham's two-party duopoly, also standing are Benjamin Loryman for the Green Party and Jess McGuire for Labour.†

North Ormesby

Middlesbrough council, North Yorkshire; caused by the resignation of independent councillor Ashley Waters.

We now travel north to another area which, like Nettleham, Andrew's Previews last visited in September 2012. There the similarities end.

If you were asked to visualise the most run-down Victorian housing imaginable, you might end up with a mental image which looks not unlike North Ormesby. As with much of Middlesbrough, this area was effectively a late-Victorian new town built for workers at the Middlesbrough docks just to the north. We're less than a mile to the east of the town centre here, and only a few hundred yards away from the shining Riverside Stadium of Middlesbrough FC.

Middlesbrough is the centre of a conurbation which was based on heavy industry, and which is looking for a new future with the decline of heavy industry. The census stats bear this out. In 2011 the ward of North Ormesby and Brambles Farm had the eleventh-highest unemployment rate (12.5%) of any ward in England and Wales. For those who had jobs, the employment profile was extremely working-class: the ward was in the top 90 for "routine occupations" (23.8%) and in the top 70 for those who have never worked or are long-term unemployed. The entire ward hovers very close to the bottom of the deprivation indices. Despite some spectacularly cheap house prices—in October 2017 the average house here was reported to be worth just £36,000—a lot of residents have upped sticks and left for somewhere where they can get a job, leading to significant depopulation. The council's response to this has simply been to demolish a fair chunk of the ward's housing.

North Ormesby was split off from the Brambles Farm estate in 2015 to be-

* *Andrew's Previews 2016*, page 210. † *West Lindsey, Nettleham*: LD 585 C 374 Lab 116 Grn 71 [LD gain from C]

Parliamentary constituency: Middlesbrough
May 2019 result Ind 371 Lab 142 C 17
May 2015 result Lab 389 Ind 314 C 74

Figure 213: Middlesbrough, North Ormesby

come a ward of its own. Its first election returned a Labour councillor, but that changed in 2019. The 2019 election in Middlesbrough was dominated by independent candidate Andy Preston, who won the town's elected mayoralty in a landslide; and a large number of independent councillors were elected on Preston's coat-tails. The latest available composition has 24 independent members of Middlesbrough council (plus this vacancy) against 18 Labour and 3 Conservatives; the independents are divided into three groups on the council with varying degrees of support for and opposition to Mayor Preston. It's really quite hard for an outsider to keep track of what is going on in the Boro.

The North Ormesby ward was carried by the independent tide in May 2019, with independent candidate Ashley Waters defeating the incumbent Labour councillor by the wide margin of 70–27. Waters subsequently joined Mayor Preston's cabinet with the regeneration portfolio, something rather important to his constituents.

In January this year it emerged that Ashley Waters was living and working in France, where he was regenerating the ruined 18th-century Château de Lalacelle in Normandy, along with his partner and his partner's parents. They plan to turn the château into an upmarket bed-and-breakfast. He wasn't exactly being discreet about this: the team had posted a number of videos on the internet detailing their progress on the renovation. Waters had continued to attend council meetings online from France.

Andrew's Previews has covered a number of similar cases recently. In this column's opinion, if *everybody* is dialling into council meetings remotely—as was happening until May this year for pandemic-related reasons—then really it doesn't make much difference whether you're dialling in to Middlesbrough council meetings from Normandy or Normanby. However, once council meetings went back in-person from May, that no longer applied. Waters came under mounting criticism for his absences from Middlesbrough, and in November he resigned as councillor for North Ormesby to spend more time at his French château.

I never expected to write the words "North Ormesby" and "French château" in the same sentence.

One independent candidate has come forward to replace Waters: he is Mark Horkan, a volunteer with the White Feather Project which helps local people in food poverty. Horkan is associated with the Middlesbrough Independent Group, the larger of the council's two main independent factions. The Labour candidate is Nicky Gascoigne, another charity volunteer who lives in the ward and has recently graduated from Teesside University. Also standing are Val Beadnall for the Conservatives and Ian Jones for the Liberal Democrats.*

Hexham East

Northumberland council; caused by the resignation of Conservative councillor Cath Homer.

For our final English by-election of the week we travel to the Tyne valley and the town which, last month, was voted by the property website Rightmove as the happiest place to live in Britain. The history of Hexham goes back to the 7th century, when Hexham Abbey was founded by St Wilfrid; the present Abbey building dates from the 11th and 19th centuries, but the crypt of Wilfrid's monastery still survives. The town's major industry in the 18th and 19th centuries was the manufacture of leather gloves; today the Egger chipboard factory is a major employer, while the town's location and good transport links to Newcastle and Carlisle mean that it is a good base for tourism in western Northumberland. Hadrian's Wall is only a few miles to the north.

The town gives its name to a parliamentary seat which has been in Conservative hands continuously since 1924, with the exception of 1943–51 when Hexham's MP Douglas Clifton Brown was the Speaker of the Commons. It is divided between three divisions of Northumberland council. Hexham East covers about half of Hexham's urban area, with landmarks including the town's general hospital, the Old Gaol (dating from the fourteenth century and one of the first purpose-built prisons in England) and the Moot Hall, a well-preserved mediaeval courthouse.

Hexham East division has been in Conservative hands for many years as well. Cath Homer was first elected as the division's councillor in 2013 in what was then a very safe Conservative seat. The Conservatives finished one seat short of a majority on Northumberland council in the 2017 election, and Homer served as the Northumberland cabinet member for culture, arts, leisure and tourism until the summer of 2020.

At that point Northumberland council was rocked by a scandal, in which the chief executive was suspended after blowing the whistle on alleged wrongdoing by the then council leader Peter Jackson. Homer resigned from the cabinet,

* *Middlesbrough, North Ormesby*: Lab 172 Ind 32 C 20 LD 7

Parliamentary constituency: Hexham
May 2021 result C 687 LD 557 Lab 323
May 2017 result C 941 LD 218 Lab 206 Grn 68
May 2013 result C 623 Lab 300 UKIP 207 LD 205
May 2008 result C 903 Lab 223 LD 203
May 2005 Northumberland county council result C 1064 Lab 636 LD 491

Figure 214: Northumberland, Hexham East

indicating that she would comply with independent investigations which were going on. Jackson was subsequently no-confidenced by the council.

In the May 2021 Northumberland elections it appears that the Lib Dems had a go at Hexham East, and they sharply cut the Conservative majority here. Shares of the vote were 44% for the Conservatives, 36% for the Liberal Democrats and 21% for Labour. Cath Homer resigned from the council six months later, citing social media abuse; however, the local press have also reported that her behaviour may have breached the council's code of conduct.

Which gives us a crucial by-election. If the Northumberland Conservatives lose this seat, their majority on Northumberland council will go with it. The council currently has 33 Conservative members plus this vacancy, against 21 Labour, 7 independents, 3 Lib Dems and 2 Greens.

Defending for the Conservatives is Stephen Ball, a Hexham town councillor who has twice served as deputy mayor of the town. Ball was appointed MBE in the 2021 Birthday Honours for services to mental health charities. The Liberal Democrats have reselected their candidate from May, Suzanne Fairless-Aitken. The Labour candidate is Jonathan Wheeler, a GMB union steward and town councillor in Prudhoe, down the Tyne valley. Completing the ballot paper is Hexham town councillor and writer Lee Williscroft-Ferris, who is standing as an independent candidate.*

Lomond North

Argyll and Bute council, Scotland; caused by the resignation of Conservative councillor Barbara Morgan.

We now come to what will be the penultimate by-election of this Scottish local council term. There is one more poll to come in January, and then that will be it until the next Scottish local elections in May.

It's back to the Highlands for this one, as we come to a ward on the deeply-indented Argyll coast which is dominated by the military. The Lomond North

* *Northumberland, Hexham East*: LD 584 C 370 Lab 154 Ind 127 [LD gain from C]

ward includes the naval bases at Faslane (on Gare Loch) and Coulport (on Loch Long), which together form the home of the Royal Navy's submarine fleet and the British nuclear deterrent.

Before the Navy took over this area, Coulport was a favoured location for wealthy Glasgow merchants who had holiday homes here. Coulport was the original home of the Kibble Palace, a large glasshouse which now stands in the Glasgow Botanic Gardens; the Kibble Palace was named after John Kibble, who commissioned it. There were similar large villas further down the Rosneath peninsula in Cove and Kilcreggan, which were easily accessible from Glasgow by steamer. Even now Kilcreggan's railhead is Gourock, on the far side of the Firth of Clyde, to which there is a regular passenger ferry connection.

The Lomond North ward runs north and east from Roseneath and Garelochhead to take in much of the western bank of Loch Lomond, the village of Arrochar at the head of Loch Long and the mountain pass at Rest and be Thankful. Nearly all of that area is part of the Loch Lomond and the Trossachs National Park. Although it is often impassable in winter, the Rest and be Thankful is the only link between this area and the Argyll and Bute council offices in Lochgilphead.

Lochgilphead was formerly the home of Argyll county council, but until the 1970s almost all of Lomond North ward was part of Dunbartonshire rather than Argyll. For Scottish Parliament purposes, this ward is still part of the Dumbarton constituency.

Following the 2021 Holyrood elections Dumbarton remains one of a handful of constituencies to have voted Labour at every Scottish Parliament election. However, there are very few Labour voters in Lomond North ward. The first election to this ward, in 2007, returned three independent candidates: Billy Petrie, Danny Kelly and George Freeman. In 2012 Petrie retired, Freeman was re-elected at the top of the poll, Kelly lost his seat and the two new councillors were Maurice Corry of the Conservatives and independent Robert MacIntyre. On both occasions, the SNP finished as runner-up.

The Nationalists finally broke through here in May 2017, defeating MacIntyre. Top of the poll was the new Conservative candidate Barbara Morgan, who polled 29% of the first preferences and was elected on the first count. The SNP's Iain Paterson polled 20%, George Freeman was re-elected with 17%, independent candidate Fiona Baker was runner-up with 12%, and MacIntyre was eliminated in fifth place with 11%.

The Argyll and Bute elections that year returned 11 SNP councillors, 10 independents, 9 Conservatives and 6 Lib Dems. An anti-SNP coalition, with the pretentious title of "The Argyll, Lomond and the Islands Group", is running

Parliamentary constituency: Argyll and Bute
Scottish Parliament constituency: Dumbarton
May 2017 first preferences C 989 SNP 678 Ind 587 Ind 407 Ind 359 Lab 212 LD 133
May 2012 first preferences Ind 847 C 544 SNP 406 Lab 376 Ind 358 ind 237 Ind 129
May 2007 first preferences Ind 794 Ind 734 Ind 616 SNP 557 C 484 LD 395

Figure 215: Argyll and Bute, Lomond North

the council.

Barbara Morgan resigned for personal reasons in October, a month before the six-month rule was due to kick in. Accordingly, there is just time for a by-election to replace her. If we rerun the 2017 count for a single vacancy then Morgan comes out on top, with a lead of 1,304 to 1,275 votes over George Freeman; so the Tories can go into this by-election with some confidence.

All four candidates in this by-election are based on the Rosneath peninsula. Defending for the Conservatives is Paul Collins, who lives and runs a business in Rosneath itself. You cannot count out independents here, and there are two of them standing in this by-election. Mark Irvine, the husband of the *Antiques Road Trip* and *Bargain Hunt* expert Roo Irvine, is a businessman from Kilcreggan; while Rosneath resident Robert MacIntyre, who lost his seat here in 2017, is seeking to resume a very long local government career which started with his election to the former Helensburgh Landward District Council in 1968. Completing the ballot paper is Ken Smith, a quantity surveyor from Clynder, who was the runner-up here in 2012; he stands again for the Scottish National Party. Remember the usual Scottish disclaimers: Votes at 16 and the Alternative Vote apply here.*

* *Argyll and Bute, Lomond North*: first preferences C 742 SNP 459 Irvine 418 MacIntyre 204; top 3 C 786 Irvine 494 SNP 489; final C 805 Irvine 711

23rd December 2021

Before we start this week, this column would also like to send best wishes to the staff involved in last week's by-election count for Telford and Wrekin, at which results were declared for the Dawley and Aqueduct by-election and a separate by-election to Dawley Hamlets parish council. Following the declarations, I regret to report that count staff were attacked by a group of men while leaving the count in Dawley Town Hall, and the ballot papers from the parish council by-election were stolen. The incident took place at around 11:50pm on Thursday; anybody who may have witnessed anything relating to the incident is asked to contact West Mercia Police.

There is one by-election on 23rd December 2021 to finish the year off...

Bransgore and Burley

New Forest council, Hampshire; caused by the resignation of Conservative councillor Mark Steele.

For the last council by-election of 2021 we have come to the New Forest National Park. The New Forest isn't all trees: the word "Forest" in the name is used in its mediaeval sense of royal hunting territory, which encompassed both woodland and heathland. It's in this heathland that we can find the village of Burley, located to the east of Ringwood around 13 miles north-east of Bournemouth.

Just outside the National Park boundary is Bransgore, whose eponymous parish includes a number of villages just outside Christchurch: Neacroft, Waterditch and Hinton are all part of this ward. Christchurch used to be part of Hampshire, but it was transferred to Dorset in the 1974 reorganisation. As part of that reorganisation the new Hampshire–Dorset boundary was drawn through the middle of what was then Christchurch East parish, and Bransgore parish is the part of that area which remained in Hampshire. The ward includes Hinton Admiral railway station on the northern edge of Christchurch's built-up area; not far from the station is the Office Field Solar Farm, which has been generating electricity for the National Grid (in sunnier months than December) since 2013.

This ward was drawn up for the 2003 election to New Forest council, which is one of England's largest two-tier districts by population. The council area is not as rural as it looks at first sight. As well as the Forest itself, the district takes in the towns of Ringwood and Lymington, the Southampton suburb of Totton and a densely-populated and industrial area on the western bank of Southampton Water.

Bransgore and Burley is one of the few genuinely-rural wards in the New Forest district, and it has returned Conservative councillors at every election this century. In 2019 the Conservative slate was opposed here only by a single Labour candidate, who lost 72–28. The ward is part of the Brockenhurst division of Hampshire county council, which isn't much less safe; and it's part of the New Forest West parliamentary seat represented by COVID sceptic Sir Desmond Swayne. Swayne lives in this ward, and he has signed the nomination papers of the Conservative candidate for this by-election. His partner in the awkward squad Sir Christopher Chope, the MP for the neighbouring seat of Christchurch, is also an elector in this ward.

This by-election is one from the Councillors Behaving Badly file, although I should stress right at the beginning that the resigning councillor Mark Steele is *not* the one behaving badly. Steele was first elected in this ward in 2015, and he served on the council's cabinet with the partnering and leisure portfolio.

At the time the leader of the council was Barry Rickman of the Conservatives, who had taken on the top job in 2008. Rickman served in that post for over twelve years, before being brought down by a scandal over his business affairs. For those readers who think politics is a dumpster fire at the moment, well...in the case of Rickman, that almost literally happened.

Along with his brother Robert, Barry Rickman owned a scrapyard in Sway, within the New Forest National Park, which was in the business of breaking up and disposing of old cars. Following a complaint that burning was taking place on the site, the police and the Environment Agency found that Rickman's scrapyard was operating without the necessary environmental permits. The Environment Agency launched a prosecution.

In March 2021 the Rickmans appeared before Southampton magistrates and pleaded guilty to one charge each under the Environmental Permitting (England and Wales) Regulations 2016. The district judge delayed sentencing to allow them the opportunity to clean the site up; after a number of missed deadlines for doing this the Rickmans were eventually sentenced in November. Councillor Barry Rickman, who was not involved in the day-to-day running of the scrapyard, was fined £2000 plus costs for knowingly permitting the operation of an illegal

Parliamentary constituency: New Forest West
Hampshire county council division: Brockenhurst
May 2019 result C 1002/964 Lab 385
May 2015 result C 2386/1805 Grn 740 Lab 464
December 2014 by-election C 834 UKIP 171 Lab 74
May 2011 result C 1789/1539 LD 536 Lab 386
May 2007 result C 1335/1164 Ind 888 LD 430
May 2003 result C 961/886 Ind 880 LD 678

Figure 216: New Forest, Bransgore and Burley

waste site; Robert received a four-month suspended sentence for operating the site. Both of them have been also ordered by the court to remove all remaining cars and waste from the land within 12 months.

Following Barry Rickman's guilty plea he resigned as leader of New Forest council, and he was subsequently kicked out of the ruling Conservative group. The new council leader, Edward Heron, then proposed that Rickman be removed as one of the council's representatives on the New Forest National Park Authority.

This plan was opposed by Mark Steele, who went so far as to make a complaint to the council's monitoring officer that Heron was seeking to bully him into voting for Rickman's removal. The monitoring officer rejected the complaint, following which Steele resigned from the council.

That leaves us with a tasty by-election to take us into the Christmas break, although the form book says this should be an easy win for the new Conservative candidate Sarah Howard. She is fighting her first election campaign, and she is a professional chef and member of the Royal Academy of Culinary Arts. The only other party to stand here last time was Labour, whose candidate James Swyer works for the Game and Wildlife Conservation Trust. Outgoing councillor Steele has signed the nomination papers for independent candidate Richard Frampton, a farmer and cider maker who has previously sat both as a Conservative and as a Liberal Democrat member of New Forest council: Frampton, then with the Conservative nomination, won a by-election here in December 2014 and served this ward until 2019. Completing the ballot paper is Lucy Bramley for the Green Party.*

As stated, this is the last council by-election of 2021. But fear not! It's Christmas, and as a Christmas bonus we have a ghost story to tell you: the by-election that never was...

* *New Forest, Bransgore and Burley*: Ind 617 Grn 459 C 258 Lab 59 [Ind gain from C]

CHRISTMAS BONUS TRACK: Paisley Southeast

Renfrewshire council, Scotland; caused by... er...

We finish for the year in Scotland's largest town. This is Paisley, which despite having a population approaching 80,000 has never had city status. Instead this is an old industrial town to the west of Glasgow, with the traditional industry here being textiles. The town gave its name to the Paisley pattern, a teardrop-shaped textile design which Renfrewshire council has adopted as its logo.

The Paisley Southeast ward is a suburban area running along the main road towards Barrhead. It includes the conservation area of Thornly Park and part of the postwar housing estate of Glenburn. The ward also includes Dykebar Hospital, a secure psychiatric unit. It is represented on Renfrewshire council by three councillors: Marie McGurk of the SNP, Eddie Devine of Labour, and independent councillor Paul Mack.

Paul Mack does not come across from press reports as a particularly nice person. Way back in 1994 he was forced to resign as deputy leader of the Labour group on the former Renfrew district council, after being found guilty of assaulting his ex-girlfriend and causing a breach of the peace. The *Herald*'s press report* records that Paisley Sheriff Court fined him £200, after Mack's lawyer told the sheriff that the guilty verdict would have serious repercussions, including "the end of his political career."

Not so. In fact Mack became leader of Renfrewshire council, which shortly afterwards replaced Renfrew district council as part of the 1990s Scottish reorganisation. However, he was subsequently expelled from the Labour party in the controversy following the 1997 suicide of the Paisley South MP Gordon McMaster, who had named Mack (along with a number of other Renfrewshire Labour politicians, including the neighbouring MP Tommy Graham) in his suicide note. Mack lost his seat in the 1999 council elections and didn't get back until 2012, when he was elected as an independent councillor for Paisley South ward. He transferred to the successor Paisley Southeast ward in 2017.

Mack was rather lucky to be re-elected on that occasion. Paisley South was a four-seat ward, but Paisley Southeast only has three councillors, which meant he needed to put together 25% of the vote to secure re-election rather than 20% as previously. On first preferences the SNP led with 37%, Labour polled 27%, the Conservatives 15% and Mack started in fifth place in the count with 14%, 16 votes behind the second SNP candidate. The SNP (ex-Lib Dem figure Marie

* `tinyurl.com/2p8dw3vr`

McGurk) and Labour (Eddie Devine) had a safe seat each, but on those figures the final seat would be difficult to call.

In the event the SNP failed to balance their candidates, and after Mack picked up transfers from Labour the second SNP candidate was eliminated 17 votes behind Mack and 37 votes behind the Conservatives. Mack then picked up the SNP transfers to beat the Conservatives for the final seat rather easily. If Mack had been eliminated instead of the SNP, his transfers would probably have elected the Conservative candidate although it's difficult to be certain about this.

Readers of this column in recent months will have noted a large number of entries in the Councillors Behaving Badly file, some of which I shall touch on in the next section. There used to be a national tribunal in England for ruling on complaints against councillors' behaviour, but the Standards Board for England and its associated Adjudication Panel disappeared in the Coalition's bonfire of the quangos. However its Scottish equivalent, the Standards Commission for Scotland, still exists.

The Standards Commission for Scotland must by now be sick of the sight of Paul Mack. In October 2016 they suspended him from Renfrewshire council's Education and Policy Board for three months for offensive behaviour in a council meeting. In October 2017 they suspended him from all Renfrewshire council meetings for seven months for further offensive behaviour in a council meeting.

In September 2020 Mack's case came before the Standards Commission again. This time they disqualified him from public office until February 2022 for "behaving repeatedly in an unwarranted and offensive manner towards two other councillors, as well as to the Chief Executive and other officers". The Commission found that he had run a long and relentless hate campaign against his Labour ward colleague Eddie Devine, and had also made offensive and demeaning remarks about Conservative councillor Alistair Mackay. I won't go into the details here, but the Standards Commission have set out all the complaints made in their eventual decision notice*.

The document I've referenced in the footnote was not the first decision by the the Standards Commission in this case. Their panel reached that original decision in Councillor Mack's absence, having been advised during their deliberations that Mack was unable to attend because he was isolating as a close contact of someone who had tested positive for COVID. Mack appealed against the panel's decision, and in February 2021 Paisley Sheriff Court ruled that the Commission was wrong to proceed without Mack present. He was reinstated as a councillor and the case was sent back to the Standards Commission for re-hearing.

Following a fresh hearing, held online in May 2021, the Standards Com-

* tinyurl.com/4ch5awws

mission for Scotland disqualified Paul Mack as a councillor again, this time for 14 months until September 2022. Again, Mack was not present at the hearing. Again, he appealed. This time Paisley Sheriff Court rejected his appeal.

By now we were in October 2021, over a year after the initial disqualification, and Renfrewshire council jumped at the chance to finally rid themselves of Mack. There was just time to hold a by-election, and a polling date of Tuesday 14th December 2021 was quickly announced. Six candidates were nominated: Bruce Macfarlane for the SNP, Jamie McGuire for Labour, Alec Leishman for the Conservatives, Kyle Mitchell for the Greens, John Craft for the Lib Dems and Duncan Grant for the Libertarian Party. Polling stations were booked, and postal votes were sent out. Thousands of pounds of council taxpayers' money was spent: the latest estimate is £15,823 with one large invoice from Royal Mail still to come in. Democracy costs money, you know.

And then it all went wrong. On 25th November, three weeks before polling day, Renfrewshire council cancelled the by-election. It appears that the returning officer had overlooked that Mack still had the option of appealing his disqualification to the Court of Session, and Mack has done just that. After taking legal advice, the returning officer concluded that the poll could not safely go ahead. And there won't be time for another by-election now, because the May 2022 Scottish local elections are just around the corner.

This news came through too late to be included in the 25th November 2021 edition of Andrew's Previews, which by coincidence included two other cases where by-elections have been affected, or potentially affected, by dubious council legal advice. On that occasion I had a go at Wigan council for first accepting an invalid resignation and having to call off a by-election in 2018, then trying not to accept a valid resignation three years later *from the same councillor*. There was also the Peter Little case in Allerdale. To quote from what I wrote about the Little case four weeks ago (page 520):

> Workington magistrates... sentenced Peter Little to six weeks in prison for the threatening communication *and* activated [a previous] 12-week suspended sentence for... public order offences, the two sentences to run consecutively.
>
> You can't really blame the Allerdale council staff for wanting to get Little off their council as soon as possible. The council added 6 weeks and 12 weeks together, noticed that the sum came to more than the 13-week threshold, and promptly pronounced him to be disqualified. A by-election was just as promptly called to replace him.

I will admit to having some concern when I heard what Allerdale council had done there. The worrying word in the above quote is "promptly". Yes, the Local

Government Act 1972 does provide that councillors sentenced to three months' imprisonment (including suspended sentences) are disqualified. However, as this column has pointed out on a number of occasions, the disqualification doesn't kick in until the time for appealing against the conviction or sentence expires. Little had three weeks to appeal against sentence; but Allerdale council pronounced him to be disqualified, and published a Notice of Vacancy, on 20th October just two days after his sentencing hearing. On this occasion, it would appear that they got away with it and the passage of time means that Little is definitely disqualified now.

Back in Paisley, Paul Mack is still a Renfrewshire councillor. Depending how quickly the Court of Session get around to his appeal, he might still be eligible to stand in the May 2022 local elections. This column will keep an eye on matters and report back if there are further developments in Renfrewshire. But that will be a job for next year.

Review of the Year

"The same procedure as last year, Miss Sophie?"

Thus ends the busiest year on record for Andrew's Previews, and as usual I will sign off for 2021 with some personal notes and votes of thanks to conclude the year. It's time to toast the new year, bid farewell to the old, and wonder whether the change of year will herald an improvement.

Well, on the face of it 2021 was certainly better than the unmitigated catastrophe which was 2020. In 2020 this column talked about just thirty-six polls, and when I wrote this piece last year I was looking at a list running to over 260 vacancies in our local councils. There was no plan to fill those vacancies except to wait for May's local elections.

A year on, the backlog has been caught up. A quick countup reveals that Bransgore and Burley is the 450th council by-election or postponed poll which Andrew's Previews has covered this year. This is a record, by quite a long way.

Also in this column in 2021 we brought to you the context for six Parliamentary Specials, in Hartlepool, Airdrie and Shotts, Chesham and Amersham, Batley and Spen, Old Bexley and Sidcup, and North Shropshire; four council governance referendums, in Newham, Sheffield, Tower Hamlets and Croydon*; and two Police and Crime Commissioner Specials, in Wiltshire and North Yorkshire.

* The Croydon mayoral referendum was not actually covered in Andrew's Previews at the time, but a note on its result has been written for this book: see page 417.

It has all added up to a enormous amount of work. The research time involved in producing this year's Previews has come to hundreds if not thousands of hours. The source files in my archives for this year come to around two million keystrokes. No wonder my laptop looks knackered.

And that just represented the attention I gave, as an interested observer, to the 450 local by-elections and all the rest of the polls this year. Those local by-elections attracted 1,889 candidates between them; the six parliamentary by-elections had 73 candidates nominated, and there were ten candidates in the two Police and Crime Commissioner by-elections. The vast majority of these candidates will have put some sort of effort into and spent some money on their campaign. Across all these elections, millions of votes were cast.

But all this pales in comparison with the effort put in by your local council's electoral services team to keep this show on the road for your benefit. This column is forever in their debt, and I cannot thank them enough. Those small teams, who might not be well-paid or even full-time, who maintain the electoral register all year round; who have to negotiate with school and venue operators, ballot paper printers and Royal Mail for every May's local elections and for any other polls which may turn up at unexpected times; who book, train and equip staff and polling stations; who organise counts, declare a winner and sort out all the paperwork. They have to get it right, every time. Let's be clear that the failures I have mentioned in this week's column are rare exceptions, and it's an enormous tribute to the professionalism of our electoral services that so few problems are reported with our electoral processes. Thank you.

This particularly applies to a local election on the scale of May 2021, which I hope I never see the like of again. The whole of Great Britain went to the polls, with most voters having multiple ballot papers to juggle. In exceptional cases, up to five polls were taking place simultaneously. The counting took four days to finish.

But it's these same hardworking electoral professionals who are under direct threat from the Department of Vacuous Slogans, Housing and Communities. Our electoral services teams are employed and paid by our local councils, for which a decade of austerity is apparently not enough cuts if rumours are to be believed. Rumours abound of further reorganisations, which would inevitably result in what is already the most remote local government in Europe becoming even more remote. It would also inevitably result in redundancies in our electoral service teams, in the loss of knowledge and experience, at the same time as they are called on to perform more functions as more and more posts become subject to election. This column has not forgotten what happened in Newcastle-under-Lyme in June 2017, which was a clear demonstration that loss of knowledge and experience has the potential to put our elections in danger. And we would all suffer from that.

I wrote in last year's review that "at some point the madness has to stop". Oh no. 2021 was a year when the madness and weirdness of local government was on full display.

It's such a shame that there was no column upon which I could hang a timely dissection of that infamous Handforth Parish Council Planning and Environment Committee meeting when it went viral in February, but the Previews did come back to Handforth in September to see what the fallout was. To cut a long story short, John Smith—the sane councillor in the video—is now running the show and the badly-behaved councillors have all resigned now. The last of them to go was Brian "you have no authority, Jackie Weaver" Tolver. This column doesn't cover parish or town council by-elections, but it would be rude not to note that the by-election to replace Tolver is taking place today in Handforth's South ward.

In May we brought you the by-election for Chessington South ward in Kingston upon Thames, where the Official Monster Raving Loony Party put up thirteen candidates in a feat which really should have won them the Turner Prize. In the summer heatwave of July, one presiding officer decided to use their initiative in the hot weather to set up a polling station in the open air of a school playground.

Only last week an attempt by the Conservatives and independents to depose an SNP administration on Moray council failed in bizarre circumstances. The vote was tied, and the convenor decided to draw lots to resolve the tie. Representatives of the two sides cut a pack of cards. The SNP ended up with the higher card (the jack of spades) and remain in control of the council.

We also had rather a lot of Councillors (and Other Elected Representatives) Behaving Badly. As well as the ones already covered in the Christmas Bonus Track above, in July we told you of the story of the South Tyneside councillor who resigned "by mistake", after being repeatedly disciplined by the council for being an idiot on social media. In August we had the Wiltshire Police and Crime Commissioner election, which had to be rerun after the Conservatives put up a candidate in May who was disqualified from being a PCC; last week Labour did the same thing at a by-election in Walsall. In September we told the tale of the South Tyneside councillor who was disqualified after being given a suspended sentence for carrying a knife into a court building, which he was attending to answer a drink-driving charge. In November we had the by-election to replace the North Yorkshire Police and Crime Commissioner who caused outrage with his comments on the Sarah Everard murder. In December we reported on the Conservative councillor who was forced to resign after being revealed to be a supporter of a far-right white nationalist group. And that's without even mentioning the Owen Paterson case.

The madness doesn't just end there, of course. Every Thursday when the column goes out, my Twitter lights up. And when the results come in of a Thursday night, the level of outrage from whoever is on the losing side this week is something to behold.

There are, of course, kinder people out there both on the Twitter and in real life. Professor Michael Thrasher, who has been writing about local elections since before I was a lad, was kind enough to describe Andrew's Previews as "wonderful reports" to an online meeting I attended. The European edition of *Politico*[*] were kind enough to spend time profiling me in April, in advance of the local elections, and I also found myself giving an interview to Talk Radio as the results came in. In addition, I was very grateful to see this endorsement earlier this month, from the Twitter of political scientist Paula Surridge:

> Reading the tea-leaves on Westminster by elections is dangerous, for local by elections even more so, but you won't find a better way to engage in this dangerous behaviour than by following these previews.

Paula Surridge has a book out at the moment, and *The British General Election of 2019* is firmly on your columnist's Christmas list. I'm eagerly waiting to read it.

Looking forward to 2022, next year's local election festival of democracy is scheduled for Thursday 5th May. It won't be as complicated as this year's. On that day we will have polls for the elected mayoralties of South Yorkshire, Hackney, Lewisham, Newham, Tower Hamlets and Watford, the inaugural mayoral election in Croydon, local elections for all councillors in London, Scotland and Wales, polls in those English districts which renew a third or a half of their council at each election, votes for some form of new unitary structure in Cumbria, North Yorkshire and Somerset, and the next scheduled election to the Northern Ireland Assembly. The English local elections are mostly to renew councillors elected in May 2018, an election which was very close between Theresa May's Conservatives and Jeremy Corbyn's Labour; the last Scottish and Welsh local elections were in May 2017, while the current Stormont Assembly was elected at a snap poll in March 2017 following the Renewable Heat Incentive scandal.

Before then we have the last piece of electoral business which has been delayed by the pandemic: the next scheduled elections to the Corporation of the City of London, for which polling will take place on Thursday 24th March. These elections were postponed by a year from March 2021, due to the work-from-home

[*] `tinyurl.com/2p9ct5ah`

lockdown advice causing havoc with the City's business-heavy franchise rules. There will also be the first elections since December 2019 to the City's Court of Aldermen. City Aldermen are technically elected for life, but are expected to seek re-election every six years and retire at the age of 70; Aldermanic elections are not synchronised and take place in each ward as and when necessary. Four current Aldermen were last elected or re-elected over six years ago, at least three will have reached 70 by the new year, and there is also a vacancy to fill following the death last year of former Lord Mayor Sir Roger Gifford. Accordingly, we can expect at least eight Aldermanic elections in 2022.

Also at some point in 2022, the forthcoming sixth annual collection of these columns, *Andrew's Previews 2021*, should hit the virtual shop window. The editing process has already started, and the page count is heading for a record high of something like 600 (last year's collection was just 136 pages), so this is going to take some time to polish. It'll be ready when it's ready. In the meantime, the five earlier paperback volumes in their fetching teal covers are and will remain available from Amazon at your convenience. The royalties from the books will go towards future Previews, while you are also welcome to contribute a smaller or more regular sum towards the research. Which is of course fine, but if you go down that route you won't have the permanent reminder of your donation on your bookshelves.

Self-publishing these books has not made your columnist a rich person. If I received a small sum of money for every copy sold...oh, actually I do. Instead, it's the nice comments I receive back on the Previews which make the hard work of researching and writing them worthwhile. And they clearly have a large readership, judging from the comments I get every week that "this isn't working" as everybody tries to read that week's issue at once and overloads the Britain Elects server. To all who have read and enjoyed the Previews every week, whether you agree with me or not, whether your side won or lost that week, thank you.

Thanks are also due to the very hard-working team at Britain Elects who bring the other aspects of this site to life: the poll aggregation, the video streams, the behind-the-scenes work that people don't notice. You are the most wonderful hosts. Thank you for continuing to kindly give Andrew's Previews a home.

Britain Elects will of course be ready for the 2022 local elections as they happen, and so will this column. We stand ready, yet again, to go through the same procedure as every year.

> "The same procedure as last year, Miss Sophie?"
>
> "The same procedure as every year, James!"

There's only one thing left for Andrew's Previews to do now, and that is to close down for the year in the form of words which has become traditional. This column will return in time for the first local by-election of 2022, to be held in Carlton, Nottinghamshire on Thursday 6th January; until then, on behalf of all at Britain Elects may I wish you a very merry Christmas, and may your 2022 be an improvement on your 2021.

The Roll of Honour

Date	*Council*	*Ward or division*	*Result*	*Winning candidate(s)*
4 Mar	N. Lanarks.	Fortissat	Lab gain from SNP	Peter Kelly
		Thorniewood	Lab gain from SNP	Helen Loughran
11 Mar	Highland	Aird & Loch Ness	Ind gain from C	David Fraser
	Sc. Borders	Leaderdale & Melrose	C gain from SNP	Jenny Linehan
	W. Lothian	Livingston S.	SNP hold	Maria Macaulay
18 Mar	Argyll & Bute	Helensburgh & Lomond S.	C gain from LD	Gemma Penfold
		Isle of Bute	Ind hold	Liz McCabe
	Conwy	Eirias	Ind hold	Gail Jones
	Denbs.	Corwen	PC hold	Alan Hughes
	Glasgow	Baillieston	SNP gain from Lab	David Turner
		Partick E./Kelvindale	Lab gain from C	Jill Brown
	Wrexham	Maesydre	PC gain from Lab	Becca Martin
25 Mar	Gwynedd	Llanrug	PC hold	Beca Brown
	Midlothian	Midlothian E.	SNP hold	Stuart McKenzie
	Perth and Kinross	Almond & Earn	C gain from SNP	Frank Smith
1 Apr	Mons.	St Kingsmark	C hold	Christopher Edwards
8 Apr	Torfaen	Abersychan	Lab gain from Ind	Lynda Clarkson
		Cwmyniscoy	Lab hold	John Killick
		New Inn	C hold	Keith James
6 May	Allerdale	Aspatria	Ind gain from Putting Cumbria First	Kevin Thurlow
		Christchurch	C gain from Lab	Alan Kennon
		Ellen & Gilcrux	C gain from Lab	Patrick Gorrill
		St John's	Lab gain from Ind	Antony McGuckin
		Seaton & Northside	C hold	Colin Sharpe
	Arun	Brookfield	C gain from LD	David Chace
		Pevensey	C gain from LD	Joan English
	Ashfield	Annesley & Kirkby Woodhouse	Ashfield Ind hold	Jamie Bell
		Skegby	Ashfield Ind hold	Will Bostock
	Ashford	Beaver	C gain from Lab	Trevor Brooks
	Babergh	Great Cornard	C hold	Simon Barrett

Date	Council	Ward or division	Result	Winning candidate(s)
6 May	Barking & Dagenham	Thames	Lab hold	Fatuma Nalule
	Barnet	E. Barnet	C gain from Lab	Nicole Richer
		Edgware	C hold	Nick Mearing-Smith
	Barrow-in-Furness	Hindpool	Lab hold	Jo Tyson
		Roosecote	C hold	Jay Zaccarini
	Bassetlaw	Ranskill	C gain from Lab	Gerald Bowers
		Sutton	C gain from Ind	Denise Depledge
		Tuxford and Trent	C hold	Lewis Stanniland
	Bexley	Longlands	C hold	Lisa-Jane Moore
	Birm'ham	Billesley	Lab hold	Katherine Carlisle
		Hall Green N.	Lab hold	Saima Suleman
		Oscott	C gain from Lab	Darius Sandhu
		Quinton	C gain from Lab	Dominic Stanford
	Blaby	Stanton & Flamville	C hold	Mike Shirley
	Blackpool	Highfield	C hold	Bradley Mitchell
		Norbreck	C gain from Ind	Julie Sloman
	Bolsover	Bolsover N. & Shuttlewood	Lab hold	Donna Hales
		Pinxton	Lab gain from Ind	Stan Fox
	Boston	Skirbeck	C gain from Ind	Katie Chalmers
	B'mouth, C'church & Poole	Canford Heath	C gain from LD	Sean Gabriel
		Commons	Christchurch Ind hold	Vanessa Ricketts
	Braintree	Hatfield Peverel & Terling	C hold	Darren White
		Witham S.	C hold	William Korsinah
	Brent	Brondesbury Pk	Lab hold	Gwen Grahl
	Bridgend	Nant-y-moel	Ind hold	Mary Hughes
	Brighton & Hove	Hollingdean & Stanmer	Grn gain from Lab	Zoë John
		Patcham	C hold	Anne Meadows
	Bromley	Crystal Palace	Lab hold	Ryan Thomson
	Broxtowe	Beeston Rylands	Lab hold	Shaun Dannheimer
		Stapleford S.W.	Lab hold	Sue Paterson
	Canterbury	Swalecliffe	C hold	Mark Dance
		Westgate	Lab hold	Pip Hazelton
	Carlisle	Cathedral & Castle	Lab hold	Pete Sunter
		Harraby S. & Parklands	C gain from Lab	Linda Mitchell
		Newtown & Morton N.	C gain from Lab	Neville Lishman
	Castle Pt	Boyce	C hold	Jack Fortt
		St George's	C hold	Sue Mumford
	Chelmsford	Moulsham Ldg.	C gain from LD	Robert Gisby
	Ches. E.	Crewe W.	Lab hold	Connor Naismith
	Ches. W. & Chester	Frodsham	C hold	Christopher Basey
		Neston	Lab hold	Keith Millar
	Copeland	Whitehaven C.	Lab hold	Joseph Ghayouba
	Cotswold	Fosseridge	C hold	David Cunningham
	Craven	Barden Fell	Ind hold	David Pighills
		Penyghent	C hold	Robert Ogden

Date	*Council*	*Ward or division*	*Result*	*Winning candidate(s)*
6 May	Croydon	Kenley	C hold	Ola Kolade
		New Addington N.	Lab hold	Kola Agboola
		Park Hill & Whitgift	C hold	Jade Appleton
		S. Norwood	Lab hold	Louis Carserides
		Woodside	Lab hold	Michael Bonello
	C'bria CC	Brampton	C hold	Mike Mitchelson
		Cockerm'th N.	C gain from LD	Catherine Bell
		St John's & Gt Clifton	C gain from Ind	Debbie Garton
		Ulverston W.	Grn gain from C	Judy Filmore
	Dacorum	Leverstock Grn	C hold	Neil Harden
		Tring C.	LD hold	Sheron Wilkie
	Darlington	Hummersknott	C hold	Jack Sowerby
		Red Hall and Lingfield	C gain from Lab	David Willis
	Dartford	Darenth	C hold	Maria Kelly
		Wilmington, Sutton-at-Hone & Hawley	C hold	Ellenor Palmer
	Derbyshire Dales	Masson	C gain from Lab	Dermot Murphy
		Wirksworth	Lab hold	Dawn Greatorex
	Dover	Mill Hill	C gain from Lab	David Hawkes
	Ealing	Ealing Bdwy	C hold	Julian Gallant
		Hanger Hill	C hold	Fabio Conti
		Hobbayne	Lab hold	Louise Brett
	E. Devon	Whimple and Rockbeare	C gain from Ind	Richard Lawrence
	E. Hants.	Bramshott & Liphook	C hold	Nick Sear
		Grayshott	C hold	Tom Hanrahan
	E. Herts.	Bishop's Stortford All SS.	LD hold	Richard Townsend
	E. Lindsey	Chapel St Leonards	C hold	Graham Williams
	E. Riding	S.E. Holderness	C hold	Claire Holmes
		S.W. Holderness	C hold	David Winter
	E. Staffs.	Eton Park (2)	1 Lab hold, 1 Lab gain from Ind	Thomas Hadley Louise Walker
	E. Suffolk	Beccles & Worlingham	Grn hold	Sarah Plummer
		Framlingham	C hold	Lydia Freeman
	Eastbourne	Hampden Park	LD hold	Josh Babarinde
		Sovereign	C hold	Kshama Shore
	Eden	Hartside	C hold	Raymond Briggs
		Skelton	C hold	Colin Atkinson
	Enfield	Chase	C gain from Lab	Andrew Thorp
		Jubilee	Lab hold	Chinelo Anyanwu
		Southbury	Lab hold	Ayten Guzel
	Erewash	Hallam Fields	C gain from Lab	Jon Wright
		Nottingham Rd	C gain from Lab	Bryn Lewis
	Fenland	Lattersey	C hold	Jason Mockett
	Flints.	Gwernymynydd	Ind hold	Andy Hughes

Date	*Council*	*Ward or division*	*Result*	*Winning candidate(s)*
6 May	Forest of Dean	Berry Hill	Ind hold	Jamie Elsmore
		Cinderford E.	Lab hold	Shaun Stammers
	Gravesham	Westcourt	C gain from Lab	Samir Jassal
	Great Yarmouth	Claydon	C gain from Lab	Bob Price
		Ormesby	C gain from Ind	Ron Hanton
	Greenwich	Glyndon	Lab hold	Sandra Bauer
		Greenwich W.	Lab hold	Pat Slattery
		Kidbrooke with Hornfair	Lab hold	Odette McGahey
		Shooters Hill	Lab hold	Clare Burke-McDonald
	Guildford	Friary & St Nicolas	LD hold	Cait Taylor
		Pirbright	C hold	Keith Witham
		Send	Guildford Greenbelt Group hold	Guida Esteves
	Hackney	Hoxton E. & Shoreditch	Lab hold	Anya Sizer
		King's Park	Lab hold	Lynne Troughton
		Stamford Hill W.	C hold	Hershy Lisser
		Woodberry Dn	Lab hold	Sarah Young
	Harboro'	Market Harborough—Little Bowden	C hold	Peter Critchley
	Herefs.	Newton Farm	C gain from Ind	Ann-Marie Probert
	Hertsmere	Borehamwood Kenilworth	Lab gain from C	Dan Ozarow
		Bushey N.	LD hold	Alan Matthews
	Hillingdon	Charville	C hold	Darran Davies
	House of Commons	Hartlepool	C gain from Lab	Jill Mortimer
	Horsham	Trafalgar	LD hold	Martin Boffey
	Hounslow	Cranford	Lab hold	Devina Ram
		Hounslow Hth	Lab hold	Madeeha Asim
	Hunts.	Huntingdon N.	Lab hold	Marion Kadewere
		St Ives E.	C hold	Craig Smith
		St Ives S.	C hold	Rianna d'Souza
		Warboys	C hold	Michael Haines
	Isle of Anglesey	Caergybi	Ind hold	Jeff Evans
		Seiriol	PC hold	Gary Pritchard
	Islington	Bunhill	Lab hold	Valerie Bossman-Quarshie
		Highbury W.	Lab hold	Bashir Ibrahim
		Holloway	Lab hold	Jason Jackson
		Mildmay	Lab hold	Angelo Weekes
		St Peter's	Lab hold	Toby North
	Kingston (Thames)	Chessington S.	LD hold	Andrew Mackinlay
	Lancaster	Bulk	Grn hold	Jack Lenox
		Kellet	C gain from LD	Stuart Morris
	Leicester	N. Evington	Lab hold	Vandevi Pandya
	Lewes	Seaford E.	C hold	Richard Turner
		Seaford W.	C hold	Linda Wallraven
	Lewisham	Bellingham	Lab hold	Rachel Onikosi
		Catford S.	Lab hold	James Royston

Date	*Council*	*Ward or division*	*Result*	*Winning candidate(s)*
6 May	Lewisham	New Cross	Lab hold	Samantha Latouche
	(*cont.*)	Sydenham	Lab hold	Jack Lavery
	Lichfield	Summerfield & All SS.	C gain from Lab	Heather Tranter
	Luton	High Town	Lab hold	Umme Ali
		Round Grn	LD gain from Lab	Steve Moore
	Maldon	Heybridge E.	C hold	Bruce Heubner
		Tollesbury	Ind gain from C	Emma Stephens
	Mansfield	Oakham	C hold	Robert Elliman
	Mendip	Wells St Thos'	C gain from LD	Tanys Pullin
	Merton	St Helier	Lab hold	Helena Dollimore
	Mid Devon	Castle	C gain from LD	Elizabeth Slade
		Taw	C hold	Peter Heal
		Westexe	C gain from Ind	Stephen Pugh
	Mid Sussex	Copthorne & Worth	C gain from Ind	Bruce Forbes
	Neath Port Talbot	Aberavon	Lab hold	Stephanie Lynch
	Newark & Sherwood	Boughton	C hold	Tim Wildgust
	Newham	East Ham C.	Lab hold	Farah Nazeer
	Newport	Victoria	Lab hold	Farzina Hussain
	N.E. Derbys.	Eckington S. & Renishaw	C gain from Lab	Philip Wheelhouse
		Killamarsh E.	C hold	David Drabble
		Killamarsh W.	C hold	Alex Platts
	N. Kesteven	Bassingham & Brant Broughton	C gain from Lincs Ind	Russell Eckert
	N. Lincs.	Ashby	C gain from Lab	Joanne Saunby
		Bottesford	C hold	Janet Longcake
		Broughton & Appleby (2)	2 C holds	Carol Ross Janet Lee
	N. Norfolk	Coastal	C gain from LD	Victoria Holliday
		Holt	C hold	Eric Vardy
	N. Somerset	Portishead E.	Portishead Ind hold	Caroline Goddard
	N. Warks.	Atherstone C.	C gain from Lab	Mark Jordan
		Curdworth	C hold	Sandra Smith
		Polesworth E.	C gain from Lab	Dan Hancocks
	N.W. Leics.	Ibstock E.	C gain from Lab	Jenny Simmons
		Worthington & Breedon	C hold	Raymond Morris
	N. Yorks. CC	Harrogate Bilton & Nidd Gorge	C gain from LD	Matt Scott
		Ribblesdale	C hold	David Staveley
	Redbridge	Loxford	Lab hold	Sahdia Warraich
		Seven Kings	Lab hold	Pushpita Gupta
	Redcar &	Guisborough	C hold	Andrew Hixon
	Cleveland	Hutton	C hold	Stephen Waterfield
		Longbeck	C hold	Andrea Turner
	Rhondda	Llantwit Fardre	C hold	Sam Trask
	Cynon Taf	Penrhiwceiber	Lab gain from Cynon Valley Party	Ross Williams

Date	*Council*	*Ward or division*	*Result*	*Winning candidate(s)*
6 May	Ribble Valley	Billington & Langho	C hold	Steve Farmer
		Mellor	C hold	Robin Walsh
		W. Bradford & Grindleton	C hold	Kevin Horkin
	Richmond (Thames)	Hampton Wick	LD gain from Grn	Petra Fleming
	Rother	Eastern Rother	C hold	Lizzie Hacking
	Rushcliffe	Sutton Bonington	C hold	Matt Barney
	Selby	Camblesforth & Carlton	C gain from Yorkshire Party	Charles Richardson
	Sevenoaks	Brasted, Chevening & Sundridge	C hold	Keith Bonin
	Somerset W. & Taunton	Trull, Pitminster & Corfe	LD hold	Dawn Johnson
	S. Cambs.	Girton	LD gain from Ind	Corinne Garvie
		Harston and Comberton	LD hold	Fiona Whelan
		Melbourn	LD hold	Sally Hart
		Milton & Waterbeach	LD hold	Paul Bearpark
	S. Derbys.	Church Gresley	C hold	Roger Redfern
		Hilton (2)	2 C holds	Gillian Lemmon Peter Smith
		Seales	C hold	Simon Ackroyd
	S. Glos.	Frenchay & Downend	C hold	Liz Brennan
	S. Hams	Ivybridge W.	C hold	Louise Jones
	S. Kesteven	Glen	C hold	Penny Robins
	S. Lakeland	Broughton & Coniston	LD gain from C	Heather Troughton
		Furness Peninsula	C hold	Ben Cooper
		Grange	LD hold	Pete Endsor
		Kendal Rural	LD hold	Ali Jama
	S. Oxon.	Didcot N.E.	C gain from Ind	Andrea Warren
		Forest Hill & Holton	LD hold	Tim Bearder
	S. Ribble	Longton & Hutton W.	C hold	Julie Buttery
		St Ambrose	Lab hold	Kath Unsworth
	Spelthorne	Staines S.	C gain from LD	Sinead Mooney
	Staffs. M'lands	Cheadle N.E.	C gain from Ind	Stephen Ellis
		Cheadle S.E.	C gain from Ind	Peter Jackson
	Stirling	Forth & Endrick	C gain from SNP	Jane Hutchison
	Stockton-on-Tees	Billingham W.	C gain from Ind	Lee Spence
		Bishopsgarth & Elm Tree	C gain from LD	Hugo Stratton
		Hartburn	C hold	Niall Innes
		Western Parishes	C hold	Steve Matthews
		Yarm	C hold	Dan Fagan
	Stoke-on-T.	Moorcroft	C gain from Lab	Tariq Mahmood
	Surrey Hth	Bagshot	C gain from LD	Mark Gordon

Date	*Council*	*Ward or division*	*Result*	*Winning candidate(s)*
6 May	Swale	Sheerness	C gain from Lab	Oliver Eakin
	Swansea	Castle	Lab hold	Hannah Lawson
		Llansamlet	Lab hold	Matthew Jones
	Telford & Wrekin	Dawley & Aqueduct	Lab hold	Ian Preece
		Donnington	C gain from Lab	Jay Gough
	Tendring	Eastcliff	Ind gain from Holland-on-Sea & Eastcliff Matters	Andy Baker
		W. Clacton & Jaywick Sands	C gain from UKIP	Jayne Nash
	Test Valley	Andover Millway	C gain from Andover Alliance	Jim Neal
		Andover St Mary's	C gain from Andover Alliance	Jan Budzynski
		Chilw'th, Nursling & Rownhams (2)	2 C holds	Mike Maltby Terese Swain
	Tewkesb'ry	Cleeve Hill	C hold	Keja Berliner
	Thanet	C. Harbour	Grn gain from Lab	Tricia Austin
		Dane Valley	C gain from Thanet Ind	David Wallin
		Newington	C gain from Lab	Trevor Shonk
	Torbay	Clifton with Maidenway	LD hold	Cat Johns
	Waltham Forest	Hatch Lane	C hold	Justin Halabi
	Uttlesford	Newport	Residents for Uttlesford hold	Judy Emanuel
		The Sampfords	C gain from Residents for Uttlesford	George Smith
	V. of White Horse	Grove N.	C gain from LD	Ben Mabbett
	Wandsw'th	Bedford	Lab hold	Hannah Stanislaus
	Warwick	Leamington Clarendon	Lab hold	Colin Quinney
	Wealden	Hailsham N.	LD gain from C	Paul Holbrook
		Hailsham S.	C hold	Kevin Balsdon
		Heathfield N.	C hold	Mike Baker
		Heathfield S.	C hold	Tom Guyton-Day
	W. Lindsey	Kelsey Wold	C hold	Peter Morris
	W. Suffolk	Abbeygate	Grn hold	Julia Wakelam
		Clare, Hundon & Kedington	C gain from Ind	Nick Clarke
		Lakenheath	C gain from Ind	Colin Noble
		Moreton Hall	C gain from Ind	Birgitte Mager
		Southgate	C hold	Sarah Stamp
		Whepstead & Wickhambrook	C hold	Sarah Pugh
	W'minster	Churchill	Lab hold	Liza Begum
	Wychavon	Elmley Castle & Somerville	C hold	Emma Kearsey
13 May	House of Commons	Airdrie & Shotts	SNP hold	Anum Qaisar-Javed

Date	Council	Ward or division	Result	Winning candidate(s)
10 June	Waltham Forest	Grove Green	Lab hold	Uzma Rasool
		Lea Bridge	Lab hold	Jennifer Whilby
17 June	Aberdeen-shire	E. Garioch	C gain from LD	David Keating
	Caerphilly	Aber Valley	PC hold (*unopposed*)	Charlotte Bishop
	House of Commons	Chesham & Amersham	LD gain from C	Sarah Green
	Kent CC	Elham Valley (*postponed from 6 May*)	C hold	Susan Carey
	Mid Devon	Upper Culm	C hold	James Bartlett
	N'folk CC	Sewell (*postponed from 6 May*)	Lab hold	Julie Brociek-Coulton
	Norwich	Sewell (*postponed from 6 May*)	Grn gain from Lab	Gary Champion
	Somerset W. & Taunton	Old Cleeve & District	LD hold	Steve Griffiths
	Tandridge	Felbridge (*postponed from 6 May*)	Ind gain from C	Judy Moore
24 June	Chichester	Chichester E.	LD gain from Lab	Bill Brisbane
	Gwynedd	Harlech	PC gain from Ind	Gwynfor Owen
	Is. of Scilly	Bryher	Ind hold (*unopposed*)	Andrew Frazer
	N. Lanarks.	Murdostoun	Ind hold	Robert McKendrick jnr
	Rugby	Wolvey & Shilton	C hold	Becky Maoudis
	Somerset W. & Taunton	N. Curry & Ruishton	LD hold	Barrie Hall
	Swindon	Priory Vale	C hold	Kate Tomlinson
1 July	Chelmsford	Writtle	C hold	Andrew Thorpe-Apps
	Elmbridge	Cobham and Downside	LD gain from C	Robin Stephens
	Enfield	Bush Hill Park	C hold	Peter Fallart
	House of Commons	Batley & Spen	Lab hold	Kim Leadbeater
	Islington	Tollington	Lab hold	Mick Gilgunn
	Newark & Sherwood	Bridge (2)	2 C gains from Ind	Jack Kellas Simon Haynes
	N.E. Lincs.	Heneage	C gain from Lab	Catherine Hogan
	Stoke-on-T.	Penkhull and Stoke	C gain from City Ind	Dean Richardson
8 July	E. Devon	Feniton	C gain from Ind	Alasdair Bruce
		Honiton St Michael's	Lab gain from LD	Jake Bonetta
	Harlow	Mark Hall	C gain from Lab	John Steer
	Hunts.	St Neots E.	Ind gain from Lab	Ben Pitt
	M. Sussex	Ardingly & Balcombe	Grn gain from C	Jenny Edwards
	W. Suffolk	Aldeburgh & Leiston (2)	1 Grn gain from C, 1 C hold	Thomas Daly (Grn) Russ Rainger (C)
15 July	Sandwell	Tividale	C gain from Lab	Emma Henlan
22 July	Camden	Fortune Green	LD hold	Nancy Jirira

Date	*Council*	*Ward or division*	*Result*	*Winning candidate(s)*
22 July	Dover	Alkham and Capel-le-Ferne	C hold	Martin Hibbert
	Leicester	Humberstone & Hamilton	C gain from Lab	Daniel Crewe
	N. Somerset	Congresbury & Puxton	Grn gain from LD	Phil Neve
	Rhondda Cynon Taf	Tyn-y-nant	Lab hold	Julie Barton
	Spelthorne	Staines	Grn hold	Malcolm Beecher
	Thanet	Cliftonville E.	C hold	Charlie Leys
	Wirral	Liscard	Lab hold	Daisy Kenny
29 July	Basildon	Pitsea N.W.	C gain from Lab	Stuart Terson
	Bassetlaw	E. Retford S.	C gain from Lab	Mike Introna
	Harrogate	Knaresborough Scriven Park	LD gain from C	Hannah Gostlow
	N'folk CC	Gaywood S.	LD gain from C	Rob Colwell
	S. Tyneside	Fellgate & Hedworth	Lab gain from Ind	Jay Potts
5 Aug	W. Lothian	E. Livingston & E. Calder	SNP gain from Lab	Thomas Ullathorne
12 Aug	E. Suffolk	Orwell & Villages	C hold	Mick Richardson
	Highland	Inverness W.	LD gain from Ind	Colin Aitken
		Wick & E. Caithness	LD gain from Ind	Jill Tilt
	N. Ayrs.	Dalry & W. Kilbride	C gain from SNP	Ronnie Stalker
	S. Lakeland	Grange	LD hold	Fiona Hanlon
	Tr Hamlets	Weavers	Aspire gain from Lab	Kabir Ahmed
19 Aug	Aberdeens.	Mid Formartine	C gain from SNP	Sheila Powell
	Ashford	Downs N.	Grn gain from C	Geoff Meaden
	Dover	Sandwich	C hold	Dan Friend
	E. Riding	E. Wolds and Coastal	C hold	Charlie Dewhirst
	Ribble Valley	Littlemoor	LD hold	Gaynor Hibbert
		Primrose	LD hold	Kerry Fletcher
	Rutland	Oakham S.	LD gain from C	Paul Browne
	Wilts. PCC	—	C hold	Philip Wilkinson
26 Aug	C'bria CC	Corby & Hayton	LD gain from Ind	Roger Dobson
	Medway	Princes Park	C hold	Robbie Lammas
		Strood N.	Lab gain from C	Zöe van Dyke
	Newport	Graig	C hold	John Jones
2 Sept	Calderdale	Park	Lab hold	Mohammed Shazad Fazal
		Ryburn	C gain from Ind	Felicity Issott
	Ches. E.	Wilmslow Dean Row	Residents of Wilmslow hold	Lata Anderson
9 Sept	Newcastle upon Tyne	Castle	LD hold	Thom Campion
	N.E. Derbys.	Barlow & Holmesfield	C hold	Bentley Strafford-Stephenson
		Killamarsh E.	Lab gain from C	Tony Lacey
	N. Tyneside	Camperdown	Lab hold	Tracy Hallway
	S. Derbys.	Seales	Ind gain from C	Amy Wheelton

Date	*Council*	*Ward or division*	*Result*	*Winning candidate(s)*
9 Sept	S. Tyneside	Cleadon & E. Boldon	C hold	Stan Wildhirt
16 Sept	Ealing	Hobbayne	Lab hold	Claire Tighe
	M'vern Hs.	Tenbury	Ind gain from C	Lesley Bruton
	Middlesbrough	Ladgate	Ind gain from Lab	Tony Grainge
	Sheffield	Firth Park	Lab hold	Fran Belbin
23 Sept	Charnw'd	Shepshed W.	C hold	Ian Williams
	E. Cambs.	Soham N.	C gain from LD	Mark Goldsack
	E. Devon	Exe Valley	LD hold	Jamie Kemp
	Epsom & Ewell	Cuddington	Res Assoc of Cuddington hold	Graham Jones
	H'smith & Fulham	Wormholt & White City	Lab hold	Frances Umeh
	S. Lakeland	Kendal N.	LD hold	Jonathan Cornthwaite
28 Sept	Broadland	Brundall (2)	2 Grn gains from C	Jan Davis Eleanor Laming
		Old Catton & Sprowston W.	C hold	Richard Potter
30 Sept	E. Hants.	H'dean Downs	Grn gain from C	Blossom Gottlieb
	E. Staffs.	Tutbury & Outwoods	C hold	Russell Lock
	Eden	Penrith W.	LD gain from C	Roger Burgin
	Sunderland	Hetton	Lab hold	Iain Scott
	Swale	Priory	LD hold	Michael Henderson
	W. Suffolk	The Rows	C gain from Ind	Lance Stanbury
7 Oct	Flints.	Penyffordd	Lab gain from Ind	Alasdair Ibbotson
	Nott'ham	St Ann's	Lab hold	Corall Jenkins
		Sherwood	Lab hold	Nayab Patel
	Rushcliffe	Musters	LD hold	Vicky Price
	Somerset CC	Comeytrowe & Trull	LD hold	Dawn Johnson
	Somerset W. & Taunton	Wilton & Sherford	LD hold	Tom Deakin
	Waverley	Cranleigh E.	LD hold	Philip Townsend
14 Oct	Falkirk	Falkirk S.	SNP gain from Lab	Emma Russell
	Harrow	Pinner S.	C hold	Hitesh Karia
	Surrey Hth	Frimley Green	C gain from LD	Stuart Black
	Wigan	Leigh W.	Lab hold	Samantha Brown
21 Oct	Birm'ham	Yardley E.	LD hold	Deborah Harries
	Horsham	Forest	LD hold	Jon Olson
	Newark & Sherwood	Rainworth S. & Blidworth	Ind gain from Lab	Tina Thompson
28 Oct	Bolton	Bromley Cross	C hold	Amy Cowen
	Carlisle	Currock & Upperby	Lab gain from UKIP	Christopher Wills
	Luton	South	Lab hold	Fatima Begum
	S. Kesteven	Grantham Arnoldfield	C hold	Kaffy Rice-Oxley
		Stamford All SS.	Ind gain from C	Richard Cleaver
	S. Staffs.	Kinver	C hold	Geoff Sisley
		Wombourne S.E.	C hold	Mark Evans
	Wrexham	Gresford E. & W.	C hold	Jeremy Kent

Date	*Council*	*Ward or division*	*Result*	*Winning candidate(s)*
4 Nov	Gloucester	Longlevens	LD gain from C	Sarah Sawyer
	Hunts.	Huntingdon E.	LD hold	Michael Shellens
	Rutland	Oakham N.W.	Lab gain from Ind	Leah Toseland
	Salford	Blackfriars & Trinity	Lab hold	Roseanna Wain
	W. Lancs.	N. Meols	C hold	John Howard
	W. Sussex CC	Bourne	LD gain from C	Andrew Kerry-Bedell
11 Nov	Cardiff	Heath	Lab gain from Heath & Birchgrove Ind	Julie Sangani
	Denbs.	Llandrillo	PC hold	Gwyneth Ellis
	Lancaster	University & Scotforth Rural	Lab hold	Sayeda Askari
	Melton	Melton Dorian	C hold	Timothy Webster
	N. Kesteven	Metheringham (2)	1 Lincs Ind hold (*on drawing of lots*), 1 C gain from Lincs Ind	Fran Pembery (C) Amelia Bailey (Lincs Ind)
		Sleaford Castle	C gain from Lincs Ind	Malcolm Offer
	Thanet	Thanet Villages	Grn hold	Abi Smith
18 Nov	Canterbury	Gorrell	Grn gain from Lab	Clare Turnbull
	Liverpool	Anfield	Lab hold	Tricia O'Brien
		Clubmoor	Lab hold	Matthew Smyth
		Kirkdale	Lab hold	Dave Hanratty
	Manchester	Chorlton	Lab hold	Mathew Benham
	Ryedale	Cropton	Lib hold	Alasdair Clark
	S. Ribble	Bamber Bridge E.	Lab hold	Patricia Hunter
	Tewkesb'ry	Brockworth E.	Ind hold	Charlotte Mills
	W. Devon	Bere Ferrers	C gain from LD	Angela Blackman
25 Nov	Allerdale	Maryport S.	Lab gain from Ind	Bill Pegram
	Basildon	Lee Chapel N.	Lab hold	Terry Webb
	Halton	Halton Castle	Lab hold	Sharon Thornton
	Hambleton	Raskelf & White Horse	C hold	Philippa James
	Lancaster	Carnforth & Millhead	Lab hold	Luke Taylor
	Newcastle (Lyme)	Knutton	C gain from Lab	Derrick Huckfield
	N. Yorks. PCC	—	C hold	Zoë Metcalfe
	Nuneaton & Bedw'th	Bar Pool	C gain from Lab	Jamie Hartshorn
	Tunbridge Wells	Speldhurst & Bidborough	Tunbridge Wells Alliance gain from C	Matthew Sankey
	Wandsw'th	Bedford	Lab hold	Sheila Boswell
	W. Suffolk	Horringer	C hold	Nick Wiseman
	Wigan	Bryn	Lab gain from Ind	Samuel Flemming
	Wirral	Oxton	LD hold	Orod Osanlou
30 Nov	Wyre Forest	Franche & Habberley N.	C gain from Health Concern	David Ross
2 Dec	Adur	Hillside	C hold	Leila Williams
	Breckland	Hermitage	C hold	Robert Hambidge
	Highland	Fort William & Ardnamurchan	SNP gain from C	Sarah Fanet

Date	*Council*	*Ward or division*	*Result*	*Winning candidate(s)*
2 Dec	House of Commons	Old Bexley & Sidcup	C hold	Louie French
	Lancaster	Bare	LD gain from C	Gerry Blaikie
		Upper Lune Valley	LD gain from C	Ross Hunter
	Newport	Victoria	Lab hold	Gavin Horton
	N. Norfolk	Stalham	C gain from LD	Matthew Taylor
	Warwick	Whitnash	Whitnash Res Assoc hold	Adrian Barton
	Wealden	Hartfield	Grn gain from C	Rachel Millward
	Worthing	Marine	Lab gain from C	Vicki Wells
9 Dec	Bracknell Forest	Old Bracknell	Lab gain from C	Paul Bidwell
	Rotherham	Anston and Woodsetts	LD gain from C	Drew Tarmey
		Aughton and Swallownest	Lab gain from C	Robert Taylor
	Tonbridge & Malling	Castle	Grn gain from C	Anna Cope
		Kings Hill	C hold	Dan Harman
		W. Malling & Leybourne	LD gain from C	Paul Boxall
	Torridge	Northam	C gain from Ind	Carrie Woodhouse
14 Dec	Renfs.	Paisley S.E.	*Cancelled*	—
16 Dec	Argyll & Bute	Lomond N.	C hold	Paul Collins
	Ashford	Highfield	Grn gain from C	Dawnie Nilsson
	Bridgend	Caerau	Ind gain from Lab	Chris Davies
	Horsham	Roffey S.	LD gain from C	Sam Raby
	House of Commons	N. Salop.	LD gain from C	Helen Morgan
	Lichfield	Armitage with Handsacre	C hold	Richard Cross
	Medway	Rochester E.	Lab hold	Lauren Edwards
	Middlesbrough	N. Ormesby	Lab hold	Nicky Gascoigne
	Northumberland	Hexham E.	LD gain from C	Suzanne Fairless-Aitken
	Telford & Wrekin	Dawley & Aqueduct	Lab hold	Bob Wennington
	Walsall	Pleck	Lab hold	Simran Kaur Cheema (*returned while ineligible*)
	W. Berks.	Tilehurst S. & Holybrook	C hold	Akinbiyi Oloko
	W. Lindsey	Nettleham	LD gain from C	Jaime Oliver
23 Dec	New Forest	Bransgore and Burley	Ind gain from C	Richard Frampton

Index

Printed in Great Britain
by Amazon

84318700R10363